Principles of Marketing Research

Principles of Marketing Research

Edited by Richard P. Bagozzi

Copyright © Basil Blackwell Ltd, 1994

First published 1994

Reprinted 1996

Blackwell Publishers Inc.
238 Main Street
Cambridge, Massachusetts 02142
USA

Blackwell Publishers Ltd
108 Cowley Road
Oxford OX4 1JF
UK

All rights reserved. Except for the quotation of short passages for the purposes of criticism and review, no part of this publication may be reproduced, stored in a retrieval system, or transmitted, in any form or by any means, electronic, mechanical, photocopying, recording or otherwise, without the prior permission of the publisher.

Except in the United States of America, this book is sold subject to the condition that it shall not, by way of trade or otherwise, be lent, resold, hired out, or otherwise circulated without the publisher's prior consent in any form of binding or cover other than that in which it is published and without a similar condition including this condition being imposed on the subsequent purchaser.

Library of Congress Cataloging-in-Publication Data

A CIP Catalog record for this book is available from the Library of Congress.

ISBN 1-55786-548-5

British Library Cataloguing in Publication Data

A CIP catalogue record for this book is available from the British Library.

Typeset in 10.5 on 12.5 pt Times by Pure Tech Corporation, Pondicherry, India.
Printed in the UK by T.J. Press (Padstow) Ltd., Padstow, Cornwall

This book is printed on acid-free paper

Contents

List of Figures	vii
List of Tables	x
List of Contributors	xiii
Acknowledgments	xiv
Introduction *Richard P. Bagozzi*	xv
1 Measurement in Marketing Research: Basic Principles of Questionnaire Design *Richard P. Bagozzi*	1
2 Qualitative Marketing Research *Bobby J. Calder*	50
3 Sampling *Seymour Sudman*	73
4 Mail and Telephone Surveys in Marketing Research: A Perspective from the Field *Daniel C. Lockhart and J. Robert Russo*	116
5 Regression Analysis for Marketing Decisions *Dipak Jain*	162
6 Experimental Design: Generalization and Theoretical Explanation *Brian Sternthal, Alice M. Tybout, Bobby J. Calder*	195
7 Analysis of Experimental Data *Dawn Iacobucci*	224
8 Classic Factor Analysis *Dawn Iacobucci*	279

9	Structural Equation Models in Marketing Research: Basic Principles *Richard P. Bagozzi*	317
10	The Evaluation of Structural Equation Models and Hypothesis Testing *Richard P. Bagozzi and Hans Baumgartner*	386
	Index	423

List of Figures

1.1	The structure of theory	4
1.2	Illustration of the structure of theory applied to the effects of source credibility	7
1.3	Examples of the semantic differential	13
1.4	Examples of ratio scales	16
1.5	A multitrait-multimethod matrix for three traits and three methods	21
1.6	Types of error in research	27
1.7	Some processes respondents go through when answering attitude questionnaire items	34
2.1	Opposing definitional models of qualitative research	68
3.1	Examples of BRR designs for 16 and 20 pairs	98
4.1	Price elasticity for individuals who see product prices displayed in different orders	123
4.2	Relationship of number of call-backs to costs per completed survey and sampling error	134
4.3	Change in responses to dichotomous questions as they relate to number of call-backs and percentage response rate	136
4.4	Return rate by incentive level	141
4.5	Differences between returners and non-returners by physician specialties	143
4.6	Hypothesized combination of Triandis (1977) and Fishbein and Ajzen (1976) models that best predicts mailed questionnaire returning behavior	144
4.7	Alpha distribution (standard pattern of mailed questionnaire returns)	146
4.8	Alpha distribution (with effect of reminders included)	146
5.1	Estimated regression line and the breakdown of the total variation in Y	167
5.2a	No evidence of heteroscedasticity	178

LIST OF FIGURES

5.2b	(Absolute) magnitude of residual increases as X increases	179
5.3a	Positive autocorrelation	179
5.3b	Negative autocorrelation	180
6.1	The effects of knowledge and price on brand sales/evaluation	200
6.2	The effect of complexity and message repetition on product judgments	207
6.3	Expanded parka study design findings	214
6.4	Dependent measures varying in proximity to the independent variable	216
7.1	F-tests seen intuitively as a comparison of between-group differences to within-group differences (F3 > F1 > F2)	230
7.2	Two 2×2 designs: one with an interaction, one without	235
7.3	Simple effects	247
7.4	The power of MANOVA over ANOVA	257
7.5	Plot of "service satisfaction" data	260
8.1	Venn diagram representing variances and covariances of p original measures and single composite	283
8.2	Eigenvectors in $p = 2$-dimensional scatterplot	285
8.3	Example of principal components	287
8.4	Causality assumed in factor analysis	289
8.5	Relationships among common and unique factors	290
8.6	Structure of underlying factors	292
8.7	Scree tests	295
8.8	Example of $r = 2$ and $r = 3$ common factors	296
8.9	Graphical rotations	298
8.10	Graphical factor rotation	299
8.11	An example	302
8.12	Example of a higher-order factor analysis	306
9.1	The elements and structure of the holistic construal	318
9.2	The congeneric measurement model for four measures of a single construct	324
9.3	The congeneric measurement model for two constructs, each indicated by two measures	328
9.4	Multidimensional expectancy-value attitudes	336
9.5	Multidimensional expectancy-value attitude model with additive and multiplicative effects	338
9.6	Second-order confirmatory factor analysis model for beliefs about the consequences of giving blood	340
9.7	Confirmatory factor analysis-model for MTMM design with three traits and three methods	344
9.8	The correlated uniqueness model for three traits and three methods	351
9.9	Guidelines for the analysis of MTMM matrix data	359
9.10	The effects of measurement error on tests of hypotheses: illustration of a means for correcting for the consequences of random error	364

9.11	Full model with measurement error taken into account in attitudes, subjective norms, and intentions	366
9.12	Some consequences of omitted variables	370
9.13	Further consequences of omitted variables: parallel exogenous causes	372
9.14	Simple non-recursive and recursive models	374
9.15	Causal models of reciprocal causation	376
10.1	Summary of model specifications	411

List of Tables

1.1	Criteria for convergent and discriminant validity in the Campbell and Fiske multitrait multimethod matrix (three traits and three methods)	23
1.2	Pearson product–moment correlations among measures of the use of computers by wholesale-distribution companies in four areas as judged by the chief executive officer (method 1) and subordinates (method 2)	25
1.3	Variables affecting size and direction of context effects	36
1.4	Norms for writing questions and queries to address in this regard	40
3.1	Examples of clusters	84
3.2	Typical sample sizes used for consumer and industrial marketing research	111
4.1	Most commonly used survey methodologies	121
4.2	Mail, telephone, and focus group methods compared	127
4.3	Costs per interview for a national and local survey conducted by three different methods	128
4.4	Major costs for telephone and mail surveys	129
4.5	Results of first dialing attempts	131
4.6	Disposition of dialings in a Lavrakas study and a recent marketing research study on hospital decision-making	131
4.7	Disposition of call sheets in Lavrakas study	132
4.8	Regression equations predicting expected return rate from two US studies	139
4.9	Return rates for physicians and pharmacists using three levels of incentives and two levels of contacts	141
4.10	Return rates for difficult to reach populations	142
4.11	Hypothesized stages of mailed questionnaire response	145
4.12	Number of mail, telephone, in-person, and focus group studies participated in during 1991	149
4.13	Factor loadings and suggested names for importance items with acceptable internal consistency	150

4.14	Factor loadings and suggested names for importance items with unacceptable internal consistency	151
4.15	Reliability (standardized Chronbach's Alpha) of 13 factors on importance scale and each (reliable) method's importance rating	152
4.16	Performance of four survey methods on items	153
6.1	Diagnostic measures of response	219
7.1	Small one-way ANOVA example: data and computations	231
7.2	Customer satisfaction data for illustration of ANOVA, MANOVA, and MANCOVA	237
7.3	Univariate analyses of variance on the data in Table 7.2	239
7.4	The ANOVA table for a 3-factor factorial	241
7.5	ANOVA on 2×3 ad x price example	243
7.6	Univariate analyses of covariance	252
7.7	Relationships between models covered in this chapter	253
7.8	Numerical example of one-sample and two-sample Hotelling's T^2	255
7.9	Multivariate ANOVA: computation of H's and E for a 2-factor factorial	258
7.10	Multivariate analysis of variance of service satisfaction data	259
7.11	Multivariate analysis of covariance of service satisfaction data	262
7D.1	Univariate ANOVA table for a 1-factor within-subjects design	270
7D.2	Repeated measures as a function of raw data (y_i's) or difference scores ($y_{i-1} - y_i$'s)	272
9.1	Correlation matrix of four measures of attitude toward giving blood – aroused sample ($n = 110$)	326
9.2	Findings for goodness-of-fit indices, parameter estimates, and reliability indices for one-factor congeneric, tau-equivalent, and parallel forms models applied to the data in Table 9.1 (aroused sample)	326
9.3	Correlation matrix of four measures of attitude toward giving blood – unaroused sample ($n = 110$)	329
9.4	Findings for goodness-of-fit indices, parameter estimates, and reliability indices for two-factor congeneric and parallel forms models applied to the data in Table 9.3 (unaroused sample)	329
9.5	Correlation matrix for seven measures of beliefs about the consequences of giving blood ($n = 127$)	340
9.6	Partitioning of variance for second-order confirmatory factor analysis example	341
9.7	Findings for confirmatory factor analysis of supplier influence on wholesale distributors using data from Phillips (1981)	347
9.8	Parameter estimates for correlated uniqueness model applied to the data in Arora (1982)	352

xii LIST OF TABLES

9.9	Illustration of the direct product model applied to data from Foxman, Tansuhaj, and Ekstrom (1989)	356
9.10	Summary of pros and cons with regard to contemporary procedures for assessing construct validity	361
9.11	Variance–covariance data matrices for coupon usage study	367
9.12	Key parameter estimates for the models in Figure 9.10 and sample A in Table 9.11	368
9.13	Data for reciprocal causation example	377
10.1	Summary of overall goodness-of-fit indices	398
10.2	Observed variance–covariance matrix	413
10.3	Overall goodness-of-fit measures and model comparisons	414
10.4	Results for the target model	415

List of Contributors

Richard P. Bagozzi, Dwight F. Benton Professor of Behavioral Science in Management and Marketing, School of Business Administration, University of Michigan

Hans Baumgartner, Assistant Professor, School of Business Administration, Pennsylvania State University

Bobby J. Calder, Montgomery Ward Professor of Marketing and Professor of Psychology, Kellogg Graduate School of Management, Northwestern University

Dawn Iacobucci, Associate Professor of Marketing, Kellogg Graduate School of Management, Northwestern University

Dipak Jain, Professor of Marketing, Kellogg Graduate School of Management, Northwestern University

Daniel C. Lockhart, Senior Marketing Research Scientist, Boehringer Mannheim Corporation, Indianapolis

J. Robert Russo, Professor of Psychology, Department of Psychology, Southern Illinois University

Brian Sternthal, General Foods Professor of Marketing, Kellogg Graduate School of Management, Northwestern University

Seymour Sudman, Walter A. Stellner Professor of Marketing, Department of Business Administration and Survey Research Center, University of Illinois, Champaign

Alice M. Tybout, Harold T. Martin Professor of Marketing, Kellogg Graduate School of Management, Northwestern University

Acknowledgments

Appreciation is expressed to the School of Business Administration, the University of Michigan for support in preparation of this monograph and to Mrs Carolyn Maguire and Mrs Joan Walker for help in word-processing and administrative details. Special thanks go to the following scholars who reviewed at least one, and in many cases, two or more chapters: Elizabeth Edwards (Eastern Michigan University), Hans Baumgartner (Pennsylvania State University), Frank Andrews (deceased, University of Michigan), Donald Barclay (University of Western Ontario), Terry Elrod (University of Alberta), Joel Huber (Duke University), Peter Lenk (University of Michigan), Wayne De Sarbo (University of Michigan), and Clifford Clogg (Pennsylvania State University).

In addition, many authors have acknowledged the help of others in footnotes to their chapters.

Introduction

Richard P. Bagozzi

This volume reflects the confluence of a number of currents in contemporary marketing research. One of these is the explosion in new techniques and novel ways of looking at old methods. The chapters cover the latest developments in classic areas of marketing research. Much of the content is not to be found in contemporary tests. Current treatments tend to be either short (and often out-of-date), "me-too" introductions to marketing research or superficial overviews of the field in handbook form. The present volume is more firmly grounded in statistics and basic knowledge in methodology than current texts.

A second theme emerging in the field is the integration of philosophy of science criteria with research methods. Researchers are beginning to realize that the quality of their data, the reliability and validity of measures, and the usefulness of results are intimately bound up with the philosophical underpinnings of the methods they employ. Many of the chapters to follow explicitly consider these issues.

A third and final current in the field concerns the relationship between the research questions one asks and theory. For historical and pedagogical reasons, texts and courses in research methods have been segregated from the substantive issues to which they are applied. The lacuna makes the research enterprise more of a hit or miss affair than it should be. Special attention is given in this text to ways for better linking research to the practical and theoretical knowledge that it is designed to inform.

The primary audiences to which this book is directed are threefold: first, Ph.D. students, faculty, and researchers who desire an in-depth tutorial in the latest developments in basic research methods. Second, some instructors may find the volume useful in the MBA marketing research course. Although a more advanced treatment than customarily found, this volume can be handled by most MBA students.

The topics covered in this volume address the foundation topics in marketing research: questionnaire design, qualitative methods, sampling, mail and telephone surveys, regression analysis for marketing decisions, experimental design, the analysis of experimental data, classic factor analysis, and structural equation modeling. For coverage of more specialized topics, the reader may find the companion volume, *Advanced Methods of Marketing Research*, helpful. *Advanced Methods* considers the analysis of panel data, partial least squares, the multivariate analysis of categorical data, marketing segmentation with chi-square automatic interaction detection, cluster analysis, multidimensional scaling, conjoint analysis, multiple correspondence analysis, and latent structure analysis.

Chapter 1, "Measurement in Marketing Research: Basic Principles of Questionnaire Design" by Richard P. Bagozzi, introduces the idea of quantification of information. Philosophical and classical statistical issues in measurement are discussed, different types of measurement scales scrutinized, reliability, validity, and threats to accurate measurement considered. The chapter ends with a recommended procedure for scale and questionnaire construction.

Bobby Calder, the author of Chapter 2 ("Qualitative Marketing Research"), gives a thorough overview of focus group interviews, personal interviews, and projective techniques – methods that inform, complement, and indeed at times even outperform the more quantitative procedures discussed in this text. Emphasis is placed on how to approach qualitative research to make the research endeavor more fruitful. An interesting perspective is provided on contrasts between qualitative and quantitative research.

Sampling is the topic of Chapter 3 by Seymour Sudman. A taxonomy of sampling methods is introduced and criteria for evaluating different frames offered. Stratification and clustering are highlighted. Non-sampling errors and procedures for determining sample sizes are then discussed. The reader is given a more comprehensive, in-depth coverage than that found in contemporary texts and handbooks, yet insightful examples make the details come to life.

Daniel Lockhart and J. Robert Russo survey issues with mail and telephone surveys and compare them to other methods in Chapter 4. They begin by discussing the different constraints faced by marketing research practitioners and academic researchers. Particular attention is then given to the advantages and disadvantages of mail and telephone surveys. In addition to providing a thorough coverage of the literature, the authors present original research supporting their conjectures. Although this chapter stresses practical issues faced by practitioners, it should prove illuminating for basic researchers as well.

Regression analysis has a long history and is a workhorse of marketing researchers. In Chapter 5, Dipak Jain takes this venerable technique and shows how it is useful in managerial decision-making. At the same time, he focuses upon assumptions, specification and estimation issues, and hypothesis testing. Categorical variables, various diagnostic checks, dummy variable regression, and alternative functional forms round-out the presentation. The author shows how regression is a tool for explanation and understanding, as well as forecasting.

Brain Sternthal, Alice Tybout, and Bobby Calder examine the logic of experimental designs as generators of knowledge in marketing research (Chapter 6). They begin by considering two approaches: generalization and theoretical explanation. Next they address the context for experimentation, which is marked by the extremes of laboratory and field experiments. Following this, sample selection and the choice of independent and dependent variables are discussed. The issues raised by the authors and their recommendations have seldom been made explicit in the literature.

Chapter 7, "Analysis of Experimental Data", by Dawn Iacobucci, covers the basics of analysis of variance, analysis of covariance, multivariate analysis of variance, and multivariate analysis of covariance. The presentation of techniques is most lucid, and the examples help to point out nuances and stress key interpretational issues. Readers will find the discussions of sample size issues, contrasts, simple effects, repeated measures, fixed versus random effects, and effect-size very useful.

Dawn Iacobucci introduces the essentials of classic factor analysis in Chapter 8. After beginning with an intuitive example of measurement and a brief history of the technique, she gives a thorough presentation of principal components analysis and contrasts it to the general factor analytic model. For the latter, detailed discussion are made of the determination of the number of factors, rotations, and sample size issues. Such advanced topics as higher-order factor models, confirmatory factor analysis, and the factor analysis of binary data are touched upon. The Appendix contains example inputs for SPSSX and SAS.

In Chapter 9, Richard Bagozzi covers structural equation models in marketing research. The role of philosophy of science issues, introduced in Chapter 1, is given further treatment here to set the stage for the use of structural equation models in measurement and hypothesis testing. Much of the chapter focuses on reliability and validity because applied and substantive research can be no better than the measurements used in research. The chapter ends with a discussion of the goals of explanation, prediction, and control and their fulfilment in structural equation models. Such topics as the implications of measurements error, intervening variables, moderating variables, and reciprocal causation are considered.

Richard Bagozzi and Hans Baumgartner discuss and illustrate how structural equation models can be evaluated in Chapter 10. The issues involved are complex and still evolving. Nevertheless, the need for guidelines has never been stronger, as more and more marketing researchers discover the versatility and power of structural equation models. After treating measurement, model specification, identification, and statistical assumptions, the chapter turns to data screening issues. Next, model estimation, assessment of overall model fit, assessment of the measurement and latent variable submodels, model modification, residual analysis, cross-validation, and model equivalence are addressed.

At the end of each chapter, a set of questions can be found. These are designed to measure one's comprehension of the material, provide opportunities to apply the knowledge gained, and in general, challenge the reader. Answers to the questions can be obtained by writing to Richard P. Bagozzi, School of Business Administration, University of Michigan, Ann Arbor, Michigan, 48109–1234, USA.

1

Measurement in Marketing Research: Basic Principles of Questionnaire Design

Richard P. Bagozzi

Introduction

Marketing research, whether basic or applied, is designed to solve problems. Consider the following scenarios:

> A marketing researcher for a food manufacturer is asked to forecast demand for a new frozen canoli dessert. As this information is needed quickly in the concept development and business analysis stages of the new product development process, the researcher decides to rely upon responses from a sample of 100 consumers as proxies for making a forecast. She conducts a field study where consumers are provided with free samples from a number of different products (a soft drink, potato chips, the canoli) and then asked to express how strongly they intend to try each product when each becomes available. Based on data for the company's long-standing sales of cake mixes and similar surveys of intentions, norms are developed relating the likelihood of trial and repeat purchasing to different magnitudes of intentions. What is the best way to measure intentions? How do we know whether the measures are good or not?

> A brand manager is asked to provide guidance to the advertising agency which handles his dual cassette VCR. The ad agency wants to know what to emphasize in its ads and which media to use. The brand manager decides to survey 500 potential customers to measure their attitudes toward copying and editing films and their beliefs about, and importance of, product attributes upon which these attitudes are based, as well as socio-demographic data. This information will be used to suggest key product attributes and the attitudinal tone to place in ads, and to identify different market segments for media selection. How should attitudes, beliefs, and importances be measured?

> An advertising account executive is asked by her client to demonstrate which of two proposed ad executions will be more effective. She commissions a vendor to do a controlled test with real consumers and to measure attitudes

toward the ad, the spokesperson, and the focal brand. Reactions to the ads of competitors are also obtained. What kinds of measures and how many are needed? How do we know the measures indicate what they are supposed to indicate and that the concepts they reflect are really distinct?

In this chapter, we will explore ways of quantifying phenomena such as those illustrated above. For simplicity, the term "attitudes" will be used as an umbrella to stand for such affective and cognitive responses as preferences, feelings, emotions, beliefs, expectations, judgments, appraisals, and intentions. All of these obviously have different meanings, but most of the principles presented below apply to them as well as to attitudes classically defined.

We begin with a philosophical discussion of measurement to place things in perspective. Next, four types of scales and examples are presented. Following this, the concepts of reliability and validity are introduced, including common threats to effective scale construction and the interpretation of results. Finally, the chapter closes with a model of how people respond to questions, and a procedure is presented for scale and questionnaire construction.

Measurement

A definition

An early view defined measurement as a procedure for assigning numerals to objects, events, or persons according to a rule (e.g. Campbell, 1928; Stevens, 1951). More specifically, it can be said that "(m)easurement is not only the assignment of numerals, etc. It is also the assignment of numerals in such a way as to correspond to *different degrees of quality* (emphasis in original) . . . or property of some object or event" (Duncan, 1984, p. 126). For example, a person's attitude toward a political candidate might be placed somewhere on a continuum from +3 to −3, where "+3" indicates "very positive," "0" stands for "indifferent," and "−3" signifies "very negative."

When people hear the word "measurement", they often think of such empirical operations as placing a checkmark on a questionnaire, recording the galvanic skin response of a subject as he or she watches an advertisement, or cataloging one's weekly purchases on a scanner at the supermarket. Actually, to focus only on the operations associated with any particular measurement is to ignore important elements of measurement and risk forming misleading inferences.

The scientific community now thinks of measurement in a broad sense in that the meaning of any measurement is part conceptual and part empirical (Bagozzi, 1984; Oliva and Reidenbach, 1987). Measurements achieve meaning in relation to particular theoretical concepts embedded in a larger network of concepts, where the entire network is used to achieve a purpose. The purpose may be to solve such problems as noted above for marketing researchers, brand managers, and advertising account executives. More broadly, the purpose is to obtain understanding, explanation, prediction, or control of some phenomenon. We do this by developing theories, testing them, and implementing the results.

The structure of theory

Some visual imagery helps place these ideas in perspective:

> (a) scientific theory might... be likened to a complex spatial network: Its terms are represented by the knots, while the threads connecting the latter correspond, in part, to the definitions and, in part, to the fundamental and derivative hypotheses included in the theory. The whole system floats, as it were, above the plane of observation and is anchored to it by rules of interpretation. These might be viewed as strings which are not part of the network but link certain points of the latter with specific places in the plane of observation. By virtue of those interpretive connections, the network can function as a scientific theory: From certain observational data, we may ascend, via an interpretive string, to some point in the theoretical network, thence proceed, via definitions and hypotheses, to other points, from which another interpretive string permits a descent to the plane of observation. (Hempel, 1952, p. 36).

Thus, a scientific theory is a system of ideas and observations, all related among themselves in a meaningful way (e.g. Feigl, 1970).

Figure 1.1 presents a graphical interpretation of the so-called orthodox conceptualization of scientific theory. Notice first that there are three possible types of terms or concepts in any theory: theoretical, derived, and empirical concepts. The first two are unobservable to a researcher in the sense that they cannot be perceived by the senses. A consumer's judgment about how reliable a new model car would be or a customer's attitude toward the service at a hotel are two examples. The third concept, the empirical, is observable in the sense that it can be perceived by the senses and is capable of intersubjective verification (e.g. Hempel, 1965, p. 22). For example, the amount of time a customer spends reading nutrition labels while grocery shopping might be an empirical concept in a theory of health consciousness.

Theoretical concepts are the building blocks of hypotheses. They are abstract entities represented by the terms in the sentence constituting a hypothesis and express an idea or thought of a researcher. Common synonyms of theoretical concepts employed by marketing researchers and found frequently in journal articles include primitive concepts, theoretical constructs, unobservable variables, latent variables, and hypothetical constructs. Consumer attitudes, brand equity, and sales force satisfaction are examples. Derived concepts, like theoretical concepts, are abstract, and obtain their meaning through their relation to theoretical concepts

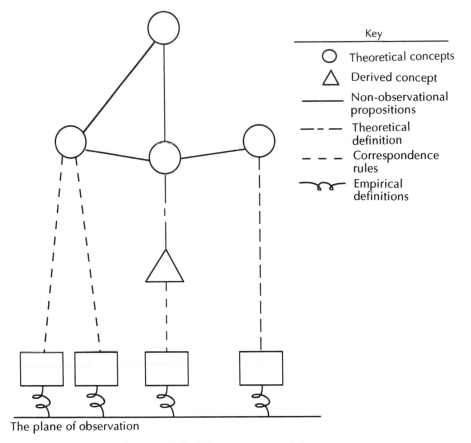

Figure 1.1 The structure of theory

(e.g. through nominal definitions). Derived concepts are less abstract, and generally more detailed, than the theoretical concepts to which they are connected. An example of a derived concept for the theoretical concept of attitude toward an act (Aact) might be the summation of the products of beliefs (b_i) about the consequences of acting times evaluations (e_i) of the consequences ($\sum b_i e_i$).

A second, broad point to note about Figure 1.1 is that there are four possible types of relationships that link concepts in any theory. The first, which is depicted by solid line segments in Figure 1.1, connects only theoretical concepts and is termed a non-observational proposition. Non-observational propositions are often expressed as logical, mathematical, functional, or causal relationships. Common synonyms used by researchers for non-observational propositions include theoretical laws, hypothetical laws, non-observational hypotheses, theoretical hypotheses, and causal relations. An example of a non-observational proposition is: "visual distraction introduced into a television commercial will inhibit counter-argumentation toward the selling points in the message." In this example, it is assumed that distraction and counter-argumentation are theoretical concepts and that each may be operationalized. The former might be a manipulated variable in an experiment, the latter cognitive responses generated from a thought listing exercise performed after a consumer sees the ad. Counter-argumentation might, in turn, be related in a non-observational proposition to attitude toward the brand depicted in the ad. The hypothesis might be: "the greater the counter-argumentation, the less favorable the attitude." The rationale for this hypothesis can be found in the Elaboration Likelihood Model (Petty and Cacioppo, 1986).

The second type of relationship expressed in Figure 1.1 is the theoretical definition. A theoretical definition connects a theoretical concept (a primitive term) to a derived concept. The nominal definition and reforming definitions are two common types. The former, which was illustrated with attitudes earlier, introduces a new term (i.e. Aact $\stackrel{d}{=} \sum b_i e_i$), whereas the latter stipulates new meaning for an existing term. An example of a reforming definition is: "consumer A's self-efficacy is his/her confidence that he/she can operate the controls on the CD cam-recorder."

Correspondence rules are the third type of relation found in any theory. As shown in Figure 1.1, correspondence rules express a relationship between theoretical concepts and empirical concepts. They provide empirical significance to theoretical terms. One of the first formal representations of correspondence rules was proposed by the Nobel prize-winning physicist, Percy Bridgman, and has come to be known as the operational definition model: "we mean by any concept nothing more than a set of operations; *the concept is synonymous with the corresponding set of operations*" (Bridgman, 1927, p. 5). Formally, the operational definition model can be written as: $P(x) \equiv (E(x) \rightarrow R(x))$, which in words reads, "x has theoretical property P by definition, if and only if, when x is subjected to experiment test E, it yields result R." According to this model, every theoretical concept has, indeed must have, one and only one operation associated with it. One shortcoming of this model is that any new measurement operation implies a new theory. Not only does this result in a proliferation of theories and difficulty in establishing generalities, but it precludes multiple operationalization of theoretical concepts. Yet as we shall see in this and later chapters, multiple operationalizations are needed to determine internal consistency reliability and construct validity (e.g. Campbell, 1969). For these reasons, the operational definition model is no longer advocated by philosophers of science. Nevertheless in marketing research, the operational definition model is still the most frequently applied approach. Whenever a theory is tested on observations, and each observation is defined as an operationalization of a single theoretical concept (and vice versa), the operational definition model is implicitly being employed. This model may not be a significant shortcoming in applied research, but it does constitute a problem for basic research, where the interplay between theory and observations plays an important role in theory development and testing.

The partial interpretation model of correspondence rules was proposed to overcome shortcomings of the operational definition model. This model can be expressed: $E(x) \rightarrow (P(x) \equiv R(x))$ and in words reads, "If x is subjected to experimental test procedure E, it will exhibit theoretical property P, if and only if it yields result R" (Carnap, 1956). It is called a partial interpretation because the meaning of a theoretical term is only specified under particular test (i.e. measurement) conditions. In the absence of test conditions, the theoretical term has no meaning. On the positive side, the model allows any theoretical term to have multiple operationalizations, and thus it is meaningful to determine internal consistency reliability and construct validity. Among other problems, however, the partial interpretation model does not permit theoretical terms to have semantic content over and above that provided by the rule, and any change in a measurement will change the meaning of the corresponding theoretical term (Petrie, 1971; Suppe, 1977, pp. 102–4).

The most widely accepted correspondence rule in management and the social sciences is the causal indicator model (e.g. Keat and Urry, 1975). Specifically, the causal indicator model can be depicted through: $(P(x) \rightarrow (E(x) \rightarrow R(x)))$, which reads, "If x has theoretical property P, then if experimental test procedure E is applied, it will yield result R." Here a causal link is specified between a theoretical term (or network of terms) and a test operation(s) and its result(s). A phenomenon or state represented by a theoretical term is thought to imply or explain observations. The correspondence rule, then, functions as a scientific law linking theoretical term to experimental test procedure to observed results (Schaffner, 1969; Sellars, 1961). Notice that the correspondence rule is not part of the theory or the observations to which it is linked. Rather, it is an auxiliary hypothesis concerning theoretical mechanisms existing between theoretical terms and observations. Suppes (1962) suggests that a hierarchy of theories links theoretical terms and implied observations: a physical theory (e.g. of the instrumentation), the theory of the experiment, the theory of experimental design, the theory of data, and ceteris paribus conditions. One drawback with the approach is that some observations can be produced by different or multiple theories and/or experimental procedures. Thus, a certain degree of ambiguity exists. One way to lessen the ambiguity is to examine the construct validity of measures in any test of a theory (Bagozzi, 1980, 1981).

The final relationship to note in Figure 1.1 is the empirical definition. The empirical definition gives meaning to an empirical concept by equating it with actual physical events in the world of sense experience. For instance, the phrase, "a checkmark placed adjacent to one of the following descriptors: very satisfied, satisfied, dissatisfied, or very dissatisfied," might be given as an empirical definition of "expressed satisfaction."

A simple example

To make the meaning of the structure of theory more concrete, let us take an illustration from consumer research. Consider the effect of source credibility in a persuasive communication on attitudes toward the brand in an ad. Classic work in the communication literature suggests that greater source credibility leads to more positive attitudes. Figure 1.2 presents one way to pictorially represent the structure of theory.

The central hypothesis of the theory is expressed in sentence form and depicted as ℓ_t a non-observational proposition. Generally, non-observational propositions are intended to be statements about actual or potential law-like generalizations. Two theoretical terms – V_{T_1} and V_{T_2} – are contained

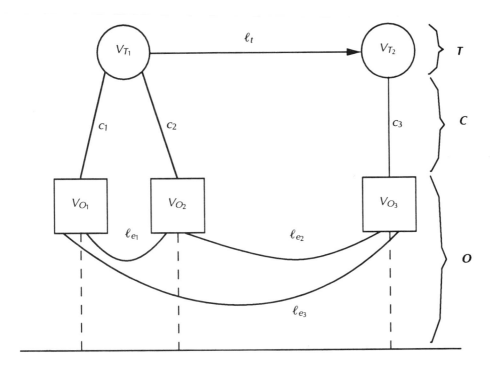

Key
- V_{T_1} source credibility
- V_{T_2} attitude
- V_{O_1} experimental manipulation of source credibility
- V_{O_2} manipulation check
- V_{O_3} operationalization of attitude
- ℓ_t theoretical (i.e. nonobservational) proposition: the greater the source credibility, the more favorable the attitude
- c_1, c_2, c_3 correspondence rules
- ℓ_{e_1} proposition of empirical association
- ℓ_{e_2}, ℓ_{e_3} propositions of empirical generalization

Figure 1.2 Illustration of the structure of theory applied to the effects of source credibility

in ℓ_t and stand for source credibility and attitude, respectively. Although not shown in Figure 1.2, V_{T_1} and V_{T_2} would each typically be defined with primitive terms. For example, source credibility might be defined in terms of expertise and trustworthiness, whereas attitude might be conceptualized as particular affective responses toward the brand in the ad. All together, V_{T_1}, V_{T_2}, their primitive terms, ℓ_t, and the theoretical rationale behind ℓ_t can be termed the theoretical postulates, T, of the effect of source credibility on attitude. In a full exposition of T, we might have primitive terms, definitions, axioms, theorems, and non-observational propositions.

The V_T in Figure 1.2 are given empirical meaning through Cs, correspondence rules. Looking first at V_{T_1}, we see that it has two observational terms attached to it, V_{o_1} and V_{o_2}. The first might be the experimental manipulation(s) used to create the images of different levels of credibility. For instance, a common procedure is to employ different spokespersons for experimental and control groups such that each person possesses varying levels of knowledge, skill, experience, etc. with the issues at hand. The second observational term might be a manipulation check consisting of measures of perceived expertise taken on subjects exposed to the ad. Similarly, V_{T_2} is shown connected to V_{o_3}, where the latter might be physiological, self-report, or other measures of attitude. Next, notice that the V_o are shown interconnected by ℓ_e, i.e. empirical propositions. These are statements linking the respective observational terms. For V_{o_1} and V_{o_2}, the proposition (i.e. ℓ_{e_1}) is expressed as an empirical association, to reflect the fact that the concepts should covary as a consequence of their common content in meaning. The remaining propositions (i.e. ℓ_{e_2} and ℓ_{e_3}) are represented as empirical generalizations, to indicate that covariation here occurs as an observational consequence of underlying laws linking different concepts. Finally, notice that each V_o is tied to the plane of observation with dashed lines. This is intended to stand for the actual physical sensations or sense extending data through which the empirical concepts implied by V_o are monitored. This might be a visual movement noted by an experimenter, an "x" placed in a box on a questionnaire, a change in a transducer measuring muscle movements in the face, or a whole host of other types of observational recording procedures. For additional comments on this example as well as an extension, see Bagozzi (1984).

Further comments on the structure of theory

A number of points deserve mention with respect to the portrayal of the structure of theory discussed above. First, if a researcher were to deal exclusively with empirical concepts and their associations among each other, then this would be an example of raw empiricism. Although such a practice might prove useful in certain exploratory senses (e.g. as a means of discovering empirical laws), it is limited and can induce misleading inferences. For example, empirical associations among observed things need not correspond with the true causal or functional relations existing between theoretical concepts because of measurement, specification, or methodological errors. Yet, observed associations reflect these latter confounds as well as the theoretical forces one desires to discover. Raw empiricism deals entirely with measurements, i.e., the lower stratum of entities in Figure 1.1.

At the opposite extreme is the practice of dealing only with theoretical concepts and the relationships between them – the upper stratum of Figure 1.1. Strictly speaking, these activities are the domain of mathematics and logic, because, by themselves, they are internally consistent and true by definition. They tell us nothing about the structure of the world of experience and thus cannot serve as a basis for scientific explanation. Activities of this sort might be termed sterile tautologies.

Most of the research conducted in marketing is neither purely empirical nor purely tautological. Rather, research in marketing often mixes the two in a manner reminiscent of Figure 1.1, but with the correspondence rules omitted or poorly specified. That is, the practice has been to segregate the conceptual stage of research from its test. Theoretical structures are first developed, and then hypotheses are tested on data which are only loosely tied to the theoretical structures. Rarely are correspondence rules formally stated. Perhaps the best example of this segregation can be found in applications of microeconomic theory in marketing. Typically, the conceptual stage of this research consists of a utility function, budget constraint equations, and an optimization procedure which are used to derive a demand equation. The test of the demand equation is then conducted entirely on empirical concepts in a regression equation. The correspondence between empirical model and theory is left implicit. As a result, one never knows fully the adequacy of any test when conducting research along these lines. Significant coefficients and a failure to reject the regression equation provide only limited insight because one does not know how well observations represent theoretical constructs. Similarly, a rejection of the empirical model is not very helpful because one cannot ascertain whether the failure is due to inadequate measurements, a misspecified theory, or both.

What is required for making valid research conclusions is an approach which integrates the conceptual phase of inquiry with its test. The structure of theory attempts to do this in a formal sense. The key element in this conceptualization is that aspect of the measurement process which is reflected in correspondence rules. However, it should be stressed that measurement is not limited to this relationship because, as Figure 1.1 illustrates, correspondence rules, the concepts they connect, and other entities in a theory are all interrelated through a complex network of relations. The meaning of any theoretical concept, then, depends not only on its link to empirical concepts, but also on the entire pattern of relationships to which it is directly and indirectly connected. Many of the techniques introduced in this book strive to implement the structure of theory in a way lending itself to the evaluation, testing, and development of theories.

Scales of Measurement

Most of the techniques described in this book are used either in scale construction (i.e. to examine the reliability and validity of measures) or in hypothesis testing, where the variables entering hypotheses are based on measurements from individual items or scales on questionnaires or from information provided on firms, products, brands, or other phenomena in the marketplace. Because so much of the data marketing researchers collect and analyze is based on responses of consumers or managers, it is useful to review the most common measurements in this regard. Below we consider four primary scales used in questionnaires and provide illustrations: nominal, ordinal, interval, and ratio scales. Although these scales constitute formal or structured ways of obtaining measurements, it should be remembered that it is often possible to recode unstructured data such as derived from open-ended responses, thought listing exercises, participant observation, analyses of narrative material, or key informant judgments into one or more of the four scale types.

Nominal scales

A nominal scale is a procedure for assigning a number to an object, property, or concept in order to identify or label the thing to be measured. For example, researchers often desire to discover differences in consumption based on gender and therefore assign a "1" to males and "2" to females in analyses. This yields a one-to-one correspondence between gender and the particular numbers attached to them. Of course, any number could be assigned to males and females such as "11" = male and "57" = female, since the only property conveyed by a nominal scale is membership in a category.

A nominal scale makes the least restrictive assumptions of the four scale types, but is not suitable for computing operations with the usual parametric statistics such as means, standard deviations, and Pearson product–moment correlations. It permits us to count the number of things in each category and make statements about which category has more instances than the others. But a nominal scale says nothing about order or distance and has no origin. Some tests can be performed telling us about the likelihood that a member in one category is also a member in another, as we shall see in later chapters. In addition, nominal scales are used to identify groups of members for separate analyses on each group where the analyses are performed on other measures (e.g. based on interval scales) and comparisons are made on parameters across the groups. These kinds of analyses will also be addressed in later chapters.

In addition to gender, other nominal scales are frequently used in marketing research. Common ones include: buyer-nonbuyer; current user-past user – never used; market segments A, B, C, and D; and married, widowed, divorced, never married.

Ordinal scales

Ordinal scales assign responses of people (or properties of things) to categories such that scores in a higher category possess more of a focal characteristic than scores in a lower category. Ordinal scales are sometimes called ranking scales because objects are rank-ordered in a particular direction on a property of interest. For example, a respondent might be asked the following:

> "Please rank-order the following headache remedies in order of your personal preference. Use a '1' to indicate your most preferred brand, a '2' your second most preferred brand, and so on."

Brand name	Your ranking
Bayer Aspirin	————
Excedrin	————
Tylenol	————
Bufferin	————
Advil	————

Although an ordinal scale does not permit one to make conclusions about the differences between the things being ranked (e.g. we can say that one brand of headache remedy is preferred to another in the above example, but we cannot say anything about how much more one is preferred over another), it does allow more statistical operations to be performed than nominal scaled data. For instance, the median, quartile, and percentile are meaningful for ordinal scaled data; and measures of association can be computed such as the polyserial correlation between ordinal and interval scaled variables and the polychoric correlation between ordinal scaled variables, when latent variables with normal bivariate distributions are assumed to underlie the measured variables (Jöreskog and Sörbom, 1988). When one prefers not to make assumptions about the underlying distributions of responses, the analysis of qualitative data by log-linear models and related methods are appropriate. Alternatively, asymptotic free distribution methods may be appropriate with large samples (e.g. Bentler, 1989; Jöreskog and Sörbom, 1989). All of the above options are discussed in this text and the companion volume, *Advanced Methods of Marketing Research* (Blackwell Publishers, 1994).

Besides the rank order of preferences for brands, other uses for ordinal scales occur in marketing research. For instance, occupations can be ordered by prestige or socioeconomic status (Miller, 1991, pp. 327–65); social class is sometimes categorized into lower, middle, and upper;

product usage is broken into groupings of no, light, medium, and heavy; and education is ranked by elementary, high school, associate degree, bachelors degree, and graduate degree.

Interval scales

Interval scales are arguably the most frequently used measures in marketing research. In the typical interval scale, numbers are assigned to indicate differences in degree of a property along a continuum, such that the differences from number to number are equal across the range of the scale.

An example can be used to illustrate the properties of the interval scale. Imagine that a researcher is interested in measuring the attitudes of consumers toward a new brand of athletic shoes, and the following item is used to do this:

"Please inspect the shoes on this table and express your reactions toward brand A on the following scale:

"My attitude toward brand A can be best summarized as (circle the appropriate number):"

Very negative	Negative	Neither negative nor positive	Positive	Very positive
1	2	3	4	5

This scale only approaches an interval scale in the sense that the difference, say, between "2" (negative) and "3" (neither negative nor positive) is approximately half the difference between between "3" and "5" (very positive). Differences between points on a true interval scale are multiples of each other (e.g. the centigrade scale for temperature). Interval scales do not have absolute zero points, and therefore it is not permissible to conclude that a person scoring a "4" on the above scale, say, is twice as positive as a person scoring a "2." In other words, we cannot compare the absolute magnitudes of scores, only their differences. This comment applies even when, as often happens, the researcher presents the scale along with a zero point assigned to one of the scale points (e.g. a zero is sometimes assigned to neither negative nor positive in the above example). In this case, the zero point is arbitrary.

An important property of an interval scale that is not held by either nominal or ordinal scales is its ability to maintain its measurement for any linear transformation of the form $y = a + bx$ for a any constant and $b > 0$ and where x is the original number on the scale and y is the new, transformed number.

It is meaningful to apply the arithmetic mean, standard deviation, Pearson product–moment correlation, and parametric statistics (e.g. factor analysis, multiple regression) to interval scaled data. But a caution is in order. Some techniques require normality or even multivariate normality

MEASUREMENT IN MARKETING RESEARCH

for the distribution of measured variables. It is not so much an issue to ask whether one has ordinal or interval scaled measures, *per se*, in order to apply these techniques, as it is to inquire about the distributional properties such as univariate and multivariate skewness and kurtosis. More will be said on these topics in later chapters (see also Jöreskog and Sörbom, 1988, 1989; Mardia, 1970; and Olsson, 1979 a,b).

Many formats are used to create scales that are approximately interval in character. One of the most popular and effective is called the *semantic differential*. In the typical application, the semantic differential consists of seven-point bipolar scales anchored with adjectives such as pleasant–unpleasant, good–bad, or useful–useless. Figure 1.3 shows common variations of the semantic differential. The first example is the form recommended by attitude researchers (e.g. Ajzen and Fishbein, 1980). Notice that

1. My feelings toward abortion can be expressed as:

favorable :____:____:____:____:____:____:____:unfavorable
         extremely quite slightly neither slightly quite extremely

2. I intend to purchase brand X of cereal within the next two weeks:

unlikely ____ ____ ____ ____ ____ ____ ____ likely
          1   2   3   4   5   6   7

3. With respect to its effect on my stomach, Pain Reliever X is for me:

[ ]   [ ]   [ ]   [ ]   [ ]
very   gentle   neither   upsetting   very
gentle   gentle nor   upsetting
                    upsetting

4. Graphic feature #2 on word processing package L is

                                   neither
                                   useless
                                   nor
         very   somewhat slightly useful   slightly somewhat very
useless ____   _____ _____ _____   _____ _____ ____ useful

5. Exercising at Health Club Y is

pleasant :____:____:____:____:____:____:____:unpleasant

6. The carbonation in fruit juice K is

bad ____ ____ ____ ____ ____ ____ ____ good
    −3   −2   −1   0   +1   +2   +3

Figure 1.3 Examples of the semantic differential

each scale step between the end-points has a modifier attached to it (i.e. "extremely", "quite", etc.). These tend to make the scale interval-like in character (e.g. Cliff, 1959; Howe, 1962; Messick, 1957), although the version shown in example 5 in Figure 1.3 without adverbs often works equally well. The semantic differential serves well in the measurement of attitudes toward political issues or persons (example 1), attitudes toward objects, services, products, or brands (examples 4 and 5), intentions to buy (example 2), beliefs about the consequences of product use (example 3), and evaluations of product attributes or the consequences of use (example 6). Notice also that numbers are often included to aid in data entry (example 2) or to create an artificial zero point (example 6). Finally, although seven-point scale steps are the most common, five-point (example 3) or even nine-point or eleven-point scales (not shown) are sometimes used. Some research indicates that at least five points should be used, so that some assurance is gained that the distributional properties of responses will be satisfactory (Olsson, 1979b). Most applications of the semantic differential employ multiple items (e.g. wise–foolish, like–dislike, favorable–unfavorable) for each attitude, intention, etc. to be measured. A total score is then computed for each respondent as the sum of responses to the multiple items.

The semantic differential is simple to use, versatile, and shows strong face validity. Research reveals that people make hundreds of fine-grained evaluations; at least language is spiced with hundreds of evaluative terms. Nevertheless, most evaluations tend to reflect either a relatively pure evaluative dimension or either a potency or activity dimension (Osgood, Suci, and Tannenbaum, 1971; Snider and Osgood, 1969). For example, in most cases pleasant–unpleasant, like–dislike, and good–bad load on an evaluative factor; strong–weak, large–small, powerful–powerless load on a potency factor; and fast–slow, excited–unexcited, and aroused–unaroused load on an activity factor. Interestingly, the semantic differential has shown amazing applicability and consistency across cultures (e.g. Osgood, May, and Miron, 1975). For additional research on the semantic differential, see Chapman, McCrary, Chapman, and Martin (1980) and Mann, Phillips, and Thompson (1979).

Another popular scale that is approximately interval in character is the *Likert* or *summated rating scale*. A Likert scale is a series of statements regarding an attitudinal object for which a respondent is asked to agree or disagree. For example, one item from a scale measuring attitude toward dieting might read:

"Please express your extent of agreement or disagreement with the following:

"1. Controlling the amount of fat in one's diet is important for maintaining a healthy life-style (circle number corresponding to your reaction to this statement):"

1	2	3	4	5
Strongly disagree	Disagree	Neither disagree nor agree	Agree	Strongly agree

Kuhl, J. 1985: Volitional mediators of cognition-behavior consistency: self-regulatory processes and action versus state orientation. In J. Kuhl and J. Beckmann (eds), *Action Control: From Cognition to Behavior*, New York: Springer, 101–28.

Lessler, J. T. and Kalsbeek, W. D. 1992: *Nonsampling Error in Surveys*, New York: Wiley.

Likert, R. 1967: The method of constructing an attitude scale. In M. Fishbein (ed.), *Readings in Attitude Theory and Measurement*, New York: Wiley, 90–5.

Lodge, M. 1981: *Magnitude Scaling: Quantitative Measurement of Opinions*, Beverly Hills, CA: Sage Publications.

Lord, F. M. and Novick, M. R. 1968: *Statistical Theories of Mental Test Scores*, Reading, MA: Addison-Wesley.

Mann, I. T., Phillips, J. L. and Thompson, J. L. 1979: An examination of methodological issues relevant to the use and interpretation of the semantic differential, *Applied Psychological Measurement*, 3, 213–29.

Mardia, K. V. 1970: Measures of multivariate skewness and kurtosis with applications. *Biometrika*, 57, 519–30.

McClendon, M. 1991: Acquiescence and recency response – order effects in interview surveys. *Sociological Methods of Research*, 20, 60–103.

Messick, S. J. 1957: Metric properties of the semantic differential. *Educational and Psychological Measurement*, 17, 200–6.

Michell, J. 1986: Measurement scales and statistics: a clash of paradigms. *Psychological Bulletin*, 100, 398–407.

Miller, D. C. 1991: *Handbook of Research Design and Social Measurement*, 5th edn, Newbury Park, CA: Sage Publications.

Nicholls, J. G., Licht, B. G. and Pearl, R. A. 1982: Some dangers of using personality questionnaires to study personality. *Psychological Bulletin*, 92, 572–80.

Oliva, T. A. and Reidenbach, R. E. 1987: Extensions of Bagozzi's holistic construal. In A. F. Firat, N. Dholakis and R. P. Bagozzi (eds), *Philosophical and Radical Thought in Marketing*, Lexington, MA: Lexington Books, 135–53.

Olsson, U. 1979a: Maximum likelihood estimation of the polychoric correlation coefficient. *Psychometrika*, 44, 443–60.

Olsson, U. 1979b: On the robustness of factor analysis against crude classification of the observations. *Multivariate Behavioral Research*, 14, 485–500.

Osgood, C. E., May, W. H. and Miron, M. S. 1975: *Cross Cultural Universals of Affective Meaning*. Urbana, IL: University of Illinois Press.

Osgood, C. E., Suci, G. J. and Tannenbaum, P. H. 1971: *The Measurement of Meaning*. Chicago, IL: University of Illinois Press.

Parkes, K. 1990: Coping, negative affectivity, and the work environment: additive and interactive predictors of mental health. *Journal of Applied Psychology*, 75, 399–409.

Paulhus, D. L. 1984: Two-component models of socially desirable responding. *Journal of Personality and Social Psychology*, 46, 598–609.

Paulhus, D. L. 1989: Social desirable responding: some new solutions to old problems. In D. M. Buss and N. Cantor (eds), *Personality Psychology: Recent Trends and Emerging Directions*, New York: Springer Verlag, 201–9.

Payne, S. 1951: *The Art of Asking Questions*, Princeton: Princeton University Press.

Petrie, H. G. 1971: A dogma of operationalism in the social sciences. *Philosophy of the Social Sciences*, 1 (May), 145–60.

Petty, R. E. and Cacioppo, J. T. 1986: *Communication and Persuasion: Central and Peripheral Routes to Attitude Change*, New York: Springer-Verlag.

Putnam, H. 1962: The analytic and the synthetic. In *Minnesota Studies in the Philosophy of Science*, Vol. 3, H. Feigl and G. Maxwell (eds), Minneapolis: University of Minnesota Press, 350–97.

Ray, J. J. 1983: Reviving the problem of acquiescent response bias. *Journal of Social Psychology*, 121, 81–96.

Rosenthal, R. and Rosnow, R. L. (eds) 1969: *Artifact in Behavioral Research*, New York: Academic Press.

Rugg, D. 1941: Experiments in wording questions: II. *Public Opinion Quarterly*, 5, 91–2.

Schaffner, K. F. 1969: Correspondence Rules. *Philosophy of Science*, 36 (September), 280–90.

Scheier, M. F. and Carver, C. S. 1985: The self-consciousness scale: a revised version of use with general populations. *Journal of Applied Psychology*, 15, 687–99.

Schuman, H. and Presser, S. 1981: *Questions and Answers in Attitude Surveys*, New York: Academic Press.

Schwarz, N. and Wyer, R. 1985: Effects of rank ordering stimuli on magnitude ratings of these and other stimuli. *Journal of Experimental Social Psychology*, 21, 30–46.

Sellars, W. 1961: The language of theories. In *Current Issues in the Philosophy of Science*, H. Feigl and G. Maxwell (eds), New York: Holt, Rinehart, and Winston, 57–77.

Sheatsley, P. 1983: Questionnaire construction and item writing. In P. Rossi, J. Wright and A. Anderson (eds), *Handbook of Survey Research*, New York: Academic Press, 195–230.

Siegel, S. 1956: *Nonparametric Statistics*, New York: McGraw-Hill.

Silk, A. J. 1990: Questionnaire design and development. Teaching Supplement No. 9–590–015, Boston, MA: Harvard Business School.

Snider, J. G. and Osgood, C. E. (eds) 1969: *Semantic Differential Technique: A Sourcebook*, Hawthorne, NY: Aldine.

Snyder, M. 1974: The self-monitoring of expressive behavior, *Journal of Personality and Social Psychology*, 30, 526–37.

Stevens, S. S. 1951: Mathematics, measurement and psychophysics. In S. S. Stevens (ed.), *Handbook of Experimental Psychology*, New York: Wiley.

Stone, E. F., Stone, D. L. and Gueutal, H. G. 1990: Influence of cognitive ability on responses to questionnaire measures: measurement precision and missing response problems. *Journal of Applied Psychology*, 75, 418–27.

Sudman, S. and Bradburn, N. M. 1974: *Response Effects in Surveys*, Chicago: Aldine.

Sudman, S. and Bradburn, N. 1982: *Asking Questions: A Practical Guide to Questionnaire Design*, San Francisco: Jossey-Bass.

Suppe, F. 1977: *The Structure of Scientific Theories*, 2nd edn, Urbana, IL: University of Illinois Press.

Suppes, P. 1962: Models of data. In *Logic, Methodology, and Philosophy of Science: Proceedings of the 1960 International Congress*, E. Nagel, P. Suppes and A. Tarski (eds), Stanford, CA: Stanford University Press, 252–61.

Torgerson, W. S. 1958: *Theory and Methods of Scaling*, New York: Wiley.

Tourangeau, R. and Rasinski, K. A. 1988: Cognitive processes underlying context effects in attitude measurement. *Psychological Bulletin*, 103, 299–314.

Tversky, A. and Kahneman, D. 1973: Availability: a heuristic for judging frequency and probability. *Cognitive Psychology*, 5, 207–33.

Watson, David, and Clark, L. A. 1984: Negative affectivity: the disposition to experience aversive emotional states. *Psychological Bulletin*, 96, 465–90.

Watson, David, and Clark, L. A. 1991: "Self-versus peer ratings of specific emotional traits: evidence of convergent and discriminant validity. *Journal of Personality and Social Psychology*, 60, 927–40.

Watson, David, and Clark, L. A. 1992: Affects separable and inseparable: on the hierarchical arrangement of the negative affects. *Journal of Personality and Social Psychology*, 62, 489–505.

Watson, Dorothy 1992: Correcting for acquiescent response bias in the absence of a balanced scale: an application to class conciousness. *Sociological Methods and Research*, 21, 52–88.

Winkler, J. D., Kanouse, D. E. and Ware, Jr., J. E. 1982: Controlling for acquiescence response set in scale development. *Journal of Applied Psychology*, 67, 555–61.

Wyer, R. and Hartwick, J. 1984: The recall and use of belief statements as bases for judgments: some determinants and implications. *Journal of Experimental Social Psychology*, 20, 65–85.

Zaltman, G., Pinson, C. R. A. and Angelmar, R. 1973: *Metatheory and Consumer Research*, New York: Holt, Rinehart Winston.

Zerbe, W. J. and Paulhus, D. L. 1987: Socially desirable responding in organizational behavior: a reconceptualization. *Academy of Management Review*, 12, 250–64.

2

Qualitative Marketing Research

Bobby J. Calder

Qualitative research is epitomized in marketing practice by the focus group interview. Typically 8–12 people are seated around a table. They are usually recruited from a database of willing people supplied by the local facility where the session takes place. The participants may have been screened to reflect characteristics such as product usage. A "moderator" conducts the session by raising a series of issues and eliciting comments from the participants. Representatives of the client sponsoring the research often watch from behind a one-way mirror. The client may also receive a report describing the results across several of these sessions.

This is the prototypical focus group. On any given day in the United States, some 700 or more focus group sessions take place. With some differences, focus groups are common in Europe as well. The products involved range from common consumer package goods to the most specialized and sophisticated products and services. An example of the latter would be focus groups with physician subspecialists concerning expensive medical devices. The variety of this activity is indicated by the fact that lawyers even use focus groups to anticipate jury decisions, not to mention using them as a source of expert evidence and for marketing their own services. Clients range from companies to governments and political candidates to not-for-profit organizations such as charities and hospitals.

No reliable estimate exists for the economic scope of focus groups and other qualitative marketing research activities. But rough estimates converge on something over $400 million a year in the US. (See for instance *Advertising Research Foundation* (1992) that puts qualitative research at about 17 percent of total spending for external research services.) Goldman and McDonald (1987) put this activity in perspective by noting that it undoubtedly exceeds the gross domestic product of many small countries.

The extent of qualitative research, and the ubiquity of the focus group interview, is thus inescapable. So much so that one might think that such usage carries with it the presumption of usefulness. Yet there are many questions and concerns about the use of qualitative marketing research in general and focus groups in particular. Among some marketers the subject is even controversial and can engender rather heated debate.

This discussion deals with the issues that must necessarily confront the marketer who uses qualitative research. Various approaches for both the focus group interview and individual interviews and projective techniques are discussed. Based on this, implications are drawn for conducting qualitative research. This chapter does not, however, provide detailed procedural guidance for those unfamiliar with qualitative methods. For this the reader should consult the references below.[1] Concern here is with how to approach qualitative methods in a sophisticated way. The conclusion of the chapter broadens the discussion from considering specific methods to appreciating the distinction between qualitative and quantitative marketing research.

Background Insight

Much insight into the current use of qualitative research, and the ideas marketers have about it, can be gained from exploring the historical development of the field. In one way this development was quite definite; in another, it was highly diffuse. The definite side occurred during World War II when two social scientists, Robert Merton and Paul Lazarsfeld, developed an interview technique in the course of their research on the impact of war-related communications (Merton, 1987). Initially the interview was used to assess a radio program intended to build morale. As participants listened to the program they pressed a red button when they had a negative reaction and a green button when they had a positive one. Afterward the interviewer used a cumulative record across all the participants to question people about their reactions to parts of the program that were especially negative or positive. They came to call this technique the "focussed interview."

The key to the technique, and Merton's original inspiration, was focusing the participants on particular stimuli and getting their specific reaction to the stimuli. This focusing made the participants' comments more understandable. Without it people's comments would be more general and vaguer. Moreover, knowing what people were reacting to made it much easier to understand what they were saying. In the course of their research Merton and Lazarsfeld used the focussed interview in many settings, both with groups and individuals. A description of it was published first as an article (Merton and Kendall, 1946) and then as a book in 1956 (now available as Merton, Fiske, and Kendall, 1990).

The focussed interview found its way into marketing research, though exactly how is something of a mystery. Merton (1987, p. 564) describes the process as more one of "intellectual continuity" than "explicitly realized historical continuity" and as "obliteration by incorporation" (someone adopted the technique, then someone else took it from there, but later users did not explicitly realize the original use). In any event the name was eventually shortened to "focus group," though the term "focused group" still has some use (the double ss in focussed was dropped early by Merton's editors).

Besides its (dubious) linguistic triumph in creating the name "focus group," the Merton–Lazarsfeld idea of focusing so as to better understand people's comments was an important one and continues to be so. Much current focus group research relies directly on this idea. In some cases this reliance mirrors the original work. Kolbert (1992), for instance, describes focus groups for George Bush during the 1992 presidential campaign in which participants first listened to a speech during which they recorded their reactions by turning a dial and then discussed their reactions. More generally, it is still common to show people things (products, concept statements, ads) in focus groups and then to discuss their reactions.

Often the question is raised as to what is the advantage of interviewing people in groups. One of the most important advantages is little recognized. This is that groups are inherently focusing. Even without being presented with anything, people in a group must focus on the topic and what is being said in order to interact. They are not as free to wander in their comments as they would be individually. The group necessarily provides a strong context which has a focussing effect.

The name "focus group" might best be interpreted at this point in time as underscoring the self-focusing character of groups. The relevant comparison is not simply between interviewing people in combination or singly. It is between using groups to help focus people's comments versus allowing people more freedom in an individual context (which also can be useful). The term "focus group" is a way of emphasizing why the group is useful.

If the "focussed interview" was a definite contribution to the "focus group," it is also clear that present practice was also affected by more diffuse developments. One was simply the sociological tradition of interviewing people in the "field" in an open-ended, participative way. An obvious analog to this for marketers was to interview people in groups of their peers in a situation in which people would react as they would in their daily lives. Into the 1960s it was thus common to hold focus groups in the home of a participant or the person who recruited the group. And even with the increased use of facilities, many (especially on the East Coast) focus group rooms were designed in living-room style. More recently conference-room style dominates, but attention is still given to homey touches. Participants are routinely offered snacks, etc. and an effort is made to use first names. But the focus group, however inspired by the sociological tradition, became isolated from methodological work in sociology and anthropology. The tradition served more to legitimate than instruct focus group work. There is a need, and I will return to this, to connect qualitative marketing research to sociological and anthropological thinking.

Focus groups were also linked early on with the "Motivation Research" school of marketing research. The driving idea behind this school of thought was the goal of uncovering hidden, or deeper seated motivations underlying people's behavior. Research should probe beyond simply what is said to get at these deeper motivations, which might even be unconscious or otherwise outside of people's awareness. Projective tests were thus widely used. Not surprisingly, another approach that came into use was patterned after the group therapy session. Focus groups were often conducted by psychiatrists or psychologists and sought to reveal deeper motivations as well as capture what was expressly said in the interview. This use of group interviewing was eventually detailed by Goldman (1962) who labeled it the "Group Depth Interview" (in a futile if commendable effort to avoid confusion with other focus group orientations).

The third, and most diffuse, development was the use of focus groups for efficiency and economy. Marketers saw in focus groups a quicker way to obtain information than conducting sample surveys and one that was less expensive. Linked to this was the idea that focus groups should ideally be followed up by a survey but that sometimes this might not be possible. According to Goldman and McDonald (1987), some of the very earliest group interviews were conducted for products such as Pablum for just these reasons.

We see then that the ubiquitous focus group is a product of diverse ideas. It carries with it the idea of focusing people through the use of stimuli and the group context itself. It also carries with it the sociological notion of the open-ended, participative interview in an everyday setting. There is the notion too of probing beyond surface reaction. And finally there is the thought, repeated and stressed in marketing research textbooks, that focus groups should be followed by survey work unless there are budgetary or time constraints.

Types of Focus Groups

This review of its historical development should make it obvious that there is no such thing as *a* focus group. The focus group is a product of diverse ideas, all of which are still present in current practice. But any one piece of research may be more or less influenced by any one of these ideas. The manager who says, "Let's conduct some focus groups," is likely to get almost anything. That most researchers would gather a group of people around a conference table is only a superficial similarity and a convention. What really matters is the approach taken, and this can vary depending on the researcher's particular idea of the focus group.

Phenomenological interaction centered focus groups

In 1977, I proposed that at least three approaches to focus groups needed to be distinguished in marketing research practice. More recently the Advertising Research Foundation's Qualitative Research Council incorporated this classification into their guidelines for qualitative research

(*Focus Groups: Issues and Approaches*, 1985). Of the three types, I consider one to be the most important – I have labeled it the "phenomenological approach."

The term "phenomenological" was drawn from the philosophical and sociological literature (see Calder, 1977, pp. 358–60). I have suggested that a simpler term might be "interaction centered" (Calder, 1988). In any event, this approach tries to understand people in terms of their own experience – an experience that is necessarily shared in large part with others who are peers with respect to the issues on which the group is focused. The only way this can be done is for the researcher to experience people's shared perspective and to describe that experience. The focus group enables the researcher to experience the experience of people in the group, to enter their world.

The phenomenological focus group has one overriding objective: to allow the researcher to share, participatively, the experience of a group of people. The focus group interview *per se* is thus a way of approximating a longer, more direct involvement in people's lives. It must involve natural interaction among the participants through which the researcher is able to take the role of the participants. This does not mean the researcher must act like a participant in the group session. It means the researcher must acquire the ability to see the world from the participants' point-of-view, to experience their experience.

The contribution of this approach is to serve as a bridge between the world of the participant and the world of decision-makers. It is the job of the researcher to make the decision-maker understand how marketing decisions appear in the world of participants. Decision-makers must see that it is people's own experience that leads to their behavior and that this experience may not be at all apparent from the perspective of the decision maker, who typically has a different perspective.

An example may help to make the use of phenomenological focus groups clear. Take the case of low income (at or below the poverty line) consumers who are focused on issues regarding the consumption of electricity. In a series of focus groups, comments such as those below were heard.

> Well, you know what it is, people don't make enough to pay all these things . . .
>
> Because I remember, I had car insurance, rent and that was it and everybody was like "Why you always broke? Well, what do you expect? You know it's like you never have anything to spend."
>
> It's hard, but what are you going to do. You have to pay it. You can't live without it [electricity].
>
> Well, I agree with what she says. You've got enough to pay your rent and that's it.
>
> Every month I get my shut off notice and I run over there. I don't get my check until the 2nd or the 3rd, maybe sometimes the 4th or the 5th, the last minute, run it over to pay that bill.

It's expensive in my old age, but what's going to happen. It's a necessary evil ... It's something you can't get along without especially if you're alone; you need to have a phone. You certainly need electricity. That's the necessary part. What makes it a necessary evil? Well, the fact that you have to pay so much for it.

The fact that everything is so high. And I feel that we are being ripped off.

From these comments and others it becomes apparent to the researcher that low income consumers are not just "price sensitive." In their experience paying for electricity is a trap. They have to have electricity no matter how little income they have, so they see their bills as not only "too high" but as "unfair" as well. Paying for electricity is akin to paying for air. It is unfair for such a necessity to take up so much of their income and to demand regular payment.

This view fits with a lack of knowledge about how electricity is produced. It seems like air in that it is readily available. Moreover, many aspects of utility service reinforce people's general point-of-view. Electric bills for instance are seen as arbitrary and incomprehensible.

The only thing I can figure out is that I use more kilowatts from one month to the next.

And you complain, I mean I can't picture a kilowatt; I don't know if it's a half cup or a full cup. All I know is I'm charged more than I think I should be charged. I don't have a legitimate complaint because I can't say I got so much and it cost me so much more. So get your bill and pay it.

But what are kilowatts? I mean, how can you say if you used this many kilowatts when you don't know what a kilowatt is?

I look at the bill but I really don't understand what they are charging us for.

They sent information about how to figure it out, but why go to all that trouble 'cause you just have to pay it anyway.

Once the researcher comes to understand the experience of these consumers, their hostility becomes understandable. This understanding can be conveyed to decision-makers who can then use this knowledge in marketing the service.

Consider another case in which focus groups revealed a strong opportunity in the market place (from Calder and Bjorling, 1981). A for-profit hospital chain was opening a new 100-bed facility in a town with two existing and much larger hospitals. Hospital planners worried that the new hospital's small size and lack of reputation might make it unattractive to the community.

Focus group sessions were held in the city's major neighborhoods. Although few people had any direct experience with the new hospital, it was not perceived negatively. Its smaller size and limited facilities were recognized. However, its size created the expectation that the hospital would be friendlier and more personal than the established hospitals. This perception led people to interpret practices such as serving wine with meals as personal attention. Although such practices might otherwise have seemed frivolous, they reinforced the perception of friendliness.

> Very friendly and you get a lot of good care there, The others are a little big for that kind of care.
>
> From what I hear, it has more personalized service. Mealwise, otherwise. You even get wine. It's more of a personalized hospital.
>
> I understand it has quite an excellent menu to choose from. Wine. They have the time to take care of you.

Another theme running through the group interaction was a feeling of identifying with the new hospital. People saw it as struggling against the bigger hospitals.

> The new hospital is on the outside looking in. It has to do a good job.
>
> I don't know whether they've been full even. They're fighting the battle against the city hospitals. They have to try harder.

In their minds, the new hospital *had* to offer more.

Although the perception of limited facilities was worrisome, this did not reflect on the entire hospital. Instead, this limitation was largely offset by reports that the hospital had extensive provisions for consulting with specialists in the event of complications:

> They have a good idea. They can draw from their video on doctors all over the country. They can call on a doctor clear out in California. They can talk to the doctor and he can watch.
>
> They have this thing where you can call around the whole countryside in case you have something they need to find out about.

From their point of view, people reacted to the new hospital as an alternative having benefits that the older hospitals, for all their superior facilities, lacked. Instead of ignoring the new hospital, it became apparent that new services and public relations should be considered to address this opportunity.

Phenomenological focus groups can also be very useful with professionals who are involved in a buying process. Doctors for example are sometimes resistant to presentations for a new drug that rely heavily on information from clinical trials. Focus groups reveal in some cases that doctors weigh their own results with a drug very heavily. They often counter research studies used in selling a different drug with the argument that "in my hands" the drug I am using does this or that. That they are not persuaded by larger samples than their own usage might seem puzzling. But it is entirely explicable when it also becomes clear from focus groups that doctors view medicine as art as much as science. The experience of the professional is another world that, as with any other, needs to be understood in its own terms.

These examples illustrate how focus groups reveal patterns of experience. They also illustrate the utility of such findings for decision-making. Many other issues can be explored through focus groups. Indeed, the studies above dealt with several other focal issues besides the ones mentioned. Phenomenological focus groups are applicable any time there is a need to understand the way a product or service fits into the user's world.

Clinical focus groups

The hallmark of the clinical approach to focus groups is that the researcher goes beyond understanding how participants view issues from their own experience. The researcher instead develops an understanding that participants could not articulate. And, beyond this, the understanding reached is qualitatively different from the participants' understanding. This approach traces back to the motivation research and depth interviews described earlier. The goal is usually seen as going deeper, beyond surface comments, to the real, underlying causes of behavior. These causes are assumed to be beneath the conscious experience of the participant. Obviously this approach is very compatible with a psychotherapy orientation (hence the label clinical focus group).

The important thing to realize with clinical focus groups is that the findings depend on both what is said in the group and on the researcher's interpretation of what is said. This interpretation is guided by the psychodynamic theory applied by the researcher. This theory guides the search for underlying causes of behavior. Furthermore, the researcher should be employing a particular psychodynamic theory, so that it is important for the decision-maker to subscribe to that theory. If the decision-maker does not buy into the theory, he or she should not accept the findings of the research.

Sometimes the researcher is not guided by a particular, detailed psychodynamic theory. The researcher is guided only by vaguely Freudian ideas – for example, that unconscious thoughts are primary, that they are rooted in early experience. There is a potential problem with this. It is not that these ideas might be wrong. They may be, as with any theory. The problem is that the guiding ideas may be so vague that the researcher has great latitude in reaching a conclusion. The researcher concludes for instance that some behavior reflects an effort to gain approval of the sort given by parents earlier in life. This may be true, but without more link to theory it is difficult to see why the researcher came to the conclusion. Clinical focus groups done in this way can thus have an ad hoc, arbitrary character.

Considerable caution is necessary in using clinical focus groups. The main requirement is that decision-makers appreciate the theoretical basis for the researcher's interpretation. This is not, however, to belittle the potential contribution of this approach. Many decision-makers have found clinical focus groups valuable. Some cases are in fact legendary in the folklore of marketing research. For instance, Ernest Dichter, a well-known advocate of the clinical approach, had women participants in groups focus on issues involving their resistance to adopting a non-dairy coffee creamer. The women were asked to role-play in the groups, a technique often used to get people to reveal more than they know. (Groups in which people role-play are sometimes referred to as "psychodramas.") Half of the women in the creamer groups were asked to role-play coffee, the other half, the creamer. When role-playing coffee, the women acted tough and strong. When role-playing the creamer, they were much softer, embracing others. This was interpreted in terms of underlying masculine–feminine personality dynamics. The successful recommendation was to feminize the creamer's packaging and to show male–female interaction in the advertising.

Exploratory focus groups

The exploratory approach to focus groups has been perhaps the most common one in marketing research practice. It is rooted in the notion described earlier that groups represent a convenient way to quickly interview people at a lower cost than a sample survey. With the increasing efficiency of telephone surveys, this cost advantage is not always as apparent today. But groups are still seen as quick and easy. One needs only to prepare a moderator's guide (list of issues to be focused on) and results are immediately available (indeed decision-makers can observe the group). Along with this view that the focus group is a quick and easy technique, there is also the thought that focus groups are necessarily either preliminary to a survey or even a substitute for one. This status is justified by considering focus groups to be "exploratory."

There are several versions of the exploratory approach. One is literally to conduct the focus group as a mini-survey. Questions are posed to participants, often in serial fashion around the table. The focus group becomes a quick substitute for a survey. With this approach it is seen as a poor substitute, however, and one that must be regarded as less than definitive, hence exploratory. If there is the possibility of doing a survey, focus groups are often conducted with the idea of testing the questions. The focus group can indicate which questions are good ones and whether the questions are understandable; however, it cannot reveal the answers to the questions. The focus group explores the questions, which are then used in the survey to obtain definitive results.

Another version of the exploratory approach is to view focus groups as a way of generating ideas. The moderator enlists participants' help in coming up with new ideas about product features, service requirements, and copy, etc. Such focus groups are in many cases conducted as brainstorming sessions. The groups explore issues to come up with things the researcher has not thought of. Further marketing research is necessary to assess how many people think an idea is a good one and to answer other questions about the ideas.

There is a third, more subtle variant of the exploratory approach. Here, focus groups are not conducted to generate new ideas *per se*. Rather the groups are used to stimulate decision makers. Their value is to let decision-makers "see" the customer so that the decision-maker gets new ideas. Advertising agencies, for example, commonly believe that having copywriters watch focus groups directs their ideas and sharpens their creativity. The goal is not finding out about the experience of the customer as would be true with the phenomenological approach. (Although in many ways the phenomenological focus group would be a logical extension of this approach.) With this approach, focus groups are exploratory in that they are a way of expanding the decision-maker's mind.

The exploratory approach, in all three of its variants, treats focus groups as if their value were limited – limited either to testing survey questions or generating (but not validating) new ideas or insights. Conducting focus groups in this way can be useful. Marketing research folklore contains many examples of successes such as the idea of marketing microwave ovens as a way to cook food extremely fast. On the other hand, the exploratory approach unnecessarily limits the use of focus groups and characterizes the method as preliminary to surveys. I return to this issue later in discussing the distinction between qualitative and quantitative research.

Very specifically I would resist the tendency to use focus groups as only an idea generation technique. If nothing else, there are many brainstorming techniques such as the nominal group, the Delphi procedure, and leaderless discussion groups that have been especially developed for this purpose. Moreover, it seems likely that focus groups might not be very effective for participant generated new ideas. The very focus provided by the group may inhibit such creativity. And while the group is useful in anchoring a discussion in people's experience, this is a drawback for fresh ideas. Fern (1982) even provides data that group, as compared to individual, interviews do not yield more or better ideas. This should not be taken as a criticism of focus groups, however. It is a mistake to use focus groups primarily as an idea generation technique.[2]

Other approaches

The three approaches to focus groups described here, the phenomenological/interaction centered, the clinical, and the exploratory, are readily encountered in marketing research practice. There may be other approaches as well, and this would not be surprising given the background origin of the focus group. Certainly new approaches may arise from the increased interest of marketers in semiotics and anthropology. In all, a diversity of approaches is healthy as long as researchers and decision-makers realize their differences.

Sometimes the development of new approaches is driven by the need of researchers to differentiate their services and of decision-makers to try something new. This leads to focus group innovations that are really not distinct approaches but procedural twists. Such innovations can potentially obscure the basic approach being followed.

There was, for instance, a recent swell of interest in the so-called "mini-focus group." These groups were composed of four people or so and supposedly combined the advantages of group and individual interviewing. While it is reasonable to adjust the size of a focus group under some conditions (say a smaller group for a more technical subject), the mini-focus group begs the question of how group size constitutes a distinct approach and how this approach might differ from those discussed here.

One troubling aspect of the different approaches to focus groups is that some researchers mix approaches and even mix them within the same session. This approach (if it can be called that) can be problematic. Consider a focus group following the phenomenological approach in which participants are interacting naturally and enacting their everyday experience. Suddenly the researcher switches from this mode to brainstorm new marketing ideas. Or the researcher injects a clinical probe of the sort, "Could you see yourself using the product in situation X?" where X is outside the participant's experience. Obviously this mixed-bag approach can lead to confused focus groups and confusing results.

Finally, our discussion of approaches to focus group interviewing would not be complete without recognizing that style also enters into practice. Specifically, there are several problem approaches that are routinely encountered. I have identified some of these as follows (Calder, 1988, p. 26):

- theater-in-the-round groups where the moderator puts on a show for the observers and participants;
- intrusive groups where the moderator's biases are forced on the group;
- professional groups in which people (who may have been in many groups before) are allowed to act out their fantasies as to how they would market a product.

Procedural issues and analysis

The references cited at the beginning of this chapter provide information about the practical steps involved in conducting focus groups. Although this information will be helpful to those new to the technique, it must also be said that much of this is due more to convention that to any methodological necessity. This is why I have emphasized the importance of the approach being taken. Being clear about the approach being taken is the best guide to actually doing focus group interviewing. Calder (1971, pp. 360–3) provides an overview of the implications for each of the three approaches.

There are some procedural issues that commonly arise in connection with any approach. One such issue is that participants vary greatly in the sheer amount of time they talk. The concern is that this makes the discussion somehow unrepresentative. It is necessary, however, to realize that uneven participation is a characteristic of any natural group discussion. Usually what happens is that some people talk with a great deal more redundancy that others. Also, it has been shown that some participants play a functional or socioemotional role in a group (e.g. Bales, 1953). They encourage and otherwise facilitate the group process as opposed to always contributing to content.

Thus, in my view, it is not alarming that participation is uneven in a focus group. Particularly in the case of phenomenological focus groups, this natural phenomenon is just what you would want. Extreme probing aimed at forcing participants to talk more is only likely to interfere with the group process and make the group experience more artificial. Likewise, people who talk, more, even up to 40 percent of the time, are not inherently "pests," as they are often labeled. Both the low talker and high talker can contribute equally to the content of the group discussion.

Beyond amount of participation, decision-makers often worry about the potential for conformity effects. "Someone says something, then everyone else goes along" is a common assessment of focus groups. Now there is no doubt that conformity can occur in groups. Studies demonstrate that it can even affect perceptions of the length of a line. But it would be a mistake to conclude that people always conform. Conformity may well be unlikely in groups in which people are peers with respect to the issue being discussed. Here people, especially in the course of an extended discussion, may well choose to discuss differences of opinion. In fact normal conversation probably gravitates to differences. It is also the case that a moderator can point out that what someone says suggests that they do not really agree with others, even if they have seemed to acquiesce at some point. In my view, conformity is something the researcher must watch out for. It is not the rampant problem that some take it for.

Whereas unequal participation and conformity are often overemphasized as problems, this is not to say that there are not issues that deserve procedural attention. One class of these is, I believe, particularly important and can be called "polarization" effects. A great deal of research indicates that groups can make people more extreme, either positively or negatively, than people would be alone. At a minimum this means that if people like something a lot in a focus group, they are likely to like it less in an individual situation. A moderator can perhaps avoid polarization by anchoring people (focusing on details) in the marketing situation of interest. The effects of polarization may nonetheless be varied and subtle.

Once the focus groups have been completed, analysis is commonly done using tape recordings. Stuart and Shamdasani (1990) provide a good discussion of the practices usually followed. Typically the researcher looks for patterns of material that form content themes that relate to the issues of interest. The electric bill and hospital case examples described earlier illustrate what is meant by a content theme. Verbatim quotes are often used to convey the exact tenor of people's comments.

The strength of the traditional focus group analysis is that it makes for a readable report that is geared to the needs of decision-makers. Its weakness is a lack of methodological rigor. There is no guarantee that a different researcher would identify the same content themes. And there is no way to check the conclusions since they depend so heavily on the researcher's judgment.

It may be that computers can be used to make the analysis of focus groups more systematic. Systems are available that find key words in a transcript and display that word in context. The length of the context can be controlled by the researcher. Key words, however, may not be sufficient to identify rich patterns of thematic content. More likely to be useful are chunking and coding programs. Here the researcher assigns codes to segments of the transcript. The programs can then search for and display a given code or combination of codes. An overview of relevant issues and presently available software is contained in Fielding and Lee's *Using Computers in Qualitative Research* (1991).

The use of chunking and coding programs would be a step toward greater methodological rigor. But in themselves these programs do not replace the judgement of the researcher. They only assure a complete search of the data.

Nor is it clear that trying to objectify the researcher's judgement is, even in principle, an entirely good idea. It may be that an attempt to develop more data-analytic techniques might lead to more superficial conclusions. Richards and Richards worry that "the computer offers a Trojan horse for infiltrating into qualitative research the narrowest goals of quantitative sociology" (1991, p. 40).

The dangers of more systematic analysis need to be weighed against the reality that focus groups are often analyzed almost casually in marketing research practice. Researchers "debrief" decision-makers after the group and/or submit a summary report without even listening to a tape of the groups. While this may sometimes be dictated by business situations, it hardly represents good research practice.

A Call for Research

The above discussion highlights the real need for research on focus group research. That such research has been almost nonexistent is staggering given the widespread use of focus groups.

In particular, research needs to be done to validate the basic premise that the group does focus participants on the issues. This could be done by comparing transcripts of focus groups and individual interviews. Codes could be developed for the degree of issue – relatedness of people's comments. Alternatively, experiments could be done to determine how people respond to cues in groups versus individual interviews. The cues could be designed to lead people into more idiosyncratic thinking.

Obviously, a host of studies are needed around the procedural issues that arise with focus groups. Although there is a rich literature on small groups, it should be remembered that most of this research does not cover natural groups. Moreover, it is usually concerned with task-oriented groups.

Studies of conformity in focus groups would be especially useful due to the concern with this. Confederates programmed to behave in certain ways could be inserted into focus groups for this purpose. Conformity should be investigated both with respect to majority influence and minority influence. The literature suggests that minority influence might be more troubling in that it causes people to actually change their opinions rather than to just comply with the group (which is easier to detect).

The possible effects of polarization need to be investigated. Studies comparing what people have said in groups to their behavior in other (say, purchasing) situations would be valuable. This work might lead to interventions that minimize polarization.

Beyond this, descriptive research that simply shows what happens in focus groups might lead to new hypotheses. Coding systems already exist for describing interaction in groups. Bales (1950) Interaction Process Analysis is a well-known example, but there are many others. These systems could be customized to focus groups and might even become part of focus group analysis.

It is amazing how little we know, beyond the experience of individual moderators, as to what actually happens in focus groups.

Individual Interviews

Focus groups have dominated qualitative marketing research for several decades. Yet many researchers believe that individual interviews, often called one-on-ones, are as useful if not more so. The reasons they have not been used more, besides the visibility of focus groups, are logistical. One-on-ones take more time to conduct and are difficult for decision-makers to observe.

There are several advantages to individual interviews. A major one is that more information can be collected. Group interviews must fit within a short time period (usually one and a half to two hours, though in Europe longer groups are the norm). A five group study might yield at most ten hours of material. A series of twenty one-on-ones could easily yield twice this. And, as Levy (1979) points out, the issue is more than just the quantity of information: in focus groups "ideas are expressed that take up a disproportionate amount of time and are not useful to the general discussion" and focus groups "often have much repetition, get hung up on certain issues, and may not permit a balanced analysis" (p. 36). With individual interviews it is easier for the moderator to control the time spent on each issue.

One-on-ones also avoid some of the concerns about focus groups discussed above. Obviously the potential for group conformity is not a problem. And the less talkative person can more easily be drawn out.

It is also thought that people are more spontaneous in individual interviews. They are less considered about what they say and more likely to say whatever comes to mind. People relate to their own life in responding rather than to the comments of others. Their personal hopes, aspirations, fears are accordingly more likely to come through.

Individual interviews lend themselves to projective techniques too. People can be given ambiguous pictures and asked to fill in balloon captions. They can be asked to draw pictures about the product or its use. In one recent case that received some publicity women were asked to draw pictures in connection with a roach spray. The pictures portrayed the roaches as decidedly male. People can be led to project in all kinds of ways: to make up stories; sort photographs into groups that fit the product or not; or match products with animals, colors, places, or music. They can be asked to make up collages that go with a product, to act out expectations (pretend you were using this at a party), to make clay models, or even to write the obituary for a product.

These advantages suggest that individual interviews should be used more. The problem is that there is little to guide this use in practice. Certainly some researchers have an explicit approach to individual interviews. For most of these, this approach is clinical, some have a more semiotic orientation. Overall, however, most researchers seem to have no guiding approach at all.

The following case illustrates how problematic the approach to individual interviews can be. At this writing several companies, including General Motors, use "blindfolded one-on-ones."

People's eyes are covered during the interview. It is thought that this causes then to concentrate better. Probably it does do this (not to mention what else it might do). But if this is the rationale, why not use focus groups to achieve more considered responses? Blindfolded one-on-ones may or may not be useful. The point is that the rationale, as with the use of individual interviews in general, is not very clear.

One possible guiding approach lies in viewing individual interviews as the complement of the phenomenological focus group. The focus group seeks the shared meaning of social experience. Individual interviews, in contrast, would seek the world of personal experience. The goal would be to bring the researcher in touch with the more idiosyncratic thinking of the individual and the individual's personal situation. This approach might be called an "ideographic approach" to individual interviews.

An illustrative study

Sidney Levy and I (1990) conducted a study for the US Army that illustrates the possibilities of an ideographic approach. The study concerned all aspects of the recruiting process for high school students. Some prospective recruits were interviewed individually and some in focus groups at different points in the recruiting process including just after induction. The issues were the same for both – the role of family, friends, the school; contacts with recruiters in various facilities (including the Military Entrance Processing Station (MEPS) used for examinations); exposure to advertising and direct mail.

In many instances the findings of the individual interviews and the focus groups overlapped. They also tended to yield different information. The focus groups revealed more about the social process and how it involved various people. The individual interviews were more revealing of personal reactions.

The focus groups make it clear that the type of person targeted by the Army faced strong expectations that they would go to college immediately after high school. Most potential recruits feel that it is assumed that they will go to college. They see this as the social norm for their situation.

> It was always assumed that I would go to college if I could.
>
> It is almost assumed that you will go to college. You only won't if you can't. Everyone puts it that way.
>
> I talked to an older friend in college. Found out what it was like. I think you start out with college in mind. With that on your mind, you talk to people . . . find out if you can go.
>
> They have a (computer) system. You can plug in location, what you can afford . . . It'll give you a list of schools. That's what people do, come up with a list of schools. That's what they're looking for.
>
> My counselor was good. She knew all about schools . . . whether you could get in . . . She knew I wanted to get away from home. She could tell me about a small school that would be just right. She knew all that stuff.

Looking for a job is not a realistic alternative to college. Any job they could get would be a dead-end, low-paying one. This is easy to see from other people around then.

> You know people who graduated like last year. They have jobs but they're not making any money. You know what I mean. Plus they're so bored.
>
> People who get jobs are not on the right track. They're going nowhere, in trouble . . . Doesn't matter if I take a drink, know what I mean.
>
> The first day of school I saw five guys who graduated last year. Got jobs. And they were at school.
>
> My boss at work. I see he's going to community college at night. He can't make it, wife, kids.
>
> I know like one of my neighbors went out and got a job after high school. Now she is going to go back 'cause you just don't make the money. It's not really an option – just to get a job.

The focus groups indicated that prospective recruits first come to question going to college, usually for financial reasons or because they dislike school.

Since getting a job does not appear to be an alternative, they are led to consider the military as a fallback. The consequence of this is that they feel pushed toward the military.

> About my junior year I thought about college. Decided I couldn't go. So now I am undecided about what I want to do. Maybe I'll look at the military.
>
> The Army is a fall back basically... not something you compare to college.
>
> It (service) comes across as an alternative. But after, like something to fall back on.
>
> I look at it like this. If I don't go to school right now, then I'll spend four years or two years doing something else (service). But I'll make that decision when I have to.
>
> I started thinking of the military the summer after I graduated. I was supposed to go to Loyola, but didn't have the money... I'm still not set on it. Might go to UIC. But maybe if I go into military it'll give me a chance to think, get experience before deciding to go to college. Anyway, I'm thinking about it since I wouldn't go to Loyola.

The individual interviews make it clear that the experience of being pushed toward the military is an unsettling one. When asked to anticipate what a recruiting station would be like (before they had visited one), many expressed intimidation and apprehension.

> The feeling I would get is that I'm going to be locked up for two years.
>
> A not so friendly feeling.
>
> Kind of cold atmosphere, not friendly, mostly.
>
> It would give me a lonely feeling.
>
> I would feel small, scared, cold, alone.
>
> I get a bad feeling, because they would try to get me to sign something I did not want to yet.

Those interviewed after visiting a recruiting station were reassured if the station was a smaller one. Even if the station seemed makeshift, this made it cozier and less intimidating. The larger stations and the MEPS seemed institutional and impersonal. Here prospective recruits experienced nervousness and a sense of being lost. The larger stations were described as follows.

> A building with a lot of books and posters, and information about the Army. They are going to try to convince you as much as possible to join.
>
> Just a basic building. Lot of people in uniform, lot of nervous people sitting around.
>
> Big building reminded me of school, what will be expected of me.
>
> A big airport or bus station, everybody is behind the counters.
>
> Like a school administration building. When I first arrived, I felt like everyone would be in service, but not everyone working here was in the service.

Prospective recruits were shown pictures in the individual interviews of scenes depicting Army situations such as a uniformed older person standing in front of people their age dressed in street clothes. Among other things this revealed a fear of failure underlying the nervousness about the Army.

> The drill instructor is trying to get them into shape. From the looks on their faces, a couple of them will probably be kicked out.
>
> The recruits are preparing for basic training the next day. A few will be kicked out because of attitude problems and the rest will get through training OK.

In the individual interviews people were asked, "If you were to think of the Army as an animal, which of these animals would it be most like?" They picked two choices from a list and explained their choices. The most popular choices were, in order: tiger, lion, bull, wolf, and bear. The least popular were, in order: mule, horse, dog, squirrel, elephant, cow, and cat. The Army is symbolized by the wild and more predatory animals. The fear of failure experienced by recruits is one of confronting something that is strong, tough, aggressive, powerful, big, and dominating.

Eventually the fear of prospective recruits is resolved into highly personalized expectations of triumph. Just after induction enlistees were asked to recount "a dream last night about what you would be doing a year from now."

> Be in Germany, find a nice lady to settle down with, have some kids. I'll be happy, making the best of it, working on tanks.
>
> I'm in a German pub, definitely very drunk with a lot of girl friends. We're on our way to ski the Alps tomorrow.
>
> I'm in Europe meeting important people in the Army while interviewing them, since I will be in journalism. I will be on the verge of getting into overseas television. I'm very happy and happy with myself.
>
> On active duty, working on my job. Sitting at a desk, probably in Texas. It's a whole new dramatic experience, and I feel good about it. I've accomplished something.
>
> Be overseas, hopefully into mechanics, having a good time. Will be in Germany and there is a lot to see there. More discipline and turn into a man and am able to handle more responsibilities.
>
> I'm in California attending the Defense Language Institute. Have a new car, lots on money saved, dating some cute, smart rich guy . . . happy, thrilled actually.
>
> I'd be over in West Germany or Korea or somewhere overseas enjoying the clubs and the food and all the great features of where I'd be and just expanding my horizon . . . and learning who I am in the process.

In sum, the focus group interviews most clearly conveyed the social situation of recruits. They are expected to go directly to college. If this does

68 BOBBY J. CALDER

not seem possible, they face no alternative but to fall back on the military. The individual interviews most clearly conveyed the sense of intimidation and nervousness that accompanies this. The fears of prospective recruits must eventually be resolved into positive expectations for them to enlist.

It may be that focus groups can obtain the same results as individual interviews, and vice versa. Nonetheless, it is my hypothesis that the two methods differ in the ease with which they can investigate social versus personal experience.

The Qualitative–Quantitative Distinction

In concluding I would like to turn from specific methods to the general qualitative–quantitative distinction. The view of many marketers is graphically portrayed in the left side of Figure 2.1. Qualitative research is defined by negative contrast to quantitative marketing research, typified by the sample survey. Qualitative contrasts in employing small, unrepresentative samples. Questions are not standardized for comparison across respondents and respondents may contaminate each other. Results cannot be numerically coded and subjected to statistical analysis and therefore are not reliable. There is in short a schism between qualitative and quantitative research.

At best the schism model fits and, no doubt, fosters the attitude that qualitative research is preliminary and expedient. It implies that qualitative research requires follow-up quantitative studies for validation. Indeed

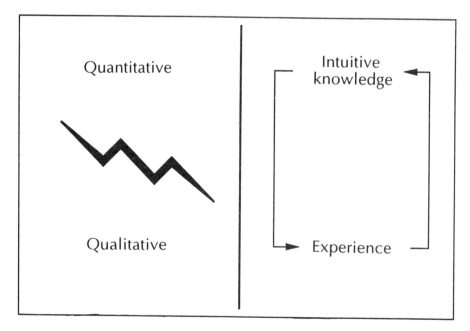

Figure 2.1 Opposing definitional models of qualitative research

qualitative studies often carry caution labels to this effect. It implies that decisions should not be based on qualitative research alone. And indeed companies have been known to bar product managers from even seeing qualitative research. At worst the schism model simply rejects qualitative research as worthless.

The schism view of qualitative research is, in my view, wrong. The reason for this is that the distinction it makes between qualitative and quantitative research is a false distinction.

All research methods are fallible. None ensures the right answer that will explain and predict people's behavior.[3] Each method has its strengths and weaknesses. Sample surveys and associated statistical analyses certainly have strengths. These methods also have real weaknesses. Briefly: Sampling may ensure that a sufficiently large and representative number of people are contacted. It does not ensure that the people, say, at the other end of a phone are paying attention equally or are otherwise reacting similarly. Moreover, it is now known that response errors due to question wording, order of questions, and many other factors may extend the error range of surveys well beyond sampling error (Bradburn, 1983).

It is therefore misleading to use only the strengths of quantitative research to define qualitative research as the absence thereof. What is instructive is to compare the weaknesses of quantitative research with the strengths of qualitative research. Qualitative research does not interview people in a constrained question and answer fashion. Most importantly, it does not assume that respondents merely have to output a thought fixed in their minds. There is a voluminous literature after all that shows people construct responses, that they think about questions, and that they can respond very differently based on situational cues. Qualitative methods are geared to following people's thought processes.

Neither space nor appropriateness permit a full critique of the schism definition and of its historical and economic roots. The point here is that the distinction between qualitative and quantitative research that it gives rise to is highly problematic. A more productive definitional model of qualitative research is needed.

Defining qualitative research

At any point a decision-maker has a certain level of knowledge about a customer. This is the intuitive knowledge gained through previous experience with customers. If this is not sufficient for the decision at hand, she or he will need to learn more about customers. This means that the decision-maker requires additional experience with customers. If much is already known, or if what is not known is very explicit, this experience can be gained via a simple interaction with customers. A survey might well be in order. If little is known, or if issues are vague or complex, more extensive interaction with customers may be required to gain the necessary experience. Focus groups or one-on-ones may be appropriate and new methods such as prolonged "ethnomethodological" encounters with customers may be desirable.

In some cases more than one method may be useful. In any case there is no great distinction to be drawn between methods. Both qualitative and quantitative methods can be useful. There is no question of *inherent* methodological supremacy. It so happens that some methods are qualitative and some are quantitative. All are in need of improvement. None will ever be the magic answer.

As portrayed on the right in Figure 2.1, qualitative research is one way of giving decision-makers experience with customers so as to increase their knowledge.

Questions

1 Explain what the term "focus" means in the name focus group interview.
2 How are focus groups and one-on-one interviews different? Describe a marketing problem that would call for focus groups and one that would call for one-on-one interviews.
3 Describe how focus groups and one-on-one interviews can complement each other. Which approach to focus groups best fits with this?
4 Distinguish between qualitative and quantitative marketing research. What are the implications for marketing research practice?

Notes

1 One valuable source of information about procedural issues is the publication *Focus Groups: Issues and Approaches* (Advertising Research Foundation, 1985). It is based on an assessment of current research practices. More expository descriptions are given by Goldman and McDonald (1987) and Stewart and Shamkasani (1990). Krueger (1988) and Morgan (1988) also provide basic procedural guidance, though geared more to social science than marketing research.
2 As an aside, it may be tempting for academic researchers to construe focus groups as an idea generation technique. This provides an easy unit for analyzing focus groups. It leads, however, to an overemphasis on idea generation in the literature and a lack of appreciation of other approaches to focus groups.
3 The present discussion is in reference to common marketing research practice. The role of theoretical studies is not considered. See Calder, Phillips, and Tybout (1981); Sternthal, Tybout, and Calder (1987); and Calder and Tybout (1987) for a discussion of theoretical and applied research.

References

Advertising Research Foundation 1985: *Focus Groups: Issues and Approaches*, Advertising Research Foundation, New York.

Advertising Research Foundation 1992: *The ARF Qualitative Research Market Study*, Advertising Research Foundation, New York.
Bales, Robert 1950: *Interaction Process Analysis: A Method for the Study of Small Groups*, Addison-Wesley, Cambridge.
Bales, Robert 1953: The equilibrium problem in small groups. In T. Parsons, R. Bales, and A. Shils (eds), *Working Papers in the Theory of Action*, Free Press, Glencoe, Ill., 111–61.
Bradburn, Norman 1983: Response effects. In P. Rossi, J. Wright and A. Anderson (eds), *Handbook of Survey Research*, Academic Press, New York.
Calder, Bobby 1977: Focus groups and the nature of qualitative marketing research. *Journal of Marketing Research*, 14, 353–64.
Calder, Bobby 1986: Exploratory, clinical, and interaction centered focus groups. *Journal of Data Collection*, 26, 24–7.
Calder, Bobby and Bjorling, Judy 1981: Marketing research for better planning: focus groups. *Hospital Management Quarterly*.
Calder, Bobby, Phillips, Lyn, and Tybout, Alice 1981: Designing research for application. *Journal of Consumer Research*, 8, 197–207.
Calder, Bobby and Tybout, Alice 1987: What consumer research is . . . . *Journal of Consumer Research*, 14, 136–40.
Fern, Edward 1982: The use of focus groups for idea generation: the effects of group size, acquaintanceship, and moderator on response quantity and quality. *Journal of Marketing Research*, 19, 1–13.
Fielding, Nigel and Lee, Raymond 1991: *Using Computers in Qualitative Research*, Sage, London.
Goldman, Alfred 1962: The Group Depth Interview. *Journal of Marketing*, 26, 61–8.
Goldman, Alfred and McDonald, Susan 1987: *The Group Depth Interview*, Prentice Hall, Englewood Cliffs, NJ.
Kolbert, Elizabeth 1992: Test-marketing a president. *The New York Times Magazine*, August 30, 18–72.
Krueger, Richard 1988: *Focus Groups: A Practical Guide for Applied Research*, Sage, Newbury Park, Ca.
Levy, Sidney 1979: Focus group interviewing. In J. Higginbotham and K. Cox (eds), *Focus Group Interviews: A Reader*, American Marketing Association, Chicago, 29–37.
Levy, Sidney and Calder, Bobby 1990: *Total Marketing: A Study of Image*, US Army Recruiting Command, Fort Sheridan, Ill.
Merton, Robert and Kendall, Patricia 1946: The focused interview, *American Sociological Review*, 51, 541–57.
Merton, Robert, Fiske, Marjorie, and Kendall, Patricia 1990: *The Focused Interview*, 2nd edn, Free Press, New York.
Merton, Robert 1987: The focused interview and focus groups: continuities and discontinuities. *Public Opinion Quarterly*, 51, 550–66.
Morgan, David 1988: *Focus Groups As Qualitative Research*, Sage, Newbury Park, Ca.
Richards, Lyn and Richards, Tom 1991: The transformation of qualitative method: computational paradigms and research processes. In N. Fielding and R. Lee (eds), *Using Computers in Qualitative Research*, Sage, London, 38–53.

Sternthal, Brian, Tybout, Alice, and Calder, Bobby 1987: Confirmatory versus comparative approaches to judging theory tests, *Journal of Consumer Research*, 14, 114–25.

Stuart, David and Shamdasani, Prem 1990: *Focus Groups: Theory and Practice*, Sage, Newbury Park, Ca.

3

Sampling

Seymour Sudman

Introduction

The focus of this chapter is on the use of careful probability sampling methods to produce estimates of the behavior and attitudes of a specified population. There is a place for loose sampling procedures such as focus groups to generate ideas about products or to help develop questionnaires, but it is foolhardy to think that a focus group, or even several such groups, can accurately reflect a total population.

Probability samples are defined as samples of a specified population in which every element has a known, non-zero probability of selection. Probability samples require that chance mechanisms such as tables of random numbers be used to select sample units. It should be recognized, however, that judgment is not excluded from the process of sample design. Much of sampling consists of designing optimum samples that either maximize information or minimize costs. To accomplish this requires some knowledge of the characteristics of the population as well as good judgment.

The chapter first describes a taxonomy of possible sampling methods based on where and how the data collection is to be done, and whether or not sampling frames exist. All sampling frames have problems, and the second section of the chapter describes how to evaluate frames and what to do about limitations. As an example, we discuss in the next section how careful samples would be selected for surveys involving telephones.

The next section deals with methods for increasing the value of a sample by stratification to reduce sampling variances, and by clustering and specialized screening procedures to reduce costs. Examples are given of shopping mall sampling and location of a geographically clustered ethnic group. This is followed by a discussion of how sampling variances are computed for these complex designs.

It is important to recognize, however, that non-sampling errors may often be more important than sampling errors. The next section discusses how these sample biases may be measured and corrected. The final section of the chapter discusses how sample sizes are determined using a Bayesian framework that relates the value of information for decision-making to its cost. It is obvious that a single chapter cannot go into the detail of a full book on sampling. For this reason, the chapter closes with a discussion of the major sampling texts available for additional reading.

A Taxonomy of Possible Sampling Methods

The market researcher faced with the task of designing an optimum sample for a specific study will usually have a range of options available. In this section we discuss these design alternatives and the criteria for selecting the best design. Of course, even before making this decision, the researcher will need to have clearly in mind the population that is being studied. Does this population consist of households, individuals within households, business establishments, college students, etc.? It will be important to recognize that the population and the source of information may or may not be the same. Thus, when individuals report about themselves, the population and respondent are identical; when individuals report about a household, the population is not the same as the respondent. Similarly, business executives may sometimes be the population, and other times be the source of information about firms.

The definition of a population also includes specifying inclusion and exclusion characteristics. Thus, with individuals, there will usually be specifications of age, so that individuals below a given age are excluded. There may also be specifications on many other factors such as geography, buying behavior, income, gender, etc. Similarly, for business establishments, there may be criteria on minimum number of employees or of minimum annual sales.

Mode of data collection

How and where market research data are collected will have a significant effect on what sample designs are possible, and what design is optimum. As a basic principle, most researchers use the cheapest data collection mode that is capable of obtaining the data required. Mail methods are very cheap, but are limited by the size and complexity of the questionnaire. If a mail method is used, it will be necessary to have addresses that identify the respondent, preferably by name. A common problem in sampling of organizations is to have a list of the organizations, but not of people within the organization. Sending the questionnaire simply to the company or to the president usually results in its being thrown away before reaching the person who has the required information.

Personal interviews can be conducted either by telephone or face-to-face, and in homes, central locations such as malls, or at business offices. Obviously, phone surveys require that the respondent have a phone available, although as we shall discuss below, phone directory listings may not be required. Face-to-face, or self-administered surveys in central locations require lists of such locations, plus a procedure for sampling within location. Household samples require a method for identifying sample households and the person within the household to be interviewed.

The availability of sampling frames

One of the most critical factors in determining a sample design is the availability of a sampling frame. If such a frame is available, the task of sample selection is significantly reduced. If no frame is available, researchers will essentially need to construct their own frames, a difficult, costly, and time-consuming task. It is not necessary that an available sampling frame be perfect. Indeed, almost all sampling frames have some problems. The next section discusses evaluating the adequacy of sampling frames and what to do if there are problems. It must be recognized, however, that some frames are so essentially flawed that it is better to ignore them and develop a new frame. Thus, for example, if one wished to study drug use among teenage boys, a sampling frame consisting of members of the Boy Scouts of America would not be appropriate.

It may be useful to give examples of frames that are, and are not, available. There is no good frame that lists all individuals or households in the United States. Such a frame is maintained by the US Bureau of the Census, but is unavailable to anyone else because of privacy concerns. There is a frame of all telephone numbers in working exchanges, although some of these numbers may not yield the desired population of households. There is a good frame of business establishments maintained by Dun and Bradstreet. There is also a good frame of all colleges and universities, but no good frame of all college students, although there are lists of students available for most individual colleges. There are frames available for members of professional organizations such as physicians, attorneys, and accountants. A first step in the design of any sample is to explore for the availability of existing sample frames. Consulting directories such as Gale's *Directory of Associations* is often useful.

Evaluating the Adequacy of Sampling Frames

Sampling frames may differ from the population in three ways:

(1) *The frame may contain ineligibles*, elements that are not members of the population. Thus, for a study of households or individuals, a telephone directory will contain ineligible numbers of businesses, government agencies and other organizations. The Dun and Bradstreet list of businesses will contain names of firms that are no longer in

existence. A list of students in a school may contain names of students who have graduated, transferred, or dropped out.

(2) *The frame may contain duplicate listings.* Some elements of the population are listed two or more times, because of how the frame was constructed. Frames are often constructed by combining lists. Thus, a researcher might construct a list of marketing professionals by combining lists of the American Marketing Association, the Marketing Section of the American Statistical Association and The Association for Consumer Research. Someone who belonged to all three organizations would have a triple chance of being selected in a sample from this frame. In a sample of respondents selected in shopping malls, frequent shoppers have higher probabilities of selection relative to less frequent shoppers.

(3) *The frame may omit units of the population.* This is by far the most serious problem. For example, the frame of marketing professionals described above omits all marketers who, for whatever reason, belong to none of the three professional organizations included in the frame. The Dun and Bradstreet list of businesses omits those that have just started and have not yet established credit records. A telephone sampling frame omits those without phones, and a frame of shopping mall customers omits those who never shop in malls.

Correcting frame problems

Some frame problems are easy to correct, such as frames with ineligible units. The simple solution in this case is to omit the ineligible units from the sample. Of course, this means selecting a larger sample initially to account for the ineligible units. Thus, if a sample of n is required, an initial sample of n/e should be selected where e is the fraction eligible in the frame. If e is not known from previous use of the frame, it can be estimated by a small sample of the frame, before the main sample is selected. A widely used method for sampling from lists is to take every ith item on the list. This procedure is called systematic sampling. When a sample of size n is required from a frame of size N, and the eligibility rate is e, the sampling interval $i = Ne/n$.

Duplication problems are relatively easy to correct. One way is simply to go through the frame and remove all duplicate listings. This procedure is satisfactory for small frames, but becomes costly and time consuming for large frames. For large frames, two methods are possible. The first is to select a sample from the frame and check all units selected in the sample for duplications. For sampling units listed n times in the frame, a subsample of $1/n$ is selected at a second stage, i.e. half of all units listed twice, 1/3 of all units listed three times and so on. This method gives all units in the frame an equal probability of selection.

It is sometimes impossible to determine duplications until after the interview is conducted. A household with multiple listings under the names of individuals in the household is one such example. Another example is shopping mall sampling where the probability of selection of a person depends on the frequency with which that person visits the mall. In such cases, weighting is necessary to obtain unbiased estimates. The weight is $1/t$ where t is the number of times the individual is in the frame, where t is determined from the interview.

The most serious frame problem, the omission of population elements, is the hardest one to solve. Essentially, three solutions are possible:

(1) Ignore the omissions from the frame and accept the possible biases that result:
(2) Discard the frame, and use a different frame or generate a new frame.
(3) Use the frame, but combine with another frame.

Suppose a frame exists that includes 93 percent of the total population, but omits the other 7 percent. This is the case for a frame of all working household telephone numbers since only 7 percent of households do not have a telephone. Virtually all market researchers would use such a frame and ignore the households without telephones. It might be argued that households without telephones are unlikely to be a significant factor in the purchasing of branded goods, especially durables. There is also the issue of cost of frame preparation. A complete frame of households requires interviewers to list and contact households face-to-face, and this is far more expensive than the phone frame.

For some purposes, however, the biases of such a sample would be serious. If one were attempting to study poverty households, or households without health insurance, a telephone frame would be inadequate. This illustrates the fact that the ultimate decision on the use of a frame depends not only on its completeness, but also on the purpose of the study. For market research purposes, however, frames with 10 or even 20 percent of the population omitted are often used. (We discuss below the estimation of and correction for sample biases from such frames.)

Some frames are clearly inadequate if used alone. These are frames that contain only a small fraction of the population, usually with some known biases. Some examples of clearly biased frames for the total population are subscribers to a magazine or members of an organization. Similarly, the Fortune 500 is a biased list of all business establishments since it consists only of the largest ones. A famous example of a biased frame was that used by the *Literary Digest* to predict the 1936 Presidential Election. This frame consisted of subscribers to the magazine, automobile owners and households with telephones, at a time when many people had neither cars nor phones. The *Literary Digest* predicted a victory for Republican Alf Landon, but the actual result was a landslide for President Franklin D. Roosevelt.

The decision whether to use such a frame and supplement it with another frame, or to discard the frame entirely, is based on cost-efficiency considerations. If using the frame can substantially reduce costs, as is the case with the business sample (see below), then it obviously makes sense to do so. If the use of the frame does not save any money, and may actually increase costs, it should not be used. Thus, for a sample of US adults, it would not be sensible to start with the subscription list of *Reader's Digest* and supplement it with a frame of telephone numbers.

Telephone Sample Frames

One of the two most popular sampling procedures currently is the use of telephone frames. The use of telephone *directories* is not satisfactory, especially in larger cities, because of the high percentage (sometimes 50 percent or more) of non-listed numbers. It is, however, possible to generate a frame that includes all working telephone numbers. This can be accomplished by using the list of working area codes and exchanges provided by AT and T. and attaching four random numbers to the sampled exchanges. The exchange list is updated twice a year.

The problem with this procedure is that while it includes all working household numbers, it also generates a very high percentage, about 80 percent, of non-working and non-household numbers. The methods currently used attempt to reduce the fraction of ineligible numbers while omitting only a small fraction of working numbers.

Most market researchers use computer-generated samples that are supplied by several firms such as Survey Sampling. These samples are obtained by taking all listed numbers in US telephone directories and sorting them into numerical sequence. It is then easy to determine the sequence of working numbers and to omit the remainder. The list is then also sorted against a list of business establishment numbers so that such numbers are omitted. This frame is not perfect. It still includes non-working numbers within a bank of working numbers and other non-household numbers that have not been screened out, but the majority of numbers in the frame are eligible. Since the frame is based on the most recently published directories, there are always some new banks of numbers that are excluded. Estimates of the percentage of excluded numbers are in the range of 2–3 percent.

An alternative method that includes all working household numbers, but is slightly more costly and includes somewhat more non-eligible numbers is the Waksberg–Mitofsky method (Waksberg, 1978). With this procedure, a four-digit random number is attached to a working exchange. If this number is a working number, calls are made until k additional working numbers in the same bank of 100 numbers are selected. (That is, the last two numbers of the dialed number are replaced by other random numbers.) If the number is not a working number, no additional calls are made off that stem.

The major advantage of this procedure is to reduce the number of calls to non-working banks of numbers. The method produces a two-stage self-weighting sample. The probability of a bank being selected initially is proportional to p, the percentage of working numbers in the bank of 100.

At the second stage, the probability of a household being selected = $k/100p$. Thus, the joint probabilities of all households are equal.

Sample Optimization

The information that is obtained from a sample is inversely proportional to the sampling variance. An optimum sample is one that minimizes sampling variance (maximizes information) for a given cost. Optimum samples can be accomplished by stratification procedures that minimize sampling variances and by clustering and screening procedures that minimize cost. These are not exclusive methods. Some samples utilize both stratification and clustering. In this section, we first discuss when stratification is useful and optimum stratified designs. This is followed by a discussion of clustering and screening procedures that reduce cost.

Stratification

There are four major reasons for optimum stratification:

1. The analysis consists of comparisons between strata.
2. Variances differ between strata.
3. Costs differ between strata.
4. Prior information differs between strata.

Comparisons between strata

It is often the case that one wishes to segment a market by demographic, psychological or purchase characteristics or by media usage or life-style. This segmentation is done by comparing across subgroups or "strata." The null hypothesis is that there are no group differences. It is usually the case that the within group variances are roughly equal, even though the means may differ. If this is the case, it is easy to show that the power of the test is maximized when the sample sizes in each of the groups are equal. For comparing two groups, this means that the standard error of the difference is minimized when the two groups are the same size.

Proof: $\sigma_d^2 = \sigma^2[1/n_1 + 1/(n - n_1)]$ where $n_1 + n_2 = n$.

To find the minimum, differentiate this function with respect to n_1 and set equal to zero. This yields the equation:

$-1/n_1^2 + 1/(n - n_1)^2 = 0$, and the solution is that $n_1 = n_2 = n/2$.

Since, in general, the strata will not be of equal size this means that smaller strata will need to be oversampled, and this will require some initial screening. To be specific, suppose one wished to compare African-American and white households on purchase behavior. It will be necessary to screen households by race and oversample the African-American population by a factor of about nine. In general when comparing two groups, the less common group is oversampled at the rate p/q relative to the more common group where p is the proportion of the more common group and q of the less common group.

Variances differ between strata

In sampling business establishments and other organizations, there is typically enormous variation in size of establishments and organizations that translates into large differences in variances when these organizations are grouped by size. That is, the variances on almost all measures of marketing interest such as sales and marketing activities and expenditures are much larger between the largest firms than between the smallest firms. In a proportional sample, the small number of large firms contribute a very large proportion of the total sampling error.

In a classic paper, Neyman (1934) proved that sampling variances are minimized if the sample for a stratum h is proportional to $N_h \sigma_h$. That is:

$$n_h^* = n(N_h \sigma_h) / \sum_h N_h \sigma_h \quad \text{or} \tag{3.1}$$

$$n_h^* = n(\pi_h \sigma_h) / \sum_h \pi_h \sigma_h \tag{3.2}$$

where N_h = total elements in the population in stratum h
π_h = proportion of total population in stratum h
σ_h = standard deviation in stratum h
n = total sample size
n_h^* = optimum sample size in stratum h

Proof: The proof uses the method of Lagrange multipliers to obtain the minimum sampling variance under the constraint that $\sum n_h = n$. The Lagrange function is the variance of the stratified sample, which is to be minimized, $+\lambda(\sum n_h - n)$. The optimum values for n_h are found by taking the partial derivatives of this function with respect to each of the n_h and setting them equal to zero.

$$F = (1/N^2) \sum_L (N_h^2)(1 - n_h/N_h)(\sigma_h^2/n_h) + \lambda\left(\sum n_h - n\right) \tag{3.3}$$

$$\partial F / \partial n_h = (-N_h^2/N^2)(\sigma_h^2/n_h^2) + \lambda = 0 \quad (h = 1, 2, \ldots) \tag{3.4}$$

$$n_h = N_h \sigma_h / N \lambda^{1/2} \tag{3.5}$$

$$\sum n_h = n = (1/\lambda^{1/2}) \sum N_h \sigma_h / N \tag{3.6}$$

$$1/\lambda^{1/2} = Nn/\sum N_h \sigma_h \qquad (3.7)$$

so $\quad n_h^* = n(N_h \sigma_h)/\sum N_h \sigma_h$

It will often be the case in surveys of establishments or organizations that the optimum allocation using any size measure would indicate a sample size in the largest stratum that exceeds the actual number of units in that stratum. The simple solution is to take *all* the units in that stratum. If this is done, then there is no sampling variance in that stratum, and the total sampling variance is very substantially reduced.

The ongoing Surveys of Business conducted by the US Bureau of the Census are examples of the use of this optimum design. In these surveys all of the establishments in the largest size stratum are sampled continuously while smaller businesses are sampled at a much lower rate and stay in the sample for only a limited time. This method reduces the sampling variance in these business surveys by about half, since the largest establishments account for about half of all the activity (sales, production, etc.).

If one is conducting a continuous survey on a specific topic, or has previous experience, then direct estimates of stratum variances will be available. If these direct measures are unavailable, more general size measures will be used. If multiple size measures are available, the one most highly correlated to the variable of interest should be used. Thus, in studying distribution systems, annual sales data would be used; in studying salesforce compensation or benefit plans, one would use size of salesforce if available, and if not, size of total marketing staff. Almost all size measures are highly correlated, however, so that any size measure will yield a far more efficient sample than using simply a proportional sample.

Costs differ by stratum or method

In discussing omissions from frames, a suggested solution was the use of combined procedures. It is generally the case that some of the procedures are much more expensive than others. Combined procedures may also be used with a single frame when cooperation rates by an inexpensive method are too low. The most common application of combined methods is for follow-up to mail surveys. Mail surveys are inexpensive, but sometimes yield relatively low cooperation rates with the possibility of significant biases by respondents most interested in the topic. A telephone follow-up to non-respondents sharply increases the cooperation rate and reduces biases, but is, of course, more expensive. Another illustration of differential costs by strata is in screening for special populations that are geographically clustered. Thus, it is much easier and cheaper to locate Hispanic respondents in certain Texas border cities, as well as in some neighbourhoods in New York City, than in suburban or rural areas.

In his same classic paper, Neyman (1934) demonstrated that optimum sampling when costs differ by strata is inversely proportional to the square root of costs, i.e.:

$$n_h^* = n(\pi_h \sigma_h / c_h^{1/2}) / \sum (\pi_h \sigma_h / c_h^{1/2}) \qquad (3.8)$$

Most applications for which costs differ deal with human populations where the variances are about equal in the strata and formula (3.8) reduces to

$$n_h^* = (n\pi_h / c_h^{1/2}) / \sum (\pi_h / c_h^{1/2}) \qquad (3.9)$$

Proof: The proof again uses Lagrange multipliers. The only difference is that the constraint is now C, the total cost of the survey, where $C = \sum c_h n_h$. It is possible to find the optimum h_h in terms of n, and then to find n in terms of C.

$$F = 1/N^2 \left[\sum (N_h^2)(1 - n_h/N_h) \right] (\sigma_h^2 / n_h) + \lambda \left(\sum c_h n_h - C \right) \qquad (3.10)$$

$$\partial F / \partial n_h = (-1/N^2)(N_h^2 \sigma_h^2) / n_h^2 + \lambda c_h = 0 \qquad (3.11)$$

$$n_h = (1/\lambda^{1/2})(N_h \sigma_h) / (N c_h^{1/2}) \qquad (3.12)$$

$$\sum n_h = n = (1/\lambda^{1/2}) \left[\sum (N_h \sigma_h / c_h^{1/2}) \right] (1/N) \qquad (3.13)$$

$$n_h^* = n(N_h \sigma_h / c_h^{1/2}) / \sum (N_h \sigma_h / c_h^{1/2}) \qquad (3.14)$$

To find n, note that $C = \sum c_h n_h$

$$C = n \left(\sum N_h \sigma_h c_h^{1/2} \right) / \sum (N_h \sigma_h / c_h^{1/2}) \qquad (3.15)$$

so
$$n = C \sum (N_h \sigma_h / c_h^{1/2}) / \sum N_h \sigma_h c_h^{1/2} \qquad (3.16)$$

Example 3.1 A computer software firm sends out information and a sample disk for a new software package to a sample of businesses and asks for an evaluation of the new product and potential willingness to buy. About a third of all sampled firms respond and reactions are very positive. Unfortunately, one cannot trust the results to apply to all businesses since it is likely that firms that were negative or uninterested simply threw the survey away.

A telephone follow-up is conducted with a sub-sample of non-respondents. Since costs of this phone survey are about nine times greater than the cost of the mail survey, a subsample of 1/3 is selected. This is optimum since taking a larger sample by phone would have meant that many fewer cases could have been obtained by the cheap mail method for a fixed budget C. The worst mistake in this situation would have been to spend all of the money on the mail survey. This would have yielded a larger, but dangerously misleading, sample.

Prior information differs between strata

In the last section of this chapter we discuss how to determine the value of information, and thus optimum total sample sizes for decision-making. We make the obvious point that the value of information depends on what the decision-maker already knows. If enough is already known, no additional sampling may be required. This also applies if the decision-maker has differential information available by strata. The optimum solutions in this case are described and proved by Ericson (1965), and are beyond the scope of this chapter. We give an example, however, to demonstrate an application.

Example 3.2 A manufacturer of electrical motors has developed a new motor that is more durable, but also more expensive and wishes to conduct a survey to get market reactions. His customers can be grouped into two strata: About fifty firms account for half of all his current sales volume, while the remaining several thousand firms account for the rest. Based on what we said earlier, one would expect that the manufacturer would survey all the big firms, and sample the others, but instead the survey is only of smaller firms. Why?

The reason is that the manufacturer has already been in steady informal communication with the big firms while the new motor was being developed. Indeed, their imput may well have shaped the specific design decisions. Thus, there is no need to survey them formally at this time. Similar decisions are often made by marketers who define a target buying population for a product by omitting certain demographic and geographic segments of the population.

Clustering to Reduce Costs

Clusters are units of the population that are found in close geographic proximity. A two-stage sampling scheme that first identifies and samples clusters and then samples within clusters can significantly reduce costs and, thus, make it possible to select a larger sample for the same budget. As we shall show, however, clustering increases sampling variance as compared to a simple random sample. Optimum cluster designs produce the smallest sampling variance for a fixed budget.

Table 3.1 gives examples of clusters that are of interest in marketing research.

Survey costs

In general, survey costs can be grouped into three categories:

1 overhead costs that are independent of sample size;

Table 3.1 Examples of clusters

Population elements	Possible clusters
US adult population	Counties
	Localities
	Census tracts
	Blocks
	Households
US telephone households	Exchanges
	Banks of 100 numbers
US shoppers	Shopping malls
	Day/time
Grocery shoppers	Stores
College students	Colleges and universities
High school students	High schools
Businesses	Localities
	Plants, stores, offices
Business employees	Businesses
Airline travelers	Airports
	Planes

2 costs that are related to the number of clusters;
3 costs that are directly related to the total sample size n.

The costs directly related to the sample size are the interviewer charges plus those sampling and data processing costs that depend on the number of units processed. Costs related to the number of clusters depend on the method of data collection. For mall samples, there will typically be an access charge of several thousand dollars to pay for the facilities plus an additional charge for each interview conducted. In sampling of schools or universities or airports, the cluster costs include payments to someone to obtain or generate the sample and to supervise the data gathering at those locations. Interviews conducted at multiple clusters require that interviewers be hired, trained and supervised at each location. Of course, these interviewers may be then be used for multiple studies.

A simple cost function that expresses the cost of interviewing, omitting overhead costs, is:

$$C_t = ac_1 + nc_2 \tag{3.17}$$

where C_t = total cost of study
a = number of clusters

c_1 = average cluster costs allocated to the given study
n = total sample size for the study
c_2 = average unit costs per interview.

This cost function suggests that survey costs can be reduced for a fixed sample size by reducing the number of clusters and increasing the sample size of each cluster. Typically, however, as the average cluster size increases, there is an increase in the sampling variance for a fixed sample size.

Effects of clustering on sampling variances

The cliché that "birds of a feather, flock together" reflects the fact that two units within a geographic cluster are more like each other on many characteristics than would be two units selected at random from the population. This similarity is called cluster homogeneity or correlation and is represented by ρ. Some marketing examples (and counter-examples) may be useful.

Example 3.3 Brand and product choice is a function of where people live and shop:

1. In given localities and at specific stores, not all brands and products are available. Consumers can only choose from among available brands. Thus, most dairy products are local or regional.
2. Brand and product choice is a function of income level of the household and, because of the cost of housing, neighboring households are likely to have similar incomes.
3. Ethnicity and race impact purchase decisions. Ethnic and racial communities tend to be clustered geographically.
4. Even widely distributed products such as Coca-Cola and Pepsi-Cola, or Chevrolet and Ford show regional differences in market shares that may be a function of climate or other historical factors.

Counter-example For some activities such as purchasing prescription drugs there may be little or no effect of location. Purchase of a drug depends on someone having an acute or chronic illness, and studies have shown zero or minute correlations between where people live and illnesses. Similarly, there is little evidence that network television viewing is much affected by geography.

An important assumption of simple random sampling is that the observations are independent. If everyone in a cluster is identical on a given variable, then regardless of the sample size from that cluster, there is only one unit of independent information. The actual information from a cluster depends on the cluster size and ρ the intra-cluster correlation; ρ is a measure of the degree of similarity between two randomly selected elements within the cluster and typically ranges between zero and one. Hansen,

Hurwitz and Madow (1953) showed that the sampling error of a cluster sample of size $m\bar{n} = n$ (where m is the number of clusters and $\bar{n}$ is the average cluster size, assuming the clusters are all of about equal size) to that of a simple random sample of the same size may be approximated by the formula

$$\sigma^2_{\text{cluster}} = \sigma^2_{\text{srs}}[1 + \rho(\bar{n} - 1)] \tag{3.18}$$

Proof: (Simplified by assuming number of clusters and cluster sizes in the population are sufficiently large so that finite correcction terms may be ignored.)

The total variance for a population may be split into two parts, a between cluster variance B^2 and a within cluster variance W^2 so that:

$$\sigma^2 = B^2 + W^2 \tag{3.19}$$

The sampling variance for a cluster sample may be expressed as:

$$\sigma^2_{\text{cluster}} = B^2/m + W^2/m\bar{n} \tag{3.20}$$

This can be seen by first assuming that all units are selected within sampled clusters. Then $\sigma^2_{\text{cluster}} = B^2$ since the within term vanishes. Similarly, if all clusters are sampled, the between term vanishes and $\sigma^2_{\text{cluster}} = W^2/m\bar{n}$.

The intercluster correlation ρ is defined as B^2/σ^2 and

$$B^2 = \rho\sigma^2 \tag{3.21}$$

$$W^2 = \sigma^2 - B^2 = \sigma^2(1 - \rho) \tag{3.22}$$

So $\quad \sigma^2_{\text{cluster}} = \rho\sigma^2/m + \sigma^2(1 - \rho)/m\bar{n} = \sigma^2(\rho\bar{n} + 1 - \rho)/m\bar{n}$

$$= \sigma^2_{\text{srs}}[1 + \rho(\bar{n} - 1)] \tag{3.23}$$

A researcher would usually compute the cluster sampling error directly at the end of a study using the methods we discuss below for estimation of sampling errors from complex samples. It is then possible to estimate ρ and to use this estimate for planning of future studies. The ratio of the variance of any sample design to the variance of a simple random sample of the same size has been called the design effect by Kish (1965). The idea of a design effect is useful in planning complex studies, but it does depend on the cluster sample size.

Optimum cluster size

Considering only cost, one would want to have a few large clusters; considering only sampling variance one would want no clustering. Obviously, there must be some level of clustering that provides the maximum information for a given cost. Using the cost function in Equation 3.17 and an estimated value of ρ, Hansen, Hurwitz and Madow (1953) showed that an optimum sample size within each cluster was:

$$\bar{n}_{opt.} = [(c_1/c_2)(1-\rho)/\rho]^{1/2} \qquad (3.24)$$

Given an optimum $\bar{n}$ it is possible to find the number of clusters and sample size for a fixed C or to find C if the total size n is fixed.
Proof: As with our earlier optimization proofs, the proof involves the use of Lagrange multipliers to minimize the cluster sampling variance subject to a total cost constraint C.

$$F = B^2/m + W^2/m\bar{n} + \lambda(c_1 m + c_2 m\bar{n} - C) \qquad (3.25)$$

$$\partial F/\partial m = -B^2/m^2 - W^2/m^2\bar{n} + \lambda(c_1 + c_2\bar{n}) = 0 \qquad (3.26)$$

$$\partial F/\partial \bar{n} = -W^2/m\bar{n}^2 + \lambda c_2 m = 0 \qquad (3.27)$$

$$\lambda m^2 = W^2/c_2\bar{n}^2 \qquad (3.28)$$

Multiplying equation 3.26 by m and equation 3.27 by $\bar{n}$ and subtracting, the difference is:

$$-B^2/m + \lambda m c_1 = 0 \quad \text{or} \quad \lambda m^2 = B^2/c_1 \qquad (3.29)$$

Therefore, from Equations 3.28 and 3.29:

$$B^2/c_1 = W^2/c_2\bar{n}^2 \qquad (3.30)$$

Solving for $\bar{n}_{opt.}$:

$$\bar{n}_{opt.} = [(c_1/c_2)(W^2/B^2)]^{1/2} = \{[c_1/c_2][\sigma^2(1-\rho)]/\sigma^2\rho\}^{1/2}$$
$$= [(c_1/c_2)(1-\rho)/\rho]^{1/2} \qquad (3.31)$$

Example 3.3 Sample sizes within shopping malls

It is often the case that the fixed cost of collecting data in a mall is about 100 times as large as the cost of an interview. Thus, the cluster cost c_1 might be \$2,000 while the cost per interview c_2 is \$20. If the study involves a nationally distributed brand the mall intercluster correlations might be fairly small, say around 0.02. In this case an optimum sample size for each mall would be $[(2{,}000/20)(0.98/0.02)]^{1/2} = 70$. The total number of malls m that could be afforded is easily found as:

$$m = C/c_1 + c_2 \bar{n}_{opt.}$$

Thus, each mall sampled costs $2,000 + (20)(70) = $3,400, and if $C = $17,000 one could afford to sample five malls.

Cluster Sampling with Unequal Cluster Sizes

To this point, we have made the assumption that clusters are all about the same size. As may be seen in Table 3.1, however, natural clusters may vary enormously by size and this variation can lead to increases in sampling variance if ignored. That is, if clusters are chosen with equal probabilities, and elements within all clusters are also chosen with equal probabilities, and sample sizes within small clusters will be small and the large sampling variance in these small clusters will sharply increase the total sampling variance.

The minimum sampling variance is obtained when the sample sizes in each cluster are the same. This means, however, that there are different sampling rates by size within cluster, with smaller clusters having higher within sampling rates. If the sample is to be self-weighting, the clusters are not selected with equal probabilities, but with probabilities proportionate to their size (PPS). The within cluster sampling rate is inversely proportional to the cluster size so that the sample is self-weighting. To see that this yields equal sizes within each cluster, let:

P_T = overall probability of selection = n/N
$P_{cluster}$ = probability of a cluster being selected = $MOS_{cluster}/(N/n)$
where $MOS_{cluster}$ is the measure of size for the cluster
$P_T = P_{cluster} X P_W$ where P_W = the probability of selection within the cluster

Solving for P_W:

$$P_W = P_T/P_{cluster} = (n/N) X (N/m\ MOS_{cluster}) = (n/m)(1/MOS_{cluster})$$

The estimated number of cases from a cluster is the number of units in the cluster times $P_W = (MOS_{cluster}) X (n/m)(1/MOS_{cluster}) = n/m$.

Note that this method does not guarantee exactly equal sample sizes in each cluster. If the measure of size is outdated or incorrect, the actual sample selected in a cluster may be higher or lower than expected. Large changes in measures of size over time increase sampling variability, but small errors in the size measures for a few clusters have little effect. Alternatively, in situations where it would be difficult or impossible to obtain a current size measure, the researcher may opt for a method that insures equal sample sizes within each cluster, recognizing that this may result in some small sample bias.

How to sample PPS

Sampling with probabilities proportionate to size (PPS) involves assigning to each cluster a sequence of random numbers equal to its size and then sampling systematically. The following steps yield a PPS sample:

1. Arrange the clusters in a desired order to obtain possible benefits from stratification by region, economic or other variables. (Arranging by size is unnecessary when sampling PPS.)
2. Obtain a size measure for each cluster.
3. Cumulatively sum the size measures over all clusters.
4. Compute a sampling interval s which is the total sum of all size measures divided by m, the number of clusters desired.
5. Choose a random start $r < s$. The selection numbers are r, $r + s$, $r + 2s, \ldots, r + (m - 1)s$.
6. A cluster is selected if the selection number falls into its sequence of numbers; that is, the selection number is greater than the cumulative sum of all previous clusters, but less than or equal to the cumulative sum including the designated cluster.

Example 3.4 Shopping center selection

A list of shopping centers is available that contains 32,500 units. We wish to select a sample of ten malls and 500 persons for testing a new consumer product. We do not have any estimates of the number of customers or visits at a mall, but do have two other size measures for each unit, either gross leasable area or annual retail sales. The sales measure seems slightly better for our purposes. The total sales at all shopping centers is estimated at $640 billion so s, the sampling interval is 640/10 or $64 billion. A center with annual sales of, say, $128 million would have a selection probability of 0.02. At each selected shopping center, 50 shoppers would be selected by the methods described in the next section.

Example 3.5 Shopping mall sampling

Shopping mall sampling is an example of cluster sampling discussed in the previous section with special problems because the population is mobile. The discussion in this section is limited to careful sampling within a shopping mall. Frames exist that list all shopping malls by size and location, so that there is no theoretical problem in selecting a sample of malls. The major practical problem in mall selection is that malls are private locations and sampling within them requires permission of the mall management, and payment of a fee. Many malls do not permit surveys, so that any sample of malls is subject to potential non-response biases. Controlling for region and city-suburban location helps to reduce, but does not eliminate, potential biases. Also, only about half of all shoppers in a mall are willing to be interviewed, and this creates the possibility of additional sample biases that may be partially controlled by controlling for gender and age.

Time sampling

The characteristics of persons visiting malls varies by time of day and day of week. Each day/time period must have a non-zero probability of selection, but efficient samples select periods with probabilities proportionate to the number of customers expected to shop in that period. Then, within that time period, the probability of a shopper being selected is inversely proportional to the number of customers expected, so that the sample is self-weighting to that point. The number of interviews in each day/time period will be approximately the same, but not identical, since the actual number of customers will vary from the expected number of customers for uncontrollable reasons such as weather and special events or sales.

It is typically assumed that customers sampled in the time period during which the study is conducted represent shoppers at other seasons. If this assumption cannot be made, separate surveys will need to be conducted at different times of the year.

Location within mall

It is easiest to sample shoppers as they enter or leave the mall. As with time, entrances should all have a non-zero probability of selection since different types of shoppers may enter at different points. Again, efficient sampling would select these entrances (exits) with probabilities proportionate to the expected number of shoppers who use them. Note that an entrance would typically be sampled at a specific day/time. It is not necessary that the interview be conducted at the entrance. If more convenient, sampled shoppers may be invited to a central facility within the mall where the interview is conducted.

If sampling at entrances is not possible or allowed, it is possible to sample locations within the mall, typically corridors. It should be possible to divide the mall into defined areas, and to sample such areas with probabilities proportionate to the traffic over them. The use of a single site in one part of a mall should be avoided since it will result in a sample biased toward customers of stores in that part of the mall.

Probability of visit

While almost everyone shops in a mall once in a while, there is enormous variation in the frequency of mall shopping by age, gender, and other characteristics, such as employment in the mall. Frequent shoppers have much higher probabilities of selection than do less frequent shoppers. It is possible to correct for this by asking, as part of the interview, how frequently the person shopped at the mall in the past two weeks and weighting the respondents' data inversely by their reported shopping frequencies. The two week period is used because it yields reasonably accurate reports of shopping behavior.

If the sampling is done within the mall, rather than at an entrance, a shopper's probability of selection will also depend on how long the shopping visit has lasted, assuming the shopper moves in a random way through the mall. In this case, an unbiased sample can be obtained by also asking shoppers at what time they arrived at the mall, and weighting inversely by the time between arrival and the interview.

Example 3.6 Area probability sampling

The use of area probability samples for face-to-face interviews with individuals or households is now uncommon in marketing research because of costs, but is still the method used by the Census Bureau and by others conducting large-scale government surveys. Such samples are really multi-stage cluster samples that use the sampling PPS procedures discussed in this section.

The selection stages in sampling are:

(1) Selection of Primary Sampling Units (PSUs) from all the counties or Standard Metropolitan Statistical Areas (SMSAs) in the United States, region or state being studied. These PSUs are selected PPS based on the most recent census data available. The number of PSUs selected is determined by decisions on the total sample size, and the optimumum sample size within PSU based on costs and homogeneity. It is often the case that optimum cluster sizes within PSUs average around 25 households or individuals. Thus, for a total n of 1,200, one would use approximately 48 PSUs.

An exception arises because very large metropolitan areas, such as New York, Los Angeles and Chicago, fall into the sample with certainty. Then, the sample selected from the New York metropolitan area with about ten percent of the population would be about 120 units in a total sample of 1,200.

(2) Within each PSU, specific places are selected, again PPS. These are cities, towns, unincorporated places or minor civil divisions.

(3) Segments are selected within places, also PPS. In cities these segments are usually blocks within census tracts. In rural areas, Census Enumeration Districts are often used.

(4) Individuals or households are selected within segments with equal probability. At this stage, it is usually necessary that all households in the segment be listed unless the segment had been listed earlier or good city directory information is available.

Decisions on the number of households to sample per segment determine the number of segments and places to be sampled. In many cases, it is found that average sample sizes of five per segment are optimum. This would mean that if the optimum PSU sample is 25 then five segments should be selected.

Note that in area probability sampling, it is a sampling rate that is specified at each stage and not an exact number of cases. It is possible that some of the census data used at each stage of selection may be outdated. That is, some areas have grown while others have shrunk. In this case, the actual sample selected will vary from the expected sample. Fixing the sample size based on outdated information leads to biases against growing areas.

There is a final stage of sampling if individuals, rather than households, are the sampling units. Household members must be listed and samples of respondents chosen. Since household size varies considerably, a sample of one member per household is biased toward smaller households. Either the data must be weighted by household size, or a household sampling rate, usually 0.5, is used. Thus, one person would be selected from the typical two adult household, but two would be selected if there were four adults. Households with only one adult would be excluded half the time.

Screening for Special Populations

It is frequently necessary to study small sub-samples of the total population for which no sampling lists exist. Thus, for many market research purposes one might be interested in certain ethnic groups such as African-Americans or Hispanics or high income households or households with a computer or recreational fishermen.

In such cases, screening of the general population will be necessary, and the costs of screening may equal or far exceed the actual costs of data collection. Even more with special than with general populations, the temptation is to use ad hoc convenience samples, but these are usually totally inadequate for making careful estimates about the special population. There are some methods now available for improving screening efficiency, depending on whether or not the special population is, or is not, geographically clustered, and is fixed or mobile (Sudman, Sirken, and Cowan, 1988).

Geographically clustered samples

Many special populations such as ethnic and religious groups or high income households are not spread evenly across the United States, but are found in a limited number of geographic clusters. There is a large fraction of geographic segments in which no members of the special population are located. Standard cluster procedures in such a case require large numbers of contacts in these zero segments that yield no eligible respondents.

SAMPLING 93

If the zero segments can be determined in advance from Census data or other sources, and can be eliminated from the sample, substantial cost savings are possible. If these zero segments are not known in advance, it is still possible to make substantial savings by the use of a modified Waksberg procedure. This modified procedure requires that initially a single unit be screened (usually by telephone) within a geographic segment. If that unit is a member of the special population, additional screenings are conducted in the segment until a predetermined cluster sample size $k + 1$ is reached. If not, no additional screenings are made. This eliminates all the zero clusters after a single call.

Among nonzero clusters, the probability of selection of cluster $i = N_i/S$ where N_i is the number of special population units in cluster i and S is the total size of the special population. The overall probability of selection of a unit of the special population in a cluster is:

$$(N_i/S)(k + 1/N_i) = (k + 1)/S.$$

As with determining an optimum cluster size, it is possible to compute an optimum value of $k + 1$ that minimizes the sampling variance for a given cost. In many applications this value of $k + 1$ is between 5 and 10. When the proportion of the total population in zero segments with no special population members is around 0.9, cost savings of 70 percent or more are possible. On the other hand, there are no cost savings when the proportion of zero segments is less than 0.5.

Use of incomplete lists

Even incomplete lists may be useful in identifying areas where the special population is located. Suppose one were interested in sampling Jews and had a list of members of Hadassah. This is the largest Jewish women's organization in the United States, but not all Jewish women belong. In the simplest case, assume that a random or systematic sample of starting points is chosen from the list and screening continues until k additional eligible units are located in the cluster. This procedure is almost identical to the procedure just discussed, and yields self-weighting samples. For telephone sampling, the telephone exchange of the unit selected from the list would be the natural cluster, while for face-to-face interviews the block or zip code would be the natural cluster.

Such a sample is biased if there are geographic clusters with eligible units, but none of them appears on the list. Such clusters have zero probabilities of selection. It is possible to measure the undercoverage from using a list for starting points if there is an independent estimate of the total size of the special population. This is done by estimating from the list the number of nonzero clusters and from the screening the average number eligible per nonzero cluster. The product is an estimate of the number of persons in the special population who have a nonzero probability of selection. The difference between this product and the known size of the special population is the estimated bias.

Dual frame methods

An alternative procedure for use of an incomplete list is to combine a sample from such a list with a sample screened from the total population. The total population sample is unbiased, but costly. The list sample is biased, but cheap. Hartley (1962, 1974) demonstrated that efficient, unbiased estimators are possible by combining the estimates, a procedure that he called dual frame estimation. It is possible, given the kinds of cost functions that have been discussed, to minimize the variance of the dual frame estimates by optimum allocations between the two frames.

Variations in density of special populations in nonzero clusters

It will often be the case that most members of a high income or an ethnic group live in a few area clusters with high proportions of the special population, but others are thinly spread over the remaining nonzero clusters. In those clusters where special population members are rare, screening costs will be much higher than in clusters where the special population is concentrated. It is possible to estimate the total costs of screening and interviewing for these different types of clusters and to sample them at rates inversely proportional to cost. Using this optimum allocation, major cost savings are possible if more than 80 percent of the special population are in high density clusters (Kalton and Anderson, 1986). A cheaper, but slightly biased sample may be obtained simply by omitting entirely those clusters where the special population is less than a specified small percentage of the population.

Non-Geographically Clustered Special Populations

It is usually more difficult and costly to screen for rare special populations that are not geographically clustered. One effective procedure is to use large previously collected samples or to add the screening questions to ongoing or future surveys of the general population conducted for other purposes. In marketing research, the use of one or more of the commercial mail panels for screening is also an alternative. Such mail panels have unknown biases caused by the very low initial cooperation rates, but have been balanced by major geographic characteristics. For special samples consisting of purchasers of a given product, sample biases may not be very serious. Thus, the Federal Trade Commission used mail panels consisting of about 300,000 households to obtain a sample of recent purchasers of hearing aids to determine if there was major consumer dissatisfaction with the products and how they were sold.

Network samples

In many surveys, information is obtained about all household members from one household informant. This information might be about ownership of products such as motorcycles or boats, behavior such as playing golf or fishing and sometimes even attitudes. This information is used for locating members of special populations. In theory, an informant could be asked about relatives, neighbors and co-workers living at a different location. Of course, since people have different network sizes, weighting is necessary for a network sample to be unbiased.

People who are eligible to be reported by n others are weighted by the reciprocal $1/n$, as was seen above in the treatment of units listed n times on a sample frame. An example may be helpful. Suppose a sibling network is defined as all households where the respondent or a sibling lives. Someone without brothers and sisters could be selected only if that person's household was selected and would have a weight of 1. Someone with 3 brothers and 3 sisters, all in separate households, would have $3 + 3 + 1 = 7$ chances of selection, and would get a multiplicity weight of 1/7.

There are two prerequisites for the use of network sampling. The first is that network informants are able to provide reasonably accurate information about all persons in the network on the screening characteristic. Past experience with the procedure has shown that this is the case with reports of demographic information and serious chronic illnesses such as cancer (Czaja et al., 1986; Sirken et al., 1975; Nathan, 1976). There is limited information on network accuracy of ownership and usage of products. The more visible and expensive the product, the better the reporting is likely to be. Thus, yacht ownership would be better reported than ownership of a garbage disposal unit.

The second prerequisite is less obvious; it is necessary to have an accurate estimate of the network size. This is very straightforward when the network consists only of close relatives, but becomes more difficult when more distant relatives are included and even more problematic when large networks of neighbors or friends are used. The most global question "do you know anyone who has . . .?" is useless because the network size is completely undetermined. There is some evidence, however, that good data may be obtained about persons in a work group (Sudman, 1985b, 1988).

Practically, most network studies use close relatives such as parents, children, brothers and sisters. This reduces the amount of information that is obtained, but still frequently cuts screening costs in half. Larger networks are still cheaper, but problems with data quality make their use questionable.

Mobile special populations

Suppose one wishes to study fishermen to determine how many there are at specific locations, what equipment they have been using and what they caught, or airline passengers to learn the purpose of the trip and why they selected a particular flight. Some of this information can be obtained by household surveys where the information is recalled, but often recall data are unreliable. In this case, site sampling of mobile populations is necessary. The methods used are simply generalizations of the procedures that have been discussed earlier for shopping mall sampling.

At the first stage, it is essential to have a good frame of the sites. Then for efficient sampling, it is necessary to have information on traffic patterns at the site so that days, times of day, and (if necessary) entrances and exits to the site may be selected with probabilities proportionate to size. Finally, if one is interested in distinct individuals and not trips to the site, it is necessary to obtain information from the sampled respondents about frequency of visits to the site so that the data can be weighted.

Computing Sampling Errors from Complex Samples

The procedures we have described for optimizing sampling design are intended to have an effect on sampling errors. Obviously, it is inappropriate to use simple random sampling error formulas for such procedures, as well as for complex estimates that involve ratios or parameters for linear models. There are several procedures available for estimating sampling variances from complex samples that are described in this section. The procedures all involve the use of computer algorithms, but are all about equally efficient unless the sample sizes are very large (over 50,000 cases). For most purposes, a researcher will use that sampling error program that is linked to the software package being used.

One important warning. All of the programs depend on identification of the cluster and stratum in which each sample unit is located. It is easy to put this information into a record in advance if one plans to compute sampling variances. The researcher who decides after all the data have been analyzed that sampling errors are needed will often find that the necessary sorting information is missing and will need to spend much more time and money on computations.

If the sample involves any clustering, the sampling error programs all use data aggregated at the primary sampling unit (PSU) level. Usually, these m PSUs are grouped into $m/2$ strata each containing 2 PSUs. If there are more than two PSUs per stratum, these are combined into two groups for simplicity. If, for efficiency reasons, strata consist of only one PSU, two adjacent strata are combined to make variance estimation possible. In this case, the estimate of variance is biased slightly upward.

For linear statistics of the form $\Theta = \sum_i \sum_j \sum_k \sum_l u_{ijkl}$

$$v(\Theta) = \sum_i (u_{h1} - u_{h2})^2 \qquad (3.32)$$

Note that the computer programs can handle either weighted or unweighted data.

Taylorized deviations

Many non-linear statistics may be approximated as polynomials by Taylor Series expansions computed from the partial derivatives of the functions. The approximate variance of the function can be obtained using only the linear terms of the expansion. This makes the solution similar to that given above. It is necessary that partial derivatives exist, but this is generally the case for statistical parameters used in market research. Given a reasonably large number of strata, a general form of the central limit theorem would apply. In practice, the method of Taylorized deviations is very widely used by the US Bureau of the Census and many other organizations with no evidence that the assumptions are not met.

Woodruff (1971) devised a computer algorithm for obtaining a first-order Taylor series approximation to compute the variance of any complex statistic, and programs for Taylorized deviations are available from Hidiroglou, Fuller and Hickman (1980); Holt, (1977); Shah, 1974 or Woodruff and Causey (1976).

Independent replications

One way to avoid any assumptions is to draw two or more independent samples in exactly the same way from the population. The basic definition of sampling variance is simply the variance between such repeated samples selected from the same population. This is a procedure that is sometimes used when work on a study is divided between two different data gathering organizations. Then, it is natural to compare the results between the two organizations as both a measure of sampling variance as well as of possible organizational affects.

The practical problem with this technique is that it makes it more difficult to design an optimum sample, because each independent replication is smaller. Also the number of independent replications is small so that the estimate of the variance will itself have a high variance.

Pseudoreplication

It is possible to reduce the variance of the estimated variance by selecting multiple pseudoreplications. For a single replication one of the two PSUs within a stratum is selected at random. Over all strata this yields a half sample. This process can be repeated many times (typically 50–100) yielding many pairs of half samples. The variance between these many samples gives an estimate of the variance (McCarthy, 1966).

Even greater precision is possible using a procedure called balanced repeated replication, BRR (McCarthy, 1969; Kish and Frankel, 1970). These procedures based on experimental designs proposed by Plackett and Burman (1946) are almost as reliable as doing all possible replications for

N–16

Replication	\	\	\	\	\	\	\	Pair	\	\	\	\	\	\	\	\
	1	2	3	4	5	6	7	8	9	10	11	12	13	14	15	16
1	+	−	−	−	+	−	−	+	+	−	+	−	+	+	+	−
2	+	+	−	−	−	+	−	−	+	+	−	+	−	+	+	−
3	+	+	+	−	−	−	+	−	−	+	−	−	+	−	+	−
4	+	+	+	+	−	−	−	+	−	−	+	+	−	+	−	−
5	−	+	+	+	+	−	−	−	+	−	−	+	+	−	+	−
6	+	−	+	+	+	+	−	−	−	+	−	−	+	+	−	−
7	−	+	−	+	+	+	+	−	−	−	+	−	−	+	+	−
8	+	−	+	−	+	+	+	+	−	−	−	+	−	−	+	−
9	+	+	−	+	−	+	+	+	+	−	−	−	+	−	−	−
10	−	+	+	−	+	−	+	+	+	+	−	−	−	+	−	−
11	−	−	+	+	−	+	−	+	+	+	+	−	−	−	+	−
12	+	−	−	+	+	−	+	−	+	+	+	+	−	−	−	−
13	−	+	−	−	+	+	−	+	−	+	+	+	+	−	−	−
14	−	−	+	−	−	+	+	−	+	−	+	+	+	+	−	−
15	−	−	−	+	−	−	+	+		+	−	+	+	+	+	−
16	−	−	−	−	−	−	−	−	−	−	−	−	−	−	−	−

N–16

Replication	\	\	\	\	\	\	\	\	\	Pair	\	\	\	\	\	\	\	\	\	\
	1	2	3	4	5	6	7	8	9	10	11	12	13	14	15	16	17	18	19	20
1	−	−	+	+	−	−	−	−	+	−	+	−	+	+	+	+	−	−	+	−
2	+	+	−	+	+	−	−	−	−	+	−	+	−	+	+	+	+	−	−	−
3	−	+	+	−	+	+	−	−	−	−	+	−	+	−	+	+	+	+	−	−
4	−	−	+	+	−	+	+	−	−	−	−	+	−	+	−	+	+	+	+	−
5	+	−	−	+	+	−	+	+	−	−	−	−	+	−	+	−	+	+	+	−
6	+	+	−	−	+	+	−	+	+	−	−	−	−	+	−	+	−	+	+	−
7	+	+	+	−	−	+	+	−	+	+	−	−	−	−	+	−	+	−	+	−
8	+	+	+	+	−	−	+	+	−	+	+	−	−	−	−	+	−	+	−	−
9	−	+	+	+	+	−	−	+	+	−	+	+	−	−	−	−	+	−	+	−
10	+	−	+	+	+	+	−	−	+	+	−	+	+	−	−	−	−	+	−	−
11	−	+	−	+	+	+	+	−	−	+	+	−	+	+	−	−	−	−	+	−
12	+	−	+	−	+	+	+	+	−	−	+	+	−	+	+	−	−	−	−	−
13	−	+	−	+	−	+	+	+	+	−	−	+	+	−	+	+	−	−	−	−
14	−	−	+	−	+	−	+	+	+	+	−	−	+	+	−	+	+	−	−	−
15	−	−	−	+	−	+	−	+	+	+	+	−	−	+	+	−	+	+	−	−
16	−	−	−	−	+	−	+	−	+	+	+	+	−	−	+	+	−	+	+	−
17	+	−	−	−	−	+	−	+	−	+	+	+	+	−	−	+	+	−	+	−
18	+	+	−	−	−	−	+	−	+	−	+	+	+	+	−	−	+	+	−	−
19	−	+	+	−	−	−	−	+	−	+	−	+	+	+	+	−	−	+	+	−
20	−	−	−	−	−	−	−	−	−	−	−	−	−	−	−	−	−	−	−	−

Figure 3.1 Examples of BRR designs for 16 and 20 pairs

means and are thus highly efficient for computer application. A computer program for computing variances using BRR is available at the Survey Research Center, University of Michigan.

For each pair, one of the two PSUs is chosen at random to be "plus" while the other member of the pair is "minus." The first replication is chosen at random with a plus or minus selected from each pair, except that a minus is always chosen in the last pair. For the next replication, the sign of the $n-1$st pair on replication 1 becomes the sign of the first pair on replication 2, the sign of the first pair on replication 2 becomes the sign of the second pair on replication two, the sign of the second pair on replication one becomes the sign of the third pair on replication two and so on. The process continues until the number of replications equals the number of pairs. For illustration, Figure 3.1 gives examples of BRR designs for 16 and 20 pairs.

Extrapolating estimates of sampling variance

Even though the methods given above are efficient and relatively inexpensive, it is unlikely that sampling variances will be computed for all variables in a study, or for all subgroups. Usually, sampling variances for subgroups will be estimated by assuming design effects for the subgroup are identical to those for the total population so that an estimate of a statistic for a subgroup that is p percent of the total population will have a sampling variance V/p where V is the computed sampling variance for the total population.

For all statistics for which sampling variances are computed, it is possible to estimate a design effect by comparing the computed V to that under the assumption of simple random sampling. These design effects will, of course, not be identical, but should form roughly normal distributions for items with similar properties. Thus, it is possible to estimate average design effects for variables when they have not been computed directly, and to estimate sampling variances by multiplying the design effects by the simple random sample variances for those items.

As mentioned earlier, these design effects may also be used for planning new studies. Remember, however, that design effects depend on cluster size. If cluster size is different, it will be necessary to first estimate ρ before computing a design effect based on the new cluster size.

Non-Sampling Errors

In many research applications, non-sampling errors may be substantially larger than sampling errors and need to be measured and, where possible, corrected. In this section we discuss first how sample biases and measurement errors can be estimated, and then the alternative methods of correcting for them.

Measuring sample cooperation

A first step, but only a beginning, to the process of measuring sample biases is a careful measure of the fraction of the eligible sample that actually participated in the study. Biases may result from sampled units that are never contacted as well as units that are contacted and refuse to cooperate. Measuring sample cooperation becomes more difficult, however, when one wishes to sample a special population that requires screening.

The question then is how to treat households who are never contacted or refuse to supply screening information. What is unknown is what fraction of such households would have been eligible if they had provided the screening information. The estimate that is usually adopted assumes that the screening rate for those households who did provide screening information is equal to the screening rate of those who did not. It is obvious that the ultimate cooperation rate for rare special populations is very sensitive to this assumption.

Users of survey data need to be sure what measure of sample cooperation is provided. Since low cooperation is often a sign of poor quality, some researchers will use a sample cooperation rate that ignores all non-contacts or households that were not screened. This artificially raises the cooperation level. At the least, any measure of sample cooperation should clearly specify how it was obtained. The lack of any information on sample cooperation is a strong warning that severe sample biases are likely.

Measuring demographic biases

The next stage in assessing sample quality is to compare the demographic characteristics of the sample to those from a validation source, usually the US. Census or a large Census survey such as the Current Population Survey. In many cases, these comparisons will reveal major differences by gender, age, race, income, education or other variables. It must be stressed, however, that the absence of biases on major demographic characteristics is not, in itself, sufficient to ensure that no sample biases exist on unmeasured variables. Similarly, for business surveys, one would wish to examine the sizes of cooperating firms with Census data on establishments and to compare sales data estimates.

Measuring purchase biases

For marketing research studies, it will often be the case that purchase validation information is available from a syndicated service or from manufacturer shipments. This validation information can be compared to total purchases reported in a survey if such information is obtained. If there is strong agreement between the survey and validation information, one would be much less concerned about major sample biases on non-measured variables.

It must be noted that reported purchase data are subject to both sample biases and measurement error. Thus, almost all surveys asking respondents to report liquor consumption obtain a much lower level of purchases than validation information based on tax records. Most of this difference is likely caused by respondents finding such questions socially threatening. Care must also be used in evaluating the validation data that may have problems of their own. Thus, shipment data may include shipments to non-households or out of the country; store scanner data are subject to their own sample biases and measurement errors.

Bounding the effects of sample biases

It is sometimes useful to think of a worst case scenario and to estimate the maximum effects of sample biases. This is easily done for binomial variables where the cooperation rate is c and the proportion in the sample for some variable V is p. An upper bound for this proportion is to assume that all non-cooperators possess variable V; the lower bound is to assume that none does. Thus the upper and lower bounds are:

Upper bound: $cp + (1 - c)$ Lower bound: cp
Thus, if $p = 0.5$, $c = 0.6$, the range would be 0.3 to 0.9.

For continuous variables such as number of units purchased or media viewing, a lower bound of zero is used. There is no finite upper bound, but it is possible to assume rates r times those of the cooperating sample and to see what would happen if $r = 2, 3$, etc. Note that as c gets lower and lower, the bounds become very wide and not very useful for decision-making. On the other hand, for high cooperation rates, the bounds may be sufficiently narrow so that biases caused by non-cooperation may be ignored.

Correcting for sample biases by post-stratification

The standard procedures for correcting for sample biases are called post-stratification. They involve sorting the sample by several demographic characteristics into strata, and giving each stratum a weight based on Census data. The larger the number of strata, and the greater the range of strata weights, the greater will be the effect of weighting on bias; unfortunately, bias reductions are accompanied by an increase in sampling variance caused by the weights. These potentially large sampling variances become especially problematic if one is attempting to measure trends.

As a rule of thumb, strata with fewer than 20 observations tend to be unstable, unless those observations are a large fraction of the total units in the population, as with large businesses. Thus, the total number of strata used are limited to about 5 percent of the total sample size. As with all stratification, one would wish to stratify on those variables where weighting would have the greatest effect on the variables of interest such as purchasing. Many surveys of consumer expenditures have shown that household size and total household income are the two variables most closely related to purchasing behaviour and if the sample is biased on these two characteristics, it will be useful to post-stratify by them. Additional post-stratification variables would be selected for their incremental effects on the estimates of interest. Efforts are often made to stratify by geography, but these usually have minor effects on estimates, both because the geographic biases are not large, and because geography is often only weakly related to purchase behavior.

Ratio estimates

The other principal adjustment procedure is an aggregate ratio estimate adjustment, based on validation data or past experience. Thus, a large food manufacturer uses a standard procedure of mall testing for new products. They have learned from past experience that estimates based on such samples overstate the percentage of new buyers an average of about one-third. They simply reduce estimates for any new product tested by this percentage. The assumption, of course, is that biases for estimates of the new product sales will be identical to those for previous products. To the extent that there is variation in bias estimates, this variation becomes an additional source of measurement error.

The Value of Information Approach to Sample Size Determination

The "classical" approach to computing a sample size is to specify the desired width of the confidence interval at a given probability level. This makes it possible to compute a sample size required to obtain that confidence interval. However, this method has significant weaknesses. It is seldom clear what criteria should be used in specifying a confidence interval, and in practice one often notes specifications that are unreasonably small given the resources available. The classical approach ignores costs and resources.

The "value of information" approach to sample size calculation, in contrast, explicitly considers costs and attempts to estimate the value of the information obtained. Again using an optimizing perspective, a sample size is selected that maximizes the net gain in value of information minus the cost. This approach is decision oriented, and consequently especially appropriate for marketing research.

Why information has value

To understand the value of information approach to sample size, we first must understand why research has value. Every manager makes decisions, and marketing managers are no exception. These decisions are not always right. Because of uncertainty in the marketplace, even the most experienced and judicious of managers are sometimes wrong. The value of information is that it enables managers to be right more often and thus to increase overall profits for a company.

Suppose, for example, that a marketing manager makes 100 new product introduction decisions. Given the manager's experience and judgment, suppose that the manager can make the right decision 65 percent of the time without conducting marketing research. Let us assume that marketing research will allow the manager to make the right decision 75 percent of the time (research information is never perfect and competitors may react in unexpected ways).

What, then, is the value of information? Assume for simplicity that the profit from a correct decision is $1,000,000 for a specified time period and the loss of a wrong decision is a negative $1,000,000. Simple arithmetic suggests that being right 65 times makes the firm $65,000,000 while being wrong 35 times loses $35,000,000. The net profit is $30,000,000. With information, and a 75 percent rate of correct decisions, the net profit is ($75,000,000 − $25,000,000) or $50,000,000. Thus, the use of information earns the firm an additional $20,000,000. If the cost of information is less than $20,000,000, there is a net gain for the firm.

Note that the company does not make $200,000 from each research project. On average, this is true, but the value of any given research project can vary. Also, the value of any given project is not really known in advance. Information has value in a specific project only if it causes a change from an incorrect to a correct decision, and, of course, one doesn't know in advance when this will happen.

Factors related to the value of information

The following factors are related to the value of information:

(1) *Prior uncertainty* about the proper course of action. How much would you pay for information on the direction the sun will rise tomorrow morning? Most people would be unwilling to pay anything for this information because they already know the answer.

We have often seen managers who are sure that they know what is happening in the market. They will not accept research findings that contradict their preconceptions. Those preconceptions may be incorrect, but, even so, new information has no value for these managers, and marketing research should not be done.

(2) *Gains or losses* available from the decision. Who will pay more for a research project: General Motors in studying reactions to a new electric car or a hardware store owner in studying customers' perceptions about service at the store? The answer is "General Motors," and the reason is that GM has far more money at stake than the local hardware store dealer. Tooling

up for and marketing a new car model can cost hundreds of millions of dollars.

Note, by the way, that the value of information does not depend on ability to pay. It is not that GM has more money to spend, it is that they have more to gain or lose from a decision.

(3) *Nearness to breakeven* This indicates the likelihood that research affects the decision. Suppose, for example, that a company is introducing a new home appliance and has computed the breakeven point to be 100,000 units. A manager is asked for his best "pre-research" estimate of potential sales for the new product. Research will be more useful if the manager's estimate is 110,000 units than if the manager's estimate is 1,000,000 units.

When the estimate is near the breakeven point, whether below or above, new information has a high likelihood of affecting the decision. On the other hand, when the estimate is substantially above or below the breakeven point, it is unlikely the decision will be affected. New information might change the specific estimate of profits resulting from a product introduction, but the decision to introduce the product is less and less likely to change as we go farther from breakeven.

Estimating the value of information for a specific project

For decisions such as whether or not to market a new product, it is possible to quantify prior uncertainty, gain or loss potential, and nearness to breakeven, and to compute a dollar value for information.

Assume a simple profit function for marketing a new product:

$$R = (kx - K) \qquad (3.33)$$

where R is the total profit or return on investment realized within some time period, K is the fixed cost necessary to market the product, k is the contribution to profit of each item sold (the difference between the selling price and variable costs), and x is the actual number sold in the specified time period. Given this profit function, the breakeven sales volume is

$$X_b = K/k \qquad (3.34)$$

For research planning purposes, the fixed cost, K, should not include "sunk costs." It should include expenditures for new plants and new equipment, if needed, and for introductory marketing costs, but it should not include costs of existing plants or R and D costs spent in developing the product. These costs have already been incurred regardless of whether the product is marketed, and thus should play no role in the decision to market.

Estimating Prior Uncertainty

The first step in estimating the value of information for new product research is to get the decision-maker to provide explicit estimates regarding (1) the number of units of the new product which can be sold and (2) a measure of uncertainty regarding this estimate. The uncertainty measure directly indicates prior uncertainty, and the uncertainty measure along with the sales estimate allow the calculation of nearness to breakeven.

Sales estimates usually are easy to get from managers. A manager is likely to have some idea of market size, competitive environment, and competitors' sales volumes in the product category (this information comes from the company's marketing information system). Knowing the advantages of the new product and its proposed selling price, the manager can make a preliminary estimate of sales. We label this estimate X_p.

It is more difficult to get decision-makers to quantify their uncertainty, but this is also possible. One can start by asking about the shape of the distribution around the best estimate. The question might be "Is it equally likely that sales will be higher or lower than your best estimate?" Usually, this will be the case, and this implies that the decision-maker's prior distribution is symmetric. The most widely known and easiest distribution to use is the normal distribution. It is not necessary that the decision-maker's distribution be normal, or even symmetric, but since it greatly simplifies discussion and computation of the value of information we shall assume normality.

The normal distribution is fully described by two parameters, the mean and standard deviation. A natural measure of the decision-maker's uncertainty is the standard deviation, The larger the standard deviation, the greater the uncertainty. Decision-makers often lack the statistical knowledge to answer a question such as "What standard deviation would you associate with the distribution of decision outcomes?," but it is not necessary to ask the question in this form. Any statement about the probability of some point other than X_p on the prior distribution is sufficient to determine σ_{prior}, the standard deviation of the decision-maker's estimate. For example, if the decision maker says that chances are about two out of three that estimated sales will be between $(X_p - a)$ and $(X_p + a)$, then the value of $\sigma_{prior} = a$. If the decision-maker says that the chances are 95 out of a 100 that sales will be between $(X_p - b)$ and $(X_p + b)$, then $\sigma_{prior} = b/2$.

Gains and losses

In calculating sample size under the value of information approach, potential gains and losses are simply expressed by k, the per unit contribution to profit. A decision not to market a product will result in an opportunity loss (lost potential contribution to profits).

Distance from breakeven

Given the manager's sales and uncertainty estimates, distance from breakeven is defined as:

$$D = |X_p - X_b|/\sigma_{\text{prior}} \tag{3.35}$$

That is, D is not simply expressed as the absolute distance between the prior estimate and the breakeven point: it is expressed relative to uncertainty. If breakeven is 250,000 units, and we think chances are 95 out of 100 that sales will be between 150,000 and 200,000, then we are far from breakeven and are unlikely to seek new information or market the new product; on the other hand, if we believe that chances are two out of three that sales will be between 100,000 and 300,000, then we are closer to breakeven.

The Value of Perfect Information for Two-Action Problems with Linear Costs and Gains

The situation we have described is essentially a two-action problem (market/don't market) with linear costs and gains. For this case, Robert Schlaifer has defined the value of information in his classic book *Probability and Statistics for Business Decisions* (1959) as:

$$V = [k] \times [\sigma_{\text{prior}}] \times [G(D)] \tag{3.36}$$

Where V is the value of perfect information, k is the per unit profit contribution, σ_{prior} is the standard deviation of the sales estimate, D is the distance from break-even, and $G(D)$ is the unit normal loss integral, a function first defined and used by Schlaifer. Tables of the unit normal loss integral are found as Appendix 1 for this chapter.

Note, in Appendix 1, that $G(D)$ becomes smaller as D gets bigger. Therefore, the value of information declines as the distance from breakeven increases. However, the value of information increases as k (the gain or loss associated with the decision) and σ_{prior} (the prior uncertainty) increase. Thus, V simply quantifies our earlier discussion concerning the value of information.

To illustrate the calculation of V, suppose a decision-maker is considering the introduction of a new home appliance. The firm plans to sell this appliance at about $40 with a unit profit $k = \$10$. Their fixed costs K for production and marketing are estimated at $5,000,000. Thus their breakeven is $X_b = 500,000$ units (K/k). The decision-maker's prior distribution as to the number that can be sold is normal with an expected value (mean) of 450,000 and a standard deviation of 100,000. What is the value of information?

First, compute $D = |500{,}000 - 450{,}000|/10{,}000 = 0.50$. Next, find $G(D)$ in Appendix 1; in this case, $G(D) = 0.1978$. Finally, calculate $V = \$10 \times (100{,}000) \times (0.1978) = \$197{,}800$.

As noted earlier, V does not really indicate how much money will be made or or lost for a specific decision. V is a long-run estimate of how much more you could be made per decision over many decisions of this type if there were *perfect* information (which, of course, is never available.)

What, then, is V good for? As we will show below, V can be used to measure the gain in information if new research is done. V then can be used to determine whether gathering new information is justified and, if so, how much new information to get.

How Much Research Should Be Done?

From Equation 3.36, one can see that the value of information declines as you get more of it. As you get more information, σ_{prior} becomes smaller and D becomes larger (because the denominator becomes smaller). As D gets larger, $G(D)$ becomes smaller. Therefore, since σ_{prior} and $G(D)$ become smaller, V, the value of perfect information becomes smaller. This should be no surprise if we consider information as an economic good similar to chocolate ice cream. We may love chocolate ice cream and be willing to pay a lot for the first pint if we haven't had any for weeks, but we aren't willing to pay as much for the tenth pint.

As you may remember from basic economics, the solution to maximizing the net value of any good is to purchase the good until marginal gain equals marginal cost. This same principle holds for information. The marginal cost is simply the variable cost of information – in a survey, variable costs would include interviewer time, telephone tolls, coding and data processing. The marginal gain is more complex to compute. It requires that we re-compute the value of information V' after gathering information, with the difference $(V - V')$ being the gain. There is no easy algebraic solution to this problem, but Schlaifer has computed a graph which provides the data needed to optimize n, the sample size. See Appendix 2. We describe how to compute an optimum n and then continue our example.

Computing an Optimum n

To compute an optimum n it is necessary to estimate the following terms:

- k, the unit contribution to profit;
- σ_{prior}, the prior uncertainty;
- σ, the population standard deviation (this would usually be known or estimated from earlier research on similar products);

- D, the distance from breakeven;
- c, the variable cost (per observation) of research.

The difference between σ and σ_{prior} is the same as the difference between the standard deviation of a population and the standard error of a mean. You will probably remember that the standard error of the mean is defined as:

$$\sigma_x = \sigma/n^{1/2} \qquad (3.37)$$

From this equation, if we treat σ_{prior} as a form of σ_x, we can solve for n, which in this case, since σ_{prior} represents our prior information about the market, is the "sample size equivalent" of our prior knowledge. The solution for n is $n = (\sigma/\sigma_{prior})^2$. If new information is obtained from an optimum sample of size $n_{opt.}$, then n', the posterior sample size equivalent, will be the sum of this new sample size plus the n equivalent from our prior information. That is, $n' = n_{opt.} + (\sigma/\sigma_{prior})^2$.

To compute the size of the new optimum sample, $n_{opt.}$, one must do the following:

1. Compute the value $Z = (\sigma_{prior}/\sigma)(k\sigma/c)^{1/3}$.
2. Then compute the value D as defined in equation 3.35.
3. Use the graph in Appendix 2 with the appropriate values for D and Z to find the value of h. This graph taken from Schlaifer (1959) is derived from Taylor series expansion of the "Gain in Information" function to find maximum values.
4. The optimum sample size, $n_{opt.} = (h) \times (k\sigma/c)^{2/3}$

To illustrate these calculations, continue with the previous example, in which the decision-maker considers the introduction of a new home appliance.

- Assume $\sigma = 1,000,000$
- Assume $c = \$10.00$
- Then $z = [(100,000/1,000,000) \times (10 \times 1,000,000/10)]^{1/3} = 10$
- $D = 0.5$ (as before)
- $h = 0.125$ (from Appendix 2)
- Therefore $n_{opt.} = 0.125 \times (100)^2 = 1,250$

Is research justified?

In the example above, we have computed an optimum sample size, but have not yet determined whether or not to do research at all. This decision will be based on the total costs of research including fixed costs C that we have not considered up to now. We will need to perform the following steps to determine if research is justified:

1. Compute a new $V' = [k\sigma_{posterior}] \times [G(D')]$, where $\sigma_{posterior}$ is calculated as $\sigma/(n')^{1/2}$ and D' is calculated as $D/\sigma_{posterior}$.
2. Compute the gain in value of information $= V - V'$
3. Compute total research cost $= C + cn_{opt}$, where C is the fixed cost of research and c is the variable cost per observation.
4. Compute the net gain due to research, calculated as:

$$(V - V') - (C + cn_{opt}) \qquad (3.38)$$

If the net gain is positive, research is justified; if not, then research is not justified.

Returning to our appliance introduction example:

- Suppose $C = \$10,000$
- We first compute a new $\sigma_{posterior} = \sigma/(n')^{1/2}$
  Here $\sigma_{posterior} = 1,000,000/[1250 + (10)^2]^{1/2}$.
  $= 1,000,000/36.74 = 27,218$.
- We now compute $D' = 50,000/27,218 = 1.84$
- We now compute $V' = 10 \times (27,218) \times G(1.84)$
  $= 272,180 \times (0.01290) = \$3,511$
- Next we calculate the total research cost,

$$(C + cn_{opt}) = \$10,000 + \$10(1,250) = \$22,500$$

- Finally, the net gain from research:

$$\$197,800 - \$3,511 - \$22,500 = \$171,789$$

The net gain is positive, so in this example research is justified with an optimum sample size of 1,250.

You may wonder what are the components of the fixed cost C. These are of two kinds. The first group are costs of the market research organization for developing the study design, training interviewers and all the aspects of the study whose costs are not dependent on the sample size, including overhead and profits. The second are costs to the company developing the new product. Primarily these are in the form of possible foregone profits if the new product is a success. The time required to conduct and analyze the study is time that can be used by competitors to catch up. As the competition introduce their versions of the new product, profits generally decline, so all firms want to have as much lead time as possible.

It is rational for firms to consider possible foregone profits when deciding whether or not to do a new market study. It is irrational, however, to never do research because of concerns about competitors catching up. Under such a strategy, there will be many more new product failures that will ultimately lead to poorer overall performance by the firm.

Alternative Methods for Setting Sample Size

Since a value of information approach to determining sample size does require valuable management time, several alternative approaches for determining sample size are used. These include:

- Setting the sample size according to previous practice.
- Setting the sample size according to typical practice.
- Setting the sample size according to resource limitations.

Using previous sample sizes

It is common for companies that do repetitive research to set sample sizes according to what has worked in previous projects. The simple approach of repeating sample sizes works well if situations are similar and the previous sample size was optimum. It is easy to show that this method remains optimum if prices change because of inflation, but all else remains the same. It is important to recognize, however, that different situations may require different sample sizes. Simply doing the same thing each time can lead to spending too much or too little on information relative to what it is worth.

Using typical sample sizes

A related approach to setting sample size is to "follow the crowd," and use sample sizes similar to what other companies have done. Table 3.2 gives some typical sample sizes which can be used in this regard. Copying sample sizes has the same logic as repeating your own sample sizes – "if it worked before, it should work again" – and the same possible pitfalls. Different situations may require different sample sizes.

Table 3.2 Typical sample sizes used for consumer and industrial marketing research

Number of subgroup analyses	Consumer		Industrial*	
	National	Regional/ special	National	Regional/ special
None/few	800–1200	200–500	200–400	50–200
Average	1200–2000	500–1000	400–800	200–400
Many	2000+	1000+	800+	400+

* Assumes total population size large relative to these sample sizes.

Using Resource Limitations

In real-world settings, a decision-maker may fix the budget for a research project on the basis of resources available and competing needs for research funds. Once the budget is fixed, the sample size is determined based on the data collection methods that will be used. Just as statistical calculations must be checked against a budget to see whether the sample is affordable, it is desirable to check a budget based sample size against information needs to see whether the sample will be satisfactory and efficient.

There is often not too much harm if the sample size is less than optimum based on a "value of information" approach. The decision-maker can evaluate the results of the smaller sample, and request an additional wave of sampling if still uncertain. The problem with sampling in stages is that it delays the time of the final decision and may impact on profits. There are also some additional costs of field work if the interviewing is done at different times.

The more serious problem is conducting an unnecessary study or making the sample size too large simply because the budget exists. Ultimately, market researchers who conduct studies that are not used for decision-making lose their credibility within the organization as well as costing their firms money.

Questions

1   Choose one of the following four populations whom you wish to study:
    (a) all university and college faculty in the USA (or some other country);
    (b) business school faculty in the USA (or some other country);
    (c) all university and college students in the USA (or some other country);
    (d) all business school students in the USA (or some other country).
1.1 Describe the purpose of the study you wish to conduct.
1.2 Carefully define your population based on study objectives.
1.3 Assuming no list of the population is available, you will need to start with a list of universities or business schools. Find such a list and evaluate its completeness.
1.4 Assuming limited resources (say, $25,000), you will need a sample of schools. If the cost to obtain a list from a school is $500 (personal persuasion is necessary) and the cost of each sample unit is $10 (using mail methods), and you estimate that homogeneity between sample units within a school is 0.04 (based on a pilot study), what is the optimum number of schools and units per school, and the total sample size?
1.5 Since schools vary substantially by size, sampling with probabilities proportionate to size (pps) is most efficient. Using your list, select a sample of schools pps.
2   You wish to sample owners of home computers to determine interest in a new software package. You decide on a telephone survey using Random Digit Dialing. Describe how you would obtain your sample. (*Note*: Telephone screening is required.) Would you be concerned about non-telephone households?
3.1 You wish to sample businesses to determine their interest in a new software package, again using telephone methods. Describe how you would obtain your sample. (You may, if you wish, limit your study to specific industries.)

3.2 Note that these establishments will vary enormously in size. How would you handle this in your sample? (*Hint*: Consider stratification and disproportionate sampling.)

3.3 How would you determine whom in the organization to contact for information?

4.1 Visit a local mall and observe its entrances and layout. Obtain from the management or by observation, information on number of people who shop at different times and on different days, and who use different entrances.

4.2 Prepare a detailed plan for sampling from this mall during a one-week period, specifying times, locations, and number of cases to be obtained. Assume the purpose is a taste test of a new snack.

4.3 Discuss how you would treat mall employees. Would you be concerned about frequency of shopping at the mall? Why or why not? If you are concerned about frequency, how would you handle this in sampling?

5 For many media and market research studies, one aim is to finish as rapidly as possible with an exact number of cases. Calls are made, and no answers or busy signals are discarded with new numbers selected until the target sample is reached. What are the problems with this procedure? How can these problems be reduced or eliminated?

Suggested additional reading

The classic texts on sampling that anyone who does sampling will want are:
Morris, H., Hurwitz, William N., and Madow, William G. 1953: *Sample Survey Methods and Theory*, New York: Wiley, 2 vols.
Kish, Leslie 1965: *Survey Sampling*, New York: Wiley.
An elegant book for those interested in the mathematical foundations of sampling is Cochran, William 1962: *Sampling Techniques*, 2nd edn, New York: Wiley.
The classic exposition of the use of surveys for decision-making is Schlaifer, Robert 1959: *Probability and Statistics for Business Decisions*, New York: McGraw-Hall.
An extended description of the material in this chapter is in my book: Sudman, Seymour 1976: *Applied Sampling*, New York: Academic.
For a careful discussion of the analysis of complex surveys including the computation of sampling errors, see Skinner, C. J., Holt, D. and Smith, T. M. F. 1989: *Analysis of Complex Surveys*, New York: Wiley.
Good discussions of non-sampling errors in surveys are found in:
Biemer, Paul *et al.* (eds) 1991: *Measurement Errors in Surveys*, New York: Wiley.
Groves, Robert M. *et al.* (eds) 1988: *Telephone Survey Methodology*, New York: Wiley.
Groves, Robert M. 1989: *Survey Errors and Survey Costs*, New York: Wiley.

References

Czaja, Ronald F., Snowden, Cecelia B. and Casady, Robert J. 1986: Reporting bias and sampling errors in a survey of a rare population using multiplicity counting rules. *Journal of the American Statistical Association*, 81, 411–19.

Ericson, William A. 1965: Optimum stratified sampling using prior information. *Journal of the American Statistical Association*, 60, 750–71.

Fuller, Wayne A. 1986: *PC CARP*, Ames: Iowa Statistical Laboratory, Iowa State University.

Hansen, Morris H., Hurwitz, William N. and Madow, William G. 1953: *Sample Survey Methods and Theory*, New York: Wiley, 2 vols.

Hartley, H. O. 1962: Multiple frame surveys. *Proceedings, Social Statistics Section, American Statistical Association*, 203–6.

Hartley, H. O. 1974: Multiple frame methodology and selected applications. *Sankyha C*, 36, 99–118.

Hidiroglou, M. A., Fuller, Wayne A. and Hickman, R. D. 1980: *SUPER CARP* 6th. edn, Ames, Iowa Statistical Laboratory, Iowa State University.

Holt, M. M. 1977: SURREGR: standard errors of regression coefficients from sample survey data. Research Triangle Institute, Research Triangle Park, North Carolina.

Kalton, Graham and Anderson, D. 1986: *Sampling rare populations. Journal of the Royal Statistical Society*, 149, 65.

Kish, Leslie 1965: *Survey Sampling*, New York: Wiley.

Kish, Leslie and Frankel, Martin 1970: Balanced repeated replications for standard errors. *Journal of the American Statistical Association*, 65, 1071–91.

McCarthy, Philip J. 1966: *Replication: An Approach to the Analysis of Survey Data from Complex Samples*, Washington DC: US National Center for Health Statistics, Vital and Health Statistics, Series 2, No. 14.

McCarthy, Philip J. 1969: *Pseudoreplication: Further Evaluation and Application of the Balanced Half-Sample Technique*. Washington DC: US National Center for Health Statistics, Vital and Health Statistics, Series 2, No. 31.

Nathan, Gad 1976: An empirical study of response and sampling errors for multiplicity estimates with different counting rules. *Journal of the American Statistical Association*, 71, 808–15.

Neyman, Jerzy 1934: On the two different aspects of the representative method: the method of stratified sampling and the method of purposive selection. *Journal of the Royal Statistical Society*, 97, 558–606.

Plackett, R. L. and Burman, P. J. 1946: The design of optimum multifactorial experiments. *Biometrika*, 33, 305–25.

Schlaifer, Robert 1959: *Probability and Statistics for Business Decisions*, New York: McGraw-Hill.

Shah, B. V. 1974: STDERR: standard errors program for sample survey data. Research Triangle Institute, Research Triangle Park, North Carolina.

Sirken, Monroe G. 1970: Household surveys with multiplicity. *Journal of the American Statistical Association*, 65, 257–66.

Sirken, Monroe G. *et al.* 1975: Household sample surveys of diabetes: Design effects of counting rules. *Proceedings, Social Statistics section, American Statistical Association*, 659–63.

Sudman, Seymour 1980: Improving the quality of shopping center sampling. *Journal of Marketing Research*, 17, 423–31.

Sudman, Seymour 1985: Efficient screening methods for the sampling of geographically clustered special populations. *Journal of Marketing Research*, 22, 20–29.

Sudman, Seymour 1985: Experiments in the measurement of the size of social networks. *Social Networks*, 7, 127–51.

Sudman, Seymour 1988: Experiments in measuring neighborhood and relative social networks. *Social Networks*, 10, 93–108.

Sudman, Seymour, Sirken, Monroe G. and Cowan, Charles D. 1988: Sampling rare and elusive populations. *Science*, 240, 991–5.

Waksberg, Joseph 1978: Sampling methods for random digit dialing. *Journal of the American Statistical Association*, 73, 40–6.

Woodruff, Ralph S. 1971: A simple method for approximating the variance of a complicated estimate. *Journal of the American Statistical Association*, 66, 411–14.

Woodruff, Ralph S. and Causey, B.D. 1976: Computerized method for approximating the variance of a complicated estimator. *Journal of the American Statistical Association*, 71, 315–21.

Appendix 3.1

Unit normal loss integral $G(u) = P'_N(u) - uP_N(\bar{u} > u)$

D	0.00	0.01	0.02	0.03	0.04	0.05	0.06	0.07	0.08	0.09
0.0	0.3989	0.3940	0.3890	0.3841	0.3793	0.3744	0.3697	0.3649	0.3602	0.3556
0.1	0.3509	0.3464	0.3418	0.3373	0.3328	0.3284	0.3240	0.3197	0.3154	0.3111
0.2	0.3069	0.3027	0.2986	0.2944	0.2904	0.2863	0.2824	0.2784	0.2745	0.2706
0.3	0.2668	0.2630	0.2592	0.2555	0.2518	0.2481	0.2445	0.2409	0.2374	0.2339
0.4	0.2304	0.2270	0.2236	0.2203	0.2169	0.2137	0.2104	0.2072	0.2040	0.2009
0.5	0.1978	0.1947	0.1917	0.1887	0.1857	0.1828	0.1799	0.1771	0.1742	0.1714
0.6	0.1687	0.1659	0.1633	0.1606	0.1580	0.1554	0.1528	0.1503	0.1478	0.1453
0.7	0.1429	0.1405	0.1381	0.1358	0.1334	0.1312	0.1289	0.1267	0.1245	0.1223
0.8	0.1202	0.1181	0.1160	0.1140	0.1120	0.1100	0.1080	0.1061	0.1042	0.1023
0.9	0.1004	0.09860	0.09680	0.09503	0.09328	0.09156	0.08986	0.08819	0.08654	0.08491
1.0	0.08332	0.08174	0.08019	0.07866	0.07716	0.07568	0.07422	0.07279	0.07138	0.06999
1.1	0.06862	0.06727	0.06595	0.06465	0.06336	0.06210	0.06086	0.05964	0.05844	0.05726
1.2	0.05610	0.05496	0.05384	0.05274	0.05165	0.05059	0.04954	0.04851	0.04750	0.04650
1.3	0.04553	0.04457	0.04363	0.04270	0.04179	0.04090	0.04002	0.03916	0.03831	0.03748
1.4	0.03667	0.03587	0.03508	0.03431	0.03356	0.03281	0.03208	0.03137	0.03067	0.02998
1.5	0.02931	0.02865	0.02800	0.02736	0.02674	0.02612	0.02552	0.02494	0.02436	0.02380
1.6	0.02324	0.02270	0.02217	0.02165	0.02114	0.02064	0.02015	0.01967	0.01920	0.01874
1.7	0.01829	0.01785	0.01742	0.01699	0.01658	0.01617	0.01578	0.01539	0.01501	0.01464
1.8	0.01428	0.01392	0.01357	0.01323	0.01290	0.01257	0.01226	0.01195	0.01164	0.01134
1.9	0.01105	0.01077	0.01049	0.01022	0.0^29957	0.0^29698	0.0^29445	0.0^29198	0.0^28957	0.0^28721
2.0	0.0^28491	0.0^28266	0.0^28046	0.0^27832	0.0^27623	0.0^27418	0.0^27219	0.0^27024	0.0^26835	0.0^26649
2.1	0.0^26468	0.0^26292	0.0^26120	0.0^25952	0.0^25788	0.0^25628	0.0^25472	0.0^25320	0.0^25172	0.0^25028
2.2	0.0^24887	0.0^24750	0.0^24616	0.0^24486	0.0^24358	0.0^24235	0.0^24114	0.0^23996	0.0^23882	0.0^23770
2.3	0.0^23662	0.0^23556	0.0^23453	0.0^23352	0.0^23255	0.0^23159	0.0^23067	0.0^22977	0.0^22889	0.0^22804
2.4	0.0^22720	0.0^22640	0.0^22561	0.0^22484	0.0^22410	0.0^22337	0.0^22267	0.0^22199	0.0^22132	0.0^22067
2.5	0.0^22004	0.0^21943	0.0^21883	0.0^21826	0.0^21769	0.0^21715	0.0^21662	0.0^21610	0.0^21560	0.0^21511
2.6	0.0^21464	0.0^21418	0.0^21373	0.0^21330	0.0^21288	0.0^21247	0.0^21207	0.0^21169	0.0^21132	0.0^21095
2.7	0.0^21060	0.0^21026	0.0^39928	0.0^39607	0.0^39295	0.0^38992	0.0^38699	0.0^38414	0.0^38138	0.0^37870
2.8	0.0^37611	0.0^37359	0.0^37115	0.0^36879	0.0^36650	0.0^36428	0.0^36213	0.0^36004	0.0^35802	0.0^35606
2.9	0.0^35417	0.0^35233	0.0^35055	0.0^34883	0.0^34716	0.0^34555	0.0^34398	0.0^34247	0.0^34101	0.0^33959

Source: Schlaifer, 1959, pp. 706–7, Table IV). By permission of McGraw-Hill Book Co., Inc.

Appendix 3.2

Nomograph for computing optimum sample size
Source: Schalifer (71, p. 712, Chart II). By permission of McGraw-Hill Book Co., Inc.

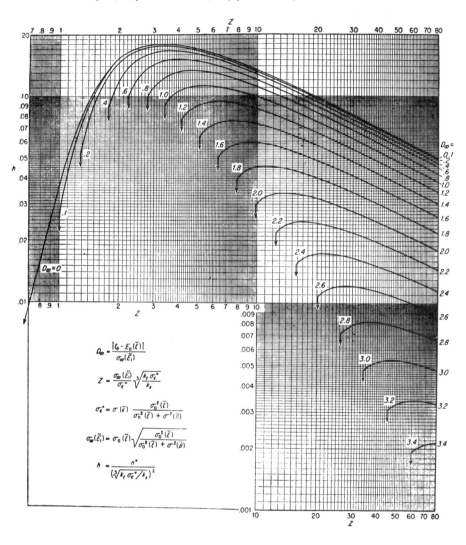

4

Mail and Telephone Surveys in Marketing Research: A Perspective from the Field*

Daniel C. Lockhart
and
J. Robert Russo

This chapter presents the perspective that mail and telephone surveys used in marketing research are different than surveys used by governments and academics. Marketing research surveys have fewer items measuring constructs, are more likely to use convenience samples, are completed in less time, rely more on multivariate (as opposed to univariate) analyses, and are more concerned with external as opposed to internal validity. These differences affect the application of both mail and telephone surveys in marketing research.

We begin with a discussion of the differences between academic survey research and the application of survey techniques in the corporate environment. Following that is a section that compares the advantages and disadvantages of mail and telephone surveys. Empirical evidence comparing different survey approaches is then presented. Each section is summarized by one or more hypotheses. Some of these hypotheses are based on relevant literature while others are speculative. The major purpose of these hypotheses is to challenge the reader to further examine the issues that have been presented.

Our intent is to present mail and telephone surveys as two of many survey research techniques used in marketing research. These techniques are used in a unique manner in marketing research organizations. Unlike academic researchers, there are usually many layers of individuals associated with a marketing research survey. These individuals include those who require the information, the individuals who arrange for the information to be collected, the people who manage the data collection, those who collect the data, and individuals who create and clean the data, those who analyze the data, and the people who present the results of the data analyses.

Marketing Research in the Corporate World

Surveys are one source of data collection in marketing research. Survey research texts are normally written by individuals connected with an academic institution (Dillman, 1978; Rossi, Wright, and Anderson, 1983; Alreck and Settle, 1985; Schuman and Presser, 1981). These authors frequently teach classes on survey research and many conduct surveys. Surveys done by academics typically use well trained personnel with little time pressure and no profit motive.

The professors who write such books are up to date with the research literature and often maintain contact with individuals who use the survey method in marketing research. The contact between these authors and the field professionals is not random. Such contact is with those individuals who are most interested in applying the up-to-date methods presented in such texts. These field professionals are likely to be among the marketing researchers who are best at using surveys in marketing research.

Like the texts on survey research, books on marketing research are normally written by individuals connected with an academic institution. Such texts present one chapter on surveying in general followed by chapters on sampling, question writing, measurement scales, and occasionally a chapter on collecting data by questionnaire (e.g. Aaker and Day, 1990; Churchill, 1991, 1992; Dillon, Madden and Firtle, 1990). Rarely is the student informed about the tight time frames and budget limitations that will confront them when conducting marketing research using the survey method in an applied setting.

Individuals who write textbooks have a different reinforcement structure than individuals who conduct marketing research studies. Professors are reinforced for teaching classes, publishing books, and sometimes consulting. Individuals who work in marketing research are reinforced differently depending on whether they are clients or suppliers. Marketing researchers who work for client organizations are rewarded by: (a) securing contracts, (b) producing high profit products, and (c) reducing production costs. The marketing researchers who supply these clients are reinforced by producing: (a) low cost, timely results, (b) numbers with face validity, and (c) results that appear to increase the clients' sales. The reinforcement structure for all three of these groups have little in common.

What follows is a perspective that is usually not presented in textbooks. The authors of this chapter represent a unique combination. Lockhart is a marketing researcher who has spent most of his professional career designing, conducting, and analyzing marketing research surveys. He works on the client side of marketing research – not the supplier side. Russo, a professor and principle in a supplier organization, has focused much of his activity on federal government contracts – e.g. Office of Inspector General.

Each of these perspectives is neither more nor less correct. Our goal is to step back and present a perspective that the student does not normally see.

It is our hope that such an applied orientation assists the reader in improving both the future of survey research techniques applied to marketing research as well as the application of such techniques to his or her professional life.

A little history

Bradburn and Sudman (1988) report that surveys have been conducted since Biblical times. William the Conqueror recorded a general census of England during the eleventh century. Censuses were taken during the Renaissance in Venice and Florence. The first US census, done in 1790, was stimulated by the need to apportion territory into constituencies roughly equal in size (Rossi, Wright, and Anderson, 1983). The addition of questions to the original head count grew out of a developing consciousness that running the state required more than counting the number of people.

Nineteenth-century surveys attempted to resemble censuses. Later, straw poles were conducted by magazines and newspapers to estimate election results and answer other relevant questions. Gallup conducted the first pre-election polls in North Carolina and Delaware in 1824 (Smith, 1990). The Literary Digest polls, dating back to 1916, mark the beginning of modern survey methods.

Perhaps the most famous survey is the Literary Digest Survey of 1936 that predicted a landslide victory by Landon over Roosevelt. Dillman (1978) reports that this débacle was in part the result of using telephone listings as a sample frame at a time when only about 35 percent of US households had telephones. This bias was increased due to strong class distinctions in households that did and did not have telephones. Also, Republicans tended to be more affluent and had an increased probability of having a telephone.

Mail and telephone surveys have changed considerably over the past 60 years. In the 1930s, survey research was dominated by the door-to-door methodology. Today, door-to-door surveys are rarely performed. Telephone surveys, a methodology once frowned upon due to inadequate representation by many populations, have become the method of choice to conduct survey research.

This change has been brought about by the wide distribution of households with telephones and the invention of methodologies such as random digit dialing (RDD). Conducting a survey by sending the interviewers out to obtain a representative sample of respondents has become too costly. In addition, acceptable samples are generally easy to obtain by telephone.

Although little is known about early marketing research, Greenbaum (1987) speculates about the environment. He suggests that early store owners probably overheard individuals talking about a product they wanted to have and then the store owner went about procuring this product for his/her customers. Greenbaum suggests that modern marketing research began in the late 1940s or early 1950s. He asserts that it probably began with the concept of a product manager who dedicated his complete attention to his product. This product manager sought to improve sales of his or her product by seeking information and feedback that could improve the sales, marketing, and perception of the attributes of the product.

Currently marketing research data is not limited to that data which a product manager can use. Many businesses rely on survey research information for other aspects of the organization. In addition to obtaining information on potential products, surveys may be conducted to determine customer satisfaction, to determine employee satisfaction, and to improve the human factors related to manufacturing and production. It is not uncommon for every department in an organization to work with the marketing research group for assistance in gathering research data for purposes other than marketing.

Surveys in the context of marketing research

The decision to use the survey method depends upon the context and the goals of the individuals who desire the information. Frequently, the information desired serves to solve a problem and aid the decision-making process by reducing uncertainty. Sometimes the marketing researcher can reduce uncertainty without conducting a survey.

The first goal in a marketing research project is to formulate the problem (Churchill, 1991). The methodology used depends on the questions to be answered. Habits are powerful determinants of behavior. Research suppliers and marketing research managers that have been successful in the past with certain techniques may routinely employ the same method. Two common methods are the mail and telephone survey techniques presented in this chapter. However, mail and telephone survey methods represent only two of many methods used to collect data in marketing research. Other data collection methods include secondary sources, syndicated sources of purchase data, field experiments, and qualitative interviewing. In addition to working with the various sources of data, most marketing researchers serve as management consultants by using a variety of techniques to improve a company's position in the market place.

As a management consultant, the marketing researcher uses the mail or telephone survey as one view of the population of individuals to whom the company sells (or desires to sell) products. The information collected is generally designed to answer one of two question sets: (a) questions related to a specific problem which are of immediate tactical importance, or (b) questions that track an issue of long-term interest to the company. The data may feed a decision/analytic procedure, a projection model, or may be used only once to answer a particular question.

Secondary sources include data collected for a purpose other than a specific marketing research need. The US census, professional society publications, and telephone directories are examples of secondary sources.

Syndicated sources of purchase data include the largest marketing research organizations in the US and represent some of the greatest marketing research expenditures. Examples of companies providing this data are Nielsen, IRI, and Migliara-Kaplan, and IMS.

Field experiments frequently involve a limited test where a product is released to a particular market to estimate sales in a larger market area. Similar experiments and quasi-experiments are conducted to determine advertising effectiveness.

Mail and telephone surveys are sometimes used to enhance these methods. Lists of individuals whose data are represented in secondary and syndicated sources can sometimes be obtained. Similarly, field experiments can include the use of survey methods to provide information on experimental variables and co-variates of the sample included in the syndicated data.

As one can see from the variety of chapters in this book, survey research methods represent only two of many methods that can be used by marketing researchers. The valid use of these tools is frequently dependent on a marketing researcher's understanding of the products, the questions to be answered, and the audience that makes the buying decision. Regardless of how good the survey methods are, the survey will fail if the researcher does not understand the problem, ask the correct questions, and present the study in a manner that is appropriate for the audience.

Survey methodologies

Most of the research on survey methodologies is conducted by public opinion survey organizations connected to colleges and universities. Yet, organizations that conduct marketing research surveys are quite diverse in nature. They range in size from one and two person companies to multi-million dollar firms. The individuals who manage these firms frequently have academic degrees related to the type of customer they service rather than in a field related to marketing research. These individuals have considerable experience conducting marketing research surveys. They are trained on the job and in professional workshops.

Table 4.1 shows the relative popularity of survey methodologies as assessed by the research directors of the largest marketers of products and services for consumers. Telephone studies are most commonly used (Dillon, Madden, and Firtle, 1990).

Despite the popularity of telephone surveys, research on the telephone survey has lagged far behind that of other survey methodologies. Dillman (1978, p. 9) reports that "research literature on telephone surveys is as thin as that of mail questionnaires is thick." Rossi, Wright, and Anderson's (1983) book on surveys suggests a similar bias by including a chapter by Dillman (1978) on mail surveys but nothing on telephone surveys. Dillman claims the increased popularity of telephone surveys has been without the benefit of published work.

Table 4.1 Most commonly used survey methodologies

Method	Percent of time listed among the top two or three methods
Central WATS (telephone surveys)	61%
Mall intercept	51%
Focus groups	35%
Mail panels	15%
Scanner panels	12%
Cold Mail	9%
Diary panels	8%
Door to door	8%
Trade surveys	7%

Source: Based on data provided in Dillon, Madden, and Firtle (1990).

Although less popular, the methodology of mail survey benefits from much published research. This research has enabled us (e.g. Russo, Lockhart, and Paulsmeyer, 1989) to obtain return rates of 80, 90, or even 98 percent when required. However, we are concerned that this research has not answered the more serious questions regarding biases obtained by inappropriate sampling and by the differences between respondents and non-respondents.

Despite the lack of published research on telephone surveys many books on survey methodology (e.g. Alreck and Settle, 1985; Bradburn and Sudman, 1988; Warwick and Lininger, 1975; Schuman and Presser, 1981) focus on face-to-face and telephone interviews. The reasons cited for using telephone methodology include the advantages of having a well-trained interviewer, creating a permissive atmosphere for discussion, greater flexibility in asking questions, and lack of dependence on literacy.

Such books tend to deal with the well-designed and executed survey conducted under minimal management and time constraints. Marketing research surveys do not fit into this category. The authors who write survey books generally are motivated by knowledge gains. The surveys are well-designed to answer a specific question for which there is often previous research.

In contrast, the typical marketing research survey is constructed under management and time constraints. The individual designing, directing, and conducting such surveys has not spent a lifetime studying survey methodology. Those who do the interviewing are usually paid close to minimum wage.

A few specific biases Other texts present experimental results on question form, wording, and presentation method. For example, Schuman and Presser's (1981) book describes differences in item responses using face-to-face and telephone interviewing methods. No difference in responses was found from a telephone survey versus those obtained in a face-to-face interview. They found similar effects for both methodologies when offering and not offering a middle-of-the-road category.

Schuman and Presser found that the number of neutral responses to a question (in a telephone survey) depends on the content of the question being asked and whether or not a neutral response option is provided by the interviewer. For example, on a liberal-conservative question, the number of middle-of-the-road responses depends on whether a neutral response is offered or not. Middle-of-the-road responses decline from about 54 percent (when offered) to about 13 percent (when not offered). In contrast, a question regarding more strict penalties for marijuana use had 19.6 percent of respondents report "About the same as now" when the category was offered and 7.9 percent of respondents when the category was not provided by the interviewer. That is, respondents are more likely to volunteer a netural response if the interviewer offers it as an option. When the interviewer does not provide the option respondents are less likely to provide a neutral response.

A study by Peterson and Wilson (1992) found that higher levels of customer satisfaction were obtained when using personal and telephone methods as opposed to mail and other self-administered methods. Presumably respondents feel that the individual administering the survey want respondents to be satisfied. When compared to self-administered methods, respondents appear to provide an inflated satisfaction rating in the presence of an interviewer or interviewer's voice.

Another manner in which responses can be biased is less related to the presence or absence of an interviewer and more related to the order of the item in a questionnaire. Tourangeau and Rasinski (1988) provide a summary of the research on the cognitive processes underlying responses to attitude questions. They hypothesize four cognitive stages: interpret the question, retrieve the relevant information, render a judgement, and report the answer.

Prior items in a survey can bias later responses in three ways. First, responses to an earlier question can prime particular beliefs and make them more accessible. Second, responses to earlier items can serve as a standard of comparison for later items. Finally, earlier responses can serve as a source for consistency pressure on later responses.

Biased responses reduce the validity of any marketing research study. For example, our research with pricing questions indicates that greater price sensitivity is found when individuals are asked to respond to a low price first followed by successively higher prices. In contrast, the reverse order (i.e. high price to low) results in considerably less price sensitivity (see Figure 4.1). This effect has been seen in mail surveys, telephone surveys, focus groups, and surveys at major conventions.

Monroe (1990) suggests that this is due to greater sensitivity to losses than gains. This suggestion comes from prospect theory (Kahneman and Tversky, 1979; Thaler, 1985) which states that if respondents are asked to respond to a low price first followed by a higher price, then the higher price is perceived as a loss from the base established at the lower price. A gain

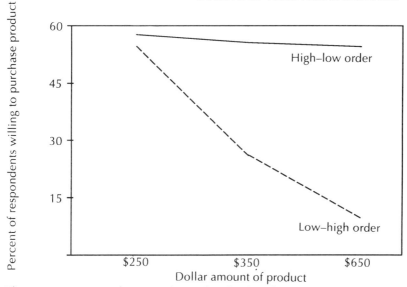

Figure 4.1 Price elasticity for individuals who see product prices displayed in different orders

is perceived if the respondent replies to the high price first followed by a lower price.

Potential reinforcements for biasing surveys Responses to surveys may be biased by both structure and administration. Knowledge of these potentially biasing variables can aid the surveyor in preventing or facilitating such bias. For example, a contractor may use a high to low order in a study for a marketing research client who has committed to showing little price sensitivity. After completing the study, the client then shows upper management that a survey supports their view that customers are not very sensitive to price. The client then looks good to management for showing the advantages to be gained by price increases.

In this case, management may have turned to marketing research to support their view for price increases. The result is that the marketing research manager looks good for supporting upper management's position. The bias results in reinforcements for everyone concerned.

However, upper management may never know that the survey, conclusion, and recommendations were all severely biased. These biases may result in reduced profits. However, the guilty parties may never be discovered. Individuals who have "bottom-line" responsibilities will pay for the poor research. The advertising agency may be fired for poorly presenting the price increase. Marketing may be blamed for improperly marketing the product. Sales may be blamed for not selling the product.

One perspective of the marketing research profession

Monahan and Walker (1990, p. 104) report that

It is notoriously easy for one survey expert to tear apart the methodology of a survey taken by another. However, one must keep in mind that there is no such thing as a perfect survey. Like any scientific method related to statistics and social sciences, every survey, no matter how carefully constructed and conducted, has some potential flaws.

Quality in the marketing research survey Three variables operate to reduce the quality of research results: (1) too many people in survey research positions with minimal training; (2) the tradeoff of flaws against costs when designing studies; and (3) large sums of money involved in the marketing research industry.

Chemists, engineers, and sales people frequently run marketing research departments and are the clients for much of the marketing research. From a position in marketing research, one is occasionally promoted to a line position such as sales or marketing manager. The typical marketing research manager has had one class in marketing research as part of an MBA program. This person's only exposure to survey methodology is the chapter that they were assigned to read in their marketing research text. The attitude in many organizations is that anyone can do marketing research.

Many successful marketing research firms conform their survey methodologies to the needs of these customers. The needs of these customers are based on business decisions. Too many individuals making such decisions have minimal knowledge of interest in the effects their decisions may have on the precision of the results obtained in the survey. They are primarily interested in a number that they can report (as the result of the survey).

Because most managers are unaware of any other type of validity, the numbers produced must have face validity. Success if not achieved by criterion related validity or by internal consistency. Success is all too frequently gauged by being on-time, under budget, and providing politically correct answers.

An environment that compromises quality The marketing research environment compromises the quality of marketing research surveys because there is: (a) a lack of firm guidelines on how to conduct a specific survey, (b) a lack of an organization capable of enforcing such guidelines, (c) a large sum of money spent in total by all of the firms conducting marketing research studies, and (d) only a small amount of money available for any particular study.

Many professional organizations related to the survey research and marketing research process have codes of ethics and standards (Bowers, 1991). Four such organizations are the American Association for Public Opinion Research (AAPOR), Council of American Survey Research Organizations (CASRO), the American Marketing Association (AMA) and the Advertising Research Foundation. However, the large number of marketing research organizations coupled with the constant changes in marketing research technology, make the systematic application of a common code of ethics impossible.

The changes in technology are rapid. A decade ago perceptual maps were new. Now there are many different types of multidimensional scaling, factor, discriminant, and correspondence analysis maps. A few years ago conjoint analysis was new. Now there are many variations of conjoint analysis: full profile; rating; ranking; computer adaptive; etc. Discrete choice analysis, decision analysis, structural equation modeling, and other techniques are all revolutionizing the manner in which questions are asked and answered in marketing research.

Many marketing research surveys are conducted by individuals who have never read a book or had a class in mail or telephone survey design. Suppliers providing the lowest bid often use minimally trained interviewers, instruments that are not pilot tested or revised, and dialing techniques that are rushed. Typically these activities occur at a facility trying to reduce costs and meet tight time schedules. Mail surveys are conducted to save costs and rarely use return rate enhancement techniques that can result in response rates of 80 percent or greater.

This criticism is not to suggest that all marketing research surveys provide inaccurate data. That certainly is not the case. Our purpose is to raise the level of awareness of the environment in which marketing research surveys are being conducted. We have worked with several high quality, low cost marketing research suppliers. We have had contact with a few suppliers that appear to be high cost–low quality. In general, however, our experience is that "you get what you pay for."

Hypotheses for your consideration

Hypothesis 1 Mail surveys are biased by non-respondents who: (a) are illiterate; (b) are not interested in the survey topic; (c) receive large amounts of mail; and (d) are extremely pressed for time.

Hypothesis 2 Respondents provide more positively biased data when surveys are administered by telephone or a face-to-face interviewer.

Hypothesis 3 Reinforcement structures reinforce marketing researchers to focus on variables that reduce the quality of the answers obtained in marketing research studies: time and money.

Advantages and Disadvantages of Each Method

Frequently the methodology chosen is more dependent on the bias of the individuals managing or conducting the study than the requirements of the study. Many researchers seem to rely exclusively on telephone surveys and focus groups. These methods have the advantage of relative instant gratification (i.e. results) resulting in their frequent use.

Most researchers believe that the appropriate survey methodology is dependent upon the needs of the survey. For example, time constraints may dictate telephone methodology while monetary constraints may force the use of a mail methodology. However, from a marketing research supplier's perspective who has a staff of full-time telephone interviewers, telephone methodology is viewed as more advantageous. In contrast, the supplier having a staff to do mailing and owning envelope printers, stuffers, and stampers would see more advantages in using the mail survey technology.

Regardless of which survey methodology one uses, there are about a dozen basic steps:

1. Specifically define the client's "problem."
2. Build questions designed to get data related to the "problem."
3. Identify a population from whom "answers" can be obtained.
4. Select a sampling frame.
5. Write introduction/cover letter and probes/follow-ups.
6. Write questionnaire/interview.
7. Field test questionnaire/interview.
8. Train interviewers/survey handlers.
9. Revise questionnaire/interview based upon field test and training results.
10. Conduct interviews/do mailing and monitor proceedings.
11. Code, enter, check/verify, and analyze data.
12. Write and present results that "answer the problem."

The clarity and specificity of the problem definition will not only determine the quality of the questions and the data generated, but also the quality of the final results and the presentation method(s) to the client. Time spent at this step, clearly identifying the problem or area of uncertainty, pays dividends through the rest of the survey process.

Often the questions to be answered will define the population to be sampled. The sampling, if one uses the random digit dialing technique, is defined by that technology. Occasionally, the sampling frame will be limited by available data. For example, if only addresses are available for the target population, mail surveys may be the method of choice. Likewise, if only telephone numbers are available, telephone methodology may be dictated.

Although not routinely done, we encourage the use of a field test of either the interview or questionnaire. Occasionally field testing can be accomplished by integrating it into the training program for either the surveyors or interviewers. When computer aided telephone interviewing (CATI) programs are employed, it is essential that time be allowed for the detailed software programming which is required for this technology and that programming be in place and field tested in advance of staff training. When CATI is used, the coding and data checking step is eliminated because CATI programs create the data set as the telephone interview is being conducted.

Mail, telephone, and focus groups compared

The information in Table 4.2 was integrated from three primary sources referenced under the table heading. The reader should remember that the texts providing the source material were not aimed at providing guidelines to marketing researchers in applied settings. Their primary audience was the researcher operating with well-trained interviewers and fewer management and time constraints. Some of the differences between these methodologies disappear when operating in the typical marketing research environment. For example, under severe time constraints, telephone surveys do not permit re-contacts and the sample biases are inflated.

Table 4.2 Mail, telephone, and focus group methods compared

	Mail	Telephone	Focus group
Population	High likelihood respondents being located. High likelihood or reduced socially desirable responses.	High likelihood locating selected respondents. High control of respondent selection within sampling unit. Availability heterogenous samples.	High level client involvement. High control over respondent selection within sampling units.
Biased response	Avoidance of interviewer distortion and subversion. Respondents have time to give thoughtful answers.	High likelihood that unknown bias from refusals will be avoided. High likelihood that contamination from others avoided.	Ability to gain quick feeling reaction to new products, packages and programs. Idea generation for new products.
Item construction	Most careful development of questions and response categories due to lack of additional information.	High success with: open-ended questions screening questions; controlling sequence; and avoiding item nonresponse. Ability to rotate items, rotate response scales and skip patterns.	High success with: open-ended questions; screening questions; controlling sequence; and with tedious and boring questions.
Costs	Potential for low costs per response. Insensitivity of costs due to geographical dispersion. Personnel requirements minimal.	Supervision and quality control potentially more costly than mail. Cost related to number of call backs and dependent upon list quality if not RDD.	Depends largely on travel and per diem; honorarium; videotaping or transcription service and facility rental.

Table 4.2 (*Cont.*)

	Mail	Telephone	Focus group
Speed	Up to 10 weeks if high response rate desired.	Data available on a daily basis especially if CATI is used.	"Quick and dirty" if panel selection, planning, and conduct is well done.
Other	Relative insensitivity to length. Avoids bias when asking sensitive questions (Peterson and Wilson, 1992). Visual stimuli (e.g. pictures) may be included.	Interviewer control may include auditory cues. FITD and LB possible.	Provides opportunity for respondents to stimulate each other. Skillful facilitators can "branch" in unplanned directions.

Source: Dillman, 1978; Frey, 1983; and Fowler, 1988.

Goodfellow *et al.* (1988) compared the bias of telephone and mail surveys in a two-stage data collection procedure (telephone first, then mail). Their results, using a sample of Pennsylvania Pharmaceutical Assistance Contract for the Elderly (PACE) program participants, indicate that telephone refusers tended to be very old, not married, and to take fewer medicines. Their mail nonresponders tended to be nonwhite, lower income, and in poorer health. They suggest that surveys of populations that include these types of subjects should include a sampling method that targets these potential nonrespondents.

Costs Dillman (1978) reports the costs for a national and a local survey when performed by three different methods. These estimates are based on a 45-minute interview. One can only speculate on the costs today as compared with those used in the 1978 report. Table 4.3 shows that the costs for a face-to-face or a telephone interview drop considerably when the distribution of respondents changes from national to local scope.

Table 4.3 Costs per interview for a national and local survey conducted by three different methods

Sample distribution	Face-to face	Telephone	Mail
National	$100	$20	$6
Local	$10	$7	$6

Source: based on data provided in Dillman (1978).

The decrease in costs (associated with a local sample) are due to lower costs for connecting the interviewer with the respondent. These costs include personnel time for both methodologies, travel for face-to-face interviews, and long-distance telephone charges for telephone surveys. The mailing charges are relatively constant regardless of location of surveyor and respondent.

What this table does not reveal is the decrease in quality associated with each methodology. For example, when moving from face-to-face to telephone interviewing one gives up the advantage of probability sampling within neighborhoods. When moving from telephone to mail survey methods, one gives up the possibility of RDD with the advantages of that method which will be discussed in a few pages.

Table 4.4 provides the factors which have the biggest influence on the cost of the survey. In telephone surveys the major cost factor is long-distance expenses. One must pay both a long-distance charge and an interviewer's salary for the length of the survey.

Table 4.4 Major costs for telephone and mail surveys

Telephone	Mail
Long distance calling	Data processing
Interviewers	Mailing
Preparation (CATI or paper)	Postage
Data processing	Printing

Currently, several marketing research firms specialize in locating the hard to find respondent for both mail and face-to-face contact. These firms are useful in obtaining a sample in some settings. However, most marketing research using person-to-person interviews use the mall intercept as opposed to the door-to-door method.

Other Methods Nowell and Stanley (1991) report that the mall intercept interview has been increasing in popularity and is now second only to telephone surveys in popularity (see Table 4.1). They report the following advantages to mall intercept interviews: (a) convenience of using a central location, (b) access to target populations, and (c) large number of available subjects.

Nowell and Stanley indicate that sample biases occur due to frequency with which various individuals shop at the mall and the length of time these individuals remain in the mall. They suggest that the expected length of stay at the mall can be used to correct for such biases.

Telephone surveys

Lehman (1989) reports that the most popular marketing research survey technique is telephone surveys. One of the primary reasons for the popularity of telephone surveys are high response rates. Response rates above 50 percent are considered very good by most mail surveyors. This same completion rate in a telephone survey would be considered very poor. Response rates of 80 percent or more are considered extraordinary in mail surveys. An 80 percent completion rate is frequently considered the norm in telephone surveys.

One advantage of telephone surveys is the behavioral norms associated with the telephone. Lavrakas (1987) suggests that there are several "behavioral norms" associated with answering a telephone: a ringing telephone is answered (90 percent of the time before eight rings), the caller determines the duration of the call, and interviewers can sense the veracity of the respondent. These norms work to the researcher's advantage. The probability that a telephone will be answered is high. The probability that the respondent will cut the call short is low. Finally perceptions of how the questions were answered can be reported by the interviewer.

Random Digit Dialing (RDD) One of the advantages of telephone surveys is the capability to get a random sample of subjects without a list. This advantage is due to Random Digit Dialing. There are other methods of telephone sampling (calling from prepared lists and calling from telephone directories), but RDD and its variations cannot be duplicated with mail surveys.

RDD enables nearly all homes with telephones to have an equal probability of being included in a sample. One exception to this rule is that homes with multiple telephone numbers have a greater probability of being included. RDD enables households with telephones to be sampled regardless of whether or not their telephone number is listed in a telephone directory. This technique reduces biases caused by areas (such as Las Vegas) that have more than 50 percent of telephones that are unlisted.

One note about RDD is that most marketing research studies do not require random samples of the general public. Most organizations do a few tracking studies of the general public but many more studies are designed to answer specific issues based on a subset of the general population. Having access to a particular subset relevant to a company's business offers a significant advantage to a marketing research firm. Such access reduces the costs associated with making the telephone calls. Quick access is also a service that consumer panels can provide.

Impending government regulation of telemarketing in nearly half of the states will affect RDD. South Carolina has already passed legislation limiting telemarketing and telephone surveys after 7:00 p.m. Many other states are in the process of developing such regulation. These laws may have a detrimental impact on the use of RDD in telephone surveys. Individuals who conduct RDD studies will need to monitor the effect of these laws. HR 280 (introduced 1.3.91) would establish a federal individual's privacy protection board.

Disposition of calls The disposition of telephone dialings represents the major expense in a telephone survey. Telephone surveys of the general public may have increased costs associated with telephone dialings that fail to result in a completed survey. The major reasons why a telephone dialing may fail are: (1) no answer after eight rings, (2) busy after redial, (3) answering machine, (4) respondent does not speak English, (5) answered by nonresident, (6) refusal, (7) disconnected/nonworking phone, (8) no one meets criteria, and (9) respondent unavailable.

Table 4.5 shows the results of first dialings (Churchill, 1991 based on Kerin and Peterson, 1983). Of those at home, 15 percent refused to be interviewed and 85 percent completed the interview. Of much greater concern than refusals are no one answering the telephone, no eligible respondents available, and out-of-service numbers.

Table 4.5 Results of first dialing attempts

Result	Probability of occurrence (%)
No answer	35
No eligible person	29
Out-of-service	20
At home	10
Business	4
Busy	2

Source: Kerin and Peterson (1983).

Lavrakas (1987) reports on the work of Skogan (1978) which tends to agree with Churchill. He reports the disposition of calls in a random digit dialing survey. These results are shown in Table 4.6 along with the results of a recent hospital decision making study.

Table 4.6 Disposition of dialings in a Lavrakas study and a recent marketing research study on hospital decision-making

Disposition of dialing	Lavrakas call dispositions %	Hospital call dispositions %
No answer or busy	38	7
Nonworking telephone	16	0
Household/hospital refusal	12	0
Ineligible/intended respondent transferred	9	18
Completed interview	9	21
Answered by nonresident or child	6	0
Nonresidential telephone	4	—
Contact only	2	0
Intended respondent refusal	1	5
Other/non-English speaking/partial interview	3	0
Respondent not available	—	43
Answering machine	—	4
	56,093	2,331

Source: partially from Lavrakas (1987).

One may note several differences in the results of the cumulative work reported by Lavrakas and the recent study on a hospital's decision-making.

The heavy time constraints on the hospital study were so severe that several contractors refused to bid on the proposal. These time constraints had severe effect on the completion rate (compare Lavrakas' 85 percent response rate to the hospital's 21 percent response rate). The time constraint also affected the respondents not available.

Since the hospital study was conducted using a telephone list from the American Hospital Association (AHA) Guide there were few numbers that were not in service. In addition few hospitals had telephones that were not answered. Our other category was greatly increased due to 18 percent of the individual decision-makers, for the product under investigation (the sample frame), had transferred out of the hospital. Another 4 percent of the other includes connecting to answering machines.

Obtaining a completed interview is frequently the result of more than one telephone attempt. This process can include scheduling call-back times with either the intended respondent or another individual living in the household. The call sheets represent all calls to a particular telephone number in the sample.

Table 4.7 reports the final disposition of call sheets in a RDD survey (Lavrakas, 1987). With the Lavrakas studies one may note that with up to 10 call-backs and scheduling of later interview times completion rates go up to 34 percent. No answer or busy drops to only 3 percent. What one sees is that the combination of refusals and inability to reach the intended respondent together drop to only 23 percent of the final dispositions. Similar percentages, discussed later, were reported by Berdie (1991).

Table 4.7 Disposition of call sheets in Lavrakas study

Final disposition of call sheets	Lavrakas percent of all dialings
Completed interview	34
Numbers not in service	33
Business/group number (screened out)	11
Household/hospital refusal	6
Selected respondent never reached	4
Intended respondent refusal	4
No answer after 10 calls	3
Needed foreign language interviewers	3
Incomplete interview	2
Other	1
	5,436

Source: Lavrakas (1987).

Completion rates Weaver, Holmes, and Glenn (1975) indicated that in a study with an overall 10 percent refusal rate, refusals by black respondents were 42 percent. Tyebejee (1979) reports that significant populations were under-represented in households having telephones. Even though over 80 percent of all rural households had telephones, less than half of rural, black households had telephones. Tyebejee adds other populations that are similarly under-represented.

O'Neil (1979) identified individuals whom he classified as those amenable to responding to a telephone survey and those he classified as resistant. The resistors tended to: (a) have less education, (b) lower incomes, and (c) be in older age brackets. The resistors over-represented blue-collar and service workers, especially skilled craftsmen. In contrast white-collar professionals and managers were under-represented in the resistors category. Similarly, Appel and Baim (1992) found that 82 percent of the variance in response rate was accounted for by median home value, the extent of urbanization, and the proportion of householders that were relatively well off or retired.

Lavrakas (1987) indicates that telephone surveys have changed considerably due to, among other things, the proportion of US households that have telephones. He indicates that during the 1970s this proportion went above 90 percent and by 1981 it was 96 percent. He suggests that the advantages of telephone survey methods (quality control, cost efficiency, and speed of data collection) outweigh the disadvantages (limitation on the type and length of questioning). Lavrakas reports that some states have high and others have low percents of households with telephone service. He note that a high percent of homes in the Northeast have telephone service and a low percent of homes in the Southeast have telephone service.

Frey (1983) reports that refusal rates in telephone surveys have stabilized around 24 percent. He indicates that refusal conversion rates can only reduce this number to about 21 percent (which is slightly better than those experienced by door-to-door interviewers). NFO reports refusals to participate in telephone surveys have increased from 15 percent in 1982 to 36 percent in 1990. Baim (1991) suggests that there are substantial declines in telephone response rates in the United States, Britain, and France. He suggests that response rates in large cities are the main problem. He suggests that these declines have not been found in Germany and Switzerland.

However some variables are working to increase participation. Tuckel and Feinberg (1991) note that individuals with answering machines are more reachable and willing to participate in telephone surveys. NFO further reports that the use of answering machines has increased from 13 percent in 1988, to 22 percent in 1990 and is up to 33 percent in 1992.

NFO adds that telemarketing calls significantly outnumber telephone survey calls 13 to 1. While Sunenshine (1992) suggests that "the methodology preferred by respondents, far and away, was mail with telephone a distant second." This suggests that telemarketing may be having a negative effect on telephone survey participation.

An argument for high return rates In addition to the differences cited above (i.e. Weaver, Holmes, and Glenn, 1975), Tyebejee (1979) cites

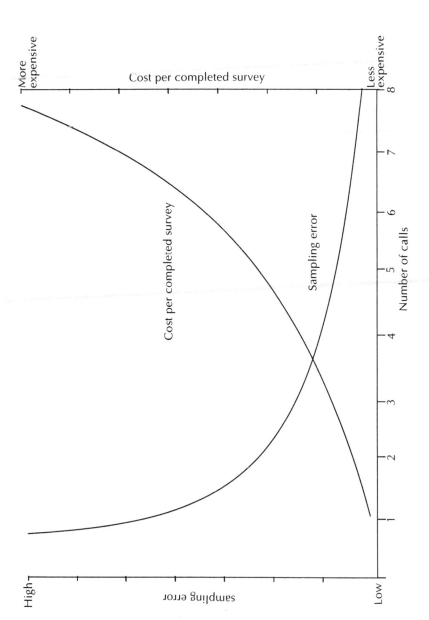

Figure 4.2 Relationship of number of call-backs to costs per completed survey and sampling error

research that suggests that the following biases may be evident when the telephone return rate is insufficient by the over-representation of (a) the over-64 age group, (b) lower education segments, (c) lower income segments, (d) housewives, and (e) retired persons. He further suggests that residents of large SMSAs may be under-represented. Using telephone interviews followed by face-to-face contact with nonrespondents, Swan, O'Connor and Seung (1991) found that even after four call-backs, the respondent sample differed from the population estimate by more than 10 percent.

Hornik, Zaig, and Shadmon (1991) report high rates of refusal to answer long telephone surveys on sensitive topics (i.e. sexual behavior, personal income, use of drugs, criminal behavior, etc.). They indicate that the foot-in-the-door (FITD) technique and the low ball (LB) technique are both effective at enhancing compliance to requests for information about sensitive behaviors. However, they indicate that a combination of these two techniques was more effective than either alone. The combined technique had subjects first commit to responding to a later survey (LB) then the subject was asked "While we are on the phone could you please respond to three short questions concerning personal matters" (FITD). At the specified time, a second call and interview was conducted with these subjects. Donsbach and Brosius (1991) suggest other techniques that have been successful in Europe.

An argument against paying for high return rates In contrast, Berdie (1991) indicates that the allocation of resources to achieve a response rate beyond 65 to 75 percent in telephone surveys may be unwise. He suggests that response rate is a more useful goal than number of callbacks. Using a telephone research panel, Donsbach and Brosius (1991) found that the representativeness of the achieved sample did not vary with the number of call-backs. Unfortunately, the number of call-backs is a billable unit of relatively known cost. This known cost is useful to both the marketing research supplier and client because it helps estimate costs when making a bid to perform the research. Figure 4.2 shows a hypothesized relationship between number of call-backs and both sampling error and cost per completed survey.

Berdie suggests that resources may be better spent elsewhere rather than increasing return rate beyond this range. He claimed that "reductions in nonresponse error associated with increasing response rate beyond the 75 percent level does not usually justify the cost of such additional effort." Berdie concludes that the data begins to converge at 50 percent response rate and with response rates in the 65 percent to 75 percent range they very closely approximate the total sample. Figure 4.3 shows that data generated from these high response rates closely approximates data from samples with higher response rates.

Smead (1980) explored ring policies and suggests that the number of rings preceding a telephone being answered follows a gamma distribution.

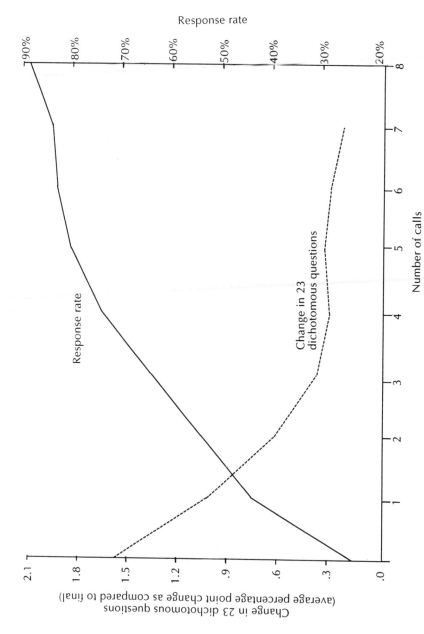

Figure 4.3 Change in responses to dichotomous questions as they relate to number of call-backs and percentage response rate

They found that 88 percent of individuals that were at home were reached after 3 rings, 4 rings resulted in 97 percent and 5 rings in 99 percent.

There are no known methods to inexpensively access a random sample of the general public with mailed questionnaires. This shortcoming considerably reduces the usefulness of mailed questionnaires to many survey research professionals. This limitation has resulted in telephone surveys being the cost-effective methodology of choice for reaching the general public.

As stated earlier most marketing research studies do not require a random sample of the general public. Most marketing research studies require specific populations. For example they frequently require individuals who purchased a specific product. It is usually too expensive to reach these individuals by seeking responses from the general public.

Mail surveys

Mail surveyors who are satisfied with the typical (35 percent or lower) return rate are presenting results of samples that sometimes vastly differ from those that would be obtained from the population. These types of return rates lead Dillon, Madden, and Firtle (1987) to consider mail surveys nonprobability or convenience samples. Those surveyors, however, who use techniques such as Dillman's (1978, 1983, 1984) "total design method" do not consider sampling error as much a disadvantage. They are frequently achieving return rates well over 70 percent with many segments of the population. However, not even these techniques can help a mail survey if complete lists of respondents are not available.

Mail panel studies Poor sampling lists lead many marketing research firms to use national panels for the mail surveys. These nationally representative samples are maintained by firms such as Market Facts (Arlington Heights, Illinois), NFO (Toledo, Ohio), and the National Purchase Diary (NPD) Group (Port Washington, New York). These organizations maintain a list of individuals that are both representative of the nation and are willing to respond to surveys (mail, telephone, focus group, etc.). These vendors take great care to insure that their samples reflect national norms.

The companies that maintain these panels also collect a considerable amount of additional information on their panels. This information includes telephone number, ages of individuals in the household, incomes of individuals in the household, types of products purchased, medications taken on a regular basis, and other types of information.

Most mail survey marketing research is conducted using these mail panels. The advantages of using mail panels include: reduced costs for identifying specific respondents, increased capability to follow the subjects longitudinally, and the capability to obtain new subjects that match those used in a previous study (that have not been contaminated by the previous study).

Only about one-third of mail surveys are conducted using direct mail to subjects other than those in panels. Consumer mail panels offer another significant advantage: the panel members would not be subject to impending legislation regarding the conduct of telephone surveys. Since mail panel members have previously agreed to complete surveys, contact can be made with them. Such contact with individuals who have not signed such an agreement may be limited by future legislation.

In addition to the major consumer panels, other organizations also maintain panels for specific purposes. Dillman and Ferber (1979) report that panels are also maintained by Market Research Corporation of America (MRCA), Marketing Information Center, A. C. Nielsen, and Slade Research. Presumably as a guide for an individual who would desire to set-up his/her own panel these authors provide information about cooperators and noncooperators. They suggest that cooperators in panels tend to be from households with two or more members and younger wives in upper income brackets.

Return rate enhancement Only the dedicated surveyor using return rate enhancement techniques can consistently obtain mail survey response rates above 90 percent. This type of dedication produces mail survey samples as representative as those typically obtained by telephone. Occasionally researchers report return rates over 95 percent (Altshuld and Lower, 1984) when using a variety of return rate enhancement techniques. On several occasions, we have obtained return rates over 90 percent when we have had sufficient time and resources to support a variety of return rate enhancement techniques. Such return rates are generally unheard of in telephone surveys.

The time it takes to conduct a mail survey severely limits their usefulness in many marketing research projects. All too frequently marketing research projects are not well designed, need to be conducted under restricted time frames, and have to meet short-term goals. These conditions are set up by management knowing little about marketing research methodologies but a great deal about their own immediate information needs.

Low return rates and long time frames are perhaps the most maligned qualities of mailed questionnaires. These qualities have led many researchers to pursue methods to increase return rates. Unfortunately there is little research to suggest that increasing return rates deceases bias.

Dillman (1991) recently examined two decades of research on techniques to increase mailed questionnaire return rates. He cites four types of error in mail surveys: sampling, noncoverage, measurement, and nonresponse. He claims significant progress has been made in reducing measurement and nonresponse error. Sampling error creates no special problems. Noncoverage error represents a significant gap in the mail survey research literature.

Noncoverage error occurs when members of the population are not included in the sampling frame. This is not a problem with sampling frames that include students at a particular university, members of a professional society, employees of a company, or other samples where acceptable population lists are available. However, in surveys of the general public such lists are inadequate. Telephone books do not include individuals with unlisted numbers. Similarly city directories and drivers' license lists are also incomplete. Techniques analogous to random digit dialing or plus one dialing are not available for the mail surveyor. Techniques to reduce nonresponse error by telephone are widely available.

Baumgartner and Heberlein (1984) report on several quantitative studies regarding mail return rate enhancement techniques. Table 4.9 presents the results of two quantitative studies reported by them. This table shows that Government sponsorship was the variable that most increased the return rate in these studies. The salience of the topic was the quality that had the second strongest positive effect on the return rate. You may note that sponsorship by a marketing research organization is the quality that most decreased the return rate. Heberlein and Baumgartner included university sponsorship under the general heading of government sponsorship. Recent research by Faria and Dickinson (1992) supports the advantages of university sponsorship over commercial firms.

Return rates can be enhanced by very simple procedures. A study we presented at the Midwestern Psychological Association (Lockhart and Russo, 1980) found an increase in return rate from 5 percent to 23 percent by simply adding a cover page on the questionnaire. It simply had a plain white cover with a border and the logo of the sponsor. A study by Frey (1991) recently used cover pages and two postcard reminders in a low budget study and obtained return rates over 50 percent. His results also suggest that the type of cover page is not as important as the presence of a cover page.

Table 4.8 Regression equations predicting expected return rate from two US studies

Attribute	Study 1	Study 2
Base rate	36.3	24.7
Government organization	10.2	13.7
Salience of topic	7.3	12.2
Total number of contacts	7.4	7.8
Incentive first contact	6.1	7.5
School or army population	9.9	6.3
Special third contact	8.6	4.3
Number of pages	−0.4	−0.4
General population	−7.5	−1.1
Market research background	−10.1	−1.6

There are some procedures that are very well researched and are known to work in almost all mailed surveys. For example there are a myriad of studies documenting the increased return rates associated with additional follow-ups. Recently Yammarino, Skinner, and Childers (1991) reported a meta-analysis of response rates on 184 effects in 115 studies. They conclude that the average manipulation increased return rates by 6.5 percent. They indicate that the greatest effects were found for: repeated contacts (including preliminary notification, and follow-ups); types of appeals; inclusion of a return envelope; postage paid; and monetary incentives.

Other research by Kallis and Giglierano (1992) report that express mail can be a cost-effective means of decreasing the cost per respondent when the recruiting costs per respondent are greater than $23. Two-way express delivery also increases the speed of response. One-way express delivery is justified if the per respondent recruiting costs are more than $10. Express mail delivery represents one of the many new methods being investigated for using a traditional survey technique.

Biner and Barton (1991) report, in a survey of the general public in a Midwestern city, that a $1.00 incentive was more effective than a $0.25 enclosure. They also report that a cover letter that emphasizes an obligation to respond (the money is to make it clear that you are now obligated to return the questionnaire to us immediately) was more effective than a cover letter that emphasizes appreciation (the small gift to show our appreciation and thanks).

Return rate enhancement with different populations Our recent research using physicians and pharmacists suggests that different rules may apply to the use of return rate enhancement techniques with different populations. Lockhart (1991) demonstrated the effect of increasing monetary incentives with physicians as shown in Figure 4.4.

This work shows that return rates from physicians show a logarithmic relationship with the dollar value of an enclosed incentive. This logarithmic relationship is shown with each of three physician subsamples. One may note the effect of interest in the topic by the height of each line. Endocrinologists and diabetologists (diabetes specialists) would be expected to be more interested in the diabetes topic of the survey than general practice (GP), family practice (FP) and internal medicine (IM) physicians. An article by Sobal et al. (1990) also notes differences in return rates for physicians in different specialties.

Table 4.10 shows three significant different return rates for physicians and one for pharmacists. These results suggest that monetary incentives are an effective means of increasing return rates for physicians. In contrast increasing contacts was an effective means of increasing return rates for pharmacists.

Internal medicine physicians who received three contacts were more likely to return the questionnaire if they received fifteen rather than five dollars. Both level of contacts for endocrinologists were more likely to return the questionnaire if they received fifteen rather than five dollars. For pharmacists the only significant effect was for those who received a five dollar incentive. Pharmacists who received three contacts were more likely to return the questionnaire than those who received only one contact.

Table 4.9 Return rates for physicians and pharmacists using three levels of incentives and two levels of contacts

Sample	Physicians				Pharmacists	
	IM		Endocrinologist			
Number of contacts:	One	Three	One	Three	One	Three
Amount of incentive:						
$5	30	21	43	41	36	46
$10	40	33	48	52	45	49
$15	34	42	59	55	46	46

These results indicate that the different types of health care professionals responded in a different manner to the questionnaire. That is, the endocrinologists had a consistently higher return rate than did internal medicine physicians. This effect was consistent regardless of monetary incentive or number of follow-ups. In contrast the pharmacists appear to have been more influenced by the number of contacts than did either group of physicians.

Since the topic of the physician surveys was specifically methods in which the doctor deals with diabetic patients, then it seems likely that the diabetes

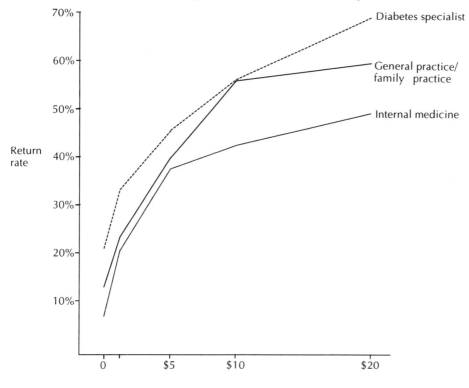

Figure 4.4 Return rate by incentive level

specialists would be most interested in the topic. These results suggest that each group responds to the survey and the incentives differently.

Subsequent research suggests that these increased response rates are not associated with decreased bias. Figure 4.5 shows the bias in this survey about diabetes in terms of type of physicians responding. This figure shows that nonrespondents consistently wrote fewer diabetes prescriptions than did respondents. This trend remained regardless of return rate or incentive amount used. O'Neil (1979) provides some suggestions for estimating this type of nonresponse bias.

Sudman and Bradburn (1984) report return rates for a few difficult to reach populations. They indicate that the busy schedule and number of questionnaires sent to physicians has a decremental effect on their return rate. They note, however, that when the topic of the survey is particularly salient to the physician, higher return rates can be obtained. This can be noted in the dental hygienists samples included in Table 4.8.

Table 4.10 Return rates for difficult to reach populations

Population	Return rate %	Mid-range average %
Accountants	81	81
Teachers	71–88	80
Dental hygienists (in ADHA)	76	76
Physicians	50–80	69
Attorneys	66	66
Dentists	63	63
Dental hygienists (not in ADHA)	62	62

Presumably those who are members of the American Dental Hygienists Association (ADHA) are more interested in a survey on dental hygiene than nonmembers. This interest level is reflected in the higher return rate observed. If Sudman and Bradburn had broken out the physician sample and the topics of the surveys, then presumably one could have identified some of the reasons for the variance in physicians' return rates. The current authors will present a more complete summary of their research with physicians later in this chapter.

Other researchers have found that personalization techniques are successful in obtaining responses from professional populations. Moss and Worthen (1991) found that handwritten salutations elicited more responses. Maheux *et al.* (1989) found a more personalized mailout resulted in higher response rates from a sample of Canadian physicians. Diamantopoulos *et al.* (1991) also investigated the effect of personalization with a sample of United Kingdom industrial surveys.

Nonresponse bias Our own research has demonstrated that techniques that increase the return rate do not necessarily decrease biased responding. One hypothesis is that individuals who are more interested in the topic of

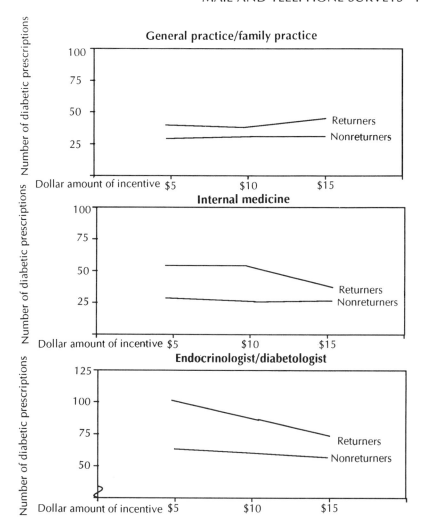

Figure 4.5 Differences between returners and non-returners by physician specialties

the survey are more likely to respond. Return rate enhancement techniques may increase response rate by encouraging responses from additional individuals who are interested in the topic of the survey and not affect responses from those who are not interested in the topic of the survey.

Recent models presented at the annual meeting of the American Psychological Association (Lockhart, 1991) suggest a model similar to that shown in Figure 4.6. That is, the best predictor of returning mailed questionnaires is past behavior of returning, mailed questionnaires. If there is no measure of past returning, then intentions to return a questionnaire significantly predict future mailed questionnaire returning behavior. Attitudes in the Fishbein and Azjen (1976) model and affect in the Triandis (1977) model were good predictors of intentions to return a mailed questionnaire. The social

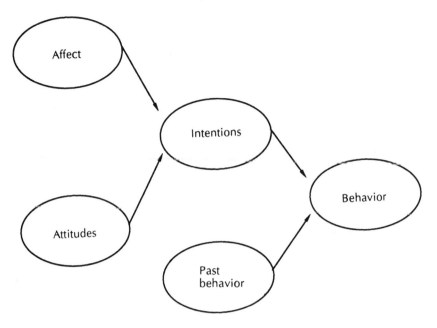

Figure 4.6 Hypothesized combination of Triandis (1977) and Fishbein and Ajzen (1976) models that best predicts mailed questionnaire returning behavior

norms, subjective norms, and perceived consequences measures in these theories did not add significant predictive power to the structural equations.

A recent article by Bagozzi, Baumgartner, and Yi (1992) suggests that the past behavior measure may best be broken into two components. One of these components is a recency measure and one is a frequency measure. In addition these authors delineated processes intervening between intentions and behavior.

Another hypothesis is that nonrespondents to mail surveys either (a) have difficulty answering the questions or (b) feel that they do not know enough about the topic of the survey. In some instances this nonresponse bias is good because subjects disqualify themselves based on the relevance of the category to them. In other instances this characteristic results in surveys that are not representative of the average individual in the initial sampling frame. The result is that attempts to generalize to the population from a mail survey are frequently difficult.

The nonrespondents, therefore, tend to over-represent those individuals who are not interested in the product or product category. This hypothesis implies that respondents to a mailed marketing research questionnaire are those who are more likely to purchase the product. This bias would suggest that marketing research surveys conducted by mail methods alone tend to overstate purchase intent.

Lockhart (1984) presented a stage theory of mailed questionnaire responding. Table 4.11 provides an update of these stages including techniques that can be used to aid respondents in completing each of the stages. Respondents must complete five stages and possibly a sixth stage (dealing with reminders) if the researcher is to obtain valid responses to mailed questionnaires. Frey (1991) suggests that the first question serves as a representative of the difficulty of responding to the entire questionnaire. A difficult or uninteresting first question increases the probability that a questionnaire will not be completed.

Table 4.11 Hypothesized stages of mailed questionnaire response

Stage	Techniques to improve
Receiving the questionnaire	Accurate sampling lists Accurate addresses Proper addressing and stamping
Opening the mail	Organizational affiliation Personalizing address Type name and address on envelope
Forming an overall impression	Quality of paper used Using commemorative stamp Cover page
Answering the questions	Well written questions Questions appropriate to audience Providing an 800 number
Dealing with reminders	Send several stages of mail reminders Provide a second questionnaire Use telephone reminders
Returning the questionnaire	Provide self addressed stamped envelope Use a commemorative stamp Questionnaire fits in return envelope

Other issues in mail surveys Figures 4.7 and 4.8 provide our hypothesized distribution of questionnaire returns in a mail survey. Figure 4.7 shows the distribution of questionnaire returns without reminders. Note that after 5 days of returns about half of the final questionnaire return rate is obtained. Figure 4.8 shows the returns with 3 reminders.

Other methods

There are a variety of research methods that are used in addition to (and as a supplement to) mail and telephone surveys. Mall intercept interviews are sometimes conducted as a prelude to a product trial followed by an immediate telephone interview and a long term follow-up using a mail survey. Similarly, subjects in a scanner panel, diary panel, or convention study can be given an 800 number to call after using a product to participate in another survey.

The one-on-one interview has changed considerably throughout the 1990s. Early in the century these interviews were conducted by surveyors

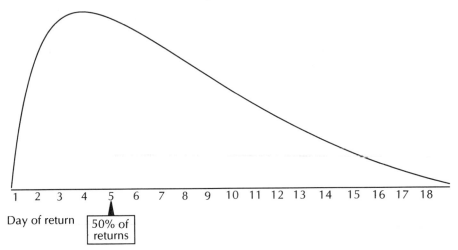

Figure 4.7 Alpha distribution (standard pattern of mailed questionnaire returns)

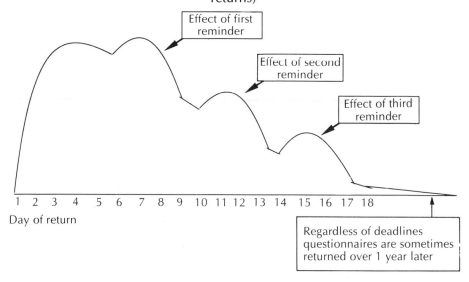

Figure 4.8 Alpha distribution (with effect of reminders included)

going to households. Currently, most involve the surveyors setting-up in one location and having the respondents come to them. These interviews are conducted by the myriad of marketing research suppliers available in every metropolitan area in the country.

Recently scanner panels have been maintained by marketing research suppliers. The suppliers keep a longitudinal data base on all the purchases of the panel members. Firms such as Arbitron, IRI, and Nielsen have subjects maintain diaries or keep meters that measure their radio listening and television watching behaviors. The diaries are used by radio and television stations to determining share of market for various programs. These shares then translate into advertising rates.

Some companies, such as Hallmark, conduct many mall intercepts. They recruit subjects who have just left a Hallmark store to determine what products they noticed, what ones they looked at, and what ones they purchased.

Focus groups represent a major form of qualitative marketing research. They are treated in depth in another chapter by Calder. Focus groups usually involve a group of four to twelve individuals gathered in one place to discuss a product, concept, or service. The group is facilitated by one or more moderators. The moderators normally have a discussion guide that is followed. Frequently clients watch the group through a one-way glass and the encounter is videotaped. The authors of this chapter have found that focus group members are more comfortable when told that the session will be taped and that the tape is to improve the accuracy of notes that are being taken by the facilitators. Although this use is rare, mail or telephone surveys are occasionally used to follow-up focus group discussions.

Research at trade conventions usually consists of the use of a booth where respondents complete surveys in exchange for gifts. For example, some firms specialize in collecting data at medical conventions. These firms recruit individuals who pass by their booth to answer a survey. Paper and pencil is usually used to obtain the responses from the medical professionals. Occasionally computers are used to conduct the interview.

Hypotheses for your consideration

Hypothesis 4 Telephone surveys lose some of the advantages mentioned above when conducted under tight time frames.

Hypothesis 5 RDD is the most economical method of reaching a random sample of the general population.

Hypothesis 6 More laws will be passed which limit the use of telephone surveys.

Hypothesis 7 Respondents to telephone surveys tend to over-represent gregarious individuals.

Hypothesis 8 Return rate enhancement techniques are successful with specific populations.

Hypothesis 9 Respondents to mail surveys are more (a) frequent purchasers of products in a category, (b) familiar with the specific product(s) being evaluated, and (c) interested in the topics included in the survey.

Hypothesis 10 Mail survey results are biased toward a more favorable image of the product and product category.

Hypothesis 11 Respondents who delay returning a questionnaire tend to be more interested in the topic than those who return the questionnaire immediately. The respondents interest conflicting with other pressures for the time slot resulted in them holding the questionnaire to a later time and eventually returning it. These individuals are the opposite of nonrespondents.

Hypothesis 12 Slow respondents to a mailed questionnaire have attitudes opposite those of nonrespondents.

A Survey of Surveyors

This section presents the results of a survey of surveyors we conducted in preparation for this chapter. These comparisons represent the first empirical comparison of the four major methodologies (mail, telephone, focus group, in-person interview) commonly used in marketing research. It is based on our perception that there is too little data on the survey research process in marketing research. This perception is based on the belief that much of the data regarding marketing research surveys is in the files and heads of the individuals who conduct these surveys. This study was conducted to translate some of these perceptions into data.

As a pilot study we view these results as suggestive and not definitive. There were four primary goals for this study. First, we intended to identify suggested factors regarding the importance of major survey factors to the success of a survey effort. Second, we sought to determine a rank ordering of these factors in terms of importance of each to the success of the survey process. Third, we intended to obtain information regarding the relative advantages and disadvantages of each methodology. Finally, we sought to determine if academics, suppliers, and clients viewed the importance factors differently.

The sample

The initial mailed questionnaire was sent to a sample of 228 and 66 returned it in time to be included (a 29 percent overall return rate). The sample included 82 individuals from academic institutions, 71 from marketing research suppliers, and 75 managers or directors of marketing research departments of major corporations (clients).

The sample for this mailing was hand selected based on either (a) their knowledge of survey research or (b) their position of responsibility for marketing research surveys. Many of the people included in the initial population list are referenced in this chapter. No return rate enhancement techniques were used in conducting this survey.

Thirty percent of the individuals from academic institutions returned the survey. Twenty-three percent of the individuals from marketing research suppliers returned the survey. Thirty-three percent of the individuals from marketing research departments of major corporations returned the survey. The survey included 200 5-point likert type scales questions plus a page of demographic data. The 200 5-point likert type scales consisted of 40 questions each regarding the importance of selected attributes to the success of a survey and the relative advantage or disadvantage of each of the four methodologies on these attributes. The four methodologies chosen were mailed surveys, telephone surveys, in-person interviews, and focus groups.

Table 4.12 provides a description of the respondents in terms of number of surveys during 1991 in which they participated. As one can see, the respondents to this pilot study are experienced in the survey field.

Table 4.12 Number of mail, telephone, in-person, and focus group studies participated in during 1991

	Average	Sum of all respondents
Mail	69	4,522
Telephone	100	6,561
In-person interview	47	3,062
Focus group	54	3,490

Based on some of the telephone and mail responses we received from this survey it may be very difficult or impossible to have these three types of respondents answer the same questions about the four types of surveys investigated. We have concerns that the same attribute list does not apply to all methodologies. We also have concerns that these three populations do not have a perspective to answer all of the questions for any one methodology. For example, some respondents found it difficult to rate the relative advantages of mailed surveys on "personnel requirements: interviewers." One client called and indicated that he could not distinguish between the various cost components.

Finally, a few respondents called and talked at length about how their survey process may be different from our intentions or the norm for the particular survey category. For example, one client indicated that all of their in-person interviews were conducted in a mall. Another client indicated that all of their in-person interviews were conducted by computer. This is to say that there is considerable variation in interpretations for each of these categories (mail, telephone, in-person, and focus group).

What is important when conducting surveys

Table 4.13 shows the reliable factors obtained from the exploratory factor analysis. Several rotations and numbers of factors were explored. Nine reliable factors were identified based on eigenvalues, scree plots, Chronbach's Alpha, and subjective interpretation of face validity.

Table 4.13 Factor loadings and suggested names for importance items with acceptable internal consistency

Factor items	Varimax loading
Nonresponse	
Refusal rate	0.85
Response rate: general public	0.78
Bias due to refusals	0.70
Noncontact/nonaccessibility	0.67
Effective probing	
Ability to use open-end responses	0.88
Ability to probe when necessary	0.89
Ability to clarify answers	0.73
Success with screening questions	0.47
Cost versus biased responses	
Confidentiality	0.69
Total cost	−0.65
Ability to obtain responses to sensitive items	0.63
Interviewer distortion of response	0.57
Interviewer control of respondents	0.51
Per interview costs	−0.46
Boring and tedious questions	
Success with boring questions	0.88
Success with tedious questions	0.86
Item nonresponse	0.61
Length of survey	
Allowable length of questionnaire	0.85
The effect of length of a survey	0.74
Complexity of questions	0.66
Personnel costs	
Personnel costs: interviewers	0.85
Personnel costs: supervision	0.70
Per interview costs	0.54
Timeliness	
Time to conduct after implementation	0.88
Time from concept to implementation	0.82
Consultation	
Ability of respondent to consult with others	0.83
Ability to consult financial and other documents	0.63
Success with controlling sequence of questions	0.43
Ability to locate selected respondents	0.45
Ability to obtain responses from an elite group	0.43
Sampling	
Sample coverage when population lists available	0.77
Sample coverage	0.71

1 = extremely important, 4 = not at all important.

In addition to the nine reliable factors four factors with lower reliabilities were obtained. Table 4.14 shows the items and their loadings from an exploratory factor analysis.

Table 4.14 Factor loadings and suggested names for importance items with unacceptable internal consistency

Factor items	Varimax loading
Biased responses	
Ability to obtain responses from a particular respondent	0.80
Social desirable responses	−0.53
Ability to locate selected respondents	0.48
Success with screening questions	0.42
Group contact	
Ability to use visual aids	0.73
Contamination of responses due to other individuals	−0.69
Time to enter data after implementation	0.44
Survey modification	
Ability to modify questionnaire	0.83
Dealing with complex skip patterns	0.67
Success with controlling sequence of questions	0.36
Locating respondents	
Substitutability of respondents within a household	0.72
Ability to obtain responses from an elite group	−0.59
Success with controlling sequence of questions	0.49

1 = extremely important, 4 = not at all important.

Some items loaded on more than one factor in the factor analyses. The following is a list of some items that had multiple factor loadings.

- "Per interview costs" loaded negatively on the "cost versus biased responses" factor and positively on the "cost factor."
- "Success with controlling sequence of questions" loaded about equally on the "consultation" and "locating respondents" factors. It also had high loadings on the "survey modification" factor.
- "Ability to locate selected respondents" loaded on the "consultation" factor and the "biased responses" factors.
- "Success with screening questions" loaded on the "biased responses" and the "effective probing" factors.
- "Ability to obtain responses from an elite group" loaded on the "consultation" and the "locating respondents" factors.

"Per interview" costs represents both the cost side of the costs versus bias factor and the positive side of the costs factor. Interview costs represent one of the major costs in conducting telephone surveys. If one raises these costs by hiring well trained (and more expensive) interviewers then one can usually reduce biased responding. This is a trade-off that anyone conducting or paying for research must make. All too frequently cost containment issues force this item into the cost side of the equation. When included as only a cost it is something that can be adjusted to reduce costs. When included as a cost versus bias item it is something to be traded off against bias. This trade-off of the location of this item represents one of our major areas of concern when individuals with less training in research methods manage the marketing research process.

Table 4.15 shows the Chronbach's alphas and the respondents' rank order of importance for the thirteen scales. Since this is a pilot study we have lowered the criteria for an acceptable scale to 0.6. One scale we had to adjust to make it obtain an acceptable reliability, survey modification. By dropping the item "success with controlling sequence of questions" we obtained ten factors with an Alpha greater than 0.6. These ten factors are used in all further analyses.

Table 4.15 Reliability (standardized Chronbach's Alpha) of 13 factors on importance scale and each (reliable) method's importance rating

Importance rank	Factor	Chronbach's Alpha	Importance rating
1	Sampling	0.72	1.82
2	Length of survey	0.74	1.97
3	Non-response	0.72	2.09
4	Timeliness	0.80	2.11
5	Survey modification	0.60	2.26
6	Biased responses	0.56	—
7	Cost versus bias	0.65	2.29
8	Effective probing	0.82	2.30
9	Personnel costs	0.69	2.33
10	Locating respondents	0.41	—
11	Group contact	0.53	—
12	Boring questions	0.74	2.58
13	Consultation	0.69	3.17

We believe that the "biased responses" factor will be found in future research. The items in the pilot study probably did not sufficiently represented this factor. Items that may load better on this factor could include ability to identify false responses, anonymity of responses, and trust of interviewer. Several of the items related to biased responding loaded better on the cost versus bias factor. Items such as interviewer distortion and confidentiality were possibly viewed as an effect of poorly trained and paid interviewers.

Table 4.15 also displays the rank order of these ten factors in terms of their rated importance when conducting a survey. Only 31 subjects completed all of the items that loaded into all of these factors. Success with boring and tedious questions was rated as having significantly lower importance than were sampling and length of survey. Consultation was rated as significantly less important than all of the other factors.

How does each method perform?

Table 4.16 shows the average rating given to each methodology on each item. When comparing only the ratings for telephone and mail there was a significant difference in the rating given for mail and telephone surveys on seven of the ten factors. Mail and telephone surveys were not rated significantly different on three of the factors: length of survey, cost versus bias, and boring and tedious questions. Most of these differences support the advantages of telephone surveys over mail surveys.

Table 4.16 Performance of four survey methods on items

Factor/items	Mail	Tele'	One-on one	Focus groups	Sig.
Nonresponse (+)					
Refusal rate	4.10	3.09	3.15	3.63	+
Response general public	3.98	2.52	3.07	3.61	+
Bias due to refusals	3.98	3.12	3.37	3.73	+
Noncontact	3.78	3.39	3.55	3.57	+
Effective probing (+)					
Open-end responses	3.21	2.10	1.46	1.29	+
Probe	4.46	1.57	1.40	1.35	+
Clarify answers	4.11	1.78	1.42	1.36	+
Screening questions	3.49	1.86	2.23	2.62	+
Cost versus biased responses					
Confidentiality	2.52	3.15	3.37	3.98	*
Total cost	1.87	2.86	4.56	2.75	*
Sensitive items	2.34	3.27	3.17	3.23	*
Distortion of responses	2.18	3.70	3.72	3.47	*
Control of respondents	3.85	2.15	1.83	1.96	+
Boring and tedious questions					
Boring questions	3.44	3.00	2.21	2.52	+
Tedious questions	3.52	2.81	2.09	2.32	+
Item nonresponse	3.71	2.55	2.41	2.88	+
Survey modification (+)					
Modify questionnaire	3.82	2.07	2.48	1.53	+
Complex skip patterns	4.38	1.67	2.23	2.54	+
Length of survey					
Length of questionnaire	2.82	3.37	2.12	2.67	
Effect of length	3.53	3.55	2.38	2.50	
Complexity of questions	2.98	3.05	1.88	1.98	
Personnel costs (*)					
Interviewers	1.97	3.47	4.15	2.94	*
Supervision	2.17	3.10	3.84	2.85	*
Per interview costs	1.97	2.88	4.56	3.69	*

Table 4.16. (*Cont.*)

Factor/items	Mail	Tele'	One-on one	Focus groups	Sig.
Timeliness (+)					
After implementation	4.05	1.97	3.50	2.01	+
Concept to implement	3.37	1.75	3.16	2.11	+
Consultation (*)					
Consult with others	3.01	3.04	2.94	2.83	
Financial documents	1.78	3.61	2.75	4.00	*
Sampling (+)					
With population lists	2.47	2.26	2.96	3.92	
Sample coverage	2.98	2.19	3.24	4.26	+

1 = major advantage, 3 = not sure, 5 = major disadvantage.
* = significant advantage of mail over telephone.
+ = significant advantage of telephone over mail.

Five factors were rated as being significantly more of an advantage for telephone surveys than for mailed surveys: non-responses, effective probing, timeliness, sampling, and survey modification. Two of the differences supported the advantage of mail surveys over telephone surveys: personnel costs and consultation. These results show telephone surveys are considered to have more advantages than mailed surveys. Not only are telephone surveys considered to have more advantages, but the advantages occur on factors that are considered more important.

Mail and telephone surveys were not rated significantly different on three of the factors: length of survey, cost versus bias, and boring and tedious questions. Most of these differences support the advantages of telephone surveys over mail surveys.

The two methodologies have about equal advantage on "length" and "consultation (with records and other individuals)". This table shows that telephone surveys have advantages on every single item that loads on nonresponse, effective probing, success with boring and tedious questions, survey modification, and timeliness. Telephone surveys are also considered to have an advantage on sample coverage. Mail surveys have an advantage on all of the items that load on cost. They also have advantages on cost versus biased responses except control of respondents. Keep in mind that total cost loads negatively on this scale.

These results suggest that respondents view the relative advantages of each survey methodology similar to those provided by Dillman, Frey, and Fowler (presented in Table 4.3). The only area of difference regards the effect of length. These authors do not indicate that the effects of length are an advantage for mailed surveys.

Comparison of sub-populations

This pilot study suggested that certain qualities of a survey are more important to individuals from an academic institution than those from nonacademic institutions. Academics view the following qualities as more important and less important than did the other respondents:

More important	Less important
Substituting respondents	Time from concept to implement
Socially desirable responses	Visual aids
Consulting records	Locate selected respondents

This study further suggests qualities of a survey that are more important to individuals from supplier organizations than those that who are not suppliers. Suppliers view the following qualities as more important and less important than did the other respondents:

More important	Less important
Per interview costs	Socially desirable responses
Response from particular respondent	
Locate selected respondent	

Finally this study suggests that individuals from client organizations view different qualities of a survey as more important. Clients view the following qualities as more important and less important than did the other respondents:

More important	Less important
Time from concept to implementation	Per interview costs
Visual aids	Response from particular respondent
	Locate selected respondents
	Substitute respondents
	Consulting records

Hypotheses for your consideration

Hypothesis 13 Academics view timelines and visual aids as less important when conducting surveys than do individuals from applied settings.

Hypothesis 14 Individuals from supplier organizations view sampling as a more important issue than do individuals from academic and client organizations.

Hypothesis 15 Clients view timelines as a greater disadvantage in conducting mail surveys than do individuals from academic and client organizations.

Hypothesis 16 Clients view the cost versus bias of telephone surveys as being more of an advantage than do individuals from academic and client organizations.

A Brief Summary and a Glimpse at the Future

Survey methods are changing every day. International computer networks, increasing computer expertise, fax machines, and other components of technological sophistication are all causing considerable changes in the methods by which marketing research is conducted. For example, with computer scanner technology, sales data can be generated daily and even hourly. Telephone surveys currently lead in popularity and will most likely continue to gain in popularity.

The two biggest marketing research companies in the country, Nielsen and IMS, are not known for surveys: their business is providing store audits. These audits inform manufacturers of category sales and shares. Most marketing research or marketing science departments spend more money on market tracking than on surveys. The belief is that behavioral data is superior to attitudinal data. Attitudinal data is used in a very broad sense to include any data collected by asking individuals questions.

Phone-mail-phone procedures are common. Face-to-face interviews where the respondent comes to the interviewer (rather than the interviewer going to the respondent) are also common. Face-to-face interviews conducted at focus group facilities are considerably more common than face-to-face interviewing conducted door-to-door. Other common methods include the computer interview, the warranty card survey, the fax survey, the lock box method, and the convention floor survey.

Russo (1984) explored the use of mailed questionnaires to collect qualitative data. The combinations of qualitative and quantitative research will probably continue with advances in each method stimulating advances in the other. A combination of focus group technology and telephone surveys played a prominent role in the 1992 Presidential election.

Mail, telephone, and face-to-face surveys can be used effectively in both academic research and business settings. The choice of survey methods will continue to depend on the trade-offs that must be made between timeliness, accuracy, and economy. Regardless of the method selected, a large sample size of qualified individuals, a high response rate, and a high level of sophistication in the people conducting the survey is likely to produce highly valid and reliable results.

Continued computerization and networking will lead to many more individuals using computers. Easier to use and less expensive computers will further increase the representativeness of individuals sampled through computers. Certainly some populations can already be surveyed by computer or disk. For example, representative samples of software engineers, computer scientists, and marketing researchers can be obtained using disk by mail methods. We have no doubt that the list is larger than this and growing. It is conceivable that in the future computer surveys will obtain representative of samples.

Questions

1 In what ways do marketing research surveys usually differ from those conducted by the government or universities?
2 What are the differences in the reinforcement structures for academics who write marketing research texts, clients who sponsor marketing research surveys, and suppliers who conduct marketing research surveys?
3 What flawed survey is one of the most infamous?
4 What common bias is found to a greater extent in telephone and in-person surveys than in mail surveys?
5 What common differences exist between individuals who respond to telephone surveys and those who do not respond to telephone surveys?
6 What are the advantages of using mail panels?
7 What key disadvantage limits the usefulness of mail surveys in marketing research?
8 What techniques can most influence return rates in a mail survey?
9 What methodology is preferred when there is a concern about respondents providing socially desirable responses?
10 Use the following formula to predict physician return rate for a mailed questionnaire.

Formula for physician return rate =

+   12.65
+   9.89 × square root of incentive
+   −2.79 × number of pages
+   23.54 × percent that responded to previous surveys
+   9.11 × specialty interested in topic (Coded 0 or over)
+   15.51 × inclusion of a gift
+   −4.80 × internal medicine specialty (Coded 0 or 1)

Calculate expected return rate for each questionnaire A through D.

Incentive	Number of pages	Response to previous survey (%)	Interested specialty	Gift	Internal medicine
A. $10	6	10	Yes	Yes	No
B. $20	10	20	Yes	Yes	No
C. $20	8	30	Yes	Yes	No
D. $10	2	40	No	No	Yes
E. $5	8	10	No	No	Yes
F. $5	12	20	No	No	Yes
G. $10	12	20	No	No	Yes

11 What is the total cost, number of completed surveys, and cost per completed survey in question 10? Make the following assumptions:

1,000 physicians in the sample
Cost of $15 for mailing and return of each survey sent
Cost of $5 for processing of each completed survey
8 percent of physicians cash their checks without completing the survey
Gifts cost $2 and are mailed to all 1,000 physicians

Notes

* Thanks to Keith Chrzan, Mary Ann Lockhart, Bill Maxey, Joe Staten, Stuart Greenberg, Scott Boggs, and Rick Bagozzi for comments on an earlier draft of this chapter.

References

Aaker, D. A. and Day, G. S. 1990: *Marketing Research*, 4th edn, New York, NY. Wikey & Sons.

Alreck, P. L. and Settle, R. B. 1985: *The Survey Research Handbook*, Homewood, IL.: Richard D. Irwin.

Altshuld, J. W. and Lower, M. A. 1984: Improving mailed questionnaires: analysis of a 96% return rate. In D. C. Lockhart (ed.), *Making Effective Use of Mailed Questionnaires: New Directions in Program Evaluation # 21*. San Francisco: Jossey-Bass.

Appel, V. and Baim, J. 1992: Predicting and correcting response rate problems using geodemography. *Marketing Research: A Magazine of Management and Applications*, 4, 22–8.

Bagozzi, R. P., Baumgartner, H., and Yi, Y. 1992: Appraisal processes in the enactment of intentions to use coupons. *Psychology and Marketing*, 9, 469–86.

Baim, J. 1991: Response rates a multinational perspective. *Marketing and Research Today*, 19, 114–19.

Baumgartner, R. M. and Heberlein, T. A. 1984: Recent research on mailed questionnaire response rates. In D. C. Lockhart (ed.), *Making Effective Use of Mailed Questionnaires: New Directions in Program Evaluation # 21*. San Francisco: Jossey-Bass.

Berdie, D. R. 1991: Telephone survey response rates: How high is high enough? *Marketing Research: A Magazine of Management Applications*, 3, 35–44.

Biner, P. M. and Barton, D. L. 1991: Justifying the enclosure of monetary incentives in mail survey cover letters. *Psychology and Marketing*, 7, 153–62.

Bowers, D. K. 1991: The inconvenience of change. *Marketing Research: A Magazine of Management and Applications*, March, 62–3.

Bradburn, N. M. and Sudman, S. 1979: *Asking Questions*, San Francisco, CA: Jossey-Bass.

Bradburn, N. M. and Sudman S. 1983: *Improving Interview Method and Questionnaire Design*, San Francisco, CA: Jossey-Bass.

Bradburn, N. M. and Sudman, S. 1988: *Polls and Surveys: Understanding what They Tell Us*, Jossey-Bass: San Francisco, CA.

Churchill, G. A. 1991: *Marketing Research: Methodological Foundations*, 5th edn, Chicago: Dryden.

Churchill, G. A. 1992: *Marketing Research: Methodological Foundations*, 5th edn, Chicago, IL: Dryden Press.

Diamantopoulos, A., Schlegelmilch, B. B., and Webb, L. 1991: Factors affecting industrial mail response rates. *Industrial Marketing Management*, 20, 327–39.

Dillman, D. A. 1978: *Mail and Telephone Surveys: The Total Design Method*, New York, NY: Wiley-interscience.

Dillman, D. A. and Ferber, R. 1979: *Consumer Panels*, Chicago, IL: American Marketing Association.

Dillman, D. A. 1983: Mail and other self administered questionnaires. In Rossi, P. H., Wright, J. D. and Anderson, A. B. (eds) *Handbook of Survey Research*, Orlando, FL.: Academic Press.

Dillman, D. A. 1984: The importance of adhering to details of the total design method (TDM) for mail surveys. In D. C. Lockhart (ed.) *Making Effective Use of Mailed Questionnaires: New Directions in Program Evaluation # 21*, San Francisco: Jossey-Bass.

Dillman, D. A. 1991: The design and administration of mail surveys. *Annual Review of Sociology*, 17, 225–49.

Dillon, W. R., Madden, T. J., and Firtle, N. H. 1987: *Marketing Research in a Marketing Environment*, Homewood, IL: Irwin.

Donsbach, W. and Brosius, H. 1991: Panel surveys by telephone: how to improve response rates and sample quality. *Marketing Research Today*, 19, 143–50.

Faria, A. J. and Dickinson, J. R. 1992: Mail survey response, speed, and cost. *Industrial Marketing Management*, 21, 51–60.

Fishbein, M. and Azjen, I. 1976: *Beliefs, Attitudes, Intentions, and Behavior: An Introduction to Theory and Research*, Boston, MA.: Addison-Wesley.

Fowler, F. J. 1988: *Survey Research Methods*, revised edn, Beverly Hills, CA.: Sage.

Frey, J. H. 1983: *Survey Research by Telephone*, Beverly Hills, CA: Sage.

Frey, J. H. 1991: The impact of cover design and a first question on response rates for a mail survey of skydivers. *Leisure Sciences*, 13, 67–76.

Goodfellow, M., Kiernan, N. E., Ahern, F., and Smyer, M. A. 1988: Response bias using two-stage data collection: a study of elderly participants in a program. *Evaluation Review*, 12, 638–54.

Greenbaum, T. L. 1987: *The Practical Handbook and Guide to Focus Group Research*, Lexington, MA: Lexington Books.

Hornik, J., Zaig, T., and Shadmon, D. 1991: Reducing refusals in telephone surveys on sensitive topics. *Journal of Advertising Research*, 31, 49–56.

Kahneman, D. and Tversky, A. 1979: Prospect theory: an analysis of decisions under risk. *Econometrica*, 47 (March), 263–91.

Kallis, M. J. and Giglierano, J. J. 1992: Improving mail response rates with express mail. *Industrial Marketing Management*, 21, 1–4.

Kerin, R. A. and Peterson, R. A. 1983: Scheduling telephone interviews. *Journal of Advertising Research*, 23, 41–7.

Lavrakas, P. J. 1987: *Telephone Survey Methods: Sampling, Selection, and Supervision*, Beverly Hills, CA: Sage.

Lehman, D. R. 1989: *Market Research and Analysis*, 3rd edn, Homewood, IL.: Richard D. Irwin, Inc.

Lockhart, D. C. and Russo, D. C. 1980: The effect of different colored color pages on the return rate of a mailed evaluation questionnaire. *Midwestern Psychological Association Annual Meeting*, May, St Louis MO.

Lockhart, D. C. 1984: The stages of mailed questionnaire returning behavior. In D. C. Lockhart (ed.), *Making Effective Use of Mailed Questionnaires: New Directions in Program Evaluation # 21*, San Francisco: Jossey-Bass.

Lockhart, D. C. 1991: Mailed surveys to physicians: the effect of incentives and length on the return rate. *Journal of Pharmaceutical Marketing and Management*, 6(1), 107–21.

Maheux, B., Legault, C., and Lambert, J. 1989: Increasing response rates in physicians' mail surveys: an experimental study. *American Journal of Public Health*, 79, 638–9.

Monahan, J. and Walker, L. 1990: *Social Science in Law: Cases and Materials*, Westbury, NY.: The Foundation Press.

Monroe, K. B. 1990: *Pricing: Making Profitable Decisions*, McGraw Hill: New York, NY.

Moss, V. D. and Worthen, B. R. 1991: Do personalization and postage make a difference on response rates to surveys of professional populations. *Psychological Reports*, 68, 692–4.

Nowell, C. and Stanley, L. R. 1991: Length-biased sampling in mall intercept surveys. *Journal of Marketing Research*, 28, 475–9.

O'Neil, M. J. 1979: Estimating the nonresponse bias due to refusals in telephone surveys. *Public Opinion Quarterly*, 43, 218–32.

Peterson, R. A. and Wilson, W. R. 1992: Effects of advertised customer satisfaction claims on consumer attitudes and purchase intention. *Journal of the Academy of Marketing Science*, 20, 61–71.

Rossi, P. H., Wright, J. D., and Anderson, A. B. 1983: *Handbook of Survey Research*, Orlando, FL.: Academic Press.

Russo, J. R. 1984: Using mailed questionnaires in negotiation consulting. In D. C. Lockhart (ed.), *Making Effective Use of Mailed Questionnaires: New directions in Program Evaluation # 21*, San Francisco: Jossey-Bass.

Russo, J. R., Lockhart, D. C., and Paulsmeyer, D. L. 1989: *Social Security Client Satisfaction Survey: Fiscal Year 1989*, Office of Inspector General/HHS.

Schuman, H. and Presser, S. 1981: *Questions and Answers in Attitude Surveys: Experiments on Question Form, Wording, and Context*, Orlando, CA.: Academic Press.

Skogan, W. G. 1978: *The Center for Urban Affairs Random Digit Dial Telephone Survey*, Evanston IL.: Center for Urban Affairs and Policy Research.

Smead, R. J. 1980: Ring policy in telephone surveys. *Public Opinion Quarterly*, 44, 115–16.

Smith, T. W. 1990: The first straw: a study of the origin of election polls. *Public Opinion Quarterly*, 54, 21–36.

Sobal, J., DeForge, B. R., Ferentz, K. S., Muncie, H. L., Valente, C. M., and Levine, D. M. 1990: Physician responses to muliple questionnaire mailings. *Evaluation Review*, 14, 711–22.

Sudman, S. and Bradburn N. 1984: Improving mailed questionnaire design. In D. C. Lockhart (ed.), *Making Effective Use of Mailed Questionnaires New Directions in Program Evaluation # 21*, San Francisco: Jossey-Bass.

Sunenshine, H. 1992: Industry image study. *American Marketing Association's Marketing Research Conference*, Atlanta, Sept. 13–16.

Swan, J. E., O'Connor, S. J., and Seung, D. L. 1991: A framework for testing sampling bias and methods of bias reduction in a telephone survey. *Marketing Research: A Magazine of Management Applications*, 3, 23–34.

Thaler, R. 1985: Mental accounting and consumer choice. *Marketing Science*, 4, 199–214.

Tourangeau, R. and Rasinski, K. A. 1988: Cognitive processes underlying context effects in attitude measurement. *Psychological Bulletin*, 103, 299–314.

Triandis, H. C. 1977: *Interpersonal Behavior*. Monterey, CA.: Brooks/Cole.

Tuckel, P. S. and Feinberg, B. M. 1991: The answering machine poses many questions for telephone researchers. *Public Opinion Research*, 55, 200–17.

Tyebejee, T. 1979: Telephone survey methods: the state of the art. *Journal of Marketing*, 43 (Summer), 68–78.

Warwick, D. P. and Lininger, C. A. 1975: *The Sample Survey: Theory and Practice*, New York, NY.: McGraw Hill.

Weaver, C. N., Holmes, S. L., and Glenn, N. D. 1975: Some characteristics of inaccessible respondents in a telephone survey. *Journal of Applied Psychology*, 60, 260–2.

Yammarino, F. J., Skinner, S. J., and Childers, T. L. 1991: Understanding mail survey response behavior: a meta-analysis. *Public Opinion Quarterly*, 55, 613–39.

5

Regression Analysis for Marketing Decisions

Dipak Jain

Abstract

Regression analysis is a widely popular technique in marketing research. It examines the nature of relationship between a *criterion* (or dependent) and one or more *explanatory* (or independent) variables. Such a relationship helps in *understanding* the effects of the explanatory variables on the criterion variable and is therefore useful in evaluating the effectiveness of various marketing efforts. Further, it is also used as a *forecasting tool* because, based on the underlying relationship, one can predict the value of the criterion variable for a given set of values of the explanatory variables.

This chapter deals with (a) issues pertaining to the specification of the regression model, (b) assumptions about the error terms, (c) procedures for estimating the model parameters, (d) statistical tests for determining the significance of the parameter estimates and their effects, (e) diagnostic checks for the validity of assumptions, (f) methods for including categorical variables in a regression model and (g) alternative model specifications and comparisons.

The objective is to focus on the usefulness of regression analysis for *managerial decision-making*.

Introduction

Managers are often interested in examining the effectiveness of their firm's marketing efforts. This provides them with an understanding of the influence of the various marketing-mix variables under their control (e.g. price, advertising expenditures, sales force size and promotional programs among others) on the sales of their product. Such an understanding helps marketing managers in *strategic planning, resource allocation decisions*, and in *predicting* the sales of the product for a particular *marketing plan*.

Another problem of considerable managerial interest involves understanding consumers' preference for a particular product/service. For example, given a set of attributes for a new product/service and the demographic and socio-economic characteristics (e.g. age, income, gender and education level) of consumers, a manager might be interested in estimating the likelihood of purchase of the new product/service.

Based on these two scenarios, some pertinent questions can be raised as follows:

1. How does one investigate the effectiveness of marketing efforts? In other words, what is an appropriate methodology for analyzing the impact of marketing-mix variables on sales?
2. How can one predict the likelihood that a consumer will purchase a new product based on his/her age, income, marital status, etc.?

Before we can attempt to answer these questions, it would be useful to see if there is something *common* between them. A close examination may reveal that both problems involve the investigation of some kind of *relationship*. The first question deals with the relationship between sales of a product and the marketing-mix variables associated with it, and the second question involves relating consumers' attitudes toward a product to their demographic and socio-economic characteristics. Hence, an appropriate technique for answering these two questions would be one that enables marketing researchers or practitioners to understand the *nature of relationship* between variables. *Regression analysis* is one such technique that provides answers to such questions.[1]

In this chapter, our objective is to illustrate the framework of regression analysis, its use in marketing decision-making and also mention some of its limitations. Our intent is not to focus on the statistical/mathematical aspects of regression analysis but to take the perspective of an applied researcher and emphasize the applications of regression analysis in marketing research. A rigorous discussion on regression analysis is available in standard texts on econometrics (e.g. Johnston 1984, Pindyck and Rubinfeld 1981, among others). An excellent discussion on management applications of regression analysis is available in Wittink (1988).

The proposed outline of this chapter is as follows. In the next section, we describe the technique of regression analysis and the assumptions made in formulating a simple regression model. In section 3 we extend the framework of simple regression to multiple regression models. Section 4 deals with the diagnostic checks for the validity of the assumptions underlying a regression model and their implications for statistical inferences on the regression parameters. In section 5 we present the technique of dummy variable regression followed in section 6 by a discussion on competing regression models in applied research. Section 7 provides a summary of the key issues in applying regression models to managerial decision making.

2 Linear Regression Model

Regression analysis deals with examining the nature of relationship between a criterion (or dependent) variable and one or more predictors (or independent variables). Referring to our earlier example, the manager would be interested in understanding the relationship between sales (the dependent variable) and the marketing-mix variables such as a price, advertising expenditures, sales force size, etc. (the set of independent variables).

For expositional clarity, we first discuss the relationship between a dependent variable (say sales) and a single independent variable (say price). In other words, we consider sales as a function of price, i.e.

$$Sales = F(Price)$$

A pertinent question that one may raise at this point is: What is the functional form of F? There may not be a clear answer to this question in all marketing situations. Researchers may propose a relationship based on some underlying economic/behavioral theory or determine the nature of relationship empirically from the data.[2] For example, if one believes that sales is linearly related to price, then the functional relationship between sales Y and price X can be expressed as

$$Y_i = \alpha + \beta X_i + U_i \tag{5.2.1}$$

where Y_i and X_i denote the ith observation on sales and price respectively, α is the intercept term, β is referred to as the slope coefficient and U_i is a random error term. The intercept α represents the estimated sales Y when $X_i = 0$. The slope coefficient β represents the change in the estimated value of Y for a unit change in price. Equation (5.2.1) is generally known as a simple *linear regression model*.

At this stage it is essential to know what is meant by the term *linear* in the context of a regression model. The most common interpretation of linearity is that the regression model representing the relationship between Y and X is a straight line. An alternative interpretation deals with the notion that the regression model is linear in the parameters α, β; it may or may not be linear in the independent variable X. This means that in a linear regression model the parameters α and β cannot be expressed as $\sqrt{\beta}$, β^3 or β/α. In this chapter, we would refer to a linear regression model as one that is linear in the parameters; it may or may not be linear in the independent variables.

Random error term

The error term in equation (5.2.1) is unobservable but its magnitude can be estimated from observed data. It is included in equation (5.2.1) for the following reasons (Wittink, 1988):

1 *Omitted variables*: It is meant to capture the effects of any omitted variables that affect sales but for some reasons have not been included in the regression model (5.2.1).
2 *Functional form*: Very often, the 'true' relationship between Y and X may be unknown and the proposed one is considered as an approximation to the actual relationship. The error term in that case captures the deviation between the proposed and the actual relationship.
3 *Measurement errors*: The error term may represent the measurement errors associated with the observations on the criterion and predictor variables.

A good discussion on the reasons behind the inclusion of a random error term in the regression model is also available in Gujarati (1988).

Before we discuss the assumptions made about the error term in a linear regression model, we want to emphasize that we start with the assumption that the regression model presented in equation (5.2.1) is *correctly specified* in terms of the proposed *functional form F* and the *variables* included in the model.

Assumptions underlying the error term

In a linear regression model, we make the following assumptions regarding the random error term:

(1) The mean value of U_i is zero for any given value of X_i, i.e.

$$E(U_i) = 0 \quad \text{for all } i$$

This assumption implies that the expected value of Y_i for any given X_i is equal to $\alpha + \beta X_i$, i.e.

$$E(Y_i | X_i) = \alpha + \beta X_i.$$

(2) The variance of U_i for each X_i is a constant σ^2, i.e.

$$\text{Var}(U_i) = \sigma^2 \quad \text{for all } i$$

This is known as the assumption of *homoscedasticity*. If the variance of U_i changes with X_i then it is referred to as *heteroscedasticity*.

(3) The random error terms associated with any two different observations are uncorrelated, i.e.

$$\text{Cov}(U_i, U_j) = 0 \quad \text{for all } i \neq j$$

where i and j refer to two different observations and Cov represents the covariance. This is also known as the assumption of no *autocorrelation* or (*serial correlation*) between the error terms.

(4) The error term U_i is normally distributed for each X_i. This implies that the dependent variable Y is also normally distributed with mean $\alpha + \beta X$ and variance σ^2. It is important for drawing statistical inferences on the regression parameters.

(5) The error term U_i is uncorrelated with X_i, i.e.

$$\text{Cov}(U_i, X_i) = 0$$

This assumption follows from assumption (1) if X's are fixed (i.e. non-stochastic) because in that case

$$\text{Cov}(U_i, X_i) = E(U_i X_i) = X_i E(U_i) = 0 \quad \text{for all } i.$$

It is needed in cases where X_i is also a random variable.

The question that now arises is – how to estimate α and β from the observed values of Y_i and X_i. We discuss this below.

Estimation of regression parameters

Given the data on sales and price, the most common statistical method for estimating the values of the intercept and slope coefficients is known as the *least-squares* procedure. This method determines the values of α and β such that the sum of squared deviations of the observed value of Y_i from their estimated values $\hat{Y}_i$ referred to as the *residuals* e_i, i.e.

$$\sum e_i^2 = \sum (Y_i - \hat{Y}_i)^2 \tag{5.2.2}$$

is a minimum, where

$$\hat{Y}_i = \hat{\alpha} + \hat{\beta} X_i \tag{5.2.3}$$

In other words, the least squares procedure finds the straight line that is 'closest' to the actual scatter of observations on Y_i and X_i. A graphical display of the observed values of Y and X is presented in Figure 5.1

Substituting the expression for $\hat{Y}_i$ from equation (5.2.3) in equation (5.2.2), differentiating the resulting equation with respect to α and β, and setting the derivatives to zero (to obtain the necessary minimum), we get

$$\sum Y_i = n\hat{\alpha} + \hat{\beta} \sum X_i \tag{5.2.4}$$

$$\sum X_i Y_i = \hat{\alpha} \sum X_i + \hat{\beta} \sum X_i^2 \tag{5.2.5}$$

where n denotes the available number of pairs of observations on Y and X_i. These equations are known as the *normal equations*. Solving them simultaneously, we obtain the following expressions for the estimates of α and β:

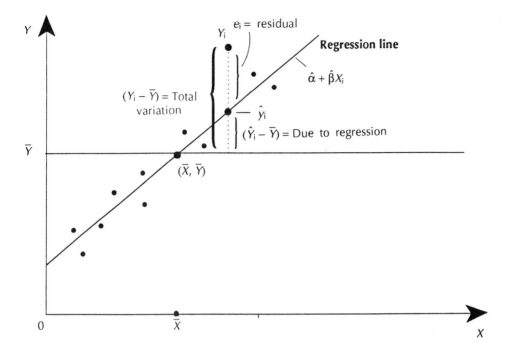

Figure 5.1 Estimated regression line and the breakdown of the total variation in Y

$$\hat{\beta} = \frac{n \sum X_i Y_i - \left(\sum X_i \right)\left(\sum Y_i \right)}{n \sum X_i^2 - \left(\sum X_i \right)^2} \qquad (5.2.6)$$

$$\hat{\alpha} = \bar{Y} - \hat{\beta}\bar{X} \qquad (5.2.7)$$

where $\bar{Y}$ and $\bar{X}$ denote the sample means of Y and X. All quantities on the right hand side of equations (5.2.6) and (5.2.7) are known from the available data on Y and X and hence $\hat{\beta}$ and $\hat{\alpha}$ can be easily computed. After the estimates $\hat{\beta}$, $\hat{\alpha}$ are obtained, one can predict the values of Y for a given value of X.[3]

It is clear from Figure 5.1 that the estimated regression line passes through the point $(\bar{X}, \bar{Y})$, the sample means of X and Y. Further, it is easy to prove that the sum of the residuals is zero.

Strength of relationship

So far we have discussed how one can estimate the parameters of the regression equation (5.2.1) and predict Y for a given value of X, but we have not answered the question – how well does X predict Y? Stated differently, we do not know how strong is the relationship between X and Y. In the context of regression analysis, this question can be stated as – how 'good' is the fit between the regression model and the observed set of data on Y and X.

To answer the question, we consider a measure R^2 commonly referred to as the *coefficient of determination*, which tells us how well the regression equation fits the observed data. This measure represents what proportion of the total variation in the observed values of Y around its mean value can be accounted for by the variation in X. Formally, it is defined as

$$R^2 = \frac{\text{variance explained by the regression model}}{\text{Total variation in } Y}$$

$$= \frac{\sum (\hat{Y}_i - \bar{Y})^2}{\sum (Y_i - \bar{Y})^2} \qquad (5.2.8)$$

Note that if $\hat{Y}_i$ predicts Y_i perfectly, i.e. $\hat{Y}_i = Y_i$ then $R^2 = 1$ since in that case the numerator in equation (5.2.8) is equal to the denominator. However, if the value predicted from the regression equation $\hat{Y}_i$ is no better than the mean value $\bar{Y}$, in that case the numerator will be equal to zero and hence R^2 will also be zero. Consequently R^2 lies between 0 (complete lack of fit) and 1 (perfect fit)[4]. If for a given situation, R^2 is 0.81, we would interpret that 81 percent of the total variation in Y has been accounted for by the regression model (or by the variation in X).

A larger value of R^2 would imply a "good" fit of the regression line and a low value of R^2 a "poor" fit. A frequently asked question in applied research is – What is a "good" value of R^2? There is no such value of R^2 that can be considered as "good" for all situations. It depends on the particular situation as well as on the nature of available data. As noted by Pindyck and Rubinfeld (1981):

> In time series studies, however, one often obtains high values of R^2 simply because any variable growing over time is likely to do a good job of explaining the variation of any other variable growing over time. In cross-section studies, on the other hand, a lower R^2 may occur even if the model is a satisfactory one, because of the large variation across individual units of observations which is inherently present in the data.

A low value of R^2 may result because either X is not a good predictor for Y or because X alone may not be adequate to account for all the variation in Y.

Statistical testing of the regression model

Rather than making a decision on the "goodness of fit" of the regression model based on the obtained value of R^2, it is useful to examine the statistical significance of the regression model. In other words, one would

REGRESSION ANALYSIS FOR MARKETING DECISIONS 169

be interested in learning if the observed value of R^2 is merely due to chance or is significantly different than zero. The statistical test used to examine the existence of a linear relationship between Y and X is given by

$$F = \frac{R^2}{(1-R^2)/n-2} \qquad (5.2.9)$$

where the test statistic F follows the F distribution with 1 and $n-2$ degrees of freedom. It is clear from equation (5.2.9) that the higher the value of R^2 the greater will be the value of the F-statistic and it is more likely that one would reject the null hypothesis that $R^2 = 0$.

An alternative way to examine if there is significant relationship between X and Y would be to test the following hypothesis about the slope parameter:

Null hypothesis $H_0 : \beta = 0$
Alternative hypothesis $H_1 : \beta \neq 0$

An appropriate test statistic for this hypothesis is

$$t = \frac{\hat{\beta} - 0}{s_{\hat{\beta}}} \qquad (5.2.10)$$

where $\hat{\beta}$ denotes the estimate of β and $s_{\hat{\beta}}$ is the estimate of the standard error of β and it is defined as

$$s_{\hat{\beta}} = \frac{s}{\sqrt{\sum(X_i - \bar{X})^2}} \qquad (5.2.11)$$

where s^2 is the estimate of the error variance σ^2. The statistic t follows the t-distribution with $n-2$ degrees of freedom. If the calculated value of this statistic is greater than the critical value at some chosen level of significance (say α) in *absolute* value then the null hypothesis is rejected. Note that in order to apply the t-test the assumptions about the error term discussed previously must hold.[5]

Given the uncertainty associated with the regression parameters, sometimes one may be interested in estimating a confidence interval for the slope parameter in order to determine the range of values that contain the true parameter estimates. A confidence interval for the slope parameter is given by

$$\hat{\beta} \pm t_c \cdot s_{\hat{\beta}}$$

where t_c is the critical value of t for a chosen level of significance, say α.[6]

As stated earlier, regression analysis is also used for prediction purposes. For a given value of the predictor X say X_0 we can use equation (5.2.3) to predict the value of the criteria variable Y_0 such that

$$Y_0 = \hat{\alpha} + \hat{\beta} X_0$$

Note that Y_0 is a point estimate of Y for given X_0 and it may be affected by the uncertainty associated with the estimated regression parameters and the error component (Wittink, 1988). A confidence interval for Y_0 would take into consideration such uncertainty and hence may be a useful tool. The confidence-interval formula is given by (Wittink, 1988):

$$\hat{y}_0 \pm t_c s_{\hat{y}_0}$$

$$\text{where } s_{\hat{y}_0} = s \sqrt{1 + \frac{1}{n} + \frac{(X_0 - \bar{X})^2}{\sum (X_i - \bar{X})^2}}$$

Hence, rather than use the point estimate $\hat{Y}_0$, one may use the interval estimator for $\hat{Y}_0$ in making effective marketing decisions.[7]

Before we extend the framework of a simple regression (i.e. two-variable) model to a multiple regression model, we would like to answer the following questions about regression analysis in general:

1 How would the results change if the simple regression model does not have an intercept-term?
2 Are the regression results sensitive to the units in which Y and X are measured?

Regression model with no intercept term

In the simple regression model discussed so far we have assumed the existence of the intercept term α. In some marketing situations, an appropriate specification of the regression model would be one in which the intercept term is zero, i.e. the regression line passes through the origin. In that case equation (5.2.1) reduces to

$$Y_i = \beta X_i + u_i$$

We can use the method of least squares to determine the estimate of β and an estimate of the error variance σ^2. However, one needs to be careful in interpreting the value of R^2 for a no-intercept regression model. The formula of R^2 is derived based on the presence of the intercept term and hence when the intercept term is dropped from the model, the formula for R^2 needs to be modified. Gujarati (1988) shows that the value of R^2 for a non-intercept regression model can be negative which is not possible in the with-intercept regression model. It is generally recommended to use a regression model with an intercept term unless the underlying theory dictates the need for a non-intercept based regression model.

Units of measurement

Consider the following regression model

$$Y_i = \alpha + \beta X_i + u_i$$

Define new variables Y and X such that

$$Y'_i = k_1 Y_i$$
$$X'_i = k_2 X_i$$

Consider the regression model for Y'_i and X'_i

$$Y'_i = \alpha' + \beta' X'_i + u'_i$$

It can be easily shown that (Gujarati, 1988)

$$\hat{\alpha}' = k_1 \hat{\alpha}$$

$$\hat{\beta}' = \left(\frac{k_1}{k_2}\right) \hat{\beta}$$

$$\hat{\sigma}'^2 = k_1 \hat{\sigma}^2$$

Therefore, if we know the scaling constants then using the estimates of the regression parameters based on a particular scale of measurement, we can easily derive the estimates under any other scale of measurement. An interesting observation is that the value of R^2 remains the same after the transformation. This is due to the fact that the correlation coefficient between X and Y is unaffected by any transformation of the origin and scale of measurement.

3 Multiple Regression Model

We now extend the framework of a *simple regression model* (consisting of one independent variable) to a *multiple regression model* that contains two or more independent variables. In marketing applications, we frequently encounter situations that involve examining relationships between one dependent variable and two or more independent variables. In a *sales response* model, sales (the dependent variable) may not only depend on price but also on advertising expenditures, number of sales force, among other explanatory variables. Hence, we want to build a functional relationship between sales and the set of explanatory variables, i.e.

Sales = F (Price, Advertising, Salesforce, ...)

As discussed previously, the commonly proposed functional relationship F is one that is *linear*. Accordingly, the relationship is expressed as:

$$Y_i = \alpha + \beta_1 X_{1i} + \beta_2 X_{2i} + \ldots + \beta_K X_{Ki} + U_i \quad (5.3.1)$$

where Y is the dependent variable (sales), X's represent the independent or explanatory variables (Price, Advertising, ...), U_i the random error term and i denotes the ith observation (e.g. X_{1i} represents the ith observation on price). Equation (5.3.1) is generally referred to as a *multiple regression model*.

The term α in equation (5.3.1) is the *intercept* term which represents the sales level when all explanatory variables are set to zero. The β's are called the *regression coefficients*. In equation (5.3.1) for example, β_2 indicates the change in Y(sales) for each unit change in X_2 (e.g. advertising expenditures) when all the other variables are *held constant*.[8] One may similarly interpret the other terms.

As in the case of a simple regression model, the *linearity* assumption in a multiple regression analysis implies that the model is linear in the parameters α, β's; it may or may not be linear in the explanatory variables. The interpretation of the regression coefficients, however, depends on the specification of the explanatory variables.

The assumptions behind a multiple regression model are similar to those made for a simple regression model. We start with the assumption that the regression model (5.3.1) is *correctly* specified. For the error term U_i we assume zero mean, constant variance (homoscedasticity), no autocorrelation, zero covariance with each explanatory variable. In addition, we assume that there does not exist any *exact* linear relationship between the X's, technically referred to as the assumption of no *multicollinearity*.

The parameters α and β's of the multiple regression model are estimated using the principle of least squares or also referred to as *ordinary least squares* procedure. As in the simple regression model we obtain those values of α and β's that minimize the residual ($e_i = Y_i - \hat{Y}_i$) sum of squares defined as

$$\sum e_i^2 = \sum (Y_i - \hat{Y}_i)^2 \qquad (5.3.2)$$

where

$$\hat{Y}_i = \hat{\alpha} + \hat{\beta}_1 X_{1i} + \hat{\beta}_2 X_{2i} + \ldots + \hat{\beta}_K X_{Ki} \qquad (5.3.3)$$

For expositional clarity, we do not provide the mathematical expressions for $\hat{\alpha}$ and the $\hat{\beta}$'s here. Generally, they are derived using matrix algebra which is beyond the scope of this chapter. Further, various statistical software packages (e.g. SAS, SPSS etc.) are available to estimate the regression parameters. A detail discussion on the properties of the ordinary least squares estimators for a multiple regression model is available in Johnston (1984), Pindyck and Rubinfeld (1981), among others.

In addition to the estimate of regression coefficients, an important measure for the influence of explanatory variables on the dependent variable is *elasticity*, the effect of a percentage change in the explanatory variables on the dependent variable. For example, if X_2 represents advertising expenditures then the advertising elasticity for observation i may be computed as

$$\eta_2 = \frac{\text{percent change in } Y_i}{\text{percent change in } X_{2i}}$$

$$\eta_2 = \frac{\hat{\beta}_2}{Y_i} \cdot X_{2i}$$

Rather than calculating elasticities at each point, they are calculated at the mean value of the variables. A value of 0.5 for η_2 would mean that a 1 percent increase in advertising expenditures will lead to 0.5 percent increase in sales. Elasticities are unit free and can be easily compared across different explanatory variables to determine those variables to which the dependent variable is highly responsive.

Another measure used to evaluate the relative importance of the explanatory variables in a regression model is the *beta coefficient* β^*, the regression coefficient obtained from a regression model in which all the variables are standarized.[9] In reality, it is not necessary to conduct additional regression analysis to derive the beta coefficients. They can be easily computed from the regular regression coefficients β's using the following relationship

$$\hat{\beta}_j^* = \hat{\beta}_j \frac{S_j}{S_y} \quad j = 1, 2, \ldots K$$

Note that $\hat{\beta}_j^*$ are unit-free and if the beta coefficient of X_1 is greater in magnitude than the coefficient of X_2, it would imply that X_1 has more impact on Y than X_2 and therefore it is more *important*.[10] A value of 0.5 for β_2^* (the coefficient for advertising) would mean that if advertising expenditures change by 1 standard deviation then sales would change by 0.5 standard deviations. This measure is often used in reporting regression results from survey research (Wittink, 1988).

The goodness of fit of the multiple regression model is measured by R^2, the proportion of the variation in Y which is accounted for by the multiple regression equation (5.3.1). The closer R^2 is to 1 the better is the fit of the model to the observed data. The measure R^2 always increases with the number of explanatory variables. Hence, based on R^2 values, a regression model with more explanatory variables would always be preferred to one with fewer variables. This is because the measure R^2 does not take into account explicitly the number of explanatory variables (and hence the number of estimated parameters) in the model specification. A better measure is the adjusted $R^2(\bar{R}^2)$ that adjusts for the number of explanatory variables included in the model. It can be computed using the estimated value of R^2 as follows

$$\bar{R}^2 = 1 - (1 - R^2) \frac{n-1}{n-K} \qquad (5.3.4)$$

where n is the total number of observations and K is the number of explanatory variables. Note that if $K = 1$, $\bar{R}^2 = R^2$. Further $\bar{R}^2$ can be negative whereas R^2 is always positive. Intuitively speaking, $\bar{R}^2$ imposes a penalty on the goodness of fit every time an additional variable is included in the model.

Significance of the regression parameters

Once the parameters α and β's are estimated and the goodness of fit measure R^2 computed, we would like to test the statistical significance of the regression model as a whole as well as the individual regression coefficients. What does this mean in a managerial sense? If a manager finds that the advertising coefficient, for example, is not significantly different from zero, then his/her decisions on advertising budget would be different than if s/he had found it to be significantly different. In other words, statistical significance of the parameters estimates has important implications for managerial decision-making.

We first discuss the statistical test used for testing the overall significance of a multiple regression model. In this case, the null hypothesis implies no effect of any explanatory variable on the dependent variable or effects of all explanatory variables are *jointly* zero, i.e.

$$H_0 : \beta_1 = \beta_2 = \ldots = \beta_K = 0 \qquad (5.3.5)$$

and the alternative hypothesis H_1 is that at least one explanatory variable affects the criterion variable. Alternatively, the above hypotheses can be restated in terms of R^2 as follows:

$$\begin{aligned} H_0 &: R^2 = 0 \\ H_1 &: R^2 > 0 \end{aligned} \qquad (5.3.6)$$

To test these hypotheses, we use the following statistic

$$F = \frac{R^2/K}{(1-R^2)/n-K-1} \qquad (5.3.7)$$

Under the null hypothesis H_0, F follows an F-distribution with degrees of freedom K and $n - K - 1$. This value of F is compared to the critical value of $F_{\alpha, K, n-K-1}$ at a significance level α (the commonly used value for α is 0.05) and if the calculated value is greater than the critical value, we reject the null hypothesis that the regression coefficients are jointly zero. In that case, one would conclude that the regression model as a whole is statistically significant.

REGRESSION ANALYSIS FOR MARKETING DECISIONS 175

Once the overall significance of the model is established, then one would be interested in testing whether *each* individual regression coefficient $\beta_i (i = 1, 2, \ldots K)$ is significantly different from zero. In that case, the null and alternative hypotheses are stated as follows:

$$H_0 : \beta_i = 0$$
$$H_1 : \beta_i \neq 0 \quad (5.3.8)$$

If the assumptions about the error term hold, then the test statistic is

$$t = \frac{\hat{\beta}_i - 0}{s_{\hat{\beta}_i}} \quad (5.3.9)$$

where $\hat{\beta}_i$ is the estimated value of β_i, $s_{\hat{\beta}_i}$ is the estimated standard error of $\hat{\beta}_i$. This test-statistic is similar to the one used in case of a simple regression model; however, the expressions for $\hat{\beta}_i$ and $s_{\hat{\beta}_i}$ are different. The statistic t follows a t-distribution with $n - K - 1$ degress of freedom. The null hypothesis would be rejected if the calculated value of t is greater than the critical value of t (for a *two-tailed* test) for $n - K - 1$ degrees of freedom at a significance level of α.[11]

There exist situations when a researcher is neither interested in testing whether all regression coefficients are jointly zero nor on testing any single coefficient but might want to test the joint significance of a subset of regression coefficients. For example, consider a regression model where the sales of a firm's product depends on both its own marketing efforts (price and advertising expenditures) as well as on the competitor's marketing efforts. The product manager wants to develop a marketing plan for his/her product and would like to examine the statistical significance of the marketing actions of the competitor on its product's sales. In order to know, s/he first starts the multiple regression model

$$Y_i = \alpha + \beta_1 X_{1i} + \beta_2 X_{2i} + \beta_3 X_{3i} + \beta_4 X_{4i} + U_i \quad (5.3.10)$$

where X_{1i}, X_{2i} denote the firm's own price and advertising expenditures, and X_{3i}, X_{4i} denote those of the competitor's. This is referred to as the *unrestricted* model. Now, s/he wishes to test whether the regression coefficients pertaining to the competitor (i.e. β_3 and β_4) are jointly equal to zero. Hence, the null and alternative hypotheses can be stated as

$$H_0 : \beta_3 = \beta_4 = 0$$
$$H_1 : \text{at least one coefficient is different from zero}$$

Under the null hypothesis, the model in (5.3.10) can be written as

$$Y_i = \alpha + \beta_1 X_{1i} + \beta_2 X_{2i} + U_i \quad (5.3.11)$$

This is referred to as the *restricted* (by the null hypothesis) model. If the null hypothesis is true, then dropping the two variables from the equation should not have any significant effect on the explanatory power of the regression model. Accordingly, the statistical test would involve the comparison of the R^2 values for the restricted (R_R^2) and the unrestricted model (R_{UR}^2) specifications, after taking into account the number of restrictions (i.e. the number of coefficients restricted to zero). One such test-statistic is given by

$$F = \frac{(R_{UR}^2 - R_R^2)/2}{(1 - R_{UR}^2)/n - 5}$$

where the statistic F follows the F distribution with 2 and $n - 5$ degrees of freedom. In general, for a K-variable regression model if we impose h restrictions (i.e. set h regression coefficients equal to zero) then the degrees of freedom would be h and $n - K - 1$ and the F-statistic can be written as

$$F = \frac{(R_{UR}^2 - R_R^2)/h}{(1 - R_{UR}^2)/n - K - 1} \qquad (5.3.12)$$

It is interesting to note that the previously discussed F test for the overall significance of the regression model (equation (5.3.7)) is a special case of this test. In that case the null hypothesis is that K coefficients are zero and therefore the number of restrictions becomes K. Further, under the null hypothesis R_R^2 would be equal to zero and the above F-test values to

$$F = \frac{R_{UR}^2/K}{(1 - R_{UR}^2)/n - K - 1}$$

which is identical to expression (5.3.7).

In fact, the F statistic presented in equation (5.3.12) is a general test statistic that can be used for testing hypotheses that deal with several regression coefficients.

Another, commonly encountered situation is one in which the manager would be interested in knowing if the effects of two marketing variables (e.g. advertising and sales force size) on product sales are equal. In that case, the restriction involves setting the coefficients of those two variables equal. To illustrate this further, consider the unrestricted model as

$$Y = \alpha + \beta_1 X_{1i} + \beta_2 X_{2i} + \beta_3 X_{3i} + U_i \qquad (5.3.13)$$

where X_{1i}, X_{2i} and X_{3i} denote the firm's price, advertising and sales force size variables. The hypotheses to be tested are:

$$H_0 : \beta_2 = \beta_3$$
$$H_A : \beta_2 \neq \beta_3$$

Under the null hypotheses, the regression model in (5.3.13) reduces to

$$Y = \alpha + \beta_1 X_{1i} + \beta_2 X_{2i} + \beta_2 X_{3i} + U_i$$

or

$$Y = \alpha + \beta_1 X_{1i} + \beta_2 (X_{2i} + X_{3i}) + U_i \qquad (5.3.14)$$

which is a restricted version of equation (5.3.13). Now the F-test statistic presented in equation (5.3.12) can be used for this hypotheses where $h = 1$ (only 1 restriction) and $K = 3$. Hence, the test statistic in equation (5.3.12) has significant practical importance.

4 Diagnostic Checks in Regression Analysis

In previous sections we discussed the assumptions about the error term in a regression model. In addition, we also emphasized the assumption that the regression model is correctly specified. This is an important assumption and its validity depends on whether the researcher has significant information and knowledge to specify correctly the *two* critical components of a regression model: (a) the explanatory variables to be included in the model and (b) the appropriate functional form of each explanatory variables as well as the nature of relationship between the criterion and the explanatory variables. Very often, the assumptions pertaining to the error term may be violated because the researcher omitted some relevant explanatory variables from the model and/or specified an inappropriate functional form of the model. Hence, it is critical that the researcher spends considerable time on these issues prior to the empirical analysis (Wittink, 1988). We now discuss the implications of the assumptions about the error term below.

The first assumption about the error term is that its expected value should be zero. In case it is not zero (due to model misspecification or other reasons) *only* the estimate of the intercept term in the regression model will be affected by it, and it would be difficult to partial out the true estimate of the intercept term and the non-zero value of the error term. The violation of this assumption is not considered serious because in practical situations we are more interested in drawing inferences on the regression coefficients β_i's than on the intercept term α.

The assumption of constant error variance or homoscedasticity may not be valid in some marketing contexts. For example, when analyzing cross-sectional data on consumer behavior, the variance associated with different types of consumers may be different. In general, the problem of nonconstant error variance (or heteroscedasticity) is likely to be more present in cross-sectional than time-series data.

If the errors are not homoscedastic, the least-square parameter estimates are still unbiased and consistent but they don't have the minimum variance (i.e. not be efficient). Further, the variance of the estimated parameters will also be biased. Hence, one may draw incorrect inferences on the significance of the parameter estimates if heteroscedasticity is not accounted for. This problem is commonly dealt with by using a *weighted least squares* (or *generalized least-squares*) procedure where the weight assigned to each observation is inversely proportional to its variance. Note that in ordinary least-squares procedure observations are assigned the same weight. A detail discussion on heteroscedosticity is available in Pindyck and Rubinfeld (1981).

For detecting heteroscedasticity a plot of the residuals (e_i) against the estimated values of the criterion variable ($\hat{Y}_i$) may be helpful. If there is no systematic pattern between e_i and $\hat{Y}_i$ as depicted in Figure 5.2(a) then perhaps no heteroscedasticity is present. Also, as shown in Figure 5.2(b), one may plot the residuals against each explanatory variable to determine which variable exhibits a relationship with the residuals. This information can be used to transform the variables such that the error variance is constant. Plots are an *informal* way to detect heteroscedasticity, there also exist *formal* statistical tests for this purpose in the literature (Gujarati, 1988).

The assumption that errors are not autocorrelated may be violated due to model misspecification in the sense that a relevant explanatory variable is omitted from the regression model. Generally, autocorrelation is likely to be present in time-series data. For example, in examining advertising-sales relationship it is common to believe that current advertising as well as advertising in previous time periods affect current sales and if those *lagged* effects are not included in the model specification then errors in earlier time periods will carry over into future periods resulting in autocorrelation. A scatterplot of the residual against time can be used to detect

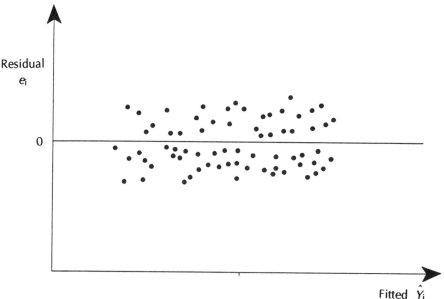

Figure 5.2a No evidence of heteroscedasticity

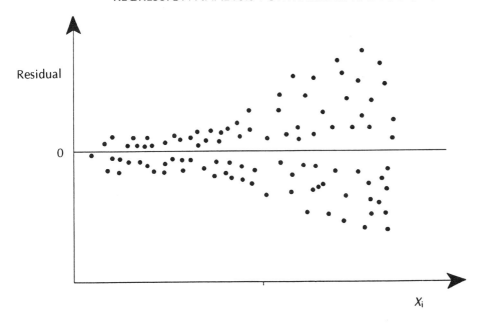

Figure 5.2b (Absolute) magnitude of residual increases as X increases

autocorrelation (see Figures 5.3(a) and 5.3(b)). If the residuals vary systematically with time then there is an evidence for autocorrelation.

In the presence of autocorrelation, the ordinary least squares estimators are still consistent and unbiased but the estimates of the standard errors for the parameters as well as the estimates of the error variance are biased. If the correlation is positive than the estimated standard errors will be

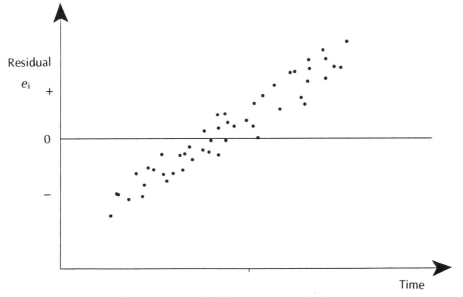

Figure 5.3a Positive autocorrelation

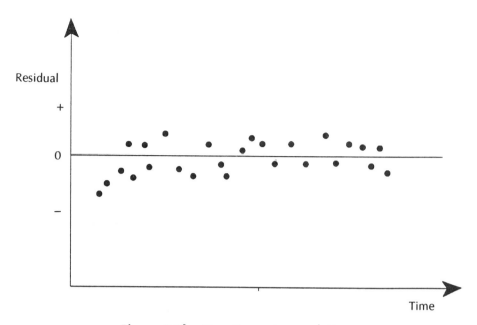

Figure 5.3b Negative autocorrelation

smaller than the true standard errors and therefore they may lead to larger t-values. Consequently, one may tend to conclude that certain explanatory variables have significant impact on the criterion variable which in fact may not be correct. Hence, in the presence of autocorrelation one needs to execute caution in inferring the significance of the parameter estimates.

There are various procedures (e.g. Cochrane-Orcutt, generalized least squares) to correct for autocorrelation. A discussion of these procedures is beyond the scope of this chapter. Interested readers may consult Johnston (1984).

Finally, the assumption that the error terms follow a normal distribution is critical from the statistical inference point of view. The tests of several hypotheses about the regression coefficients are based on this assumption. The validity of this assumption can be examined by constructing a histogram of the residuals (Wittink, 1988). Generally, before we check the validity of this assumption it is essential to see if the regression model is correctly specified and that the errors are neither heteroscedastic nor autocorrelated.

An additional assumption we make in multiple regression analysis is that there does not exist an exact linear relationship between the explanatory variables in the model. In other words, the explanatory variables are not perfectly collinear. In practical situations, existence of such extreme collinearity is unlikely; however, we face situations where there is a "high" degree of linear relationship (i.e. *multicollinearity*) among the explanatory variables. A natural question is – What are the consequences if multicollinearity is present? We would like to emphasize that multicollinearity is essentially a *sample* phenomenon (or a problem with observed sample data) and the statistical properties (e.g. unbiasedness, consistency and efficiency) of the parameter estimates are still preserved in the presence of multicollinearity. The major concern lies in the interpretation of the regression coefficients because we cannot associate a high degree of reliability to them. The standard errors of the regression coefficients are very sensitive to multicollinearity. Generally speaking, high collinearity between two explanatory variables (e.g. price and advertising) would increase the estimated standard errors of their coefficients dramatically. Consequently, the value of the t-statistic would be smaller for these variables implying that these coefficients are not significantly different from zero. One would in that case be tempted to conclude that price and advertising do not have a significant impact on sales whereas it may not be the correct inference.

The following rules of thumb indicate when multicollinearity is likely to be a problem:

1 if the correlation coefficient between two explanatory variables is larger than the correlation between them and the criterion variable;
2 if the correlation coefficient between two explanatory variables is high (0.8 or more);
3 if we find that the value of R^2 is high and the overall regression model is statistically significant but very few of the individual regression coefficients are significantly different from zero;
4 if several of the regression coefficients have high standard errors and dropping of one or more explanatory variables from the regression model considerably lowers the standard errors of the remaining variables.

These rules are by no means collectively exhaustive for detecting multicollinearity. Further, multicollinearity is not an issue if the purpose of regression analysis is to develop a forecasting model (Wittink, 1988).

We state below some possible ways of dealing with multicollinearity. Our intent is not to provide a rigorous discussion but to mention some commonly used rules of thumb in practice (see also Wittink, 1988 and Gujarati, 1988).

1 Since multicollinearity is a sample problem, it may be useful to obtain additional relevant data if possible. More data may result in a lower degree of multicollinearity. In practice, this may not be an easy solution.
2 Drop one of the two explanatory variables that are highly correlated and re-estimate the model parameters. The common practice is to drop the one that has the lowest t-value because either it means that it is truly statistically insignificant or it is not possible to obtain a reliable estimate for it because of multicollinearity. Dropping a variable from the model may lead to *specification bias* because if theory suggests that both variables are critical to the problem dropping one of them would make the model misspecified.

3 Respecify the model to eliminate any potential source of multicollinearity. In some situations, if two variables are highly correlated, there may be a way to combine them into a single variable (and redefine them) provided they measure the same underlying construct. Statistical methods such as *principal component analysis* and/or *factor analysis* can be used for this purpose.
4 A commonly used procedure is *ridge* regression (Chatterjee and Price, 1977). This method provides *biased* estimates for the coefficients but results in considerably lower standard errors than the least squares procedure.

To summarize, we see that one of the reasons behind the violations of the assumptions is model misspecification. Hence, before doing anything else we need to thoroughly examine if the regression model is correctly specified. Further, the major consequences resulting from the violation of the assumptions is biased estimates for the standard errors of the regression coefficients and the error terms. Hence, the validity of the assumptions should be checked before drawing any statistical inference on the regression parameters.

5 Dummy Variable Regression

In marketing studies, we frequently collect information on the demographic and socio-economic characteristics of the consumers. Part of this information is collected through variables that are *quantitative* and can be measured using an interval or a ratio scale (e.g. income, age, family size, etc.); while the remaining information is collected through variables that are usually categorical in nature and measured either on a nominal or ordinal scale (e.g. gender, race, education level, etc.). Both types of variables may be useful predictors about consumers' preferences or their purchase intentions. Any variable measured on an interval or ratio scale can be easily included in the regression model as it is. A question one may raise is – how to include a categorical variable in the regression model? This is an important issue since one may be interested in determining whether the preferences are different between males and females? A categorical variable identifies a particular consumer as either having or not having a particular characteristic, e.g. considering *gender* as a variable then either the consumer is a male or a female. One common approach for "quantifying" such a variable is to represent it using an *indicator* variable which takes a value of 1 to *indicate* that the particular characteristic is "present" in the consumer and 0 otherwise. For example, 1 may indicate that the consumer is a male and 0 a female. Therefore, using indicator variables (also referred to as *dummy variables*) one can include categorical variables in a regression model as easily as *quantitative* variables.

Consider the following regression model

REGRESSION ANALYSIS FOR MARKETING DECISIONS

$$Y_i = \alpha + \beta D_i + U_i \tag{5.5.1}$$

where Y_i denotes the overall preference (for a product) of the ith consumer and D_i is a dummy variable.

$$D_i = \begin{cases} 1 & \text{if the ith consumer is a male} \\ 0 & \text{if the ith consumer is a female} \end{cases} \tag{5.5.2}$$

The model in equation (5.5.1) would enable us to determine whether gender makes any difference to consumers' preference for a particular product.[12] Using least squares procedure, we can estimate the model parameters and suppose the estimated model is

$$\hat{Y}_i = \hat{\alpha} + \hat{\beta} D_i \tag{5.5.3}$$

If we want to predict the mean preference of a female, we substitute 0 for D_i and get

$$\text{Mean preference of female } \hat{Y}_F = \hat{\alpha} \tag{5.5.4}$$

Similarly, substituting 1 for D_i we get the mean preference for male, i.e.

$$\text{Mean preference of male } \hat{Y}_M = \hat{\alpha} + \hat{\beta} \tag{5.5.5}$$

Therefore, the *intercept* term $\hat{\alpha}$ represents the mean preference of females and the sum of the *intercept* and *slope* terms represents the mean preference of males. Substracting equation (5.5.4) from (5.5.5) we get

$$\hat{Y}_M - \hat{Y}_F = (\hat{\alpha} + \hat{\beta}) - \hat{\alpha} \tag{5.5.6}$$
$$= \hat{\beta}$$

implying that the *slope* coefficient measures how much the mean preference of a male differs from that of a female. Consequently, to test if there is any difference in the mean preference values between males and females, we state the hypotheses as:

$$\begin{aligned} H_0 &: \hat{\beta} = 0 \\ H_1 &: \hat{\beta} \neq 0 \end{aligned} \tag{5.5.7}$$

Therefore, a test of the null hypothesis that $\hat{\beta} = 0$ provides a test of the hypothesis that there is no difference in the mean preference values associated with males and females. If the assumption pertaining to the error terms hold, then one can use the following t-statistic

$$t = \frac{\hat{\beta} - 0}{s_{\hat{\beta}}} \qquad (5.5.8)$$

were $s_{\hat{\beta}}$ denotes the standard error of $\hat{\beta}$ and t follows a t-distribution with $n - 2$ degrees of freedom (n being the total number of observations in the data set). Thus, the t-value for the dummy variable's coefficient can be used to test the difference between the mean values of the two categories represented by the dummy variable.

The above discussion pertains to a categorical variable with only two categories (e.g. male/female). We now consider variables which may have more than two categories. Consider a situation where a firm is interested in testing the effectiveness of three different commercials for a new consumer packaged good. A random sample of individuals (i.e. users of the product category) is selected and the sample is then split randomly into three groups. Individuals within each group are shown a different commercial and they are asked to express their likelihood of buying the advertised brand on a 10-point scale ranging from 1 (very unlikely) to 10 (very likely). In this case, the criterion variable Y_i is the *likelihood of purchase* and the explanatory variable is the *type of commercial*. It is clear that the explanatory variable is categorial in nature and has three categories – say A, B and C. We show below that two dummy variables would be needed to account for the variable *type of commercial* in a regression model. We use the following model specification

$$Y_i = \alpha + \beta_1 D_{1i} + \beta_2 D_{2i} + U_i \qquad (5.5.9)$$

where Y_i = likelihood of purchase by the ith individual

$D_{1i} = \begin{cases} 1 & \text{if the ith individual is shown commercial A} \\ 0 & \text{otherwise} \end{cases}$

$D_{2i} = \begin{cases} 1 & \text{if the ith individual is shown commercial B} \\ 0 & \text{otherwise} \end{cases}$

Then the three commercials are represented by the following combination of values of the dummy variables

Commercials	D_1	D_2
A	1	0
B	0	1
C	0	0

(5.5.10)

Using the least squares procedure, the estimated regression model can be expressed as

$$\hat{Y}_i = \hat{\alpha} + \hat{\beta}_1 D_{1i} + \hat{\beta}_2 D_{2i} \qquad (5.5.11)$$

Substituting the values of D_{1i} and D_{2i} from equation (5.5.10) in (5.5.11) we get

$$\hat{Y}_i = \begin{matrix} \hat{\alpha} & \text{when } D_{1i} = 0 \text{ and } D_{2i} = 0 \text{ for all } i \\ \hat{\alpha} + \hat{\beta}_1 & \text{when } D_{1i} = 1 \text{ and } D_{2i} = 0 \text{ for all } i \\ \hat{\alpha} + \hat{\beta}_2 & \text{when } D_{1i} = 0 \text{ and } D_{2i} = 0 \text{ for all } i \end{matrix}$$

Note that both $D_1 = 0$ and $D_2 = 0$ imply that the type of commercial C and hence the intercept term $\hat{\alpha}$ in equation (5.5.11) represents the mean likelihood of purchase under commercial type C. The first slope coefficient β_1, associated with variable X_1, is the difference in the mean likelihood of purchase when commercial C is replaced by commercial A. Similarly, the second slope coefficient β_2 increases the difference in the mean likelihood of purchase between commercial types B and C. In other words, the intercept term accounts for the affect of commercial type C and the two slope coefficients measure the predicted difference between choosing commercial type C and another type of commercial. Thus, with two dummy variables, the regression model can measure the effect of all three types of commercials on individuals' likelihood of purchase of a packaged good. In general, for a categorical variable with k categories we require only $k-1$ dummy variables in the regression model. The choice of the *base* category (commercial C in the present case) is *arbitrary* and has no bearing on the regression results.[13]

A test of the null hypothesis that there is no difference in the mean likelihood of purchase values across the three types of commercial i.e.

$$H_0 : \beta_2 = \beta_3 = 0$$

can be performed using the following F statistic

$$F = \frac{R^2/2}{(1-R^2)/(n-3)}$$

where R^2 is the value of the coefficient of determination for the model in (5.5.11) and n is the total number of sample observations. The statistic F follows an F-distribution with 2 and $n-3$ degrees of freedom.

A t-test of the null hypothesis that $\beta_2 = 0$ will determine if there is any significant difference in the mean likelihood values between commercial types A and C, while a similar test on the coefficient β_3 will enable us to compare the effects of commercial types B and C on the likelihood of purchase.

We now consider the case in which the regression model consists of both *categorical* and *quantitative* explanatory variables. We extend the model in (5.5.9) to include *age* of the individuals and express it as:

$$Y_i = \alpha + \beta_1 D_{1i} + \beta_2 D_{2i} + \beta_3 X_i + U_i \qquad (5.5.12)$$

where $\qquad X_i = $ *age of the ith individual*

Equation (5.5.12) contains a quantitative variable (age of the individual X) and a categorical variable (type of commercial – represented by two dummy variables D_1 and D_2). Further, the model assumes a linear relationship between Y and X. What is the meaning of equation (5.5.12) and how does one interpret the coefficients α, β_1, β_2 and β_3? The estimated version of the model (5.5.12) can be represented as

$$\hat{Y}_i = \hat{\alpha} + \hat{\beta}_1 D_{1i} + \hat{\beta}_2 D_{2i} + \hat{\beta}_3 X_{3i} \tag{5.5.13}$$

The mean likelihood of purchase under the three types of commercials can be expressed as

Commercial C: $\hat{Y}_i = \hat{\alpha} + \hat{\beta}_3 X_{3i}$
Commercial A: $\hat{Y}_i = (\hat{\alpha} + \hat{\beta}_1) + \hat{\beta}_3 X_{3i}$
Commercial B: $\hat{Y}_i = (\hat{\alpha} + \hat{\beta}_2) + \hat{\beta}_3 X_{3i}$

The coefficient β_1 measures the difference in the mean likelihood values between commercials A and C after accounting for age, an extraneous factor commonly referred to as a *covariate*. Similarly, one may interpret β_2. The coefficient β_3 measures the change in the mean likelihood value for a year change in the age variable provided the gender is held constant. The effect of the type of commercial variable is to shift the line of relationship between likelihood of purchase and the age of the individual.[14]

In general, a regression model can include any number of quantitative and dummy variables. The interpretation of the coefficients associated with such variables will, however, be different. Note that if there exists a qualitative variable with several categories, including it in a regression model will involve a large number of dummy variables and therefore few degrees of freedom for the error term. One should always weigh the number of dummy variables to be included in a regression model against the number of available observations.

6 Functional Forms of Regression Models

In sections 2 and 3, while discussing the properties of a simple and multiple regression models, we mentioned that the term *linear* in a regression model refers to a model that is linear in the parameters and not necessarily in the explanatory variables. However, all the illustrations we have provided so far in this chapter dealt with cases where the explanatory variables were also linearly related to the dependent variable. In this section we consider commonly used regression models that are either *nonlinear* in the explanatory variables but *linear* in the parameters or are *nonlinear* in form but can be reduced to a model that is linear in the parameters by suitable transformations of the dependent and the explanatory variables. This is an important issue since if the true regression model is nonlinear in the explanatory variables imposing a linear relationship involves a specification error and it may also lead to biased and inconsistent parameter estimates (Pindyck and Rubinfeld, 1981).

Consider the following model that represents experience curve effects

$$Y_i = \alpha X_i^\beta \, e^{U_i} \qquad (5.6.1)$$

where Y denotes the marginal cost of observation, X the cumulative production, U the random error term, α and β are constants, and e is the base for natural logarithms. Equation (5.6.1) is a nonlinear specification, however, by taking natural logarithms on both sides of equation (5.6.1), we obtain

$$ln\, Y_i = ln\, \alpha + \beta\, ln\, X_i + U_i \qquad (5.6.2)$$

since $ln\, e = 1$. By redefining certain terms, equation (5.6.2) can be expressed as

$$Y_i^* = \alpha^* + \beta\, X_i^* + U_i \qquad (5.6.3)$$

where
$$\begin{aligned} Y_i^* &= ln\, Y_i \\ \alpha^* &= ln\, \alpha \\ X_i^* &= ln\, X_i \end{aligned} \qquad (5.6.4)$$

Equation (5.6.3) is linear in the parameters α^* and β, and also linear in the natural logarithms of the variables Y and X. Consequently, one can use ordinary least squares to estimate α^* (and therefore α) and β. The estimates of α would however, be biased (Gujarati, 1988).

An interesting feature of the specification in equation (5.6.2) is that the slope coefficient β also measures the *elasticity* of Y with respect to X. In other words, equation (5.6.2) implies a constant elasticity model since the change in $ln\, Y$ per unit change in $ln\, X$ remains the same at each value of the explanatory variable X. In an empirical situation, the simplest way to decide about using an equation in the form (5.6.2) is to see if the scatterplot of $ln\, Y$ against $ln\, X$ indicates a straight-line pattern of points.

As an extension of equation (5.6.1), we may consider the model

$$Y_i = \alpha\, X_{1i}^{\beta_1} X_{2i}^{\beta_2} e^{U_i} \qquad (5.6.5)$$

where, say Y denotes the sales; X_1, X_2 denotes the price and advertising; U represents the error term, and α, β_1, β_2 are constants. Note that equation (5.6.2) specifies a *multiplicative* relationship between Y and X's. As shown for equation (5.6.1), we can obtain a linear additive formulation of equation (5.6.5) which will be linear in the natural logarithms of the Y and X's, i.e.

$$\ln Y_i = \ln \alpha + \beta_1 \ln X_{1i} + \beta_2 \ln X_{2i} + U_i \quad (5.6.6)$$

Equation of the type (5.6.6) is generally referred to as *double-log* or *log-linear* regression models. It also implies constant price and advertising elasticities for sales.

An alternative specification is the following *semilog* model in which *only* the X's are in the natural logarithms form:

$$Y_t = \alpha + \beta_1 \ln X_{1t} + \beta_2 \ln X_{2i} + U_i \quad (5.6.7)$$

In this model the slope coefficient β_1, say measures the absolute change in the mean value of Y for a given relative change in the X's.

Other Commonly Used Model Specifications

(i) Exponential form

$$Y_i = \exp[\alpha + \beta X_i] U_i \quad (5.6.8)$$

By taking natural logarithms on both sides of (5.6.8), we get

$$\ln Y_i = \alpha + \beta Y_i + \ln U_i \quad (5.6.9)$$

In this model the slope coefficient β measures the relative (or percentage) change in Y for a given absolute change in X. If the variable X represents time, then β can be interpreted as a *growth* rate ($\beta > 0$) or decay rate ($\beta < 0$). Equation (5.6.9) is also referred to as a *growth* model (Gujarati, 1988). Wittink (1988) illustrates the use of an alternative specification of equation (5.6.9) in studying the diffusion of touch-tone telephones. He proposes the following model

$$\ln Y_i = \alpha + \frac{\beta}{X_i} + U_i \quad (5.6.10)$$

where Y_i is the penetration level of touch-tone telephones and X_i is the length of availability of touch-tone service in territory i. In this case if $X \to \infty$ i.e. the service has been available for a long time, then $1/X \to 0$ and therefore

$$\ln Y_i = \hat{\alpha}$$

The antilog of $\hat{\alpha}$ would represent the maximum possible level of penetration.

(ii) Reciprocal form

$$Y_i = \alpha + \frac{B}{X_i} + U_i$$

One application of this form in marketing is in investigating the relationship between demand and price. An illustration of this relationship is available in the case *E. T. Phone Home Inc: Forecasting Business Demand* (Harvard Business School, 1983).

(iii) Polynomial form

$$Y_i = \alpha + \beta_1 X_i + \beta_2 X_i^2 + U_i \tag{5.6.12}$$

This equation specification implies a nonlinear relationship between Y and X. Clearly, if we fail to reject the null hypothesis that $\beta_2 = 0$ then the relationship reduces to a linear one. The following particular form of equation (5.6.12) is widely used in marketing to study the diffusion of new consumer durables:

$$S_t = pm + (q-p)X_{t-1} - \frac{q}{m} X_{t-1}^2 + u_t \tag{5.6.13}$$

where

S_t = rates in time period t
X_{t-1} = cumulative sales up to time period $t-1$
p = coefficient of innovation
q = coefficient of imitation
m = market potential

Equation (5.6.13) is the famous Bass diffusion model (Bass, 1969). Note that it is not linear in the parameters p, q and m. Alternatively, equation (5.6.13) can be written as

$$S_t = \alpha + \beta_1 X_{t-1} + \beta_2 X_{t-1}^2 + U_i \tag{5.6.14}$$

which is linear in the parameters and hence ordinary least squares procedure can be used to estimate α, β_1 and β_2. Once these parameters are estimated one can easily obtain the estimates for its diffusion parameters p, q and m.

One may be tempted to think that for polynomial regression models multicollinearity may be a serious problem since the explanatory variables being all powers of X are highly correlated. Note that the explanatory variables are *nonlinear* functions of X and hence strictly speaking do not violate the no multicollinearity assumption (Gujarati, 1988).

(iv) Distributed-lag form

$$Y_t = \alpha + \beta_1 X_t + \beta_2 X_{t-1} + \beta_3 X_{t-2} + U_t \tag{5.6.15}$$

In this specification, the effect of X_t (say advertising at time period t) on Y_t (sales) is expected to last beyond the current period t. Equation (5.6.15) allows for the lagged effects of advertising X_{t-1} and X_{t-2}. How many lagged terms should be included in the model specification? One can resort to some underlying behavioral theory about the effects of advertising for an answer. Alternatively, one can abstract himself out of this issue (the number of lagged terms) and use a Koyck type specification as presented below in which the coefficients of the lagged terms are expressed as a fraction of β_1, the current effect:

$$Y_t = \alpha(1 - \lambda) + \beta_1 X_t + \lambda Y_{t-1} + U_t \tag{5.6.16}$$

where $U_t = U_t + \lambda U_{t-1}$ and λ is referred to as the decay rate. Marketing applications for the Koyck model are available in Lilien, Kotler and Moorthy (1992).

v Interaction form

$$Y_i = \lambda + \beta_1 X_{1i} + \beta_2 X_{2i} + \beta_3 (X_{1i} X_{2i}) + U_i \tag{5.6.17}$$

Under this specification, the third explanatory variable is the product of the first two and is referred to as an *interaction* term. The presence of this term in the model implies that the impact of X_1 on Y (or X_2 on Y) is not the *same* at all levels of X_2 (or X_1). In fact, the effect of X_1 on Y is $\beta_1 + \beta_3 X_2$. For example, if X_1 denotes price, X_2 advertising expenditures and Y sales then equation (5.6.17) will imply that the effect of price on sales depends on the amount of advertising. Failing to reject the null hypothesis that $\beta_3 = 0$ would imply that there is no interaction effect and the effect of price does not depend on advertising.

In practice, researchers are often faced with the problems of determining which model specification is most consistent with the available data. A discussion on this issue is beyond the scope of this chapter. There exists statistical tests for comparing different model specifications. A detailed discussion on such tests is available in Jain and Vilcassim (1989) and Balasubramanian and Jain (1993).

7 Summary

Regression analysis is a widely used technique in marketing research. The key idea behind developing a regression model is to determine the nature of relationship between the criterion variable and the explanatory variables. Regression models provide an understanding of how the explanatory variables affect the criterion variable and therefore may be used for *control* purposes. For example, if the marketing manager has a good understanding of the relationship between the demand for his/her product and the advertising expenditures then s/he could use this knowledge to control advertising expenditures to produce a desired sales level. In other words, regression models will help in developing effective advertising strategies. It is to be noted that a statistically significant regression does not necessarily imply a *cause-and-effect* relationship between the criterion and the explanatory variables (Parasuraman, 1991).

A regression model is also a good *prediction* or *forecasting* tool in the sense that once the relationship between the criterion and explanatory variables is established, we can use such relationship to predict the value of the criteria variable based on specified values of the explanatory variables. For example, suppose the firm is interested in cutting down its advertising budget. What will be the effect of this cut on sales? The regression model can easily predict the sales level at a given advertising expenditure level provided it is *within the ranges* of the values used in estimating the regression model.

The usefulness of a regression model is contingent on the appropriate specification of the criterion variable and the explanatory variables and also on the specification of the functional form that shows how the criterion variable is related to the independent variables.[15]

Diagnostic checks for heteroscadesticity and autocorrelation in regression models can be performed by a close examination of the residuals. A *systematic* pattern exhibited by the variables is a sign of alarm. The researcher in that case has to investigate the sources behind this pattern and re-examine the functional specification of the regression model. Multicollinearity, although a sample problem, should be checked before making any misleading inferences.

Dummy variable regression enables a researcher to include categorical variables into a regression model. This technique is very useful in analyzing marketing data. Specifically, it has become a popular method for estimating the *partworths or utility values* of different levels of various attributes in *conjoint* analysis.

There are situations in marketing where no economic or behavioral theory exists to guide researchers in specifying an appropriate functional form of the regression model. In that case, the researcher may consider more than one functional form and see which specification is most consistent with observed data. Various statistical tests are available that can be used in determining the appropriateness of the model specification.

In this chapter, we have discussed the conceptual framework of simple *multiple* regression analysis. In our presentation, the focus has been on the applications of this technique in *managerial decision-making*. We have made an attempt to highlight the pertinent issues that we encounter in applied research. However, it is not possible to discuss all the issues at length in a single chapter. In order to get a comprehensive understanding of regression analysis, readers should consult some of the texts cited in the references.

Questions

1. State the assumptions behind a linear regression model. Which of these assumptions are essential for obtaining the least squares estimates of the parameters?

2(a) Consider the following two simple regression models:

$$Y = \alpha + \beta X$$
$$X = a + bY.$$

Show that the product of the estimates of the regression coefficients β and b is equal to r^2, where r is the coefficient of correlation between X and Y.

2(b) Show that the correlation coefficient between X and Y is independent of transformation of these variables, that is, if X and Y are transferred as

$$X' = a_0 + a_1 X$$
and $$Y' = b_0 + b_1 Y$$

then the correlation coefficient between X' and Y' is the same as that between X and Y.

3. Consider the model

$$Y = \beta_0 X_1^{\beta_1} X_2^{\beta_2} \varepsilon$$

Show that the regression coefficients β_1 and β_2 are the elasticities of Y with respect to X_1 and X_2 respectively.

4. How would you estimate the parameters of the following model and interpret them?

$$Y = \exp(\alpha + \beta_1 X_1 + \beta_2 X_2 + \varepsilon)$$

5. You have been assigned to test whether the mean rate of consumption of beer is the same for graduate business students, liberal arts students, natural science students and law students. How would you do this using regression analysis?

Notes

Financial support provided by the Marketing Science Center of the Kellogg Graduate School of Management, Northwestern University is greatly appreciated.

1. Note that the two questions are by no means the only marketing problems suitable for regression analysis. These examples are chosen for purpose of illustration – one from firms' and the other from consumers' perspective. Further, the first example deals with time-series data while the second involves analyzing cross-sectional data.
2. For the case of a simple regression analysis dealing with only two variables, one can determine the nature of relationship from a scatterplot of the data on the two variables. The scatterplot of data points is generally referred to as a scatter diagram or a scattergram.
3. We should not use a regression model to predict the value of Y for a given value of X which is "far" beyond the range of the observed values of X used in estimating the parameters of the regression model.
4. In case of a simple regression model, the square root of R^2 is known as the coefficient of correlation r ($\pm \sqrt{R^2}$) which is a measure of the degree of *linear* association between the two variables Y and X. This measure lies between -1 and 1. A *positive* value of r means that as X increases, the value Y also increases, whereas a negative value of r would imply that if the value of X is increased, Y goes down in value. A *zero* value for the correlation coefficient means that the two variables are not *linearly* related. A complete discussion on the properties of the correlation coefficient is available in standard texts on statistics or econometrics (e.g. Gujarati, 1988).
5. A similar procedure exists for testing the hypothesis about the intercept term α. We do not discuss it here but interested readers may refer to Wittink (1988).
6. One can also use the confidence interval to test the null hypothesis that $\beta = 0$. It is rejected if the value zero does not lie within the confidence interval.
7. We note that the standard error of $\hat{Y}_0$ depends on the deviation of X_0 from the sample mean $\bar{X}$. This suggests that the predictive ability of a regression model may be seriously affected if X_0 is chosen far from $\bar{X}$. Hence, one should be careful in using (5.2.3) model to predict Y_0 for a given value of X_0 which is quite distant from $\bar{X}$.
8. Holding all other variables constant means controlling for the effect of other variables on Y in order to measure the impact of a unit change in X_2 on Y.
9. A variable is standardized by subtracting its mean and diving by its standard deviation.
10. An alternative way to determine the relative importance of the explanatory variables is to compare the absolute values of the t-statistics for these variables. The variable with the largest t-value is considered the most significant predictor for Y.
11. One can also easily obtain the 95 percent confidence interval for $\hat{\beta}_i$ by using the expression

$$\hat{\beta}_i \pm t_{\alpha/2}\, s_{\hat{\beta}_i}$$

where $\alpha = 0.05$ and test the null hypotheses.

12. This statement, however, assumes that all other variables (e.g. age, education level etc.) have been held constant.
13. If we add an additional variable D_3 for commercial type C such that

$D_3 = 1$ if the ith individual is shown commercial C
$ = 0$ otherwise,

to the regression model (5.5.9), then it can be easily shown that

$$D_{1i} + D_{2i} + D_{3i} = 1 \quad \text{for all } i$$

indicating the presence of *perfect collinearity*, a violation of one of the critical assumptions of a multiple regression model.
14 A regression with only dummy variables is also referred to as an *analysis of variance* (ANOVA) model. If it also includes covariates that account for the effects of extraneous factors then it is similar to an *analysis of covariance* (ANCOVA) model.
15 By the term appropriate *specification* of the variables in a regression model we mean that it includes issues about the definitions and measurements of the criterion as well as the explanatory variables, the set of relevant explanatory variables, and the nature of appropriate data required for the analysis.

References

Balasubramanian, S. K. and Jain, D. C. 1993: Simple approaches to evaluate competing non-nested models in marketing. *International Journal of Research in Marketing* (forthcoming).
Bass, F. M. 1969: A new product growth model for consumer durables. *Management Science*, 15, 215–27.
Chatterjee, S. and Price, B. 1977: *Regression Analysis by Example*, New York: John Wiley & Sons, Inc.
Gujarati, D. 1988: *Basic Econometrics*, International edn, Singapore: McGraw-Hill Book Company.
Jain, D. C. and Vilcassim, N. J. 1989: Testing functional forms of market share model using the Box-Cox transformation and the Langrange multiplier approach. *International Journal of Research in Marketing*, 6, 95–107.
Johnston, J. 1984: *Econometric Methods*, New York: McGraw-Hill Book Company.
Lilien, G. L., Kotler, P. and Moorthy, K. S. 1992: *Marketing Models*, New Jersey: Prentice Hall.
Parasuraman, A. 1991: *Marketing Research*, Reading, Massachusetts: Addison-Wesley Publishing Company.
Pindyck, R. S. and Rubinfeld, D. L. 1981: *Econometric Models and Economic Forecasts*, New York: McGraw-Hill Book Company.
Wittink, D. R. 1988: *The Application of Regression Analysis*, Boston: Allyn and Bacon, Inc.

6

Experimental Design: Generalization and Theoretical Explanation

Brian Sternthal
Alice M. Tybout
Bobby J. Calder

The goal of marketing research is to increase the understanding of buyers. This knowledge can be used to make more informed marketing decisions. One way of doing marketing research is to ask people questions about why they buy what they do, how they make buying decisions, what features of the product are important, etc. Such questions attempt to capture the knowledge that people have about their own behavior. Another way of doing marketing research is to see what buyers do or say when confronted with a real or simulated setting of marketing interest. Thus some people might be given one product alternative and others a second alternative. They are then asked how much they like the product alternative, or whether they would buy it. This is the experimental way of doing marketing research.

The difference between the two ways of doing marketing research is obvious (and should not be obscured by the fact that using what people say can be part of both). The first way, asking questions, is relatively easy to do and can yield rich information. But it is limited by people's insight into their own behavior and by their willingness and ability to reveal what they know. The second approach to research circumvents this disadvantage. Knowledge comes not from people's own insight but from what they do or say in response to what they are presented with in the experiment. Knowledge comes from observed causality – when given X, people do or say Y.

The observation of causality is the defining aspect of the use of experiments (see Cattell, 1988). Knowledge from experimental marketing research is based on this. As such, experiments are not just another choice of "technique". Experimentation is a fundamentally different way of trying to understand buyers.

Although the observation of causality is basic, we must go beyond this in understanding how experiments can increase our knowledge. There are in fact two approaches to producing knowledge from experiments. One approach we term *generalization* and the other *theoretical explanation.* In this chapter, we describe both approaches and point out their differing implications for designing experiments. In this analysis the notion of experimental design is conceived broadly to include (a) the context or setting in which the experiment is conducted, (b) the characteristics of the sample used, (c) the selection of independent variables, (d) the selection of dependent variables. Our discussion focuses on how the generalization and theoretical explanation approaches aim to produce knowledge. The narrower conception of experimental design, which involves an assessment of how particular comparisons between experimental groups are made (factorial or otherwise), is mentioned only in passing because sources of information on this topic are readily available.

The Generalization Approach

An intuitively plausible approach to producing knowledge from experiments is to reason as follows: There is a particular situation of marketing interest. Before we decide what to do in this situation, let us conduct an experimental test of alternatives. The alternatives will constitute different variables and the levels of these variables in the experimental design. The test will be conducted so as to correspond to the actual marketing situation in critical respects. An example will clarify this approach.

An example study

A manufacturer of winter apparel had recently begun to advertise a line of ski parkas. Although this expenditure seemed questionable because all brands of parkas are similar, it was considered necessary because competitors were promoting their lines in advertising. The challenge was to create interest or "news" for a brand in a category composed of parity items.

The parka manufacturer's strategy was to promote features common to all parkas and to distinguish the brand by its alpine down fill. Although the brand was unique in having alpine down fill, this attribute was inconsequential: Alpine down fill is no different than any other down fill. The alpine brand was priced competitively with other parkas. Nevertheless, sales increased substantially with the alpine ad campaign.

Management's pleasure with this outcome was tempered by several questions that they could not answer with confidence. Would the alpine feature be more attractive at a different price point than the competitive price being charged? Some felt that a lower price would underscore the value of alpine down fill and thus enhance sales. Others believed that charging a premium in relation to competitive brands would reinforce the perception of alpine down fill's superiority. Further, might different types of consumers respond to price differently? In particular the market was known to be segmented according to repeat buyers versus first-time buyers.

A field study was conducted to address these issues.[1] While continuing to run the campaign advertising the alpine down fill, management persuaded each of three retail outlets to employ different pricing strategies. In the first store, the parkas were priced below competitive brands. In the second store, they were priced at parity with competitive brands. And, in a third store they were priced at a premium relative to competitive brands. In addition, all customers purchasing parkas in these stores were asked whether or not they owned a parka. Sales of the manufacturer's parka line were tracked by store and by customer type.

When the data were analyzed using an analysis of variance statistical technique, a significant interaction between store and customer type was found. For first-time buyers, sales increased as price increased and sales were greatest for the store charging the highest prices. For repeat buyers the relationship between price and sales was nonmonotonic: Sales were greater when the target brand was priced competitively than when it was priced either below or above the competition. Based on these findings, management decided to continue the ad campaign and implement a strategy whereby the parkas were priced competitively at specialty stores likely to be frequented by experienced parka buyers and were priced at a premium in department stores where first time buyers were thought to shop.

Variable relationships

As a starting point in assessing whether the parka experiment conforms to the requirements of the generalization approach, the presence of causal relations must be determined. Such relations are thought to exist when a causal agent precedes the outcomes observed, when there is covariance between the causal agent and outcome variables and when plausible alternative causal agents do not exist. When these conditions are met, a causal relationship between the agent and outcome variables is inferred and the experiment is said to have *internal validity* (Cook and Campbell, 1975).

The parka study appears to satisfy these conditions. The causal agents, price and type of buyer, preceded the product's sales, there was covariation between the causal agents and sales, and plausible rival causes for the pattern of effects on product sales are not apparent. Note, however, that this study is a quasi-experiment. Buyers were not randomly assigned to either the price or type of buyer variable conditions (rather buyers self-selected to the conditions). This heightens the possibility of threats to internal validity, as would occur if the store variable correlated with something in addition to price. Even so, any experiment is merely the *opportunity* to infer causality, and this particular study might be judged to be adequate in this regard if possible threats can be dismissed.[2]

Once the researcher is satisfied with internal validity, the generalization approach proceeds as follows. The experimental test is compared to the marketing situation of interest. If the two seem analogous, the observed relation between the variables in the experiment is assumed to hold for the market situation. The two are deemed analogous if they match on what the researcher takes to be the critical points of comparison. For example, if the people in the test are representative of the target buying population and the variables reflect the critical factors in the market, then the analogy may be considered acceptable. The study is viewed as having external validity and the results are thought to be generalizable to the marketing situation. Assessing the analogy thus involves considering the potential for threats to external validity (i.e. differences between the two settings that seem likely to affect the outcomes). If such threats are not apparent, then the analogy is sound.

Although this logic is intuitively reasonable, it raises several concerns. One is how do we determine whether a match is good. Statistical sampling techniques may be of help (e.g. by selecting a probability sample of buyers), but the criterion for a match can still be ambiguous. In the parka study, how can we be sure first-time buyers are analogous to buyers who shop at department stores?

Perhaps of even greater concern is how we can be sure that we have made the appropriate matches on all of the key characteristics. There could always be one that we have overlooked. In the parka study, it may be that the size of the store is crucial and that our test stores did not reflect either the specialty stores or the department stores in the marketing situation.[3] We shall return to these issues after considering the theoretical explanation approach.

The Theoretical Explanation Approach

The key to the generalization approach is to equate the variable relationships in the test experiment to the marketing situation via an analogy. Although the approach is intuitively appealing, as we have seen, it is not without problems. An alternative approach is to use experiments to test a theoretical explanation, and then to apply the explanation to marketing situations. We begin with another illustrative study. The example is also intended to afford a comparison with the above generalization study.

An example study

After the initial ad campaign for the alpine parka, interest turned to a determination of *why* such a response had occurred. It was speculated that the favorableness of consumers' responses to the parka was determined by their ability and motivation to assess its value. Specifically, consumers' ability to evaluate the parka was thought to be enhanced by the knowledge that the alpine down fill feature was inconsequential in distinguishing the parka from competitive brands. Consumers' motivation to process the parka information was assumed to increase as the price of the parka increased.

These assumptions implied two predictions. One was that the judgments of consumers who were uninformed about the value of alpine fill would become more favorable as price increased. This was because as price increased these consumers would process the parka features, including its unique (and presumably valuable) alpine down fill, in greater detail. By contrast, the judgments of consumers who were informed that alpine down fill was inconsequential were expected to follow a nonmonotonic pattern whereby the competitive price would result in a more favorable evaluation than either a low price or a premium price. This was because increasing price from a low to a competitive level would enhance evaluation by motivating attention to the fact that the parka possessed a unique feature, alpine down fill. However, further increasing price to a premium level was expected to prompt sufficient processing for this unique feature to be discounted as inconsequential.

To test this explanation, an experiment was conducted that included elements both similar to and different from the study described earlier. A convenience sample of college students was brought to a laboratory where they evaluated four ski parkas. All of these parkas were described similarly in terms of attributes such as weight, length, and color. But only one of the parkas claimed to have alpine down fill (i.e. the target brand). Which parka served as the target brand was varied for different subjects. Further, students were randomly assigned either to the informed condition, where they were told that the alpine down fill was no different than other down fill, or to the uninformed condition where this fact was not made known. They also were randomly assigned to one of three price conditions. For some the target parka brand was priced lower than other brands, for others it was competitively priced, and for still others the target parka was priced at a premium in relation to other brands. Thus, a 2×3 experiment was designed with two levels of knowledge about the value of alpine down fill (informed, uninformed) three levels of price (low, competitive, premium). Students' evaluations of the brands on a set of attitudinal measures served as the dependent variable. In the discussion that follows, we shall refer to this experiment as the laboratory study to distinguish it from the earlier described field experiment.

An analysis of variance revealed a significant interaction between knowledge and price. Subjects who were uninformed about the value of alpine down fill evaluated the target brand more favorably the higher its price, whereas informed subjects evaluated the target brand more favorably when it was competitively priced than when it was priced either above or below the competition (see Figure 6.1). These findings imply that the earlier theorizing about how ability and motivation affect judgment processes is viable and that, until contrary evidence emerges, this explanation of subjects' evaluations is applicable in other contexts.

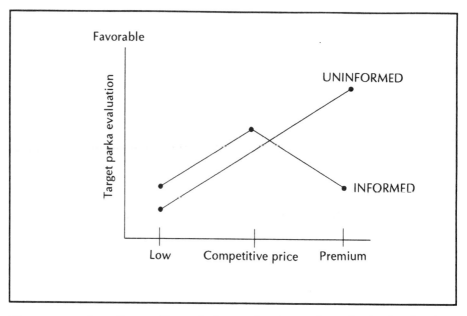

Figure 6.1 The effects of knowledge and price on brand sales/evaluation

Theoretical relationships

Whatever the specific problem that motivates testing a theoretical explanation, the questions posed for research deal with causal relations among *constructs*. A construct is an abstract notion. It cannot be observed. Rather, its existence is inferred from examination of the relationships between variables. For example, people's ability and motivation to process information are constructs, as is the notion of an attitudinal judgment. When a construct is hypothesized to cause some effect in another construct, this relationship is referred to as a nomological network. Thus in the laboratory experiment, the nomological network specifies how the constructs of the cause, ability and motivation to process information jointly determine the construct of the effect, judgment.

Theories are represented by constructs in a nomological network. These relations among abstract notions are tested by introducing variables that represent the constructs. Whereas a construct is abstract, variables are concrete. When the variable is thought to represent or influence a causal agent, it is referred to as an independent variable. In the laboratory parka experiment, knowledge and price are the independent variables. Knowledge was hypothesized to influence ability to assess information (i.e. informed consumers were expected to be better able to assess the value of alpine down fill than uninformed consumers), and price was thought to represent the construct of motivation to process information (i.e. as price increased motivation to process the information about the parka was assumed to increase). Research participants' evaluations of the parka on attitudinal scales such as good/bad and like/dislike are dependent variables that represent judgment.

To avoid confusion about whether a concept represents a construct or a variable, it is important to remember the distinction between them. Constructs are abstractions that have implications for underlying processes (i.e. nomological networks), whereas variables are simply descriptions of events. Thus, repetition of an advertisement is an independent variable, while the construct represented by this variable might be the extent to which people generate associations to the product in the ad.

How is a concept such as the vividness of information in communications classified? It is more abstract than variables such as the presence or absence of pictures, or the use of concrete versus abstract words but because its operation in a nomological network is unspecified it is not appropriate to consider it to be a construct. Vivid stimuli might, however, serve to operationalize a construct such as the extensiveness of associations that are activated.

An important feature of constructs is that they always can be represented by multiple variables. So consumers' motivation to process a communication such as an ad may be prompted by their involvement with or knowledge of the product category. But motivation to process the ad may also be affected by whether the ad employs a credible or a noncredible spokesperson, or by whether a known liability of the advertised product is acknowledged. Moreover, from a theoretical perspective, the experimenter is indifferent to which operationalization is selected, provided that it represents or affects the construct of interest.

Not only can a construct be operationalized by many variables, but variables also can represent many constructs. Consider a variable such as repetition. What construct does it represent or affect? It could affect people's ability to process information, their motivation to process information, feelings toward the communicator, or some other factor. The construct represented by a variable may vary by people, by settings, and over time. Thus, it is not possible to determine which construct is influenced by a variable in the absence of data.

The construct implied by a variable must be inferred from an examination of the experimentally generated relationships between independent and dependent variables. Alternative explanations are developed by assuming that the variables represent different constructs. The explanation requiring the fewest constructs that can account for all of the data is the one that is preferred. We refer to this explanation as the most parsimonious.

What if there are several explanations that are equally efficient or parsimonious in accounting for the relationships observed between independent and dependent variables? When this occurs additional data are needed to discriminate between the explanations. Such data may be uncovered by searching the existing literature or may be generated by conducting further research. However the data are obtained, data collection proceeds until one explanation can be said to provide a more parsimonious account than all other available explanations. This implies that *construct validity* has been achieved (Cook and Campbell, 1975). Thus a unique explanation for phenomena is the stopping rule when research involves testing theoretical relationships.

The findings of a successful theory testing program are applied in a specific way. The theorist seeks a general and, ultimately, universal explanation.[4] As a consequence, generalizability of the relationship between the variables is not of interest. Rather what the theorist attempts to generalize is the relationship that is inferred to exist among the constructs. The variables are merely a vehicle for doing this. Moreover, the task of generalizing is never complete. This is because theories cannot be proven true. There are always new theoretical propositions to test and there are always new ways to test existing propositions. Thus the notion of parsimony is the *momentary* result that a set of relations is uniquely explained. This result is either sustained by subsequent experimentation, in which case the theory maintains its status as the most parsimonious or is replaced by a more parsimonious view. Knowledge is advanced in this way.

To illustrate this theory testing experimentation process, let us consider an alternative explanation for the laboratory experiment, in which knowledge is assumed to operationalize the motivation to process information. Specifically, suppose consumers who were unaware that the alpine down fill was no different than other down fills devoted few resources to evaluating the parkas. This might result in their employing a price-quality heuristic such that the higher the price, the higher the assumed quality of the distinctive alpine down fill and, thus, the more favorable the parka evaluation. Further, assume that consumers who were aware that alpine down fill was no different than any other down fill devoted more resources to the task. This might lead to evaluating the parka most favorably in the competitive price condition because this price would be consistent with their knowledge of the parka's true value. Relative to the competitive price, low price would be evaluated less favorably because it would raise questions about the quality of the alpine fill and high price would be evaluated less favorably because it would exceed the known value of the alpine down fill.

This alternative interpretation and the original interpretation of the data reported in Figure 6.1 seem equally parsimonious. In such circumstances, when internal validity is established (i.e. there is agreement that the variables, knowledge and price, are causal variables for the outcomes on judgment), but multiple interpretations of the constructs represented by these variables are plausible (i.e. in the original interpretation knowledge represents the *ability* to assess information and in the alternative explanation it represents the *motivation* to process information), the experiment is said to lack construct validity (Cook and Campbell, 1975). The absence of construct validity implies that conclusions cannot be drawn about the causal relationship *between theoretical constructs* and, thus, the theory test is not rigorous. Another experiment is needed if theoretical progress is to be made. The goal of the additional study is to determine which of the alternative explanations is most parsimonious.

Suppose in a follow-up experiment, the procedures used in the laboratory study are replicated, but a recall measure is added to the evaluation measure previously taken. If it is found that the data shown in Figure 6.1 are replicated on the evaluation measure, and there is greater recall of descriptive facts about the target parka as price increased, the original explanation would be preferred. This is because that explanation interprets price as varying the motivation to process information. By contrast, if recall were greater in the informed condition than in the uninformed one, the alternative explanation outlined above would be preferred because it assumes that knowledge, not price, varies the motivation to process information.

The demonstration that the pattern of outcomes that independent variables have on multiple dependent variables can be accounted for by one theory better than by others is one procedure for demonstrating parsimony. It involves showing that only one explanation can efficiently account for disparate outcomes. This approach is referred to as dependent variable triangulation because the unique explanation emerges by virtue of outcomes on multiple dependent variables.

An alternative approach to triangulation entails selecting independent variables that vary in many ways from one to another but share a particular characteristic that offers a unique explanation for observed outcomes. For example, suppose that in the laboratory experiment varying repetition of the information about the target parka or varying product involvement produced the same outcomes as were found when knowledge about the value of alpine down fill was varied. It could be argued that the only feature these variables share is that they are likely to affect the motivation to process information, a construct that uniquely explains the outcomes observed.

An important implication of considering parsimony as the criterion for judging the rigor of tests of theoretical relationships is that *post hoc* explanations are just as compelling as predicted explanations. As long as a unique account is available it would seem immaterial when it was conceived (Brinberg, Lynch, and Sawyer, 1992; Sternthal, Tybout, and Calder, 1987).

It should be noted that this conclusion is not universally held. Many researchers believe that even unique explanations are problematic if they are generated *post hoc*. The contention is that a test of a theoretical relationship is only rigorous when the theory uniquely *predicts* an outcome. If the explanation is made *post hoc*, it is incumbent on the researcher to conduct another experiment in which a successful prediction is made. Thus special status is given to accurate prediction. Accurate prediction is seen as the appropriate criterion because it seems to limit the possibility that researchers would be unduly influenced by the phenomena they found in articulating their theoretical views.

The logic for considering prediction as the criterion for a successful experimental program can be questioned from several perspectives. As a practical matter, it is often difficult to know whether an investigator made a prediction or developed a *post hoc* explanation and it seems rather arbitrary to designate the rigor of an experiment on the basis of whether or not prediction is claimed.

The preference for prediction can also be questioned because it appears to be based on the assumption that the empiricist is more trustworthy than the theorist. *Post hoc* explanation is discredited because theorists might use their knowledge of the data to generate the theory. Undoubtedly this can happen. But there is also strong evidence that data can be influenced to conform to the predictions of theory (see Rosenthal, 1969).

The foregoing analysis suggests that prediction holds no advantage over *post hoc* explanation. There are, however, grounds for preferring *post hoc* accounts. When a prediction is tested, the opportunity to assess whether alternative explanations offer as good accounts for the data as the favored view is limited. When tests are *post hoc*, rival explanations have had such an opportunity. Brush (1989) makes this point in his discussion of two types of evidence for Einstein's theory of relativity: light bending which was predicted before it was observed, and Mercury's orbit which was explained after it was observed:

> rather than light bending providing better evidence because it was predicted before the observation, it actually provides less secure evidence for that very reason... Because the Mercury orbit discrepancy had been known for several decades theorists had already had ample opportunity to explain it... and had failed to do so... Light bending, on the other hand, had not previously been discussed theoretically,... but now that the phenomenon was known to exist one might expect that another equally or more satisfactory explanation would be found (p. 1126).

Thus when the goal of research is to establish causal theoretical relationships, a program of research is complete when there is a unique theoretical account of the available data (i.e. when both internal and construct validity exist). It does not matter whether this explanation emerges before the data are collected or after, though there might be greater certitude on the basis of *post hoc* explanation because it has already withstood challenges from alternative views.

In the following sections, we discuss experimental design in greater detail. Emphasis is given to the considerations that underlie the choice of context, subjects, and procedures. Within each of these issues, the concerns unique to researchers employing generalization and theoretical explanation are examined separately. Readers less interested in the details of design may wish to skip the next four sections and go to a comparison of the two approaches.

Choice of Context

The settings or contexts in which experiments are conducted can be represented on a continuum. At one end of this continuum is a laboratory setting where the independent variables are introduced in an impoverished background. To the extent possible, all factors that are not being manipulated are either eliminated or are held constant. At the other end of the continuum is the field study. Here the causal relations are examined in a setting that more or less represents the richness of some real world context in which the problem being investigated occurs.

The decision of whether to conduct a laboratory or field experiment depends on the researcher's priorities. If an experiment employs a theoretical explanation approach, a laboratory setting is often preferred. Because a laboratory offers an environment where factors extraneous to the relationship of interest may be eliminated or held constant, it reduces the chances that theoretically predicted outcomes will not emerge when the theory is correct (i.e. it reduces Type II error). For example, in the laboratory parka experiment, the setting allowed factors such as the presence of displays, crowds, shopping companions and the like to be held constant while variables thought to operationalize the constructs of interest, knowledge and price, were manipulated. This increased the likelihood that any effects of these variables on judgments would be detected. Had the same study been conducted in a field setting, the variance in responses created by factors that were not of theoretical interest might have overwhelmed the effects of these variables. The theory thus would fail to make accurate predictions even if it were true.

It seems that a laboratory experiment offers the preferred environment in which to test theoretical relationships because it facilitates control over nontheoretical sources of variance that might otherwise obscure causal relations. However, it is sometimes argued that a laboratory is too artificial an environment even for theory testing purposes (Wells, 1993). The concern is that the independent variables and other procedures used in a laboratory will not generalize to real world environments where researchers might hope to apply the theory.

It is true that in many cases the procedures employed in a laboratory will not parallel or be appropriate in other contexts. And even when similar procedures are employed in the field, laboratory findings may not be replicated. This is because, as noted earlier, the constructs operationalized by variables may vary as a function of people, settings, and time. It should be noted, however, that generalization of this sort is not germane when the researcher focuses on theoretical relationships. If a theoretical explanation for phenomena is accepted on the grounds that it is the most parsimonious explanation available, then it is this abstract relationship (i.e. the nomological network), and not the variable-level outcomes that is applied within the domain of the theory. Such application may provide a basis for speculating about how variables thought to represent the theoretical constructs will operate in some real world context. However, precise predictions about these outcomes cannot be made without further research that examines the operation of these variables under conditions where other factors that may influence outcomes in the real world are also present (see Calder, Phillips, and Tybout, 1981 for their discussion of theory-based intervention testing).

A more frequent motivation for conducting field experiments is to ascertain how much of particular variables are needed to produce a strategically desired outcome (i.e. to examine and generalize variable relationships). In marketing, such concerns are typically investigated using field experiments in the form of test markets. The level of ad spending, price, promotion, or some other marketing factor is varied between markets and sales performance is compared between test areas. Causal inferences are then made about which independent variables and at what levels the best outcomes are likely to obtain. An assumption is made that the test areas are representative of the population to which generalization will be made and the strategy producing the most favorable outcomes is instituted on a regional or national scale.

Although this analysis implies that field settings may be appropriate when a generalization approach is followed, it is important to emphasize that they are not always necessary. If interest is in the specific price points at which various outcomes would obtain, then a field study is required. However, if the researcher is only interested in generalizing relationships, such as how variations in price moderate people's response to an irrelevant attribute, then a laboratory experiment such as that described earlier might serve the purpose. More generally stated, the laboratory is a convenient context for identifying the nature of causal relationships among constructs where generalization pertains to the nomological network. A field setting is valuable when examining causal relationships between variables as it provides a basis for estimating the level of response likely to result from particular levels of the independent variables.

The failure to consider the goals of an experiment in selecting a research context can have severe consequences. Consider, for example, the procedures commonly used to pretest advertising effectiveness. People are recruited to participate in an evaluation of a new TV program. When they arrive at the theater, they are told that they might win a prize for their participation, and for this purpose they are asked to indicate how much they like specific brands in several different categories. This survey includes the brand of interest, which we shall refer to as the target brand. Next, a pilot TV program is shown that includes several exposures (usually three) to a commercial for the target brand as well as commercials for other brands. At the conclusion of the program, research participants are asked to evaluate the new program, assess their preferences for the target and other brands anew, and recall the advertising they have seen. The extent to which a target commercial is recalled and the extent to which people switch brands are measured.

This theater testing procedure is commonly used to decide between two different commercials that an advertiser is considering. If commercial A dominates commercial B on measures of recall and switching, then A is selected. It is recognized that the magnitude of difference in recall and brand switching found in the theater test might not be sustained in real world settings, but it is assumed that the superiority of A would be sustained at some level.

This approach to commercial pretesting is likely to provide valid inferences in only a limited set of circumstances. The problem is not that the theater (i.e. laboratory) setting is inappropriate. In fact, the cost of a comparable field study often makes the theater test the more viable alternative. But in conducting a theater test it is important to assess the viability of the assumptions being made as a basis for projecting commercial performance in a theater to performance in the market place. For example, a key assumption made in the procedures described above is that any difference in the performance of the A and B commercials will be constant regardless of the number of times an audience is exposed to the commercials. If this assumption is false, then inferences about which ad to select on the basis of a theater test are suspect.

To elaborate on this point, we shall briefly review current knowledge about the effect of ad exposures on brand evaluations. A repeated finding is that ad exposures are nonmonotonically related to brand evaluations (Anand and Sternthal, 1990; Cacioppo and Petty, 1979; Calder and Sternthal, 1980). Initial exposures enhance the processing of the ad content and thus result in increased agreement with the advertiser's claims. Beyond a certain point, adding exposures prompts a scrutiny of the ad content that often causes a reduction in the favorableness of brand evaluations. Moreover, as Figure 6.2 shows, this effect of exposures is moderated by the complexity of the advertiser's message. For an ad that is moderately difficult to comprehend, the nonmonotonic pattern described above is found. For an ad that is easy to comprehend, people learn its content quickly and engage in its scrutiny after relatively few exposures. Finally, for an ad that is difficult to comprehend, people are still attempting to

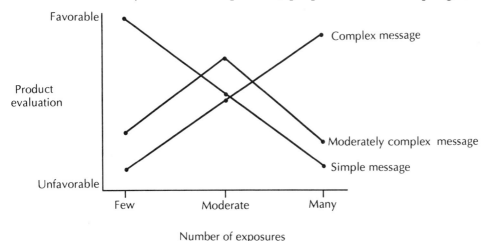

Figure 6.2 The effect of complexity and message repetition on product judgments

process the ad content at high level exposures and so increasing exposures enhances brand evaluations.

These observations question the assumption typically made in using theater tests: that is, there is a constant difference in ad performance across different levels of ad exposures. While in some cases it may be valid to infer that if commercial A dominates commercial B at some low exposure level, it will also do so at other exposure levels, there are other situations in which this outcome will not occur. If A is an easy to process commercial and B is a difficult one, A may dominate B at the low exposure levels often used in theater tests, but the reverse will occur at the higher exposure levels typically used in the market place (see Figure 6.2). Thus if a laboratory study is to be conducted to evaluate alternative commercials, it is important that the alternative ads be equated on complexity and more generally on the cognitive resources they require to process.

In sum, when a laboratory test is to be used to select between alternative strategies, it is important to represent factors that are likely to moderate the outcomes. Theoretical deductions are often useful in selecting the moderators. When financial resources are available, a field experiment might be undertaken to decide between alternative strategies. This entails either assessing outcomes in response to various levels of a strategy, or selecting the specific level of the strategy that is likely to be used in the marketplace. The advantage of this approach over the less expensive laboratory test is that it offers an estimate of the level of demand that is likely to obtain at different levels of a strategy.

Sample Selection

Once the context is established, the sample is selected. A focal issue in making this decision is whether the sample should be composed of members of a readily available homogeneous group such as students or members of a church group, or whether it should be more representative of some relevant population. As in our discussion of context, a critical determinant of the appropriate sample is whether the research goal is generalization or theoretical explanation.

When the researcher is interested in theoretical explanation, a homogeneous sample is the preferred option. The purpose of such experiments is to determine whether the relations hypothesized among constructs offer a unique explanation for some data. Thus it is desirable to minimize the variation in people's responses that might undermine observations of the theoretical relations being investigated. The more similar research participants are to each other, the greater are the chances that the experimental treatments will have the same impact on all participants. Lowering intersubject variance in this way enhances the likelihood of finding support for the theory when the theory is true. In such instances, student samples or other homogeneous groups are preferred.

Applying these notions to the laboratory study described earlier, it might be noted that a homogeneous sample is appropriate because the goal of the research was to assess how consumers' ability and motivation to process information influenced their evaluations of the parka. More representative samples might also be used, but they would be less desirable if, say, these participants varied substantially in their knowledge about parkas. This diversity would undermine the chances of finding the theoretically predicted outcomes when they exist. Although this problem could be overcome by increasing the power of the test (i.e. the number of people participating in the research), this is often an expensive remedy.

Critics of student and other homogeneous samples often dismiss this sampling approach by noting what is considered a critical flaw. It is that average responses reported by homogeneous samples often differ from those provided by a more representative sample (Ferber, 1977). Although such demonstrations underscore the fact that different groups will respond differently, this is not an issue when the objective is theoretical explanation. The demonstration of group differences in some response does not undermine the possibility that the relations among constructs are universal. Rather the critical issue is whether the same theoretical explanation can account for the outcomes observed across various samples. As an example, it might be found that student subjects in the parka study are reliably more favorable than a representative sample of potential parka purchasers. At the same time, if it were shown that increasing price resulted in a more favorable parka evaluation by uninformed respondents and a nonmonotonic pattern for informed respondents for both students and a representative sample of parka purchasers, the choice of a particular sample would not compromise the test of the theoretical explanation.

An alternative approach to sample selection when the research goal is theoretical explanation involves the choice of research participants who vary on dimensions thought to represent the constructs of interest. Along these lines, both men and women might be sampled if knowledge is of theoretical interest and the genders are known to vary in their knowledge about the topic being examined (e.g. fashion or football). Similarly, if the speed of new information acquisition were being investigated a sample might be designed to include younger and older people on the assumption that the processing of new information slows with age. At this point in the discussion, we shall only note that this is a valid approach to sample selection. A discussion of the merits of representing causal agents in terms of individual differences is deferred until we discuss independent variable strategies.

A different set of standards apply when the researcher in concerned with generalization. Here, it is appropriate to select a sample that is representative of the population of interest. This sample may be a homogeneous one composed of students, a heterogeneous sample that includes several strata, or some other segmentation scheme that represents the population to which generalization is to be made. For example, in the first parka study, it might be appropriate to sample only people living in cold weather climates.

In sum, there is no universally appropriate sample. Sample selection is guided by the goal of the research. When the objective is to examine theoretical explanations, it is appropriate to select a homogeneous sample of research participants. This increases the likelihood that the causal relations of interest will be observed when they exist. An alternative strategy of sampling people who differ on theoretically-relevant factors but who, ideally, are homogeneous on other dimensions also can be employed. Here the effect of the inter-subject differences is of interest. When generalization is the goal, the criterion for sample selection is its representativeness of the population of interest.

Selecting Independent Variables

Experiments involve assessing the impact of one or more causal agents on certain outcomes. The independent variables are the causal agents. When the goal is theoretical explanation, the independent variables are of interest as a means of inferring how constructs operate in a nomological network, whereas when the goal is generalization interest is in the independent variables *per se*. Several issues require resolution in selecting independent variables: Should the independent variables be manipulated or measured, how many independent variables should be examined in an experiment, and what levels of an independent variable are appropriate? These questions are first addressed in the context of research examining theoretical explanations and then in the context of research intended for generalization.

Theoretical explanations

Manipulated vs. measured One decision that must be made routinely in theoretical experiments seeking explanation is whether to employ manipulated or measured independent variables. *Manipulated* independent variables are constructed by introducing two or more levels or conditions of a variable and randomly assigning research participants to the different levels. Both knowledge and price were manipulated independent variables in the laboratory parka study. The other type is a *measured* independent variable. Here research participants naturally vary on, or self-select themselves to a level of an independent variable depending on some personal state, experience, or disposition such as their gender, expertise, or motivation. One school of thought is that manipulated independent variables are preferred to measured ones when the researcher is interested is examining theoretical relationships. The logic for this assertion is that by manipulating levels of the independent variable it is possible to assign respondents randomly to treatments. This procedure allows the researcher to rule out factors other than the independent variable as the cause for the outcomes observed and, thereby establishes internal validity. For example, in the laboratory parka study subjects in the informed and the uninformed knowledge conditions may differ in their exposure to advertisements for parkas, ability to afford a parka, and many other factors. Random assignment, however, makes it unlikely that the experimental conditions will, on average, differ on these extraneous factors. Thus any differences in outcomes associated with the different knowledge levels can be attributed to knowledge differences.

Following this same line of reasoning, it seems logical to conclude that a measured independent variable is necessarily flawed. This is because there are numerous factors that might correlate with the measured factor and could account for the outcomes observed. For example, if people were asked about their knowledge of parkas and this information was used to categorize them as either informed or uninformed, it would be unclear whether the brand evaluations associated with the different levels of knowledge were due to knowledge differences or to some other variable that happened to be correlated with knowledge (say, income or gender).

As logical as the preference for manipulated independent variables may seem, in actuality when examining theoretical relationships the choice is primarily a matter of researcher taste or convenience. To see why this might be, recall our earlier observation that every variable can represent many constructs. This applies to manipulated as well as measured independent variables. Thus, there are rival interpretations for every independent variable. So although random assignment can establish *which variable* caused an effect (internal validity), it is not sufficient to establish *what construct* that variable represents (construct validity). The construct represented by a variable is judged on the basis of its ability to account for the data more parsimoniously than alternative constructs. Such inferences are not necessarily enhanced by random assignment, but are facilitated by introducing the independent or dependent variable triangulation procedures that are successful in offering a unique explanation for the data at hand.

Although theoretical relationships can be inferred from either manipulated or measured independent variables, there are circumstances when manipulated independent variables are preferred. This would occur when the range of the measured variable available is not likely to represent enough variance in the construct to permit observation of a significant effect that might otherwise occur. For example, suppose an experiment was conducted to examine the effect of motivation to process information on evaluation of a product offered at different prices. Motivation to process information might be influenced by a measured variable such as individuals' need for cognition (Cacioppo and Petty, 1982), with the logic that those with a high need for cognition might be more motivated to process a message than those with a lower need for cognition. If, however, the pool of research participants was composed of highly motivated subjects (perhaps, say, graduate students), then their range in the need for cognition might represent only a narrow spectrum of the construct motivation to process information. In turn, the failure to represent a sufficient range may result in the absence of an effect on evaluation, even though one would have existed had a larger range of motivation to process information been sampled. In this instance, it may be easier to achieve the needed differences in levels of the construct of the cause by using a manipulated independent variable, such as an instruction to process the information carefully or casually, to create levels of motivation to process information.

Number of levels How many levels of an independent variable are necessary to test a theoretical explanation? In most instances, only two levels of an independent variable are required. When the theory predicts a nonmonotonic relationship, as was the case for motivation to process information among consumers with the ability to evaluate the information in the laboratory parka study, it is appropriate to include a third level of the independent variable operationalizing the construct (in this case, price). This is not, however, the only procedure for addressing anticipated nonmonotonicity. It can also be handled by introducing two independent variables that represent the same construct. Instead of using three levels of price to create three levels of motivation to process, two levels of price and two levels of another variable also thought to influence motivation would be included in the experimental design. For example, subjects might be told that they would be entered in a lottery and either they would receive the parka they evaluated most favorably if they won, or they would receive a fixed sum of cash if they won. The low price and the cash lottery would represent low motivation, high price and the parka lottery would represent high motivation and mixed levels of price and lottery would represent moderate motivation. In essence, three levels of a *construct* are needed to check a nonmonotonic prediction. This can be achieved either by using one independent variable with three levels or two independent variables with two levels each.

In selecting levels of the independent variable, some investigators use a no treatment control as one of the levels. For example, in the parka study the treatments might be low, competitive, and premium price and the control might be the absence of price information. Although in some instances such no treatment controls turn out to be useful in explaining treatment effects, they have the potential of contributing more to confusion than to clarity.

The limitation of no treatment controls in tests of theoretical relationships is straightforward. In designing a test of such a relationship, the researcher has the notion that some construct is causally related to another. Operationally this is achieved by selecting two levels of a variable: One level that prompts something to happen and the other that blocks this occurrence. When a no treatment control is used to represent the absence of a causal construct, the respondents may interpret this treatment in any way they deem appropriate. This latitude often makes the outcomes difficult to interpret.

To illustrate, consider a situation in which the impact of a credible spokesman is being investigated. Credibility is thought to influence the construct, extent of counter-argumentation, and thereby the persuasive impact of a message. To investigate this premise, two levels of credibility are introduced. A highly credible spokesperson presents the communication in the treatment condition and the source is not identified in the no treatment control.

Faced with this scenario, subjects are invited to respond in any number of ways in the no source control. They may assume that the spokesman was not very credible, on the logic that otherwise he would have made his credibility known. In this event, a credibility effect would probably have been found such that people exposed to the highly credible spokesperson were more influenced than those exposed to no spokesperson. But it seems just as likely that subjects could make some other inference about the absence of the source. They might reason that the experimenter is the spokesperson and, assuming that the experimenter was held in high regard, subjects would respond to the message in the same way as those in the high credibility condition. In this case, the absence of an effect may be attributable to the fact that an experimental condition necessary to prompt counter-argumentation was absent.

Thus, when testing theoretical explanations it is appropriate to avoid using no treatment control groups. This is not because no treatment controls will always undermine the ability to make inferences about the construct operationalized by an independent variable. The problem is that a no treatment control provides an ambiguity that unnecessarily offers the respondent latitude in selecting the construct to be represented. A superior approach is to vary actively all levels that are intended to represent a construct. For example, if high credibility is to reduce counter-argumentation to a message, the appropriate control is a treatment that is likely to prompt counter-argumentation such as a low credibility spokesperson.

Number of independent variables How many independent variables are necessary to test a theoretical explanation? This question is most easily addressed by identifying conditions that are not adequate for such purposes. Experiments that include only one independent and one dependent variable necessarily are open to multiple interpretations. This follows from the fact that a single variable can always represent two or more constructs, whereas an inference about a theoretical relationship requires unique specification of the construct at work.

One way to address this problem is to add a second independent variable. This procedure provides an opportunity to identify a unique explanation for the data, but it does not ensure this outcome. As we noted in discussing the laboratory parka study, the two independent variables employed, consumer's knowledge of the value of alpine down fill and price, were inadequate to establish a theoretical relationship because it is possible to generate at least two explanations for the study's results. When this occurs, an additional variable may be added to the design in an effort to discriminate between the explanations. For example, suppose the study design is expanded to include the manipulation of task involvement described in the previous section; subjects are told that they will be entered in a lottery in which the prize is either the parka they evaluated most favorably or a fixed sum of cash. If the results depicted in Figure 6.3 were obtained, then the original explanation for the parka study results would be preferred over the alternative explanation. This is because telling subjects they might receive the parka they evaluated most favorably produces the same outcome as the high price level in the original laboratory study (i.e. uninformed subjects evaluate the parka more favorably than informed subjects). This pattern of data is consistent with the inference that task involvement and price operationalize the same construct, motivation to process information. Further, the data are inconsistent with the assumption underlying the alternative view, that knowledge rather than price affects motivation (i.e. knowledge does not affect evaluation in the same manner as task involvement, making it difficult to argue that both variables operationalize motivation).

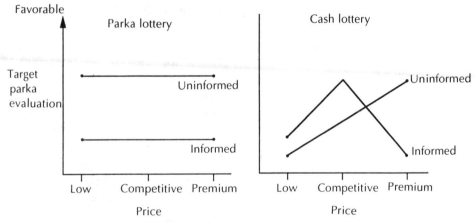

Figure 6.3 Expanded parka study design findings

Generalization

When the purpose of an experiment is to establish causal relations between variables as a basis for generalization, a different set of considerations emerge. Contrary to situations in which theoretical explanations are being examined, where any independent variable may be used that is likely to represent a construct of interest, in generalization research the choice of independent variables is usually more selective. The list of appropriate independent variables is restricted to ones that the researcher can implement and that might offer some barrier to competitive retaliation.

Consider the parka study conducted in retail stores which was described at the outset of the chapter. The results of this study suggested that a competitive pricing strategy offers the most favorable judgment of the alpine down fill brand among people who are repeat buyers. From a theoretical explanation perspective, this result is no more or less interesting than if personal relevance of the product category or repetition of an ad for the alpine parka were employed. In contrast, a generalization researcher may not be indifferent to these alternatives. Message repetition might be the preferred independent variable if it were subject to greater strategic control than product relevance. The point is that alternative independent variables are often not considered equally viable. This implies that the researcher's primary focus will be on establishing which *variable* caused the outcome (i.e. internal validity), and that little attention may be devoted to employing multiple independent variables in an effort to triangulate on an underlying construct (i.e. construct validity).

The criteria that guide the researcher's selection of the levels of the independent variable also are different from those that apply when the researcher examines theoretical explanations. Implementation of a strategy entails choosing specific levels of the independent variables. And choosing optimal levels of these variables requires that their effects on the dependent variables or outcomes of interest be known. Thus, in conducting an experiment, the researcher selects levels of the independent variable that might actually be employed. One implication of this orientation is that no treatment control groups may be of interest. For example, it is useful to know whether or not an ad expenditure of say $1 million results in a significantly different level of demand than no expenditure.

Another concern is that a sufficient number of levels of the independent variables be examined for accurate interpolation of points that lie between them. For example, in the parka study conducted in retail stores, three levels of price were required to detect the nonmonotonic relationship between price and evaluation that exists for informed consumers. Had only two levels been used, say competitive price and high price, the result could have been an erroneous inference that consumers respond more favorably the lower the price, and this influence might have led management to price below the optimal competitive price.

Selecting Dependent Measures

People's responses can be measured in a variety of ways. In the parka study conducted in retail stores, for example, consumers' behavior was monitored unobtrusively by observing whether or not they purchased the target brand of parka. More intrusive measures, such as consumers' evaluations of the parka's attributes, their perceptions of who might use it and their notions about the occasions of use could also have been solicited. Whatever the measures taken, they are generally administered with one of two purposes in mind. One is to determine the impact of an independent variable on some relevant criterion. The other goal is to gain some understanding about the relationships observed. In examining approaches to achieving these goals, we discuss the special considerations related to whether the goal of the research is theoretical explanation or generalization.

Theoretical explanations

To test any theoretical explanation one or more dependent measures is administered and the impact of the independent variables on these measures is examined. In the parka study, the theoretical researcher might include dependent measures such as people's perception of the appropriateness of the price, recall of the message, thoughts about the message advocacy, attitude toward the parka and willingness to buy it. Whatever the dependent measures used, they are always measures of some state. Dependent measures cannot directly tap a process. Process is necessarily inferred by examining the impact of independent variables on a state indicated by a dependent variable.

To see this point, first consider a dependent variable such as attitude toward the target parka, as described in the laboratory parka study discussed earlier. This measure reflects a psychological state or predisposition. By examining how price and knowledge affect people's attitude toward the brand we were able to make inferences about the process at work. Similarly, consumers' thoughts while reading the parka description capture a psychological state from which inferences can be made about process. If people report that they "thought the parka sounded superior," this thought is a description of a state they experienced. It does not explain either the process by which the thought was generated or the process by which it might affect a subsequent state such as attitude. However, like other measures of state, it can be used to *infer* process by relating the response observed to the independent variable(s) producing it.

In selecting dependent measures in theoretical research, it is often useful to include measures that vary in their psychological proximity to the causal agent (see Figure 6.4). The most proximal measure is often termed a manipulation check. The goal in administering a manipulation check is to assess the likelihood that the state intended by an independent variable was induced. For example, suppose that in the laboratory parka study, subjects' knowledge about the implications of alpine down fill was manipulated with the intent of varying the extent to which they scrutinized the

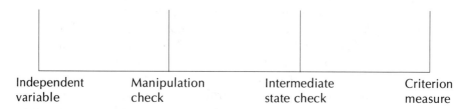

Figure 6.4 Dependent measures varying in proximity to the independent variable

product information. A measure of recall might serve as a manipulation check. If greater knowledge was associated with better recall it would be consistent with the notion that the knowledge variable operated in the manner intended.

Observing the expected effect on a manipulation check *per se* does not prove that an independent variable created *only* the desired state. All that can be claimed for a successful manipulation check is that the desired state is among those states the independent variable might have prompted; other unmeasured states may also have been created. As noted earlier, either additional measures or multiple independent variables are necessary to rule out alternative interpretations. Thus, manipulation checks have the same status as other measures; they are valuable to the extent that they help rule out alternative interpretations.

Sometimes a measure that is more distal to the causal agent than a manipulation check but more proximal to it than the criterion measure is administered (see Figure 6.4). These measures are commonly termed "measures of process." Such terminology is misleading because, as we have already observed, dependent measures can only measure states. Processes must be *inferred* from these states. Accordingly, we shall refer to such measures as intermediate state checks.

To illustrate the use of an intermediate state check, consider the laboratory parka study condition in which subjects are informed about the value of alpine down fill. To tap their reactions, subjects are instructed to record their thoughts. This involves a listing of all ideas, feelings, and other thoughts that come to mind. These thoughts might be classified in terms of whether they are more or less faithful representations of the information that subjects were given about the parka or counter-arguments to it. If it were found that the former type of thought increased as price was raised from a low to a competitive level and counter-arguments increased with a further rise in price, it might be inferred that price initially prompted message processing and then scrutiny of the message.

The measure most distal to the independent variable is termed the criterion. It represents an indicator of the outcome deduced from theory. As is true for other measures, a criterion is an indicator of some state from which process can be inferred. The criterion in the laboratory parka study was brand evaluation, though other indices such as intention to purchase or brand choice could also have been used.

Thus we can conceive of dependent measures as tapping a psychological continuum of states that occur after a stimulus presentation. All dependent measures, regardless of how proximal or distal they are to an independent variable share two facets. They are measures of some state and the state measured can be used to infer the process at work.

In testing a theoretical explanation, a decision must be made about the number and type of dependent variables that will be included. At first glance, it might seem as though the optimal strategy is to include measures of all types: manipulation checks, intermediate state checks and criterion measures. But this approach is not without cost. When multiple questions are asked responses to initial questions can influence the answers to subsequent questions (Feldman and Lynch, 1988). Such reactivity can be controlled by varying the order in which questions are administered. But if the order of manipulation checks, intermediate state checks, and criterion measures is varied so that each is administered first, the requirements in terms of research participants is likely to be costly. Such an approach treats order as an additional independent variable and the expanded design is likely to increase the sample size required. Moreover, additional measures of states do not always yield greater insight. This is because the theoretical process may affect multiple measures in the same manner. When this occurs, the additional measures may be of little value in achieving the goal of ruling out rival explanations.

A preferred approach involves administering a limited set of measures that are disassociated from each other. Measures that are expected to prompt different patterns of outcomes in response to the independent variables are selected for this purpose. As we illustrated earlier, when the pattern of effects of the price manipulation differed for recall and evaluation, a unique interpretation of the construct related to price was possible. In general, the use of multiple disassociated measures is valuable because the more complex the pattern of data that a theory can predict, the harder it is generate an alternative explanation.

It is important to note that the inclusion of manipulation checks, intermediate state checks and criterion measures does not make a test of theory rigorous, nor does the absence of a manipulation check or an intermediate state check necessarily compromise rigor. The adequacy of a theory test is not determined by the number or type of dependent measures but by whether the resulting pattern of data is uniquely explained.

Because the adequacy of a dependent variable strategy depends on whether a parsimonious explanation results, it is not possible to evaluate the adequacy of the test before data are collected. Only when the outcomes are examined for the availability of rival hypotheses is it possible to know whether the dependent variables selected were adequate to provide a rigorous theoretical test.

Thus what determines the dependent variable strategy selected is the investigator's decision-making style. Risk-averse researchers are likely to incur the costs attendant to administering manipulation checks, intermediate state checks and criterion measures. Their assumption is that the pattern of outcomes produced by these measures will be sufficiently complex so as to rule out rival explanations. Risk-taking researchers might prefer to administer only one or two measures. Whether either or both of these strategies results in strong causal inferences about the theoretical process at work depends on whether the data can be explained uniquely.

Although we have suggested that parsimony is the criterion for judging the adequacy of the dependent variables selected, sometimes other criteria are evoked. One of these pertains to the distribution of responses on dependent measures. Specifically, suppose that mean responses for two experimental treatments are 5 and 6.5 on a 7-point semantic differential type scale in Study A and 3.5 and 5 on the same scale in Study B. In both cases let us assume that the differences are significant. It might be contended that Study B provides a more rigorous test than Study A because in the former the means were on different sides of the mid-point, in effect producing high and low responses.

This argument reflects a lack of understanding of the properties of scales such as Likert and semantic differential. In these scales the mid-point is arbitrary. It does not divide favorable from unfavorable responses. The only assumption that can be made is that equal scale distances are equal (i.e. the scales are interval, not ratio). Thus the distance between 1 and 2.5 is interpreted in the same way as is the distance between 3.5 and 5 or 5 and 6.5.

Generalization

Like the theoretical researcher, the researcher interested in generalization selects dependent variables for their diagnostic power. Criterion measures are used to assess the viability of some strategy and measures more proximal to the stimulus are introduced to determine the reason for the criterion performance. Along these lines, sales may serve as the criterion and brand awareness, preference and trial and repeat may serve as the diagnostics.

To illustrate how these measures can be used to diagnose the impediments to sales, consider the first scenario in Table 6.1. Suppose there are 100 people in a sample drawn from a target population of which 30 percent are aware of the brand. Further, 20 of the 100 (or two-thirds of those aware) prefer the brand, 10 percent have tried it and 5 percent have purchased it more than once. This scenario offers guidance to the researcher by suggesting that response is being constrained by a lack of brand awareness. Strategies such as increased media expenditure or better media targeting are suggested.

Table 6.1 Diagnostic measures of response

	Case 1	Case 2	Case 3	Case 4	Case 5
Awareness	30	80	80	80	80
Preference	20	20	40	40	40
Trial	10	10	10	30	25
Repeat	5	5	5	20	5

In Case 2, this has been achieved. The problem now is to stimulate those who are aware of the brand to prefer it. This may require a change in brand position, or a modification of the product may be needed. Apparently this has been achieved in Case 3 as indicated by the preference scale. Trial, however, still is low. These outcomes imply that the product is difficult to find or some other distribution-related problem exists. Alternatively, the price of the brand may be causing resistance.

Once these problems are addressed, Case 4 might emerge. It is a typical scenario for a niche brand. While a large majority of people are aware of the brand, only a subset find it sufficiently appealing to purchase it with some regularity. If action is to be taken, it probably should be in terms of new product development.

Finally, Case 5 reflects a scenario where a substantial number of people have been prompted to try the brand, but have found it lacking. This may occur because the brand is not on par with alternative offerings. Or, it may be a parity product that people were motivated to buy because of some incentive such as low price. When the incentive is later withdrawn, a major motivation for purchase also becomes absent and repeat purchase declines.

Thus, as in experiments examining theoretical explanations, experiments focused on generalization involve the selection of dependent variables that vary in their proximity to an independent variable. And as in theoretical experimentation, the dependent variables in generalization experiments can be used to make inferences about the process at work. However, in contrast to theoretical research, where any number of dependent measures may be equally suitable representatives of a construct, in generalization research specific dependent measures are preferred. For example, in theoretical work, attitude, preference and purchase may all be viewed as equally valuable indications of a person's disposition. However, for generalizations, sales may be the criterion on which alternative strategies are assessed and alternative measures are not as appropriate.

Comparing Generalization and Theoretical Explanation

Although we have discussed generalization and theoretical explanation as distinct enterprises, this separation was motivated by the need to articulate the properties of each rather than by the belief that generalizations and theoretical explanation are unrelated. In fact, it is doubtful that any researcher actually does pure generalization.

To illustrate this point, consider how a researcher chooses variables for an experimental test. It may seem as if the task is to represent the marketing situation of interest. But how does the researcher know what aspects of the situation to represent? Consider the parka study conducted in retail stores where the variables price (store) and types of consumer were examined. Why were these variables selected? Presumably, the researcher had a reason for thinking that the alpine fill attribute might affect consumers' response to price. And certainly there had to be some thought as to why first-time buyers might react differently to price than repeat buyers. Otherwise, why study these variables as opposed to others inherent in the situation? Why not investigate the design of the alpine fill logo or point-of-sale material or anything else? The researcher's logic for believing that the selected variables might affect purchase behavior constitutes a theoretical explanation of the variable relationships. While this explanation may be couched very close to the language of the variables it is nonetheless a theoretical explanation.

Given that the researcher must have had an implicit theoretical explanation, we see that this compounds the problems discussed earlier of matching the marketing situation. Not only is the process of assessing the analogy inherently subjective, but it is in fact based on a theory that remains untested, and essentially unstated. The explanatory approach may seem too ambitious to undertake, but actually it is unavoidable. The alternative is the implicit theory that remains untested with the generalization approach.

While theoretical explanation seems mysterious and possesses an aura of impracticality to many marketers, we subscribe to the dictum that there is nothing so practical as a good theory. We can never escape theory to deal purely with observations in creating knowledge.

Marketing researchers should realize that theory development is a logical process, though a poorly understood one. It is a result of *abduction* (Thagard, 1988, 1992). In its simplest form, it is an inference of the form:

Q is be explained
If P then Q

Therefore, hypothetically p

Abduction results in a hypothesis about theoretical constructs, P, that explains a variable relationship, Q. The nature of abduction leads naturally to hypothesizing the existence of an unobserved entity (e.g. motivation to process information) as a theoretical construct. This should be seen as enhancing the power of explanation in that explanation is not limited to known or observable entities. It is definitely not the stepping away from the real marketing situation that many associate with theory. Theory involves an effort to understand that situation.

Rather than treating them as competing alternatives, resulting in potential confusion about design issues, a better approach would be to link the generalization and theoretical explanation approaches. Along these lines, some studies would be close to the variable relationship level. It is not that these studies would be non-theoretical. They would involve theory, based on abduction, and in need of testing against alternative theoretical interpretations. But the theory would employ constructs that follow literally from the variable (e.g. the variable, number of words in the ad, and the construct, comprehension difficulty). External validity and matching would not be an issue. Any application would be based on the theory and not the variable relationships.

The link with theoretical explanation based on even higher-order abduction of the theoretical constructs would be that the above studies could serve to ground the higher order abduction studies. Several studies close to the variable level could be integrated into a single explanation resulting from higher-order abduction. The link is one of stimulating increasingly powerful theories.

A benefit of linking the generalization and theoretical explanation approaches would be an end to the schism between academic and practitioner marketing researchers as discussed by Wells (1993). At present many practitioners do not appreciate the need for or the role of theory. Under the view articulated here of integrating generalization and theoretical explanation, there is a basis for cooperation and synergy between the two approaches.

Questions

1. What similarities are there in the procedures used for theoretical explanation and generalization? What are the differences? Consider sample, context, and variable selection in addressing these questions.
2. Why is post hoc explanation preferred to prediction? If *post hoc* explanation is preferred, then why is it important to make theoretical predictions when designing research?
3. Why is it generally preferable to conduct experiments aimed at theoretical explanation in laboratory settings? What considerations would prompt a researcher to conduct theoretical explanation research in a real-world marketing context?
4. Consider the data shown in Figure 6.2. Suppose that two measures were administered in addition to evaluation. One was a recall measure, where it was found that increasing the number of message exposures caused an increase in recall for all levels of complexity. The other measure was a thoughts measure, where subjects listed their favorable and unfavorable thoughts about the message information. Here it was found that favorable thoughts exhibited the same pattern as that shown in Figure 6.2 for evaluation, whereas unfavorable thoughts were the mirror image of evaluation responses (e.g. for the complex message unfavorable thoughts declined with increasing exposures).

   Provide a rationale for administering the thoughts and recall measures and offer a logic for considering one of these measures to be the more critical.

   Would it be more important to vary the order in which the recall and evaluation measures were administered or the thoughts and evaluation measures were taken?

Notes

1. This study was motivated by Carpenter, Glaser and Nakamoto (1994).
2. Statistical validity is also an issue and techniques such as the analysis of variance protect against interpreting chance as causality.
3. On purely logical grounds, even *if* the test setting exactly mirrored the marketing situation, the two must still differ due to time, the former at t_1 and the latter necessarily at t_2.

4 Although we attempt to identify universal relationships, universality is unlikely to be achieved and can never be proven. It is the striving toward universal explanation that provides guidance in the conduct, interpretation, and application of theoretical research.

References

Anand, Punam and Sternthal, Brian 1990: Ease of message processing as a moderation of repetition effects in advertising. *Journal of Marketing Research*, 27, 345–53.

Brinberg, David, Lynch, Jr., John G., and Sawyer, Alan G. 1992: Hypothesized and confounded explanations in theory tests: a Bayesian analysis. *Journal of Consumer Research*, 19 (September), 139–54.

Brush, Stephen G. 1989: Prediction and theory evaluation: the case of light bending. *Science*, 246, 1124–9.

Cacioppo, John T. and Petty, Richard E. 1979: Effects of message repetition and position on cognitive response, recall, and persuasion. *Journal of Personality and Social Psychology*, 37, 97–109.

Cacioppo, John T. and Petty, Richard E. 1982: The need for cognition, *Journal of Personality and Social Psychology*, 42, 116–31.

Calder, Bobby, J., Phillips, Lynn W. and Tybout, Alice M. 1981: Designing research for application. *The Journal of Consumer Research*, 8, 197–207.

Calder, Bobby J. and Sternthal, Brian 1980: Television commercial wearout: an information processing view. *Journal of Marketing Research*, 17, 173–86.

Carpenter, Gregory, Glazer, Rashi, and Nakamoto, Kent 1994: Meaningful brands from meaningless differentiation: the dependence on irrelevant attributes. Working Paper, Northwestern University.

Cattell, Raymond B. 1988: The principles of experimental design and analysis in relation to theory building. In John R. Nesselroade and Raymond Cattell (eds), *Handbook of Multivariate Experimental Psychology*, New York: Plenum Press, chap. 2, 21–67.

Cook, Thomas and Campbell, Donald 1975: The design and conduct of experiments and quasi-experiments in field settings: In Martin Dunnette (ed.), *Handbook of Industrial and Organizational Research*, Chicago: Rand McNally & Co.

Feldman, Jack M. and Lynch Jr., John G. 1988: Self-generated validity and other effects of measurement on belief, attitude, intention and behavior. *Journal of Applied Psychology*, 73, 421–35.

Ferber, Robert 1977: Research by convenience. *Journal of Consumer Research*, 4 (June), 57–8.

Rosenthal, Robert 1969: Interpersonal expectations: effects of the experimenter's hypothesis. In Robert Rosenthal and Ralph L. Rosnow, *Artifact in Behavioral Research*, New York: Academic Press, 182–277.

Sternthal, Brian, Tybout, Alice M., and Calder, Bobby J. 1987: Confirmatory versus comparative approaches to judging theory tests. *Journal of Consumer Research*, 14 (June), 114–25.

Thagard, Paul 1988: *Computational Philosophy of Science*, Cambridge, Ma.: MIT Press.

Thagard, Paul 1992: *Conceptual Revolutions*, Princeton, N.J.: Princeton University Press.

Wells, William D. 1993: Discovering-Oriented Consumer Research. *Journal of Consumer Research*, 19 (March), 489–504.

7

Analysis of Experimental Data*

Dawn Iacobucci

Analysis of Experimental Data

This chapter illustrates the analysis of variance (ANOVA) and related techniques including the analysis of covariance (ANCOVA), the multivariate analysis of variance (MANOVA), and the multivariate analysis of covariance (MANCOVA). The analysis of variance will be introduced as a simple extension of the t-test, but as the title of this chapter implies, it is when these methods are applied to experimental data that their full potential can be realized. Thus, the emphasis in this chapter is on data that might arise from experiments.

Experiments have been used both in the laboratory and in the field to study an enormous variety of phenomena. Lab experiments are most often used by scientists interested in theory testing, studying basic, conceptual topics such as: information processing and attitude formation, perception and preference, and antecedents of behaviors and behavioral intentions. Lab studies can also be used to investigate more applied questions, such as the impact of color perception on packaging, and preferences in product taste tests. Field experiments are most often used by practioners interested in applications to the marketplace, studying such topics as: price elasticities, promotion effectiveness, and media exposures via split-cable technology in test markets.

The simplest basic inferential statistics (e.g. z, t) are used to test hypotheses, or *a priori* guesses, about population parameters (e.g. $H_0 : \mu = \mu_0$, where μ represents the population mean on some variable of interest, and μ_0 is a constant – your hypothesized value of μ). Inferential statistics, therefore, test whether the characteristics of the sample support the plausibility of the hypotheses regarding the characteristics of the total population. The first extension of the basic test statistics is from one group to two. That is, rather than ask research questions of the form, "Does μ equal μ_0?", researchers ask, "Are the respondents in group 1 like those in group 2?" and test hypotheses of the form, $H_0 : \mu_1 = \mu_2$ (i.e. a two-sample t-test). In field studies, these groups may be naturally existing (e.g. men and women), or self-selected (e.g. marketing and finance majors, users and non-users of some brand). In comparison, experimentation contrasts groups created by the researcher. For example, a small (two-group) experiment might test the persuasiveness or likeability of two different advertisements, ad copy "A" or "B".[1]

Subjects (i.e. participants in the experiment) would be *randomly assigned* to either group, with the assumption that doing so equates the groups on any irrelevant, extraneous variables prior to their differential experimental treatment. The experimenter would then treat the two groups identically, except for the focal manipulated factor. Any resulting group differences can be attributed to that manipulated factor.[2] Clearly this research method is a powerful approach to scientific progress, and is considered by many researchers to be the only true means of establishing causality.

When the experimenter creates *three or more* groups (e.g. in testing a null hypothesis about 3 or more ads, $H_0 : \mu_1 = \mu_2 = \mu_3$), one might imagine that the group means could be compared via a series of 2-sample t-tests. However, such an approach would be inappropriate because the multiple tests are not independent – the data would be used more than once, and doing so would not provide unique information (e.g. $\bar{y}_1 > \bar{y}_2$ and $\bar{y}_2 > \bar{y}_3$ *implies* $\bar{y}_1 > \bar{y}_3$). Furthermore, the pairwise tests would not be as powerful as the proper analytical procedure (ANOVA); if 30 subjects were randomly assigned to each of 3 groups, the comparison of any 2 groups via a 2-sample t-test would use only 60 data points. When the data are used simultaneously, as in an ANOVA, all 90 data points contribute to the *power* of the test statistic. That is, the likelihood of discovering even subtle patterns in the data increases.

Finally, ANOVA may also be considered to be a generalization of t-tests in another sense – in ANOVA, not only may two or more groups be compared, but those groups can be the result of having manipulated more than one factor. For example, consumer reaction might be investigated as a function of both ad copy (as in the single factor design described previously) and price sensitivity. Thus, the researcher would create all combinations of the factors (e.g. ad "A" or "B", crossed with "low", "medium", or "high" pricing strategies) in order to investigate the effects of the factors, both independently and jointly.

Accordingly, the presentation of analysis of variance in this chapter is organized as follows. First, the relationship between the t-statistic and ANOVA is demonstrated, and then the ANOVA is extended to more than two groups, and to more than one factor. The variants on ANOVA are then described (e.g. MANOVA), and several data sets serve as examples throughout the chapter.

Analysis of Variance

One-sample *t*-test

To briefly review the basic inferential t-statistic, we begin with a population (usually assumed to be normally distributed) which can be described sufficiently with two parameters, μ_y and σ_y (the mean and standard deviation, indicators of central tendency and dispersion, respectively).[3] We draw a sample of "n" independent observations from the population, and compute $\bar{y}$ and s_y, estimates of the parameters, to test hypotheses about μ_y, where:

$$\bar{y} = \sum_i y_i/n, \quad \text{and} \quad s_y^2 = \sum_i (y_i - \bar{y})^2/(n-1) \tag{7.1}$$

(The variance estimate can also be written in a general form that will be useful later, as $s_y^2 = SS_y/df_y$, where "SS" represents the "sum of squares" (i.e. sum of squared deviations about the mean) and "df" represents the "degrees of freedom", a term that will be described more completely shortly.)

The null hypothesis, $H_0 : \mu_y = \mu_0$ is tested against the alternative, $H_a : \mu_y \neq \mu_0$, by comparing the sample mean $\bar{y}$, to the "sampling distribution of means," the analytical distribution that describes all sample means that could have been derived from the population with mean μ_0 drawing a sample of size n. Its mean is $\mu_{\bar{y}} = \mu_y$, and its variance is $\sigma_{\bar{y}}^2 = \sigma_y^2/n$. This distribution is "better behaved" than the population or sample, because its variance is smaller, and with sample sizes of at least n, we can be more confident that the "central limit theorem" applies, thus ensuring the normal shape.

If the null hypothesis is true (i.e. $\mu_y = \mu_0$), then 95 percent of the time a mean is computed (based on a sample size of n drawn from the population), it would fall within the limits $\mu_0 \pm (t_{0.025;n-1})(s_{\bar{y}})$. We would expect to observe values further from μ_0 (in either direction) much less frequently. Stated differently, we can compute the test statistic:

$$t = \frac{\bar{y} - \mu_0}{s_{\bar{y}}} \tag{7.2}$$

and compare it to tabled critical values. If the observed t exceeded the critical $t_{\alpha/2;n-1}$ (where $(1-\alpha) * 100\%$ represents the confidence level of the test, and $n-1$ are the degrees of freedom), we would reject H_0, concluding that the observed $\bar{y}$ is too far from μ_0 (relative to $s_{\bar{y}}$) for H_0 to be plausible.[4]

Note that the t-test is a function of three components: (1) the "effect size," or the extent to which the sample mean deviates from the population mean (i.e. which makes H_a looks more plausible), (2) the sample variability, and (3) the sample size:

$$t = \frac{\bar{y} - \mu_0}{s_{\bar{y}}} = \frac{\bar{y} - \mu_0}{s_y/\sqrt{n}} = \frac{\sqrt{n}(\bar{y} - \mu_0)}{s_y}. \tag{7.3}$$

The first two factors might be difficult to control (though clean, standardized experimental procedures and manipulations should help increase the sensitivity of detecting a difference of $\bar{y}$ from μ_0, and simultaneously decrease the variability), but the sample size is always under the experimenter's control. This equation (7.3) demonstrates how an increase in sample size increases the power of the test (i.e. the likelihood that the computed t will exceed the critical value). This relationship is the major reason why larger sample sizes are preferred to smaller sample sizes. It is also the reason some researchers have criticized significance tests – any nonzero effect in the population can be made to be significant with a sufficiently large sample (even if the effect is small and "unimportant" in size). These critics recommend including measures of "effect size" (described later in the chapter), which do not increase as a function of sample size.

Two-sample t-test

Now imagine drawing observations from two independent populations (e.g. men and women) with means μ_1 and μ_2 and standard deviations σ_1 and σ_2 (e.g. on some "likelihood to purchase" scale).[5] The sample statistics ($\bar{y}_1$, $\bar{y}_2$, $s_{\bar{y}1}$, and $s_{\bar{y}2}$) would be used to test the null hypothesis $H_0 : \mu_1 = \mu_2$ (or $(\mu_1 - \mu_2) = 0$) versus the alternative $H_a : \mu_1 \neq \mu_2$ using the statistic:

$$t = \frac{(\bar{y}_1 - \bar{y}_2) - (\mu_1 - \mu_2)}{s_{(\bar{y}_1 - \bar{y}_2)}} \quad \text{on } (n_1 - 1) + (n_2 - 1) \, df, \quad (7.4)$$

where $s^2_{(\bar{y}_1 - \bar{y}_2)} = s^2_p \left(\frac{1}{n_1} + \frac{1}{n_2} \right)$ and $s^2_p = \frac{\sum_i (y_{1i} - \bar{y}_1)^2 + \sum_i (y_{2i} - \bar{y}_2)^2}{(n_1 - 1) + (n_2 - 1)}$,

which is an estimate of within-group variability that is pooled over the two groups.

Note the two-sample t-test has the same basic form as the one-sample t-test: it is a comparison of data (e.g. $\bar{y}$ or $(\bar{y}_1 - \bar{y}_2)$) to "theory" (e.g. μ_0 or $(\mu_1 - \mu_2)$) relative to some indication of variability ($s_{\bar{y}}$ or $s_{(\bar{y}1 - \bar{y}2)}$). The numerator is the "effect size" (i.e. the size of the group differences when comparing two means), and these between-group differences can be judged large or small (i.e. significant or not) only relative to the within-group differences, which appear in the denominator.

One-Way ANOVA

The logic of the t-test is easily extended to three (or more) independent populations. For example, imagine comparing the sales figures for three test markets, in which different pricing strategies have been implemented.[6] In this example, price is manipulated by the researcher, so it is called an experimental "factor" (or "independent variable"), and sales is the variable measured by the researcher that is expected to be affected by the price variation, so it is called the "dependent variable".[7] In other words, the values exhibited by the dependent variable are hypothesized to *depend* upon the different values of the independent variable, which are purposefully manipulated. A "one-way" ANOVA implies that only a single factor has been manipulated. ANOVAs involving multiple factors are described later in this chapter.

The null hypothesis for the one-way analysis of variance is $H_0: \mu_1 = \mu_2 = \ldots = \mu_a$ (where a is the number of levels of the factor, such as $a = 3$ pricing levels randomly assigned across the test markets) versus the alternative, H_a: at least one μ_i is different from the other μ_i's. The one-way ANOVA test is based on the following model and assumptions:

$$y_{ij} = \mu + \alpha_i + \epsilon_{ij}, \qquad (7.5)$$

where y_{ij} is the score of the jth observation ($j = 1, 2, \ldots, n$) in group i ($i = 1, 2, \ldots, a$). ("n" is the sample size in each group, so the total sample size is $a * n$. Note that the equal cell sizes imply a "balanced" design, which is especially important for designs with two or more factors. The issue of unbalanced data is discussed later in this chapter.) μ is the grand mean (i.e. the mean across all $a * n$ observations), the α_i is the incremental difference between group i's mean and the grand mean, and ϵ_{ij} is the error term (i.e. the extent to which y_{ij} varies from group i's mean). The α_i's are usually the focus of the analysis – μ simply adjusts for the "scaling" of the dependent variable (e.g. if the three test markets had mean sales figures of \$40,000, \$45,000, and \$50,000, the estimate of μ would be \$45,000, and while that is information (e.g. it is different from \$250,000), it is usually of greater import that the groups might be different (the estimates of α_1, α_2 and α_3 are $-5{,}000$, 0, and $5{,}000$). The α_i's are constrained to sum to zero, so if the null hypothesis were true ($\mu_1 = \mu_2 = \ldots = \mu_a$) all the α_i's would equal zero.

Assumptions Based on sampling theory, the ϵ_{ij}'s are assumed to be random, which make the y_{ij}'s random. The specific assumptions on the ϵ_{ij}'s are three: (1) the ϵ_{ij}'s are independent (e.g. one subject's score does not affect another's); (2) the ϵ_{ij}'s are normally distributed with a mean of 0 (i.e. the errors cancel each other); and (3) each group shares a common variance (i.e. "homogeneity of variance"): $\sigma_1^2 = \sigma_2^2 = \ldots = \sigma_a^2 = \sigma_\epsilon^2$. The first assumption is most critical (because the test statistic is fairly robust to violations of the second and third assumptions), but it usually holds (unless group data are passed off as individual observations, for example).

Estimation Computation begins with the group means ($\bar{y}_{1.}, \bar{y}_{2.}, \ldots, \bar{y}_{a.}$, where a "." represents the subscript over which the means were computed, thus $\bar{y}_{1.}$ is the mean for group 1, $\bar{y}_{2.}$ is the mean for group 2, and so on), and the overall, grand mean, $\bar{y}_{..}$, which serves as the estimate of μ. The estimates of the group effects, α_1, α_2 and α_3, are computed as the difference between the group mean and the overall mean (i.e. $\hat{\alpha}_1 = (\bar{y}_{1.} - \bar{y}_{..})$, $\hat{\alpha}_2 = (\bar{y}_{2.} - \bar{y}_{..})$, $\hat{\alpha}_3 = (\bar{y}_{3.} - \bar{y}_{..})$, respectively). The error terms reflect individual differences, or variability within a group – even though all subjects in a condition are treated similarly, they are unlikely to yield identical responses $(y_{ij} - \bar{y}_{i.})$.

Sums of squares If we replace the parameters in the model statement with these estimates, we have:

$$y_{ij} = \mu + \alpha_i + \epsilon_{ij} = \bar{y}_{..} + (\bar{y}_{i.} - \bar{y}_{..}) + (y_{ij} - \bar{y}_{i.}). \qquad (7.6)$$

Note that the total variability of each y_{ij} is equal to $(y_{ij} - \bar{y}_{..})$, which can be broken into two parts, $(\bar{y}_{i.} - \bar{y}_{..})$ and $(y_{ij} - \bar{y}_{i.})$. If we square these differences and sum terms across all y_{ij}'s, we have the following "sums of squares" equation:

$$\sum_i \sum_j (y_{ij} - \bar{y}_{..})^2 = \sum_i \sum_j (\bar{y}_{i.} - \bar{y}_{..})^2 + \sum_i \sum_j (y_{ij} - \bar{y}_{i.})^2. \qquad (7.7)$$

In words, the total variability of the dependent variable (SS_{total}) may be decomposed into two parts – the variability *between* each group relative to the grand mean ((SS_A or SS_{between}), and the variability *within* each group relative to the group mean (SS_{error} or SS_{within}). SS_A is explainable by the effect of the manipulated factor, and SS_{error} is attributed to chance.

Degrees of freedom Equation (7.1) demonstrated that $\hat{\sigma}^2 = SS/df$. Here too, the sums of squares must be normed by their degrees of freedom (a scaling process to facilitate comparison). Degrees of freedom are defined as the number of data points less the number of parameters estimated (and/or number of constraints on those estimates). For example, $df_{\text{total}} = a*n - 1$ (the total sample size, $a*n$, minus 1 df used for the estimation of μ).[8] The $df_A = a - 1$ (the number of levels of factor A minus 1 df because the α_i's are constrained to sum to zero). The $df_{\text{error}} = a(n-1)$ (for each of the a groups, there are n data points that are constrained by the group's mean, $\bar{y}_{i.}$).

Mean squares and F Together, these sums of squares and degrees of freedom form the "mean squares" for each source of variability: $MS_A = SS_A/df_A$, and $MS_{\text{error}} = SS_{\text{error}}/df_{\text{error}}$. The ratio of the between-group source of variance to the within-group variance is the "F"-statistic, $F = MS_A/MS_{\text{error}}$, which is compared to the critical value from an "F" table with df_A and df_{error}.

Understanding the F-test The logic of the F-test can be understood in several ways – intuitively, by its relationship to the t-statistic, and most precisely, using the concept of "expected mean squares". Intuitively, the F-test is simply a ratio of between- to within-group differences. Figure 7.1 displays several possible outcomes for three samples. Compare panels I and II. The differences between the groups' means are the same (i.e. $\bar{y}_{i.} - \bar{y}_{..}$ in I equals $\bar{y}_{i.} - \bar{y}_{..}$ in II), so the numerators of the F-tests in studies I and II would be the same. However, the within-group variability is greater in

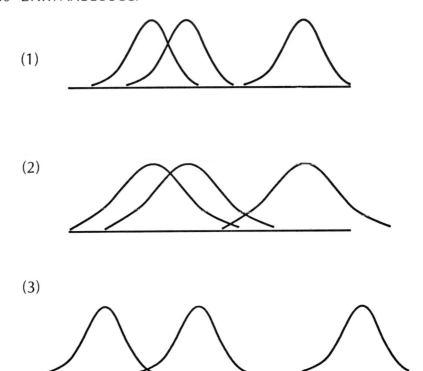

Figure 7.1 F-tests seen intuitively as a comparison of between-group differences to within-group differences (F3 > F1 > F2)

panel *II* (i.e. the dispersion of the individual y_{ij}'s around each group mean is greater in *II* than *I*), so the denominator of the *F* for *II* would be larger than that for panel *I*. Thus, the overall value of the *F* for *II* would be smaller than the *F* for *I* – the *F* in *I* would be more likely to be significant. Similarly, compare panels *I* and *III*. The scenarios are identical in their within-group variability (so the two *F*'s would have the same value in their denominators), but the differences between the groups' means are larger for the distributions in panel *III* (so the corresponding *F* would have a larger numerator). Thus, the *F* in *III* is more likely to be significant.

The *F*-statistic has a simple relationship to the two-sample *t*-statistic. Square the *t* in equation (7.4), and the result $\{(\bar{y}_1 - \bar{y}_2)^2 / s^2_{(\bar{y}_1 - \bar{y}_2)}\}$ has SS_A / df_A (= $SS_A/1$) in the numerator, and a pooled estimate of the within-group variance in the denominator. Formally, $t^2_{2(n-1)} = F_{1, 2(n-1)}$. Thus when there are only two groups, the *F*-test and the *t*-test will yield the same qualitative judgment regarding the rejection of H_0. When there are more than two groups, the *F*-test is used as the generalization of the *t*-test.

Finally, the "expected mean square" (EMS) is another approach to understanding the logic of the *F*-test. Imagine taking a sample of size *n*, computing the various statistics (e.g. MS_A), setting the value aside, tossing the data back and drawing another sample (i.e. sampling with replacement).

ANALYSIS OF EXPERIMENTAL DATA 231

The mean (or "expected value") of the theoretical distribution of MS_A's is $E(MS_A)$, where:

$$E(MS_A) = n \sum (\alpha_i)^2/(a-1) + \sigma_\epsilon^2, \text{ and } E(MS_{\text{error}}) = \sigma_\epsilon^2. \quad (7.8)$$

That is, $E(MS_{\text{error}})$ is an unbiased estimate of the error variance, but $E(MS_A)$ is also affected by the treatment effects (the α_i's). If the null hypothesis were true, $\mu_1 = \mu_2 = \ldots = \mu_a$, or $\alpha_1 = \alpha_2 = \ldots = \alpha_a = 0$, then $E(MS_A)$ would also be an (independent) estimate of σ_ϵ^2. The F-ratio compares $E(MS_A)$ against $E(MS_{\text{error}})$, or $[n\sum(\alpha_i)^2/(a-1) + \sigma_\epsilon^2]$ against $[\sigma_\epsilon^2]$, so when the null hypothesis holds, F would be $[\sigma_\epsilon^2]/[\sigma_\epsilon^2]$. Thus, when H_0 is true, F is approximately equal to one, and when H_0 is false (i.e. the groups differ), F will be significantly larger than one. Appendix A contains further information on EMSs.

Example Table 7.1 contains a hypothetical data set for a one-way ANOVA, in which the factor has three levels ($a = 3$). The number of subjects per condition ($n = 4$) is too small to be realistic, but the size of the data set will allow us to track the computations easily.[9] The group means appear different ($\bar{y}_{1.} = 5, \bar{y}_{2.} = 6, \bar{y}_{3.} = 10$), but the F-test will indicate whether they are statistically *significantly* different. Note that, as stated previously, the sums of squares add properly ($SS_{\text{total}} = 62.00$, $SS_A = 56.00$, and $SS_{\text{error}} = 6.00$), as do the degrees of freedom ($df_{\text{total}} = 11$, $df_A = 2$, $df_{\text{error}} = 9$). $MS_A = 56/2 = 28$, $MS_{\text{error}} = 6/9 = 0.667$, and $F = 28/0.667 = 41.98$. This observed test statistic exceeds the critical value ($F_{0.05;2,9} = 4.26$), so we would reject $H_0 : \mu_1 = \mu_2 = \mu_3$ (in favor of H_a: at least 1 μ is different), which indicates the means are significantly different. The intermediate computations are shown in Table 7.1, and the results are compiled into what is known as an "ANOVA table". The total variability is decomposed into its various "sources", and the "SS", "df", "MS" and "F" are summarized in the table. Sometimes journal articles will report an entire ANOVA table, but more frequently, writers simply incorporate the F and p (significance level) into the text (e.g. "The effect for factor A was significant ($F_{2,9} = 41.98, p < 0.05$)").

Table 7.1 Small one-way ANOVA example: data and computations

(I) Data y_{ij} : 's

Subject ID#	Factor A	Y	
1	1	4	
2	1	5	$\bar{y}_{1.} = 5$
3	1	6	
4	1	5	
5	2	5	
6	2	6	$\bar{y}_{2.} = 6$
7	2	6	
8	2	7	

9	3	9	
10	3	10	$\bar{y}_{3.} = 10$
11	3	11	
12	3	10	$\bar{y}_{..} = 7$

(II) Computation of SS's:

$SS_{total} = \sum_i \sum_j (y_{ij} - \bar{y}_{..})^2$
$= (4 - 7)^2 + (5 - 7)^2 + (6 - 7)^2 + (5 - 7)^2$
$+ (5 - 7)^2 + (6 - 7)^2 + (6 - 7)^2 - (7 - 7)^2$
$+ (9 - 7)^2 + (10 - 7)^2 + (11 - 7)^2 + (10 - 7)^2 = 62.00$

$SS_A = \sum_i \sum_j (\bar{y}_{i.} - \bar{y}_{..})^2$
$= (5 - 7)^2 + (5 - 7)^2 + (5 - 7)^2 + (5 - 7)^2$
$+ (6 - 7)^2 + (6 - 7)^2 + (6 - 7)^2 + (6 - 7)^2$
$+ (10 - 7)^2 + (10 - 7)^2 + (10 - 7)^2 + (10 - 7)^2 = 56.00$

$SS_{error} = \sum_i \sum_j (y_{ij} - \bar{y}_{i.})^2$
$= (4 - 5)^2 + (5 - 5)^2 + (6 - 5) + (5 - 5)^2$
$+ (5 - 6)^2 + (6 - 6)^2 + (6 - 6)^2 + (7 - 6)^2$
$+ (9 - 10)^2 + (10 - 10)^2 + (11 - 10)^2 + (10 - 10)^2 = 6.00$

(Note these SS were computed using the "definitional" formulae. "Computational" formulae can be faster, and they are provided in many texts, such as Keppel, 1991.)

(III) Computation of df's:
$df_{total} = a * n - 1 = 3 * 4 - 1 = 11$
$df_A = a - 1 = 3 - 1 = 2$
$df_{error} = a(n - 1) = 3(4 - 1) = 9$

(IV) ANOVA summary table:

(IV.A) In general:

Source (of variation)	SS	df	MS	F
Factor A (between groups)	$SS_A = \sum_i \sum_j (\bar{y}_{i.} - \bar{y}_{..})^2$	$(a - 1)$	SS_A/df_A	MS_A/MS_{error}
Error (within groups)	$SS_{error} = \sum_i \sum_j (y_{ij} - \bar{y}_{i.})^2$	$a(n - 1)$	SS_{error}/df_{error}	
Total	$\sum_i \sum_j (y_{ij} - \bar{y}_{..})^2$	$an - 1$		

(IV.B) For these data:

Source (of variation)	SS	df	MS	F
Factor A (between groups)	56	2	28.000	41.98
Error (within groups)	6	9	0.667	
Total	62	11		

Note that at this point, all the analyst knows is that the group means (5, 6 and 10) are not statistically equal. It may be that 5 is approximately

ANALYSIS OF EXPERIMENTAL DATA   233

equal to 6, and only 10 is different, or it could be that all three means are distinct. More specific information is needed, and it is obtained by computing follow-up "contrasts," which are discussed later in the chapter.

Two-way ANOVA

In this section, we consider the ANOVA methods for analyzing data that result from experiments in which two factors have been manipulated. The most common two-factor design is known as the "completely randomized, two-factor factorial." "Completely randomized" means that each subject is drawn from the same population but is *randomly* assigned to one (and only one) of the experimental conditions (when subjects are exposed to more than one condition, the proper analysis is "repeated measures" ANOVA, discussed later in this chapter). "Two-factor factorial" means that the two factors included in the study are being manipulated simultaneously, thus creating all possible combinations of the levels of the independent variables.[10] Such a design is said to be "completely crossed."

For example, in addition to varying price levels as one factor (e.g. "low," "medium," and "high"), the test marketers might add the factor of ad copy (e.g. ad "A", and "B"). If every test market is randomly assigned to one of the six combinations of these factors, this design would be a completely randomized two-factor factorial, or a "three by two factorial" for short. All levels of factor A are crossed with all levels of factor B, so there are $a * b$ cells in the design, and $a * b * n$ total subjects in the data. (This logic and notation are easily extended to three or more factors; e.g. a "$3 \times 2 \times 4$ factorial," etc.)

Advantages We might imagine running two studies, one focusing on the pricing levels, and another focusing on the advertisement factor, and analyze either data set using a one-way ANOVA. However, manipulating the factors simultaneously in a single factorial design affords two major advantages over a series of single factor experiments: (1) "economy," and (2) the ability to study "interactions." Factorial designs are more economical because fewer subjects are necessary to maintain equivalent power. For example, in a 2×2 design, only 60 subjects (15 per cell) would be needed for a comparison between a_1 and a_2 (or b_1 and b_2) based on $n = 30$ for each level of the factor. But running these as two separate one-factor designs (with comparable power) would require 120 total subjects.

More important than the economical advantage is the more theoretically-relevant advantage of being able to estimate and examine the "interaction" between the two factors – any joint effect resulting from the two factors that may be non-additive. The ANOVA on a two-factor factorial allows studying the effects of both factors (*A* and *B*) separately as well as together. Their separate effects are known as "main effects," and their joint influence on the dependent variable is the "interaction." For example, in the 3×2 design, it may be clear that one ad is always preferred to another (i.e. a main effect for ad), and it may be clear that one price is always preferred to another (i.e. a main effect for price), but it might instead be the case that some combination of price and ad appears to be particularly effective or a combination to avoid (i.e. an interactive effect for ad and price). For example, if one ad targets "upscale" purchasers, the combination with high price might be effective in sending a consistent signal regarding "quality." Similarly, an interaction in the data might suggest that an ad emphasizing "value" would be used best in conjunction with the lower price.

Interactions An interaction is best represented in a plot of the cell means. Consider Figure 7.2, which contains the cell means for two 2×2 designs, one that demonstrates an interaction, and one that does not. In these diagrams, note that the dependent variable serves as the vertical axis, and either factor may be drawn as the horizontal axis. The second factor is represented by the different profiles in the plot. If the factors do not "interact" in terms of their effect on the dependent variable, the graphs will contain parallel lines; that is, the effect of factor B (comparing b_j to $b_{j'}$) is the same for any level of factor A, or vice versa (the effect of factor A (comparing a_i to $a_{i'}$) is the same for any level of factor B). Conversely, note that the interaction is represented by lines that are not parallel (the lines will converge, cross-over, or diverge, depending on the range of values chosen when manipulating the factors). To establish significance, the non-parallelism must be tested via an F-test, which will be described shortly. Finally, note that the interpretations of the lower-order effects (i.e. the main effects) are "qualified" by the higher-order interactions (i.e. the two-factor interaction). Focusing upon main effects would result in misleading conclusions about causality. Interactions yield a more precise understanding of how a particular type of outcome is enacted. For example, the main effects (in the top of Figure 7.2) suggest that A_2 results in higher scores than A_1, and that there is no main effect for factor B. However, with the presence of the interaction in the first data set, A_2 does not always yield greater scores than A_1, and B_1 is not always equal to B_2. The highest scores on the dependent measure occur in the (A_2, B_1) cell, and lowest scores occur with the combination of A_1 and B_2.

Interactions are often the effects of greatest interest in an experiment. Especially when studying phenomena as complex as human or market behavior, we cannot expect to accurately model such behavior by studying only a single factor at a time. Furthermore, interactions allow more effective scientific progress because theories that predict interactions are easier to test and refute than theories that make predictions only about main effects – the latter are simpler in form, and thus allow more alternative explanations (Sternthal, Tybout, and Calder, 1987). Some experimental designs (other than factorials, which are the main focus of this chapter) do not allow for the estimation of certain interactions. Clearly if the interactions are of interest, a more suitable design (e.g. a factorial) must be executed.

The two-way model and analysis The two-factor ANOVA model, and the computation of the relevant statistics can be seen as a generalization of

(I) Cell means and marginal means:

	With an interaction				With no interaction		
	b1	b2			b1	b2	
a1	3	7	$\bar{y}1. = 5$	a1	5	5	$\bar{y}1. = 5$
a2	11	7	$\bar{y}2. = 9$	a2	9	9	$\bar{y}2. = 9$
	$\bar{y}.1 = 7$	$\bar{y}.2 = 7$			$\bar{y}.1 = 7$	$\bar{y}.2 = 7$	

(II) Interaction plots:

        With an interaction   With no interaction

(A) Version 1:

 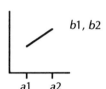

(B) Version 2:

(III) The shape of an interaction (divergence, convergence, or crossover) depends on the range of levels chosen for the independent variables. If the interaction in the population looks like.

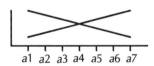

a divergence would appear if the factor was manipulated only at levels 5, 6, and 7; convergence for levels 1, 2, and 3; and a crossover for levels 3, 4, and 5 (or 1, 4, and 7, etc.).

Figure 7.2 Two 2 × 2 designs: one with an interaction, one without

the one-way ANOVA. The data y_{ijk} represent the kth subject ($k = 1, 2, \ldots n$) in the ith level of factor A ($i = 1, 2, \ldots, a$) and j^{th} level of factor B ($j = 1, 2, \ldots, b$), and is modeled as follows:

$$y_{ijk} = \mu + \alpha_i + \beta_j + \alpha\beta_{ij} + \varepsilon_{ijk}, \tag{7.9}$$

where μ represents the overall, grand mean, α_i is the differential effect of factor A, β_j is the effect of factor B, the $\alpha\beta_{ij}$'s represent the interaction between factors A and B, and the ϵ_{ijk}'s are the within-group deviations (with the constraints that $\sum_i \alpha_i = \sum_j \beta_j = \sum_i \alpha\beta_{ij} = \sum_j \alpha\beta_{ij} = 0$). These parameters are estimated by: $\bar{y}_{...}$ for μ, $(\bar{y}_{i..} - \bar{y}_{...})$ for α_i, $(\bar{y}_{.j.} - \bar{y}_{...})$ for β_j, $(\bar{y}_{ij.} - \bar{y}_{i..} - \bar{y}_{.j.} + \bar{y}_{...})$ for $\alpha\beta_{ij}$, and $(\bar{y}_{ijk} - \bar{y}_{ij.})$ for ϵ_{ijk}. In comparison to the model for a one-way ANOVA, the only term that is new in form is the interaction, which can be thought of as the effect left in the data after subtracting off all lower-order effects (the main effects and the grand mean); i.e.

$$(\bar{y}_{ij.} - \alpha_i - \beta_j - \mu) = (\bar{y}_{ij.} - (\hat{Y}_{i..} - \bar{y}_{...}) - (\bar{y}_{.j.} - \bar{y}_{...}) - \bar{y}_{...}) = (\bar{y}_{ij.} - \bar{y}_{i..} - \bar{y}_{.j.} + \bar{y}_{...}).$$

The model in (7.9) contains three sets of parameters which may be tested in the following hypotheses: First, is there a main effect for factor A ($H_0 : \alpha_1 = \alpha_2 = \ldots = \alpha_a = 0$, vs. H_a: at least 1 $\alpha_i \neq 0$)? Second, is there a main effect for factor B ($H_0 : \beta_1 = \beta_2 = \ldots = \beta_b = 0$, vs. H_a: at least 1 $\beta_j \neq 0$)? Third, is there an interaction ($H_0 : \alpha\beta_{ij} = 0$ for all i and j, vs. H_a: at least 1 $\alpha\beta_{ij} \neq 0$)? Each hypothesis is tested via an F-test that is a ratio of mean square terms. To that end, the SS_{total} is computed as $\sum_i\sum_j\sum_k(y_{ijk} - \bar{y}_{...})^2$, which can be decomposed into the following structural components:

$$SS_A = \sum_i\sum_j\sum_k(\bar{y}_{i..} - \bar{y}_{...})^2,$$

$$SS_B = \sum_i\sum_j\sum_k(\bar{y}_{.j.} - \bar{y}_{...})^2,$$

$$SS_{A*B} = \sum_i\sum_j\sum_k(\bar{y}_{ij.} - \bar{y}_{i..} - \bar{y}_{.j.} + \bar{y}_{...})^2,$$

and

$$SS_{\text{error}} = \sum_i\sum_j\sum_k(\bar{y}_{ijk} - \bar{y}_{ij.})^2.$$

The degrees of freedom are as follows: $df_A = a - 1$ and $df_B = b - 1$ (degrees of freedom for main effects equal the number of levels of that factor minus one), $df_{A*B} = (a-1)(b-1)$ (degrees of freedom for interactions equal the product of the df for the factors involved in the interaction), $df_{\text{error}} = a*b*(n-1)$ (within-group variability yields $(n-1)$ df for each of the $a*b$ cells), and df_{total} is their sum, $a*b*n - 1$. The mean squares are computed as the $SS_{\text{effect}}/df_{\text{effect}}$ (e.g. $MS_{A*B} = SS_{A*B}/df_{A*B}$). The forms of the F-ratios are determined by their expected mean squares:

$$E(MS_{\text{error}}) = \sigma_\epsilon^2, \quad E(MS_A) = \sigma_\epsilon^2 + bn\sum(\alpha_i)^2/(a-1),$$

$$E(MS_B) = \sigma_\epsilon^2 + an\sum(\beta_j)^2/(b-1),$$

$$E(MS_{A*B}) = \sigma_\epsilon^2 + n\sum\sum(\alpha\beta_{ij})^2/[(a-1)(b-1)].$$

ANALYSIS OF EXPERIMENTAL DATA

The idea is to compare two terms (one that has the effect to be tested (e.g. $\alpha\beta_{ij}$), and one that does not), to judge whether the additional term had a substantial effect in the data. Thus, the F-tests are: MS_A/MS_{error}, MS_B/MS_{error}, and MS_{A*B}/MS_{error} to test the main effects for A, B, and the interaction, respectively.

An example Table 7.2 contains a data set that will be analyzed here via ANOVA, and later in the chapter via ANCOVA, MANOVA, and MANCOVA. The scenario is as follows. One of the characteristics that researchers often point to when distinguishing the marketing of goods from the marketing of services is that services involve people more – both the consumers and the service providers. Therefore, in addition to purchasing the "core" of some service (e.g. legal advice), customer satisfaction is thought to also be a function of the goodness of the "relationship" between the client and service provider (cf. Crosby and Stephens, 1987). However, clearly this effect will be on a continuum, varying with industry. For example, while a good interpersonal relationship might be critical in dealing with a psychotherapist, it might not be so important in dealing with a service provider such as a bank teller. Thus, imagine testing these simple propositions using the following experiment.

Table 7.2 Customer satisfaction data for illustration of ANOVA, MANOVA, and MANCOVA

A	B	Y1	Y2	X	A	B	Y1	Y2	X
1	1	1	1	1	2	1	4	5	4
1	1	2	1	2	2	1	5	5	5
1	1	1	2	1	2	1	4	6	5
1	1	2	2	2	2	1	5	6	6
1	1	3	2	3	2	1	6	6	6
1	1	4	2	2	2	1	7	6	7
1	1	2	3	2	2	1	5	7	6
1	1	3	3	3	2	1	6	7	7
1	1	4	3	3	2	1	7	7	7
1	1	5	3	4	2	1	8	7	8
1	1	2	4	3	2	1	6	8	7
1	1	3	4	4	2	1	7	8	8
1	1	4	4	4	2	1	8	8	9
1	1	5	4	5	2	1	8	9	9
1	2	5	1	4	2	2	3	5	5
1	2	7	1	4	2	2	4	5	4
1	2	5	2	4	2	2	2	6	5
1	2	6	2	3	2	2	3	6	4
1	2	8	2	4	2	2	5	6	3
1	2	5	3	3	2	2	3	7	5
1	2	6	3	3	2	2	4	7	4
1	2	7	3	4	2	2	5	7	4
1	2	8	3	5	2	2	6	7	3

Table 7.2 (Cont.)

A	B	Y1	Y2	X	A	B	Y1	Y2	X
1	2	9	3	5	2	2	4	8	6
1	2	6	4	4	2	2	5	8	4
1	2	7	4	3	2	2	7	8	3
1	2	9	4	3	2	2	5	9	4
1	2	8	5	5	2	2	6	9	3

Factors:
   A = Relationship described was good ($a = 2$) or not ($a = 1$)
   B = Relationship important in industry? Yes ($b = 1$), No ($b = 2$)
Dependent variables:
   Y1 = Overall satisfaction
   Y2 = Attitude toward service provider
Covariate:
   X = Need for affiliation

The experimenter created stories about service encounters that have varied (manipulated) properties, and asked a random sample of subjects (who have been randomly assigned to the written stimulus conditions) for their reactions. The experimenter manipulated two factors. Factor A was whether the relationship between the service provider and client described in the story was good ($a = 2$) or not ($a = 1$), and factor B was whether the relationship is expected to be relatively important in that industry ($b = 1$, a psychotherapist) or not ($b = 2$, a bank teller). Subjects' reactions were measured on several variables, including their "overall satisfaction" with the encounter ($Y1$, which presumably includes satisfaction with the "core" service and also with the "relationship" component) and their "attitude toward the service provider" ($Y2$, which presumably focuses on the relationship component). Finally, the researchers also asked the subjects to fill out a questionnaire that measured their "need for affiliation" (X), with the idea that the importance of a good relationship with a service provider to customer satisfaction might be tempered by the extent to which a subject had a social, outgoing orientation.

First, we will apply the univariate ANOVA to each of the dependent variables ($Y1$ and $Y2$) separately. Later in the chapter, we will use the multivariate ANOVA to model the dependent variables simultaneously. Finally, we will use the X variable later as a "covariate" in the ANCOVA and MANCOVA analyses.

Table 7.3 contains the results for the ANOVA on $Y1$ (overall satisfaction) and $Y2$ (attitude toward service provider).[11] Note the factors have different effects on these two dependent variables. The ANOVA for $Y1$ indicates a significant main effect for B ($F_{1,52} = 8.94, p = 0.0042$) and an interaction ($F_{1,52} = 58.08, p = 0.0001$) on "overall satisfaction". The ANOVA for $Y2$ indicates only a main effect for A ($F_{1,52} = 168.39, p = 0.0001$) on "attitude toward the service provider". A comparison of the means indicates the direction of the effects and allow for their interpretation: for "overall

ANALYSIS OF EXPERIMENTAL DATA   239

satisfaction", $\bar{y}_{.1.} = 4.536$, $\bar{y}_{.2.} = 5.643$, and $\bar{y}_{11.} = 2.929$, $\bar{y}_{12.} = 6.857$, $\bar{y}_{21.} = 6.143$, $\bar{y}_{22.} = 4.429$ (the interaction is also plotted at the bottom of Table 7.3). These results suggest ratings of overall satisfaction were higher for the bank teller than for the psychotherapist (which may be a stimulus calibration difference and/or a result of something such as the "importance" attached to the latter service – this is the problem with trying to use main effects for theoretical advancement – many alternative explanations are possible (Dominowski, 1989; Sternthal et al., 1987)). The significant interaction suggests that satisfaction is lowest when the relationship component is bad (i.e. $a = 1$) in an industry where the relationship is important (i.e. $b = 1$). For Y2, the means for factor A were: $\bar{y}_{1..} = 2.786$ and $\bar{y}_{2..} = 6.893$, which effectively serves as a manipulation check, indicating the relationships described as stronger indeed generated significantly more positive attitudes toward the service provider. The substantive interpretations of these effects may have some theoretical support, but what is more important for these purposes is an understanding of how and why effects are judged to be significant.

Table 7.3 Univariate analyses of variance on the data in Table 7.2

(I) Dependent variable: Y1 = Overall satisfaction

Source	DF	Sum of squares	Mean square	F value	p
A	1	2.161	2.161	1.13	0.2935
B	1	17.161	17.161	8.94	0.0042
A * B	1	111.446	111.446	58.08	0.0001
Error	52	99.786	1.919		
Total	55	230.554			

(II) Dependent variable: Y2 = Attitude toward service provider

Source	DF	Sum of squares	Mean square	F value	p
A	1	236.161	236.161	168.39	0.0001
B	1	0.446	0.446	0.32	0.5750
A * B	1	0.018	0.018	0.01	0.9106
Error	52	72.929	1.403		
Total	55	309.554			

(III) The general ANOVA table for this 2-factor design

Source	DF	Sum of squares	Mean square	F value
A	$(a-1)$	$\sum_i\sum_j\sum_k(\bar{y}_{i..} - \bar{y}_{...})^2$	SS_A/df_A	MS_A/MS_{error}
B	$(b-1)$	$\sum_i\sum_j\sum_k(\bar{y}_{.j.} - \bar{y}_{...})^2$	SS_B/df_B	MS_B/MS_{error}
A * B	$(a-1)(b-1)$	$\sum_i\sum_j\sum_k(\bar{y}_{ij.} - \bar{y}_{i..} - \bar{y}_{.j.} + \bar{y}_{...})^2$	SS_{A*B}/df_{A*B}	MS_{A*B}/MS_{error}
Error	$ab(n-1)$	$\sum_i\sum_j\sum_k(y_{ijk} - \bar{y}_{ij.})^2$	SS_{error}/df_{error}	
Total	$abn-1$	$\sum_i\sum_j\sum_k(y_{ijk} - \bar{y}_{...})^2$		

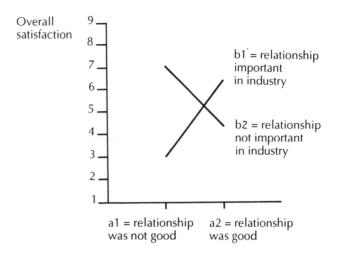

Three-way and higher-order ANOVAs

The analysis of variance for a three-factor factorial is a straightforward generalization of a two-factor ANOVA, and factorials with four or more factors are similarly easily extended. With three factors, A, B, and C, the model allows the study of three main effects (A, B, C), three two-factor interactions ($A * B$, $A * C$, $B * C$), and one three-factor interaction ($A * B * C$). First, we consider the interpretation of the three-way interaction, and then we proceed to the model and analytical details.

The concept of a three-factor interaction is no more complicated than a two-factor interaction. The interpretation of a two-factor interaction is that the effect of one factor (A or B) varies depending on the level of the other factor (B or A). Similarly, a three-factor interaction means that the relationship between two of the factors varies depending on the level of the third. For example, a three-way interaction exists if there is an interaction between factors A and B for c_1 but not for c_2. Or, a three-way interaction exists if there is a divergent-appearing interaction between factors A and C for b_1 but a crossover-appearing interaction for b_2, etc. This property generalizes to any k-factor factorial design, and while a six-factor interaction term might sound intimidating, its interpretation is logically no more complicated than that of a two-factor interaction.

The model is also a straightforward generalization of the simpler ANOVAs. Each data point is labeled $y_{ijk\ell}$, for the ℓth subject ($\ell = 1, 2, \ldots, n$) in the ith level of factor A ($i = 1, 2, \ldots, a$), j^{th} level of factor B ($j = 1, 2, \ldots, b$), and k^{th} level of factor C ($k = 1, 2, \ldots, c$), and is modeled as follows:

$$y_{ijk\ell} = \mu + \alpha_i + \beta_j + \gamma_k + \alpha\beta_{ij} + \alpha\gamma_{ik} + \beta\gamma_{jk} + \alpha\beta\gamma_{ijk} + \varepsilon_{ijk\ell}, \quad (7.10)$$

where μ is the grand mean, α_i's, β_j's, and γ_k's are the main effects for factors A, B, and C, respectively. The $\alpha\beta_{ij}$'s, $\alpha\gamma_{ik}$'s, and $\beta\gamma_{jk}$'s represent the

ANALYSIS OF EXPERIMENTAL DATA 241

$A*B$, $A*C$ and $B*C$ two-way interactions. The $\alpha\beta\gamma_{ijk}$'s reflect the three-way interaction, and the $\varepsilon_{ijk\ell}$'s are the within-group deviations. (Again, these parameters carry the constraints that

$$\sum_i \alpha_i = \sum_j \beta_j = \sum_k \gamma_k = \sum_i \alpha\beta_{ij} = \sum_j \alpha\beta_{ij} = \sum_i \alpha\gamma_{ik} = \sum_k \alpha\gamma_{ik} = \sum_j \beta\gamma_{jk}$$
$$= \sum_k \beta\gamma_{jk} = \sum_i \alpha\beta\gamma_{ijk} = \sum_j \alpha\beta\gamma_{ijk} = \sum_k \alpha\beta\gamma_{ijk} = 0.)$$

The sums of squares and degrees of freedom formulae are listed in Table 7.4.

Table 7.4 The ANOVA table for a 3-factor factorial

Source of variability	df	SS	H_0 tested
A	$(a-1)$	$SS_A = \sum_i\sum_j\sum_k\sum_\ell (\bar{y}_{i...} - \bar{y}_{....})^2$	all $\alpha_i = 0$
B	$(b-1)$	$SS_B = \sum_i\sum_j\sum_k\sum_\ell (\bar{y}_{.j..} - \bar{y}_{....})^2$	all $\beta_j = 0$
C	$(c-1)$	$SS_C = \sum_i\sum_j\sum_k\sum_\ell (\bar{y}_{..k.} - \bar{y}_{....})^2$	all $\gamma_k = 0$
$A*B$	$(a-1)(b-1)$	$SS_{A*B} = \sum_i\sum_j\sum_k\sum_\ell (\bar{y}_{ij..} - \bar{y}_{i...} - \bar{y}_{.j..} + \bar{y}_{....})^2$	all $\alpha\beta_{ij} = 0$
$A*C$	$(a-1)(c-1)$	$SS_{A*C} = \sum_i\sum_j\sum_k\sum_\ell (\bar{y}_{i.k.} - \bar{y}_{i...} - \bar{y}_{..k.} + \bar{y}_{....})^2$	all $\alpha\gamma_{ik} = 0$
$B*C$	$(b-1)(c-1)$	$SS_{B*C} = \sum_i\sum_j\sum_k\sum_\ell (\bar{y}_{.jk.} - \bar{y}_{.j..} - \bar{y}_{..k.} + \bar{y}_{....})^2$	all $\beta\gamma_{jk} = 0$
$A*B*C$	$(a-1)(b-1)(c-1)$	$SS_{A*B*C} = \sum_i\sum_j\sum_k\sum_\ell (\bar{y}_{ijk.} - \bar{y}_{ij..} - \bar{y}_{i.k.} - \bar{y}_{.jk.} + \bar{y}_{i...} + \bar{y}_{.j..} + \bar{y}_{..k.} - \bar{y}_{....})^2$	all $\alpha\beta\gamma_{ijk} = 0$
Error	$abc(n-1)$	$SS_{error} = \sum_i\sum_j\sum_k\sum_\ell (y_{ijk\ell} - \bar{y}_{ijk.})^2$	
Total	$abcn-1$	$\sum_i\sum_j\sum_k\sum_\ell (y_{ijk\ell} - \bar{y}_{....})^2$	

All mean squares are computed as: $MS_{effect} = SS_{effect}/df_{effect}$, and the F-tests are of the form: MS_{effect}/MS_{error}.

Sample size issues

There are three important points to make regarding sample size. First, the previous discussions have assumed that all cells (i, j) have n subjects. When cell sizes are unequal (e.g. $n_{ij} \neq n_{i'j'}$) the design is "unbalanced," and special care must be taken with the data analysis.[12] (See Iacobucci (1992) for further details.)

Second, when statisticians advise using sample sizes of "30 or more," this rule applies to the computation of *any* mean. For example, if there are 15 subjects in each cell of a 2×2 design, the hypothesis tests of either main effect would involve comparing two means, each of which would have been computed over 30 subjects. However, the interaction is based on a comparison of the four cell means, each of which would have been computed over only 15 observations. Thus, ideally, researchers would run studies collecting 30 or more subjects *per cell*. Practical constraints usually dictate much smaller cell sizes, but the data may then have insufficient power to detect any significant differences (Cohen, 1977).

Third, an important issue arises if there is only a single subject in each cell. Without replications, within-cell variance is zero, MS_{error} is conceptually zero, and the denominators of the F-tests would be zero. This might seem to be a sure-fire way to get significant F's (they would equal infinity), but corresponding degrees of freedom are also lost. To illustrate, consider the degrees of freedom for a two-factor factorial: $df_A = (a-1)$, $df_B = (b-1)$, $df_{A*B} = (a-1)(b-1)$, $df_{error} = ab(n-1)$, $df_{total} = abn - 1$. The df_A, df_B, df_{A*B}, and df_{total} are fine, but the $df_{error} = ab(n-1) = ab(1-1) = 0$ is problematic. And while a true error term cannot be estimated (degrees of freedom have been depleted), clearly some MS needs to serve as a denominator if an F is to be computed, so the highest-order term (in this case, the $A*B$ interaction) usually performs this function. This is simply an assumption, and is not without its own drawbacks (namely, while it allows the testing of the main effects, the interaction term becomes non-testable because it is functioning as the error term – the interaction effect and the error variability are confounded). Thus, interactions cannot be studied unless n, the sample size in each cell, exceeds one.

Fixed- vs. random-effects

All F-tests are of the form MS_{effect}/MS_{error}, where MS_{effect} is simply the MS for whatever "effect" is being tested in the null hypothesis (such as MS_A to test a main effect of factor A, $H_0: \alpha_1 = \ldots = \alpha_a = 0$). All the F-tests discussed thus far have used the within-group variability as the source of error variance (e.g. $\sum_i\sum_j\sum_k(\bar{y}_{ijk} - \bar{y}_{ij.})^2$ on $a*b(n-1)$ df for a two-factor factorial). However, the form of the F-test can be different (e.g. MS_A/MS_{A*B}), depending on two things: (1) the experimental design, and (2) whether the factors are "fixed or random." This chapter focuses on the sort of F-tests reported in most published research (i.e. "factorial designs," and "fixed factors"). However, many other experimental designs exist (e.g. within-subjects designs, which are discussed later in this chapter, and "blocking" designs, "latin squares," "nested factors," and "fractional factorials," among others, which are discussed in Box, Hunter, and Hunter (1978), Cochran and Cox (1957), and Kirk (1982)), and the issue of fixed vs. random factors (and its effect on the F-test) is discussed in Appendix A.

Contrasts

In a two-way design, three separate null hypotheses are tested: (1) $H_0: \alpha_1 = \alpha_2 = \ldots = \alpha_a = 0$; (2) $H_0: \beta_1 = \beta_2 = \ldots = \beta_b = 0$; and (3) $H_0:$ all $(\alpha\beta)_{ij} = 0$. Say we learn there is a significant main effect for factor A. From this we know that not all of the means for the different levels of A are equal.

However, if there are more than two levels of A (i.e. $df_{\text{effect}} > 1$), we do not know specifically which mean(s) differ from the others. For example, if $a = 2$ and we reject $H_0 : \alpha_1 = \alpha_2 = 0$, and we know that $\bar{y}_{1..} = 5.0$ and $\bar{y}_{2..} = 3.5$, then we know $\bar{y}_{1..}$ is *significantly* greater than $\bar{y}_{2..}$. However, if df_{effect} exceed one, the data must be examined at a more microscopic level than the omnibus F-statistic that tests $H_0 : \alpha_1 = \alpha_2 = \ldots = \alpha_a = 0$. For example, if $a = 3$ and we reject $H_0 : \alpha_1 = \alpha_2 = \alpha_3 = 0$, and the means are $\bar{y}_{1..} = 5.0$, $\bar{y}_{2..} = 4.5$, and $\bar{y}_{3..} = 4.3$, we might suspect that the first group has a significantly higher mean than the other two groups, and that the latter groups are not significantly different. However, depending on the magnitude of MS_{error}, it could also be that 5.0 is not significantly different from 4.5, but that 5.0 is significantly different from the average of the latter two means $((4.5 + 4.3)/2)$, or that all three means are significantly different. This more detailed information is obtained using follow-up tests that are called "contrasts." Contrasts simply enable single degree of freedom comparisons among the group means, so that the results regarding multi-level factors can be interpreted with no ambiguity.

For example, consider the mean sales data in Table 7.5. These data resulted from the 3×2 factorial on varying price and advertisement. The p-values (which indicate the likelihood of an F as large or larger than the observed F, and therefore indicate significant effects if they are less than 0.05) indicate that only the main effect for price was significant. That is, the consumers seemed to be indifferent to the advertisements, and there appeared to be no particular combination of ad interacting with price which gives especially high (or low) yields. The means on the price factor are ordered, but the question is, what is the precise nature of the means' differences that led to the rejection of the null hypothesis ($H_0 : \mu_{\text{low price}} = \mu_{\text{med. price}} = \mu_{\text{high price}}$). Contrasts will allow a precise answer.

Table 7.5 ANOVA on 2×3 ad $\times$ price example

(I)

Means:			Price			
		low	medium	high		
Ad	A	21.4	10.6	10.4	$\bar{y}_{1..} = 14.133$
	B	21.0	11.2	9.6	$\bar{y}_{2..} = 13.933$
		$\bar{y}_{.1.} = 21.2$	$\bar{y}_{.2.} = 10.9$	$\bar{y}_{.3.} = 10.0$	

(II) ANOVA table

Source	df	SS	MS	F	p
Ad	1	0.300	0.300	0.12	0.7321
Price	2	774.467	387.233	154.89	0.0001*
Ad × price	2	2.600	1.300	0.52	0.6011
Error	24	60.000	2.500	—	—
Total	29	837.367			

*$p < 0.05$ indicates a significant effect.

Table 7.5 (*Cont.*)

(III) Contrasts to followup significant effects

Source	df	SS	MS	F	p
Price	2	774.467	387.233	154.89	0.0001
Contrasts:					
High vs med.	1	4.050	4.050	1.62	0.2153
H&M vs low	1	770.417	770.417	308.17	0.0001

Each contrast can be thought of as a comparison between two means, such as $H_0 : \mu_2 = \mu_3$ or $H_0 : \mu_1 = (\mu_2 + \mu_3)/2$. A contrast is written as a linear combination of the group means and contrast coefficients ($\psi = \sum_i c_i \mu_i$): contrast$_1 = \psi_1 = 0 * \mu_1 + 1 * \mu_2 - 1 * \mu_3$, and $\psi_2 = 1 * \mu_1 - 0.5 * \mu_2 - 0.5 * \mu_3$. (The contrast coefficients must sum to zero, $\sum_i c_i = 0$, but not all c_i's can equal zero.) Each follow-up hypothesis ($H_0 : \psi = 0$) is easily tested: $SS_{\text{price}-\psi 1} = a * n(\sum_j c_j \bar{y}_{.j.})^2 / \sum_j c_j^2$, $df_{\text{price}-\psi 1} = 1$ (as for all contrasts), so $MS_{\text{price}-\psi 1} = SS_{\text{price}-\psi 1}/1$. The F takes this MS as its numerator, and the denominator is the same error term that was used to test the omnibus hypothesis of the price main effect.

Demonstration For example, return to the pricing main effect. The first contrast tests whether 10.9 is significantly greater than 10.0.

$$SS_{\text{price}-\psi 1} = 2 * 5(0 * 21.2 + 1 * 10.9 - 1 * 10.0)^2 / (0^2 + 1^2 + (-1)^2) = 4.05.$$
$$F_{\text{price}-\psi 1} = (SS_{\text{price}-\psi 1}/1) MS_{\text{error}} = 4.05/2.50 = 1.62.$$

This value does not exceed the critical $F_{0.05;1,24} = 4.26$, so we would conclude that the medium and high price test markets responded similarly. Therefore, in the subsequent analysis (ψ_2), it is legitimate to aggregate the data from these two groups and compare whether they differ from group 1.

$$SS_{\text{price}-\psi 2} = 2 * 5(1 * 21.2 - 0.5 * 10.9 - 0.5 * 10.0)^2 / (1^2 + (-0.5)^2 + (-0.5)^2)$$
$$= 770.417,$$
$$F_{\text{price}-\psi 2} = 770.417/2.50 = 308.17.$$

Because this F-statistic exceeds the critical value, we conclude the mean sales for the low price markets were significantly greater than for the other price levels. The variability due to the manipulated price factor has been decomposed into two sources – the high-medium comparison, and the low-other comparison. Clearly the latter contrast is the source of the price main effect.[13]

Interpretation The findings for this 3 × 2 test market design are easy to make practicable. A manager choosing a price point using these results could choose "low price" because this level of the pricing factor led to highest sales. However, if the manager wished to price higher (e.g. the low price is not sufficiently profitable, or it is inconsistent with the product's intended image), the choice would be the "high" price. There would be no reason to stay at the medium price level; raising prices from the medium to high levels did not cause significant reduction in purchases, so the higher profits might as well be reaped. In this same practical spirit, the proper response to the manager choosing between the advertisements is, "it doesn't matter." Ad A might be chosen because its mean is slightly higher, but recall that it was not significantly different from that for ad B.

Orthogonality This example demonstrated the utility of contrasts in further partitioning variance until the patterns in the data are understood precisely. In this example, the sums of squares for each contrast totaled the sums of squares for the main effect (i.e. $SS_{price-\psi 1} + SS_{price-\psi 2} = 4.050 + 770.417 = 774.467 = SS_{price}$). This property holds whenever the degrees of freedom are depleted using mutually "orthogonal" contrasts. Two contrasts ψ_k and $\psi_{k'}$ are orthogonal if the sum of their cross product is equal to zero, that is, $\sum_i c_{ik} c_{ik'} = 0$. In the example, the coefficients for ψ_1 were 0, 1, -1, and for ψ_2, 1, -0.5, -0.5, and the test indicates they are orthogonal: $(0)(1) + (1)(-0.5) + (-1)(-0.5) = 0$. If fewer than df_{price} contrasts were estimated, then not all the variability due to price would be explained. More than df_{price} ψ's would provide redundant information (although an entirely different set of orthogonal contrasts may be computed to view the data from a different perspective). The property of orthogonality is not critical; it merely provides this mathematical nicety that the $\sum SS_{contrasts} = SS_{main\ effect}$. Theoretical interests might motivate the choice of contrasts that are not orthogonal, and clearly in such circumstances, theory should override the summation property. The results will be a bit trickier to understand however, given that non-orthogonal contrasts explain overlapping sources of variability (i.e. causing an interpretation problem like multicollinearity).

Planned vs. post-hoc Many statisticians distinguish between contrasts that are "planned" *a priori* (i.e. driven by theoretical expectations developed before examining the data), and *post hoc* comparisons that occur after seeing the data (i.e. driven by empirical concerns). They argue that statistical tests for the latter should be more conservative (i.e. be more difficult to reject) than those for the former, because the *post hoc* comparisons could be "capitalizing on chance". That is, *post hoc* contrasts are tested because the researcher has seen the means and already knows which differences are likely to be significant. Similarly, statisticians are concerned that researchers do not test "too many" contrasts, because doing so also increases the likelihood of making type I errors (declaring randomness to be significant). If 100 contrasts are tested, and all null hypotheses are true, "α" of them (e.g. 5 percent) would be rejected due to chance alone.

The solutions to these issues are several. For true *planned* comparisons, some statisticians would recommend the (ψ) tests just described, with no alterations. Others would recommend that the same statistic be computed, but that it should be compared against a critical value of $F_{\alpha/C;\, df\,\text{effect},\, df\,\text{error}}$. That is, the significance level (e.g. 0.05) is divided by the number of contrasts conducted (e.g. $C = 5$) producing a smaller α-level (e.g. 0.01). The smaller α-level is the "per comparison" significance level, and the larger α is the "family-wise" significance level (i.e. for the "family" of related hypotheses). This adjustment is applied per omnibus hypothesis; that is, 0.05 may be the family-wise significance level for both main effects A and B, but the adjusted per-comparison α-level would be smaller for factor A than B if more constrasts were analyzed in examining A than B.

For *post hoc* contrasts, statisticians agree that the tests must be made more conservative – this is done either by adopting a smaller α, or by selecting a larger critical value for F. The Scheffe test is a conservative test that no statistician would find objectionable. The same F-statistic is computed, but the critical value is multiplied by the degrees of freedom for the effect being tested. For example, an F computed for a *post hoc* contrast on factor A would be compared to the adjusted critical value $(a - 1) * F_{\alpha;\, (a-1),\, df\,\text{error}}$. As a increases, this new critical value increases, in order to protect for the fact that the number of combinations and possible contrasts increases.

Other contrasts Special types of contrasts may be estimated when circumstances are appropriate. For example, the "Dunnett" test is appropriate when a factor consists of $(a - 1)$ experimental conditions and one control condition to which each of the others will be compared. (The Scheffe test could also be used, but it would be more conservative.) The "Honestly Significant Difference" test by Tukey is used when all pairs of means will be compared (but no comparisons combining groups, such as $H_0 : \mu_1 - (\mu_2 + \mu_3)/2 = 0$, are allowed). "Trends" are contrasts that can be tested with "quantitative" factors (e.g. 1, 3, 5 ad exposures, or $1.99, 3.49, 4.99 prices, as opposed to a qualitative factors like Ad A vs. B). Trends are like standard contrasts, except the contrast coefficients are predetermined to resemble linear, quadratic, cubic (etc.) trends. For a factor with a levels, a function may be fit with up to $(a - 1)$ inflection points; a curve is fit using component trends of maximum $(a - 1)$ power (e.g. for $a = 3$, the linear trend coefficients are $-1, 0, 1$, and the quadratic contrast is tested using c_i's: $1, -1, 1$). For example, many consumer behavior phenomenon may have "linear" predictions (i.e. "more is better," such as more time to study an ad will produce more positive affect toward the product) and competing explanations that are "nonmonotonic" (i.e. "some amount is optimal," and too much is not good) – a linear and quadractic trend could be fit to such data to tease the explanations apart. Many other types of contrasts exist (cf. Hochberg and Tamhane, 1987).

Simple effects

Just as contrasts are useful in pursuing significant main effects, so is the analysis of "simple effects" useful in understanding an interaction in greater detail. For example, consider the plots in Figure 7.3. In panel I, it appears that the 2 × 2 interaction is driven by the point labeled "x"; it looks different from the rest. However, before such a result can be interpreted substantively, it must be tested statistically. The comparison of points w and x is a test of the simple effect of factor A at level 1 of factor B; i.e. is there a main effect of A for only those data where $b = 1$? Similarly, the comparison of means y and z tests the simple effects of A at level b_2. It may be illuminating to test both points of view; the comparison of w and y tests the simple effect of factor B at a_1 and x vs. z is the simple effect of B at a_2. Panel II provides another example; here the simple effect of A at b_1 should be significant, whereas the simple effect of A for b_2 should not. Finally, note in panel III, a combination of contrasts and simple effects is sometimes necessary. If the simple effect of A at b_1 was significant, we would wish to test further that $\bar{y}_{11.}$ is not different from $\bar{y}_{21.}$, but that both are different from $\bar{y}_{31.}$.

Simple effects are easily computed and tested.[14] To estimate the simple effect of factor A at level j of B, compute $SS_{A@bj} = n(\sum_i \bar{y}_{ij.}^2 - a\bar{y}_{.j.}^2)$, $df_{A@bj} = a - 1$, and $F = MS_{A@bj}/MS_{error}$. Conversely, the simple effect of B

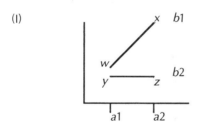

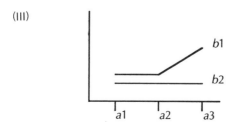

Figure 7.3 Simple effects

at $a_i = n(\sum_j \bar{y}_{ij.}^2 - b\bar{y}_{i..}^2)$ with $df_{B@ai} = b - 1$. Note that these simple effects have more degrees of freedom than the interaction terms that they are explaining. For example, in a 2×3 design, $df_{A*B} = 2$, yet each of the three simple effects of A at b_j has $(a - 1) = 1$ degree of freedom, or three in all. Similarly, both of the two simple effects of B at a_i have $(b - 1) = 2$ degrees of freedom, or four in all. These degrees of freedom result from the fact that simple effects do not partition only the SS_{A*B}. The simple effects of A at b_j are also influenced by the main effect of A, and the simple effects of B at a_i are also affected by the main effect of B. For example, in panel I of Figure 7.3, we see that the means labeled x and w will be affected not only by an interaction, but also by a main effect of A. Thus, while a contrast for a main effect for A (or B) partitions the SS_A (or SS_B), the simple effect of A at b_j (or B at a_i) partitions SS_{A*B} and SS_A (or SS_B). To summarize,

$$\sum_j SS_{A@bj} = SS_{A*B} + SS_A, \quad \sum_j df_{A@bj} = b(a-1), \quad \sum_i SS_{B@ai} = SS_{A*B} + SS_B,$$

and $\sum_i df_{B@ai} = a(b-1)$.

Finally, note that contrasts and simple effects allow researchers tremendous flexibility in the experimental designs they create. For example, it is common in a series of studies to attempt to replicate the findings of certain interesting cells, or particular combinations of factors. Yet replications of entire designs, along with new conditions can be time-consuming and costly. It is not uncommon to replicate only one or a few cells in designs like a "$2 \times 2 + 1$", where factors A and B comprise the 2×2 factorial, and the extra cell might be a_1, say, in conjunction with some previously tested manipulation, c_1, for example. Similarly, researchers might be interested in the combination of some factor (A) with several others (B, C), but have no interest in the combined effect of the other factors (e.g. $B * C$ or $A * B * C$). A design such as a 2×4 may be created, where A takes on 2 levels, a_1 and a_2, and B takes on four levels, b_1, b_2, "c_1" (b_3 really), and "c_2" (or b_4). For such a design, contrasts would focus on b_1 vs. b_2, and b_3 vs. b_4, in accordance with the experiment's structure.

Effect-size

Thus far, this chapter has described how to test whether any effect (main effects, contrasts, interactions, simple effects) in a factorial design is significant. Many researchers feel that in addition to determining an effect's significance, it is important also to determine its size; that is, an effect may be statistically significant (i.e. have a high reliability of recurrence in a replicate study), and yet have little or no substantive importance (e.g. have no predictive validity with respect to external measures). As a result, several measures of the magnitude of treatment effects have been derived, and this section describes one of the most popular measures, ω^2 (omega-squared).

ω^2 compares the size of an effect to the size of the error term. For example, the size of the main effect of factor A is defined as:

$$\omega^2 = \frac{\left(\sum \alpha_i^2/a\right)}{\left(\sum \alpha_i^2/a\right) + \sigma_\epsilon^2}. \tag{7.11}$$

Logically, this measure ranges from 0 (when H_0 is true and all population $\alpha_i = 0$) and approaches 1 as σ_ϵ^2 decreases (i.e. where the size of the effect dominates σ_ϵ^2). Practically, this measure can be shown to fall below zero and rarely exceed 0.20. The lower-bound can be negative because of the following relationship between an ω^2 and its corresponding F-value:

$$\omega_A^2 = \frac{F - 1}{F - 1 + a * n/df_A}. \tag{7.12}$$

Occasionally nonsignificant Fs can be less than 1, and as can be seen in the numerator of formula (7.12), the ω^2 would become negative. Given the ω^2's definitional formula (7.11), which resembles a ratio of variances, a negative coefficient is difficult to explain (and therefore rarely reported). However, such a result is a clear indication of a small effect. Regarding the upper-bound, rarely in behavioral research does σ_ϵ^2 (or its estimate, MS_{error}) approach 0, so rarely does ω^2 approach 1. Rules of thumb have been offered in interpreting the sizes of ω^2: $\omega^2 \geqslant 0.15$ is considered to be a "large" effect; $0.15 > \omega^2 \geqslant 0.06$, "medium"; and $0.06 > \omega^2 \geqslant 0.01$, "small" (Cohen, 1977). Keppel (1991, pp. 67) explains that ω^2's are indeed likely to be small when research is conducted in a mature discipline, in which very fine and subtle effects are being pursued. Peterson, Albaum, and Beltrami (1985) discuss typical effect sizes in consumer behavioral research.

Four possibilities of results for significance (F) and effect size (ω^2) exist. The interpretation of a nonsignificant F and a small ω^2 is straightforward (i.e. the effect is tiny or nonexistent), as is the interpretation of a significant F and a large ω^2 (i.e. the effect is substantial). However, the two remaining combinations are also diagnostic. A nonsignificant F and a large ω^2 may indicate a substantial effect that would have been significant had the sample size be large enough to afford greater power. Conversely, a significant F and a small ω^2 may indicate one of two things: either the effect is minute and had only been observed as significant because the sample size was large, or perhaps the phenomenon under study is complex, and the effect measured by ω^2 is but a small part.

Having laid the foundations of analysis of variance, subsequent sections incorporate additional predictor variables into the model (ANCOVA), or additional dependent measures (MANOVA), or both (MANCOVA).

ANCOVA is covered in the next section, and the slightly more complicated multivariate sections will follow.

Analysis of Covariance

Analysis of covariance (ANCOVA) is a technique used to increase the power or sensitivity of the ANOVA tests.[15] In ANOVA, an F-test is of the form MS_{effect}/MS_{error}; a large F-statistic can arise from a large effect and/or a small error term. Like designs with "blocking" factors, or repeated measures factors (discussed later in this chapter), ANCOVA works to reduce the size of the error term. Unlike the direct control exerted by blocking homogeneous subjects into groups or running subjects through multiple conditions, the ANCOVA exerts statistical control, extracting variability from the MS_{error} term that can be attributed to sources other than sheer error. These sources are external to the experimental design and are called "covariates."

For example, imagine an experiment that varies time available to process the information presented in an ad, and the dependent variable measures the accuracy of memory recall or recognition. It is easy to argue that subjects' intelligence could affect their ability to process and thereby remember information, regardless of the manipulated time allocation. Intelligence, then, is a "nuisance factor," an extraneous source of variability between subjects. It is not of focal interest in the study, yet will almost certainly affect the subjects' scores on the dependent variables.[16] If some indicator of intelligence is measured, that variable could serve as a covariate to statistically control this extraneous variability by partitioning the SS_{error} into a smaller SS_{error} and a $SS_{covariate}$. Each covariate costs one degree of freedom from the error term, but it is expected that this loss of one degree of freedom is much offset by the reduction in SS_{error}.

It should be noted that the ANCOVA is a powerful analytical technique than can easily be planned at the outset of the design. In practice, researchers do not tend to use covariates as a key element in their experimental design. What usually happens is that the experimental factors and the dependent measure(s) are selected, and any known covariates or other variables that might be related are assembled in a laundry list manner and measured near the end of the experiment. Then frequently the analysis begins with an ANOVA, and only if the "correct" effects are not significant are the covariates entered into the model. This process is consistent with the goal of seeking a parsimonious model, but it is rather *post hoc*. There is no reason that ANCOVA cannot be the planned analysis; it is not much more complicated than the ANOVA, as will be demonstrated.

The analysis of covariance is essentially a combination of ANOVA and regression. The covariate is regressed out of the total variability, so the covariate must be measured on an interval or ratio scale, and it must have an approximately linear relationship to the dependent variable.[17] (Although, as in regression, dummy variables are also acceptable.) Recall that in a simple regression, subjects' scores on one variable $\{x_i\}$ are used to predict their scores on another $\{y_i\}$, via a simple linear function, $\hat{Y}_i = b_0 + b_1 x_i$. The total variability of Y ($SS_y = \sum_i (y_i - \bar{y})^2$) is decomposed into a part that is explainable by the linear relationship between X and Y ($SS_{regression} = \sum_i (\hat{y}_i - \bar{y})^2$) and a part that is not ($SS_{residuals} = \sum_i (y_i - \hat{y}_i)^2$). In the AN-COVA, we can think of the later term as "$SS_{y(adj)}$", representing the sums of squares of Y remaining after adjusting for its relationship with the covariate, X. The ANCOVA model is fit in one analytical step, but loosely speaking, it is as if a regression was conducted on X (the covariate) and Y (the dependent variable), and then an ANOVA was performed on the adjusted scores $(y_i - \hat{y}_i)$. For example, consider a simple one-way design and a single covariate. The ANOVA model is $y_{ij} = \mu + \alpha_i + \epsilon_{ij}$, whereas the ANCOVA model is:

$$y_{ij} = \mu + \alpha_i + \beta(x_{ij} - \bar{x}) + \epsilon_{ij}, \text{ or } y_{ij(adj)} = y_{ij} - \beta(x_{ij} - \bar{x}) = \mu + \alpha_i + \epsilon_{ij}, \quad (7.13)$$

where x_{ij} is the score on the covariate for the jth subject in the ith level of factor A, and β is the regression coefficient representing the strength of the relationship between the covariate (X) and the dependent variable (Y). (It is the estimation of this β coefficient that costs a degree of freedom.) Note there is only a single β parameter, not one per group, and there are tests for whether the assumption that all treatment conditions share a common slope seems statistical plausible.

Example

To illustrate, the analyses of covariance for the "service satisfaction" data (in Table 7.2) are presented in Table 7.6.[18] These ANCOVA results can be compared to the ANOVA results (in Table 7.3) to understand the advantages ANCOVA makes possible. First, note the df_{error} has dropped from 52 to 51, a reduction of one degree of freedom for the single covariate. Second, note this loss is indeed offset by the reduction in SS_{error} from 99.786 and 72.929 to 80.495 and 58.336, respectively. Both reductions are significant, which is to say in both cases the covariate was significant (the F's for the effect of the covariate "X" were: $F = 12.22$, $p = 0.001$, and $F = 12.76$, $p = 0.0008$, each of which tests $H_0 : \beta = 0$). (If the covariate is not significant, it might still clarify the other F-tests, but its own lack of significance would cast doubt on whether or not it should remain in the model.) Third, note that the MS_{effect}s changed, due to the fact that the dependent variable and covariate are correlated – thus, adjusting for the covariate also adjusts the groups' means, and therefore the between-group variability. Finally, note that the ANCOVAs indeed improved the sensitivity of the hypotheses; p-values that were 0.2935, 0.0042, 0.0001, 0.0001, 0.5750, and 0.9106 under the ANOVA model became 0.1230, 0.0001,

0.0001, 0.0001, 0.0772, and 0.0192 under the ANCOVA model. Thus, as promised, the ANCOVA is simple, yet powerful.

Table 7.6 Univariate analyses of covariance

(I) Dependent variable: Y1 = Overall satisfaction

Source	DF	Sum of squares	Mean square	F-value	p
A	1	3.883	3.883	2.46	0.1230
B	1	29.061	29.061	18.41	0.0001
A * B	1	26.648	26.648	16.88	0.0001
X	1	19.290	19.290	12.22	0.0010
Error	51	80.495	1.578		
Total	55	230.554			

(II) Dependent variable: Y2 = Attitude toward service provider

Source	DF	Sum of squares	Mean square	F-value	p
A	1	71.825	71.825	62.79	0.0001
B	1	3.722	3.722	3.25	0.0772
A * B	1	6.688	6.688	5.85	0.0192
X	1	14.592	14.592	12.76	0.0008
Error	51	58.336	1.144		
Total	55	309.554			

More than one covariate can be easily modeled in an ANCOVA. In such cases, the dependent variable (Y) is simply adjusted by a multiple regression with as many predictors as there are covariates. Note that a degree of freedom is lost for each additional covariate.

Analysis of covariance is a means of clarifying the analysis of experimental data by adding information to the right-hand-side of the model (i.e. the predictors). The next section illustrates that multivariate ANOVA clarifies the data picture by adding information to the left-hand-side of the model (i.e. the dependent variables).

Multivariate Analysis of Variance

Just as the ANOVA was demonstrated to be an extension of the t-test, so too is the multivariate analysis of variance (MANOVA) an extension of simpler tests. The multivariate counterparts to one-sample and two-sample t-tests are the one-sample and two-sample "Hotelling's T^2" tests. For these multivariate tests, each subject is measured on multiple dependent variables. The null hypotheses for the multivariate tests resemble their univariate counterparts, except that the means on all dependent variables are tested simultaneously. To do this, the scores for each subject on each dependent variable (let's say there are p of them) are assembled into a $p \times 1$ vector.[19] By calculating the mean of each element of these vectors across subjects, a vector of means, $\boldsymbol{\mu}$, is obtained. The null hypothesis tested by the one-sample T^2 is $H_0 : \boldsymbol{\mu} = \boldsymbol{\mu}_0$, and the null hypothesis tested by the two-sample T^2 is $H_0 : \boldsymbol{\mu}_1 = \boldsymbol{\mu}_2$, where $\boldsymbol{\mu}, \boldsymbol{\mu}_0, \boldsymbol{\mu}_1$, and $\boldsymbol{\mu}_2$ are $p \times 1$ vectors, and each μ_j must equal its corresponding μ_{0j}, or $\mu_{1j} = \mu_{2j}$, for the null hypothesis to hold. The null hypothesis can be rejected for many reasons (e.g. perhaps groups 1 and 2 differ on variable 3, but are the same on all other variables; or perhaps they differ on the average of the first, second, and p^{th} variables, etc.), which makes these methods more complex than ANOVA. Thus, followup micro-level tests will be required to understand the precise nature of the group differences. These followup tests are conducted for the same reason that contrasts and simple effects are estimated in ANOVA, and when the T^2 test is generalized to more than two groups and a MANOVA is fit, the comparisons will need to be conducted both to contrast the groups, and to inspect the linear combinations of variables along which the groups differ.

Table 7.7 classifies the models presented in this chapter by the number of populations from which the data are drawn (1 or 2 for t and T^2, and at least 2 for ANOVA and MANOVA, etc.), the number of factors that are testable (1 for t or T^2 and at least 1 for ANOVA, etc.), the number of dependent variables modeled (e.g. 1 for ANOVA, more than 1 for MANOVA), and the number of covariates (e.g. none for ANOVA, at least 1 for ANCOVA). These models are truly close relatives, and the classification scheme presented in Table 7.7 should help clarify their relationships. The one-sample and two-sample Hotelling's T^2 statistics are described next, and then the MANOVA and multivariate contrasts are described.

Table 7.7 Relationships between models covered in this chapter

Method	Number of groups	# independent variables[a]	# dependent variables[b]	# covariates[b]
t-test	1 or 2	1	1	0
ANOVA	≥ 2	≥ 1	1	0
ANCOVA	≥ 2	≥ 1	1	≥ 1
T^2	1 or 2	1	> 1	0
MANOVA	≥ 2	≥ 1	> 1	0
MANCOVA	≥ 2	≥ 1	> 1	≥ 1

[a] Each factor must be a categorical (or categorized) variable (e.g. Ad A or B, or price low medium or high).
[b] Each must have at least interval-level properties, because means, standard deviations, and correlation coefficients are computed on these data.

One-sample Hotelling's T^2

The univariate t-test for the null hypothesis $H_0 : \mu = \mu_0$ assumes the y_i data points are independent and drawn from a univariate normal population with mean μ_0 and variance σ^2. If the t-statistic in equation (7.3) is squared (and written in what seems to be a peculiar form), it will facilitate its generalization to the one-sample T^2:

$$t^2 = \frac{(\bar{y} - \mu_0)^2}{s^2/n} = \frac{n(\bar{y} - \mu_0)(\bar{y} - \mu_0)}{s^2} = n(\bar{y} - \mu_0)(s^2)^{-1}(\bar{y} - \mu_0). \quad (7.14)$$

Using $\bar{\mathbf{y}} = (1/n)\sum_i \mathbf{y}_i$ (a $p \times 1$ vector of the means computed over the n subjects on each of the p dependent variables) as an estimate of $\boldsymbol{\mu}$, and $\mathbf{S} = (1/(n-1))\sum_i(\mathbf{y}_i - \bar{\mathbf{y}})(\mathbf{y}_i - \bar{\mathbf{y}})'$ (the sample covariance matrix) as an estimate of $\boldsymbol{\Sigma}$ (the population covariance matrix), we can simply replace these estimates in (7.14) to obtain the one-sample T^2:

$$T^2 = n(\bar{\mathbf{y}} - \boldsymbol{\mu}_0)'\mathbf{S}^{-1}(\bar{\mathbf{y}} - \boldsymbol{\mu}_0). \quad (7.15)$$

(For proofs and derivations see Anderson (1984) or Seber (1984).) This equation (7.15) closely resembles equation (7.14) except that vectors and matrices have replaced single numbers. The T^2 is easily transformed into a statistic that follows the F-distribution (i.e. approximate critical values are obtained in F-tables), with p and $n - p$ degrees of freedom:

$$F = \frac{n - p}{p(n - 1)} T^2. \quad (7.16)$$

Two-sample Hotelling's T^2

Recall that the major differences between the one-sample and two-sample t-tests were two: μ_1 and μ_2 replaced μ and μ_0, and a pooled estimate of within-group variability served as the standard error. So too does the two-sample T^2 resemble the one-sample T^2 with the analogous changes (in terms of vectors and matrices):

$$T^2 = \frac{n_1 * n_2}{(n_1 + n_2)} (\bar{\mathbf{y}}_{1.} - \bar{\mathbf{y}}_{2.})' \mathbf{S}_p^{-1} (\bar{\mathbf{y}}_{1.} - \bar{\mathbf{y}}_{2.})$$

and $$F = (n_1 + n_2 - p - 1) \frac{T^2}{p(n_1 + n_2 - 2)} \quad (7.17)$$

where each $\bar{\mathbf{y}}_{i.}$ is the $p \times 1$ vector of means on each of the dependent variables for group i, F has p and $(n_1 + n_2 - p - 1)$ degrees of freedom, and $\mathbf{S}_p$ is the pooled covariance matrix:

$$\mathbf{S}_p = \frac{1}{n_1 + n_2 - 2} \sum_i \sum_j (y_{ij} - \bar{y}_{i.})(y_{ij} - \bar{y}_{i.})'. \quad (7.18)$$

Examples Table 7.8 contains two data sets small enough to manipulate by hand to understand the T^2 better. If the first sample is considered alone, with

ANALYSIS OF EXPERIMENTAL DATA   255

a null hypothesis of say, $H_0 : \boldsymbol{\mu} = \boldsymbol{\mu}_0 = [0\ 0\ 0]'$, the $T^2 = 275.628$, $F = 30.625$, and the null hypothesis cannot be rejected $F_{0.05; p = 3, n - p = 4 - 3} = 215.70$) because the data set is too small. (The sample size n should greatly exceed the number of dependent variables, p, and for the example, $n = 4$, and $p = 3$.) When the two data sets are compared to test $H_0 : \boldsymbol{\mu}_1 = \boldsymbol{\mu}_2$, $T^2 = 10.816$, $F = 2.404$, and once again the sample size is too small to reject $H_0(F_{0.05; 3, 4} = 6.59)$. Note the intermediate computational results are given in the table.

Assumptions The assumptions underlying the two-sample T^2 are the multivariate extensions of those for the two-sample t-test (and the assumptions for the one-sample T^2 are similar). First, each vector of p pieces of information obtained for subject j in group i (i.e. $\mathbf{y}_{1j}$ and $\mathbf{y}_{2j}$) is independent of the other subjects' vectors of data. Second, these vectors, $\mathbf{y}_{ij}$ are assumed to be drawn from a multivariate normal distribution (MVN_p) with population vectors of means $\boldsymbol{\mu}_1$ and $\boldsymbol{\mu}_2$.[20] Finally, the groups are assumed to share a common covariance matrix, $\boldsymbol{\Sigma}$. This final assumption is the multivariate counterpart to the assumption of homogeneity of variances $(\sigma_1^2 = \sigma_2^2 = \sigma^2)$ in the univariate t-test. Note that the multivariate assumption $(\boldsymbol{\Sigma}_1 = \boldsymbol{\Sigma}_2 = \boldsymbol{\Sigma})$ is stricter, given that each σ_i^2 is a single value, whereas each $\boldsymbol{\Sigma}_i$ is a $p \times p$ matrix with $p(p + 1)$ unique elements, each of which must equal those in the other population.[21] If more than two groups are to be compared, or more than one factor manipulated, the T^2 is no longer sufficient, so we turn to the multivariate analysis of variance model.

Table 7.8 Numerical example of one-sample and two-sample Hotelling's T^2

Sample 1   Sample 2

(I) Data matrix:

$\mathbf{Y}_1 (4 \times 3)$ $\mathbf{Y}_2 (4 \times 3)$

$\begin{vmatrix} 3 & 4 & 11 \\ 9 & 8 & 10 \\ 3 & 7 & 6 \\ 5 & 9 & 9 \end{vmatrix}$ $\begin{vmatrix} 10 & 9 & 11 \\ 11 & 9 & 10 \\ 6 & 9 & 12 \\ 9 & 9 & 11 \end{vmatrix}$

(II) Sample means:

$\bar{\mathbf{y}}_1 = [5\ 7\ 9]'$ $\bar{\mathbf{y}}_2 = [9\ 9\ 11]'$

(III) Sample covariance matrix:

$\mathbf{S}_1 = \begin{vmatrix} 8.00 & 3.33 & 2.00 \\ 3.33 & 4.17 & -1.67 \\ 2.00 & -1.67 & 4.67 \end{vmatrix}$ $\mathbf{S}_2 = \begin{vmatrix} 4.67 & 0.00 & 1.67 \\ 0.00 & 0.00 & 0.00 \\ 1.67 & 0.00 & 2.67 \end{vmatrix}$

(IV) Computation of one-sample Hotelling's $T^2 (\boldsymbol{\mu}_0 = [0\ 0\ 0]')$:

$T^2 = n(\bar{\mathbf{y}} - \boldsymbol{\mu}_0)' \mathbf{S}^{-1} (\bar{\mathbf{y}} - \boldsymbol{\mu}_0)$

$= 4[5\ 7\ 9] \begin{vmatrix} 0.321 & -0.319 & -0.251 \\ -0.319 & 0.562 & 0.337 \\ -0.251 & 0.337 & 0.442 \end{vmatrix} \begin{vmatrix} 5 \\ 7 \\ 9 \end{vmatrix} = 275.628$

(V) Computation of two-sample Hotelling's T^2:

$$T^2 = \frac{n_1 * n_2}{(n_1 + n_2)} (\bar{y}_{1.} - \bar{y}_{2.})' S_p^{-1} (\bar{y}_{1.} - \bar{y}_{2.}) \quad \text{and} \quad F = (n_1 + n_2 - p - 1) \frac{T^2}{p(n_1 + n_2 - 2)}$$

$$= \frac{4*4}{4+4} [5-9 \quad 7-9 \quad 9-11] \begin{vmatrix} 0.204 & -0.169 & -0.066 \\ -0.169 & 0.623 & 0.205 \\ -0.066 & 0.205 & 0.443 \end{vmatrix} \begin{vmatrix} 5-9 \\ 7-9 \\ 9-11 \end{vmatrix}$$

where $S_p = \frac{1}{n_1 + n_2 - 2} ((n_1 - 1)S_1 + (n_2 - 1)S_2)$

$$= \frac{1}{6} \begin{vmatrix} 24 & 10 & 6 \\ 10 & 14 & -5 \\ 6 & -5 & 14 \end{vmatrix} + \begin{vmatrix} 14 & 0 & -5 \\ 0 & 0 & 0 \\ -5 & 0 & 2 \end{vmatrix} = \begin{vmatrix} 6.33 & 1.67 & 0.17 \\ 1.67 & 2.33 & -0.83 \\ 0.17 & -0.83 & 2.67 \end{vmatrix}$$

MANOVA

The relationship between the MANOVA and ANOVA is the same as that between the T^2 and t; rather than modeling a single dependent variable, a battery of p dependent measures are modeled simultaneously. A MANOVA is preferred to a series of p separate ANOVAs for several reasons: First, when the multivariate null hypothesis is true, the MANOVA is a single test, which protects the type I error rate to be simply α, whereas a series of p ANOVAs increases the likelihood of a type I error beyond α. Second, when the p dependent variables are correlated, the MANOVA is the more sensitive test, because it takes advantage of the correlation structure, whereas the separate ANOVAs function as if the p dependent variables are independent. If the p dependent variables are perfectly uncorrelated (i.e. no $r_{jj'}$ is significantly different from zero), the ANOVA model should suffice; not much information would be lost if the multivariate model is not fit. Similarly, if all correlations are high (i.e. the $r_{jj'}$'s are not significantly different from one), the ANOVA model might also suffice because all p variables are essentially giving the same information (e.g. an average of the p variables would be computed and that composite score would be modeled via a single ANOVA). Thus, the MANOVA is at best advantage for the cases in between, where the $r_{jj'}$'s are greater than zero and less than one in magnitude. Of course, most data sets yield correlations of this size (between 0 and 1), whether the p dependent variables are indicators of p distinct constructs interrelated in some nomological network, or represent p different facets of a single construct. Thus, MANOVA is frequently applicable.

Figure 7.4 illustrates how the MANOVA can be more informative and more powerful than p ANOVAs. The example has only two dependent variables, Y_1 and Y_2 ($p = 2$), but the principle generalizes to more dependent variables. The ellipses represent the 95 percent confidence regions for two experimental groups, I and II, and the projections of these data points on to Y_1 and Y_2 are the marginal, univariate distributions. If a univariate ANOVA is conducted on Y_1, the two groups might be significantly

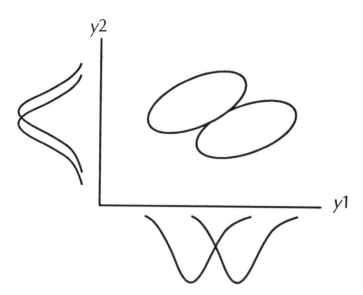

Figure 7.4 The power of MANOVA over ANOVA

different. If an ANOVA is run on the data for Y_2, the groups will not be significantly different. However, if a MANOVA is used to model both Y_1 and Y_2 simultaneously, the multidimensional information is clearer than either Y_1 or Y_2 alone. That is, there is some group overlap on Y_1, and a great deal on Y_2, but the bivariate plot shows no overlap between the groups, so the MANOVA would be more sensitive (i.e. more powerful) in detecting group differences than either ANOVA alone.

With these intuitions, we can proceed to the analytics. MANOVA, like ANOVA, is best thought of as a two-staged procedure. In stage I, omnibus tests are conducted to reveal main effects and/or interactions. If any effects are significant, follow-up comparisons are conducted in stage II. Each stage is now discussed in detail.

Computation of **H** *and* **E** In univariate ANOVA, we begin with a SS_{effect} and a SS_{error}. MANOVA is slightly more complicated; a SS_{effect} is computed for each dependent variable as well as for the crossproducts of each pair of dependent variables. That is, rather than a single value for SS_A (for example), there is a matrix of SS_A's, reflecting the p dependent variables and their intercorrelated structure. This matrix, $\mathbf{H}_A$ (H for a *h*ypothesis to be tested), is $p \times p$, with the $SS_{A(j)}$ on the diagonal (i.e. the SS_A for the jth dependent variable), and $SS_{A(jj')}$ on the off-diagonal (i.e. the SS_A for the correlation between variables j and j'). Similarly, the multivariate SS_{error} is **E**, a $p \times p$ matrix of error sums of squares. These matrices are how MANOVA "takes into account" the correlations among the dependent variables. Table 7.9 contains the formulae for these matrices (for a two-factor factorial design), and illustrates the easy generalization from a univariate ANOVA to a MANOVA. The sources of variability are the same, as are the degrees of freedom (p does not affect df, but enters the test statistics, as is described later). The computational formula of the **H** and **E** matrices resemble those of SS_{effect} and SS_{error}, except that, as usual, a vector of p values replaces a single number in multivariateland.

Table 7.9 Multivariate ANOVA: computation of **H**'s and **E** for a 2-factor factorial

Source	df	matrix
H_A	$a-1$	$\sum_i^a \sum_j^b \sum_k^n (\bar{y}_{i..} - \bar{y}_{...})(\bar{y}_{i..} - \bar{y}_{...})'$
H_B	$b-1$	$\sum\sum\sum (\bar{y}_{.j.} - \bar{y}_{...})(\bar{y}_{.j.} - \bar{y}_{...})'$
$H_{A \times B}$	$(a-1)(b-1)$	$\sum\sum\sum (\bar{y}_{ij.} - \bar{y}_{i..} - \bar{y}_{.j.} + \bar{y}_{...})(\bar{y}_{ij.} - \bar{y}_{i..} - \bar{y}_{.j.} + \bar{y}_{...})'$
E	$ab(n-1)$	$\sum\sum\sum (y_{ijk} - \bar{y}_{ij.})(y_{ijk} - \bar{y}_{ij.})'$
T	$abn-1$	$\sum\sum\sum (y_{ijk} - \bar{y}_{...})(y_{ijk} - \bar{y}_{...})'$

The matrix analog of SS_{effect}/SS_{error} is $\mathbf{HE}^{-1}$, and while $(SS_{effect}/df_{effect})/(SS_{error}/df_{error})$ is a single number (the F-statistic), $\mathbf{HE}^{-1}$ is an entire $p \times p$ matrix of values. $\mathbf{HE}^{-1}$ contains p^2 values which must be combined to obtain a statistic, like F, to indicate whether to reject H_0. However, p^2 values can be combined in different ways, each of which results in a different statistic. Thus, while there is a single uniformly most powerful test statistic for the univariate ANOVA, there are several test statistics to choose from for the multivariate ANOVA. The statistic discussed here, V, was selected because of its typically superior empirical properties, but three other statistics (Λ, T, and R) are also frequently used, and these are described briefly in Appendix C.

All the test statistics are functions of the eigenvalues[22] of $\mathbf{HE}^{-1}$. The number of unique, nonzero eigenvalues of $\mathbf{HE}^{-1}$ is the rank of the matrix, s. This rank, s, equals whichever value is smaller: p (the number of dependent variables), or df_{effect} (the degrees of freedom for the effect being tested in $\mathbf{H}$, such as $(a-1)$ for H_A, or $(a-1)(b-1)$ for H_{A*B}). That is, $s = \min(p, df_{effect})$, so $\lambda_1 > \lambda_2 > \ldots > \lambda_s > 0$, and λ_{s+1} through λ_p equal zero.

Pillai-Bartlett trace V The statistic V is defined in equation (7.19), and because λ_i is interpretable as analogous to SS_{effect}/SS_{error}, V is interpretable as SS_{effect}/SS_{total} (like a "variance accounted for"):

$$V = \sum_{i=1}^{s} \frac{\lambda_i}{1 + \lambda_i}. \quad (7.19)$$

V gets its name from its creators and from its relationship to the **H** and **E** matrices: $V = trace[\mathbf{H}(\mathbf{E} + \mathbf{H})^{-1}]$. Null hypotheses are rejected for large values of V, specifically using an F approximation:

ANALYSIS OF EXPERIMENTAL DATA 259

$$F = \frac{V[df_{error} - p + s]}{b(s - V)}, \qquad (7.20)$$

with sb and $s(df_{error} - p + s)$ degrees of freedom, and while $s = min(p, df_{effect})$, $b = max(p, df_{effect})$. In simulation studies, V has been demonstrated to be the most robust of the test statistics when the assumptions of normality and equality of covariance matrices do not hold (Olson, 1974, 1976, 1979; Bird and Hadzi-Pavlovic, 1983; Harris, 1985; even in the face of criticism (Stevens, 1979)).

Example We return to the "service satisfaction" data to fit the MANOVA model. Table 7.10 contains the $\mathbf{H}_A$, $\mathbf{H}_B$, $\mathbf{H}_{A*B}$, and $\mathbf{E}$ matrices, and the V statistics for testing whether the multivariate main effects and interaction are significant.[23] The F statistics and p-values indicate that indeed, when both dependent variables are modeled simultaneously, all three effects are significant. Recall that the univariate ANOVAs indicated a main effect for factor B and an interaction for the "overall satisfaction" variable, and the main effect for factor A was significant for the "attitude toward the service provider" variable. The data picture is clearer when the bivariate (or generally, multivariate) structure is analyzed; and for these particular data, all three effects become significant. Figure 7.5 contains the scatterplot for these data, with the 4 cells of the 2×2 design indicated. The eigenvectors of the $\mathbf{HE}^{-1}$ matrices are superimposed to indicate the linear combination of the dependent variables that best distinguishes the various experimental conditions.

Table 7.10 Multivariate analysis of variance of service satisfaction data

(I) **H** and **E** matrices:

$$\mathbf{H}_A = \begin{matrix} 2.161 & 22.589 \\ 22.589 & 236.161 \end{matrix} \qquad \mathbf{H}_B = \begin{matrix} 17.161 & 2.768 \\ 2.768 & 0.446 \end{matrix}$$

$$\mathbf{H}_{A*B} = \begin{matrix} 111.446 & -1.411 \\ -1.411 & 0.018 \end{matrix} \qquad \mathbf{E} = \begin{matrix} 99.786 & 47.857 \\ 47.857 & 72.929 \end{matrix}$$

(II) Testing the main effect for A:
Eigenvalue: 4.323
Eigenvector: [−0.061, 0.141]
$V = 0.812$, $F_{2,51} = 110.249$, p-value = 0.0001

(III) Testing the main effect for B:
Eigenvalue: 0.207
Eigenvector: [0.119, −0.058]
$V = 0.171$, $F_{2,51} = 5.273$, p-value = 0.0083

(IV) Testing the A * B interaction:
Eigenvalue: 1.657
Eigenvector: [0.121, −0.081]
$V = 0.624$, $F_{2,51} = 42.259$, p-value = 0.0001

260 DAWN IACOBUCCI

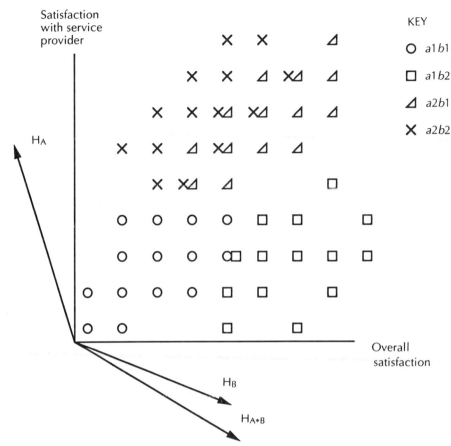

Note: The directions of the eigenvectors are superimposed on the plot, which indicate the direction in which the groups are most clearly distinguishable (i.e. the optimal linear combination of dependent variables). For example, the eigenvector for H_A is $[-.061, .141]'$, so if the data were projected onto this axis, the distribution of $a1b1$'s and $a1b2$'s would be significantly different from that of the $a2b1$'s and $a2b2$'s.

Figure 7.5 Plot of "service satisfaction" data

Contrasts and followup testing in MANOVA

Many followup procedures exist, and the property shared by the most useful analytical techniques are those which analyze the groups and variables simultaneously. For example, consider the 2×3 ad-by-pricing test market design. If sales in units and sales in dollars were to be modeled simultaneously, a MANOVA would be appropriate. If the price main effect were significant, we would need to know how the three pricing strategies varied, and on which of the two sales measures the group differences appeared. The data would be summarized in a 3×2 matrix of means, $\bar{Y}$ (3 being the number of pricing groups, and 2 is the number of dependent variables), and contrasts will examine the group differences (the rows) and the linear combinations of variables along which the groups were most different (the columns):

$$\psi = C\bar{Y}A. \tag{3.21}$$

ψ is a c by m matrix of contrasts, where element ψ_{ij} represents the ith contrast among the groups for the jth combination of dependent variables. C is a c by #groups matrix specifying the c contrasts between the groups, one per row, $\bar{Y}$ is the #groups by p matrix of means, and A is the p by m matrix declaring the form of the m linear combinations of variables, one per column. Each hypothesis ($H_0 : \psi = 0$) is tested by computing $(n(\psi)^2)/(c'ca'Ea)$.

Note that several special cases appear in (7.21). For example, if A were the $p \times p$ identity matrix, these followup comparisons would be equivalent to running p univariate ANOVAs. If a row in C defined a single degree of freedom contrast among groups that involved all p variables, the resulting statistic would be a Hotelling's T^2. If the single degree of freedom contrast involved only one variable, the resulting statistic would be a univariate t.

Repeated measures via MANOVA

Thus far, all analyses (ANOVA, ANCOVA, MANOVA) have been described as they are applicable to "between-subjects designs"; those in which each subject is randomly assigned to only one treatment condition. In comparison, "within-subjects designs" are those in which each subject yields data under more than one (and possibly all) treatment conditions. These designs are also called "repeated measures designs" because subjects are repeatedly exposed to an experimental manipulation and then measured on the response variables.

Data that are obtained through within-subjects designs may be analyzed using a univariate ANOVA, but the "repeated" nature of the data requires certain assumptions beyond the fundamental ANOVA assumptions, and these additional assumptions are often violated. While the univariate ANOVA performs well for between-subjects data, it is not terribly robust against violations of assumptions for within-subjects data. Accordingly, statisticians often recommend the application of (the less restrictive) MANOVA to the repeated measures data; even if only a single dependent variable is measured, it is measured at more than one point in time, so multiple data points exist for each subject. Details on both the univariate and multivariate treatments of within-subjects data are presented in Appendix D.

Multivariate Analysis of Covariance

In this final section, the covariate features of the ANCOVA are combined with the multivariate features of the MANOVA to produce the MANCOVA model. To put this model in some perspective, it might be noted that the *vast majority* of research publications report ANOVA results; few report ANCOVAs, few report MANOVAs, and fewer still report MANCOVAs. Given this practical observation, and the fact that the ANCOVA and MANOVA models were both presented in detail, this section on MANCOVA will be brief.

Each subject is randomly assigned to an experimental condition, and produces data on p dependent variables and say "v" covariates. The p dependent variables are regressed jointly (in a multivariate regression) on the v covariates, and the adjusted scores are modeled via the MANOVA. The presentations of the ANCOVA and MANOVA models described them as more sensitive than the basic ANOVA model because they made use of additional information (more predictors in ANCOVA and more responses in MANOVA). Accordingly, the MANCOVA should be even more powerful, given that it has the strengths of both the ANCOVA and the MANOVA. This proposition is easily demonstrated in the "service satisfaction" data.

Table 7.11 contains the results for the MANCOVA (which may be compared to the MANOVA results in Table 7.10).[24] The MANOVA results were somewhat difficult to improve upon, given that all three effects (both main effects and the interaction) were already significant, but note the improvement in the test for the main effect of factor B. The p-value was 0.0083 for the MANOVA and is 0.0004 for the MANCOVA (the p-values for the other effects remained at 0.0001). A quick glance at the three eigenvectors also indicates the MANOVA and MANCOVA were fairly convergent in the optimal linear combinations derived for the distinction among these experimental conditions. Finally, note also the H matrices for the three effects. The relationship between the two dependent variables appears clearer and stronger in the MANCOVA matrices (due presumably to the extraction of the covariate influence); that is, the off-diagonal elements in the H matrices are larger for the MANCOVA results than for the MANOVA results. The removal of the covariate even changes the direction of the relationship for the H_A matrices, evidently functioning as some sort of supressor variable. These stronger covariances are the source of the improved significance levels in the MANCOVA.

Table 7.11 Multivariate analysis of covariance of service satisfaction data

(I) H and E matrices:

H_A =   3.883   −16.700 H_B = 29.061   10.401
         −16.700   71.825   10.401   3.722
H_{A*B} = 26.648 −13.350 E = 80.495   31.079
          −13.350   6.688   31.079   58.336

(II) Testing the main effect for A:
Eigenvalue: 1.889
Eigenvector: [−0.074, 0.145]
$V = 0.654$, $F_{2,51} = 47.228$, p-value = 0.0001

(III) Testing the main effect for B:
Eigenvalue: 0.362
Eigenvector: [0.113, −0.005]
$V = 0.266$, $F_{2,51} = 9.038$, p-value = 0.0004

(IV) Testing the A * B interaction:
Eigenvalue: 0.784
Eigenvector: [0.116, −0.112]
$V = 0.439$, $F_{2,51} = 19.590$, p-value = 0.0001

Summary

In addition to the relationships among the four models discussed in this chapter (ANOVA, ANCOVA, MANOVA, MANCOVA) and presented in Table 7.7, these models may be shown to be related to still others. A classic theoretical statistical approach is to tie these four models to regression models via the "general linear model;" a general modeling statement that posits some optimal linear combination of dependent variables as a linear function of predictor variables (discrete factors in the case of ANOVA; continuous variables in the case of regression, etc.). Once the general linear model is understood, special cases such as ANOVA and regression are also easily understood. However, when learning statistically analytical techniques, it is often the case that the general models are "too" general to be didactically useful. Thus, this chapter was positioned to be more specific, and hopefully more useful, but readers interested in the more general modeling may find more information in sources such as Kirk (1982).

Another nice development is Bagozzi's recent work (cf. Bagozzi and Yi, 1989) relating structural equations models to the ANOVA model and its relatives. The former analytical framework explicitly models measurement error, which gives it great potential in the modeling of experimental data. One might argue that MANOVA accommodates errorful measures, because of its built-in derivations of optimal linear combinations of dependent variables (e.g. so measurement errors would presumably cancel each other out), but the structural equations modeling approach does so explicitly.

Finally, while this chapter was intended to be self-sufficient in its introduction to the major concepts of the ANOVA model and its relatives, there are many *excellent* references for additional information. Some of the texts that are especially easy to read, particularly for researchers with behavioral interests, include Keppel (1991), and Cliff (1987), Glass and Stanley (1970), Hays (1988), and Kirk (1982). More information on MANOVA (and other multivariate methods) can be found in Cliff (1987) and Tatsuoka (1988). Finally, the *Sage* publications are typically excellent introductions to quantitative material; ANOVA is covered by Iverson and Norpoth (1986), ANCOVA by Wildt and Ahtola (1978), MANOVA by Bray and Maxwell (1985), and repeated measures ANOVA by Girden (1992).

Appendix 7A: Effects of "Fixed vs. Random Factors" on Expected Mean Squares

A factor can be classified as "random" if the levels of the factor are selected randomly when designing the experiment, and "fixed" if the levels are chosen more purposively. The major advantage of random factors is that the results regarding those factors may be generalized to the entire population from which the levels were drawn. For example, in selecting pricing levels from the population values of $1.00 to $5.00, an experimenter might randomly select the values $1.50, $1.75, and $3.40. The results on the pricing factor may be generalized validly on statistical grounds to the entire pricing population $1.00 to $5.00. However, the disadvantage of random selection is that a "peculiar-looking" random sample is just as likely as a "meaningful" sample, especially when the number of levels selected for the factor is small. For example, another random selection of price levels would be $1.01, $1.05, and $1.10. These levels do not seem very useful – they would yield "too much" information over a small range of values, and no information over the rest of the range. Furthermore, some prices have more meaning than their sheer number value (e.g. psychologically the difference between $3.99 and $4.00 is probably much greater than that between $4.00 and $4.01). An example of a fixed-selection would be $1.99, $3.49, and $4.99.

Fixed- vs. random-effects differ in their selection procedures and in their implications for extending the findings. They also differ in a very important operational aspect. When all the manipulated factors are "fixed", all the F-tests are of the form described in the text of the chapter, MS_{effect}/MS_{error}. When *any* factor is random, some of the F-tests will take a different form. The idea is that the "randomness" introduces an additional source of variability, and this must be considered when constructing the F-ratios. The expected mean squares will differ, and they will dictate the form of the F-statistic. The rules for deriving the EMS are presented in several texts (cf. Hicks, 1982), and while the detail is too much for the purposes of this chapter, we can consider an example.

The EMS and the appropriate F-tests are listed below for a two-factor factorial, with the unique combinations of the factors being fixed and/or random.

(A) Factors A and B are both "fixed" (using the notation, $\theta_A^2 = \sum_i \alpha_i^2/(a-1)$):

Effect	EMS	F
α_i	$bn\theta_A^2 + \sigma_\epsilon^2$	MS_A/MS_{error}
β_j	$an\theta_B^2 + \sigma_\epsilon^2$	MS_B/MS_{error}
$\alpha\beta_{ij}$	$n\theta_{AB}^2 + \sigma_\epsilon^2$	MS_{A*B}/MS_{error}
ϵ_{ijk}	σ_ϵ^2	

(B) Factor A is fixed, B is random:

Effect	EMS	F
α_i	$bn\theta_A^2 + n\sigma_{AB}^2 + \sigma_\epsilon^2$	MS_A/MS_{A*B}
β_j	$an\sigma_B^2 + \sigma_\epsilon^2$	MS_B/MS_{error}
$\alpha\beta_{ij}$	$n\sigma_{AB}^2 + \sigma_\epsilon^2$	MS_{A*B}/MS_{error}
ϵ_{ijk}	σ_ϵ^2	

(C) Factors A and B are both random:

Effect	EMS	F
α_i	$bn\sigma_A^2 + n\sigma_{AB}^2 + \sigma_\epsilon^2$	MS_A/MS_{A*B}
β_j	$an\sigma_B^2 + n\sigma_{AB}^2 + \sigma_\epsilon^2$	MS_B/MS_{A*B}
$\alpha\beta_{ij}$	$n\sigma_{AB}^2 + \sigma_\epsilon^2$	MS_{A*B}/MS_{error}
ϵ_{ijk}	σ_ϵ^2	

Most experiments reported in journal articles contain only fixed factors. While random factors sound desirable because of the implication that results can be generalized, it is usually of greater importance to select levels of a factor in a way that assures coverage of a theoretically appropriate range.

It should also be noted that the introduction of random factors into a factorial design can sometimes produce a set of EMS which provide no apparent error term for some effects. In such circumstances, error terms are created as linear combinations of the other effects, the F-test is called a pseudo F (F'), and the degrees of freedom are adjusted accordingly. Finally, note that no statistical computing package makes practical use of the random- vs. fixed-factor distinction; F's are computed using within-group variability as the error term. Therefore, with random-factor designs, some computer-given F's will be incorrect. If random factors are used in a study, the researcher needs to derive the EMS in order to know the appropriate form of the F-statistics, and while the computer can yield proper MS's, the F's should be computed by hand to ensure their validity.

Appendix 7B: Matrix Algebra

This appendix reviews two matrix concepts relevant to this chapter: linear combinations of variables, and eigenvalue–eigenvector decompositions.

(1) A linear combination is simply a method of transforming p variables (e.g. $y_{i1}, y_{i2}, \ldots, y_{ip}$) into a single new variables (q_i), for subject i. Each q_i is defined by $\mathbf{q} = \mathbf{Yc}$, where $\mathbf{q}$ is the $n \times 1$ vector of new scores (one for each of the n subjects), $\mathbf{Y}$ is the $n \times p$ matrix of original scores, and $\mathbf{c}$ is the $p \times 1$ vector of weights (i.e. $q_i = c_1 Y_{i1} + c_2 Y_{i2} + \ldots + c_p Y_{ip}$). Linear transformations yield simple relationships between the means and covariance

matrices of the original variables to the new variables: $\mu_q = c'\mu_Y$, and $\Sigma_q = c'\Sigma_Y c$.

In particular, the multivariate ANOVA contrasts of the form, $\Psi = C\bar{Y}A$ are triple products, or "double linear combinations". For example, consider the matrices defined below:

$$\begin{vmatrix} 1 & -1 & 0 \\ 0 & 1 & -1 \end{vmatrix} \begin{vmatrix} \bar{y}_{11} & \bar{y}_{12} & \bar{y}_{13} & \bar{y}_{14} \\ \bar{y}_{21} & \bar{y}_{22} & \bar{y}_{23} & \bar{y}_{24} \\ \bar{y}_{31} & \bar{y}_{32} & \bar{y}_{33} & \bar{y}_{34} \end{vmatrix} \begin{vmatrix} 1/4 & 1/2 & 1 & 0 \\ 1/4 & 1/2 & 0 & 0 \\ 1/4 & 0 & 0 & 1 \\ 1/4 & 0 & -1 & 0 \end{vmatrix}. \quad (7B.1)$$

C is a 2×3 matrix, which compares groups 1 and 2 in the first contrast (the first row), and groups 2 and 3 in the second contrast. $\bar{Y}$ is the 3×4 matrix of means for the three groups/samples on the four variables, and A is a 4×4 matrix in which each column defines a different combination of dependent variables to study. (The first column computes the average of all four variables; the second comparison considers the average of the first two variables, ignoring the others; the third column defines the difference score contrasting the first and last measures; and the fourth "comparison" examines variable 3 univariately, in isolation.)

(2) While experimenters can place values in the A matrix, just as for the C matrix, the multivariate analysis of variance will derive the A matrix that maximally discriminates between the experimental groups. Consider once more the data represented in Figure 7.4. A linear combination of the p dependent variables is sought to best describe how groups I and II differ. If the linear combination was defined as $q = 0 * y_1 + 1 * y_2$ (i.e. use only y_2), the data would be projected on to this new "function" q, the vertical (y_2) axis, with the result of little discriminability between the groups. The optimal linear combination is derived analytically as follows.

First, consider what is being maximized. If p variables are transformed to a single new variable, subsequent significance tests would be univariate. The t-test is of the form: $t = (\bar{q} - \mu_0)/(s_q/\sqrt{n})$, and because $q = c_1 y_1 + c_2 y_2 + \ldots + c_p y_p$, the t is really: $t = (c'\bar{y} - c'\mu_0)/(\sqrt{(c'Sc/n)})$. To maximize t, we maximize t^2 (it is mathematically easier):

$$t^2 = \frac{[c'(\bar{y} - \mu_0)]^2}{c'Sc/n} = \frac{nc'(\bar{y} - \mu_0)(\bar{y} - \mu_0)'c}{c'Sc}, \quad (7B.2)$$

with the side constraint that $c'Sc = 1$ (which makes the variance of the new variable one, to normalize the problem, otherwise, c's could simply be chosen to make $c'Sc$ very small). This side constraint requires a LaGrangian multiplier, and the maximization requires differential calculus. The solution to this problem ($[n(\bar{y} - \mu_0)(\bar{y} - \mu_0)' - \lambda S]c = 0$, or $[nS^{-1}(\bar{y} - \mu_0)(\bar{y} - \mu_0)' - \lambda I]c = 0$ is the eigenvalue–eigenvector decomposition of the matrix $nS^{-1}(\bar{y} - \mu_0)(\bar{y} - \mu_0)'$. For the generalization to a one-way MANOVA, the c's need to be derived that maximize $\mathbf{c'Hc}/\mathbf{c'Ec}$, and it too is an eigenproblem: $(\mathbf{HE}^{-1} - \lambda\mathbf{I})\mathbf{c} = 0$, with the solution that the maximized value is the first eigenvalue of $\mathbf{HE}^{-1}$, and $\mathbf{c}_1$ is the first eigenvector of $\mathbf{HE}^{-1}$. Recall that the rank of this matrix is s, so there are s eigenvalues: $\lambda_1 > \lambda_2 > \ldots > \lambda_s$ associated with eigenvectors $\mathbf{c}_1, \mathbf{c}_2, \ldots, \mathbf{c}_s$ (and each eigenvector $\mathbf{c}_i$ is orthogonal to the previous $\mathbf{c}_1$ through $\mathbf{c}_{i-1}$ vectors). Thus, $\mathbf{c}_1$ will describe the linear combination of p variables that best distinguishes the groups, and $\mathbf{c}_2$ will describe the second best combination that is uncorrelated with the first, and so on.

Appendix 7C: MANOVA Statistics Λ, T, and R.

While the text of this chapter focuses on the V statistic, this appendix describes three other useful test statistics, Λ, T, and R.

(1) The Wilks' Likelihood Ratio Test Statistic, Λ, is defined as follows:

$$\Lambda = \prod_{i=1}^{s} \frac{\lambda_i}{1 + \lambda_i} = \frac{|\mathbf{E}|}{|\mathbf{E} + \mathbf{H}|}. \tag{7C.1}$$

If λ_i is interpretable as $SS_{\text{effect}}/SS_{\text{error}}$, then the Λ-statistic is interpretable as $SS_{\text{error}}/SS_{\text{total}}$; that is, H_0 is rejected for *small* values of Λ. The F-approximation follows (for $p * df_{\text{effect}}$ and $(mq - 0.5p(df_{\text{effect}}) + 1)$ degrees of freedom):

$$F = \frac{(1 - \Lambda^{1/q})(mq - 0.5p * df_{\text{effect}} + 1)}{\Lambda^{1/q} \, p * df_{\text{effect}}}, \tag{7C.2}$$

where $m = [df_{\text{error}} - (p + 1 - df_{\text{effect}})/2]$, and $q = \sqrt{(\{p^2 df_{\text{effect}}^2 - 4\}/\{p^2 + df_{\text{effect}}^2 - 5\})}$.

(2) The Hotelling–Lawley trace, T, and an F-approximation (on "a" and "b" degrees of freedom) are defined as follows:

$$T = \sum_{i=1}^{s} \lambda_i = tr(\mathbf{HE}^{-1}), \quad \text{and} \quad F = T/C, \tag{7C.3}$$

where $a = p * df_{\text{effect}}$, $b = 4 + (a + 2)/(B - 1)$, $c = a(b - 2)/(b(df_{\text{error}} - p - 1))$, and

$$B = \frac{(df_{\text{error}} + df_{\text{effect}} - p - 1)(df_{\text{error}} - 1)}{(df_{\text{error}} - p - 3)(df_{\text{error}} - p)}.$$

(3) While V, Λ, and T combine the s eigenvalues, the test statistic R, "Roy's greatest characteristic root," focuses on λ_1.

$$R = \lambda_1 \qquad (7C.4)$$

Thus, R ignores eigenvalues λ_2 through λ_s, and R will equal V when s equals one. If s is one, or if λ_1 is much larger than the remaining eigenvalues, then little information (contained in the latter values) would be lost in choosing the R statistic over the others.

(4) The four test statistics, R, T, Λ, and V can be compared with respect to their power and their robustness. Regarding power, whether information is lost or not (in computing R) depends on the dimensionality of the "noncentrality" structure of the data. That is, there is a "uniformly most powerful test statistic" when the number of experimental groups is 2 (Hotelling's T^2), and when p equals one (the F-test), but which of the test statistics R, T, Λ, or V is most powerful depends on how the null hypothesis is wrong. That is, when H_0 is false (the group means differ), the groups might differ along one dimension (i.e. "concentrated structure") or along several dimensions (i.e. "diffuse structure").

When the structure is concentrated (the groups differ along a single underlying dimension, $\lambda_1 >>> \lambda_2 > \lambda_3 > \ldots > \lambda_s$), R is the most powerful of the four tests (followed by T, Λ, and V). For this structure, most of the information contained in $\mathbf{HE}^{-1}$ is in λ_1 (and subsequent eigenvalues add little). Conversely, when the structure is diffused, the groups differ along several dimensions, (i.e. $\lambda_1 \approx \lambda_2 \approx \lambda_3 \approx \ldots \approx \lambda_s$), the power of the four tests rank in reverse: V, Λ, T, R. Different behavioral researchers argue that multidimensionality (Olson, 1976) or unidimensionality (Bock, 1985) is most typically expected. Certainly the eigenvalues can be inspected, and often $s = 1$, so the issue would be moot (e.g. in a 2×2 MANOVA, the df_{effect} for A, B, and $A * B$ would each equal one). The power differences are not large, and the statistics converge for large sample sizes.

The four test statistics can also be compared with respect to their robustness. Nonnormality (specifically kurtosis) has the effect of reducing the power of all four statistics, but their relative power remains unaffected. Inequality of covariance matrices, however, affect the four statistics differently. In particular, type I errors can be very high for R. V is least affected (i.e. V is most robust). In general (i.e. for all four test statistics), robustness improves as the number of dependent variables becomes fewer and as the number of groups decreases. Furthermore, when sample sizes are equal and large, all four statistics perform well.

(5) As an example, consider the "service satisfaction" data. The MANOVA results were reported in Table 7.10, using the V statistics. The design was a 2×2 factorial, so df_A, df_B, and df_{A*B} each equal 1, and $p = 2$, so $s = \min(df_{\text{effect}}, p) = 1$. As a result, the F-statistics (and thereby, p-values)

converge for the four tests, but the values of the statistics R, T, Λ, and V differ. They are as follows. For testing the main effect of A, V was 0.812, $\Lambda = 0.188$, and $T = R = 4.323$. For testing the main effect of B, V was 0.829, $\Lambda = 0.171$, and $T = R = 5.273$. For testing the interaction, V was 0.376, $\Lambda = 0.624$, and $T = R = 1.657$. These are easily confirmed, given the eigenvalues in Table 7.10. Finally, note that all four test statistics (and their F-approximations) are standard output in SAS.

Appendix 7D: The Analysis of Repeated Measures Data

This appendix describes the univariate and multivariate ANOVA modeling of repeated measures data. Repeated measures data, or data that result from within-subjects designs, are fairly common, but the logic of their requisite statistical models is somewhat different from that for between-subjects ANOVAs, so we treat the within-subjects ANOVA topic separately in this appendix. We begin with a brief introduction to the within-subjects designs, and proceed to the univariate model and its problematic assumptions, and conclude with the MANOVA alternative. (Girden, 1992 contains more details.)

One advantage of within-subjects designs over between-subjects designs is that the former are more efficient – fewer subjects are needed to attain comparable testing power. For example, for a completely randomized (between-subjects) 2×2 design with 10 subjects per cell, 40 subjects would be required in total. For a complete within-subjects 2×2 design, the 10 subjects would serve in all four conditions, so only 10 subjects would be necessary. As a third alternative, a "mixed" design could be run, in which each subject participated in, say, both levels of factor A (so factor A would be a "within-subjects" factor), but only one level of factor B (so factor B would be a "between-subjects" factor). Here only 20 subjects would be required.

Repeated measures designs are also generally more sensitive. For between-subjects designs, it is merely an assumption that random assignment makes subjects in each condition comparable (differing only as a result of the experimental manipulations). For within-subjects designs, the error term is reduced by effectively removing a source of error variability – that of individual differences. In other words, subjects are not only *assumed* to be the same across conditions, they *are* the same. In this sense, each subject serves as his/her own control, so treatment differences can be detected more easily. This point will be demonstrated analytically shortly. Lastly, within-subjects designs have proven especially useful in studying attitudinal or behavioral change (e.g. learning), because a subject's performance is tracked over time.

Within-subjects designs are not without their disadvantages. The primary potential drawback is the very source of the designs' potential advantages: each subject is used more than once. A person's memory cannot be wiped clean like a chalkboard between experimental sessions. Rather, there is likely to be some residual "carry over" from earlier conditions to later ones. Subjects can get bored, tired, and careless over time; they can get more practiced and knowledgeable over time; and more generally, the early conditions serve as a "context" for the later conditions. (Though note that Greenwald (1976) argues that between subjects designs are not without their own context effects.) Any of these can be detrimental to the soundness of the experiment, because the "carry over" effects become confounded with the latter experimental manipulations. Solutions to these difficulties have included increasing the subjects' motivation, having subjects rest between conditions, counterbalancing the treatments presented across subjects, and running a "mixed" design (i.e. one with both between- and within-subjects factors) in which within-subject factors are run only when small effects are expected (which thus require the greater sensitivity of the within subjects factor).

Consider a simple example, in which a single factor (A) is manipulated, and each subject $S_i (i = 1, 2, \ldots, S)$ serves in all a treatments. This design may be denoted "$A \times S$" (Keppel, 1991, pp. 345), because the factor A is completely crossed with the subjects factor, S (each subject S_i sees all levels of factor A). We are familiar with a two-factor factorial such as $A \times B$, in which the variability is broken down as follows: $SS_{total} = SS_A + SS_B + SS_{A*B} + SS_{error}$. In particular, $df_{error} = ab(n - 1)$, representing the variability within the ab cell. In the within-subjects version, "B" is really "S", so there is only one subject in each as cell. Recall that when there is only a single observation in each cell, the interaction term must serve as the error term (i.e. the sample size per cell, n, equals one, so $df_{error} = aS(n - 1) = a*S*0$). The ANOVA table and form of the F-statistics for this design are given in Table 7D.1.

Table 7D.1 allows us to explicitly examine the claim made earlier that within-subjects designs are generally more sensitive than between-subjects designs. We can define any SS_{error} to be the SS_{total} minus the $SS_{effects}$; in a between-subjects one-factor design, this would mean $SS_{error} = SS_{total} - SS_A$. By comparison, in a within-subjects design, the "total minus effects" would be $SS_{error} = SS_{total} - SS_A - SS_S$. Clearly the within-subjects error term has to be smaller than the between-subjects error term, because an additional terms ($SS_S \geq 0$) has been subtracted off.

Table 7D.1 Univariate ANOVA table for a 1-factor within-subjects design

Source	df	SS	F
A	$a - 1$	$\sum_i \sum_s (\bar{y}_{i.} - \bar{y}_{..})^2$	MS_A/MS_{error}
S	$S - 1$	$\sum \sum (\bar{y}_{.s} - \bar{y}_{..})^2$	MS_S/MS_{error}
"error"	$(a - 1)(S - 1)$	$\sum \sum (\bar{y}_{is} - \bar{y}_{i.} - \bar{y}_{.s} + \bar{y}_{..})^2$	
Total	$aS - 1$	$\sum \sum (y_{is} - \bar{y}_{..})^2$	

To generalize the designs, consider a complete within-subjects two-factor factorial ($A \times B \times S$); each subject is exposed to all combinations of the factors. For example, in a 2×2 design, each subject would see the a_1b_1, a_1b_2, a_2b_1, and a_2b_2 conditions (in some order). The sources of variability would be: A, B, S, $A * B$, $A * S$, $B * S$, and $A * B * S$ (with degrees of freedom just as you would think: $df_A = (a-1)$, $df_B = (b-1)$, $df_{A*B} = (a-1)(b-1)$, $df_{A*S} = (a-1)(S-1)$, $df_{B*S} = (b-1)(S-1)$, $df_{A*B*S} = (a-1)(b-1)(S-1)$). To test an effect ($A$, B, or $A * B$), the mean square for the effect is compared to the mean square for the effect that also contains "subjects" (i.e. MS_{A*S}, MS_{B*S}, MS_{A*B*S}, respectively).[D.1] Note this interesting feature of within-subjects designs – that often there are as many "error" terms in the sources of variability as there are "effects" to test.

For comparison, consider a 2×2 mixed-design in which factor A is the "between-subjects" factor, and B is the "within-subjects" factor ($A \times (B \times S)$). Thus, each subject sees a_1b_1 and a_1b_2, or a_2b_1 and a_2b_2 (so the "subjects" factor is "crossed" with B, but "nested in" $A - S(A)$). The sources of variability are: A, B, $S(A)$, $A * B$, and $B * S(A)$, and the effects A, B, $A * B$ are tested against $MS_{S(A)}$, $MS_{B*S(A)}$, and $MS_{B \times S(A)}$.[D.2]

The operationalization of the univariate repeated measures ANOVA is straightforward. The assumptions of the model include independence of observations (from one subject to another), normality, and instead of "homogeneity of variance," "homogeneity of treatment difference scores' variances and covariances." Difference scores arise because of the explicit comparison of a subject's score in one condition to his/her score in another condition. Thus, the repeated measures ANOVA should be thought of as a procedure applied not to the p dependent measures $y_1, y_2, \ldots, y_p$, but to the $p-1$ slopes of each subject's profile – the differences between adjacent measures $y_1 - y_2, y_2 - y_3, \ldots, y_{p-1} - y_p$. In the univariate ANOVA, the $(p-1) \times (p-1)$ matrix containing the variances and covariances is assumed to have the form of "compound symmetry;" all σ_i^2's are equal and all covariances $\rho\sigma_i\sigma_j = \rho\sigma^2$ are equal. However, most empirical data indicate that measures taken closer together in time are more highly correlated than measures taken at larger intervals, producing a matrix with correlations that diminish in size from the main diagonal to the corners of the matrix.

A violation of this assumption need not be severe to affect the F-test. Unfortunately, the violations tend to increase the type I error rates (rejecting H_0 when no effects really exist). Researchers have offered solutions to make the test more conservative (e.g. the "Geisser-Greenhouse" correction simply decreases the degrees of freedom, but tends to overcorrect), but usually conclude the MANOVA is prefered because it requires less restrictive assumptions.

Specifically, using MANOVA to analyze repeated measures data, the $(p-1) \times (p-1)$ matrix containing the variances and covariances of the difference scores $y_1 - y_2, y_2 - y_3, \ldots, y_{p-1} - y_p$ can take on any form. That is, every element of Σ is free: σ_i^2 need not equal σ_j^2, and the covariances similarly may vary. The "equality of covariance matrices" assumption of MANOVA still holds across conditions, of course (e.g. $\Sigma_1 = \Sigma_2$), but the structures within the Σ_i are less restricted. Table 7D.2 shows the basic form of the test statistic as a function of the raw measures (the y_i's) or the difference scores (the $y_{i-1} - y_i$'s).

Table 7D.2 Repeated measures as a function of raw data (y_i's) or difference scores ($y_{i-1} - y_i$'s)

$$\begin{vmatrix} 1 & -1 & 0 & 0 & \ldots & 0 & 0 \\ 0 & 1 & -1 & 0 & \ldots & 0 & 0 \\ 0 & 0 & 1 & -1 & \ldots & 0 & 0 \\ \cdot & & & & & & \\ \cdot & & & & & & \\ 0 & 0 & 0 & 0 & \ldots & 1 & -1 \end{vmatrix} \begin{vmatrix} \bar{y}_1 \\ \bar{y}_2 \\ \bar{y}_3 \\ \cdot \\ \cdot \\ \bar{y}_{p-1} \\ \bar{y}_p \end{vmatrix} = \begin{vmatrix} \bar{y}_1 - \bar{y}_2 \\ \bar{y}_2 - \bar{y}_3 \\ \cdot \\ \cdot \\ \bar{y}_{p-1} - \bar{y}_p \end{vmatrix}$$

$\mathbf{D}_{(p-1) \times p}$ $\bar{\mathbf{y}}_{p \times 1}$ $\bar{\mathbf{y}}\text{diff}_{(p-1) \times 1}$

Effects can be tested using the raw data and the transformation matrix, $\mathbf{D}$ ($T^2 = n(\mathbf{D}\bar{\mathbf{y}})'(\mathbf{DSD'})^{-1}(\mathbf{D}\bar{\mathbf{y}})$), or the difference scores directly ($T^2 = n(\bar{\mathbf{y}}\text{diff})'(\mathbf{Sdiff'})^{-1}(\bar{\mathbf{y}}\text{diff})$), and $F = T^2(n-p+1)/((n-1)(p-1))$ on $(p-1)$ and $(n-p+1)$ degrees of freedom.

Notes to Appendix D

D.1. To fit this model in SAS, use the following commands: proc glm; class a b s; model y = a b s a * b a * s b * s a * b * s; test h = a e = a * s; test h = b e = b * s; test h = a * b e = a * b * s; means a b s a * b a * s b * s a * b * s;.

D.2. To fit this model in SAS, use the following commands: proc glm; class a b s; model y = a b s(a) a * b b * s(a); test h = a e = s(a); test h = b e = b * s(a); test h = a * b e = b * s(a); means a b s(a) a * b b * s(a);.

Questions

1. Use SAS to analyze the data in Table 7.1 to verify the ANOVA results.
2. Draw a hypothetical interaction plot for each of these data scenarios in a 2 × 2 factorial: A significant main effect for A; both main effects but no interaction; a significant main effect for B and an interaction; an interaction but no main effects; all three significant results; and (perhaps the most common!) all null results.
3. Use SAS to analyze the data in Table 7.2 to verify the ANOVA, ANCOVA, MANOVA, and MANCOVA results presented in this chapter.
4. Using Table 7.4 as a guide, write the equations for computing the sums of squares for a 5-factor factorial.

5 If a contrast were run on a factor that had two levels, what would the relationship be between the $SS_{contrast}$ and the SS_{effect}.
6 Using the eigenvalues reported in Table 7.10, compute the R, T, V, and Λ statistics, and their respective F-approximations, to verify the reported results.

Notes

* I am grateful to Northwestern University's Marketing Department and to the National Science Foundation (Grant #SES-9023445) for research support, and to Rick Briesch, Kent Grayson, Gerri Henderson, Nigel Hopkins, Amy Ostrom, Sally White, and an anonymous reviewer for their helpful comments on this chapter. I am also grateful to Rick Bagozzi for including me in on this project and for his kind encouragement.

1 A classic medical experiment involves the random assignment of an experimental treatment or drug (e.g. vitamin C) to half of a (randomly selected) sample of healthy patients and a placebo to the other half, to observe the impact on subsequent health (e.g. incidence of colds).
2 Notice that random assignment (and therefore statements of causality) can occur only for "manipulated" factors, such as the ad copy or price level examples. Naturally occurring factors (sometimes called "measured" or "observed" factors) such as gender or educational major cannot be randomly assigned, so these groups may or may not be "equated" on a host of other variables which may impact the results, which in turn makes statements of causality more tentative.
3 If the underlying population is non-normal, the distribution of the sample mean is still approximately normal if the sample size is "large" ($n \geqslant 30$, so we could use a "z-test" (which we define shortly). However, we focus on the t-test early in this chapter (over the z) because the t, and its notion of "degrees of freedom," generalize most directly to the "F-statistic" of analysis of variance.
4 If we knew σ_y, or if $n \geqslant 30$, we would call the statistic computed in (7.2) "z" and compare it to the (univariate) normal curve, whose probability density function (which determines the area under the curve, and therefore the appropriate critical values, such as 1.96, for the chosen confidence level, such as 95 percent) follows:

$$\frac{1}{\sqrt{(\sigma_{\bar{y}}(2\pi))}} e^{-(\bar{y}-\mu)^2/2\sigma_{\bar{y}}^2} \quad \text{or} \quad \frac{1}{\sqrt{(2\pi)}} e^{-(\bar{y})^2/2} \quad \text{if} \quad \mu_y = 0 \quad \text{and} \quad \sigma_{\bar{y}} = 1.$$

By way of comparison, the t-distribution has heavier tails (and a shorter peak) than the z-distribution, to make the test of H_0 more conservative (if more area is under the curve out in the tails, a larger t will be needed to reject H_0 than a z for the same confidence level), to compensate for the small (and therefore possibly quirky) sample.
5 Tests comparing "matched" samples (i.e. non-independent groups) will be discussed later, as "repeated measures" ANOVAs.
6 Test markets are an example of experiments low in "internal validity" but high in "external validity." Internal validity is the extent to which any group (i.e. test market) differences can be attributed to the manipulated factor (e.g. the price

difference). While one's own price variation across markets can be controlled, other extraneous variables might also differ across markets (e.g. local differences, competitors' marketing variables, etc.), thereby confounding the effect of the manipulated factor. External validity is the extent to which any findings may be generalized to "the real world." Given that test markets occur in the real world, they tend to be strong with respect to this property (as long as those observations – that is, the markets – are sampled randomly from the population of markets).

7   Independent variables are also called "explanatory-" or "predictor-variables," and dependent variables are also called "response variables" or "criterion measures."

8   So, for example, if one researcher is trying to guess another's data, once the grand mean was known, only the first $a*n-1$ data points would need to be obtained.

9   To analyze these data via SAS, use the following commands: proc glm; class a; model $y = a/ss3$; means a;.

10 If the design is not completely crossed (e.g. there are no observations in one or more cells), the analyses are far more complicated. See Searle (1987) for further information on such unbalanced designs.

11 The SAS commands necessary to run the ANOVAs follow (SAS, 1985):

proc glm; class a b; model y1 = a b a * b/ss3;
means a b a * b; lsmeans a b a * b;
proc glm; class a b; model y2 = a b a * b/ss3;
means a b a * b; lsmeans a b a * b;.

12 Specifically, when using the analysis of variance on unbalanced data, use the statistical computing package *SAS*'s procedure "*GLM*" and report the *F*-statistics and *p*-values resulting from the "*Type III*" sums of squares (see Iacobucci, 1992 for additional information).

13 Contrasts are easily tested in SAS. The commands follow for the 2×3 ad-by-pricing example:

proc glm; class ad price;
model y = ad price ad * price/ss3;
contrast 'price-med. vs. high' price 0 1 −1;
contrast 'price-low vs. other' price 1 −0.5 −0.5;.

14 The commands to estimate simple effects in SAS follow for a 2×2 example:

proc glm; class a b; model y = a b a * b/ss3;
contrast 'simple effect of A at b1' a 1 −1 a * b 1 0 −1 0;
contrast 'simple effect of A at b2' a 1 −1 a * b 0 1 0 −1;
contrast 'simple effect of B at a1' b 1 −1 a * b 1 −1 0 0;
contrast 'simple effect of B at a2' b 1 −1 a * b 0 0 1 −1;.

15 The "analysis of covariance" is a close relative to the ANOVA model, and should not be confused with the technique of structural equations modeling (e.g. LISREL), which is sometimes referred to as the "analysis of covariance structures."

16 Random assignment is assumed to equate subjects across conditions with respect to these extraneous variables, but sometimes this does not work perfectly, particularly if the sample size per cell is small (e.g. $n < 10$). Also note that when the sample is fairly homogeneous on the nuisance factors (e.g. college students on intelligence), the covariate may be less effective (and therefore not necessary) due to its likely lack of variability.
17 If the level of measurement is simpler, or the expected relationship is non-linear, blocking or repeated measures factors may be more appropriate.
18 The SAS commands necessary to run the ANCOVAs follow:

   proc glm; class a b; model y1 = a b a * b x/ss3;
   proc glm; class a b; model y2 = a b a * b x/ss3; *note the covariate, x, is a predictor in the model, but is not declared as a factor in the classification statement;.

19 Most studies measure subjects' reactions on multiple measures, but only when those measures, or some subset of them, are modeled together is there a need for multivariate statistics. Certainly researchers can take p measurements on each subject and analyze each separately via a series of p univariate analyses. If the research questions are conjunctive (i.e. are groups I and II the same on Y_1 and Y_2) or compensatory (i.e. are groups I and II the same on some linear combination of Y_1 and Y_2), the multivariate models are most appropriate. If the questions are disjunctive (i.e. are groups I and II the same on Y_1 or Y_2), multivariate models may still be useful, in providing greater analytical power by incorporating explicitly into the model the correlations among the dependent variables.
20 The multivariate normal distribution (or "multinormal") with dimensionality p has the probability density function:

$$(2\pi)^{-p/2} |\Sigma|^{-1/2} \exp\{-(y_i - \mu)' \Sigma^{-1} (y_i - \mu)\},$$

where $|\Sigma|$ is the determinant of Σ (Seber 1984).
21 Note that assumptions imply that the null hypothesis we usually think we are testing, $H_0: \mu_1 = \mu_2$, is really $H_0: \mu_1 = \mu_2$, and $\Sigma_1 = \Sigma_2$ and y_{ij}'s are independent and drawn from $MVN_p(\mu_i, \Sigma)$. When the null hypothesis is rejected, we usually conclude $\mu_1 \neq \mu_2$, but this difference need not have been the source of the deviation from H_0. The good news is that T^2, like t, is indeed more sensitive to differences between means than to differences between Σ_i's or departures from normality. Many quantitative behavioral researchers and statisticians have investigated these properties, most frequently via Monte Carlo simulation methods, where μ_1 is set equal to μ_2 (cf. Algina and Oshima, 1990; Chase and Bulgren, 1971; Hakistian, Roed, and Lind, 1979; Harris, 1985; Ito and Shull, 1964; Mardia, 1975). Thus, the mean part of the null hypothesis is true, and then the shape of the distribution and the covariance matrices are varied to see if H_0 is rejected more than $\alpha\%$ of the time. These researchers' findings thus far indicate the T^2 is fairly robust to violations of these assumptions, at least if $n_1 = n_2$ and both n_i are large. Skewness is occasionally cited as problematic, so data that are multivariately skewed may need to be transformed to appear more normal. With regard to the equality of covariance matrices assumption, there are statistical tests of whether

$\Sigma_1 = \Sigma_2$ based on their estimates, S_1 and S_2, but unfortunately, these tests have the property of being "overly" powerful, rejecting the hypothesis, $H_0 : \Sigma_1 = \Sigma_2$ even in cases where the departures from equality would not have had much of an effect on the test of $H_0 : \mu_1 = \mu_2$. (In particular, these tests of Σ_i tend to be more sensitive to non-normality than the tests of the μ_i's.) Finally, no standard analytical (e.g. nonparametric) technique exists when the assumptions of normality and equal covariance matrices do not hold. Fortunately, as stated in the text of the chapter, T^2 is fairly robust.

22 For an introduction to eigenvalues and eigenvectors, see Appendix B of this chapter and the chapter on exploratory factor analysis. Briefly, an eigensolution is a means of decomposing a $p \times p$ matrix into r (usually far fewer than p) eigenvalue–vector pairs. Such a reduction simplifies the analysis without losing the essential structural information in the $p \times p$ matrix.

23 The SAS commands necessary to run the MANOVA follow:

proc glm; class a b; model y1 y2 = a b a * b;
manova h = a/printh printe; manova h = b /printh printe;
manova h = a * b/printh printe; *contrast statements have the same form as for the univariate ANOVA within proc glm;.

24 The SAS commands necessary to run the MANCOVA follow:

proc glm; class a b; model y1 y2 = a b a * b x;
manova h = a /printh printe; manova h = b /printh printe;
manova h = a * b /printh printe;.

References

Algina, James and Oshima, Takako C. 1990: Robustness of the independent samples Hotelling's T^2 to variance–covariance heteroscedasticity when sample sizes are unequal and in small ratios. *Psychological Bulletin*, 108, 308–13.

Anderson, T. W. 1984: *An Introduction to Multivariate Statistical Analysis*, New York: Wiley.

Bagozzi, Richard P., and Yi, Youjae 1989: On the use of structural equation models in experimental designs. *Journal of Marketing Research*, 26, 271–84.

Bird, Kevin D. and Hadzi-Pavlovic, Dusan 1983: Simultaneous test procedures and the choice of a test statistic in MANOVA. *Psychological Bulletin*, 93, 167–78.

Bock, R. Darrell 1985: *Multivariate Statistical Methods in Behavioral Research*, Scientific Software Inc.

Box, G. E. P., Hunter, W. G. and Hunter, J. S. 1978: *Statistics for Experimenters*, New York: Wiley.

Bray, James H. and Maxwell, Scott E. 1985: *Multivariate Analysis of Variance*, Sage.

Chase, G. R. and Bulgren, W. G. 1971: A Monte Carlo investigation of the robustness of T^2. *Journal of the American Statistical Association*, 66, 499–502.

Cliff, Norman 1987: *Analyzing Multivariate Data*, San Diego: Harcourt Brace Jovanovich.

Cochran, W. G. and Cox, G. M. 1957: *Experimental Designs*, New York: Wiley.

Cohen, Jacob 1977: *Statistical Power Analysis for the Behavioral Sciences*, New York: Academic Press.

Crosby, Lawrence A. and Stephens, Nancy 1987: Effects of relationship marketing on satisfaction, retention, and prices in the life insurance industry. *Journal of Marketing Research*, 24, 404–11.

Dominowski, Roger L. 1989: Method, theory, and drawing inference. *American Psychologist*, July, 1078.

Girden, Ellen R. 1992: *ANOVA: Repeated Measures*, Newbury Park, CA: Sage.

Glass, Gene V. and Stanley, Julian C. 1970: *Statistical Methods in Education and Psychology*, Englewood Cliffs, NJ: Prentice-Hall.

Greenwald, Anthony G. 1976: Within-subjects designs: to use or not to use?. *Psychological Bulletin*, 83, 314–20.

Hakistian, A. Ralph, Roed, J. Christian and Lind, John C. 1979: Two-sample T^2 procedure and the assumption of homogeneous covariance matrices. *Psychological Bulletin*, 86, 1255–63.

Harris, R. J. 1985: *A Primer of Multivariate Statistics*, 2nd edn, NY: Academic Press.

Hays, William L. 1988: *Statistics*, 4th edn, New York: Holt, Rinehart, and Winston.

Hicks, C. R. 1982: *Fundamental Concepts in the Design of Experiments*, New York: Holt, Rinehart, & Winston.

Hochberg, Yosef and Tamhane, Ajit C. 1987: *Multiple Comparison Procedures*, New York: Wiley.

Iacobucci, Dawn 1992: Analysis of variance on unbalanced data. Unpublished manuscript, available upon request.

Ito, Koichi and Shull, William J. 1964: On the robustness of the T^2 test in the multivariate analysis of variance when variance–covariance matrices are not equal. *Biometrika*, 51, 71–82.

Iverson, G. R., and Norpoth, H. 1986: *Analysis of Variance*, 2nd edn, Beverly Hills: Sage.

Keppel, Geoffrey 1991: *Design and Analysis: A Researcher's Handbook*, 3rd edn, Englewood Cliffs, NJ: Prentice Hall.

Kirk, Roger 1982: *Experimental Design: Procedures for the Behavioral Sciences*, 2nd edn, Belmont, CA: Brooks/Cole.

Mardia, K. V. 1975: Assessment of multinormality and the robustness of Hotelling's T^2 test, *Applied Statistics*, 24, 163–71.

Olson, Chester L. 1974: Comparative robustness of six tests in multivariate analysis of variance. *Journal of the American Statistical Association*, 69, 894–908.

Olson, Chester L. 1976: On choosing a test statistic in multivariate analysis of variance. *Psychological Bulletin*, 83, 579–86.

Olson, Chester L. 1979: Practical considerations in choosing a MANOVA test statistic: a rejoinder to Stevens. *Psychological Bulletin*, 86, 1350–2.

Peterson, Robert A., Albaum, Gerald and Beltrami, Richard F. 1985: A Meta-analysis of Effects in Consumer Behavior Experiments. *Journal of Consumer Research*, 12, 97–103.

SAS Institute 1985: *SAS User's Guide: Basics, and Statistics*, version 5, Cary, NC: SAS Institute Inc.

Searle, S. R. 1987: *Linear Models for Unbalanced Data*, New York: Wiley.

Seber, G. A. F. 1984: *Multivariate Observations*, New York: Wiley.

Sternthal, Brian, Tybout, Alice M. and Calder, Bobby J. 1987: Confirmatory versus comparative approaches to judging theory tests. *Journal of Consumer Research*, 14, 114–25.

Stevens, James 1979: Comment on Olson: choosing a test statistic in multivariate analysis of variance. *Psychological Bulletin*, 86, 355–60.

Tatsuoka, Maurice M. 1988: *Multivariate Analysis: Techniques for Educational and Psychological Research*, 2nd edn, New York: Macmillan.

Wildt, Albert R. and Ahtola, Olli 1978: *Analysis of Covariance*, Beverly Hills, CA: Sage.

8

Classic Factor Analysis

Dawn Iacobucci

In this chapter we explore the classic factor analytical model. Factor analysis is extremely important in its scientific historical role in explicitly recognizing measurement error in behavioral research, and in providing a rigorous means of conceptualizing unobservable constructs and the theoretical nomological networks in which the constructs are embedded. More recently its importance is also in its foundational role as a predecessor to the currently enormously popular structural equations modeling techniques. Finally, classic factor analysis is also still commonly used today as an exploratory method.

This chapter is organized as follows: First, the concepts of unobservable constructs and measurement error are reviewed. Second, factor analysis is distinguished from principal components analysis – these terms are often mistakenly used interchangeably even though these models have very different theoretical bases (if not empirical performances). Third, the decisions that must be made in the process of conducting a factor analysis are addressed. These issues include the "number of factors to retain" and the method of "rotation" to facilitate interpretation of the results. Finally, several advanced topics (e.g. higher-order factor analysis, multi-mode factor analysis, etc.) are discussed briefly. Several small data sets are analyzed throughout the chapter to provide examples, and the SAS and SPSSX commands necessary to run simple jobs are provided in Appendix A.

Unobservable Constructs and Measurement Error

An unobservable construct is a theoretical notion that is not directly measurable, but is useful nonetheless. For example, contrast the human characteristics of height and intelligence. One can determine immediately upon sight which of two persons is taller, but it is more difficult to determine who is the more intelligent. Intelligence is not directly observable–

it must be inferred from observing indicators, such as the individual's behaviors and performance on exams purported to measure intelligence.

Measurement theory posits that observations of either variable (height or intelligence) will be a function of the individual's true height or true intelligence score, but will also be contaminated by "measurement error" (cf. Allen and Yen, 1979). Measurement error is random variability about the true score mean. Thus, much like a simple model in statistics, whereby a data point, x_i, is posited to be a function of a population mean, μ, and a random error component, ϵ_i (i.e. $x_i = \mu + \epsilon_i$) so too is an observed measure, z_i, considered to be a function of a true score, τ, and a random error of measurement, e_i (i.e. $z_i = \tau + e_i$).

For example, if the height of Dr. X were 5' 7", and her height was measured by several persons using their most trusted measuring sticks and tape measures, it is unlikely that every measurement taken would exactly equal 5' 7". Instead, we would expect some slight differences among the observed measures, given that the persons measuring the height, and their chosen tools, may differ in their abilities to take precise measures. Nevertheless, we would hope the mean of the distribution of observed heights would be 5' 7" (i.e. that there would be no bias over all the persons and methods measuring the height). Furthermore, we would expect that the variability around that mean would be small (i.e. that the measures would yield as precise estimates as possible).

In contrast, consider the even more difficult task of these researchers measuring Dr. X's intelligence. A standard measurable unit of intelligence has not been agreed upon to the extent that is true for a unit of height (e.g. inches or centimeters). Therefore, each proposed measurement instrument is likely to be unique, tapping slightly different aspects of intelligence, and we must hope that those estimates converge on the main core of what we consider to be intelligence. For example, consider the variety of indicators of intelligence commonly used as educational selection criteria: undergraduate grade point averages, scores on standardized graduate school admissions tests, intelligence tests, and so on.

No single test can adequately measure intelligence, because the construct of intelligence is too broad and multidimensional to be captured in a single score. Therefore, we would expect that an individual's intelligence level would be estimated more precisely with multiple indicators – the battery of three tests would be preferable to any single one of them. Conversely, we must also recognize that each of the aforementioned tests does not measure only intelligence. Grade point averages also reflect in-class behavior and cooperation, standardized tests also reflect test-taking abilities under time constraints and emotional pressures, etc. That is, these measures are also imperfect indicators of intelligence because they tap other, extraneous constructs.

When multiple indicators are used to measure unobservable constructs like intelligence, we expect the irrelevancies to effectively cancel each other out. Thus, the variability in each measurement that is commonly shared (i.e. the *co*variability) would presumably tap the construct of interest, intelligence. If grade point averages measured *only* in-class behavior, and entrance exams measured *only* test-taking abilities under conditions of anxiety, these two indicators would not yield a significant correlation. A large correlation coefficient, on the other hand, would indicate that whatever one test measured was similar to what the other test measured – that they shared some common ground. This notion of "communality" is central to the factor analytical model, and will be defined more precisely shortly.

The example of intelligence just discussed was not chosen arbitrarily. The most important origin of factor analysis was the study of human abilities and intelligence tests. In 1904, Spearman posited what is usually credited to be the first true common factor model in his analysis of test scores on 36 school boys measured on a variety of school subjects.[1] He conceptualized intelligence hierarchically, with one "general intelligence" factor, overarching several "specific abilities" factors (e.g. verbal, spatial, musical, etc.), positing the score on each test (z_j) to be a function of the general factor of intelligence (G) and some effect unique to each particular test (u_j) : $z_j = b_j G + u_j$.

In contrast, the work by L. L. Thurstone at Chicago begun in the 1930s formed the basis of the logic by which we proceed today. Thurstone modified the conceptualization of intelligence factors to be more consistent with the scientific goal of parsimony. Thus, he posited no "general intelligence" factor, but rather sought to simplify the factor analytical structure into its more specific factors (yielding less overlap or redundancy in the factor space).

The first factor from a typical factor extraction usually resembles a "general" factor, in that it reflects a bit of each of the input variables (which will become clearer in the examples presented later). While Spearman would have taken such a solution as final, Thurstone would have treated that first "general" factor as unimportant, much like a grand mean in the analysis of variance, or an intercept in regression. Thus, Thurstone would have "rotated" the solution according to his rules for "simple structure" (each of these terms will be described in detail later in this chapter). Thus, a debate regarding the existence of a "general" factor is effectively a debate over whether one should rotate factors. It is currently common practice *not* to interpret the initial factor solution, but to *rotate* to enhance interpretability.

Mulaik (1972, pp. 3–15) presents a delightful discussion of the history of factor analysis, beginning with the likes of Gauss (and his analysis of individual differences in data on planet orbits), Galton (who worked on the difficulties in predicting sons' heights from fathers' heights), and Pearson (who developed the critically important product-moment correlation coefficient). He discusses Spearman and Thurstone in more detail, and proceeds through the explosion of factor analysis with the development of the "modern" computer[2] into the 1950s and 1960s, to which he refers as the "era of blind factor analysis".[3]

We now proceed to describe the factor analytical model. We begin first with a review of eigenvalues and eigenvectors, and the model of principal components.

Eigenvalues, Eigenvectors, and Principal Components Analysis

In this section, only a passing knowledge of calculus is assumed, but some knowledge of matrix algebra is necessary.[4] We begin with a data matrix, $\mathbf{X}$, with elements x_{ij}, for the jth measure on the ith subject. The matrix $\mathbf{X}$ is $n \times p$, where n is the sample size, and p is the number of variables to be analyzed. Also, for simplification in later computations, we can take $\mathbf{X}$ to be a "deviation" matrix (i.e. the mean for each variable has been subtracted from each data point).

Even though we took p measures on each of our n subjects, we might wish to condense this information to a more manageable number of data points. Furthermore, this reduction might be possible if the variables are somewhat redundant in the information they provide (i.e. they are correlated). Thus, our goal might be to find some way to combine those p original variables into a single new score that still captures the essence of the information contained in the p variables. We can posit the following linear model:

$$z_{1i} = b_1 X_{1i} + b_2 X_{2i} + \ldots + b_p X_{pi}, \quad \text{or} \quad \mathbf{Z} = \mathbf{Xb} \tag{8.1}$$

where z_{1i} is the score on the new variable for subject i, and $\mathbf{z}$ (for now) is $n \times 1$ (i.e. there is only a single new variable, but a score on it for each of the n subjects). The vector $\mathbf{b}$ is $p \times 1$ and it contains the weights to create this linear combination. The optimal values for these weights must be solved for, and this procedure is now described.

For regression, the "optimal" weights would be those that made $\mathbf{z}$ maximally correlated with some criterion variable. Instead, the goal here is to find the linear composite variable, z, that explains the maximum possible variance in $\mathbf{X}$ (i.e. our goal is to find the b's such that $\mathbf{z}$ "best represents" $\mathbf{X}$). Figure 8.1 shows a Venn diagram of the variances of the original x variables (and the overlaps represent the covariances). If the circles depicting the variances were water droplets, the linear composite variable we seek could be likened to a paper towel "soaking up" as much of that variance as possible.

We need to know the variance of $\mathbf{z}$ in order to understand what must be maximized. For univariate transformations of the form, $z = v * x$, we know $\sigma_z^2 = v^2 \sigma_x^2$. Analogously, for multivariate transformations of the form in equation (8.1), $\mathbf{s}_z = \mathbf{v}'\mathbf{S}_x\mathbf{v} = (n-1)^{-1}\mathbf{v}'\mathbf{X}'\mathbf{Xv}$ (where $\mathbf{S}$ is a covariance matrix; $\mathbf{S}_x = (n-1)^{-1}\mathbf{X}'\mathbf{X}$). One way to make the entries in $\mathbf{S}_z$ large is to make the weights (the v's) very large, but this solution is trivial. Thus, we add the

Variances and covariances
of p original variables

Variance of new composite
variable

Figure 8.1 Venn diagram representing variances and covariances of p original measures and single composite

restriction that the sums of squares of the weights must be one ($\mathbf{v}'\mathbf{v} = 1$). To maximize a function (F) simultaneously with such a constraint, we need derivative calculus and a "LaGrangian multiplier" (λ):

$$F = \mathbf{v}'\mathbf{X}'\mathbf{X}\mathbf{v} - \lambda(\mathbf{v}'\mathbf{v} - 1) \stackrel{\alpha}{=} \mathbf{v}'\mathbf{S}_x\mathbf{v} - \lambda(\mathbf{v}'\mathbf{v} - 1) \stackrel{\alpha}{=} \mathbf{v}'\mathbf{R}_x\mathbf{v} - \lambda(\mathbf{v}'\mathbf{v} - 1), \quad (8.2)$$

where $\mathbf{R}$ is the correlation matrix among the p variables. The partial derivatives of F with respect to each weight v_1, v_2 through v_p must be set to zero:

$$\partial F/\partial \mathbf{v} = 2\mathbf{R}_x\mathbf{v} - 2\lambda\mathbf{v} = \mathbf{R}_x\mathbf{v} - \lambda\mathbf{v} = (\mathbf{R}_x - \lambda\mathbf{I})\mathbf{v} = 0 \quad (8.3)$$

One way to make $(\mathbf{R}_x - \lambda\mathbf{I})\mathbf{v}$ equal to zero would be to multiply both sides by $(\mathbf{R}_x - \lambda\mathbf{I})^{-1}$ but this would imply $\mathbf{v} = 0$, which cannot be, given that $\mathbf{v}'\mathbf{v} = 1$. Thus, $(\mathbf{R}_x - \lambda\mathbf{I})$ must not have an inverse, so the determinant, $|\mathbf{R}_x - \lambda\mathbf{I}|$ must equal zero. Solving $|\mathbf{R}_x - \lambda\mathbf{I}| = 0$ results in a polynomial of power p: $(-\lambda)^p + v_{p-1}(-\lambda)^{p-1} + \ldots + v_1(-\lambda) + v_0 = 0$. All λ's that satisfy this equation are called "characteristic roots", or "eigenvalues" of $\mathbf{R}$. There will be p λ's (though they might not be distinct, and some may equal zero).[5] Each λ_k is paired with an eigenvector, $\mathbf{v}_k$. If an eigenvector premultiplies equation (8.3), we have:

$$\mathbf{v}'_k(\mathbf{R} - \lambda\mathbf{I})\mathbf{v}_k = 0$$
$$\mathbf{v}'_k\mathbf{R}\mathbf{v}_k - \lambda\mathbf{v}'_k\mathbf{v}_k = 0$$
$\mathbf{v}'_k\mathbf{R}\mathbf{v}_k = \lambda\mathbf{v}'_k\mathbf{v}_k$, and because we know any $\mathbf{v}'_k\mathbf{v}_k = 1$:

$$v_k' R v_k = \lambda. \quad (8.4)$$

Thus λ is the variance of the new composite variable formed from the old variables (in **X**) using the newly derived weights (in v_k). The eigenvectors $v_1, v_2, \ldots, v_k$ are mutually orthogonal, so the new composite variables, $z_1 = Xv_1$, $z_2 = Xv_2, \ldots, z_p = Xv_p$ are mutually uncorrelated.

By convention, the eigenvalues are ordered $\lambda_1 \geq \lambda_2 \geq \ldots, \lambda_p \geq 0$, so the first eigenvector contains those weights that would create a linear combination of the p variables that explains most of their variance, and the second eigenvector explains the most variance that remains (with the constraint that the new linear combination is orthogonal to the first), and so on. The λ's are put into a $p \times p$ diagonal matrix, Λ. The eigenvectors $v_1, v_2, \ldots, v_k$ form the columns of a $p \times p$ matrix **V** that is orthonormal (i.e. $V'V = VV' = I$; $V' = V^{-1}$). Thus, if the form of the equation for a single eigenvector was $(R - \lambda I)v_k = 0$, or $Rv = \lambda Iv_k$, then with p eigenvalues and eigenvectors, we have: $RV = V\Lambda$, or:

$$R = V\Lambda V'. \quad (8.5)$$

That is, we can decompose a correlation matrix into two unique matrices – one of eigenvalues and one of eigenvectors (and its transpose).

Eigenvalues and eigenvectors are abstract concepts that are often difficult to students of matrix algebra (matrix multiplication and inversion seem easy by comparison), so it may be useful to consider a more intuitive explanation of these concepts. Consider the simple two-dimensional scatterplot (i.e. $p = 2$) in Figure 8.2. The eigenvector v_1 defines the direction in space in which the cloud of data points is the longest. That is, if all data points were projected on to that line, that distribution would have the greatest variance, compared with projecting the data points on to any other line in any other orientation in that $p =$ two-dimensional space. The eigenvalue is the variance of the data points were they to be projected on to that new dimension defined by the eigenvector. The second eigenvector will be oriented orthogonally (perpendicularly), to explain the maximum of the remaining variance, and so on.[6]

With an eigenvalue–eigenvector decomposition of $R (R = V\Lambda V')$, we have the vectors of optimal weights to use in forming the linear combination of our p x's: $Z = XV$ (i.e. our unknown weights, **b**, are contained in the columns of **V**). Recall that **X** is an $n \times p$ matrix, and **V** is a $p \times p$ matrix, so **Z** is an $n \times p$ is an matrix. That is, there is a row in **Z** for every subject, and a column for each newly created variable. These p variables have properties that make them different from the p original scores: they are ordered with respect to the variance they explain, and they are uncorrelated. However, our goal was to find a means of data reduction, explaining the variability in our original p measures using "r", usually much smaller than p, new composite variables. The model $Z = XV$ explains all the data, but has not contributed to the goal of parsimony. Thus, we have

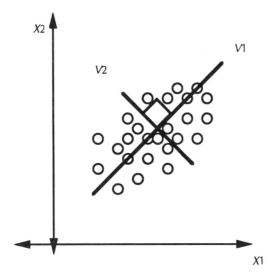

Figure 8.2 Eigenvectors in $p = 2$-dimensional scatterplot

encountered the usual conflicting goals in data analysis: trying to explain the data thoroughly, but doing so using as few parameters as possible.

Accordingly, what we will do is use only those first few (r) eigenvectors, which are associated with the r largest eigenvalues (which thereby explain the most variance) to approximate the data. That is, define Z_r to be a $n \times r$ matrix, which contains the first r columns of Z, and V_r to be a $p \times r$ matrix, containing the first r eigenvectors as columns. Then we can define $Z_r = XV_r$, or rearranging the equation, we would be approximating the data matrix using the r new variables:

$$\hat{X} \doteq Z_r V_r'. \tag{8.6}$$

We can judge the goodness of this approximation by comparing it to our data matrix, which would yield a matrix of residuals, or errors, $E = X - \hat{X}$. The least-squares criterion for finding $\hat{X}$ minimizes $\sum_i \sum_j e_{ij}^2$, and leads to the same solution as the eigenvalue-vectors maximization of the variance of the composite variables. (Note that $E = 0$ if $r = p$, or if $r < p$, but $r = \text{rank}(X)$.)

If we take the eigensolution, $R = V\Lambda V'$, or the approximation, $R \doteq V_r \Lambda_r V_r'$, and define $\Lambda^{.5}$ to be an $r \times r$ diagonal matrix containing the square roots of the eigenvalues, then we can rewrite the model to be:

$$R \doteq (V_r \Lambda_r^{.5})(\Lambda_r^{.5} V_r'), \quad \text{or defining} \quad B_r = V_r \Lambda_r^{.5}, \quad \text{then} \quad R \doteq B_r B_r'. \tag{8.7}$$

This reformulation is known as "principal components". Each element in the $p \times r$ matrix B_r is the "loading" of the original variable (the row) on the principal component (the column). For now, we can interpret "loading" as the correlation between the variable and the component, so the component is defined by those variables with the largest (positive or negative) loadings (i.e. $|b_{ij}| \geq .3$). We will see shortly that the classic factor analysis model is similar, in that it also requires an eigenvalue–eigenvector decomposition.

We can write the data matrix, $\mathbf{X}$, as a function of "standardized component scores" and the principal component loadings:

$$\mathbf{X} = (\mathbf{X}\mathbf{V}_r\Lambda_r^{-.5})(\Lambda_r^{.5}\mathbf{V}_r') \quad \text{(since the } \Lambda\text{'s and } \mathbf{V}\text{'s would cancel)}, \quad (8.8)$$

where $\mathbf{X}$ is the original data matrix, $\mathbf{X}\mathbf{V}_r$ is a $n \times r$ matrix of the scores for each of the n subjects on the r new composite variables, $\mathbf{X}\mathbf{V}_r\Lambda_r^{-.5}$ are the standardized scores (i.e. each $\sigma^2 = 1$) for each of the n subjects on the r composites, and $\Lambda_r^{.5}\mathbf{V}_r'$ is the transpose of the $p \times r$ matrix $\mathbf{B}_r$ of principal component loadings.

Figure 8.3 contains an example of a principal components analysis (Green, 1978, p. 344). All correlations in this matrix are large, so we would suspect immediately that a single composite should be sufficient for explaining most of the variance (e.g. the three variables are likely measuring the same construct). Note the ordered nature of the eigenvalues in Λ (with the first component explaining 89 percent of the variance), and the very "general" nature of the first principal component (the first column in $\mathbf{B}$).

With this basic understanding of eigensolutions and principal components, we can proceed to the factor analytic model. In transition, we compare the two.

Similarities between principal components and factor analysis

At face value, the models for principal components and factor analysis appear very similar. In principal components, we represent variable j as follows:

$$x_j \doteq b_{j1}P_1 + b_{j2}P_2 + \ldots + b_{jr}P_r.$$

For factor analysis, we represent variable j as:

$$x_j \doteq b_{j1}F_1 + b_{j2}F_2 + \ldots + b_{jr}F_r + d_jU_j. \quad (8.9)$$

The P's stand for principal components, and the F's stand for factors. The notation was kept constant across these two equations to highlight their similarity, but in general, the components loadings and factor loadings will not be equal, nor will "r", the number of components or factors be the same. The new term in equation (8.9) is a weight (d_j) for variable j on its own "uniqueness" factor. This term will be defined precisely shortly. For now, simply note the overall apparent similarity between the models. Note also that (8.9) looks similar to a regression equation, except that the F's and U's are unobservable and must be inferred from the data.[7]

(I) Correlation Matrix, **R**:

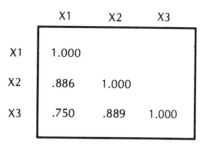

(II) Eigenvalues in Λ, and eigenvectors in **V**:

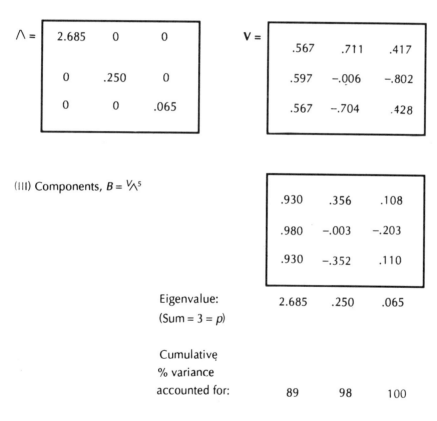

Figure 8.3 Example of principal components

A second similarity between principal components and factor analysis is that both solutions are fundamentally eigenvalue–eigenvector decompositions of the correlation matrix (for principal components) or the correlation matrix modified for the $d_j U_j$ terms above (for factor analysis). That is, the b's in both equations in (8.9) are elements in a matrix $\mathbf{B}_r$, of the form, $\mathbf{B}_r = \mathbf{V}_r \Lambda'_r$.

A third similarity between principal components and factor analysis is that frequently their empirical performance is similar. That is, from a practical, data analytical point of view, these models often convey roughly equivalent information (cf. Velicer, Peacock, and Jackson, 1982). However, recent research by Snook and Gorsuch (1989) indicates that factor analysis performs better than principal components (especially for small p and small loadings). Furthermore, the theoretical differences between the models are very important.

Differences between principal components and factor analysis

One difference between principal components and factor analysis exists in their objectives. The goal for principal components is one of data reduction, extracting as much information from p variables into r components; we seek to explain the maximum variance in the data. For factor analysis, we seek to explain the *co*variation in the data. That is, we will simply "take care" of the variances (which are in the diagonal of **S** or **R**), and model what is left – the off-diagonal terms (i.e. the covariances or correlations among the p variables). Thus, in the Venn diagram in Figure 8.1, the variances of each measure will be perfectly modeled, and the covariances (the areas of overlapping variability) are that which is to be approximated and understood.

A second difference between principal components and factor analysis is the measurement theory underlying factor analysis. Principal components analysis is a straightforward data analytical technique – no "unobservable" constructs are posited, and all parameters are strictly a function of the observed data points. Factor analysis, on the other hand, is not just a tool for "data reduction"; it proceeds via extensive underlying theory. It is the object of factor analsis to represent a variable x_j in terms of several underlying (i.e. unobservable) *factors*, or hypothetical constructs. The underlying factors that are of most interest to us are the "common" factors – those shared across variables to explain their covariances. Other underlying factors are also posited, and these explain the variability that is not shared, but is "unique" to each measure.

Introduction to the Logic of Factor Analysis

Recall from basic statistics the maxim that "correlation does not necessarily imply causation". A coefficient r_{xy} might be large because x causes y, y causes x, or some third variable causes both. In factor analysis, we assume the last case, that a common factor is the mutual cause of variables that are correlated. Thus, in Figure 8.4, we see a path diagram depicting the hypothesized causality between the unobservable constructs (i.e. factors), and the observable indicator variables (the x's). The b-weights are factor loadings (which we will derive momentarily), and the d-weights are those associated with the uniqueness factors.

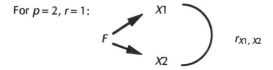

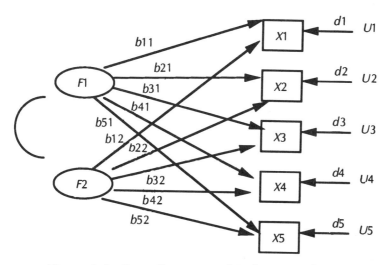

Figure 8.4 Causality assumed in factor analysis
Source: Figure modified from Kim and Mueller, 1978, p. 25 ($p = 5, R = 2$)

The uniqueness, d_j^2 is the contribution of the unique factor U_j to the modeling of variable x_j. It indicates the extent to which the common factors $(F_1, F_2, \ldots, F_r)$ fail to account for the total variance of x_j. The uniqueness factor may be further decomposed into two sources as follows:

$$d_j U_j = c_j S_j + e_j E_j, \qquad (8.10)$$

The S_j is the "specificity" factor, a source of variance that is systematic to measure x_j, whereas E_j is the "measurement error" factor, a random source of variability.[8]

Test-taking abilities under anxious conditions is an example of a "specific" factor that would influence an individual's performance on a standardized exam. While the common factor, intelligence, would affect both the standardized test scores and the grade point average, the anxiety factor would presumably influence solely the performance on the test. If examinees were tested multiple times, this specific factor would affect performance on each examination. Thus, the "specific" factor is considered to be a systematic source of variability, one that will contribute to the consistency, or reliability, of x_j. In contrast, E_j is a random source of variability, such

		In diagram factors
Total variance:	$s_j^2 = 1 = h_j^2 + c_j^2 + e_j^2 = h_j^2 + d_j^2$	1&2&3
Communality:	$h_j^2 = 1 - d_j^2$	1
Uniqueness:	$d_j^2 = c_j^2 + e_j^2 = 1 - h_j^2$	2&3
Specificity:	$c_j^2 = d_j^2 - e_j^2$	2
Measurement error variance:	$e_j^2 = 1 - r_{xx'}$	3
Reliability:	$r_{xx'} = h_j^2 + c_j^2 = 1 - e_j^2$	1&2

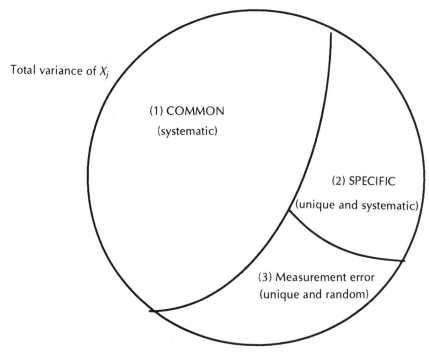

Figure 8.5 Relationships among common and unique factors

as an examinee's mood. Mood, or other temporary states, would not affect the individual's scores in the same way over multiple administrations, and therefore does not contribute to the reliability of the test.

In a correlation matrix, the variance of each measure x_j is standardized to be one. In Figure 8.5, we see the partitioning of the variance into its different sources. First, note the three major portions: common variability (due to the common factors, which are derived from the covariances), specific variance (due to systematic factors that are unique to measure x_j), and measurement error (due to random factors that are also assumed to be unique for measure x_j).

According to the relationships in Figure 8.5, the variance of x_j may be decomposed into the following parts: $s_j^2 = 1 = h_j^2 + d_j^2 = h_j^2 + c_j^2 - e_j^2$, where h_j^2 is the communality (the variance explainable by the common factors shared with the other variables in the correlation matrix), d_j^2 is the uniqueness, which equals the specificity (c_j^2) and error (e_j^2) sources. Together, the two systematic (i.e. non-measurement error) sources combine to comprise measure's reliability, $r_{xx'}$.

It is not the purpose of this chapter to delve deeply into measurement theory, but some discussion was necessary to appreciate the complexity of the factor analytical model, and the tradition from which it was developed. For more information on measurement error and classic test theory, sources such as Allen and Yen (1979), Anastasi (1982), and Ghiselli, Campbell, and Zedeck (1981) are excellent.

Conducting a Factor Analysis

For factor analysis, we are trying to model the data (x's) as a function of factors (F's and U's) and appropriate weights (b's and d's). We can use these sources to understand the structure of the factor model and the predictions it makes for data. Figure 8.6 shows the complexity of the structure of the relevant matrices. The matrix of weights is partitioned into three logical sections, the $p \times r$ matrix of factor loadings, **B**, and two $p \times p$ diagonal matrices which contain the specificities and measurement errors (the latter two are only separable if we have estimates of the variables' reliabilities). The matrix of covariances among the hypothesized factors preserve the assumptions of independence between and within the three kinds of factors. Only the common factors may be correlated (as demonstrated later in this chapter). While these partitioned matrices are large $p \times (r + 2p)$ and $(r + 2p) \times (r + 2p)$, the matrix multiplication simplifies, because there are so many zero submatrices. The multiplication results in:

$$\mathbf{R} = \mathbf{B\Phi B'} + \Xi^2 + \mathbf{E}^2 = \mathbf{B\Phi B'} + \mathbf{D}^2, \tag{8.11}$$

or, if we subtract the uniqueness terms from **R**:

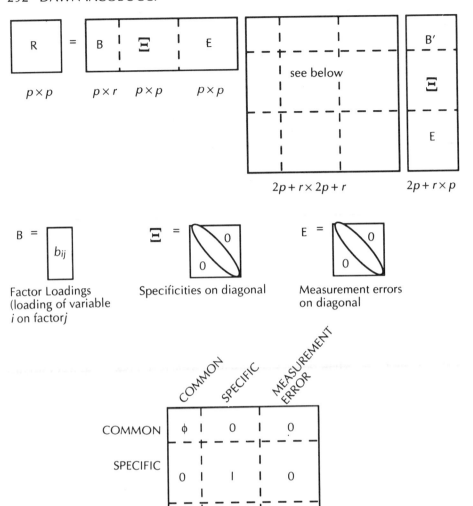

Figure 8.6 Structure of underlying factors

$$R - D^2 = B\Phi B'. \tag{8.12}$$

That is, if we adjust the correlation matrix with some estimate of the uniquenesses, then the right hand side of the model (8.12) contains only information about the common factors – their loadings (in **B**) and their intercorrelations (in **Φ**).

Thus, how do we adjust **R**? Recall that the diagonal of a covariance matrix contains $\sigma^2_{x_j}$, the variance of x_j, which is rescaled in a correlation matrix to equal one. If we take **R**, and subtract off a diagonal matrix, only the diagonal elements in **R**, will be affected. These values will equal

$1 - d_j^2 = h_j^2$. That is, if we subtract off an estimate of the uniqueness for a variable, we are left with an estimate of its communality. Alternatively, we can derive an estimate of the communality and impute it into the diagonal of R. One tried and true estimate of h_j^2 is the squared multiple correlation (SMC) coefficient derived from estimating variable x_j from all the other variables being modeled (e.g. $R^2_{x1.x2,x3,\ldots,xp}$). If the other variables predict x_j well, the SMC will be large, indicating the presence of much common variability. If the other variables do not predict x_j well, the SMC will be small, indicating more uniqueness in x_j than communality.

Thus, the first step in a factor analysis is to adjust the correlation matrix by putting SMCs into the diagonal. (This procedure is an option in most statistical computing packages.) The adjusted correlation matrix is referred to as "$\mathbf{R}_{SMC}$".[9]

The second step in a classic factor analysis is to obtain the eigenvalues and eigenvectors of the adjusted correlation matrix:

$$\mathbf{R}_{SMC} = \mathbf{V\Lambda V'}, \quad \text{or} \quad \mathbf{R}_{SMC} = \mathbf{BB'}, \qquad (8.13)$$

where $\mathbf{B} = \mathbf{V\Lambda}^{.5}$ is the "factor loadings matrix".[10] Given the usual concerns for parsimony, we take only r common factors ($\mathbf{B}_r = \mathbf{V}_r\mathbf{\Lambda}_r^{.5}$), to approximate the data. Thus, just as principal components is an eigensolution of $\mathbf{R}$, factor analysis is an eigensolution of $\mathbf{R}_{SMC}$. This solution for factor analysis is often called the "principal factors" solution, because the orientation of the first eigenvector is in the direction of the principal axis (i.e. the longest axis) of the ellipsoid of data points. In principal components, the eigenvector is in the direction that maximizes variance captured. In principal factors, no variance needs explaining – the off-diagonals reflect pairwise covariability, and the diagonals reflect aggregate common variability. Thus, the principal axis, or first eigenvector, will be in the direction explaining the maximum *covariance*.

Several decisions must be made during the process of running a factor analysis. First, we have been taking for granted the extraction of "r" common factors, but we need guidance on a good judgment of r. Second, the factor loadings matrix $\mathbf{B}_r$ has not yet been rotated, and this must be done in order to enhance interpretability. Each of these issues is discussed in turn.

Number of factors

If we knew the rank of the population correlation matrix and the true communalities, we would know r exactly (although we might still argue for taking fewer than r factors if the last eigenvalues were especially small). Usually we have access only to sample data and communality estimates, so we must make some rules about choosing r. Some of these rules are presented here.

"*Greater than one*" Probably the most popular rule for selecting r is that all factors should be retained that are associated with eigenvalues that are greater than or equal to one. This rule is popular because it is simple and because it is the default in many computing packages. This rule is a bad rule.

The theoretical basis for the rule is as follows. In a correlation matrix, each variable has been standardized to have a variance of one. We have seen that an eigenvalue is the variance of the newly formed linear composite variable. Thus, it would seem to make sense that the newly formed variable be required to account for at least as much variance as any of the old variables, hence the rule $\lambda_i \geq 1$. However, the goal of factor analysis is not to maximize *variance* accounted for.

Furthermore, and perhaps more damning, the empirical performance of the "greater than one" rule has been shown to be weak. Such tests can be made in computer simulations for which true (i.e. population) eigenvalues are known, samples drawn, and the rule applied. When the rule is applied in principal components analysis, too few components are extracted, and when the rule is applied to principal factor analysis, too many factors are extracted.

Finally, aside from the above-stated logic, the value of one is arbitrary – there is no statistical sense of values that are "close to" one. For example, Cliff (1987; p. 312) presents an example correlation matrix that shows a clear pattern requiring two factors. However, the eigenvalues are $\lambda_1 = 4.4$, and $\lambda_2 = 0.8$. Thus, by "the rule", we would mistakenly conclude that only one eigenvector would be sufficient to account for the data. (See also Cliff (1988).)

Scree tests Amateur mountain climbers might already know that "scree" is the rubble at the base of a mountain. A scree test is an ocular judgment made from a plot of the eigenvalues in their descending order. The idea is that the eigenvalues on the "mountain" represent "real" factors, but those amid the rubble represent random fluctuations. Thus, the number of factors to retain is that number before the break (or "elbow") in the curve. For example, Figure 8.7 contains several such eigenvalue plots. Imagine fitting a line through the points that form the rubble. The last eigenvalue that is above the line (at the left of the plot) is the number of factors that should be retained. (The subjectivity of this "test" can make the method difficult in real data, for which eigenvalue plots can often depict a single very large eigenvalue and then a nearly linear decline thereafter.)

Humphreys and Ilgen (1969) systematized this process. They generated numerous random, independent variables and computed their correlation matrices, for various cases of n and p. They obtained the eigenvalues for these random matrices, and suggest that the eigenvalues for "real" factors in real data should exceed the values of the eigenvalues they obtained for the random, uncorrelated variables. Clearly, it would be cumbersome to run the simulation procedure for each factor analysis, so Montanelli and Humphreys (1976) provided regression equations to predict the estimates of the random eigenvalues for a given n and p (the required linear coefficients are provided in their paper).

(I) Plot the eigenvalues in order: Eigenvalue

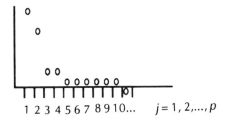

(II) Fit a line (by eye) through the points in the scree: Eigenvalue

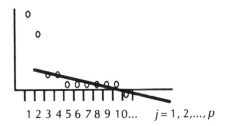

(III) Take r, the number of common factors, to be that number of eigenvalues that are above the break in the curve:

Figure 8.7 Scree tests

Chi-squared tests While the process of maximum likelihood factor analysis has not yet been described in this chapter, it should be noted that this procedure is the only factor extraction method that allows a true statistical test of a null hypothesis for r. That is, $H_0 : r = 2$ can be tested, $H_0 : r = 3$ can be tested, and so on.

A related issue It should make intuitive sense by now that if the battery of measures is changed, the number of factors to be retained would also change. That is, the set of variables with which one variable might share common variance would change. For example, consider the following "intelligence" subscales depicted in Figure 8.8: x_1 = vocabulary, x_2 = reading comprehension, x_3 = word analogies, x_4 = word problems, x_5 = algebra, x_6 = trigonometry, x_7 = Spanish vocabulary. Two common factors would be extracted (given the patterns in the correlation matrix and the content of the items). The first would resemble a "verbal" ability factor on which would load x_1, x_2, x_3 and x_4. The second would be a "quantitative" ability factor defined by x_4, x_5 and x_6. The "Spanish vocabulary" variable would likely have little in common with any of the other variables, and instead would be represented mostly by its own unique variance. In the bottom panel of Figure 8.8, one variable is added (x_8 = Spanish reading comprehension), and the number of factors would increase to three, because now x_7 and x_8 exhibit "common" variance – covariance. For reasons such as this, a researcher cannot simply lump in p variables and hope a nice factor structure results. The variables considered for inclusion should be designed carefully, otherwise "unique variance" will predominate. This problem was the source of the saying, "garbage in – garbage out"; factor analysis will not work miracles on poorly designed collections of variables.

(I) Simplistic correlation pattern for $r = 2$:

x1 = vocabulary	1.0						
x2 = reading comprehension	0.8	1.0					
x3 = word analogies	0.8	0.8	1.0				
x4 = word problems	0.4	0.4	0.4	1.0			
x5 = algebra	0.0	0.0	0.0	0.4	1.0		
x6 = trigonometry	0.0	0.0	0.0	0.4	0.8	1.0	
x7 = Spanish vocabulary	0.0	0.0	0.0	0.0	0.0	0.0	1.0

(II) Simplistic correlation pattern for $r = 3$:

x1 = vocabulary	1.0							
x2 = reading comprehension	0.8	1.0						
x3 = word analogies	0.8	0.8	1.0					
x4 = word problems	0.4	0.4	0.4	1.0				
x5 = algebra	0.0	0.0	0.0	0.4	1.0			
x6 = trigonometry	0.0	0.0	0.0	0.4	0.8	1.0		
x7 = Spanish vocabulary	0.0	0.0	0.0	0.0	0.0	0.0	1.0	
x8 = Spanish rdg comprehension	0.0	0.0	0.0	0.0	0.0	0.0	0.8	1.0

Figure 8.8 Example of $r = 2$ and $r = 3$ common factors

Rotations

The factor loadings in **B** are often plotted to get a better understanding of the common factors and the relationships among the variables. Each column (factor) of **B** becomes an axis in an r-dimensional factor space. Each row (variable) x_j is represented as a point in that space with coordinates $(b_{j1}, b_{j2}, \ldots, b_{jr})$.

For various reasons, the placement of these axes/factors might be less desirable than some other orientation in space. It is true that the derived factor matrix **B** has the mathematically nice property of the principal-axis orientation, but there may be other criteria to consider and optimize. If we are willing to forgo the principal axes property, we see that **B** may be modified in many ways (i.e. the orientation is arbitrary until some new criterion is defined). Recall that $\mathbf{R} = \mathbf{B\Phi B'} + \mathbf{D}^2$, or $\mathbf{R} - \mathbf{D}^2 = \mathbf{B\Phi B'}$, or $\mathbf{R}_{\text{SMC}} = \mathbf{B\Phi B'}$. Define $\mathbf{A} = \mathbf{BT}$ (or $\mathbf{B} = \mathbf{AT}^{-1}$), where **T** is a "transformation" matrix (or "rotation" matrix). **T** is $r \times r$ and must be nonsingular (i.e. have an inverse). If we then define $\tilde{\mathbf{\Phi}} = \mathbf{T}^{-1}\mathbf{\Phi T'}^{-1}$ (to balance the equations), then $\mathbf{B\Phi B'} = (\mathbf{AT}^{-1})(\mathbf{T}\tilde{\mathbf{\Phi}}\mathbf{T'})(\mathbf{T'}^{-1}\mathbf{A'}) = \mathbf{A}\tilde{\mathbf{\Phi}}\mathbf{A'}$; which, given its form, is also a factor solution of $\mathbf{R}_{\text{SMC}}$. That is, the "fit" of the model to the data is not affected by a transformation.

So, we know we *can* do a transformation. Next, we would want to know *why* and *how* we would rotate the factors. We do so because the results are usually much easier to interpret than the original, unrotated factors, and it is done according to Thurstone's rules for guidelines, and then demonstrate their application in rotations.

The goal of "simple structure" Thurstone's original (1947) criteria are as follows. First, each row (variable) of the factor pattern matrix should have at least one zero (or practically speaking, near-zero) loading (i.e. a variable should not load on *all* factors). Second, each column (factor) should have at least r zero elements, and the zeros for one factor should be unique from the zeros for the other factors (i.e. the second and remaining rules require that factors be linearly independent). Third, for every pair of columns (factors), there should be at least r variables with a zero coefficient in one column and a non-zero coefficient in the other. Fourth, when $r > 3$, every pair of columns (factors) should contain a large proportion of variables with zeros in both columns. And conversely, fifth, for every pair of columns (factors), there should be only a small proportion of variables with non-zeros in both columns.

Notice that his rules are not about increasing the number of large loadings defining a factor, as a novice might think, but rather the rules are about increasing the number of *zeros* in the factor loading matrix. A rotated factor pattern matrix, **A**, will be easier to interpret if more of its elements are zero than some other matrix, $\mathbf{A}^*$.

To understand how these criteria are implemented, we first discuss factor rotation "the old-fashioned way" – by hand via graphical rotation. We then discuss the modernization of these processes – the objective algorithms that are implemented in the statistical computing packages. While many algorithms exist, we focus only on the most frequently used orthogonal and oblique rotation schemas.

Graphical rotation Figure 8.9 contains a plot of 6 variables in a two-factor space. The axes labeled I and II are the unrotated factors – note the "general" nature of factor I – all variables load highly on it (i.e. their coordinates on this dimension are high). Factor II appears to contrast the two groups of variables.

(I) Orthogonal:

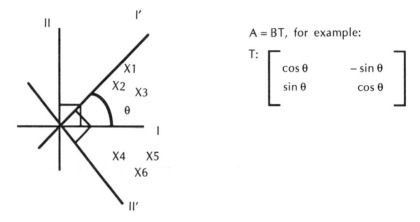

Figure 8.9 Graphical rotations

If we rotate the I–II axes by approximately 45 degrees counter clockwise, we obtain the new axes, which are labeled I' and II', and find that the variables lie closer to these rotated factors. Variables $x_1 - x_3$ would load highly on I' and rather low on II', and the reverse would be true of $x_4 - x_6$. Factors I' and II' represent the rigid orthogonal rotation – factors that have been rotated to better fit the data, while retaining the orthogonality property. The matrix, **T**, which transforms the original factor loadings (in **B**) to the orthogonally rotated factor loadings (in **A** = **BT**) is also given.

We can fit the data even better, however, if we are willing to relax the assumption that axes must be perpendicular in space.[11] The novice might think that we can send an axis through each group of points and be done, but this is not quite so (cf. Comrey and Lee, 1992). The traditional steps taken in an oblique rotation are portrayed in Figure 8.10. First, it is true that we begin by sending an axis through one group of correlated variables (points close in space), and we will call this axis "factor axis I'". For computational purposes, a "referent" axis is drawn that is orthogonal to (or "normal" to) I'. Thus, step one is to simply plot the unrotated factors. Step two is to draw a subjectively best-fitting factor axis through a group

CLASSIC FACTOR ANALYSIS 299

of points. Step three is to obtain a referent line by creating the axis perpendicular to the factor line. This continues for each factor (which can get complex working from two-dimensional plots for a three- or higher-dimensional factor solution).

In Step 6 of Figure 8.10, we see the factor axes I' and II' represent an "oblique" rotation, where the axes are not at right angles (i.e. the factors

Step 1: Plot the unrotated factors.

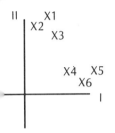

Step 2: Draw a factor axis I' through on group of points.

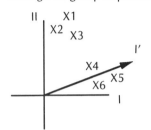

Step 3: Create a referent axis RI normal (orthogonal) to I':

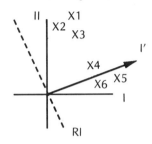

Step 4: Draw factor axis II' through a different group of points.

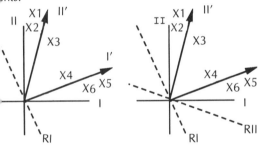

Step 5: Create referent axis RII as that axis perpendicular to II'

Step 6: $\cos \theta = \phi_{I'II'}$

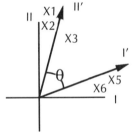

Results: Rotations were traditionally computed off the referent axes and then translated to the factor axes I' and II' to obtain:

Pattern loadings, which are the coordinates on I' and II'; parallel to the other axis (or the orthogonal) projections onto the referent axes).

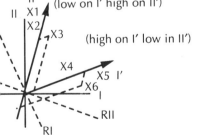

(low on I' high on II')

(high on I' low in II')

Structure coefficients, which are the projections (i.e. orthogonally) onto I' and II'. Note both groups of points will have high (or at least medium) values on both axes.

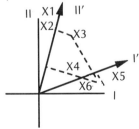

Figure 8.10 Graphical factor rotation

are correlated). Note that these new factors indeed represent an even cleaner, simpler structure than the orthogonal rotation (variables $x_1 - x_3$ would load highly on II' and *very near zero* on I', and the reverse would be true of $x_4 - x_6$).

Note also in that figure the angle θ between factors I' and II'. The cosine of the angle between I' and II' is the correlation between the two factors. (This fact is also true of orthogonal factors, for which the angle is 90 degrees, and the cosine of 90 degrees is 0; the correlation between the two factors is zero.) These factor intercorrelations are tabulated into the matrix Φ, where ϕ_{ij} represents the correlation between factors i and j.

The *coordinates* of the variables along factor axes I' and II' (with respect to – that is, parallel to – the axes II' and I') are the rotated factor loadings in **A**. **A** is also referred to as the factor pattern matrix. Alternatively, the factor loadings are also the result when the variables are projected (i.e. orthogonally) on to the referenct axes.

The (orthogonal) projections onto axes I' and II' are called the "structure coefficients". These coefficients are contained in the "factor structure matrix", Ψ, which is obtained by: $\Psi = \mathbf{A}\Phi$. Note that for an orthogonal rotation, $\Phi = \mathbf{I}$, so $\Psi = \mathbf{A}$. That is, for uncorrelated factors, the structure coefficients equal the pattern coefficients. In general, the pattern coefficients $\{a_{ij}\}$ are the coordinates (usually called loadings) of variable i on factor j, and the structure coefficients $\{\psi_{ij}\}$ are the correlations between variable i and factor j. It is the *factor loadings matrix* that is interpreted; the factor structure matrix also reflects the correlations between the factors, and so will not exhibit simple structure to the extent that the loadings matrix will (except, of course, for orthogonal factors).

Most researchers are studying constructs that are somewhat related, so it is very likely that their hypothetical factors would be correlated. Accordingly, one might expect that an oblique rotation would be more appropriate for truly describing the data than an orthogonal rotation. To decide between the two, an orthogonal and oblique rotation should be performed, and the ψ_{ij}'s examined. If *any* of these factor intercorrelations are substantial (e.g. greater than 0.3 in absolute magnitude), the oblique solution is preferred. On the other hand, if all the factor intercorrelations are near-zero, the orthogonal rotation might be the preferred, simply on the grounds of parsimony (i.e. it is a simpler model to have uncorrelated factors).

In this same spirit, the ψ_{ij}'s can also be diagnostic in another way. If all the factor intercorrelations from an oblique rotation are quite large (e.g. 0.8 or larger), one might have extracted too many factors, or one might consider performing a higher-order factor analysis, as described later in this chapter.

Objective algorithms – orthogonal and oblique Computer algorithms cannot quite perform graphical rotations, but factor analysts have developed other means of operationalizing Thurstone's simple structure criteria which are suitable for computer programming. Presented below are the two most frequently used algorithms, "VARIMAX" for orthogonal rotations, and "OBLIMIN" for oblique rotations.

If a factor pattern matrix shows simple structure upon rotation, the loadings on each factor would appear bimodal – there would be many loadings near zero, and several high loadings. A bimodal distribution has the maximum variance of any shaped distribution. Henry Kaiser used this logic in reverse – if we can maximize the variance of the loadings within each factor, that objective function should result in a factor pattern matrix that exhibits simple structure.

So we begin with the unrotated factor loadings (the eigenvectors rescaled by the square root of the corresponding eigenvalue). We note immediately that they can be positive or negative, and it is easier to maximize squared values than absolute values, so each element b_{ij} is squared. The variance, then, of these squared loadings for factor j would be:

$$\sigma_j^2 = \frac{1}{p} \sum_{i=1}^{p} (b_{ij}^2 - \overline{b_{ij}^2})^2$$

and the overall function that is maximized would be summed over all factors:

$$\sigma^2 = \frac{1}{p} \sum_{i=1}^{p} \sum_{j=1}^{r} (b_{ij}^2 - \overline{b_{ij}^2})^2. \qquad (8.14)$$

Thus, varimax *maximizes* this *variance* function.

In contrast, the oblique algorithm known as "direct oblimin" maximizes a covariance function.[12] For orthogonal rotations, there will be no covariability between factors – they are defined to be uncorrelated. For oblique rotations, the relationships between the factors must be considered. Specifically, the objective function for the oblique rotation is as follows:

$$D = \sum_{j=1}^{r} \sum_{k=1}^{r} \left[\sum_{i=1}^{p} b_{ij}^2 b_{ik}^2 - d \left(\sum_{i=1}^{p} b_{ij}^2 \sum_{i=1}^{p} b_{ik}^2 \right) / p \right] \qquad (8.15)$$

For varimax, the rotated factors are orthogonal, so the variance of each factor can be maximized separately. For oblique rotations, the resulting factors will be correlated, so the objective function involves the cross-products $((b_{ij}b_{ik})$ (which are the raw form of covariances or correlations) for each variable (i), on all pairs of factors (j and k).[13]

For these objective means of orthogonal and oblique factor rotations, the oblique rotation also yields the simpler structure. These algorithms may be best demonstrated through an example.

(I) The input correlation matrix:

	x1	x2	x3	x4	x5	x6	x7
X1 = courteous, prompt	1.000						
X2 = not arrogant, didn't talk down	.696	1.000					
X3 = seemed knowledgeable	.526	.664	1.000				
X4 = gave sound advice	.405	.523	.665	1.000			
X5 = advice sounded sensible to friend	.399	.522	.693	.612	1.000		
X6 = my case ended favorably	.419	.572	.530	.485	.520	1.000	
X7 = fees were reasonable	.464	.622	.582	.524	.558	.853	1.000

(II) The input correlation matrix:

Factor	eigenvalue
1	4.396
2	.775
3	.758
4	.389
5	.298
6	.240
7	.143

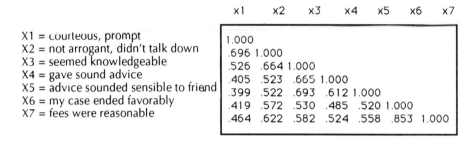

(II) The eigenvalues:

(III) The unrotated factor pattern matrix, and plots:

	I	II	III
x1	.652	.232	.361
x2	.819	.186	.330
x3	.824	.254	-.186
x4	.705	.148	-.248
x5	.735	.120	-.305
x6	.792	-.456	.024
x7	.840	-.411	.033

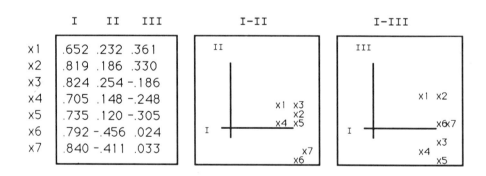

Figure 8.11 An example

(IV) Orthogonal rotation–loadings and plots:

	I	II	III
x1	.253	.202	.710
x2	.361	.332	.757
x3	.740	.252	.409
x4	.667	.268	.257
x5	.712	.305	.219
x6	.300	.826	.249
x7	.342	.818	.300

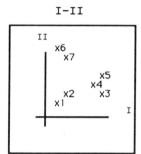

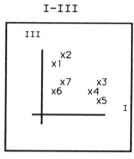

(V) Oblique rotation–loadings and plots (plotted as if orthogonal):

	I	II	III
x1	-.013	.013	.797
x2	.071	-.107	.781
x3	.802	.073	.176
x4	.751	-.018	-.003
x5	.819	-.058	-.082
x6	-.013	-.926	-.006
x7	.031	-.885	.047

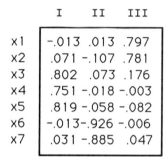

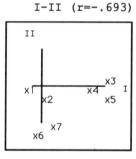

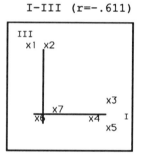

(VI) Oblique factor structure matrix, factor intercorrelation matrix, and communalities:

Factor structure coefficients

	I	II	III
x1	.530	-.465	.780
x2	.685	-.632	.895
x3	.873	-.591	.687
x4	.762	-.537	.529
x5	.802	-.575	.520
x6	.625	-.913	.550
x7	.677	-.935	.608

Factor intercorrelations

	I	II	III
I	1.000		
II	-.693	1.000	
III	.692	-.611	1.000

Communalities:

x1	.609
x2	.814
x3	.778
x4	.581
x5	.647
x6	.835
x7	.876

An example

Researchers studying services marketing often use the "relationship" between the service provider and consumer as a point of distinction from the traditional marketing of goods. Furthermore, the relationship is likely to be important in affecting customers' judgments of their overall satisfaction with the service encounter.

Consider, for example, the attorney–client relationship. In a series of ongoing exchanges, a client has many sources of information on which to base a judgment of satisfaction or dissatisfaction. Given the expected importance of their interpersonal relationship, we would include several indicator variables tapping this social psychological construct (e.g. "courteous, prompt, returned phone calls", "not arrogant, didn't talk down to me", etc.). We would certainly also expect that the rather objective "outcome" measures would be relevant to satisfaction (e.g. "did the client get off", "were the fees low", etc.). Another contributor to satisfaction may be more process than outcome, relating to the client's estimation of the goodness of the legal advice itself (e.g. "seemed knowledgeable", "advice sounded good to friends", etc.).

Figure 8.11 contains a correlation matrix for data on such measures. (The items are listed next to the correlation matrix.) The correlation matrix was adjusted using SMC's and the eigenvalue–eigenvector decomposition obtained. The eigenvalues are listed and plotted in the second panel of Figure 8.11. Three factors were retained, given the break in the scree plot curve.[14]

The third panel in Figure 8.11 contains the matrix of unrotated factor loadings, and the plots of the I–II and I–III planes. The results of the orthogonal rotations are presented in panel IV of the figure, and they indeed display simpler structure than the unrotated factors. However, simpler structure still is obtained via the oblique rotations, presented in panel V. The near-zero loadings are *very* near-zero, making it clear that Factor I is x_3, x_4, and x_5 (i.e. satisfaction with the core of the service), Factor II is defined by x_6 and x_7 (i.e. the outcome measures), and Factor III is x_1 and x_2 (i.e. the interpersonal characteristics).

The order of the factors carries no substantive meaning. The earlier factors are simply those that have more variables loading on it, and/or those that have higher loadings. It does not mean that the interpersonal factor is less important (and there is *no* information with regard to the three factors' predictability of satisfaction). It means only that of the p original variables included in the study, fewer of them tapped this construct, and/or those measures were not clear indicators of the construct.

The structure coefficients are also presented in Figure 8.11, and note they are *not* the "loadings" to interpret, nor do they display simple structure. The factor intercorrelations are all substantial, indicating that while theoretically it seems worthwhile to separate these three factors, perhaps they are all themselves driven by some over-riding grand "satisfaction" factor. Finally, the estimates of the h_j^2's (communalities) are also presented in Figure 8.11. They are all fairly large, indicating at least some covariability for each measure. At this point, the basic introduction to factor analysis is complete. In the following section, several more advanced issues are presented.

Advanced topics

Higher order factor analysis A standard factor analysis is conducted on a $p \times p$ matrix of the correlations between variables. A "higher order" factor analysis is one that is fit to the $r \times r$ matrix of *factor* intercorrelations, which results from an oblique rotation on the original p variables. Just as the previous example demonstrated, the eigenvalues of $\mathbf{R}_{\text{SMC}}$ might suggest r factors, which then turn out to be rather highly correlated themselves. High intercorrelations among factors may be indicative of having extracted too many factors. However, as in the customer satisfaction data, the original three factors were each clearly interpretable, and theoretically meaningful. Extracting only a single factor would have yielded some "satisfaction" factor on which would have loaded each variable to some greater or lesser extent. Higher order factor analyses allow researchers to have the best of both worlds – the original three satisfaction factors inform us as to the subtle differences between sources of satisfaction, and yet the higher order construct is simply, satisfaction.

Recall the factor analytic model is $\mathbf{R} = \mathbf{B\Phi B'} + \mathbf{D}^2$. In higher order factor analysis, we proceed to "factor" the $\mathbf{\Phi}$ matrix: $\mathbf{\Phi} = \mathbf{B}_2\mathbf{\Phi}_2\mathbf{B}_2' + \mathbf{D}_2^2$, or $\mathbf{R} = \mathbf{B}(\mathbf{B}_2\mathbf{\Phi}_2\mathbf{B}_2' + \mathbf{D}_2^2)\mathbf{B'} + \mathbf{D}^2$. This hierarchical logic may theoretically be continued ad infinitum. However, in practice, rarely is p so large to allow the extraction of r factors, where r is large enough to continue factoring. For example, if $p = 40$ and $r = 5$, a second order factor analysis may be fit, but a third order factor analysis would be unlikely, and if $p = 10$ and $r = 2$, it would not be sensible to even conduct the second order factor analysis.

Figure 8.12 contains an example from Jones and Iacobucci (1989) in which a sample of college students rated each of 15 politicians on 10 affect scales (e.g. "How often has he made you feel angry"), and 17 trait scales (e.g. "To what extent do you agree that he is intelligent"). The signs of the large loadings (i.e. $\geqslant 0.3$) are presented in the $p = 27 \times r = 4$ loadings matrix for the first order factor analysis. The matrix $\mathbf{\Phi}$ is $r \times r$ and clearly indicates the presence of some higher order construct. Four factors cannot support a large number of higher order factors, but one seemed sufficient. Not surprisingly, the loadings of the second order factor analysis indicate a simple halo, evaluative judgment – respondents either liked the politician or they did not. However, just to reiterate, while the four factors are related and can be described most simply by a single overarching factor, the first set of four factors allowed more detailed insight into the parts of the whole.

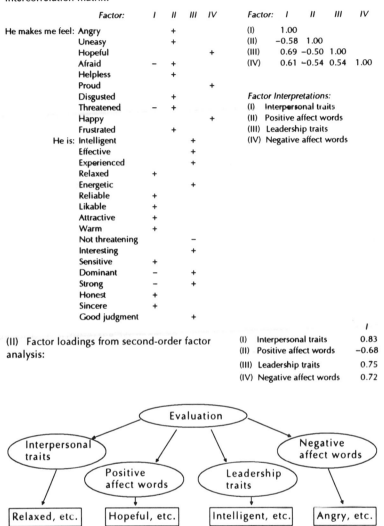

(I) Direction of large loadings from first-order factor analysis and factor intercorrelation matrix:

	Factor:	I	II	III	IV		Factor:	I	II	III	IV
He makes me feel:	Angry		+			(I)	1.00				
	Uneasy		+			(II)	−0.58	1.00			
	Hopeful			+		(III)	0.69	−0.50	1.00		
	Afraid	−	+			(IV)	0.61	−0.54	0.54	1.00	
	Helpless		+								
	Proud				+	Factor Interpretations:					
	Disgusted		+			(I) Interpersonal traits					
	Threatened	−	+			(II) Positive affect words					
	Happy				+	(III) Leadership traits					
	Frustrated		+			(IV) Negative affect words					
He is:	Intelligent			+							
	Effective			+							
	Experienced			+							
	Relaxed	+									
	Energetic			+							
	Reliable	+									
	Likable	+									
	Attractive	+									
	Warm	+									
	Not threatening	−									
	Interesting			+							
	Sensitive	+									
	Dominant	−		+							
	Strong	−		+							
	Honest	+									
	Sincere	+									
	Good judgment			+							

(II) Factor loadings from second-order factor analysis:

	I
(I) Interpersonal traits	0.83
(II) Positive affect words	−0.68
(III) Leadership traits	0.75
(IV) Negative affect words	0.72

Figure 8.12 Example of a higher-order factor analysis

Maximum likelihood estimation, exploratory vs. confirmatory factor analysis, and structural equations modeling Early in the factor analytic tradition, statisticians derived the maximum likelihood estimates for parameters like the factor pattern loadings (cf. Lawley and Maxwell, 1971). The analytics were important, but the computational details were also required, and these were developed by Joreskog (1967, 1969). Many sources provide further information on the basics of maximum likelihood estimation in general (e.g. Hogg and Tanis, 1977), and its application to factor analysis in particular (e.g. Harman, 1976, pp. 197–206; Lawley and Maxwell, 1971). Here we note simply the advantages of this approach to factor extraction.

The major advantage to this statistical approach to factor analysis is that hypotheses may be tested. That is, with the assumption of multinormality and the machinery of maximum likelihood estimation, statistical significance tests are possible. Hypotheses may concern factor loadings (b_{ij}'s), but probably the most useful hypotheses to test are those concerning "r". That is, we can examine whether extracting r factors provides a significantly better fit to the data than $r-1$ factors had.

The ability to test hypotheses allows the researcher to go beyond "exploratory", descriptive statistics, to "confirmatory", inferential statistics. For factor analysis, exploratory and confirmatory approaches to data modeling might best be thought of as existing on a continuum (see Cliff, 1987). At one end, in strictly exploratory factor analysis, the researcher does not know r (the number of factors), or the b_{ij}'s (the factor loadings). More confirmatory would be a factor analysis for which the researcher might have some prior expectation regarding r, but not regarding the loadings. Even more confirmatory would be having a hypothesis to test about r, and also specifying which variables should load on which factors (and conversely, where the zero elements should be in **A**).[15] Finally, the most strictly confirmatory analysis would require the specification of r and the value of each b_{ij}, as in, perhaps, a cross-validation study.

The maximum likelihood estimation of factor loadings is also critically important to researchers working within LISREL-like model-fitting frameworks. Structural equations modeling is comprised of a "structural" part (i.e. a path analysis, positing plausible "causal" paths from one variable to another) and a "measurement" part (which determines the loadings of the indicator variables on the hypothetical constructs, or factors), both of which are fit simultaneously, often using the maximum likelihood estimation criterion. Many sources are available for further information on structural equations modeling, including the chapters by Bagozzi and Fornell in this volume, and elsewhere, such as Bagozzi and Yi (1989), Bentler (1980), Browne (1982), Joreskog and Sorbom (1986), and McDonald (1985).

Q-factor analysis and multi-mode factor analysis The typical focus of factor analysis is in the structure that can be used to describe the relationships among variables, and respondents are simply observations over which to aggregate in order to obtain good estimates of the r_{ij}'s. Long ago, researchers considered that in addition to factor analyzing an **X'X** matrix, one could also factor analyze an **XX'** matrix, which would be essentially the correlations among the respondents, aggregating over the variables. This approach became known as "Q-analysis". The theoretical defense behind this transposition of the analytical problem was that just as in standard factor analysis, for which a factor might represent a construct – a purer version of its indicator variables – perhaps too, a factor in Q-factor analysis might represent an "idealized" type of respondent (e.g. a "verbal" person, and a "quantitative" person).

However intriguing, this method has at least two major challenges. First, a typical factor analysis proceeds by rotating to simple structure. It is not clear whether this goal is appropriate for individuals (e.g. most of us are somewhat verbal *and* somewhat quantitative). Furthermore, particularly for maximum likelihood estimation, statistical models typically assume independence between the units over which are aggregated. For Q-factor analysis, those units are the – probably correlated – variables.

Even more exciting is the work on "multi-mode factor analysis", developed by Ledyard Tucker (cf. Tucker, 1966; Lastovicka, 1981). This work began by considering three-dimensional data matrices. For example, a sample of respondents ($i = 1, 2, \ldots, n$) might give their responses on a number of scales ($j = 1, 2, \ldots, p$) to each of several stimuli ($k = 1, 2, \ldots K$) (or at several points in time, etc.). A correlation matrix among the p variables would be obtained by aggregating over i and k. Analogously, we could obtain the correlation matrix among the n respondents, and among the K stimuli. Each of these three matrices are factored for a much richer understanding of the data. In addition, Tucker derived the "core matrix", whose elements relate the variable factors to the respondent factors to the stimuli factors. (Jones and Iacobucci (1989) provide an example of a three-mode factor analysis.)[16]

Sample size Most researchers recognize that the estimation of factor loadings and the number of common factors would be more precise with large sample sizes, but the question is, "how large is large?" Some researchers have offered suggestions such as, "n must be at least 100". Others have offered recommendations regarding the ratio of n to p, such as 5 : 1 or 10 : 1. In the maximum likelihood estimation procedures, sample size is especially important, given that the distribution assumptions are based on asymptotic theory.

Recent work by MacCallum, Widaman, and Lee (1989) criticizes these rules of thumb for being simplistic – the rules are constant, not varying with any properties of the variables or factors. These researchers examined factor recovery for simulated population correlation matrices with known factor properties on sample sizes of 40, 100, 200, and 400. They manipulated several other properties: the number of common factors (3, 7); the values of the communalities (0.6–0.8, 0.2–0.8, 0.2–0.4); and the number of variables (10, 20). They found that: larger samples performed better than smaller ones, recovery was better with greater overdetermination (e.g. $p : r$ of 20 : 3 was better than 20 : 7), high communalities lent clearer results; and the two-way interactions were also significant (e.g. $n = 400$ with high communalities did even better than $n = 40$ with high communalities, etc.). However, their research also indicated several conditions for which $n = 40$ may be sufficient. For example, $n = 40$ was nearly as good as $n = 400$ when $p : r$ was 10 : 3 or 20 : 3 and the communalities were high.

Thus, the answer to the question, "how many subjects" is not so simple as a pat response. Rather, smaller samples will suffice if the factor pattern is relatively clear and many data points exist from another source (i.e. not necessarily more subjects, but more variables per factor). On the other hand, not surprisingly, larger samples are required when the "signal to noise" ratio is weaker, and the additional data points would be helpful in clarifying the factorial structure.

Number of variables A geometric figure of n-dimensions can be defined with $n + 1$ points (e.g. a line with 2 points, a plane with 1 point and a line, and so on). The points in factor space are from errorful data, so more confidence would be placed in the definition of a factor if it were "overdetermined"; i.e. had large loadings for many more variables than the minimal required geometrically.

Mathematically, the number of data points must exceed (hopefully by a large margin) the number of parameters that must be estimated. We begin with an $n \times p$ data matrix **X**, but we immediately aggregate over the n subjects to obtain an $n \times n$ matrix **R**. Thus, we begin with $p(p - 1)/2$ data points. The number of parameters we estimate in the factor model is $pr - r(r - 1)/2$. (**B** has pr elements, but any **B** can be transformed to have $r(r - 1)/2$ zero elements.) Thus, $p(p - 1)/2$ must exceed $pr - r(r - 1)/2$. This equation can be solved for the minimum value of p: $p \geq \{(2r + 1) + \sqrt{(8r + 1)}\}/2$. Thus, to extract one factor, at least 3 variables are necessary; for $r = 2$, p must be at least 5; for $r = 5$, p must be at least 9, and so forth.

There are factor analytical researchers who are even more conservative, stating that best estimates for factor loadings are obtained when p is at least 3 or 4 times the number of factors, r. By this rule, $r = 1$ would require 3–4 variables. For $r = 2$, p would need to be 6–8; for $r = 5$, p would need to be 15–20, and so on.

Binary data While Pearson product-moment correlation coefficients may be computed on binary data (i.e. resulting in "phi" coefficients) it is generally not recommended to conduct a factor analysis on binary variables. The binary nature of the data restricts the magnitudes of the correlation coefficients, and typical assumptions (e.g. linearity, normality) are not strongly defensible. Researchers have investigated how to strengthen the applicability of factor analysis to binary data (cf. Christoffersson (1975) and Muthen (1978)). Recently, a simulation study by Collins, Cliff, McCormick and Zatkin (1986) found that the use of phi coefficients could not reliably produce the "known" number of factors (r), but if r was correctly selected, the loadings were fairly well-recovered.

Summary

This chapter was intended to introduce the major concepts of the classic factor analytical model and present, at least briefly, some related issues. There are many excellent references for further reading, both at the introductory level, such as the pair of volumes by Kim and Mueller (1978a; 1978b), and Cliff (1987) and Green (1978), and also at more advanced levels, such as Comrey and Lee (1992), Harman (1976), McDonald (1985), and Mulaik (1972).[17]

Appendix 8A: SAS and SPSSX commands for factor analyses

(A.1) SAS commands, if you read in an $n \times p$ data set:
DATA MINE;
INPUT x1 x2 x3 x4 x5 x6 x7; CARDS;
– data go here –
PROC FACTOR METHOD = ML PRIORS = SMC NFACTORS = 3
ROTATE = VARIMAX;
PROC FACTOR METHOD = ML PRIORS = SMC NFACTORS = 3
ROTATE = PROMAX;
*to obtain iterated principal factors, replace METHOD = ML with METHOD = PRINIT. to obtain principal components, replace METHOD = ML with METHOD = PRINCIPAL, and PRIORS = SMC with PRIORS = ONE;

(A.2) SAS commands, if you read in a correlation matrix:
DATA CORREL (TYPE = CORR);
TYPE = 'CORR'; INPUT x1 x2 x3 x4 x5 x6 x7; CARDS;

```
1.0000   .        .        .        .        .        .
0.6961   1.0000   .        .        .        .        .
0.5256   0.6639   1.0000   .        .        .        .
0.4054   0.5232   0.6646   1.0000   .        .        .
0.3991   0.5216   0.6927   0.6119   1.0000   .        .
0.4189   0.5716   0.5305   0.4849   0.5202   1.0000   .
0.4639   0.6225   0.5824   0.5235   0.5576   0.8531   1.0000
;
```

PROC FACTOR METHOD = ML PRIORS = SMC NFACTORS = 3
ROTATE = VARIMAX;
PROC FACTOR METHOD = ML PRIORS = SMC NFACTORS = 3
ROTATE = PROMAX;
*to obtain iterated principal factors, replace METHOD = ML with METHOD = PRINIT. to obtain principal components, replace METHOD = ML with METHOD = PRINCIPAL, and PRIORS = SMC with PRIORS = ONE;

(A.3) SPSSX commands, if you read in an $n \times p$ data set:
FILE HANDLE XX / NAME = 'my data a'
TITLE 'factor analysis on the example data analyzed in this chapter'
DATA VARIABLES = x1 x2 x3 x4 x5 x6 x7
BEGIN DATA

```
-data go here-
END DATA
FACTOR
  /CRITERIA = FACTORS (3)
  /PRINT = ALL
  /EXTRACTION = PAF
  /ROTATION = NOROTATE
  /PLOT = ROTATION (1, 2) (1, 3) (2, 3)
  /ROTATION = VARIMAX
  /PLOT = ROTATE (1, 2) (1, 3) (2, 3)
  /ROTATION = OBLIMIN
  /PLOT = ROTATE (1, 2) (1, 3) (2, 3)
COMMENT   to obtain maximum likelihood estimates, replace
COMMENT   EXTRACTION = PAF with EXTRACTION = ML. to
COMMENT   obtain principal components, replace EXTRACTION =
COMMENT   PAF with EXTRACTION = PC
```

(A.4) SPSSX commands, if you read in a correlation matrix:
```
FILE HANDLE XX / NAME = 'temp out a'
TITLE 'factor analysis on the example data analyzed in this chapter'
MATRIX DATA VARIABLES = x1 x2 x3 x4 x5 x6 x7
/FORMAT = FREE
/CONTENTS = N CORR
BEGIN DATA
    100     100     100     100     100     100     100
    1.0000
    0.6961  1.0000
    0.5256  0.6639  1.0000
    0.4054  0.5232  0.6646  1.0000
    0.3991  0.5216  0.6927  0.6119  1.0000
    0.4189  0.5716  0.5305  0.4849  0.5202  1.0000
    0.4639  0.6225  0.5824  0.5235  0.5576  0.8531  1.0000
END DATA
SAVE OUTFILE XX
FACTOR MATRIX IN (COR = XX)
  /CRITERIA = FACTORS (3)
  /PRINT = ALL
  /EXTRACTION = PAF
  /ROTATION = NOROTATE
  /PLOT = ROTATION (1, 2) (1, 3) (2, 3)
  /ROTATION = VARIMAX
  /PLOT = ROTATE (1, 2) (1, 3) (2, 3)
  /ROTATION = OBLIMIN
  /PLOT = ROTATE (1, 2) (1, 3) (2, 3)
COMMENT   to obtain maximum likelihood estimates, replace
```

COMMENT EXTRACTION = PAF with EXTRACTION = ML. to
COMMENT obtain principal components, replace EXTRACTION =
COMMENT PAF with EXTRACTION = PC

Questions

1 The following exercise is adapted from Harman (1976; pp. 392–4). Complete the following table:

Variance source	Variable:	×1	×2	×3	×4	×5	×6	×7	×8
specificity		0.10	0.15	0.20	0.25	—	—	—	—
error variance		0.20	—	—	—	0.05	0.10	—	—
communality		—	0.75	—	—	0.60	—	0.50	—
uniqueness		—	—	0.35	—	—	0.45	—	0.30
reliability		—	—	—	0.85	—	—	0.75	0.90

2 Use the following factor pattern matrix to answer the next questions.

$$B = \begin{matrix} 0.7 & 0.3 \\ 0.8 & 0.0 \\ 0.7 & 0.0 \\ 0.8 & 0.6 \\ 0.6 & 0.5 \\ 0.5 & 0.0 \\ 0.6 & 0.4 \\ 0.7 & 0.6 \end{matrix}$$

(a) Compute the communality of x_8.
(b) Calculate the uniqueness of x_1.
(c) Estimate $\hat{r}_{12}$, $\hat{r}_{14}$, and $\hat{r}_{26}$.
(d) Plot the variables in this two-factor space.
(e) Will an orthogonal or oblique rotation be more useful for these data?

3 Create a rotated factor pattern matrix that does *not* exhibit simple structure. Use any number of variables and any number of factors. Use 0's and any arbitrary real numbers for the non-zero elements. Explain which of Thurstone's five criteria have been violated with the pattern created.

Notes

I am grateful to Northwestern University's Marketing Department and to the National Science Foundation (Grant #SES-9023445) for research support, and to an anonymous reviewer for comments on the chapter. I also think Rick Bagozzi is a peach of a guy for soliciting two chapters from me to include in this fine volume. This chapter is respectfully and fondly dedicated to Dr Ledyard Tucker

CLASSIC FACTOR ANALYSIS 313

as a small token of appreciation – Tuck, may you have many more years of happy rotations.

1. 36 is too small a sample to be publishable today!
2. One of Thurstone's most important students, Ledyard Tucker, has told his classes for generations that in those days, it took weeks to invert a single matrix by several persons, each of whom was working on a large adding machine. Furthermore, in those days, it was the men working at the machines who were refered to as the "compute-ers".
3. Perhaps not unlike the current status of LISREL today.
4. Excellent primers on matrix algebra include Green (1976), Kirk (1982; pp. 778–805), and Morrison (1976; pp. 37–78).
5. If all λ's are > 0, the matrix $\mathbf{R}$ is said to be "positive definite". If some λ's equal 0, the matrix is said to be "positive semidefinite". The rank of a matrix is the number of its nonzero eigenvalues.
6. Finally, consider yet another alternative analytical explanation of eigenvalues and eigenvectors. When one matrix is multiplied by another, one is being linearly transformed, and the other is providing the weights defining that linear transformation. The equation $\mathbf{R}\mathbf{a} = \mathbf{a}\lambda$ tells us that when we multiply the matrix $\mathbf{R}$ by an eigenvector, we get the eigenvector again, but it has been stretched or shrunk by multiplication of a constant, λ, the eigenvalue. Thus, we have begun with data plotted anywhere in a p-dimensional space, and the eigen-solution constrains a transformation to be in the same direction as the original data, but simply increases or decreases the data vector's length. Note too, that in the spirit of our original goal of trying to capture the essence of our p variables using a single linear composite, the $\mathbf{R}\mathbf{a} = \mathbf{a}\lambda$ equation indicates that the information contained in the *matrix* $\mathbf{R}$ is being modeled by a single *number*, λ.
7. This property is one that made statisticians nervous about factor analysis for decades. Factor analysis became slightly more acceptable to them when one of their own (as opposed to a quantitative psychologist) derived the maximum likelihood estimation model for the factor model parameters. Factor analysis has become even more acceptable in the last ten years by statisticians and even econometricians, by using the term "latent variables", rather than "underlying factors" or "unobservable constructs".
8. The factors carry the following assumptions: (1) U_j's are assumed to be mutually uncorrelated (otherwise they would provide a "common" source of variability); (2) The U_j's are assumed to be uncorrelated with the F_j's; (3) The S_j's and E_j's are all uncorrelated; and (4) when the F_j's are first derived, they will be mutually uncorrelated (but they may be transformed later to be correlated). Thus, a common misconception regarding factor analysis is that it is a means of reducing p variables to a smaller number of factors. It is true that the factor analytical model results in a smaller number of *common* factors, and these are indeed the factors of greatest interest to the researcher, but the model actually produces r common factors *and* p unique factors from the $p \times p$ correlation matrix.
9. The matrix $\mathbf{R}_{SMC}$ is reduced in rank (rank($\mathbf{R}_{SMC}$) < rank($\mathbf{R}$)), so the smaller eigenvalues of $\mathbf{R}_{SMC}$ will be negative. If a "canned" program is not being used to derive the factors, this adjustment can be performed in a matrix manipulator instead. The steps from $\mathbf{R}$ to $\mathbf{R}_{SMC}$ are as follows: First, obtain $\mathbf{R}^{-1}$. Second, create a diagonal matrix from $\mathbf{R}^{-1}$, diag($\mathbf{R}^{-1}$). Third, take the inverse of that matrix, $\mathbf{S}_e^2 = (\text{diag}(\mathbf{R}^{-1}))^{-1}$. Fourth, subtract this matrix from $\mathbf{R}$: $\mathbf{R} - \mathbf{S}_e^2 = \mathbf{R}_{SMC}$.

The off-diagonal elements of this matrix will remain untouched, but the diagonals will contain the SMCs: $R^2_{x1.x2,x3,...,xp}$, $R^2_{x2.x1,x3,...,xp}$, etc. SMCs are interpretable as the variance in x_j accounted for by all the other variables, so they serve as an ideal estimate of a communality. Furthermore, they range from 0 to 1, so the relationship $1 = h_j^2 + d_j^2$ can hold. (Occasionally in more complicated modeling, such as LISREL, one can obtain estimates of common *variance* that are negative, or larger than one (which would imply the uniqueness *variance* is negative – this is called a "Heywood case"). Both are nonsensical because variances must be greater than or equal to zero.)

10 This factor extraction technique can be modified to an iterative procedure, so that we start with $\hat{\mathbf{H}}^2 = \mathrm{diag}(\mathbf{R}_{SMC})$, and compute $\mathbf{B}$, then re-estimate $\hat{\mathbf{H}}^2 = \mathrm{diag}(\mathbf{BB'})$, then re-compute $\mathbf{B}$, and so on, until changes are minimal. Some researchers argue the iterations improve the estimates; others argue the iterations overfit the data for an exploratory data analytical technique. The iterative procedure, along with the maximum likelihood estimation procedures housed in programs such as LISREL are perhaps the two most popular techniques in use today. The popularity of the iterative procedure is probably due to the widespread use of SPSSX as a statistical computing package.

11 In doing so, we enter a very interesting world of a nonstandard geometry, in which dimensions are not necessarily at right angles with each other. This theoretical concept is no more of a logical leap than that of considering four or more dimensions, even though it is difficult to represent such complexities.

12 While the direct oblimin procedure is probably the most frequently used method for oblique rotation, simulations have shown it does not perform nearly as well as "PROMAX", the method of oblique rotation available in SAS (Tucker, personal communication). PROMAX is a simple method in which the factor loadings resulting from an orthogonal rotation are raised to a power (2 works well) so the large loadings get a little smaller, but the small and medium-sized loadings get *very* small – yielding clearer, simpler structure.

13 The argument d controls the degree to which the factors will be correlated. SPSSX uses a default of zero.

14 In data, there is almost always a huge break between λ_1 and λ_2, and then lesser breaks between subsequent λ's, but frequently more than one factor is required to understand the data. However, as these data will indicate, the three factors are indeed highly correlated.

15 This case had a logical predecessor called "Procrustes rotations", which is a method whereby the sample factor loadings matrix is rotated to match as best as possible a "target" factor structure.

16 One application of the multi-mode conceptualization has been to the "multi-trait, multi-method" matrices, as presented by Campbell and Fiske (1959). LISREL-like models have also been extremely helpful in fitting such models.

17 However, be wary of references on factor analysis by writers who were self-taught, or who work in disciplines that cannot appreciate the richness of measurement theory and behavioral data.

References

Allen, M. J. and Yen, Wendy M. 1979: *Introduction to Measurement Theory*, Monterey, CA: Brooks/Cole.

Anastasi, Anne 1982: *Psychological Testing*, 5th edn, New York: Macmillan.
Bagozzi, Richard P. and Yi, Youjae 1989: On the use of structural equation models in experimental design. *Journal of Marketing Research*, 26, 271–84.
Bentler, Peter M. 1980: Multivariate analysis with latent variables: causal analysis. *Annual Review of Psychology*, 31, 419–56.
Browne, Michael 1982: Covariance structures. In D. M. Hawkins (ed.), *Topics in Applied Multivariate Analysis*, London: Cambridge University Press, pp. 72–141.
Campbell, Donald T. and Fiske, D. W. 1959: Convergent and discriminant validation by the multitrait–multimethod matrix. *Psychological Bulletin*, 56, 86–105.
Christoffersson, Anders 1975: Factor analysis of dichotomized variables. *Psychometrika*, 40, 5–32.
Cliff, Norman 1987: *Analyzing Multivariate Data*, San Diego: Harcourt Brace Jovanovich.
Cliff, Norman 1988: The eigenvalues-greater-than-one rule and the reliability of components. *Psychological Bulletin*, 103, 276–9.
Collins, Linda, Cliff, Norman, McCormick, Douglas, and Zatkin, Judith L. 1986: Factor recovery with binary data sets: a simulation. *Multivariate Behavioral Research*, 21, 377–91.
Comrey, Andrew L. and Lee, Howard B. 1992: *A First Course in Factor Analysis*, 2nd edn, Hillsdale, NJ: Erlbaum.
Ghiselli, Edwin E., Campbell, John P., and Zedeck, Sheldon 1981: *Measurement Theory for the Behavioral Sciences*, San Francisco: Freeman.
Green, Paul E. 1978: *Analyzing Multivariate Data*, Hinsdale, IL: Dryden.
Green, Paul E. 1976: *Mathematical Tools for Applied Multivariate Analysis*, New York: Academic Press.
Harman, Harry H. 1976: *Modern Factor Analysis*, Chicago: The University of Chicago Press.
Hogg, Robert V., and Tanis, Elliot A. 1977: *Probability and Statistical Inference*, New York: Macmillan.
Humphreys, Lloyd, and Ilgen, D. R. 1969: Note on a criterion for the number of common factors, *Educational and Psychological Measurement*, 29, 571–8.
Jones, Lawrence, and Iacobucci, Dawn 1989: The structure of affect and trait judgments of political figures, *Multivariate Behavioral Research*, 24, 457–76.
Joreskog, K. G. 1967: Some contributions to maximum likelihood factor analysis: *Psychometrika*, 32, 443–82.
Joreskog, K. G. 1969: A general approach to confirmatory maximum likelihood factor analysis: *Psychometrika*, 34, 183–202.
Joreskog, Karl G. and Sorbom, Dag 1986: *LISREL VI*, Mooresville, IN: Scientific Software.
Kim, J., and Mueller, C. W. 1978a: *Introduction to Factor Analysis: What It Is and How to Do it*, Beverly Hills, CA: Sage.
Kim, J., and Mueller, C. W. 1978b: *Factor Analysis: Statistical Methods and Practical Issues*, Beverly Hills, CA: Sage.
Kirk, Roger E. 1982: *Experimental Design: Procedures for the Behavioral Sciences*, 2nd edn, Belmont, CA: Brooks/Cole.
Lastovicka, John 1981: The extensions of components analysis to four-mode matrices: *Psychometrika*, 46, 47–57.
Lawley, D. N. and Maxwell, A. E. 1971: *Factor Analysis as a Statistical Method*, New York: America Elsevier.

MacCallum, Robert C., Widaman, Keith F., and Lee, Soonmook 1989: Sample size in exploratory factor analysis. Manuscript at Ohio State University.

McDonald, Roderick 1985: *Factor Analysis and Related Methods*, Hillsdale, NJ: Erlbaum.

Montanelli, Jr., Richard G. and Humphreys, Lloyd G. 1976: Latent roots of random data correlation matrices with squared multiple correlations on the diagonal: a Monte Carlo study: *Psychometrika*, 41, 341–8.

Morrison, D. F. 1976: *Multivariate Statistical Methods*, 2nd edn, New York: McGraw-Hill.

Mulaik, Stanley A. 1972: *The Foundations of Factor Analysis*, New York: McGraw-Hill.

Muthen, Bengt 1978: Contributions to factor analysis of dichotomous variables: *Psychometrika*, 43, 551–60.

Snook, Steven C. and Gorsuch, Richard L. 1989: Component analysis versus common factor analysis: a Monte Carlo study: *Psychological Bulletin*, 106, 148–54.

Thurstone, L. L. 1947: *Multiple Factor Analysis*, Chicago: University of Chicago Press.

Tucker, Ledyard 1966: Some mathematical notes on three-mode factor analysis: *Psychometrika*, 31, 279–311.

Velicer, W. F., Peacock, A. C., and Jackson, D. N. 1982: A comparison of component and factor patterns: a Monte Carlo approach: *Multivariate Behavioral Research*, 17, 371–88.

9

Structural Equation Models in Marketing Research: Basic Principles

Richard P. Bagozzi

Introduction

Structural equation models (SEMs) are vehicles for bringing together the parts of the research enterprise in a holistic way. A full SEM specifies the key variables in any theory as latent constructs and represents the hypotheses among variables in a network of causal or functional paths. The observational content of the variables in the theory is captured through direct and indirect relationships to measurements, which are also part of the specification that comprises a SEM.

Overall, a SEM can be thought of as a methodology in its broadest sense in that its successful execution requires "forming concepts and hypotheses, making observations and measurements, performing experiments, building models and theories, providing explanations, and making predictions" (Kaplan, 1964, p. 32). If one had to characterize the general philosophy of SEMs in an ideal way, the term "theoretical empiricism" would be apt because of the need to emphasize the integration of theory with method and observations. Theoretical empiricism can be contrasted to other approaches such as raw empiricism, logical positivism, relativism, and instrumentalism. The basis for theoretical empiricism lies in scientific realism, although it shares some aspects with logical empiricism and relativism (Bagozzi, 1980a, 1984; Hunt 1991). Talcott Parsons captures the spirit of theoretical empiricism as currently practised: "science is not common sense, and its most basic theoretical ideas and frames of reference require development through complex intellectual processes which involve not only interpretations of observation but also theoretical and partly philosophical conceptualization."

In this chapter, we will consider a number of basic principles in the use of SEMs. We begin with a presentation of the underlying structure of SEMs and its philosophy of science foundations. The reader may wish to review the beginning of Chapter 1 on measurement issues in order to gain perspective. Next we turn to a series of uses of SEMs that are implied by its philosophy of science underpinnings. Reliability is the first topic in this regard followed by discussions of reflective versus formative indicators, multidimensional constructs, construct validity, and the role of SEMs in explanation, prediction, and control, three fundamental goals in basic and applied science. Our treatment of the latter goals focuses upon the use of SEMs in tests of hypotheses concerning mediating variables, moderating variables, comparisons across groups, and reciprocal causation.

The Structure of Theory and SEMs

Science might be viewed as an attempt to make sense of the past, present, and future. This is done by searching for meaning, and theories and their tests provide an important way to accomplish this. In general, there are three types of meaning inherent in the representation of any theory: conceptual meaning, empirical meaning, and spurious meaning. Together, the three types of meaning combine in an integrated way in SEMs to form the basis for theory construction and its use in explanation, prediction, and control.

Figure 9.1 summarizes the three types of meaning and is a modification of one appearing in Bagozzi (1984a). We turn to a brief description of each.

Conceptual meaning

To grasp the idea of conceptual meaning, consider the focal concept F shown at the top center of Figure 9.1. In general, the conceptual meaning

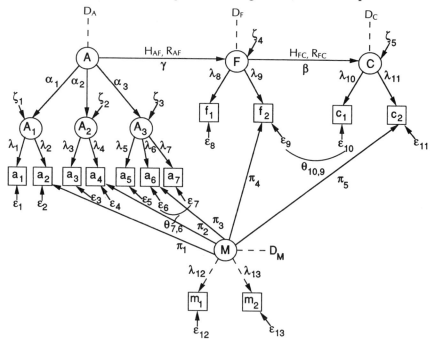

Figure 9.1 The elements and structure of the holistic construal

of F is obtained through a specification of (1) its definition, or more broadly what it is, and (2) its relation to other concepts in a larger theoretical network, that is, its relation to A and C. Notice that the meaning of F depends in part on other concepts in the theory.

The definition of a concept is a linguistic operation(s) that establishes a relationship(s) between a focal term and one or more other terms. Although the relationship(s) might be one of equivalence or identity, it may also be one of refinement, expansion, or partial specification. Typically, three types of definitions can be seen to contribute to the conceptual meaning of a theoretical concept: attributional, structural, or dispositional definitions. It is beyond the scope of this chapter to explore these definitions, but a fuller treatment with examples can be found in Bagozzi (1984a, pp. 20–1). The important point to note is that part of the conceptual meaning of any concept is given through the semantic content of the terms in the definition of the concept and the syntatic significance of their organization and relation to the definiendum (i.e. the focal concept). It is important to stress that this aspect of conceptual meaning is distinct from empirical and spurious meaning and from the other sources of conceptual meaning discussed below.

In addition to its definition, the conceptual meaning of a focal concept F is obtained through specification of (1) the antecedents, determinants, or causes of F, (2) the consequences, implications, or results of F, and (3) the associative (i.e. nonfunctional, noncausal) links to F. We briefly consider these.

As shown in Figure 9.1, some conceptual meaning of F arises through its antecedents. Whereas a definition specifies what a concept is and what it is capable of becoming and doing, its antecedents supply information as to where it has been (that is, its history and development) and/or how it is formed or influenced. The meaning is supplied through the content of the hypothesis (H_{AF}) linking A to F and its rationale (R_{AF}). The content of H_{AF} consists of a statement of the nature of the relationship of A to F and is expressed in proposition form. This might entail a relatively nonspecific statement such as "the greater the magnitude or level of A, the less the magnitude or level of F," or it might entail a more specific statement as to the functional form of the relationship or even the amount of change expected in F as a function of A. The rationale for the hypothesis is needed to complete the meaning of F provided by A. In general, a rationale for a hypothesis can be obtained through specification of the mechanism by which A influences F. Typically, this will be expressed through theoretical laws and an explication of how A produces change in F (e.g. a causal explanation).

In a parallel fashion, the meaning of F is also determined through its relations to consequences C (see Figure 9.1). That is, the implications of F supply information as to where a phenomenon is going, what it can lead to, and/or what influence it has. Again, the meaning arises through delineation of the form of H_{FC} and its rationale R_{FC}.

Finally, conceptual meaning of F occurs, at times, simply through associative or correlative links to other concepts (not shown in Figure 9.1). This expresses analogical, inductive, or deductive meaning not reflected in causal or functional relations with the concepts of interest.

To this point, we have discussed the meaning of a concept when that concept is a single entity. Actually, as implied by cluster attributional and structural definitions (see Bagozzi, 1984a, p. 20), the central concepts in a theory are often multidimensional. For example, attitudes in the theory of trying are conceived not as unidimensional responses but rather as three-dimensional reactions consisting of attitudes toward succeeding and failing to achieve a goal and the process of goal pursuit (e.g. Bagozzi and Warshaw, 1990). In addition to attitudes, many other constructs in marketing rest on multidimensional conceptualizations such as consumer satisfaction, relationships in the channel of distribution, and brand equity.

Empirical meaning

Empirical meaning refers herein to the observational content associated with theoretical terms. This is accomplished formally through correspondence rules which link theoretical terms to observations. Following the convention established in the literature, we use boxes to represent measurements. There are at least three kinds of correspondence rules – the operational definition, partial interpretation, and causal indicator models – each expressible in either point or structural forms. In the interest of brevity, only the causal indicator model will be considered here. For a fuller discussion of this model as well as the other two, see Chapter 1 and Bagozzi (1984a, pp. 21–4).

The structural form of the causal indicator model of correspondence rules can be written as $P^*(y) \rightarrow (P(x) \rightarrow (E(x) \rightarrow R(X))$ & $S(x)$, which in words reads, "y will have theoretical property P^* if (1) x having theoretical property P implies that when experimental test procedure E is applied, it will yield result R and (2) R is organized in structure S." Here a causal link is specified between a theoretical term (or network of terms) and a test operation(s) and its result(s). A phenomenon or state represented by a theoretical term is thought to imply or explain observations. The correspondence rule, then, functions as a scientific law linking theoretical term to experimental test procedure to observed results. Notice that the correspondence rule is not part of the theory or the observations to which it is linked, *per se*. Rather, it is an auxiliary hypothesis that addresses theoretical terms and observations.

Correspondence rules supply empirical meaning to theoretical terms and imply that the correspondence can be represented as a matter of degree. In Figure 9.1, the empirical implications of correspondence rules are depicted as λs, the regression parameters connecting a latent variable to measurements. It is important to stress that we do not observe an λ but rather must infer it from data. When we assess the adequacy of λ, we must not only rely on statistical criteria but also on the conceptual meaning of the correspondence rule employed. Likewise, it is important to emphasize that any correspondence rule and its associated λ are distinct entities. Research to date has tended to take correspondence rules for granted and focus only on estimates of λs. Both are needed for a full interpretation of empirical meaning. More attention is needed as well on how correspondence rules imply observations (i.e. on the rationale for specific λs in any particular piece of research).

Spurious meaning

The third type of meaning pertinent to the interpretation of any theory is spurious meaning. Two parts of spurious meaning can be identified: random error and systematic error. These issues arise when any theory is operationalized and put to test.

It is well-known that random error typically attenuates the observed relationships among variables in statistical analyses and therefore may produce errors in inference. Less well-known is the possibility that random error can actually inflate parameter estimates under some circumstances in multivariate analyses, depending on the pattern and magnitude of such errors among predictors (e.g., Bollen, 1989). In Figure 9.1, random errors in measurements are shown as εs. With respect to substantive research in tests of hypotheses, parameter estimates for causal or functional paths (i.e. γ and β in Figure 9.1) will be corrected for random error when obtained by common estimation procedures used with SEMs. This is one of the main benefits of the use of SEMs over multiple regression and other first generation statistical procedures.

A common source of systematic error in marketing research is method error. Method error refers to variance attributable to the measurement procedure(s) rather than to the concept or construct of interest. Method error may suppress or magnify relationships among variables and contribute to Type I or Type II errors if not taken into account (e.g. Bagozzi, Yi, and Phillips, 1991).

Because random and systematic errors potentially threaten the interpretation of research findings, it is important to validate measures and disentangle influences of these errors in the course of programatic research. This can be done by using multiple measures and multiple methods in measurement and hypothesis testing. We will consider the related issue of construct validity and how SEMs can be used to assess it in a later section of the chapter.

From a practical standpoint, there are at least three ways to detect and take into account systematic error. The simplest, but least satisfactory, is to merely represent the presence and effects of systematic error through correlated residuals in measurements. As shown in Figure 9.1, there are two classes of correlated residuals: correlated errors across constructs ($\theta_{10,9}$) and correlated errors within constructs ($\theta_{7,6}$). For the case of correlated errors across constructs, these errors suggest that variation in the respective measurements is produced by something in addition to the underlying causal process linking F to C (plus random error). For the case of correlated errors within constructs, these errors suggest that variation in the respective measurements is produced by something in addition to the common content implied by A_3 (plus random error). Unfortunately, the source of correlated errors will be unknown in general. The employment of correlated errors corrects for the source of the unknown systematic bias but weakens the interpretation of the structural model. Correlated errors across constructs indicate either the presence of a common method bias in f_2 and c_2 (see Figure 9.1) or an omitted variable that functions as an antecedent to both F and C. In either case, our confidence that β represents the true relationship between F and C will be weakened to the extent of the magnitude of $\theta_{10,9}$. Similarly, correlated errors within constructs such as $\theta_{7,6}$, suggest that either a_6 and a_7 share a common method bias, or A_3 is not unidimensional as hypothesized. Again, this weakens the interpretability of the model to the extent of the magnitude of $\theta_{7,6}$.

A slight improvement over the use of correlated errors as a means for addressing systematic error is the introduction of a method factor(s). A method factor is a hypothesized cause of variation in measurements in addition to that arising from random error and the contribution due to a theoretical concept. The researcher should have some grounds for hypothesizing a method factor based perhaps on identifiable methodological biases. Figure 9.1 illustrates a method factor impinging upon the second measurement of each theoretical concept in the SEM. A common type of method factor is systematic bias from a measurement procedure. For example, in Figure 9.1 it is possible that a_2, a_4, a_6, f_2, and c_2 were all obtained from key informants who exhibited characteristic biases (e.g. systematic differences in knowledge), whereas the remaining measurements might have been obtained by other methods which share no methods biases. The biases due to the method (M) shown in Figure 9.1 are reflected in the parameter estimates for the πs.

The use of methods factors goes somewhat farther and is somewhat more meaningful than the use of correlated errors. In Figure 9.1, we have drawn the arrows associated with m_1 and m_2 as dashed lines to indicate that two versions of methods factors exist: one without and one with separate measurements for the method factor. The version without separate measurements represents the effects of systematic error but does not identify the source of the error, *per se*. A researcher has suspicions here why method biases might exist but has no independent evidence about the source of these biases. The version with separate measurements represents both the source and effects of systematic error. It should be pointed out that the latter version applies not only to explicit method effects but also to the case of representation of the effects of background variables or covariates. Moreover, the latter version applies to tests of hypotheses concerning the effects of omitted variables where M is a suspected omitted variable measured with m_1 and m_2. Note, however, that the effects of covariates might be modelled as either associations with independent latent variables or determinants of them, and not necessarily as direct causes of measurements.

Reliability

In Chapter 1, we introduced two types of reliability – internal consistency and test-retest reliability–and considered the Cronbach alpha procedure for computing reliability. We turn now to the confirmatory factor analysis approach to reliability. The cases of the single-factor and two-factor models are defined and illustrated for internal consistency reliability. Test-retest reliability is reserved for the chapter on panel models in *Advanced Methods of Marketing Research*.

Single-factor model

In many published studies in marketing over the years, Cronbach alpha has been used uncritically without examination of the plausibility of its assumptions. How can the assumptions underlying Cronbach alpha be tested? Is there a better way of ascertaining reliability? We turn to a method addressing these questions.

Consider the case where a researcher has four measures believed to be indicators of a theoretical variable or construct.[1] We can express the relationships between the measures and the hypothesized construct as follows:

$$x_1 = \lambda_1 \xi + \delta_1 \quad (9.1)$$
$$x_2 = \lambda_2 \xi + \delta_2 \quad (9.2)$$
$$x_3 = \lambda_3 \xi + \delta_3 \quad (9.3)$$
$$x_4 = \lambda_4 \xi + \delta_4 \quad (9.4)$$

where x_i is measure i, ξ stands for the hypothesized construct, λ_i is a parameter relating x_i to ξ (analogous to a factor loading or regression coefficient), and δ_i is an error term (also called a residual or error in measurement). It is assumed in equations (9.1)–(9.4) that that the δ_is have zero means, are uncorrelated with ξ, and are mutually uncorrelated among themselves. Figure 9.2 presents a path diagram summarizing the relationships implied by equations (9.1)–(9.4), and has been termed the congeneric measurement model in the literature (Jöreskog, 1971).

Given a sample of observations on the x_i in equations (9.1)–(9.4), useful parameters can be estimated and a chi-square measure of goodness-of-fit computed, among other diagnostics. This can be done with computer software programs such as EzPath, EQS, and LISREL. The parameters of interest are estimates of the λ_i and the variances of the δ_i (i.e. θ_{ii}). These,

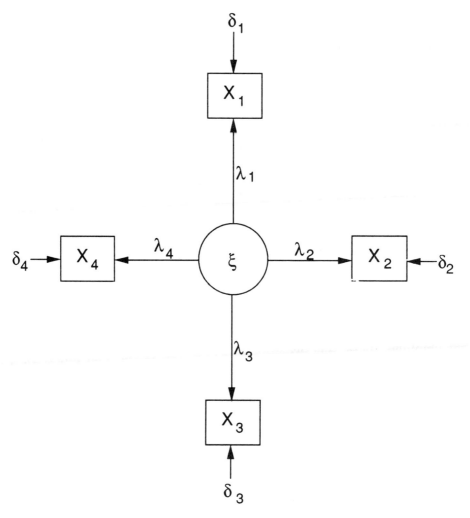

Figure 9.2 The congeneric measurement model for four measures of a single construct

in turn, can be used to compute two indices. An index of the reliability of an individual item or measure is

$$\rho_i = (\lambda_i^2)/(\lambda_i^2 + \theta_{ii}) \qquad (9.5)$$

where we have assumed that the variance of ξ is standardized at one. An index of the reliability of the composite formed by the sum of measures is

$$\rho_c = \left(\sum \lambda_i\right)^2 / \left(\left(\sum \lambda_i\right)^2 + \sum \theta_{ii}\right) \qquad (9.6)$$

where the variance of ξ is again assumed to be one. Both indices go from 0 to 1, inclusive, with higher values indicating greater reliability.

The chi-square goodness-of-fit index provides a test of the hypothesis that the four measures can be explained by a single underlying factor plus error. Large values of the chi-square index relative to its corresponding degrees of freedom suggest a rejection of the hypothesis of unidimensionality, while small values point to a failure to reject unidimensionality. A p-value greater than or equal to 0.05 for the chi-square index is taken by convention to indicate a satisfactory fit of a model to data. The next chapter addresses other measures of goodness-of-fit and additional criteria for evaluating models.

The congeneric model is a very general one useful for testing unidimensionality and estimating reliability with relatively few assumptions being made. Two other somewhat more restrictive models are worth mentioning: the tau-equivalent model and the parallel forms model, which are special cases of the congeneric model. If we begin with equations (9.1)–(9.4) and Figure 9.2 and then specify that $\lambda_1 = \lambda_2 = \lambda_3 = \lambda_4$, we have the tau-equivalent model. This model assumes that each measure relates to the true-score in an equal way and, in effect, implies that the measures have equal true-score variances. If we specify both that $\lambda_1 = \lambda_2 = \lambda_3 = \lambda_4$ and $\theta_{11} = \theta_{22} = \theta_{33} = \theta_{44}$, we have the parallel forms model. That is, all measures are assumed to have equal true-score and equal error variances. As with the congeneric model, the reasonableness of the tau-equivalent and parallel forms models for any set of data can be tested with chi-square goodness-of-fit indices.

Illustration: single-factor model

As an example, we applied the model implied by equations (9.1)–(9.4) to the data found in Table 9.1 by use of LISREL 7 (Jöreskog and Sörbom, 1989). Table 9.2 summarizes the results. The findings for the goodness-of-fit indices suggest that the congeneric and tau-equivalent models cannot be rejected, but that the parallel forms model fits poorly.[2] The parameter estimates are all significant. The individual item reliabilities for the first two measures in the congeneric model are high, but the values for the second two measures are only moderate in magnitude. Nevertheless, the composite reliability is quite high ($\rho_c = 0.88$). We see in this particular example that the four measures are indeed unidimensional and that the assumption of tau-equivalence is not overly violated. Thus, Cronbach alpha could be applied properly with a reasonable degree of confidence. However, the congeneric model appears to be the most justified model and yields more diagnostic information. With other data, it is possible that only the congeneric model will fit or that Cronbach alpha may not be appropriate at all. It should be noted that the model described herein also applies when $q > 4$ measures of a construct are available.

Table 9.1 Correlation matrix of four measures of attitude toward giving blood – aroused sample ($n = 110$)

7-point semantic differential item:				
Pleasant–unpleasant	1.00			
Comfortable–uncomfortable	0.81	1.00		
Good–bad	0.62	0.63	1.00	
Safe–unsafe	0.64	0.63	0.56	1.00

Table 9.2 Findings for goodness-of-fit indices, parameter estimates, and reliability indices for one-factor congeneric, tau-equivalent, and parallel forms models applied to the data in Table 9.1 (aroused sample)

	Goodness-of-fit data		
Model	χ^2	d.f.	P
Congeneric	1.78	2	0.41
Tau-equivalent	10.67	5	0.06
Parallel forms	23.57	8	0.00

	Parameter estimates (standard error)		
Parameter	Congeneric model	Tau-equivalent model	Parallel forms model
λ_1	0.90(0.08)	0.84(0.06)	0.80(0.06)
λ_2	0.90(0.08)	0.84(0.06)	0.80(0.06)
λ_3	0.71(0.09)	0.84(0.06)	0.80(0.06)
λ_4	0.72(0.09)	0.84(0.06)	0.80(0.06)
θ_{11}	0.20(0.05)	0.22(0.04)	0.35(0.03)
θ_{22}	0.20(0.05)	0.22(0.04)	0.35(0.03)
θ_{33}	0.50(0.08)	0.48(0.08)	0.35(0.03)
θ_{44}	0.49(0.07)	0.46(0.07)	0.35(0.03)

	Reliability estimates				
	Individual item				Composite
Model	x_1	x_2	x_3	x_4	ξ
Congeneric	0.81	0.81	0.50	0.51	0.88
Tau-equivalent	0.78	0.78	0.52	0.54	0.89
Parallel forms	0.65	0.65	0.65	0.65	0.88

Multiple-factor model

One of the shortcomings of the single-factor model considered above (which is a special case of confirmatory factor analysis) is that at least four measures are needed to yield an overidentified model for which a goodness-of-fit index can be computed. With three measures, the model is exactly identified; with two, it is underidentified.[3] Therefore, when fewer than four measures per construct are available, the researcher must pursue a different tactic, if one is to assess reliability and achieve the benefits noted above for the single-factor case.

Consider the simple case where one has two constructs and only two measures per construct. Figure 9.3 illustrates this model. The equations relating measures to constructs are similar to those found for the single-factor case except that we now have two constructs, ξ_1 and ξ_2, instead of one:

$$x_1 = \lambda_1 \xi_1 + \delta_1 \quad (9.7)$$
$$x_2 = \lambda_2 \xi_1 + \delta_2 \quad (9.8)$$
$$x_3 = \lambda_3 \xi_2 + \delta_3 \quad (9.9)$$
$$x_4 = \lambda_4 \xi_2 + \delta_4 \quad (9.10)$$

where assumptions are made similar to those noted for equations (9.1)–(9.4), and ϕ_{21} represents the correlation between the two focal constructs. For a sample of data, the model implied by equations (9.7)–(9.10) can be tested and parameters estimated. Likewise, the individual item and composite formulae for reliability can be used, but it must be remembered that the formulae apply to the measures attached to a particular construct and not to all measures across constructs.

When examining a model such as shown in Figure 9.3, at least four hypotheses may be of interest:

H_1: $\lambda_1, \lambda_2, \lambda_3, \lambda_4, \theta_{11}, \theta_{22}, \theta_{33}, \theta_{44}$ and ϕ_{21} free and unconstrained
H_2: $\lambda_1, \lambda_2, \lambda_3, \lambda_4, \theta_{11}, \theta_{22}, \theta_{33}$ and θ_{44} free and unconstrained; ϕ_{21} fixed to unity
H_3: $\lambda_1 = \lambda_2, \lambda_3 = \lambda_4, \theta_{11} = \theta_{22}, \theta_{33} = \theta_{44}$; ϕ_{21} fixed to unity
H_3: $\lambda_1 = \lambda_2, \lambda_3 = \lambda_4, \theta_{11} = \theta_{22}, \theta_{33} = \theta_{44}$; ϕ_{21} free and unconstrained.

Hypothesis H_1 is the null hypothesis for the congeneric model and corresponds directly to Figure 9.3. Hypothesis H_2 is the same as H_1 but adds the restriction that the correlation between the two constructs, ξ_1 and ξ_2, is unity (i.e. $\phi_{21} = 1.00$). Note that this correlation has random error removed from it. Hypothesis H_3 is the same as H_2 but further introduces the constraints that factor loadings and error variances are equal for measures of the same construct. This is a version of the parallel forms model. Finally, hypothesis H_4 is the same as H_3 but places no constraints on ϕ_{21} (i.e. ϕ_{21} is a free parameter). This also is a variant of the parallel forms model.[4]

Each of the above hypotheses can be examined with a chi-square goodness-of-fit test to ascertain the reasonableness of the model. In addition, two sets of hypotheses are interesting to examine, based on strategic comparisons among H_1 to H_4. To see if the two constructs, ξ_1 and ξ_2, are distinct or not, one can compare H_1 to H_2 and H_3 to H_4. The first comparison tests the hypothesis that $\phi_{21} = 1$ or not, under the assumption

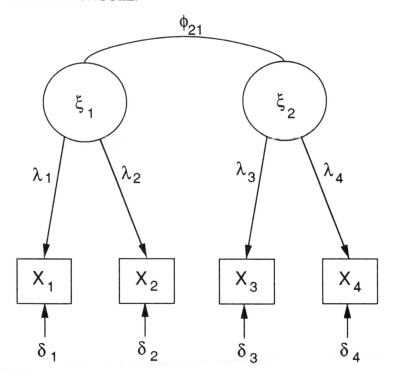

Figure 9.3 The congeneric measurement model for two constructs, each indicated by two measures

that the measures are congeneric; the second comparison tests the hypothesis that $\phi_{21} = 1$ or not, under the assumption that the measures are parallel. To see if the parallel forms hypothesis is tenable or not, we can compare H_1 to H_4 and H_2 to H_3. The former is done under the assumption that the two constructs are distinct, the latter under the assumption that they are not. Chi-square difference tests may be used to perform the above tests.

Illustration: two-factor model

The data used to illustrate the one-factor model were drawn from an experiment examining the effects of emotional arousal on attitude structure. Subjects in the experimental group were emotionally aroused and their attitudes toward giving blood measured immediately afterward, among other responses. It was hypothesized that arousal would produce a unitization of attitudinal responses, based on a spreading activation of adjacent affective reactions in memory making up one's attitude and stimulated by the arousal manipulation. The data presented in Table 9.1 are for the aroused group where we saw that a single factor indeed explained the reactions of subjects. In the nonaroused control condition, subjects were hypothesized to exhibit a two-dimensional attitude where

STRUCTURAL EQUATION MODELS: BASIC PRINCIPLES 329

pleasant–unpleasant and comfortable–uncomfortable indicate an affective factor and good–bad and safe–unsafe reflect a cognitive factor. The first two measures are thought to be more emotional in tone and constitute nearly automatic responses, whereas the last two measures are more thinking-based and comprise either moral (good–bad) or means–ends (safe–unsafe) reflections. Table 9.3 presents the data for the nonaroused group. Subjects were randomly assigned to the two conditions, and skin resistance readings showed that the two groups, in fact, differed significantly as predicted in terms of nonvoluntary physiological reactions (*t*-tests and repeated measures ANOVA were used to demonstrate this but are not reported here in the interest of brevity).

Table 9.3 Correlation matrix of four measures of attitude toward giving blood – unaroused sample ($n = 110$)

7-point semantic differential:				
Pleasant–unpleasant	1.00			
Comfortable–uncomfortable	0.72	1.00		
Good–bad	0.42	0.40	1.00	
Safe–unsafe	0.42	0.50	0.55	1.00

Table 9.4 Findings for goodness-of-fit indices, parameter estimates, and reliability indices for two-factor congeneric and parallel forms models applied to the data in Table 9.3 (unaroused sample)

Hypothesis	Goodness-of-fit data		
	χ^2	d.f	p
$H_1: \lambda_1, \lambda_2, \lambda_3, \lambda_4, \theta_{11}, \theta_{22}, \theta_{33}, \theta_{44}$, and ϕ_{21} free and unconstrained.	1.98	1	0.16
$H_2: \lambda_1, \lambda_2, \lambda_3, \lambda_4, \theta_{11}, \theta_{22}, \theta_{33}$ and θ_{44}, free and unconstrained; ϕ_{21} fixed to unity	18.26	2	0.00
$H_3: \lambda_1 = \lambda_2, \lambda_3 = \lambda_4, \theta_{11} = \theta_{22}, \theta_{33} = \theta_{44}; \phi_{21}$ fixed to unity.	18.99	6	0.00
$H_4: \lambda_1 = \lambda_2, \lambda_3 = \lambda_4, \theta_{11} = \theta_{22}, \theta_{33} = \theta_{44}; \phi_{21}$ free and unconstrained.	3.07	5	0.69

	Parameter estimate (standard error)	
Parameter	Congeneric model with ϕ_{21} free	Parallel forms model with ϕ_{21} free
λ_1	0.81(0.09)	0.85(0.07)
λ_2	0.89(0.09)	0.85(0.07)
λ_3	0.69(0.10)	0.74(0.07)
λ_4	0.80(0.10)	0.74(0.07)
θ_{11}	0.35(0.09)	0.28(0.04)
θ_{22}	0.21(0.10)	0.28(0.04)
θ_{33}	0.53(0.11)	0.45(0.06)
θ_{44}	0.36(0.12)	0.45(0.06)
ϕ_{21}	0.69(0.08)	0.69(0.08)

Table 9.4 (Cont.)

| | \multicolumn{6}{c}{Reliability estimates} | | | | | |
| Model | \multicolumn{4}{c}{Individual item} | | | \multicolumn{2}{c}{Composite} | |
	x_1	x_2	x_3	x_4	ξ_1	ξ_2
Congeneric with ϕ_{21} free	0.65	0.79	0.47	0.64	0.84	0.71
Parallel forms with ϕ_{21} free	0.72	0.72	0.55	0.55	0.84	0.71

We applied the model implied by equations (9.7)–(9.10) to the data in Table 9.3. Table 9.4 shows the results. Notice in the top of the table that the congeneric and parallel forms models with ϕ_{21} estimated freely cannot be rejected but that the same models with ϕ_{21} constrained to unity must be rejected. In other words, the factors are distinct. All parameter estimates are significant as shown in the center of Table 9.4. The individual item reliabilities are at times low, but all the composite reliabilities are high in value (see bottom of Table 9.4). In sum, the evidence supports the hypothesized two factor structure, and the reliabilities of the measures of the corresponding constructs are shown to be satisfactory.

To more formally test the hypotheses of congeneric and parallel forms and whether the two factors are distinct or not, we examine the following comparisons of goodness-of-fit indices and use chi-square difference tests to make inferences. Comparing H_1 to H_4 gives a test of whether the pairs of measures for the two constructs can be considered parallel, given the assumption that ϕ_{21} is a free parameter. The comparison yields a $\chi_d^2(4) = 1.09, p > 0.85$, which indicates that the hypothesis of parallel forms cannot be rejected. Similarly, a comparison of H_2 to H_3 gives a test of whether the pairs of measures are parallel, given the assumption that ϕ_{21} is constrained to be unity. The comparison yields a $\chi_d^2(4) = 0.73, p > 0.94$, again suggesting that the hypothesis of parallel forms cannot be rejected. Comparing H_1 and H_2 provides a test of whether $\phi_{21} = 1.00$ or not, given the assumption that the pairs of measures are congeneric. The results show that the $\chi_d^2(1) = 16.28, p < 0.001$, thus pointing to a rejection of the hypothesis that the two constructs, ξ_1 and ξ_2, are perfectly correlated, even after removing random error. Likewise, a comparison of H_3 and H_4 tests the hypothesis that $\phi_{21} = 1.00$, under the assumption that the pairs of measures are parallel. The findings reveal that the $\chi_d^2(1) = 15.92, p < 0.001$, therefore indicating that one must reject the hypothesis of perfectly correlated factors.

The estimate of ϕ_{21} is 0.69 with a standard error of 0.08. An approximately 95 percent confidence internal for ϕ_{21} is $0.53 < \phi_{21} < 0.85$, which because it is less than 1.00 shows that the factors are distinct.

In sum, the results suggest that the affective and cognitive dimensions of attitude toward giving blood are distinct under unaroused conditions. Recall that the findings for the aroused experimental group, in contrast, showed that one cannot reject the hypothesis of a single factor underlying the attitudinal responses. Bagozzi (1993a) used a spreading activation model of semantic memory to account for the unitization of affective and cognitive dimensions of attitude under arousal conditions. Arousal activates emotional concepts in memory, and the heightened excitation spreads to adjacent concepts. The effect on affective and cognitive dimensions of attitude is to increase and homogenize the association among measures, producing a fusing of dimensions into a single component. As a check on the findings for the aroused group, we applied the two-factor model to the data. The two-factor solution yields a satisfactory fit (i.e. $\chi^2(1) = 0.13$, $p \cong 0.72$), but the estimate of ϕ_{21} is 0.94 with a standard error of 0.05. Since the approximate 95 percent confidence interval includes 1.00, we can conclude that the affective and cognitive dimensions of attitude are not distinct under arousal conditions (i.e. $0.84 < \phi_{21} < 1.04$). The chi-square index for the model fixing $\phi_{21} = 1.00$ yields a value of $\chi^2(2) = 1.78$, $p \simeq 0.41$. Thus, the chi-square difference test comparing the model with ϕ_{21} free to the model with ϕ_{21} fixed to unity (i.e. $\chi_d^2(1) = 1.65, p > 0.20$) reinforces the conclusion that attitude is unidimensional under high arousal conditions.

The above development and illustration were for a two-factor model of congeneric measures. It should be obvious that the congeneric model can be easily extended to $m > 2$ factors where at least two measures are available per factor.

Reflective and Formative Indicators

The single-factor and two-factor models we illustrated in the previous section hypothesize that the variance of each measure loading on a factor is a linear function of the underlying theoretical variable plus error: $x_i = \lambda_i \xi + \delta_i$. This general approach is similar in spirit to true-score theory (e.g. Lord and Novick, 1968) and is the most frequently applied procedure for representing the relationships between theoretical variables and their measurements. Confirmatory factor analysis models of these sorts are sometimes referred to as "measurement models" because they focus on the relationships between constructs and measurements. Because diagrams depicting this approach (see Figures 9.2 and 9.3) show arrows going from latent variables to manifest variables, the measures are sometimes called reflective indicators: the measures reflect their constructs so to speak.

Reflective indicators have a particular meaning that should be kept in mind when one develops measures and specifies a model. Each reflective indicator of a theoretical variable should be regarded as a measurement of either the properties of that theoretical variable or the implications that the theoretical variable has in terms of its observable manifestations. All indicators of a particular theoretical variable measure the same thing and should covary at a high level if they are good measures of the underlying variable. The conceptual meaning of the relationship between a latent variable and each of its measures is identical, although the estimated parameter, λ_i, relating the latent variable to each measure might deviate somewhat from the others as a consequence of random error.

Reflective indicators provide a way to test hypotheses about the properties (e.g. reliability, single factoredness) and construct validity of measures. This can be done in a free-standing sense via tests of the measurement model, or in an integrated sense through tests of systems of equations consisting of both a measurement model and a theoretical model, where the latter specifies causal or functional relations among some of the theoretical variables. Hypotheses performed on systems of equations that contain both measurement and theoretical subparts pose a potential problem, known as interpretational confounding, which occurs when the properties of measurements and parameters associated with the theoretical part of a model become confounded. We will discuss this issue in the next chapter.

When a latent variable is defined as a linear sum of a set of measurements or when a set of measures of a dependant variable(s) is determined by a linear combination of measures of independent variables, the measures are termed formative indicators: the measures produce the constructs so to speak. The best example of the former is an index. Imagine that a researcher desires to study the antecedents and implications of alcohol consumption. It would not be meaningful to specify a latent variable of alcohol consumption and use the amounts of beer, wine, and hard liquor, say, as reflective indicators. Because some people drink only beer from this set, others only wine, and still others only hard liquor or different combinations of beer, wine, and liquor, separate questions asking how much one consumes of each type of alcoholic beverage would yield correlations across people with low to high values, depending on the sample and distribution of responses. Each measure could be a poor one of "alcoholic consumption", and indeed, the meaning of the latent variable is ambiguous given the inconsistent correspondence between measurements and the latent variable. For situations such as this, it is more meaningful to compute a score for each respondent corresponding to the sum (or some other combination such as a weighted sum) of the amount of alcohol consumed in a period of time for each type of alcoholic beverage. Such a score forms an index of a latent construct, termed alcoholic consumption.

Notice that each respondent given a score on the index achieves a number reflecting total consumption, and the same number for two or more people can be produced in many different ways. Person A might receive a score of 6, say, corresponding to 2 units of beer plus 2 of wine plus 2 of hard liquor; whereas Person B might receive a score of 6 based on 4 units of wine plus 2 of hard liquor. In a sense, the variance of the latent variable, the index, is an exact function of the sum of measurements. This characteristic of indexes gives the correspondence between latent variable and measurements a different meaning than found for reflective indicators. Under formative indicators, the latent variable is defined as a function of the measurements. The researcher specifies *a priori* the meaning of the latent variable and, given the validity of the specification as a premise, is most interested in how the index functions as a predictor or predicted variable. Reliability in the internal consistency sense and construct validity in terms of convergent and discriminant validity are not meaningful when indexes are formed as a linear sum of measurements. The best we can do to assess reliability and validity is to examine how well the index relates to measures of other variables (e.g. test-retest reliability; criterion related validity).

Scores on reflective indicators of a latent variable tend to be similar for any given respondent. For example, if we were to measure attitude toward an advertisement with four semantic differential items anchored by pleasant–unpleasant, nice–awful, good–bad, and favorable–unfavorable, we would expect that a person with a positive attitude would answer all four items toward the ends of the scale marked by pleasant, nice, good, and favorable. Likewise, others with a positive attitude would respond to the items toward the ends of the scale marked by pleasant, nice, good, and favorable. Those with a negative attitude would mark items toward the opposite end. Contrast this to our example of formative indicators of alcohol consumption where responses to items comprising an index need not correlate highly and people scoring high (or low) on the index can do so with vastly different responses on each item. The correspondence between reflective indicators and the latent variable they are supposed to measure is more precise than the correspondence between formative indicators and the latent variable or index they are supposed to measure. Generally, an index is more abstract and ambiguous than a latent variable measured with reflective indicators. The use of indexes is most prevalent when dealing with organizational, social, and demographic constructs where the level of analysis is that of a firm, group, or category. However, as our example of alcohol consumption implies, indexes can be used at the level of the individual respondent. Social class is an example of an individual level index commonly used in marketing where one's position in a social stratum is defined by a combination of scores on family background, education, income, place of residence, or occupation.

Our consideration of indexes has so far focused on constructs defined as a combination (e.g. sum) of scores on a set of measures. Another way that formative indicators are used is in canonical correlation analyses or in structural equation models such as the multiple indicator, multiple cause (MIMIC) model (e.g. Bagozzi, Fornell, and Larcker, 1981). At the risk of oversimplification, we can characterize these latter approaches as procedures for obtaining coefficients through the optimization of a linear combination of predicted measures as functions of predictor measures. The coefficients corresponding to the predictors are analogous to formative indicators. See the presentation on MIMIC models in *Advanced Methods of Marketing Research* (Blackwell Publishers, 1994).

In sum, the relationships between theoretical variables and their measurements can be represented in either reflective or formative senses. Because reflective indicators are the most frequently used measures in marketing, we will focus on them in this chapter. However, formative indicators are occasionally useful and the reader is referred to Bagozzi, Fornell, and Larcker (1981) for an illustration and Bollen and Lennox (1991) for further discussion.

Multidimensionality in Marketing Research

Reliability is a fundamental concept in marketing research, and as we saw earlier, reliability applies strictly to unidimensional concepts. A basic activity in marketing science is to specify well-formed concepts and develop unidimensional scales measuring these concepts. This is an essential step in the theory building and hypothesis testing phases of marketing research.

However, when one steps back and looks at the evolution of basic and applied knowledge in marketing, it becomes evident that the ideas and concepts at any one point in time represent refinements from ideas and concepts of an earlier time and will develop into new forms at a later point in time. Frequently, the progression is from a simple, unidimensional idea or concept into a more complex, multidimensional representation (Bagozzi, 1984a). For example, the concept of consumer satisfaction started-out early on as a singular affective or cognitive response (e.g. Howard and Sheth, 1969, p. 145) and was typically measured with a single item (e.g. Oliver, 1976) or multiple items thought to be unidimensional (e.g. Bearden and Teel, 1983). Soon researchers began hypothesizing multiple dimensions of consumer satisfaction (e.g. Czepiel, Rosenberg, and Akerele, 1974), and some reported evidence supporting this view (e.g. Swan and Combs, 1976). Today, consumer satisfaction is conceptualized as a multidimensional phenomenon with multiple psychological processes underlying it (e.g. Oliver, 1980, 1981; Tse and Wilton, 1988; Yi, 1990a). This progression from the simple and unidimensional to the complex and multidimensional has been repeated many times in marketing. Among other areas, it has occurred in the subfields of salesforce behavior, consumer information processing, channels of distribution, product quality, and emotional responses to advertisements.

As an example to illustrate the forms that multidimensional models can take, consider attitudes, a central concept cutting across many subfields in marketing. Classic views of attitudes have assumed one of two positions. The unidimensional school maintains that attitudes are affective reactions and can be measured on the evaluative dimension of the semantic differential (e.g. Petty and Cacioppo, 1981; Thurstone 1928). This perspective is assumed in the elaboration likelihood model (Petty and Cacioppo, 1986), the theory of reasoned action (Ajzen and Fishbein, 1980), and most other models of attitude. In contrast, the multidimensional school posits that attitudes are either tridimensional, consisting of affective-cognitive-conative parts (e.g. Bagozzi, 1992; Krech and Crutchfield, 1948) or bidimensional, existing as affective-cognitive components (e.g. Bagozzi and Burnkrant,

1979). This approach has received much less attention than the unidimensional school and has achieved mixed support to date (e.g. Bagozzi and Burnkrant, 1985; Breckler and Wiggins, 1989; Dillon and Kumar, 1985).

The debate between the unidimensional and multidimensional schools of attitude structure has focused primarily on general attitudes and has not addressed the conditions under which multidimensional attitudes function. More recently, researchers have turned to more specific representations of attitudes in multidimensional structures. Three distinct directions of research can be identified that have particular relevance for marketing. Each of these has been tested with the congeneric measurement model described in the previous section.

Expectancy-value model

The expectancy-value attitude model has received wide currency in marketing, largely because it incorporates beliefs and evaluations of either product attributes or the consequences of an action such as purchase. The most frequently used variant is the Fishbein model (Fishbein and Ajzen, 1975) which can be represented as the $\sum b_i a_i$ where b_i is one's belief that a product in question has attribute i (or an action will have consequence i) and a_i is the evaluation of the attribute (or consequence). This formulation is a unidimensional construct in that attitude is defined as the sum of the products of beliefs times evaluations.

As an alternative, multidimensional expectancy-value models have been proposed by Bagozzi (1981a, b; 1982) who studied blood donation. Figure 9.4a shows an example, where the intention to donate and the arrow going into it from the expectancy-value (EV) attitude should be ignored for the moment. Rather than forming a single expectancy-value reaction toward giving blood indicated by the seven measures shown in the figure, people had three distinguishable responses based on external physical pain, internal sickness, and anticipated costs. A practical benefit of such a model is that it permits the researcher the opportunity of discovering differential reactions to a stimulus. In the case of blood donation, the Red Cross has limited resources and needs to know which consequences of giving blood for donors are the most important and thus can be emphasized with the greatest promise at the lowest cost in its fact-to-face, direct mail, and advertising campaigns. If we regress the intention to donate on the EV attitude (see Figure 9.4a), information can be provided on the importance of the components of attitude on this decision. Multidimensional expectancy-value models have also been investigated by Oliver and Bearden (1985) in a study of the purchase of a diet suppressant and Shimp and Kavas (1984) in a study of coupon usage.

To date, marketers have used the products of beliefs and evaluations in the Fishbein model or as indicators of latent expectancy-value factors but have not partialled-out the additive effects of beliefs and evaluations necessary to derive parameters that are invariant to allowable scale transformations

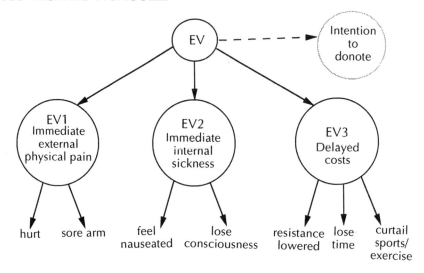

(a) Expectancy-value attitude toward giving blood

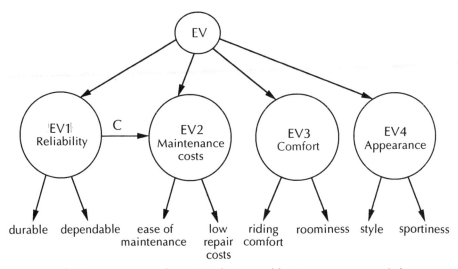

(b) Expectancy-value attitude toward buying an automobile

Figure 9.4 Multidimensional expectancy-value attitudes

(Bagozzi, 1984b). Baumgartner and Bagozzi (1993) present a structural equation methodology that yields parameters with the required properties.

Multidimensional expectancy-value models have still another managerial use. It is generally recognized that attitudes can be influenced by changing beliefs, and advertising campaigns often try explicitly to do this. However, some beliefs cannot be targeted because they are too sensitive or because they are too difficult to change. To produce a change in attitudes, then, requires that one use a different tactic. Sometimes it is possible to change a target belief, and hence attitude, by attacking another belief more vulnerable to change than the target one. Advertising, then, can be fine-tuned to influence a specific belief and then indirectly, through another belief, affect attitude. Yi (1989, 1990b) investigated the indirect effects of advertising on the network of beliefs and evaluations comprising a multidimensional expectancy-value attitude. Figure 9.4b shows the structure he examined. Beliefs about maintenance costs of a new automobile were changed by focusing on dependability in an ad (see path c in Figure 9.4b). People inferred levels of anticipated maintenance costs on the basis of information provided on dependability, given the functional connection shown in the figure. Multidimensional expectancy-value models thus provide a way to examine complex effects of advertising that the traditional unidimensional Fishbein model does not provide.

Goal-directed attitudes

A second multidimensional representation of attitudes addresses the pursuit of goals. Bagozzi and Warshaw (1990) identified three separate attitudinal reactions that accompany the pursuit of goals: attitudes toward trying to achieve a goal and succeeding, attitudes toward trying to achieve a goal and failing, and attitudes toward the process of goal pursuit, *per se*, irrespective of succeeding or failing. The first two attitudes reflect reactions to the anticipated outcomes of attaining a goal or not, while the third concerns the means followed in trying to reach the goal. Bagozzi and Warshaw (1990) studied the goal of losing weight and found that people formed three interrelated, yet distinct, attitudinal reactions toward success, failure, and the process of trying to lose weight. Similarly, Bagozzi, Davis, and Warshaw (1992) found that attitudes toward the adoption of computer technologies exist in a three-dimensional structure of success, failure, and process related reactions, and Bagozzi and Kimmel (1993) found that attitudes toward exercising and toward dieting exhibited separate success, failure, and process components. Each of the attitudinal components is a function of unique beliefs and evaluations. Advertising and sales campaigns will affect the components in different ways and need to be designed accordingly. Further, decisions and behavior can be shown to be differential functions of the attitudinal components. Structural equation models with latent variables provide a powerful means to represent these attitudinal components and their effects on preferences and choices.

Positive and negative attitudes

Burnkrant and Page (1988) proposed still a third multidimensional representation of attitudes. They suggested that expectancy-value reactions are organized in memory as separate positive and negative responses. For example, with respect to giving blood, this might mean that thoughts and feelings about fainting and getting a sore arm would load on a negative expectancy-value factor, while thoughts and feelings about being self-satisfied and having others think well of oneself would load on a positive factor. Burnkrant and Page (1988) found strong support for this model in a study of blood donation. Notice that this approach is similar to the model for goal-directed attitudes, if we assume that success and failure are analogous to positive and negative reactions, respectively. Or in a product context, both models would be similar to one where attitudes are divided into advantages and disadvantages, or alternatively, desirable and undesirable attributes.

There is no reason to restrict attitudes to positive and negative dimensions, however. The number of dimensions should reflect how information is organized in human memory, and this, in turn, will be a function of the learning experiences and cognitive styles and abilities of the individual persons under study. Some people may have global attitudes organized as a singular, summary reaction. Some may have bidimensional positive–negative attitudes. Still others may have more complex representations in their minds, perhaps with separable subdimensions under positive and negative components. Figure 9.5 illustrates a structure of attitudinal

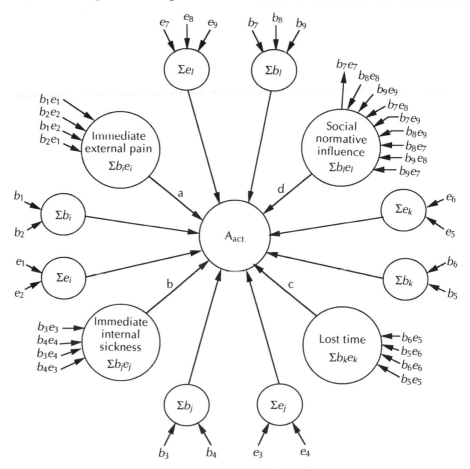

Figure 9.5 Multidimensional expectancy-value attitude model with additive and multiplicative effects

reactions found in a study of blood donation where it can be seen that three negative dimensions and one positive expectancy-value dimension represented people's attitudes (Bagozzi, 1993b). Notice in this model that formative indicators were used, which is consistent with one interpretation of attitude theory. The partial least squares procedure was used in this particular application (Wold, 1985).

Second-order confirmatory factor analysis: an illustration

One way to represent multidimensional constructs is with a second-order CFA model. Figure 9.6 presents such a model applied to seven measures of beliefs toward the consequences of giving blood. Notice that each of the seven measures is hypothesized to load on one of three first-order factors, depending on its meaning. Variance common to all measures and reflecting meaning at a higher level of abstraction is captured through the influence of a second-order factor termed "overall beliefs" in Figure 9.6. The second-order confirmatory factor analysis model is conceptually analogous to conducting a first-order factor analysis on a correlation matrix of measures, estimating correlations among the first-order factors, and then doing another factor analysis on the correlations among first-order factors to derive one or more second-order factors. However, with new advances in estimation procedures such as maximum likelihood found in EQS, LISREL, SAS, and other programs, it is possible to derive parameters for the first-order and second-order factors simultaneously. The general equations for a second-order CFA model are

$$\eta = \Gamma \xi + \zeta$$
$$y = \Lambda_y \eta + \epsilon$$

where η is a vector of first-order factors, ξ is a vector of second-order factors, Γ and Λ_y are matrices of factor loadings for second-order and first-order factors, respectively, y is a vector of measurements, and ζ and ϵ are disturbances. For the example in Figure 9.6, the equations are

$$\begin{bmatrix} \eta_1 \\ \eta_2 \\ \eta_3 \end{bmatrix} = \begin{bmatrix} \gamma_1 \\ \gamma_2 \\ \gamma_3 \end{bmatrix} \xi + \begin{bmatrix} \zeta_1 \\ \zeta_2 \\ \zeta_3 \end{bmatrix}$$

$$\begin{bmatrix} y_1 \\ y_2 \\ y_3 \\ y_4 \\ y_5 \\ y_6 \\ y_7 \end{bmatrix} = \begin{bmatrix} \lambda_1 & 0 & 0 \\ \lambda_2 & 0 & 0 \\ 0 & \lambda_3 & 0 \\ 0 & \lambda_4 & 0 \\ 0 & 0 & \lambda_5 \\ 0 & 0 & \lambda_6 \\ 0 & 0 & \lambda_7 \end{bmatrix} \begin{bmatrix} \eta_1 \\ \eta_2 \\ \eta_3 \end{bmatrix} + \begin{bmatrix} \epsilon_1 \\ \epsilon_2 \\ \epsilon_3 \\ \epsilon_4 \\ \epsilon_5 \\ \epsilon_6 \\ \epsilon_7 \end{bmatrix}$$

We applied this model to the data in Table 9.5. The findings show that this model fits well: $\chi^2(11) = 9.30$, $p \simeq 0.59$. Table 9.6 presents a partitioning of the variance in each measurement into random error, measure specificity, and common sources. These can be obtained from the following respective parameter matrices: $\widehat{\Theta}_\epsilon$, $\widehat{\Lambda_y \Gamma \Phi \Gamma' \Lambda_y'}$, and $\widehat{\Lambda_y \Psi \Lambda_y'}$.

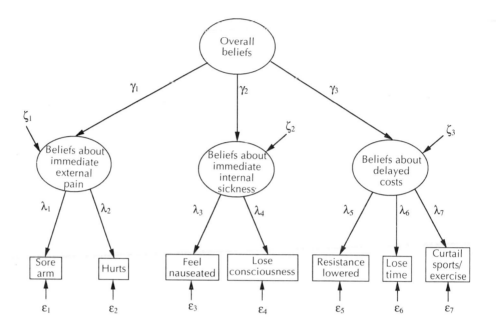

Figure 9.6 Second-order confirmatory factor analysis model for beliefs about the consequences of giving blood

Table 9.5 Correlation matrix for seven measures of beliefs about the consequences of giving blood $n = 127$

11-point probability item:							
Sore arm	1.00						
Hurts	0.76	1.00					
Nauseated	0.42	0.38	1.00				
Lose consciousness	0.42	0.44	0.79	1.00			
Resistance lowered	0.44	0.48	0.47	0.48	1.00		
Lose time	0.48	0.52	0.55	0.62	0.66	1.00	
Curtail sports/exercise	0.50	0.53	0.47	0.54	0.59	0.61	1.00

A major advantage of second-order CFA models is that the confounding of specific and random error variance is avoided. Up to this point in the chapter, the first-order confirmatory analysis models we considered contained error terms which confounded random error with measure specificity.

Table 9.6 Partitioning of variance for second-order confirmatory factor analysis example

Measure	Variance component		
	Error	Specific	Common
Sore arm	0.29	0.36	0.36
Hurts	0.19	0.41	0.41
Nauseated	0.28	0.32	0.40
Lose consciousness	0.13	0.39	0.49
Resistance lowered	0.42	−0.01	0.59
Lose time	0.29	−0.01	0.72
Curtail sports/exercise	0.42	−0.01	0.58

Measure specificity is variance unique to a measure over and above that due to an underlying latent variable and random error (where we assume there is no method or other systematic biases, a topic we discuss in the next section). Results from first-order factor analyses can be ambiguous in the sense that a low factor loading for a method or trait may be due to either substantial measurement error or a true lack of correspondence between measurement and hypothesized latent variable. The consequences of this confounding are especially important when the reliabilities of different measurements vary, because "such differences will distort inferred relations among the scales, the factor loadings on the latent . . . factors, relations among the latent factors, and summary statistics that are based on these parameter estimates" (Marsh and Hocevar, 1988, p. 108). The second-order CFA model avoids these problems and provides specific estimates for error, specific, and common variance.

Another advantage of second-order CFA models is that the dimensions of a multidimensional construct are explicitly represented and parameters related to each dimension can be used to examine useful properties of the measurements such as reliability. A final advantage of the second-order CFA model is that it can reveal the separate effects of the subdimensions of a construct on a dependent variable. This can be accomplished with a model containing a path from the second-order factor to a dependent variable (see Figure 9.4a). Bagozzi (1981a, b, 1982) presents an illustration of one of the first uses of second-order CFA models in this regard. The second-order CFA model overcomes problems of multicollinearity which occur when a dependent variable is regressed directly on subdimensions.

A final point we wish to make is that it is sometimes difficult to obtain a satisfactory goodness-of-fit for second-order CFA model solutions. This arises because the second-order CFA model is a very specific formulation and makes strong demands on data. Bagozzi, Yi, and Phillips (1991, Appendix B) present a derivation of restrictions implied by second-order CFA models which occasionally make it difficult to find satisfactory solutions. Unsatisfactory solutions (e.g. large χ^2-values, negative error variances) imply that the model is misspecified.

Construct Validity

Measures of consumer satisfaction, attitudes, beliefs, and other variables investigated in marketing reflect measurement error as well as the theoretical content presumed to underlie the measures. In turn, measurement error can be conceived to consist of random and systematic components. Thus, one might represent measure variance as the sum of true or theoretical variance, plus random error and systematic error.

A common source of systematic error in marketing research is method error. Method error refers to variance attributable to the measurement procedure(s) rather than to the construct of interest, and examples include halo effects, social desirability distortions, acquiescence tendencies, evaluation apprehension, demand artifacts, and key informant biases associated with peer or expert ratings (e.g. Campbell, 1955; Funder 1989; Ganster, Hennessey, and Luthans, 1983; Nicholls, Licht, and Pearl, 1982; Paulhus, 1989; Rosenthal and Rosnow, 1969; Seidler, 1974; Winkler, Kanouse, and Ware, 1982).

As we indicated in the beginning of the chapter, random error and method error can contribute to Type I and Type II errors. Because measurement error (i.e. random error and method variance) provide potential threats to the interpretation of research findings, it is important to validate measures and disentangle the distorting influences of these errors in the course of testing theories and doing applied research. This can be achieved by using multiple measures and multiple methods in measurement and hypotheses testing (e.g. Campbell and Fiske, 1959). Using a single measure of each variable in a theory under test does not permit one to take reliability into account in analyses. Similarly, with only a single method one cannot distinguish substantive (i.e. trait) variance from unwanted method variance, because each attempt to measure a concept is contaminated by irrelevant aspects of the method employed.

Construct validity, which is defined broadly as the extent to which an operationalization measures the concept it is supposed to measure (e.g. Cook and Campbell, 1979), is a central issue in any research endeavor. Given multiple measures obtained with multiple methods, construct validation can be assessed through an inspection of the multitrait-multimethod (MTMM) matrix, the correlation matrix for different concepts (i.e. traits) when each of the concepts is measured by different methods (e.g. Campbell and Fiske, 1959). Without assessing construct validity one cannot estimate and correct for the confounding influences of random error and method variance, and the results of theory testing may be ambiguous. That is, hypotheses might be rejected or accepted because of excessive error in measurement, not necessarily because of the inadequacy or adequacy of theory.

We introduced and illustrated Campbell and Fiske's (1959) procedure for ascertaining construct validity in Chapter 1. Now we wish to critique this approach, consider alternatives, and present a general set of guidelines.

Critique of Campbell and Fiske's procedure

How well can Campbell and Fiske's criteria be relied upon? One answer to this question can be addressed by evaluating the assumptions underlying Campbell and Fiske's criteria. Four assumptions are noteworthy: namely, the criteria are based on the premises that traits and methods are uncorrelated, methods affect all traits equally, methods are orthogonal, and measures are equally reliable (e.g. Campbell and Fiske, 1959; Schmitt and Stults, 1986). The first assumption may not be unreasonable in practice, as traits and methods are frequently unconfounded. However, one case where traits and methods can be related in marketing research is when peers or experts rate subjects and the subjects rate themselves on characteristics for which they and the key informants possess an implicit theory as to the nature or origin of the characteristics.

The other three assumptions behind the Campbell and Fiske procedure are highly unlikely in most contexts for marketing research. Measures of traits will be differentially affected by methods to the extent of heterogeneity in the traits and methods under study. Studies dealing with scale development, particularly with multifaceted constructs, and investigations into construct validation strive for heterogeneity by design. Intercorrelations among methods are difficult to avoid as well. Alternative methods based on self-reports or judgments performed by key informants typically correlate at least at moderate levels. Further, method variance and measure reliability generally vary considerably even when similar instrumentation is used to tap traits. Thus, there is reason to question the assumptions underlying the Campbell and Fiske procedure when applied in typical marketing research contexts.

Another problem with Campbell and Fiske's procedure is that no precise standards are provided for ascertaining how well the criteria are met. The rules of thumb offered as to the proportions of violations of patterns of correlations are rather arbitrary and depend on a qualitative assessment of confirming and disconfirming incidents of differences in observed correlations. By focusing on the number of times selected correlations are greater than others, Campbell and Fiske's procedure neglects the importance of the magnitudes of differences between pairs of correlations.

Reliance on the observed correlations provides a rather imprecise and potentially misleading basis for assessing construct validity. An observed correlation will reflect random error and method biases in addition to the true association among measures of traits. The Campbell and Fiske procedure provides no information as to the separate amounts of variation in measures due to traits, methods, and random error.

The CFA approach to construct validity

An alternative to the Campbell and Fiske procedure that has seen recent application (e.g. Bagozzi, 1993b; Bagozzi and Yi, 1991, 1992) is the CFA model (e.g. Jöreskog, 1974). As applied to MTMM matrix data, the CFA model hypothesizes that the total variation in measures can be written as a linear combination of trait, method, and error effects (e.g. Jöreskog, 1974).

The CFA model is perhaps best introduced by way of a diagram. Figure 9.7 presents an intuitive description of the CFA model. Three hypothesized traits and the three methods are drawn as circles. Note that each trait factor is connected to three boxes with arrows. The boxes represent the actual observed measurements, of which a total of 9 result for the three traits obtained by the three methods. Each measurement has three arrows terminating into it. The arrows from the trait factors to measures stand for variance in the measures that is due to the underlying trait; the 9 λs connected to these arrows are factor loadings relating trait factors to observed measures. The arrows from the methods to measures reflect variance that is due to the procedures used to obtain responses; the 9 λs attached to these arrows are factor loadings relating method factors to observed measures. The 9 short arrows with ϵ_i at the origins represent variation in the measures that is due to random error plus measure specificity. Finally, the curved lines connecting pairs of factors indicate correlations between factors and are designated as ψ_{jk}.

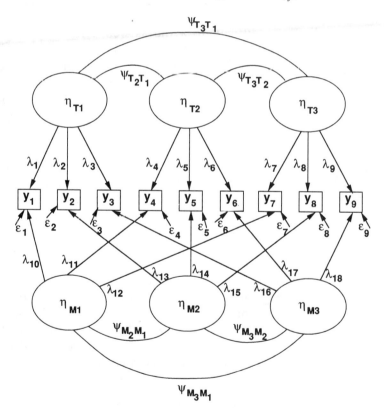

Figure 9.7 Confirmatory factor analysis-model for MTMM design with three traits and three methods

STRUCTURAL EQUATION MODELS: BASIC PRINCIPLES

If we interpret each measure as an observation whose variation we desire to explain, we can interpret the CFA model in Figure 9.7 as displaying the sources of that variation in three senses: variation due to trait (i.e. the theoretical concept of interest), method (i.e. the measurement procedures), and error (i.e. unexplained random fluctuations). More formally, the general form of the CFA model for the MTMM matrix with r traits and s methods can be expressed through two sets of equations (e.g. Jöreskog, 1974):

$$y = [\Lambda_T \Lambda_M] \begin{bmatrix} \eta_T \\ \eta_M \end{bmatrix} + \epsilon \tag{9.11}$$

$$\Sigma = \Lambda_T \Psi_T \Lambda_T' + \Lambda_M \Psi_M \Lambda_M' + \theta \tag{9.12}$$

where y is a vector of $r \times s$ observed measures for r traits and s methods, $\eta = [\eta_T \eta_M]$ is an $(r + s) \times 1$ vector of trait and method factors, ϵ is a vector of $r \times s$ residuals for y, Σ is the implied variance–covariance matrix for y, Ψ_T is an $r \times r$ correlation matrix for traits, Ψ_M is an $s \times s$ correlation matrix for methods, θ is the vector of unique variances for ϵ, $\Lambda_T = [\Lambda_1, \Lambda_2, \ldots, \Lambda_s]'$, Λ_j is an $r \times r$ diagonal matrix with trait factor loading for the r traits measured by the j-th method, and

$$\Lambda_M = \begin{bmatrix} \lambda_1 & 0 & \cdots & 0 \\ 0 & \lambda_2 & \cdots & 0 \\ \cdot & \cdot & \cdots & \cdot \\ \cdot & \cdot & \cdots & \cdot \\ \cdot & \cdot & \cdots & 0 \\ 0 & 0 & \cdots & 0 & \lambda_s \end{bmatrix}$$

where λ_j is an $r \times 1$ vector of factor loadings for the j-th method.

Four useful hypotheses to examine with respect to method and trait effects in the CFA model are the following (e.g. Widaman 1985):

Model 1 The model hypothesizing that only unique variances in measures of traits are freely estimated (i.e. the null model). This model hypothesizes that the observed measures correlate zero in the population.

Model 2 The model hypothesizing that variation in measures can be explained completely by traits plus random error (i.e. the trait-only model). This model assumes that method variance is negligible and that the measures reflect only trait and error variance.

Model 3 The model hypothesizing that variation in measures can be explained completely by methods plus random error (i.e. the method-only model). This model assumes that trait variance is negligible and that the measures reflect only method and error variance.

Model 4 The model hypothesizing that variation in measures can be explained completely by traits, methods, and error (i.e. the trait-method model). This model is the structural equation operationalization of the MTMM matrix as shown in equations (9.11) and (9.12) and Figure 9.7.

The nested hypotheses implied by Models 1–4 above can be tested by comparing chi-square values. A test of the significance of trait variance is provided by comparing chi-square tests between Models 1 and 2 and between Models 3 and 4. Similarly, a test of the significance of method variance is provided by comparing Models 1 and 3, as well as Models 2 and 4.

In addition to testing formally for trait and method effects, the CFA models can be used to partition the variance in measures in diagnostically useful ways and to estimate parameters that provide insights into measurement properties and construct validity. The partitioning of variance into trait, method, and error is revealed, respectively, in the squared factor loadings in Λ_T and Λ_M, and in θ. Further, as we illustrate in the empirical analyses below, useful information is provided in parameter estimates for correlations among traits and among methods, as well as in error variances and factor loadings.

Before we illustrate the CFA model, it is important to point-out its advantages over the Campbell and Fiske procedure. Under the CFA model, a variety of measures of fit are provided for an overall model, whereas no omnibus test exists for the Campbell and Fiske procedure. Moreover, estimates and tests of significance of parameters are derived for the CFA model, and formal tests of trait and method effects are possible. These features are not part of the Campbell and Fiske procedure. Likewise, the CFA model yields a partitioning of variance into trait, method, and error components, but the Campbell and Fiske procedure only suggests hints as to the presence of trait and method effects. Finally, with regard to the restrictive assumptions noted above for the Campbell and Fiske procedure, it should be noted that methods can correlate freely and affect measures to different degrees under the CFA model, and the reliability of measures can be freely estimated, rather than assuming that they are equal to unknown values. Indeed, by imposing certain restrictions, it is possible to estimate correlations between traits and methods.[5]

Illustration of construct validity by use of CFA

As an example of the CFA approach to construct validation, we applied the procedures to data found in Phillips (1981). Phillips collected data from 506 wholesale distribution companies and asked two or more executives in each company to provide information on the nature of supplier influence over their operations. Five traits were measured: perceived influence that the supplier had over the size of orders, the mix of orders, salesforce hiring policies, salesforce training policies, and territories served. Information provided by the chief executive officer in each company was treated as one method; while information provided by either another subordinant (in those companies where only a single additional informant was available) or the average of responses by two or more subordinants (in those companies where two or more additional informants were available) was treated as a second method. LISREL was used in the analyses.

The top half of Table 9.7 shows the results for Models 1–4 described above, as well as the comparisons among models needed to test for the significance of trait and method effects. Notice first that, on the basis of the chi-square tests, the null, method-only, and trait-only models fit poorly, but that the trait-method model, which is similar to the model shown in Figure 9.7 but with five traits and two methods, cannot be rejected. Comparisons of the null to the method-only model ($\chi_d^2(11) = 452.67$, $p < 0.001$) and the trait-only to the trait-method model ($\chi_d^2(11) = 139.63$, $p < 0.001$) reveal that method effects are significant. Likewise, comparisons of the null model to the trait-only model ($\chi_d^2(20) = 830.97$, $p < 0.001$) and the method-only model to the trait-method model ($\chi_d^2(20) = 517.93$, $p < 0.001$) show that trait effects are also significant. It appears, then, that variation in the responses of managers to questions of supplier influence over their operations can be accounted for by a model positing additive effects of traits, methods, and random error.

Table 9.7 Findings for confirmatory factor analysis of supplier influence on wholesale distributors using data from Phillips (1981)

Goodness-of-fit measures and tests of hypotheses

Null	Method	
$\chi^2(45) = 984.36$	$\chi^2(34) = 531.69$	$\chi_d^2(11) = 452.69$
$p < 0.001$	$p < 0.001$	$p < 0.001$
Trait	Trait–Method	
$\chi^2(25) = 153.39$	$\chi^2(14) = 13.76$	$\chi_d^2(11) = 139.63$
$p < 0.001$	$p \simeq 0.47$	$p < 0.001$
$\chi_d^2(20) = 830.97$	$\chi_d^2(20) = 517.93$	
$p < 0.001$	$p < 0.001$	

Decomposition of variance in measures of supplier influence

	Percentage due to		
Measure	Trait	Method	Error
size of orders, CEO	0.81	0.02	0.17
size of orders, subordinant(s)	0.27	0.09	0.64
mix of orders, CEO	0.93	0.01	0.06
mix of orders, subordinant(s)	0.18	0.09	0.73
salesforce hiring, CEO	0.14	0.65	0.21
salesforce hiring, subordinant(s)	0.55	0.28	0.18
salesforce training, CEO	0.62	0.13	0.25
salesforce training, subordinant(s)	0.22	0.24	0.54
territories served, CEO	0.64	0.06	0.29
territories served, subordinant(s)	0.52	0.06	0.43

Intercorrelations of traits and methods (corrected for attentuation)

$$\Psi_T = \begin{bmatrix} 1.00 & & & & \\ 0.32(0.07)^a & 1.00 & & & \\ 0.11(0.08) & 0.11(0.07) & 1.00 & & \\ 0.18(0.07) & 0.20(0.07) & 0.08(0.10) & 1.00 & \\ 0.09(0.06) & 0.16(0.06) & 0.39(0.10) & 0.15(0.09) & 1.00 \end{bmatrix}$$

$$\Psi_M = \begin{bmatrix} 1.00 & \\ 0.26(0.13) & 1.00 \end{bmatrix}$$

[a] Standard errors in parentheses.

The middle panel of Table 9.7 presents the decomposition of variance due to trait, method, and error. All factor loadings associated with traits were statistically significant, suggesting that convergent validity was achieved. However, an inspection of the levels of trait variance points to differences between the CEOs and subordinants across traits. The CEOs are particularly informative with respect to supplier influence over the size and mix of orders, salesforce training policies, and territories served, and much less informative with respect to salesforce hiring policies. The subordinants, in contrast, are relatively informative with regard to salesforce hiring policies and territories served, but much less informative about size and mix of orders and salesforce training policies. Method biases are generally low, except for a very high incidence of bias of the CEO in judgments of supplier influence over salesforce hiring policies and moderate amounts of bias in subordinant estimates of supplier influence over salesforce hiring and training policies. Error variance is very high for the judgments made by the CEOs concerning influence of suppliers over the size and mix of orders, and is moderately high for the estimates made by subordinants of supplier influence over salesforce training policies and territories served. The remaining error variances are small in magnitude. In sum, the variance decomposition suggests whose reports are trustworthy for which particular issues and can be used to weight judgments, revise questions, and give feedback to respondents, depending on the purposes of the researcher.

The bottom panel of Table 9.7 presents findings pertinent to discriminant validity. Notice in the matrix for intercorrelations among the five traits that each correlates at a relatively low level with the others, and in fact all correlations are much lower than 1.00. Hence, the traits achieve discriminant validity. The correlation between the two methods is also very low ($r = 0.26$), indicating that the judgments of CEOs and subordinants are relatively independent.

Critique of the CFA approach to construct validity

A major shortcoming of the application of the CFA model to MTMM matrix data is the all too frequent occurrence of ill-defined solutions. In their examination of 435 MTMM matrices based on actual and simulated data, Marsh and Bailey (1991) report that 77 percent resulted in improper solutions. Marsh (1989) identified four types of ill-defined solutions common to CFA investigations of the MTMM matrix: "underidentified or empirically underidentified models . . ., failures in the convergence of the iterative procedure used to estimate parameters, parameter estimates that are outside their permissible range values (e.g., negative variance estimates called Heywood cases), or standard errors of parameter estimates that are excessively large" (p. 339).

Negative error variances frequently occur when performing a CFA of the trait-method model. A negative error variance is, of course, impossible theoretically and points to serious problems. Often negative error variances will be non-significant, suggesting that no random error exists. One solution to the negative error variance situation in this sense is to fix the variance to zero and rerun the CFA model. However, because one normally expects at least a small amount of residual variance in marketing data, the presence of non-significant error variances should in the general case lead one to conclude that overfitting or a misspecified model is the case (e.g., Maxwell, 1977, p. 58; Van Driel, 1978). There is perhaps one exception to this generalization. When measures of factors are formed as the sum of many well-chosen items, it is possible that this will reduce considerably residual variance. Indeed, a particular measure so formed may exhibit non-significant random error. We would expect, however, that this would be a relatively rare event. Thus, while one might tolerate the occurrence of a single measure showing a non-significant error variance in CFA applications, when the measure is formed as the sum of many items, it would seem unwise to accept more than one such occurrence in a CFA application to the MTMM matrix. And when measures of factors each consist of a single item or the sum of a small number of items, we would argue that the presence of even a single non-significant error variance points to an overfitted or misspecified model.

Rindskopf (1983) proposed that negative error variances can be avoided in the CFA model by creating a new factor for each error term in the model such that the factor loading corresponding to each new factor is the square root of the error. This will guarantee that the error variance will be non-negative. One problem with this procedure is that it can lead one to accept a misspecified model. For this reason, Jöreskog and Sörbom (1989, p. 215) counsel against imposing constraints to ensure that non-negative parameter estimates for error variances do not arise. Some evidence can be found showing that the Rindskopf parameterization is equivalent to simply fixing the offending error variance to zero (e.g. Dillon, Kumar, and Mulani, 1987), which we mentioned above may not be justified. Note, however, that programs such as EQS (Bentler, 1989) derive optimal parameter estimates while assuming non-negativity.

Another shortcoming to point out with regard to the CFA model is that the partitioning of variance into trait and method components may not, in general, yield "trait-free" and "method-free" interpretations (Kumar and Dillon, 1992). This is because the individual factor loadings take on different values corresponding to the distinct trait-method pairings. For example, factor loadings concerning a trait can vary across methods, and the corresponding variation cannot be attributed solely to the trait factor. Since each factor loading is specific to the particular trait-method combination, the associated variation is not really "trait-free" or "method-free". If the correlations among traits and the correlations among methods approach zero, the variance due to traits will be reflected in the trait loadings and the variance due to methods will be reflected in the method loadings.

However, as the correlations among traits and among methods increase, trait and method variance will be confounded. For example, a general trait factor may underlie traits such that traits are highly correlated and substantial variance in measures is primarily due to traits, while methods are relatively distinct. In such circumstances, application of the CFA model can misleadingly yield highly correlated methods accounting for much variation in measures (e.g. Marsh, 1989). However, a good fitting CFA model in this case should not be believed because the apparent method effects are really confounded with trait effects from a general trait factor. That is, correlations among method factors may represent the convergence of the general trait factor. That is, correlations among method factors may represent the convergence of the general trait factor across methods, rather than true relationships among methods. Since many applications of the MTMM matrix involve substantially correlated traits and/or methods, the researcher should consider the potential confounding noted above when interpreting results from a CFA model.

A related and final issue to mention with respect to the use of the CFA model is that researchers sometimes jump to applications and interpretations of the trait-method model without considering the possibility that variation in measures could be a function of only traits and random error. That is, although true method effects may be absent, when the trait-method model is fit to data, the results may misleadingly show the presence of method effects. A good fitting model in such cases reflects confounding similar to that noted above. One way to avoid making false inferences in this sense is to carefully examine the trait-only model.

The correlated uniqueness model approach to construct validity

As a remedy for problems of overfitting and ill-defined solutions, Marsh (1989) proposed a new approach which he termed the correlated uniqueness (CU) model (see also, Kenny, 1976, 1979). Figure 9.8 presents a diagram of the CU model. The interpretation of Figure 9.8 is similar to that noted for the CFA model (Figure 9.7) except for the meaning of method effects. The effects of methods under the CU model are represented as correlations among error terms. This permits one to capture

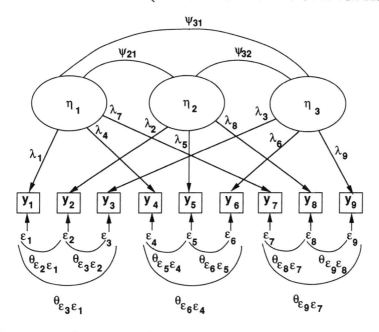

Figure 9.8 The correlated uniqueness model for three traits and three methods

differential impacts of each method on the multiple measures corresponding to that method.

Three advantages of the CU model over the CFA model are the following. Most importantly, the CU model seldom produces ill-defined solutions. For example, only 2 percent of the 435 MTMM matrixes examined by Marsh and Bailey (1991) exhibited improper solutions. A second advantage of the CU model is that methods are not assumed to be unidimensional as under the CFA model. The confounding of method variance with trait variance is avoided (when this is due to common trait variation across methods and traits are highly correlated). Finally, when four or more traits are measured with at least three methods, one can test the assumption that all correlated uniquenesses associated with one particular method can be explained in terms of a single, unidimensional method factor. This can be done by comparing goodness-of-fit indices for the alternative approaches. It turns out that the CFA model with correlations among methods constrained to be zero is a special case of the CU model. For cases where three traits and three methods are used, the models are identical. But when four or more traits are examined, more parameters are associated with each method under the CU model than the CFA model with orthogonal methods.

Illustration of the CU model

To illustrate the CU model, data originally appearing in Arora (1982) were analyzed. Arora (1982) studied the attitudes of 96 undergraduate business

Table 9.8 Parameter estimates for correlated uniqueness model applied to the data in Arora (1982)

Method–trait	Factor loadings	Correlated uniqueness			Factor correlations		
Semantic differential							
Situational involvement	0.84(0.08)[a]	0.21(0.06)			1.00		
Enduring involvement	0.90(0.08)	0.09(0.04)	0.18(0.04)		0.34(0.10)	1.00	
Response involvement	0.69(0.09)	0.16(0.06)	0.12(0.05)	0.53(0.10)	0.21(0.12)	0.36(0.10)	1.00
Likert							
Situational involvement	0.76(0.08)	0.49(0.09)					
Enduring involvement	0.84(0.08)	0.09(0.05)	0.27(0.05)				
Response involvement	0.72(0.09)	0.35(0.07)	0.10(0.05)	0.52(0.10)			
Stapel							
Situational involvement	0.81(0.09)	0.36(0.08)					
Enduring involvement	0.94(0.08)	−0.01(0.04)	0.13(0.04)				
Response involvement	0.86(0.09)	0.01(0.05)	0.10(0.04)	0.25(0.09)			

[a] Standard errors in parentheses.

students toward their university by use of three scales: semantic differential, Likert, and stapel scales. Attitudes expressed situational, enduring, and response involvement. In Bagozzi and Yi's (1991) reanalysis of Arora's data, the CFA model (see Figure 9.7) fit well: $\chi^2(12) = 15.41, p \simeq 0.22$. However, three nonsignificant error variances resulted, bringing into question the appropriateness of the model for the data at hand. Table 9.8 presents the findings for a test of the CU model shown in Figure 9.8. The CU model provides a satisfactory fit to the data: $\chi^2(15) = 21.70, p \simeq 0.12$. It can be seen in Table 9.8 that the trait factor loadings are generally quite high, revealing considerable variation due to traits and supporting convergent validity. Trait correlations are non-significant to low in value, pointing to achievement of discriminant validity. The correlated uniquenesses show that some relatively small method biases exist for the semantic differential and Likert scales, and very little method bias was found for the stapel scale.

Critique of the CU model

At least two shortcomings of the CU model should be mentioned. First, the interpretation of correlated uniqueness as method effects is not always clear. Two possible outcomes make the meaning of findings potentially ambiguous: the presence within the same method of (a) significant positive and negative correlations and (b) significant and nonsignificant correlations. The former is incongruous, since it is difficult to conceive of reasons why the same method has opposite effects on measures of different traits when the traits are expected to covary in *either* a positive or negative direction. The latter finding is possible in theory, but in practice is difficult to explain unless one has a priori methodological reasons accounting for differences in the significance and non-significance of correlated uniquenesses for a common method. In sum, whereas a CU model may fit MTMM matrix data well, the presence of one or both of the above outcomes for the correlated uniquenesses may be a consequence of capitalization on chance.

A second, broad limitation of the CU model is that it assumes that methods are uncorrelated. This may be reasonable when highly different methods are purposefully chosen in a construct validation study. But for the typical study where different self-reports constitute the methods, methods would be expected to be significantly correlated, perhaps highly so. Even in cases where self-ratings and peer or expert ratings are used, one generally anticipates at least a moderate amount of association between methods because of the common format of items, shared experiences and outlooks, and other factors. Even different methods are frequently correlated.

Construct validity and the direct product model

Up to this point, we have considered linear models where traits, methods, and error terms have additive effects on measures. It is also possible that methods may interact with traits in a multiplicative way. That is, a multiplicative interaction can occur such that "the higher the basic relationship between two traits, the more that relationship is increased when the same method is shared" (Campbell and O'Connell, 1982, p. 95). Campbell and O'Connell (1967, p. 421) implied that trait – method interactions may be the rule rather than the exception, and some of the conditions governing such interactions will be explored below after a procedure is described for modeling interactions.

Until recently, no unambiguous procedure existed for representing trait–method interactions, and Campbell and O'Connell's ideas remained little more than speculations. The foundation for a formal model representing the multiplicative interaction between traits and methods was developed by Swain (1975). Swain (1975) proposed that

$$\Sigma = \Sigma_m \otimes \Sigma_T$$

where Σ is the covariance matrix of the observed measures in a MTMM matrix design, Σ_m and Σ_T are method and trait covariance matrices, respectively, and $\otimes$ indicates a right direct (Kronecker) product. This model expresses the covariance matrix of measurements as the direct product of a covariance matrix of methods and a covariance matrix of traits. However, the model does not allow for measurement errors or different scales for different measures, oversights that limit the applicability of the model for typical MTMM matrix applications in personality research.

Browne (1984, 1989) extended Swain's (1975) approach to incorporate unique variances and scale factors and proposed the following direct product (DP) model (see also Cudeck, 1988):

$$\Sigma = Z(P_m \otimes P_T + E^2)Z,$$

where Z is a diagonal matrix of scale constants, P_m and P_T are method and trait correlation matrixes, respectively, whose elements are particular multiplicative components of common score correlations (i.e. correlations corrected for attentuation), and E^2 is a diagonal matrix of unique variances.

It is possible to give an intuitive description of the DP model as follows. The DP model hypothesizes multiplicative effects of methods and traits such that sharing a method exaggerates the correlations between highly correlated traits relative to traits that are relatively independent. That is, the higher the intertrait correlation, the more the relationship is enhanced when both measures share the same method, whereas the relationship is not affected when intertrait correlations are zero.

Two different processes lead to multiplicative effects. One might be called differential augmentation (e.g. Campbell and O'Connell, 1967, 1982).

Here, multiplicative effects are a consequence of an interaction between the "true" level of trait correlation and the magnitude of method bias. A conventional position is that method factors add irrelevant systematic (method-specific, trait-irrelevant) variance to the observed relationships among measures. In other words, sharing a method is expected to increase the correlations between two measures above the true relationship; halo effects and response sets are two common sources of such outcomes. However, not all relationships are exaggerated by sharing a common method; only those relationships that are large enough to get noticed are likely to be exaggerated. Campbell and O'Connell (1967, pp. 421-2) provide an example of such effects where ratings (e.g. self-ratings and peer-ratings) are used as methods. Each rater might have an implicit theory and set of expectations about the co-occurrence of certain traits, which lead to rater-specific biases. In such cases, the stronger the "true" associations are between traits, the more likely they are to be noticed and exaggerated, thus producing the multiplicative method-effect pattern.

A second process producing multiplicative effects is differential attenuation (e.g. Campbell and O'Connell, 1967, 1982). A conceptual basis for this view is that using different methods will attenuate the relationships between traits that are better represented when methods are held constant rather than varied. That is, methods are seen as diluting trait relationships rather than as adding irrelevant systematic variance. Not sharing a method attenuates the observed correlations differently, depending on the level of true trait relationships. Suppose, for example, that multiple occasions are used as methods in a MTMM matrix design. This approach was taken by Marsh and Hocevar (1988) in their development of the hierarchical confirmatory factor analysis (HCFA) model. The results of longitudinal studies often show that correlations are lower for longer than for shorter lapses in time, demonstrating an autoregressive process. Accordingly, a high correlation between two traits will be more attenuated over time than will a low correlation (see also, Campbell and O'Connell, 1982, pp. 100-6). In contrast, a correlation of zero can erode no further, and it remains zero when computed across methods (i.e. occasions).

The DP model can be estimated with programs such as EQS or LISREL (e.g. Wothke and Browne, 1990), but certain advantages result when the MUTMUM program is used (Browne, 1990). The MUTMUM program is less cumbersome than EQS or LISREL, provides standard errors for both trait and method correlations (a particular EQS or LISREL run only computes standard errors for trait or method correlations and must be reparameterized and run twice to yield these estimates), and accommodates constraints on both trait and method correlation matrixes.

Campbell and Fiske's (1959) original criteria for convergent and discriminant validity have the following interpretations under the DPM (e.g. Browne, 1984, pp. 9-10). Evidence for convergent validity is achieved when the correlations among methods in P_m are positive and large. The first criterion for discriminant validity is met when the correlations among traits

Table 9.9 Illustration of the direct product model applied to data from Foxman, Tansuhaj, and Ekstrom (1989)

Measures	Communalities	Error	Trait correlations			Method correlations		
			T_1	T_2	T_3	M_1	M_2	M_3
$T_1 M_1$	0.77	0.23	1.00			1.00		
$T_2 M_1$	0.81	0.19	0.63(0.10)[a]	1.00		0.31(0.09)	1.00	
$T_3 M_1$	0.79	0.21	0.63(0.10)	0.79(0.09)	1.00	0.18(0.08)	0.53(0.09)	1.00
$T_1 M_2$	0.71	0.29						
$T_2 M_2$	0.75	0.25						
$T_3 M_2$	0.73	0.27						
$T_1 M_3$	0.82	0.18						
$T_2 M_3$	0.85	0.15						
$T_3 M_3$	0.83	0.17						

[a] Standard errors in parentheses.
Note: $T_i M_j$ refers to tha appropriate trait-method pairing.

in $\mathbf{P}_T$ are less than unity. The second criterion for discriminant validity is attained when the method correlations in $\mathbf{P}_m$ are greater than the trait correlations in $\mathbf{P}_T$. The final discriminant validity criterion is satisfied whenever the DP model holds as determined, for example, by the results for goodness-of-fit indices. These interpretations follow from the specification of the DP model, and a demonstration showing this can be found in Bagozzi and Yi (1990b, pp. 549–50). More formal tests of most of these conditions as well as other useful hypotheses are possible and will be described below when we consider an example.

Illustration of the DP model

The DP model was applied to data collected by Foxman, Tansuhaj, and Ekstrom (1989) who examined 161 family triads of father, mother, and adolescent child wherein each person rated the child's general influence on purchasing. Traits consisted of influence in the areas of suggesting a price range, going shopping with parents when looking for a product for family use, and suggesting stores. Browne's (1990) MUTMUM program was used. The DP model fit the data well: $\chi^2(25) = 30.04, p \simeq 0.22$. Table 9.9 summarizes the results. Notice that the criterion for convergent validity indicates that one must reject convergent validity because two method correlations are rather small ($r_{m1m2} = 0.31$, $r_{m1m3} = 0.18$. The first criterion for discriminant validity is met in that the correlations among traits are less than 1.00, but the second criterion fails because all method correlations are in fact lower than all trait correlations. The third criterion for discriminant holds because the DP model fits well.

It is possible to examine more specific hypotheses concerning construct validity, reliability, trait effects, and methods more formally within the context of the DP model, but this will not be done herein in the interest of brevity. For derivation of specific tests and illustrations, see Bagozzi (1993c) and Bagozzi and Yi (1992, 1993).

Critique of the DP model

One drawback with the DP model is that convergent validity is assessed by a rather global standard (e.g. Bagozzi and Yi, 1990b, p. 556). The requirement that method correlations be substantial is a composite indicator of sorts for convergence of multiple measures of each trait. The criterion for convergent validity does not supply information about the degree of convergent validity or point out which measure(s) is satisfactory or not. In this sense, the DP model is less informative than the CFA model.

A related shortcoming of the DP model is that it is not possible to arrive at an estimate of variation in a method due to traits, as is possible with the CFA model. Trait and method variance are confounded in the DP model.

A final point to note is that, on occasion, the DP model and either the CFA model or the CU model can fit the same data set. Bagozzi and Yi

(1991) found, for example, that 2 of 4 data sets in their study were explained satisfactorily by both the DP and CFA models. However, because improper solutions arose for the CFA models, there is reason to reject these models and accept the DP model. On the other hand, the CU model and the DP model both fit the two data sets in question (not shown in Bagozzi and Yi, 1991). One of these data sets can be accounted for by the trait-only model (Bagozzi and Yi, 1991, p. 438), so it appears that only one data set actually can be explained by both the CU and DP models. Because the trait-only model is more parsimonious than the DP model, we might accept the former and reject the latter for the data set in question.

It thus appears that the DP model and the CFA and CU models can fit the same data on occasion, although the likelihood of this happening in practice is unknown. Unfortunately, little is known as well about the conditions under which both models will fit the same data. One decision rule that can be applied until we learn more about the relationship between the two models is to rely on differences in parsimony between the two models. From the point of view of the number of parameters to be estimated, the DP model has fewer parameters than the CU (or CFA) model. But it could be argued that linear effects are conceptually more parsimonious than multiplicative effects. A choice between the two, when both fit the same data, will depend on one's interpretation of parsimony.

Final thoughts on construct validity

The assessment of convergent and discriminant validity is a complex endeavor with many options and many pitfalls. In this book, we have considered the rationales, assumptions, and pros and cons of four leading approaches to the analysis of MTMM matrix data. Figure 9.9 presents guidelines for using the procedures in studies of construct validity.

It is useful to think of the analysis of MTMM data from the point of view of either of one of two goals, based upon whether one has strong or weak criteria for making hypotheses. When one has strong reasons for expecting a particular kind of structure underlying the data or desires information of a specific nature, either the confirmatory factor analysis model, correlated uniqueness model, or direct product model may be tried first. For example, if one has reason to believe that traits and methods interact (e.g. this might be expected when self and expert ratings are gathered of traits and respondents have an implicit personality theory which affects their judgments), then the direct product model should be examined first. If, on the other hand, one believes that traits and methods have additive effects (a likely outcome in many contexts), then either the confirmatory factor analysis model or correlated uniqueness model can be investigated. The former would be preferred when the researcher desires to partition variance into trait, method, and error components. The latter is advantageous when (a) improper solutions result in a confirmatory factor analysis or (b) trait and method variance are suspected to be confounded

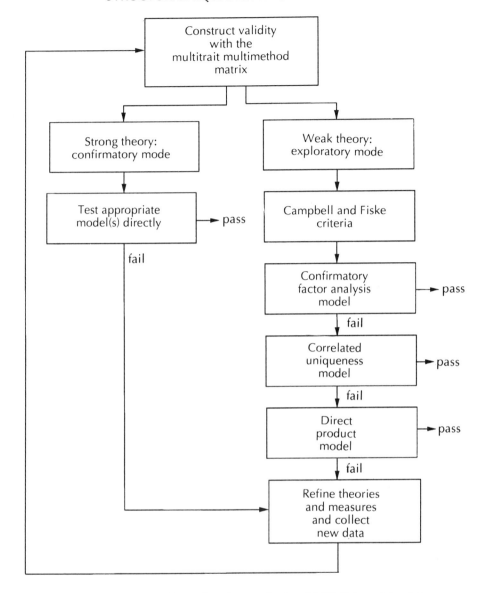

Figure 9.9 Guidelines for the analysis of MTMM matrix data

(e.g. when traits are highly correlated and a general method factor reflects trait variance).

When one lacks a strong rationale for hypothesizing an underlying structure, the exploratory sequence outlined in the right hand side of Figure 9.9 might be appropriate. It is helpful often in these cases to begin with the classic Campbell and Fiske (1959) procedure. Satisfaction of the four criteria suggested by Campbell and Fiske (1959) is incomplete, however, for making definitive conclusions, and the approach rests on unrealistic assumptions. Nevertheless, positive results from the classic analysis provide tentative criteria for concluding that a linear model might capture the relationships in the MTMM matrix. A failure to satisfy the Campbell and Fiske (1959) criteria could stem from many reasons some of which include excessive random error and unreliable measures, method effects which are highly correlated and/or nonproportional across measures of traits, and unknown relations between traits and methods.

Whether the Campbell and Fiske (1959) criteria are met or not, we recommend that the confirmatory factor analysis model be applied next in an exploratory investigation. Because the confirmatory factor analysis model overcomes so many limitations of the Campbell and Fiske (1959) approach and at the same time yields a partitioning of variance into trait, method, and error components, it is a potentially informative window into construct validity. We recommend that the trait-only model be run first in this regard. If it fits satisfactorily, then the addition of method factors should be done warily, as it will lead to overfitting and improper solutions with high likelihood. A poorly fitting trait-only model might be caused by a failure to model method effects, which the results from an analysis of a trait-method analysis should confirm.

As Marsh and Bailey (1991) show, the confirmatory factor analysis model is often unsuccessful in the sense that either iterations fail to converge and no proper solution is possible or else the solution that one finds results in improper parameter estimates such as negative or non-significant error variances. Of course, proper solutions can result but the model may deviate significantly from the data. For all these instances, the confirmatory factor analysis model must be rejected. When this happens, the correlated uniqueness model should be explored. Indeed, this model is highly robust and is likely to fit most data sets, assuming the assumptions upon which it is based are met.

In those cases where the correlated uniqueness model fails to account for the pattern of relations in a MTMM matrix, it might be a consequence of interactions between traits and methods. Here the researcher can apply the direct product model. It should be noted that none of the models may fit a particular data set if complex patterns underlie the relationships such as additive effects among some traits and methods, multiplicative effects among others. When this happens and if enough traits and methods exist, it may prove fruitful to explore different models for different subsets of measures.

All the models considered up to this point are applicable to data summarized in the classic MTMM matrix. Each trait is measured by a single indicator from each of multiple methods. A drawback common to the approaches is the property that random error is confounded with specific error in the disturbances.

Three approaches that represent both random error and measure specificity, and thus circumvent the confounding mentioned above, are the hierarchical confirmatory factor analysis (HCFA) model (Marsh and Hocevar,

1988), the first-order, multiple-informant, multiple-indicator (FOMIMI) model (Kumar and Dillon, 1990), and certain panel models (e.g. Bagozzi and Heatherton, 1993; Bagozzi and Yi, 1993). Unlike the procedures presented in this chapter, the HCFA, FOMIMI, and panel models have data requirements going beyond the classic MTMM matrix. The HCFA model uses first-order factors to represent latent trait–method combinations where two or more measures load on each trait–method factor. Thus, the correlation matrix needed for a HCFA model is at least twice as large as the traditional MTMM matrix which uses one measure for each trait–method unit. Under the HCFA model, trait and method factors are modeled as second-order latent variables. The FOMIMI model uses first-order latent variables to represent trait and method effects, as with the confirmatory factor analysis model. But to capture measure specificity, additional first-order factors are introduced. To achieve an identifiable model, at least two and preferably three measures are required for each trait–method combination (Bagozzi, Yi, and Phillips, 1991). This means that the correlation matrix required for a FOMIMI analysis is at least twice the size of a traditional MTMM matrix. Because the ratio of factors to measures in a FOMIMI model is often larger than what one would like to have in a factor analysis, the potential for overfitting and either failures to converge or improper solutions is great. This property and the large data requirements make the FOMIMI model less useful in practice. For further information on the HCFA and FOMIMI models and an illustration, see Bagozzi (1991) and Bagozzi, Yi, and Phillips (1991). Table 9.10 summarizes the advantages and disadvantages of the various approaches to construct validation.

Table 9.10 Summary of pros and cons with regard to contemporary procedures for assessing construct validity

Procedure	Advantages	Disadvantages
Campbell and Fiske (1959)	Intuitive	No precise standards for ascertaining convergent and discriminant validity.
	Easy to apply	Cannot determine degree of trait, method, and error variance.
		Assumes that traits and methods are uncorrelated, methods influence all traits equally, methods are uncorrelated, measures are equally reliable.
Confirmatory factor analysis (e.g. Widaman, 1985)	Methods can correlate freely and affect measures to different degrees.	Disturbances reflect both specific and error variances.

Table 9.10 (*Cont.*)

Procedure	Advantages	Disadvantages
	Measures of fit provided for an overall model. Estimates of tests of significance provided for parameters. Variance can be partitioned into trait, method, error components. Under certain conditions, can estimate correlations between traits and methods.	Partitioning of variance may not yield "trait-free" and "method free" interpretations. Ill-defined solutions frequently result (e.g. negative error variances). Requires at least three traits and three methods, four traits and two methods, or two traits and four methods.
Correlated uniquenesses model (e.g. Marsh, 1989)	Likelihood of ill-defined solutions low. Avoids confounding of method variance with trait variance under certain conditions. Possible to test assumption that all correlated uniquenesses associated with one method can be accounted for by a single factor (when at least four traits and three methods exist).	Confounds random error with measure specificity. Interpretation of correlated uniquenesses may be difficult. Assumes methods are uncorrelated. Requires at least three traits and three methods.
Direct product model (e.g. Browne, 1984)	Provides direct translation of Campbell and Fiske criteria. Represents interaction of traits and methods. Can work for models as small as two traits and two methods.	Confounds random error with measure specificity. Trait and method variance confounded. Degree of convergent validity difficult to interpret.
Second-order confirmatory factor analysis model (e.g. Anderson, 1987)	Random error and measure specificity estimated separately.	Assumes ratios of trait variance to measure specificity are identical for any particular measure, regardless of the method. Requires at least twice, and preferably three times, as many measures as standard procedures.
Hierarchical confirmatory factor analysis model (e.g. Marsh and Hocevar, 1988)	Random error and measure specificity estimated separately.	Assumes constant proportions for measure k for the ratios of (a) trait variance to method variance

STRUCTURAL EQUATION MODELS: BASIC PRINCIPLES

Table 9.10 (Cont.)

Procedure	Advantages	Disadvantages
		(b) trait variance to measure specificity
		(c) method variance to measure specificity.
		Requires at least twice, and preferably three times, as many measures as standard procedures.
First-order multiple-informant, multiple indicator model (e.g. Kumar and Dillon, 1990)	Random error and measure specificity estimated separately. Avoids assumptions on ratios made by second-order and hierarchical confirmatory factor analysis models.	Requires at least twice, and preferably three times, as many measures as standard procedures. Likelihood of overfitting high (i.e. failures to converge or ill-defined solutions are likely).
Panel models with multitraits (e.g. Bagozzi and Heatherton, 1993)	Random error and measure specificity estimated separately. Temporal stability and true reliability can be estimated. Applies to as few as two traits and three methods.	Needs at least two points in time for each measure.

In sum, many procedures can be used for analyzing MTMM matrix data. No single approach dominates the others. No universal procedure can be recommended. The choice of one or more models will depend on the purposes of the researcher. Nevertheless, it is important to recognize the pros and cons of the different approaches. We presented guidelines for conducting the investigation of construct validity with MTMM matrix data. A researcher must be aware of the assumptions of the different procedures and their implications for the information derived from their application. The choice of a procedure should be guided by the nature of the traits under investigation, the properties of the methods used to measure traits, the correspondence of traits and methods to the underlying rationale of the model under consideration, the assumptions of the model and its sensitivity to their violation, and the kind of information desired (e.g. partitioning of variance into components).

Explanation, Prediction, and Control

Up to this point, we have focused on measurement issues with particular attention given to reliability, the dimensions of constructs, and construct

364 RICHARD P. BAGOZZI

validity. Each of these issues is important in its own right and can be studied in isolation as a precursor to substantive research. Indeed, careful scrutiny of measurement issues in questionnaire design, pretesting, and theory development should enhance the chances that substantive inquiry will be successful. At the same time, many of the ideas discussed up to now can be formally integrated into substantive models, a topic to which we now turn.

The role of measurement error in substantive research

When we test hypotheses between predictors and dependent variables, we would like inferences to be based on relationships between true variates as

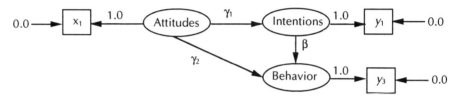

(a) Model with no provisions for meaurement error

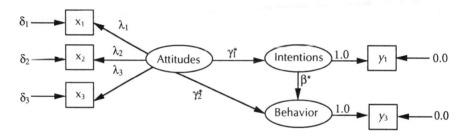

(b) Model taking into account measurement error in attitudes

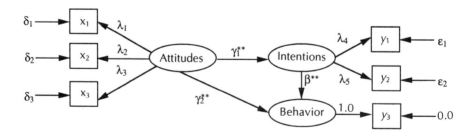

(c) Model taking into account measurement error in attitudes and intentions

Figure 9.10 The effects of measurement error on tests of hypotheses: illustration of a means for correcting for the consequences of random error

opposed to variates containing measurement error. Because most measures used in marketing contain measurement error to one degree or another, tests of hypotheses should take this error into account whenever possible. Fortunately, SEMs with latent variables provide a way to do this in a straightforward manner.

To see this, consider the model shown in Figure 9.10. Here attitudes are presented as direct and indirect (through intentions) determinants of behavior. In Figure 9.10a, all variables are shown with single indicators and thus measurement error is not taken into account (i.e. the measures are presumed to be perfectly reliable). Figures 9.10b,c present modifications revealing the effects of modeling measurement error in attitudes alone and in both attitudes and intentions, respectively. Notice that the values of key parameters among variables (the γs and βs) differ among the three situations.

We applied the models shown in Figure 9.10 to data obtained in a pretest of a study of coupon usage. Table 9.11 presents preliminary data from two samples. Sample A is from respondents identified as being action oriented in motivation; sample B is from respondents identified as being state oriented. Action versus state orientation was determined by answers to a questionnaire designed to reveal differing approaches in decision-making. The theory behind the hypotheses investigated in the study can be found in Bagozzi, Baumgartner, and Yi (1992).

Table 9.12 shows the findings for the models in Figure 9.10 applied to sample A. When measurement error in attitudes is taken into account, we see that the impact of attitudes on intentions increases by 64 percent from 0.76 to 1.25 and the effect of attitudes on behavior more than doubles from 0.24 to 0.56 (the parameter estimates shown in the table are unstandardized). This demonstrates a common consequence of measurement error in independent variables: namely, when error is not taken into account, parameters will be inconsistent and attenuated; modeling measurement error will yield parameters corrected for attenuation. However, it is important to note that error in any independent variable will be reflected throughout the parameters in a structural equation model, often in unpredictable ways. Notice in the present example that, when measurement error in only attitudes is taken into account, the coefficient linking intentions to behavior actually decreases from 0.36 to 0.28, although it still is significant.

The bottom panel of Table 9.12 shows the consequences of taking into account measurement error in both attitudes and intentions. Here we see that the effects of attitudes again increase significantly over the parameter estimates found in the top panel. The effect of intentions on behavior actually increases slightly over the situation shown in the middle panel of Table 9.12, although it still is somewhat less than that found in the top panel. Table 9.12 also reveals the consequences of measurement error on explained variance. It can be seen that the variance explained in intentions goes from 0.25 to 0.46 and the variance explained in behavior goes from 0.39 to 0.45 when we compare the model with no measurement error taken into account to the model with measurement error modelled explicitly.

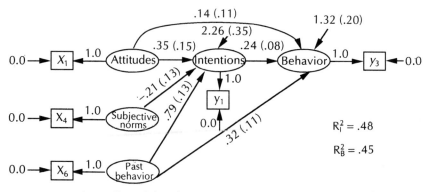

(a) Full model with measurement error taken into account

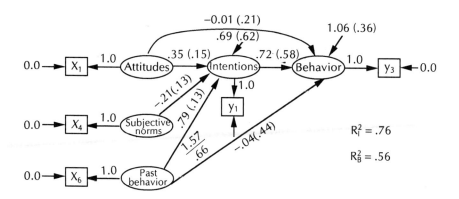

(b) Full model with measurement error taken into account in one measure of intentions

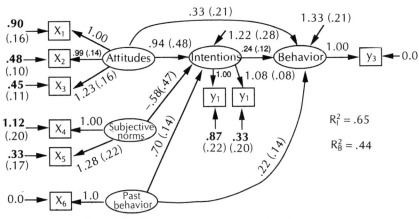

(c) Full model with measurement error taken into account in attitudes, subjective norms, and intentions

Figure 9.11 Full model with measurement error taken into account in attitudes, subjective norms, and intentions

Table 9.11 Variance–covariance data matrices for coupon usage study

Sample A: Action oriented women (n = 85)

Intentions #1	4.389								
Intentions #2	3.792	4.410							
Behavior	1.935	1.855	2.385						
Attitudes #1	1.454	1.453	0.989	1.914					
Attitudes #2	1.087	1.309	0.841	0.961	1.480				
Attitudes #3	1.623	1.701	1.175	1.279	1.220	1.971			
Subjective norms #1	0.571	0.900	0.371	0.779	0.801	0.953	1.964		
Subjective norms #2	1.056	1.258	0.767	0.928	1.130	1.192	1.085	1.718	
Past behavior	2.205	2.495	1.482	1.204	1.007	1.423	0.896	1.131	2.498

Sample B: State oriented women (n = 64)

Intentions #1	3.730								
Intentions #2	3.208	3.436							
Behavior	1.687	1.675	2.171						
Attitudes #1	0.621	0.616	0.605	1.373					
Attitudes #2	1.063	0.864	0.428	0.671	1.397				
Attitudes #3	0.895	0.818	0.595	0.912	0.663	1.498			
Subjective norms #1	1.200	1.228	0.847	0.455	0.401	0.635	1.787		
Subjective norms #2	1.095	1.064	0.779	0.560	0.714	0.790	1.147	1.587	
Past behavior	1.819	1.909	1.213	0.479	0.591	0.738	0.795	0.687	2.026

Table 9.12 Key parameter estimates for the models in Figure 9.10 and sample A in Table 9.11

Model	Parameter estimate
No measurement error taken into account	
attitudes $\xrightarrow{\alpha_1}$ intentions	0.76(0.14)[a]
attitudes $\xrightarrow{\alpha_2}$ behavior	0.24(0.11)
intentions $\xrightarrow{\beta}$ behavior	0.36(0.07)
variance explained in intentions	0.25
variance explained in behavior	0.39
Measurement error in attitudes taken into account	
attitudes $\xrightarrow{\alpha_1^*}$ intentions	1.25(0.23)
attitudes $\xrightarrow{\alpha_2^*}$ behavior	0.56(0.18)
intentions $\xrightarrow{\beta^*}$ behavior	0.28(0.08)
variance explained in intentions	0.37
variance explained in behavior	0.44
Measurement error in attitudes and intentions taken into account	
attitudes $\xrightarrow{\alpha_1^{**}}$ intentions	1.29(0.23)
attitudes $\xrightarrow{\alpha_2^{**}}$ behavior	0.48(0.20)
intentions $\xrightarrow{\beta^{**}}$ behavior	0.33(0.10)
variance explained in intentions	0.46
variance explained in behavior	0.45

[a] Standard errors in parentheses.

The model shown in Figure 9.10 is actually only part of the theory of reasoned action and thus exhibits omitted variables by definition. Figure 9.11 presents the full theory of reasoned action (attitudes, subjective norms, intentions, and behavior), where, in addition, past behavior has been added as a predictor to provide an even more complete representation. In panel a, we show the findings for the case where no measurement error is taken into account (again only sample A is investigated herein for simplicity). Attitudes influence intentions significantly and intentions influence behavior significantly, as found in the partial model, but now attitudes do not have a significant effect on behavior when subjective norms and past behavior are included as covariates. Notice that the explained variances for intentions and behavior are 0.48 and 0.45, respectively, which are moderately high for a model not taking into account random error.

Panel b presents the results for the case where measurement error in only a single measure of intentions is taken into account. Here we see that the substantive interpretation of all coefficients remains the same as in panel a except for the impact of intentions on behavior which is now in fact revealed to be nonsignificant. This finding demonstrates that the effect of one variable on another when both are part of a system of relations may be reduced when one takes into account measurement error in the antecedent. Of course, we have more information than that utilized in this subanalysis.

When all the information is used and measurement error is taken into account in attitudes, subjective norms, and intentions, the results are as shown in the bottom panel of Figure 9.11. Now we see that significant effects are found for attitudes on intentions, intentions on behavior, and past behavior on intentions. The path from attitudes to intentions increases nearly threefold when measurement error is taken into account. The path from past behavior to intentions changes slightly and the path from intentions to behavior remains the same, when comparing the cases of no measurement error to measurement error taken into account.

In sum, measurement error has complex effects in tests of hypotheses. Error in exogenous variables usually attenuates parameter estimates of the effects of these variables on other variables in a system of equations. But note that such error can contaminate the parameters representing the effects of other variables, and the direction and magnitude of this contamination depend on the nature and strength of relations among the focal variables, as well as multicollinearity among predictors. Measurement error in measures of endogenous variables may result in inflation, deflation, or no change in coefficients linking the endogenous variables to other endogenous variables dependent upon them. But the effects here are also difficult to predict and depend on the amount of error and the pattern of relations among variables. Fortunately, by modelling measurement error, we can mitigate some of the dangers of making false inferences. SEMs with latent variables represent one way to do this.

The role of intervening variables in substantive research

Structural equation models with latent variables can also be used to advantage in testing hypotheses where one or more variables are thought to intervene (i.e. mediate) between an independent variable(s) and a dependent variable(s). The benefits here are twofold. First, one gains more insight into how independent variables produce their effects, which determinants are more proximal, which more distal, and in general how a phenomenon of interest evolves and changes in response to the forces shaping it. Second, by modelling intervening variables, along with their antecedents, we avoid omitted variables and certain threats that accompany such omissions and make inferences less valid.

Figure 9.12 illustrates some of the issues. Consider first the top panel. As a baseline model, the findings for the tests of relationships among attitudes, intentions, and behavior are shown at the left. What happens when an omitted variable occurs? If intentions, an intervening variable, are omitted, the regression of behavior on attitudes will produce a coefficient

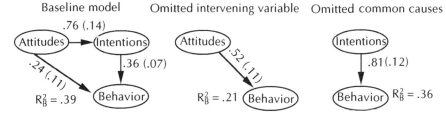

(a) Attitudes, intentions, and behavior (sample A)

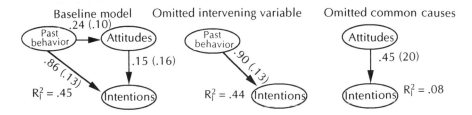

(b) Past behavior, attitudes, and intentions (sample B)

Figure 9.12 Some consequences of omitted variables (data from Table 9.11; standard errors in parentheses)

equal to the sum of the true indirect and direct effects of attitudes on behavior. As shown in the top center of Figure 9.12, the effect of attitudes on behavior is 0.52, which is 0.24 (the path from attitudes to behavior) plus 0.28 (the product of 0.76 times 0.36, the path from attitudes to intentions times the path from intentions to behavior). If attitudes, a common cause of intentions and behavior, are omitted, the regression of behavior on intentions yields a coefficient of 0.81 (see top right of Figure 9.12).

This example shows that the effects of omitted variables lead in some instances to overestimates of the impact of attitudes on behavior and the impact of intentions on behavior. For these particular data, the overestimates may not be overly misleading, since especially in the case of the omitted intervening variable, the coefficient gives a valid reflection of the total effect of attitudes on behavior. Nevertheless, we lose important explanatory information when intentions are omitted in that more of the effect of attitudes is channelled through intentions than is direct. From a managerial perspective, then, consideration must be given to intentions in any attitude change program. The effect of intentions on behavior, given an omission of attitudes, is more misleading because the results point to an inflated role for intentions.

The example shown in the top half of Figure 9.12 applies to the special case where a valid intervening variable exists and the direct and indirect effects of an antecedent are of the same sign. The omission of an intervening variable becomes even more of a problem when the direct and indirect effects are of opposite signs. Because the regression of a dependent variable on an antecedent, when an intervening variable is omitted, is the sum of true direct and indirect effects, the resulting coefficient can be less than either or both of the direct or indirect effects. Such occurrences have been termed suppressor effects in the literature, and, although perhaps rare, the researcher should be aware of the possibility. Indeed, it is possible for direct and indirect effects to cancel each other out such that a regression of a dependent variable on an antecedent, given an omitted variable, suggests no impact. In this case it is not so much that the independent variable has no effect as it is that its effects counterbalance each other. The managerial implications of counteracting phenomena will in general be different than the case of no effects.

A potentially more serious problem occurs when a variable is omitted that is a common cause of both a dependent variable and a variable that is presumed to be a cause of the dependent variable. The second panel in Figure 9.12 illustrates this situation. As shown for the baseline model at the left, past behavior determines both attitudes and intentions, with the presumed impact of attitudes on intentions failing to reach significance. The bottom center of Figure 9.12 demonstrates that the omission of attitudes, in this case a nonfunctional intervening variable, has little effect on the coefficient relating intentions to past behavior. But notice what happens when past behavior is the omitted variable and intentions are regressed on attitudes. As shown at the bottom right of Figure 9.12, a significant positive coefficient results from the regression of intentions on attitudes. This is an example of a spurious relationship. An omitted common cause of two variables that are not causally related leads to the false inference of dependence between the two variables when one is regressed on the other.

The consequences of omitted variables can be seen in still another context. Figure 9.13 presents the simple case where a single dependent variable is regressed on two independent variables. Under the baseline model, attitudes and subjective norms are both causes of intentions. The omission of attitudes, however, leads to an estimate for the effect of subjective norms on intentions that is less than the effect under the baseline model. The omission of subjective norms, in contrast, leads to an estimate for the effect of attitudes on intentions that is greater than the effect found for the baseline model. It turns out that attitudes and subjective norms are significantly associated with each other. If the association is rooted in a causal connection between the two variables, then the consequences of omitted variables will depend on which is the cause and which is the effect. Under either case, the implications parallel those discussed with respect to the models shown in the top half of Figure 9.12. Of course, these implications are different depending on which is cause and which is effect and must be traced out. Alternatively, attitudes and subjective norms could be associated because they are both dependent on one or more common causes. Here the effects of omitting attitudes or subjective norms will depend on the effects of the omitted antecedents to attitudes and intentions, as well as the significance of the paths between attitudes and intentions and between subjective norms and intentions. This complicates the analysis, but can be examined using the procedures discussed herein.

In sum, it can be seen that the role of intervening variables is quite complex, yet some generalizations are possible, at least for simple models. For more involved models, the consequences of omitting intervening processes can only be ascertained on a case by case basis. It should be noted that the examples we chose here are representative of current practice in marketing research. Consider case a in Figure 9.12. Researchers sometimes fail to measure attitudes, intentions, and behavior in their studies. Some omit intentions and regress behavior (or choice) directly on attitudes (or preference). Others omit attitudes and regress behavior on intentions. These practices are potentially misleading. With respect to case b in Figure 9.12, note that the Fishbein model fails to include past behavior in its specification, yet this variable frequently is of theoretical interest and often has strong empirical effects (Bagozzi and Warshaw, 1990). Finally, it should be stressed that the magnitude and pattern of measurement errors makes the interpretation of the role of intervening variables even more difficult to assess. Our examples of omitted variables were conducted on manifest variables. The use of structural equation models with latent variables makes it possible to explore the consequences of omitted variables and measurement error in an integrated and informative way.

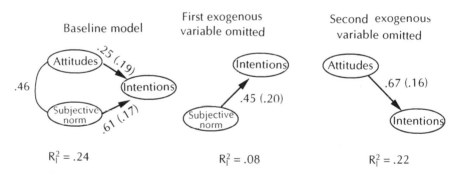

Figure 9.13 Further consequences of omitted variables: parallel exogenous causes (data from Table 9.11, sample B; standard errors in parentheses)

The role of moderating variables in substantive research

So far our discussion of substantive hypotheses has been concerned with linear effects. An important interaction effect is the operation of a moderating variable. We can think of a moderating variable as a phenomenon that affects the relationship between two or more other phenomena such that the relationship changes, depending on the level of the moderating variable. One way to study moderating effects in the context of structural equation models with latent variables, and thereby take advantage of provisions for correcting for measurement error, is to investigate a model separately for each of a set of groups of subjects corresponding to different levels of the moderating variable. Then the coefficient(s) of interest can be compared across groups to see if the focal effect(s) varies by group, thus suggesting whether the moderating variable was at work or not. The test is analogous to the Chow test used in econometrics.

As an example, we applied the model shown in the bottom panel of Figure 9.11 to the data of Table 9.11 to see if action–state orientation moderates the impact of subjective norms on intentions. The hypothesis is that subjective norms should have a greater effect on intentions for those who are state- as opposed to action-oriented. The simultaneous estimation of the model for both groups yielded a goodness-of-fit index of $\chi^2(40) = 48.73$, $p \cong 0.16$. For state-oriented people, the path from subjective norms to intentions was 0.52 with a standard error of 0.25; for action-oriented people, the path was -0.58 with a standard error of 0.46. The simultaneous group analysis with the path from subjective norms to intentions constrained to be equal across the two groups gave a $\chi^2(41) = 53.77, p \cong 0.09$. Because the chi-square difference test shows that $\chi_d^2(1) = 5.04, p < 0.05$, we can conclude that the paths do indeed differ across groups. Hence, the hypothesis is supported that the effects of subjective norms on intentions is contingent on (i.e. is moderated by) the level of action–state orientation.

A number of recent studies have examined the dependence of the attitude–behavior relationship on various moderating variables. Bagozzi and Yi (1989) investigated the degree of intention formation and found that attitudes have a direct effect on behavior and less of an indirect effect (through intentions) when intentions are ill-formed as opposed to being well-formed. When intentions are well-formed, attitudes tend to work through intentions in their influence on behavior. Bagozzi, Yi, and Baumgartner (1990) found that the level of effort required to perform a behavior moderates the attitude–behavior relation. When a large amount of effort is needed, attitudes work primarily through intentions en-route to stimulating behavior. But when the level of effort needed is very low, attitudes have less of an effect on intentions and instead operate directly upon behavior. Each of the above hypotheses for moderating variable effects was tested by use of structural equation models with latent variables. Our example of moderating variables has been necessarily brief. One issue we did not address is that one should test whether factor loadings of key latent variables are equal across groups. This should be done before testing whether causal paths are equal or not. Both tests should be performed on the covariance matrix. These and other issues in the test of moderating variables are illustrated in Bagozzi and Yi (1989).

Reciprocal causation and feedback

A final topic we wish to consider is reciprocal causation, which is also known as mutual causation, simultaneity, or non-recursive relationships. Reciprocal causation can be thought of as two variables affecting each other. For example, common sense says that the satisfaction of salespeople is a function of their performance, yet we might expect satisfaction to influence performance as well. From a conceptual standpoint, the meaning of reciprocal causation is unclear. Figure 9.14a shows a simple non-recursive model of reciprocal causation between x_3 and x_6. (The notation for Figure 9.14a, which uses x_1, x_3, x_4 and x_6, is chosen to correspond with Figure 9.14b and to facilitate subsequent comparison of parameters and their identification. Thus, no x_2 and x_5 variables appear in Figure 9.14a.) Two antecedents, x_1 and x_4, are also included as explanatory concepts and are presumed to occur at an earlier time. Figure 9.14a presents the simplest non-recursive model achieving identification and is in fact "exactly identified."

The conceptual problem with non-recursive models lies in the meaning and validity of the reciprocal paths, b_{36} and b_{63}. If one accepts modern

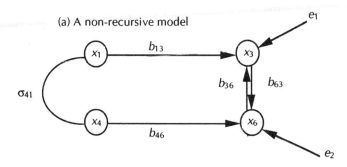

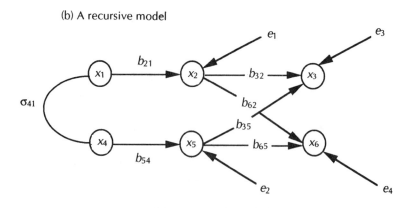

Figure 9.14 Simple non-recursive and recursive models

accounts of causality in the philosophy of science literature (e.g. Mackie, 1974; Sosa, 1975), then temporal priority of cause to effect is a necessary part of its meaning. Yet, in the cross-section, it is impossible for x_3 and x_6 to both be causes of each other and satisfy the temporal priority desideratum. This logic has lead some economists to claim that causality is an inherently recursive phenomenon, and non-recursive models are invalid on an a priori basis (e.g. Strotz, 1960; Strotz and World, 1960; cf. Basmann, 1963a, b; Strotz and Wold, 1963).

Despite the conceptual difficulties with the idea of reciprocal causation, it has frequently been advocated, and indeed, a well-developed methodology has been formulated for its analysis (e.g. James, Muliak, and Brett, 1982). To see a potential difficulty in its use at the operational level, however, one may compare the corresponding causal parameters for non-recursive and recursive models. Figure 9.14b presents a recursive representation of the causal relationships between the variables represented by x_3 and x_6 where measures of the variables at two waves permit lagged effects and thus satisfy the temporal priority requisite. For simplicity, but without loss of generality, population values of variances (σ_{ii}) and covariances (σ_{ij}) can be used to solve for the focal parameters in Figure 9.14b. Because the parameters are overidentified, four values exist for each:

$$b_{62} = \frac{\sigma_{12}\sigma_{15}\sigma_{44}\sigma_{55} - \sigma_{11}\sigma_{26}\sigma_{45}^2}{\sigma_{12}\sigma_{15}\sigma_{24}\sigma_{45} - \sigma_{12}^2\sigma_{45}^2} = \frac{\sigma_{14}\sigma_{24}\sigma_{56} - \sigma_{14}\sigma_{26}\sigma_{45}}{\sigma_{15}\sigma_{24}^2 - \sigma_{12}\sigma_{24}\sigma_{45}}$$

$$= \frac{\sigma_{12}\sigma_{14}\sigma_{15}\sigma_{56} - \sigma_{11}\sigma_{15}\sigma_{26}\sigma_{45}}{\sigma_{12}\sigma_{15}^2\sigma_{24} - \sigma_{12}^2\sigma_{15}\sigma_{45}} = \frac{\sigma_{15}\sigma_{24}\sigma_{44}\sigma_{56} - \sigma_{14}\sigma_{26}\sigma_{45}^2}{\sigma_{15}\sigma_{24}^2\sigma_{45} - \sigma_{12}\sigma_{24}\sigma_{45}^2}$$

$$b_{35} = \frac{\sigma_{11}\sigma_{23}\sigma_{24}\sigma_{45} - \sigma_{12}^2\sigma_{44}\sigma_{53}}{\sigma_{12}\sigma_{15}\sigma_{24}\sigma_{45} - \sigma_{12}^2\sigma_{45}^2} = \frac{\sigma_{14}\sigma_{15}\sigma_{23} - \sigma_{12}\sigma_{14}\sigma_{53}}{\sigma_{15}^2\sigma_{24} - \sigma_{12}\sigma_{15}\sigma_{45}}$$

$$= \frac{\sigma_{11}\sigma_{15}\sigma_{23}\sigma_{24} - \sigma_{12}^2\sigma_{14}\sigma_{53}}{\sigma_{12}\sigma_{15}^2\sigma_{24} - \sigma_{12}^2\sigma_{15}\sigma_{45}} = \frac{\sigma_{14}\sigma_{23}\sigma_{24}\sigma_{45} - \sigma_{12}\sigma_{24}\sigma_{44}\sigma_{53}}{\sigma_{15}\sigma_{24}^2\sigma_{45} - \sigma_{12}\sigma_{24}\sigma_{45}^2}$$

Similarly, for the focal parameters in Figure 9.14a, one finds

$$b_{63} = \frac{\sigma_{14}\sigma_{46} - \sigma_{16}\sigma_{44}}{\sigma_{14}\sigma_{43} - \sigma_{13}\sigma_{44}}, \quad b_{36} = \frac{\sigma_{11}\sigma_{43} - \sigma_{14}\sigma_{13}}{\sigma_{11}\sigma_{46} - \sigma_{14}\sigma_{16}}$$

It can be seen, when comparing b_{62} to b_{63} and b_{35} to b_{36}, respectively, that the recursive and non-recursive representations of causality yield quite different results for the key structural parameters. The differences persist even if one were to assume that (a) time intervals are short between cause and effect, (b) variables are stationary over time, and (c) an averaging of variables over time achieves equilibrium conditions (cf. Carlsson, 1972; James et al., 1982). For all three assumptions, key variances and/or covariances, and hence the focal causal parameters, diverge between non-recursive and recursive models.

376 RICHARD P. BAGOZZI

Therefore, not only does the notion of causality differ in a conceptual sense, but the operational and empirical representations will, except in chance circumstances, produce different outcomes in recursive and non-recursive models. As a consequence, one must question whether non-recursive models constitute valid representations of cause and effect.

An example With the above caveats in mind, we will present an illustration of reciprocal causation, but it should be remembered that longitudinal models will ultimately be needed to make definitive conclusions about the direction of causality between two variables under study. Figure 9.15 presents a causal diagram for a model designed to test whether (a) intentions influence behavior, (b) behavior influences intentions, (c) intentions and behavior influence each other, or (d) no causal relationship exists between intentions and behavior. Actually, there is even a fifth possibility that an associational relationship exists but that it is spurious in the sense of being produced by common causes. Had we modelled these common causes in Figure 9.15, we would have been able to test for spuriousness.

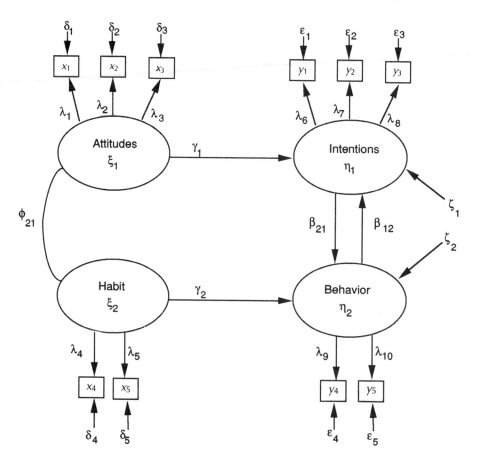

Figure 9.15 Causal models of reciprocal causation

Table 9.13 presents data for the measures presented in Figure 9.15 and is from a study of attitudes toward dieting.

We applied LISREL to the data and found that the model in Figure 9.15 fits well: $\chi^2(30) = 38.27, p \simeq 0.14$. With respect to the key paths representing reciprocal causation, it was found that intentions influence behavior ($\beta_{21} = 0.44$, s.e. = 0.09), but behavior does not influence intentions ($\beta_{12} = 0.14$, s.e., = 0.09), as attitude theory predicts. Nevertheless, we wish to reiterate that a cross-lagged panel model is needed to achieve greater confidence in these findings. For examples of reciprocal causation, see Bagozzi (1980b) and Van Loo and Bagozzi (1984). Bagozzi and Van Loo (1988) present a cross-lagged analysis. Note that, although not addressed herein, feedback effects from variables twice removed (or more) create interpretive issues similar to those arising for reciprocal causation.

Conclusion

We have considered many fundamental issues in this chapter concerning measurement and tests of functional or causal hypotheses and have shown how structural equation models can be used to advantage. The reader is urged to apply one or more of the many programs available for analyzing structural equation models to the problems presented hereafter. In the next chapter, we address how to evaluate structural equation models.

Table 9.13 Data for reciprocal causation example

Measure										
y1	1.00									
y2	0.75	1.00								
y3	0.77	0.71	1.00							
y4	0.45	0.43	0.44	1.00						
y5	0.41	0.46	0.40	0.75	1.00					
x1	0.60	0.58	0.56	0.24	0.28	1.00				
x2	0.55	0.61	0.55	0.23	0.25	0.81	1.00			
x3	0.57	0.53	0.58	0.27	0.27	0.78	0.82	1.00		
x4	0.04	0.05	0.07	0.38	0.41	0.14	0.11	0.12	1.00	
x5	0.06	0.05	0.06	0.39	0.40	0.13	0.17	0.15	0.78	1.00

$N = 152$

Questions

1 Using the data in Tables 9.1 and 9.3, test the single-factored and two-factored models. Compare findings to Tables 9.2 and 9.4.
2 Perform a second-order confirmatory factor analysis on the data in Table 9.5.
3 For the following data on measures of self-esteem, perform a trait-method confirmatory factor analysis, a correlated uniqueness model analysis, and a direct product model analysis. The sample size is 196.

Measures	A1	A2	A3	B1	B2	B3	C1	C2	C3
A. True-false inventory									
1. Global self-esteem	1.00								
2. Social self-esteem	0.58	1.00							
3. Need for order	0.17	0.14	1.00						
B. Multipoint inventory									
1. Global self-esteem	0.75	0.45	0.23	1.00					
2. Social self-esteem	0.72	0.74	0.16	0.65	1.00				
3. Need for order	0.09	0.06	0.68	0.25	0.08	1.00			
C. Simple self-rating									
1. Global self-esteem	0.58	0.53	0.14	0.62	0.68	0.09	1.00		
2. Social self-esteem	0.47	0.74	0.10	0.40	0.69	0.07	0.58	1.00	
3. Need for order	0.22	0.18	0.63	0.34	0.22	0.56	0.30	0.23	1.00

4 For a two-trait and three-method MTMM matrix, compute $P_M \otimes P_T = P_C$ in the direct product model.

5 For the following data investigating the theory of reasoned action, perform multiple group tests and determine whether the effect of intentions on behavior differs between the groups shown. Group A had ill-formed intentions, and Group B had well-formed intentions, where the degree of intention formation was determined by experimental manipulation. The model to test is

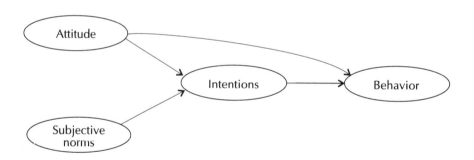

A. Ill-formed intentions ($n = 86$)

	BI1	BI2	BEH1	BEH2	BEH3	ATT1	ATT2	ATT3	SN
BI1	1.460								
BI2	1.403	1.688							
BEH1	1.010	1.615	28.653						
BEH2	0.207	0.294	5.314	2.041					
BEH3	0.773	0.697	10.359	3.837	10.975				
ATT1	0.577	0.643	1.428	0.421	1.092	1.447			
ATT2	0.726	0.695	1.796	0.530	1.068	1.087	1.623		
ATT3	0.755	0.738	2.135	0.581	1.194	1.101	1.333	1.689	
SN	0.066	0.115	−0.766	0.040	−0.188	0.145	0.238	0.002	1.748

B. Well-formed intentions ($n = 83$)

	BI1	BI2	BEH1	BEH2	BEH3	ATT1	ATT2	ATT3	SN
BI1	1.263								
BI2	1.168	1.244							
BEH1	1.985	2.128	41.484						
BEH2	0.559	0.587	6.929	2.547					
BEH3	1.038	1.128	12.763	5.486	14.435				
ATT1	0.311	0.268	−0.297	−0.224	−0.527	1.105			
ATT2	0.596	0.519	0.590	0.306	0.261	0.661	1.386		
ATT3	0.543	0.495	0.332	0.248	0.342	0.678	0.987	1.033	
SN	0.151	0.182	0.585	0.106	0.403	0.355	0.341	0.328	2.367

6. Analyze the reciprocal causation model of Figure 9.15 by use of the data in Table 9.13.

Notes

1. The terms theoretical variable, construct, true score, test score, scale, and concept are used to refer to latent (i.e. abstract or inferred) variables. The terms observable variable, measure, measurement, indicator, item, or operationalization are used to refer to manifest (i.e. observed or measured) variables.
2. Because the goodness-of-fit index for the tau-equivalent model shows a borderline p-value, an inspection was made of the standardized residuals which revealed one high value between x_1 and x_2 (i.e. s.r. = 3.25). A standardized residual is a fitted residual divided by its asymptotic standard error. A standardized residual greater than 2.58 in absolute value suggests that the hypothesized model deviates significantly from the data. Only the congeneric model had no significant standardized residuals in this example.
3. The model with three measures is overidentified when the tau-equivalent or parallel forms models are considered. The model with two measures is overidentified only for the parallel forms case. Although these applications of the models can be tested and may be meaningful in certain instances, they cannot be compared to the congeneric model to perform useful chi-square difference tests. This can only be done when four or more measures are available.
4. It is possible to develop similar hypotheses for the tau-equivalent cases, but this is not done here for the sake of simplicity.
5. For many CFA models, it is possible to permit all traits and methods to intercorrelate freely among themselves and achieve identification in a technical sense. However, in practice such a specification nearly always leads to empirical identification problems (e.g. Marsh, 1989). However, if one has reason to expect that either traits or methods are orthogonal, this can be exploited through appropriate constraints and the correlations between traits and methods can then be estimated, if desired.

References

Ajzen, I. and Fishbein, M. 1980: *Understanding Attitudes and Predicting Social Behavior*, Englewood Cliffs, NJ: Prentice-Hall.

Anderson, J. C. 1987: An approach for confirmatory measurement and structural equation modeling of organizational properties. *Management Science*, 33, 525–41.

Arora, R. 1982: Validation of an S-O-R model for situation, enduring, and response components of involvement. *Journal of Marketing Research*, 19, 505–16.

Bagozzi, R. P. 1980a: *Causal Models in Marketing*, New York: John Wiley.

Bagozzi, R. P. 1980b: Performance and satisfaction in an industrial sales force: an examination of their antecedents and simultaneity. *Journal of Marketing*, 44, 65–77.

Bagozzi, R. P. 1981a. An examination of the validity of two models of attitude. *Multivariate Behavioral Research*, 16, 323–59.

Bagozzi, R. P. 1981b. Attitudes, intentions, and behavior: a test of some key hypotheses. *Journal of Personality and Social Psychology*, 41, 607–27.

Bagozzi, R. P. 1982: A field investigation of causal relations among cognitions, affect, intentions, and behavior. *Journal of Marketing Research*, 19, 562–84.

Bagozzi, R. P. 1984a: A prospectus for theory construction in Marketing, *Journal of Marketing*, 48, 11–29.

Bagozzi, R. P. 1984b: Expectancy-value attitude models: an analysis of critical measurement issues. *International Journal of Research in Marketing*, 1, 295–310.

Bagozzi, R. P. 1991: Further thoughts on the validity of measures of elation, gladness, and joy. *Journal of Personality and Social Psychology*, 61, 98–104.

Bagozzi, R. P. 1992: The self-regulation of attitudes, intentions, and behavior. *Social Psychology Quarterly*, 55, 178–204.

Bagozzi, R. P. 1993a: The effect of emotional arousal on attitude structure. Unpublished working paper, School of Business Administration, the University of Michigan.

Bagozzi, R. P. 1993b: Multidimensional expectancy-value attitude models. Unpublished working paper, School of Business Administration, The University of Michigan.

Bagozzi, R. P. 1993c: Assessing construct validity in personality research: applications to measures of self-esteem. *Journal of Research in Personality*, 27, 49–87.

Bagozzi, R. P., Baumgartner, H., and Yi, Y. 1992: State versus action orientation and the theory of reasoned action: an application to coupon usage. *Journal of Consumer Research*, 18, 505–18.

Bagozzi, R. P. and Burnkrant, R. E. 1979: Attitude organization and the attitude-behavior relationship. *Journal of Personality and Social Psychology*, 37, 913–29.

Bagozzi, R. P. and Burnkrant, R. E. 1985: Attitude organization and the attitude-behavior relation: a reply to Dillon and Kumar. *Journal of Personality and Social Psychology*, 49, 47–57.

Bagozzi, R. P., Davis, F. D., and Warshaw, P. R. 1992: Development and test of a theory of technological learning and usage. *Human Relations*, 45, 659–86.

Bagozzi, R. P., Fornell, C., and Larcker, D. F. 1981: Canonical correlation analysis as a special case of a structural relations model. *Multivariate Behavioral Research*, 16 (October), 437–54.

Bagozzi, R. P. and Heatherton, T. F. 1993: Further evidence on the psychometric properties of the state self-esteem scale. Unpublished manuscript, the University of Michigan.

Bagozzi, R. P. and Kimmel, S. K. 1993: A comparison of models of attitude. Unpublished working paper, the University of Michigan.

Bagozzi, R. P. and Van Loo, M. F. 1988: An investigation of the relationship between work and family size decisions over time. *Multivariate Behavioral Research*, 23, 3–34.

Bagozzi, R. P. and Warshaw, P. R. 1990: Trying to Consume, *Journal of Consumer Research*, 17, 127–140.

Bagozzi, R. P. and Yi, Y. 1989: The degree of intention formation as a moderator of the attitude–behavior relationship. *Social Psychology Quarterly*, 52, 266–79.

Bagozzi, R. P. and Yi, Y. 1990a: On the Use of Structural Equation Models in Experimental Designs, *Journal of Marketing Research*, 26, 271–284.

Bagozzi, R. P. and Yi, Y. 1990b: Assessing method variance in multitrait–multimethod matrices: the case of self-reported affect and perceptions at work. *Journal of Applied Psychology*, 75, 547–60.

Bagozzi, R. P. and Yi, Y. 1991: Multitrait–multimethod matrices in consumer research. *Journal of Consumer Research*, 17, 426–39.

Bagozzi, R. P. and Yi, Y. 1992: Testing hypotheses about methods, traits, and communalities in the direct product model. Applied Psychological Measurement, 16, 373–80.

Bagozzi, R. P. and Yi, Y. 1993: Multitrait–multimethod matrices in consumer research: critique and new developments. *Journal of Consumer Psychology*, 2, 143–70.

Bagozzi, R. P., Yi, Y., and Baumgartner, J. 1990: The level of effort required for behavior as a moderator of the attitude-behavior relation. *European Journal of Social Psychology*, 20, 45–59.

Bagozzi, R. P., Yi, Y., and Phillips, L. W. 1991: Assessing construct validity in organizational research. *Administrative Science Quarterly*, 36, 421–58.

Basmann, R. L. 1963a. The casual interpretation of non-triangular systems of economic relations. *Econometrica*, 31, 439–48.

Basmann, R. L. 1963b: On the causal interpretation of non-triangular systems of economic relations: a rejoinder. *Econometrica*, 31, 451–3.

Baumgartner, J. and Bagozzi, R. P. 1993: Specification, estimation, and testing of moment structure models based on latent variates involving interactions among the exogenous constructs. Unpublished working paper, School of Business Administration, Pennsylvania State University.

Bearden, W. O. and Teel, J. E. 1983: Selected determinants of consumer satisfaction and complaint reports. *Journal of Marketing Research*, 20, 21–8.

Bentler, P. M. 1989: *Theory and Implementation of EQS: A Structural Equations Program*, Los Angeles: BMDP Statistical Software, Inc.

Bollen, K. A. 1989: *Structural Equations with Latent Variables*, New York: John Wiley & Sons.

Bollen, K. and Lennox, R. 1991: Conventional wisdom on measurement: a structural equation perspective. *Psychological Bulletin*, 110, 345–70.

Breckler, S. J. and Wiggins, E. C. 1989: Affect versus evaluation in the structure of attitudes. *Journal of Experimental Social Psychology*, 25, 253–71.

Browne, M. W. 1984: The decomposition of multitrait–multimethod matrices. *British Journal of Mathematical and Statistical Psychology*, 37, 1–21.

Browne, M. W. 1989: Relationships between an additive model and a multiplicative model for multitrait–multimethod matrices. In R. Coppi and S. Bolasco (eds), *Multiway Data Analysis*, Amsterdam: North-Holland, pp. 507–20.

Browne, M. W. 1990: MUTMUM PC user's guide. Unpublished manuscript, Department of Statistics, University of South Africa, Pretoria.

Burnkrant, R. E. and Page, T. J., Jr. 1988: The structure and antecedents of the normative and attitudinal components of Fishbein's theory of reasoned action. *Journal of Experimental Social Psychology*, 24, 66–87.

Campbell, D. T. 1955: The informant in quantitative research. *American Journal of Sociology*, 60, 339–42.

Campbell, D. T. and Fiske, D. 1959: Convergent and discriminant validation by the multitrait–multimethod matrix. *Psychological Bulletin*, 56, 81–105.

Campbell, D. T. and O'Connell, E. J. 1967: Method factors in multitrait–multimethod matrices: multiplicative rather than additive? *Multivariate Behavioral Research*, 2, 409–26.

Campbell, D. T. and O'Connell, E. J. 1982: Methods as diluting trait relationships rather than adding irrelevant systematic variance. In D. Brinberg and L. Kidder (eds), *Forms of Validity*, San Francisco: Jossey-Bass, 93–111.

Carlsson, G. 1972: Lagged structures and cross-sectional methods. *Acta Sociologica*, 15, 323–41.

Cook, T. D. and Campbell, D. T. 1979: *Quasi-Experimentation: Design and Analysis Issues for Field Settings*, Chicago: Rand McNally.

Cudeck, R. 1988: Multiplicative Models and MTMM Matrices. *Journal of Educational Statistics*, 13, 131–47.

Czepiel, J. A., Rosenberg, L. J., and Akerele, A. 1974: Perspectives on consumer satisfaction. *AMA Educator's Proceedings*, Chicago: American Marketing Association, 119–23.

Dillon, W. R. and Kumar, A. 1985: Attitude organization and the attitude–behavior relation: a critique of Bagozzi and Burnkrant's reanalysis of Fishbein and Ajzen. *Journal of Personality and Social Psychology*, 49, 33–46.

Dillon, W. R., Kumar, A., and Mulani, N. 1987: Offending estimates in covariance structure analysis: comments on the causes of and solutions to Heywood cases. *Psychological Bulletin*, 101, 126–35.

Fishbein, M. and Ajzen, I. 1975: *Belief, Attitude, Intention and Behavior: An Introduction to Theory and Research*, Reading, MA: Addison-Wesley.

Foxman, E. R., Tansuhaj, P. S. and Ekstrom, K. M. 1989: Family members' perceptions of adolescents' influence in family decision making. *Journal of Consumer Research*, 15, 482–91.

Funder, D. C. 1989: Accuracy in personality judgment and the dancing bear. In D. M. Buss and N. Cantor (eds), *Personality Psychology: Recent Trends and Emerging Directions*, New York: Springer, pp. 210–23.

Ganster, D. C., Hennessey, H. W., and Luthans, F. 1983: Social desirability response effects: three alternative models. *Academy of Management Journal*, 26, 321–31.

Howard, J. A. and Sheth, J. N. 1969: *The Theory of Buyer Behavior*, New York: John Wiley & Sons.

Hunt, S. D. 1991: Positivism and paradigm dominance in consumer research: toward critical pluralism and rapprochement. *Journal of Consumer Research*, 18, 32–44.

James, L. R., Muliak, S. A., and Brett, J. M. 1982: Causal analysis. *Assumptions, Models, and Data*, Beverly Hills, CA: Sage.

Jöreskog, K. G. 1971: Statistical analysis of sets of congeneric tests. *Psychometrika*, 36, 109–33.

Jöreskog, K. G. 1974: Analyzing psychological data by structural analysis of covariance matrices. In R. C. Atkinson, D. H. Luce, and P. Suppes (eds), *Contemporary Developments in Mathematical Psychology* (Vol. 2, pp. 1–56). San Francisco: Freeman.

Jöreskog, K. G. and Sörbom, D. 1989: *LISREL7: A Guide to the Program and Applications*, 2nd edn, Chicago: SPSS, Inc.

Kaplan, A. 1964: *The Conduct of Inquiry*, Scranton, PA: Chandler Publishing Company.

Kenny, D. A. 1976: An empirical application of confirmatory factor analysis to the multitrait–multimethod matrix. *Journal of Experimental Social Psychology*, 12, 247–52.

Kenny, D. A. 1979: *Correlation and Causality*, New York: Wiley.

Krech, D. and Crutchfield, R. S. 1948: *Theory and Problems in Social Psychology*, New York: McGraw-Hill, p. 152.

Kumar, A. and Dillon, W. R. 1990: On the use of confirmatory measurement models in the analysis of multiple-informant reports. *Journal of Marketing Research*, 27, 102–11.

Kumar, A. and Dillon, W. R. 1992: An integrative look at the use of additive and multiplicative covariance structure models in the analysis of MTMM data. *Journal of Marketing Research*, 29, 51–64.

Lord, F. C. and Novick, M. R. 1968: *Statistical Theories of Mental Test Scores*, Reading, MA: Addison-Wesley.

Mackie, J. L. 1974: *The Cement of the Universe: A Study of Causation*, London: Oxford University Press.

Marsh, H. W. 1988: Multitrait–multimethod analyses. In J. P. Keeves (eds), *Educational Research Methodology, Measurement and Evaluation: An International Handbook*, Oxford: Pergamon.

Marsh, H. W. 1989: Confirmatory factor analyses of multitrait–multimethod data: many problems and a few solutions. *Applied Psychological Measurement*, 13, 335–61.

Marsh, H. W. and Bailey, M. 1991: Confirmatory factor analyses of multitrait–multimethod data: a comparison of the behavior of alternative models. *Applied Psychological Measurement*, 15, 47–70.

Marsh, H. W. and Hocevar, D. 1988: A new, more powerful approach to multitrait–multimethod analyses: application of second-order confirmatory factor analysis. *Journal of Applied Psychology*, 73, 107–17.

Maxwell, A. E. 1977: *Multivariate Analysis in Behavioral Research*, London: Chapman & Hall.

Nicholls, J. G., Licht, B. G., and Pearl, R. A. 1982: Some dangers of using personality questionnaires to study personality. *Psychological Bulletin*, 92, 572–80.

Oliver, R. L. 1976: Hedonic reactions to the disconfirmation of product performance expectations: some moderating conditions. *Journal of Applied Psychology*, 61, 246–50.

Oliver, R. L. 1980: A cognitive model of the antecedents and consequences of satisfaction decisions. *Journal of Marketing Research*, 17, 46–9.

Oliver, R. L. 1981: Measurement and evaluation of satisfaction process in retail setting. *Journal of Retailing*, 57, 25–48.

Oliver, R. L. and Bearden, W. O. 1985: Crossover effects in the theory of reasoned action: a moderating influence attempt. *Journal of Consumer Research*, 12, 324–40.

Paulhus, D. L. 1989: Socially desirable responding: some new Solutions to old problems. In D. M. Buss and N. Cantor (eds), *Personality Psychology: Recent Trends and Emerging Directions*, pp. 201–9.

Petty, R. E. and Cacioppo, J. T. 1981: *Attitudes and Persuasion: Classic and Contemporary Approaches*, Dubuque, IA: W. C. Brown.

Petty, R. E. and Cacioppo, J. T. 1986: *Communication and Persuasion: Central and Peripheral Routes to Attitude Change*, New York: Springer-Verlag.

Phillips, L. W. 1981: Assessing measurement error in key informant reports: a methodological note on organizational analysis in marketing. *Journal of Marketing Research*, 18, 395–415.

Rindskopf, D. 1983: Parameterizing inequality constraints on unique variances in linear structural models. *Psychometrika*, 48, 73–83.

Rosenthal, R. and Rosnow, R. L. (eds) 1969: *Artifacts in Behavioral Research*, New York: Academic Press.

Schmitt, N. and Stults, D. N. 1986: Methodology review: analysis of multitrait–multimethod matrices. *Applied Psychological Measurement*, 10, 1–22.

Seidler, J. 1974: On using informants: a technique for collecting quantitative data and controlling measurement error in organizational analysis. *American Sociological Review*, 39, 816–31.

Shimp, T. A. and Kavas, A. 1984: The theory of reasoned action applied to coupon usage. *Journal of Consumer Research*, 11, 795–809.

Sosa, E. (ed.) 1975: *Causation and Conditionals*, London: Oxford University Press.

Strotz, R. H. 1960: Interdependence as a specification error. *Econometrica*, 28, 428–42.

Strotz, R. H. and Wold, H. O. A. 1960: Recursive versus nonrecursive systems: an attempt to synthesis. *Econometrica*, 28, 417–27.

Strotz, R. H. and Wold, H. O. A. 1963: The causal interpretability of structural parameters: a reply. *Econometrica*, 31, 449–50.

Swain, A. J. 1975: Analysis of parametric structure for variance matrices. Unpublished doctoral dissertation, University of Adelaide, Australia.

Swan, J. E. and Combs, L. J. 1976: Product performance and consumer satisfaction: a new concept. *Journal of Marketing*, 40, 25–33.

Thurstone, L. L. 1928: Attitudes can be measured. *American Journal of Sociology*, 33, 529–44.

Tse, D. K. and Wilton, P. C. 1988: Models of consumer satisfaction: an extension. *Journal of Marketing Research*, 25, 204–12.

Van Driel, O. P. 1978: On various causes of improper solutions of maximum likelihood factor analysis. *Psychometrika*, 43, 225–43.

Van Loo, M. F. and Bagozzi, R. P. 1984: Labor force participation and fertility: a social analysis of their antecedents and simultaneity. *Human Relations*, 37, 941–67.

Widaman, K. F. 1985: Hierarchically nested covariance structure models for multitrait–multimethod data. *Applied Psychological Measurement*, 9, 1–26.

Winkler, J. D., Kanouse, D. E., and Ware, J. E., Jr. 1982: Controlling for acquiescence response set in scale development. *Journal of Applied Psychology*, 67, 555–61.

Wold, H. 1985: Partial least squares. In *Encyclopedia of Statistical Sciences*, Vol. 6, New York: Wiley, 581–91.

Wothke, W. and Browne, M. W. 1990: The direct product model for the MTMM matrix parameterized as a second order factor analysis model. *Psychometrika*, 55, 255–62.

Yi, Y. 1989: An investigation of the structure of expectancy-value attitude and its implications. *International Journal of Research in Marketing*, 6, 71–83.

Yi, Y. 1990a: A critical review of consumer satisfaction. In V. A. Zeithaml (ed.), *Review of Marketing 1990*, Chicago, IL: American Marketing Association, 68–123.

Yi, Y. 1990b: The indirect effects of advertisements designed to change product attribute beliefs. *Psychology and Marketing*, 7, 47–63.

10

The Evaluation of Structural Equation Models and Hypothesis Testing

Richard P. Bagozzi
and
Hans Baumgartner

Introduction

Structural equation modeling with latent variables has become a popular tool in the methodological arsenal of marketing researchers. Although the potential of the technique for comprehensive investigations of both theoretical and measurement issues is great, its pitfalls are also many. The intent of this chapter is to review a variety of topics pertaining to the evaluation of structural equation models and to provide the practicing researcher with some guidelines as to how to apply the methodology in everyday research.

Up until several years ago, structural equation modeling was almost synonymous with using LISREL, the computer program developed by Jöreskog and his associates to estimate and test structural models. LISREL is now in its eighth version (Jöreskog and Sörbom, 1993a), which attests to the popularity of the technique. Owing to the surge of interest in the methodology, many other programs have recently emerged as alternatives to LISREL. Besides the implementation of LISREL in SPSSX and the PROC CALIS procedure in SAS, COSAN (McDonald, 1978, 1980; Fraser, 1980), EQS (Bentler, 1989), EZPATH (Steiger, 1989), LINCS (Schoenberg, 1987), and RAMONA (Browne and Mels, 1992) can all be used to analyze structural equation models.

Several different specifications of the general structural equation model with latent variables have been suggested in the literature (e.g. Bentler and Weeks, 1980; Browne and Mels, 1992; McArdle and McDonald, 1984; McDonald, 1978, 1980; Jöreskog, 1973). In this chapter, we will use Jöreskog's specification as implemented in LISREL. The model can be stated as follows:

$$\eta = B\eta + \Gamma\xi + \zeta \qquad (10.1)$$
$$y = \Lambda_y\eta + \varepsilon \qquad (10.2)$$

$$\mathbf{x} = \mathbf{\Lambda}_x \boldsymbol{\xi} + \boldsymbol{\delta} \tag{10.3}$$

Equation (10.1) expresses the hypothesized relationships among the constructs in one's theory and is called the latent variable (or structural) model. The $m \times 1$ vector $\boldsymbol{\eta}$ contains the latent endogenous variables and the $n \times 1$ vector $\boldsymbol{\xi}$ consists of the latent exogenous variables. The coefficient matrix $\mathbf{B}$ shows the effects of latent endogenous variables on each other, and the coefficient matrix $\boldsymbol{\Gamma}$ signifies the effects of latent exogenous on latent endogenous variables. The vector of disturbances $\boldsymbol{\zeta}$ represents errors in equations.

Equations (10.2) and (10.3) indicate how observed variables relate to latent variables. This is called the measurement model. The $p \times 1$ vector $\mathbf{y}$ contains the indicators of the latent endogenous variables, and the $q \times 1$ vector $\mathbf{x}$ consists of the indicators of the latent exogenous variables. The coefficient matrices $\mathbf{\Lambda}_y$ and $\mathbf{\Lambda}_x$ show how $\mathbf{y}$ relates to $\boldsymbol{\eta}$ and $\mathbf{x}$ relates to $\boldsymbol{\xi}$. The vectors of disturbances $\boldsymbol{\epsilon}$ and $\boldsymbol{\delta}$ represent errors in variables (or measurement error).

The variance–covariance matrices of $\boldsymbol{\xi}$, $\boldsymbol{\zeta}$, $\boldsymbol{\epsilon}$ and $\boldsymbol{\delta}$ are usually referred to as $\boldsymbol{\Phi}$, $\boldsymbol{\Psi}$, $\boldsymbol{\Theta}_\epsilon$, and $\boldsymbol{\Theta}_\delta$. Under appropriate assumptions (to be discussed later), the variance–covariance matrix $\mathbf{S}$ of the observed variables y and x can be expressed as a function of the eight parameter matrices $\mathbf{B}$, $\boldsymbol{\Gamma}$, $\mathbf{\Lambda}_y$, $\mathbf{\Lambda}_x$, $\boldsymbol{\Phi}$, $\boldsymbol{\Psi}$, $\boldsymbol{\Theta}_\epsilon$ and $\boldsymbol{\Theta}_\delta$. The goal of structural equation modeling is to account for the variances and covariances of the observed variables by relating observed variables to latent variables and by specifying theoretically interesting relationships at the level of latent variables.

The general structural equation model specified in equations (10.1) to (10.3) can be simplied to yield a variety of submodels. To cite just one example, a confirmatory factor analysis model is given by either equation (10.2) or equation (10.3). In the sequel, we will mostly deal with the full model specified in (10.1) to (10.3), but the discussion generally applies to more specific models as well. We will first discuss issues related to the initial specification of the theoretical model of interest, then deal with issues related to data screening prior to model estimation and testing, and finally consider issues related to the estimation and testing of theoretical models on empirical data. The chapter concludes with an example of structural equation modeling in which many of the points raised earlier are exemplified.

Issues Related to the Initial Specification of the Theoretical Model of Interest

Measurement and latent variable model specification considerations

Before an empirical study is ever conducted, the researcher has to think about what kinds of methodologies are best suited to answering the questions of interest. Confirmatory factor analysis and structural equation modeling with latent variables are not always the most appropriate techniques to use, and even if they are there are many issues that have to be resolved before these methods can be applied profitably.

It is useful to make a distinction between issues relating to the measurement of the constructs in one's theory and issues relating to the investigation of patterns of relationships among constructs. With respect to measurement issues, a fundamental decision has to be made about whether or not a confirmatory factor analysis model should be specified to model explicitly how empirical measures relate to theoretical constructs.[1] Generally, a positive answer to this question requires that prior studies have indicated which measures validly and reliably tap a given construct, or that pre-studies have been conducted to resolve these issues. If this is not the case, it might be preferable to specify an exploratory principle components or factor analysis model.

Even if well-developed scales for the measurement of the constructs of interest are available, there are practical limits as to how many indicators can be related explicitly to a factor. If the number goes much beyond five, disappointing results are all but guaranteed. In that case it is probably better to form a single composite of measures for each construct prior to submitting the data to a structural equations program (possibly fixing each factor loading so that the squared correlation between the single composite indicator and the factor equals reliability and adjusting the error variance accordingly), or to divide the scale in half or, better yet, thirds and use these sub-scale composites as multiple indicators of the construct of interest. For details on how to obtain the most reliable composite of measures, see the discussion of reliability below and a recent article by Lastovicka and Thamodaran (1991).

If it is decided that different measures of the same construct are to be modeled explicitly as multiple indicators of an underlying factor, a sufficient number of measures per factor has to be available. Probably more common than using too many indicators is the mistake of using too few indicators. Often, researchers measure their constructs with two indicators each so that they can say they are using multiple indicators while at the same time keeping the model as simple as possible. However, at least three indicators of each factor are needed for a model to be identified, unless another factor serves as an "indicator" (which is the case in a two-factor model with two indicators per factor, for example). Furthermore, in order for a model of modified independence, or independence at the latent variable (or structural) level, to be identified (such a model serves a very useful function in model comparison tests), there have to be three indicators per construct unless the measures are tau-equivalent or parallel.

Another decision that has to be made is whether reflective (effect) or formative (cause) indicators should be used in the analysis (see the previous chapter and Bollen and Lennox, 1991). Although researchers routinely use reflective indicators in their models, which implies that observed variables (and their variances and covariances) are regarded as manifestations of underlying constructs, this assumption does not always make sense. A case in point is the measurement of social class with indicators of income, occupational prestige, and education. If, as in this example, a "construct" is merely thought of as a summary index of observed variables and if the objective is to account for the maximal amount of variance in endogenous constructs, a formative indicator model and appropriate procedures such as PLS (Lohmöller, 1984) should be used (Fornell and Bookstein, 1982). In this chapter we will not deal with formative indicator models and assume henceforth that a reflective indicator model is appropriate.

At the latent variable level the researcher has to decide whether a recursive model (with a subdiagonal **B** matrix and/or a diagonal Ψ matrix so that no feedback loops are allowed between endogenous constructs) adequately represents the theory to be tested, or whether a non-recursive model is needed. The meaningfulness of non-recursive models in cross-sectional research has been a longstanding controversy (see previous chapter; cf. also Bassman, 1963; Strotz and Wold, 1960), and certain minimal assumptions have to be satisfied if they are to be appropriate (e.g. the system has to be in equilibrium so that the effects of variables are stable; see Schaubroek, 1990, for a recent review). Often, longitudinal studies (in the context of structural equation modeling sometimes referred to as panel studies) are better suited to investigate reciprocal causality, but alas the data requirements are often forbidding in terms of costs, time, and effort. Even if a longitudinal design is used, there is still the question of the appropriate time lag to use in the assessment of the various constructs.

One general advice that can be given for model specification at the structural level is to always entertain *a priori* a variety of possible theoretical models that can be tested against empirical data. As discussed in more detail below, it is generally not meaningful to investigate the "truth" of a single model, and the objective should rather be which one of several possible models provides the best approximation to reality.

Model misspecification

One crucial problem that applies to both the measurement and latent variable models is the issue of model misspecification. Three forms of misspecification can be distinguished: omission of relevant variables and inclusion of irrelevant ones, omission of relevant relationships and inclusion of irrelevant ones, and misspecifications of the structural form of relationships.

Omission of relevant variables is generally a more serious problem than inclusion of irrelevant ones, because while the latter may lead to inefficient estimates, the former usually results in inconsistent estimates and faulty tests of statistical significance. In particular, as seen in the previous chapter, the omission of relevant variables can lead to false inferences. The best safeguard against using the "wrong" set of variables in one's model is a well-developed theory to guide model building.

Omission of relevant relationships and inclusion of irrelevant ones is usually a less serious problem if structural equation modeling is conceived of as a process of comparing theoretically meaningful alternative models. Strong grounding in prior theory should guard against capitalization on chance, and consideration of alternate theoretical frameworks should make it less likely for relevant relationships to go undetected. Procedures for finding appropriate measurement models and determining acceptable latent variable models are described in some detail below.

The final form of misspecification – misspecification of the functional form of relationships – arises because structural equation modeling has been largely restricted to linear relationships. Although non-linearities in the measurement (e.g. Etezadi-Amoli and McDonald, 1983; Mooijaart and Bentler, 1986) and latent variable (e.g. Baumgartner and Bagozzi, 1993; Kenny and Judd, 1984; Hayduk, 1987) models have been considered by researchers, this work has not had much impact because of the complexity of the procedures and a strong belief that linear models provide a useful approximation to reality. If the distribution of the observed variables is reasonably normal, perhaps after applying an appropriate transformation, linearity may be a reasonable assumption to make, but when theory demands non-linear relationships, structural equation modeling may not be the most valid research method.

Identification

Once a set of theoretically relevant models has been specified, it is necessary to consider their identification. A model is said to be identified if all its freely estimated parameters are identified, that is, if it is impossible for two distinct sets of parameter values to yield the same population variance–covariance matrix. A model in which at least one parameter is not identified is called underidentified, and the seriousness of underidentification should be obvious when it is realized that in an underidentified model two different "solutions" for the same parametric structure with possibly widely differing theoretical implications account for the data equally well. The problem of underidentification should not be confused with the issue of model equivalence, which will be discussed toward the end of the chapter.

A model in which all of the restrictions implied by the model are needed to achieve identification is called just identified, and if there are redundant restrictions the model is said to be overidentified. An overidentified model has a positive number of degrees of freedom, and the overidentifying restrictions can be used to test the overall fit of the model by means of a χ^2 test or alternative indices.

To achieve identification, the scales of the latent variates have to be fixed. In specifying the model it is customary to set the coefficients relating the ε's to the y's and δ's to the x's to one, and indeed this is done automatically in most software programs, but for the ξ's and η's the factor loading of one observed measure also has to be set to one; alternatively, in the case of ξ the variances in Φ can be standardized. In addition, various other constraints have to be imposed to ensure identification (e.g., simple structure of the loading matrices Λ_y and Λ_x, etc.).

A necessary condition for identification is that the number of parameters freely estimated not exceed the number of distinct elements in the variance–covariance matrix of the observed variables. Except in specialized cases, easy-to-follow rules for proving identification are not available, and it is generally necessary to show "by hand" that each parameter to be estimated can be expressed as a function of the variances and covariances of the observed variables. For a full structural equation model, this is often done using the so-called two-step rule: In the first step it is shown that the measurement model (a confirmatory factor analysis model in which all constructs are allowed to freely correlate) is identified, and in the second step it is demonstrated that, given identified variances and covariances for the η's and ξ's, the structural parameters in Γ and B and the variances and possibly covariances in Ψ are identified. The rank condition is easily used for this purpose, although one has to be careful because it assumes that Ψ is estimated freely; if one is willing to specify that Ψ is diagonal, this might lead to an identified model even if the model appears to be underidentified according to the rank condition. It should also be noted that the two-step rule is a sufficient but not necessary condition for model identification (see Bollen, 1989).

A recursive model with at least three indicators per factor is theoretically identified (although there might be empirical underidentification problems). Recursive models with fewer indicators per factor may also be identified, but as already mentioned it is advisable to have at least three indicators per factor. If there is only one indicator per factor, one has to assume that the construct is measured without error or to more or less arbitrarily choose a certain level of reliability (unless the indicator is actually a composite of measures). Special care is required for the identification of measurement models that lack simple structure or contain correlated measurement errors (see, for example, Bollen and Jöreskog, 1985, for a demonstration that uniqueness of factor loadings does not imply that a factor model is identified) and for the identification of structural models that are non-recursive.

Because of the difficulties involved in identifying models, often perceived but sometimes real, empirical tests of identification are sometimes used. As suggested by Jöreskog and Sörbom (1989), a singular information matrix often hints at identification problems. If the identification of a certain parameter is in doubt, one may run a model with the parameter in question fixed to zero; if its modification index is zero, the parameter is probably not identified. Another possibility is to estimate the model whose identification is in doubt, save the estimated variance–covariance matrix, re-estimate the model on this matrix, and check whether the original parameter estimates can be reproduced; if they cannot, the model is probably not identified.

One problem with all empirical tests of identification is that they are not always accurate because of numerical problems in computer precision.

Statistical assumptions

After it has been ascertained that there are no identification problems, the researcher should check that the statistical assumptions required for estimation and testing are reasonable in the context of the given study. Besides the assumption that the model is correctly specified as discussed previously, one also has to assume that the expected values of errors in variables and errors in equations are zero, that the errors are uncorrelated with each other and with ξ, that ϵ is uncorrelated with η, that $(I-B)$ is nonsingular, and, without loss of generality, that η, ξ, y, and x are measured in deviation form. Under these conditions, the elements of the variance–covariance matrix of the observed variables are functions of the unknown parameters of the specified model. Under additional assumptions on the distribution of the observed variables (e.g. multivariate normality if maximum likelihood estimation and testing are used) and given a sufficiently large sample size, it is possible to estimate the parameters of the specified model and perform various tests on them. If there are reasons to believe that these assumptions are violated, the results of estimation and testing may not be trustworthy. In the next section, several procedures for testing the appropriateness of some of these assumptions are described.

Issues Related to Data Screening Prior to Model Estimation and Testing

Inspection of the raw data

After the empirical data are available, they should be screened carefully before a variance–covariance matrix is computed. A common mistake is to rush to model estimation and testing, with insufficient attention being paid to the quality of the raw data that go into the final variance–covariance matrix. It is important to make sure that there are no coding errors (e.g. simple descriptive statistics will indicate whether the minimum and maximum values for each variable fall within the admissible range), that variables have been recoded appropriately (e.g. if reverse coding has been used for a set of semantic differential scales in an attempt to avoid response sets, yea-saying bias, etc.), and that missing values have been dealt with appropriately. If several indicators of a construct are available and they show sizable intercorrelations, it may be possible to use a person's mean value on the remaining variables for the missing value. In other cases either pairwise or listwise deletion has to be used; the disadvantage of the former is that the elements in the variance–covariance matrix are then based on different numbers of observations and that the sample variance–

covariance matrix may not be positive definite (which implies that most estimation methods will not work), while the disadvantage of the latter is that an excessive number of cases may have to be excluded from the analysis because of a few missing values.

Outlier detection

One worrisome possibility in structural equation modeling is that the variances and covariances among the observed variables may be distorted by the presence of a few outliers. Bollen (1989) has suggested the following model-free screening test for outliers, which can be easily programmed with a matrix language package and which has been implemented in the LISRES macro for SAS (Davis, 1992). Let $\mathbf{Z}$ be a matrix of dimension $N \times (p + q)$ containing the $(p + q)$ observed variables in deviation form. Define the $N \times N$ matrix $\mathbf{A}$ as

$$\mathbf{A} = \mathbf{Z}(\mathbf{Z}'\mathbf{Z})^{-1}\mathbf{Z}', \quad (10.4)$$

with diagonal elements a_{ii}. The a_{ii} sum to $(p + q)$, so that the average size of the a_{ii} is equal to $(p + q)/N$. The a_{ii} can be interpreted as the "distance" of the ith observation from the means for all of the variables; the a_{ii} lie between 0 and 1, with cases having a_{ii} values close to 0 being "typical" observations and those with a_{ii} values close to 1 being potential outliers. The LISRES output reports all observations with significant a_{ii} values and an outlier analysis for groups of observations.

It is not recommended that outliers be routinely excluded from further analyses. However, outlier analysis may be helpful in the detection of coding errors and other mistakes, and if an observation deviates markedly from the overall mean and there are defensible theoretical reasons for excluding an outlier there might be grounds for deleting the case (see Bollen, 1989, pp. 28-32, for an example).

Assessment of normality

It is helpful to investigate the approximate normality of the observed variables by inspecting the data through histograms, stem-and-leaf displays, probit plots or other graphical means and by computing univariate and multivariate measures of skewness and kurtosis. The former statistic indicates how symmetric the distribution of a variable or set of variables is, and the latter shows how much mass the tails of the distribution contain. If the distribution of a variable is normal, its skewness will be zero and its kurtosis will have a value of three (or zero if three has been subtracted); the coefficient of relative multivariate kurtosis, which is important for elliptical estimation (see the discussion below) is one for a multivariate normal distribution. Univariate and multivariate tests of normality can also be conducted using these statistics (see Bollen, 1989 for details). EQS, PRELIS (Jöreskog and Sörbom, 1993b), and PROC CALIS all compute some or all of these statistics. The most comprehensive tests are performed by the LISRES macro which reports tests, both univariate and multivariate, that there is no excess skewness or kurtosis, either individually or jointly.

Sometimes a simple transformation is helpful in normalizing the distribution of a variable. For example, if observations are based on proportions, an arcsin transformation is often useful (i.e. $x = \sin^{-1}\sqrt{p}$ where p is a proportion); if a variable is positively skewed or skewed to the right (this is a common occurrence with response times, frequency of usage measures, etc.), a log (or possibly square root) transformation may work; if the variable is negatively skewed or skewed to the left, an inverse transformation might be appropriate. Besides reducing skewness, these transformations should also be helpful in eliminating excessive kurtosis. Furthermore, in addition to taking care of normality problems, they may also eliminate problems with some variances being much larger than others.

If the distribution is at least approximately normal, maximum likelihood and generalized least-squares estimation and testing are applicable. If there is excess kurtosis but it is uniform across variables, the distribution might be elliptical and the theory of Browne (1982), implemented in EQS and partially SAS, might be applicable. In the case of the chi-square goodness-of-fit test, the appropriate correction under elliptical estimation involves dividing the chi-square statistic by the relative coefficient of multivariate kurtosis. If there are marked non-normalities, distribution-free methods may have to be used, although they require relatively large sample sizes and are thus not always feasible (Jöreskog and Sörbom, 1989).

Measures of association

A final issue is which measure of association to use in computing the moment matrix of the observed variables. Most methods of estimation and testing assume that at least the indicators of endogenous constructs are continuously distributed. If this is the case, one may compute the usual variance–covariance matrix. If some variables are categorical, one may assume that their underlying distributions are continuous and normally distributed and estimate the strength of their association with various specialized correlation coefficients. Specifically, when the two variables are ordinal, the resulting correlation is called polychoric, when they are dichotomous it is called tetrachoric, and when one of the two variables is continuous, it is referred to as polyserial. If some variables are inherently categorical, specialized programs for structural equation modeling may have to be used (e.g. Muthén's, 1987, LISCOMP model).

Relatively little research (e.g. Babakus, Ferguson, and Jöreskog, 1987; Rigdon and Ferguson, 1991) is available to guide the researcher in the choice of appropriate measures of association if the continuity of indicators of endogenous variables is in doubt. Bentler and Chou (1987, p. 88) suggest that "[c]ontinuous methods can be used with little worry when a variable has four or more categories, but with three or fewer categories one should probably consider the use of alternative procedures."

Often, researchers use a correlation rather than a covariance matrix as input to model estimation and testing. In some cases this has no effect on the parameter estimates and the overall χ^2 goodness-of-fit test. However, the standard errors of estimated parameters may be inaccurate, and the analysis of correlation matrices is therefore not recommended (see Cudeck, 1989, for a recent discussion).

One problem that may arise in computing the sample moment matrix for the observed variables is that it is not positive definite. Most estimation methods will not work in this case. Sometimes the problem is caused by an error in the command file, but it may also result from linear dependencies among the observed variables, the use of pairwise deletion of missing values, the presence of outliers, or the use of non-standard measures of association such as tetrachoric correlations. Which remedy to apply depends on the cause of the problem, but if the data have been screened carefully and the analysis is based on variances and covariances among the variables, this problem should not occur very frequently.

Issues Related to the Estimation and Testing of Theoretical Models on Empirical Data

Model estimation

A variety of estimation methods are available to compute parameter estimates and related statistics. Besides instrumental variables and two-stage least squares, which are used to compute starting values in some computer programs (e.g. LISREL), there are unweighted least squares (ULS), generalized least squares (GLS), maximum likelihood (ML), and asymptotically distribution-free methods (Browne, 1982, 1984; referred to as generally weighted least squares, WLS, and diagonally weighted least squares, DWLS, in LISREL and arbitrary distribution theory generalized least squares, AGLS, and linearized AGLS in EQS). Browne (1982) has also considered estimation and testing under the assumption that the observed variables follow an elliptical distribution, and his method is available in EQS and partially in SAS. Extensions to the case where the marginal distributions do not have homogeneous kurtosis have also been considered (Kano, Berkane, and Bentler, 1990).

ULS produces consistent estimates irrespective of the distribution of the observed variables, but the estimates are not asymptotically efficient and they are not scale free; furthermore, the fitting function is not scale invariant. A χ^2 statistic and standard errors are available if multivariate normality of the observed variables can be assumed. ML is based on the assumption of multivariate normality of the observed variables and leads to estimates that are consistent, asymptotically unbiased, asymptotically efficient, and asymptotically normally distributed. Furthermore, in most cases the ML fitting function is scale invariant and ML estimates are scale free, which implies that the χ^2 will be the same regardless of whether a covariance or correlation matrix is analyzed and that the parameters estimated from a covariance or correlation matrix only differ by a known scale factor. GLS estimates are asymptotically equivalent to ML estimates and have the same properties under the slightly less restrictive distributional assumption that fourth-order cumulants are zero (which implies that there is no excess kurtosis; cf. Browne, 1974, 1982).

In principle, asymptotically distribution-free methods have the advantage that under mild assumptions asymptotically efficient estimates and asymptotically valid χ^2 statistics and standard errors can be obtained regardless of the form of the distribution underlying the observed variables. In practice, ADF estimation is limited by the fact that the size of the weight matrix needed for estimation increases rapidly with the number of variables in the model (e.g. when there are 20 observed variables there are over 20,000 distinct elements in the weight matrix) and that fairly large samples are required to obtain meaningful estimates of the elements of the weight matrix (which are fourth-order moments).

Simulation work has shown that ML and GLS estimation is robust to violations of the normality assumption (although the efficiency of estimation seems to suffer), but that χ^2 statistics and standard errors cannot be trusted. ADF estimates seem to be more biased than ML and GLS estimates and their usefulness in testing is in dispute (cf. Sharma, Durvasula, and Dillon, 1989).

One issue that is important in empirical work is at what sample size may one take comfort in the fact that the various estimation procedures have such nice asymptotic properties. The evidence from simulation studies is relatively limited and suggestions vary widely, but, Bentler and Chou (1987, p. 91) offer the following guidelines:

> The ratio of sample size to number of free parameters may be able to go as low as 5:1 under normal and elliptical theory, especially when there are many indicators of latent variables and the associated factor loadings are large. Although there is even less experience on which to base a recommendation, a ratio of at least 10:1 may be more appropriate for arbitrary distributions. These ratios need to be larger to obtain trustworthy z-tests on the significance of parameters, and still larger to yield correct model evaluation chi-square probabilities.

Estimation problems

Estimation problems as defined here are either difficulties in obtaining relevant estimates in the first place, or anomalies with estimates that the researcher was able to obtain. A first problem, usually referred to as non-convergence, may be that the estimation procedure fails to converge on a solution in a given number of iterations or within a given time limit. Apart from mistakes in the command file and problems with the positive-definiteness of the implied variance–covariance matrix (which is usually a result of specification errors or bad starting values), causes of non-convergence include underidentified or poorly specified models (e.g. the hypothesized model does not fit the data at all), overfitting (e.g. in multi-trait multi-method analyses the introduction of method factors may result in almost as many factors as there are observed variables), outliers (e.g. a model may fit very poorly because of a few influential anomalous cases), bad starting values (e.g. for more complex models the automatic starting values provided by LISREL may prove inadequate), insufficiently operationalized constructs (e.g. factor models with only two indicators per factor), and small sample sizes. Remedies depend on the cause of non-convergence, although sometimes simply increasing the default limit on number of iterations or time of estimation will help.

A problem closely related to non-convergence is convergence of the solution on a local, rather than global, minimum. Whereas non-convergence is indicated on the printout, locally optimal solutions are less easily detected. Useful hints are provided by serious difficulties in finding a solution or results that deviate markedly from expectations. If these situations occur, the researcher may want to re-estimate the model with different starting values.

Another problem occurs if the estimation procedure converges on a set of model estimates, but the solution is improper in the sense that the value of an estimated parameter is impossible in the population. Examples include improper variances (particularly negative error variances, called "Heywood" cases in factor analysis), correlations outside the -1 to $+1$ range, and path coefficients greater than 1 in absolute magnitude in a completely standardized solution (i.e. when both observed variables and latent constructs have been standardized). Causes of, and remedies for, improper solutions are similar to those discussed under non-convergence.

A third problem occurs if the program cannot compute standard errors for the estimated parameters, some of the standard error estimates are very large or very small, and/or some parameter estimates are very highly correlated (cf. Bentler and Chou, 1987). Technically, this happens when the information matrix is singular or close to singular. The most frequent causes of such problems are underidentified or poorly specified models, and the parameter estimates and chi-square statistics of such models should be viewed with caution.

A special problem is the case of empirical underidentification of a model (Kenny, 1979, p. 40). This happens if a parameter is identified in principle, but in practice the expression for the estimation of the parameter involves a denominator that is zero or close to zero. Empirical underidentification may be the cause of any of the three problems discussed previously. Thus, if any of these problems occurs, it is helpful to closely check the conditions under which the model is identified, because this may provide clues as to why the problem occurs.

Table 10.1 Summary of overall goodness-of-fit indices

	Definition of the index	Expression in terms of (rescaled) noncentrality parameter	Limiting form of expression in terms of noncentrality
I. Stand-alone fit indices			
Minimum of the fitting function (f)	$\chi^2/(N-1)$	$t + df/(N-1)$	τ
Scaled likelihood ratio (LHR)	$\exp[-(1/2)\chi^2/(N-1)]$	$\exp[-(1/2)(t + df/(N-1))]$	$\exp[-(1/2)\tau]$
Chi-square statistic (χ^2)	χ^2	$(N-1)t + df$	—
Chi-square over degrees of freedom ratio (χ^2/df)	χ^2/df	$(N-1)t/df + 1$	—
Rescaled noncentrality parameter (t)	$(\chi^2 - df)/(N-1)$	t	τ
Rescaled noncentrality parameter over degrees of freedom ratio (t/df)	$(\chi^2/df - 1)/(N-1)$	t/df	τ/df
McDonald's (1989) measure of centrality (MC)	$\exp[-(1/2)(\chi^2 - df)/(N-1)]$	$\exp[-(1/2)t]$	$\exp[-(1/2)\tau]$
Akaike's (1987) information criterion (AIC)	$[\chi^2 + 2r]/(N-1)$	$t + (df + 2r)/(N-1)$	τ
Schwarz's (1978) Bayesian criterion (SBC)	$[\chi^2 + r \ln N]/(N-1)$	$t + (df + r \ln N)/(N-1)$	τ
Bozdogan's (1987) consistent information criterion (CIC)	$[\chi^2 + r(\ln N + 1)]/(N-1)$	$t + [df + r(\ln N + 1)]/(N-1)$	τ
Root mean residual (RMR)	$[2\Sigma\Sigma(s_{ij} - \hat{\sigma}_{ij})^2/[(p+q)(p+q+1)]]^{1/2}$	—	—
Goodness-of-fit index (GFI)	$1 - \{[tr(S\hat{\Sigma}^{-1} - I)^2]/tr(S\hat{\Sigma}^{-1})^2]\}$	—	—
Adjusted goodness-of-fit index (AGFI)	$1 - [(p+q)(p+q+1)/2df] \cdot (1 - \text{GFI})$	—	—
Hoelter's (1983) critical N (CN)	$\{[z_{crit} + (2df - 1)^{1/2}]^2/[2\chi^2/(N-1)]\} + 1$	—	—
II. Incremental fit indices:			
Bentler and Bonett's (1980) normed fit index (NFI)	$1 - [\chi_t^2/\chi_n^2]$	$1 - [(t_t - df_t/(N-1)]/[t_n + df_n/(N-1)]$	$1 - [\tau_t/\tau_n]$
Bollen's (1988) nonnormed fit index Δ_2	$[\chi_n^2 - \chi_t^2]/[\chi_n^2 - df_t]$	$[(t_n - t_t) - (df_n - df_t)/(N-1)]/[t_n + (df_n - df_t)/(N-1)]$	$1 - [\tau_t/\tau_n]$
Bollen's (1986) normed index ρ_1	$1 - [(\chi_t^2/df_t)/(\chi_n^2/df_n)]$	$[t_n/df_n - t_t/df_t]/[t_n/df_n + 1/(N-1)]$	$1 - [(\tau_t/df_t)/(\tau_n/df_n)]$
Tucker and Lewis (1973) nonnormed fit index (TLI)	$[\chi_n^2/df_n - \chi_t^2/df_t]/[\chi_n^2/df_n - 1]$	$1 - [(t_t/df_t)/(t_n/df_n)]$	$1 - [(\tau_t/df_t)/(\tau_n/df_n)]$
Bentler's (1990) normed comparative fit index (CFI)	$1 - [\max(\chi_t^2 - df_t, 0)/\max(\chi_n^2 - df_n, \chi_t^2 - df_t, 0)]$	$1 - [\max(t_t, 0)/\max(t_n, t_t, 0)]$	$1 - [\tau_t/\tau_n]$
McDonald and Marsh's (1990) nonnormed relative noncentrality index (RNI)	$1 - [(\chi_t^2 - df_t)/(\chi_n^2 - df_n)]$	$1 - [t_t/t_n]$	$1 - [\tau_t/\tau_n]$

N = sample size, r = number of parameters estimated, $(p + q)$ = number of observed variables, z_{crit} = critical value of the normal distribution, t = sample estimate of the rescaled noncentrality parameter, τ = rescaled noncentrality parameter in the population, and the subscripts n and t refer to the null (or baseline) and target model, respectively. Note that AIC, SBC, and CIC can be defined either as given in the table or, ignoring a certain constant, as $(\chi^2 - 2df)/(N-1)$, $(\chi^2 - df \ln N)/(N-1)$, and $(\chi^2 - df(\ln N + 1))/(N-1)$, respectively; furthermore, following Cudeck and Browne (1983), the three indices have been rescaled by dividing them by $(N-1)$. The formula for GFI applies to ML estimation; analogous expressions are available for other estimation procedures. Slight discrepancies with output from available computer programs may arise because N may be used instead of $(N-1)$.

Assessment of overall model fit

Most indices for assessing the goodness-of-fit of the overall model are based on the χ^2 statistic. Theoretically, it is possible to conceive of the χ^2 as a test statistic which examines the hypothesis that the specified model correctly represents the mechanism that gave rise to the variances and covariances among the observed variables. Given an identified model and a positive number of overidentifying restrictions, and assuming that the assumptions underlying the application of the chosen estimation procedure (e.g. multivariate normality in the case of maximum likelihood estimation) are met and the sample size is large enough, the χ^2 statistic can be used to test the null hypothesis that the estimated variance–covariance matrix deviates from the sample variance–covariance matrix only because of sampling error.

In practice, the χ^2 test may be of limited usefulness for a variety of reasons (cf. Bentler, 1990). First, the assumptions on which its appropriateness is based may not be met, and there is evidence that the χ^2 test is not robust to violations of these assumptions. Second, the test is only asymptotically valid and the sample size may be too small to yield a valid test of model adequacy. A recent simulation study by Hu, Bentler, and Kano (1992) investigated the performance of various test statistics in covariance structure analysis under different violations of distributional assumptions and for different sample sizes. The test statistic based on ADF estimation performed very badly except for rather large sample sizes (i.e. 5,000). Normal-theory test statistics did poorly with nonnormal data and tests based on elliptical and heterogeneous kurtosis theory performed variably. A scaled test statistic (i.e. an adjusted ML test statistic) proposed by Satorra and Bentler (1991), which is available in EQS, did the best. Third, the sample size may be too large so that the test is powerful enough to detect even trivial discrepancies between the estimated and observed covariance matrices.

The last problem is particularly serious since a powerful test is generally desirable, but as argued by Cudeck and Browne (1983), Marsh, Balla, and McDonald (1988) and others, a hypothesized model is probably never literally true and only an approximation to reality and thus subject to rejection in a sufficiently large sample.

Because of these problems, many attempts have been made to suggest alternative measures of fit. A distinction should be made between stand-alone and incremental fit indices (cf. Marsh, Balla, and McDonald, 1988). The former assess model fit in an absolute sense (as, for example, the χ^2 statistic), while the latter compare the fit of the target model to the fit of a baseline model. The baseline model may be one of independence of the observed or latent variables (Bentler and Bonett, 1980), or a model entertained by other researchers (Sobel and Bohrnstedt, 1985).

Table 10.1 lists many of the stand-alone and incremental fit indices that have been suggested as alternatives to the chi-square statistic. Although most of these indices were designed to overcome problems with the χ^2 test (particularly its dependence on sample size), recent research has shown that, contrary to the claims of their originators, the means of the sampling distributions of many of these indices are substantially dependent on sample size.

Recently, McDonald and Marsh (1990) and Bentler (1990) have suggested new indices based on the notion of noncentrality. If the specified model is only approximately true, then the test statistics assessing overall model fit follow a non-central χ^2 distribution with non-centrality parameter τ^*. The non-centrality parameter is a measure of the discrepancy between the true variance–covariance matrix and the estimated variance–covariance matrix in the population, and it seems natural to use it to assess the degree of model misspecification, either in an absolute sense or in comparison to some baseline model. The parameter τ^* is a function of sample size and it proves convenient to rescale it by dividing through $(N-1)$ or N, yielding the rescaled noncentrality parameter τ (McDonald and Marsh, 1990). The chief advantage of measures of fit based on non-centrality is that they appear to overcome the problem of dependence on sample size.

Among the stand-alone indices based on non-centrality, McDonald's (1989) normed measure of centrality m_t can be recommended:

$$m_t = \exp[-(1/2)t_t], \qquad (10.5)$$

where t_t is an unbiased estimate of the rescaled noncentrality parameter for target model t given by

$$t_t = (\chi_t^2 - df_t)/(N-1) \qquad (10.6)$$

where χ_t^2 is the chi-square value obtained for model t, df_t are the degrees of freedom for model t, and N is the sample size.[2]

Among the relative fit indices, the comparative fit index (CFI) proposed by Bentler (1990) seems to hold the greatest promise for assessments of overall model fit:

$$\text{CFI} = 1 - (\max(t_t, 0))/(\max(t_n, t_t, 0)), \qquad (10.7)$$

where the subscripts t and n refer to the target and the baseline (or null) model, respectively. If $t_n, t_t > 0$ and $t_n > t_t$, then $\text{CFI} = 1 - t_t/t_n$, and CFI is equal to the relative non-centrality index (RNI) proposed by McDonald and Marsh (1990). CFI is normed to fall between 0 and 1 (unlike RNI) and should be independent of sample size.

One disadvantage of CFI is that it does not reflect the relative parsimony of alternative models (see Mulaik, James, Van Alstine, Bennet, Lind, and Stilwell, 1989, for a discussion). If parsimony is a criterion, one may use the Tucker and Lewis (1973) index (sometimes called the Bentler and Bonett,

1980, nonnormed fit index), which expresses noncentrality per degrees of freedom:

$$\text{TLI} = 1 - (t_t/df_t)/(t_n/df_n) \quad (10.8)$$

Some of the problems associated with the TLI are that it is not restricted to fall between 0 and 1, that its sampling variability is larger than that of CFI, and that its behavior may appear anomalous when the null model is approximately true.

Besides providing definitions of the most common stand-alone and incremental fit indices, Table 10.1 also expresses many of these indices in terms of noncentrality and shows the limiting form of the expressions in terms of noncentrality. All indices whose expression in terms of noncentrality contains N appear to be sample-size dependent. The same is true for RMR, GFI, AGFI, and Hoelter's critical N, for which no expressions in terms of noncentrality have been provided.

Several interesting observations can be made with regard to the incremental fit indices listed in Table 10.1. Marsh, Balla, and McDonald (1988) have distinguished two types of incremental fit indices, type I indices which are defined as

$$|i_t - i_n|/\max(i_t, i_n)$$

and type II indices which are defined as

$$|i_t - i_n|/|E(i_t) - i_n|$$

where i_t is the value of some stand-alone index for the target model, i_n is the value of the stand-alone index for the null model, and $E(i_t)$ is the expected value of i_t assuming that the target model is true.

When the minimum of the fitting function or the χ^2 statistic are used as the stand-alone index in a type I (type II) index, one gets Bentler and Bonett's (1980) NFI (Bollen's, 1988, index Δ_2). When the χ^2 over degrees of freedom ratio is used as the stand-alone index in a type I (type II) index, one obtains Bollen's (1986) index ρ_1 (the Tucker–Lewis Index). When the rescaled noncentrality parameter is used as the stand-alone index in either a type I or type II index, one gets CFI (and generally RNI). Finally, when the ratio of rescaled noncentrality parameter to degrees of freedom is used as the stand-alone index in either a type I or type II index, one obtains the Tucker–Lewis Index. Interestingly enough, the two recommended incremental fit indices, which are based on τ (CFI) or τ/df (TLI), eliminate the difference between type I or type II indices.

Assessment of the measurement model

After it has been ascertained that the hypothesized model represents a reasonable approximation to the data, based on the chi-square statistic or alternative fit indices, it is necessary to check the quality of construct measurement. Maybe the first thing to look at is the size and sign of the factor loadings and their level of statistical significance. Positive factor loadings, sufficiently large and statistically significant, are a minimal requirement for adequate construct measurement.

It is also advisable to compute various indices of reliability. Reliability can generally be defined as the squared correlation between a construct and its measures. Individual-item reliability for an indicator x_i of ξ_j (or y_i of η_j) is given by:

$$\rho_{ii} = [\text{cov}(x_i, \xi_j)]^2 / \text{var}(x_i) \text{var}(\xi_j) \qquad (10.9)$$
$$= \lambda_{ij}^2 \text{var}(\xi_j) / [\lambda_{ij}^2 \text{var}(\xi_j) + \theta_{ii}]$$

Some computer programs provide individual item reliabilities directly and there is no need to compute them by hand (e.g. in LISREL they are called squared multiple correlations). Although small individual item reliabilities (e.g. $\rho_{ii} < 0.4$) may point to inadequate measurement of a construct by a given indicator, it is usually more important that the construct be measured adequately by all indicators of the construct jointly. This can be assessed by computing an index of composite reliability. For a weighted composite x_c (or y_c) of measures (e.g. $x_c = w_1 x_1 + w_2 x_2 + \ldots + w_n x_n$) the formula is:

$$\rho_c = [\text{cov}(x_c, \xi_j)]^2 / \text{var}(x_c) \text{var}(\xi_j)$$
$$= \left(\sum w_i \lambda_{ij}\right)^2 \text{var}(\xi_j) / \left[\left(\sum w_i \lambda_{ij}\right)^2 \text{var}(\xi_j) + \sum w_i^2 \theta_{ii}\right] \qquad (10.10)$$

The composite with maximum reliability (i.e. the optimally weighted composite) has unit weights for parallel measures, weights proportional to $1/\theta_{ii}$ for tau-equivalent measures, and weights proportional to λ_{ij}/θ_{ii} for congeneric measures (cf. Alwin and Jackson, 1979). Often, composite reliability is computed as the squared correlation between a construct and an unweighted composite of its indicators (e.g. $x_{uc} = x_1 + x_2 + \ldots + x_n$), in which case the previous formula reduces to

$$\rho_c = [\text{cov}(x_{uc}, \xi_j)]^2 / \text{var}(x_{uc}) \text{var}(\xi_j)$$
$$= \left(\sum \lambda_{ij}\right)^2 \text{var}(\xi_j) / \left[\left(\sum \lambda_{ij}\right)^2 \text{var}(\xi_j) + \sum \theta_{ii}\right], \qquad (10.11)$$

but this is the best estimate of reliability only if measures are parallel, which is usually not the case.

An alternative measure of how well a construct is measured by its indicators is Fornell and Larcker's (1981) index of average variance extracted, which is given as

$$\rho_{\text{ave}} = \left(\sum \lambda_{ij}^2\right) \text{var}(\xi_j) / \left[\left(\sum \lambda_{ij}^2\right) \text{var}(\xi_j) + \sum \theta_{ii}\right]. \qquad (10.12)$$

Generally, composite reliability and average variance extracted have to be computed by hand from the computer output. It should be noted that the coefficient of determination reported by LISREL, which is a function of the generalized variances of the estimates of θ and Σ, is also a measure of how well all indicators jointly capture the various latent variates, but it is different from both composite reliability and average variance extracted and does not seem to be a widely used or useful measure.

Values greater than 0.6 to 0.8 have sometimes been considered adequate for composite reliability, and values greater than 0.5 have been called desirable for average variance extracted (e.g. Bagozzi and Yi, 1988). However, it is difficult to justify such guidelines without considering the context of a given measurement procedure. For example, it is not difficult to attain composite reliabilities of 0.8 when measuring attitudes with semantic differential scales such as good–bad, favorable–unfavorable, and pleasant–unpleasant; it is much more difficult to reach this level of reliability when less obviously similar indicators are used to measure a construct.

Besides looking at the factor loadings, one should also check that none of the θ_{ii} are negative. Some authors (e.g. Bagozzi and Yi, 1991) have argued that with social science data significant amounts of error variance are to be expected. If, as it often happens, negative error variances do occur, the model can be re-estimated with the offending estimate set to zero or to a small positive value (e.g. .005 for completely standardized solutions), or the error variance can be constrained to a nonnegative value using certain "trick" procedures (cf. Rindskopf, 1984); in some computer programs (e.g. EQS) this is done automatically.

A special problem arises when only one indicator of a construct is available. The most straightforward way of dealing with this difficulty is to set the appropriate factor loading to one and the corresponding error variance to zero. Some authors, however, have argued that it is better to assume some error than to posit perfect measurement. The difficulty with this proposal is that usually very little guidance about reasonable levels of measurement error are available from previous research, and assuming values for θ_{ii} essentially has the effect of assuming values for other parameters since with full-information procedures a change in one part of the model may lead to changes in other parts.

Assessment of the latent variable model

After a satisfactory measurement model has been found, attention can turn to the latent variable (or structural) model, which usually represents the hypotheses under investigation. Hopefully, structural coefficients will have the proper sign and be statistically significant. There are three ways in which statistical significance can be assessed, and two of these are commonly used. First, one may look at the z-values (sometimes called t-values) reported for each coefficient (computed as the estimated coefficient divided by its standard error); z-values larger than 1.96 are significant according to a two-sided test at $\alpha = 0.05$. The concept of z-values is based on the logic of Wald tests (i.e. the square of a z-value is equal to a Wald test). Second, one may estimate a model in which the parameter whose significance is to be assessed is set to zero and use a χ^2 difference test to see whether the constraint leads to a significant decrement in fit. The logic of this test is based on likelihood ratio tests. Third, using the constrained model from the χ^2 difference test one may conduct a Lagrange multiplier test (in LISREL called a modification index). Asymptotically, the three are equivalent, and generally they lead to the same conclusion (cf. Bentler, 1986; Buse, 1982; Vandaele, 1981).

In addition, one may also look at the squared multiple correlation for each structural equation and possibly at the total coefficient of determination for all structural equations jointly to see how much of the variance in the endogenous constructs is accounted for. Special care in the interpretation of these statistics is required if the estimated model is not recursive (i.e. if **B** is not lower triangular and/or **Ψ** is not diagonal).

It should be noted that squared multiple correlations for the endogenous constructs (variance fit) are different from χ^2 tests of overidentifying restrictions (covariance fit). It is possible for a model to fit very well but have little explanatory power at the structural level, or conversely to have a model which fits poorly but exhibits high levels of R^2.

Power

With any statistical test there is the potential for two kinds of mistakes: rejection of H_0 when it is true (type I error) or acceptance of H_0 when it is false (type II error). Power is concerned with the incidence of the latter mistake and refers to the probability that an incorrect model will be rejected. Satorra and Saris (1985) have shown how to assess the power of the likelihood ratio test in structural equation models, and Saris and Stronkhorst (1984, pp. 202–9) and Bollen (1989, pp. 338–49) describe procedures for determining power using standard output from commonly available computer programs such as EQS or LISREL. Essentially, the procedures involve calculating the moment structure implied by an alternative model (which requires that the researcher specify specific values for an alternative model) and then estimating a misspecified model in which the parameters whose power is to be assessed are constrained to zero. The resulting "chi-square" statistic provides an estimate of the required non-centrality parameter. Power values can then be obtained from tables of the non-central chi-square distribution.

As discussed by Saris, Den Ronden, and Satorra (1987), the issue of power is seldom considered when testing structural equation models. This is unfortunate because the results of tests of significance are only unequivocal if the test statistic is significant even though power is low (in which case H_0 is clearly rejected) or if the test statistic is nonsignificant even though power is high (in which case H_0 can be accepted). The decision is less clear when the test is significant and power is high (because a trivial misspecification may cause the rejection of H_0) or when the test is non-significant and power is low (because a priori the chances of finding significant results were very low). In the latter two cases adjustment of the significance level (e.g. alphas greater than 0.05) or increases in the sample size may be required to resolve the ambiguity (see Saris, Den Ronden, and Satorra, 1987, for details and examples).

Model modification

It almost never happens that the theoretical model initially specified by the researcher is the one that in the end gets reported as adequately representing the empirical data. Anderson and Gerbing (1988) have made a strong case for proceeding in two steps when estimating and testing structural equation models. They propose that researchers specify a confirmatory factor analysis model in the first step, which may have to be modified appropriately until all constructs are measured satisfactorily, and then turn to a simultaneous consideration of measurement and structural submodels in the second step. Although Fornell and Yi (1992) have criticized the two-step approach for some of its implicit assumptions, the procedure has the advantage of focusing researchers' attention on measurement issues as a prerequisite for valid theory testing.

Modifications of the measurement model may be necessitated by several reasons. First, as already mentioned, error variances may be negative, and possible solutions to this difficulty have been discussed previously. Another problem might be that the correlation between two factors is so high that the discriminant validity of the constructs in question is called into doubt. In this case a new construct may have to be specified, or better indicators of the originally posited constructs may have to be developed.

Probably the most common difficulty is that indicators do not load on the target factor, that they load on another factor, or that they load on multiple factors simultaneously (significantly and maybe substantially). If a measure does not load on any factor, it can be deleted; if it loads only on one factor (although not on the factor originally hypothesized), it can be related to the "right" factor; and if an indicator wants to load on several factors, it can be related to these factors or one may allow correlated measurement errors. The problem with allowing loadings that were not originally intended is that the approach may be motivated solely by considerations of model fit and not by theory, and the specification of multiple loadings of a single measure or correlated measurement errors sacrifices unidimensional measurement, which some authors (e.g. Anderson and Gerbing, 1988; Gerbing and Anderson, 1988; Hattie, 1985) consider to be a crucial requirement of valid measurement. As a general rule, multiple loadings and correlated measurement errors should not be used unless there is a theoretical justification for introducing them (e.g. correlated errors may be appropriate in longitudinal studies when the same construct is measured repeatedly).

Two useful tools for locating sources of misspecification in a measurement model are modification indices and residual analysis. Modification indices, which are based on the logic of Lagrange multiplier tests, provide an estimate of the expected decrease in the overall χ^2 statistic if the fixed parameter under consideration were estimated freely. For a two-sided test at $\alpha = 0.05$, a modification index greater than 3.84 indicates a significant improvement in fit as a result of freeing the parameter. In addition, one should also look at estimated parameter changes (Kaplan, 1989) because due to large power a significant modification index may not signify a substantively meaningful free parameter. It should also be stressed that model changes suggested by significant modification indices should be guided by theory since there is always the danger of capitalizing on chance (MacCallum, 1986).

An inspection of the standardized (or normalized) residuals is a second way of locating misspecifications in a measurement model. Standardized residuals greater than 1.96 (or possibly 2.58) in absolute magnitude indicate that a given variance or covariance is either overfitted (when the residual is negative) or underfitted (when the residual is positive). The pattern of over- and underfitting points to the problem. For example, an item whose loading is misspecified will have large negative residuals with other indicators of the "wrong" factor and large positive residuals with other indicators of the "right" factor. An analogous pattern emerges when a subset of indicators of one factor wants to load on a separate factor. When an item has a large number of significant residuals with other indicators and no coherent pattern is discernible, there might be grounds for eliminating this item (see Anderson and Gerbing, 1988; Steenkamp and van Trijp, 1991).

Model modification at the structural level should proceed even more carefully than at the measurement level. Simulation work by MacCallum (1986) indicates that specification searches often do not uncover the correct model (in particular, this frequently occurred because the search was terminated when the chi-square reached non-significance), and that the problems are particularly severe when the original model has many specification errors, when sample size is small, and when little theoretical guidance is available on how to proceed during the search (see also Homburg and Dobratz, 1992).

If at all possible, modeling at the structural level should constitute a comparison of a series of nested models that are theoretically meaningful, rather than an indiscriminant model modification motivated by a desire to reach acceptable levels of significance. A model M1 is nested in a model M2 if M1 can be obtained from M2 by constraining certain parameters to zero, other values, or to the value of other parameters. Anderson and Gerbing (1988) have developed a decision-tree framework for comparing the target model to a null latent variable (or structural) model (sometimes called a model of modified independence in which the latent constructs are uncorrelated), a saturated latent variable model (equivalent to a confirmatory factor analysis model in which all constructs are allowed to freely correlate with one another) and slightly more or less constrained versions of the target model. The outcome of the various model comparisons, based on sequential chi-square difference tests (which Steiger, Shapiro, and Browne, 1985, proved to be asymptotically independent), is a model that does not fit significantly worse than the saturated structural model but better than the next most likely constrained model.

It is not always possible to specify all five models required by the Anderson and Gerbing (1988) procedure, and most researchers will probably not adhere to their decision tree too religiously. The basic principle of their approach, however, seems very useful: the goal is to find the most parsimonious model which explains the data as well (or nearly as well) as the saturated structural model (which allows all possible correlations among the latent constructs and therefore lacks parsimony) and does better than the next most likely constrained (and thus more parsimonious) model. As an aside, it should be noted that at least three indicators per construct are necessary for the model of modified independence to be identified properly unless measures are tau-equivalent or parallel.

Residual analysis

A distinction should be made between residuals as the difference between the observed and estimated covariance matrices in structural equation modeling and residuals as the difference between observed and predicted values for a given observation or case. Most structural equation programs report unstandardized and standardized (or normalized) residuals in the former sense of the word, and as discussed previously they may be helpful in detecting misspecifications of the measurement model. It is also possible to evaluate the fit of a model on the basis of some summary measure of the average size of the residuals (e.g. root mean squared residual in LISREL), and stem-and-leaf and quantile plots of the standardized residuals may indicate specification errors (e.g. when there are nonlinearities in the Q-plot).

Traditionally, not much attention has been paid to individual residuals on a case by case basis. However, Bollen and Arminger (1991) have recently dealt with this issue, and their work has been implemented in the LISRES macro (Davis, 1992). Model-based residual analysis may be useful in the detection of outliers and influential cases in addition to model-free outlier detection as discussed previously. Both observed variable residuals (i.e. errors in variables) and structural equation residuals (i.e. errors in equations) can be analyzed, and LISRES reports tests of univariate and multivariate normality based on skewness and kurtosis and identifies cases with significant standardized residuals in either the measurement or structural equations. Plots of standardized residuals for each case are also provided. As stressed by Bollen and Arminger (1991), the identification of outliers allows the researcher to perform sensitivity analyses (e.g. what effect does the omission of the outliers have on parameter estimates and their level of statistical significance, measures of variation accounted for, and goodness of fit statistics), but it is necessary to explain why a case behaves anomalously before omitting it.

Cross-validation

One serious difficulty with model modifications motivated by significant modification indices or other sample-specific statistics is the potential for capitalization on chance (i.e. complexities introduced into a model based on evidence from a single sample which do not hold up in future samples). Cudeck and Browne (1983) have advocated the use of cross-validation for covariance structure models where the complete sample is split randomly into two halves (a calibration sample and a validation sample) and model selection is based on the criterion of minimum discrepancy in fit between the validation-sample observed covariance matrix and the calibration-sample estimated covariance matrix.[3] Operationally, this is accomplished by fixing all free parameters to the values obtained in the calibration sample and "estimating" this model on the validation sample. In order to make maximum use of the available data, one should use a process of double cross-validation by employing the two split half samples as both calibration and validation samples.

The goal of cross-validation is to select, from a series of possible models, the one that provides the best approximation to reality in several (at least two) samples of data. Cudeck and Browne (1983) recommend that models of different complexity be compared, ranging from a baseline model with few parameters to the saturated model with the maximum number of parameters. Cross-validation should obviously never be done blindly in a mere mechanical fashion and model interpretability should always be an important consideration, but the initial judicial selection of models to be compared through cross-validation should guard against this problem.

One disadvantage of cross-validation is that the complete sample has to be split into two halves, which may make the procedure unappealing or impossible given the need for "large" samples to begin with. In a recent article, Browne and Cudeck (1989) have proposed several adjustments to the fitting function for the calibration sample to obtain an estimate of the usual cross-validation index when a validation sample is not available. The first possible adjustment is to add a term $2r_k/(N-1)$ to the minimum of the fitting function, where r_k is the number of free parameters for model k and N is the sample size. The adjustment ignores a term of order $(N-1)^{-1}$ which may be non-negligible in smaller samples. In the special case of ML estimation and for a saturated model, the exact correction to the fitting function is given by $2r_k/(N-(p+q)-2)$, where $(p+q)$ is the number of variables in the model. Browne and Cudeck (1989) suggest that this second expression may be used as another possible adjustment for other kinds of models as well (not just saturated models).

Model equivalence

Model equivalence refers to the fact that different parametric structures may summarize the data equally well (i.e. yield the same χ^2 statistic and possibly other fit indices if the degrees of freedom are the same, etc.). This should be carefully distinguished from the issue of underidentification where different values for the same parametric structure account for the data equally well. Stelzl (1986) describes four easy-to-use rules for determining equivalent models, and Luijben (1991) presents an advanced discussion of some of the issues involved. Model equivalence signifies that tests of overidentifying restrictions can never really decide whether a model specifies the "correct" causal ordering among a number of constructs (particularly if the data come from a cross-sectional study) and points to the need for sound theory in model building.

A related issue arises when several alternative models with possibly different theoretical implications are more or less equally consistent with the data, although they are not formally equivalent. Breckler (1990) calls such models nearly equivalent. Often researchers imply that when they find a model that is in agreement with the data it is the "correct" model. In the vast majority of cases this conclusion is not warranted because there are generally many equivalent and nearly equivalent models that account for the data (almost) equally well. Glymour, Scheines, Spirtes, and Kelly (1987) have made a strong argument for considering alternative causal explanations for non-experimental data, and they have developed a computer program called TETRAD to help the researcher perform searches for alternative causal models.

An Empirical Example of Structural Equation Modeling

To illustrate the evaluation of structural equation models, we will now discuss a specific example dealing with people's patronage of fast food restaurants as a function of attitudes, subjective norms, past behavior, and behavioral intentions. A total of 246 students at the University of Michigan participated in a two-wave study in which attitudes, subjective norms, past behavior, and behavioral intentions were assessed during the first wave of data collection and actual behavior was measured by self-report two weeks later.

Attitude toward eating at fast food restaurants with friends during the next two weeks was measured with three seven-point semantic differential scales: pleasant–unpleasant (AA1), foolish–wise (AA2), and rewarding–punishing (AA3). Subjective norms were also measured with three seven-point items. Subjects indicated to what extent most people who were important to them approved–disapproved of their eating at a fast food restaurant sometime during the next two weeks (SN2) and to what extent most people who were important in their lives thought they should–should not eat at a fast food restaurant (SN3). The final item was the average of four ratings of the extent to which friends, parents, boyfriend/girlfriend, and brother(s)/sister(s) approved–disapproved of their eating at a fast food restaurant during the next two weeks (SN1). The measure of past behavior (PB) was a self-rating of how often a person had eaten with friends at a fast food restaurant last year during a typical two week period.

Behavioral intentions were measured by how likely–unlikely it was that a person presently intended to eat at a fast food restaurant with friends some time during the next two weeks (BI1) and whether there was no chance or a certain chance that they would do so (BI2). For the first item a seven-point scale was used, for the second a 10-point scale. Finally, actual behavior was assessed after two weeks with a self-report measure of how often a person had eaten with friends at a fast food restaurant during the previous two weeks (BH).

Figure 10.1 presents a diagram of the theoretical model (M_t) that was hypothesized to provide the best approximation to the empirical data. In this model, which is consistent with earlier work by Bagozzi (1981), Fredricks and Dossett (1983), and Bagozzi, Baumgartner, and Yi (1992), behavioral intentions are a function of attitudes, subjective norms, and past behavior, and future behavior is a function of behavioral intentions and past behavior.

Two other models are considered as possible alternatives. First, there is the traditional Fishbein and Ajzen (1975) framework (the so-called theory of reasoned action), which hypothesizes that attitudes and subjective norms mediate the effects of other variables (including past behavior) on behavioral intentions, and that behavioral intentions mediate the effects of attitudes and subjective norms on subsequent behavior. Model M_c, in which past behavior is allowed to covary freely with attitudes and subjective norms but otherwise has no direct effects on intentions and behavior, explicitly tests the assumption that attitudes and subjective norms are sufficient to account for variation in behavioral intentions.

In terms of overall model fit, M_c is equivalent to a model in which causal paths are specified from past behavior to attitudes and subjective norms. The example illustrates that a test of overidentifying restrictions is useless in deciding whether past behavior "causes" attitudes and subjective norms, or whether the three constructs are merely correlated. Appropriate guidelines for the "correct" specification must be gleaned from other sources (e.g. from sound theory). In the present case no causal ordering among attitudes, subjective norms and past behavior is hypothesized and the three constructs are merely allowed to correlate freely. The measure of actual behavior was collected two weeks after the assessment of attitudes, subjective norms, past behavior and behavioral intentions, so its role as the ultimate criterion variable is unambiguous. This is not the case with behavioral intentions, and the specification that attitudes, subjective norms,

(a) Model M_t:

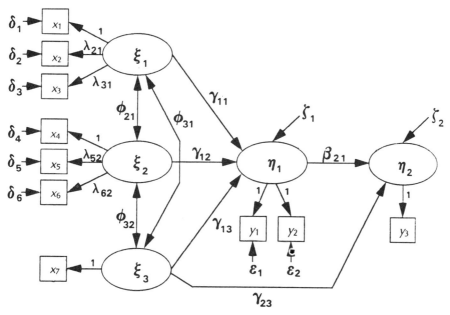

(b) Model comparisons:

Model	Measurement model parameters estimated	Latent variable model parameters estimated	degrees of freedom
M_{mi}	$\lambda_{21}, \lambda_{31}, \lambda_{52}, \lambda_{62},$ $\theta^\varepsilon_{11}, \theta^\varepsilon_{22}, \theta^\delta_{11}, \theta^\delta_{22},$ $\theta^\delta_{33}, \theta^\delta_{44}, \theta^\delta_{55}, \theta^\delta_{66},$	none	38
M_c	same as M_{mi}	$\beta_{21}, \gamma_{11}, \gamma_{12}, \varphi_{11}, \varphi_{21},$ $\varphi_{22}, \varphi_{31}, \varphi_{32}, \varphi_{33},$ ψ_{11}, ψ_{22}	32
M_t	same as M_{mi}	same as M_c plus γ_{13}, γ_{23}	30
M_u	same as M_{mi}	same as M_t plus γ_{21}	29
M_s	same as M_{mi}	same as M_u plus γ_{22}	28

Figure 10.1 Summary of model specifications

and past behavior "determine" behavioral intentions represents an assumption that cannot be tested explicitly.

Second, based on the work of Bentler and Speckart (1979, 1981), one may consider a model M_u in which past behavior has both direct effects on behavioral intentions and subsequent behavior, and in addition attitudes have direct effects on future behavior. In contrast to model M_c, which is more constrained and thus more parsimonious than M_t, M_u is less constrained and therefore less parsimonious than M_t.

For comparison purposes, two baseline (or null) models are considered—model M_{ci} which specifies all observed variables to be completely independent, and model M_{mi} which represents the assumption of modified independence or independence at the level of latent variables. The final model under consideration is the saturated latent variable model M_s.

It is easily checked that all models except one are identified if the two behavior constructs (past behavior, future behavior) are assumed to be measured without error. Model M_{mi} is not identified because there are only two indicators of behavioral intentions. However, if it can be assumed that the loadings of the two indicators of behavioral intentions are equal, even this model is identified.

The actual analysis started with an inspection of the raw data. Simple descriptive statistics suggested that there were no obvious coding errors (i.e. none of the variables had values outside of the admissible range), pairwise correlations showed that all relationships were in the expected direction after reverse-coded items had been recoded, and listwise deletion of missing values indicated that 218 observations were available for analysis.

The next step was to look for outliers and to investigate the approximate normality of all variables, using the LISRES macro in SAS. Bollen's (1989) model-free outlier detection procedure identified 4 observations which had a_{ii} values significant at the conservative Bonferroni-adjusted p-value of 0.00023 (0.05/218). Since no cogent theoretical reason suggested that these observations be excluded, they were originally retained, but sensitivity analyses were eventually conducted for the model that was found to provide the best approximation to the data.

Histograms and statistics on skewness and kurtosis showed that the distributions of most variables were roughly bell-shaped, with the exception of the behavioral measures. As found in previous research (e.g. Bagozzi, Baumgartner, and Yi, 1992), these measures were skewed to the right, with univariate skewness of 0.99 and 0.11 and univariate kurtosis of 57.86 and 8.83, respectively. To correct this problem, a square root transformation was applied to both variables, which reduced skewness (0.62 and −0.01) and kurtosis (4.63 and −0.43) substantially. Although the transformed data still showed excess multivariate skewness and kurtosis on the basis of formal statistical tests, the index of relative multivariate kurtosis of 1.27 suggested that the assumption of normality was not too badly violated.

Since all variables were measured with a minimum of seven scale steps, the data were assumed to be at least approximatedly continuous. A covariance matrix was therefore calculated which served as input to all analyses. The covariance matrix is reproduced in Table 10.2.

Table 10.2 Observed variance–covariance matrix

BI1 (y_1)	3.804									
BI2 (y_2)	2.670	3.647								
BH (y_3)	0.666	0.733	0.599							
AA1 (x_1)	0.946	0.921	0.238	1.330						
AA2 (x_2)	0.839	0.850	0.168	0.573	1.128					
AA3 (x_3)	0.711	0.814	0.179	0.666	0.563	1.345				
SN1 (x_4)	0.703	0.703	0.041	0.622	0.350	0.435	1.511			
SN2 (x_5)	0.654	0.666	0.079	0.586	0.463	0.614	1.277	2.079		
SN3 (x_6)	0.521	0.615	0.093	0.378	0.454	0.448	0.667	0.995	1.534	
PB (x_7)	0.588	0.644	0.248	0.242	0.158	0.069	0.080	0.057	0.068	0.517

Maximum likelihood was used for estimation. Depending on the specific model estimated, the ratio of sample size to number of free parameters varied from 28 : 1 to 8 : 1. For the target model the ratio is about 9 : 1. No estimation problems occurred, except in the case of model M_u where the maximization procedure apparently converged on a local minimum unless appropriate starting values were provided.

Initially, a confirmatory factor model in which the five factors were allowed to freely correlate, was estimated. This model had a χ^2 value of 44.92 with 27 degrees of freedom. Because we wanted to estimate model M_{mi}, we checked whether the loadings of the two indicators of behavioral intentions could be assumed to be equal. This was indeed the case; the revised model had a χ^2 value of 45.58 with 28 degrees of freedom and the decrement in fit was thus not significant (χ^2 difference value of 0.66 with 1 degree of freedom). A pseudo-chi-square test based on the chi-square value for model M_s and the degrees of freedom for model M_{mi} indicated that no structural model would fit the data satisfactorily based on χ^2 goodness-of-fit considerations. However, based on alternative fit indices such as CFI and TLI, it was decided that the fit of the measurement model to the data was adequate. All indicators loaded significantly and substantially on their underlying factors, providing evidence for convergent validity, and the highest correlation between constructs was 0.67, indicating that discriminant validity was achieved. Only two standardized residuals were larger than 2.58 in absolute magnitude (i.e. s.r. for SN1 and SN2 = -2.794; s.r. for PB and AA3 = -2.850). Thus, the measurement model seems adequate.

Next, all other models besides the saturated structural model (which corresponds to the confirmatory factor model considered above) were estimated. Table 10.3 presents the results for the various models and reports model comparison tests based on the chi-square statistic and CFI and TLI. All three fit measures indicate that model M_t provides the best fit to the data, although in an absolute sense the χ^2 value of 48.50 with 30 degrees of freedom points to significant discrepancies between the observed and estimated covariance matrices. Practically speaking, however, model M_t appears to be a parsimonious account of the data (i.e. if M_{ci} is used as the null model, CFI, which equals RNI in the present case, is 0.98 and TLI is 0.97, and if M_{mi} is used as the null model, CFI equals 0.93 and TLI equals 0.91).

Table 10.3 Overall goodness-of-fit measures and model comparisons

(a) Overall goodness-of-fit indices for various models:

	χ^2	df	CFI	TLI
M_{ci}	842.11	45	—	—
M_{mi}	310.52	38	0.66	0.60
			—	—
M_c	87.23	32	0.93	0.90
			0.80	0.76
M_t	48.50	30	0.98	0.97
			0.93	0.91
M_u	47.67	29	0.98	0.96
			0.93	0.91
M_s	45.58	28	0.98	0.96
			0.94	0.91

(b) Model comparisons:

	$\Delta\chi^2$	df	ΔCFI	ΔTLI
M_t vs. M_s	2.92	2	0.00	−0.01
			0.01	0.00
M_c vs. M_t	38.73	2	0.05	0.07
			0.13	0.15
M_t vs. M_u	0.83	1	0.00	−0.01
			0.00	0.00

Note: For CFI and TLI, the first line uses M_{ci} as the null model and the second line uses M_{mi} as the null model.

The next step was to assess the quality of construct measurement for the target model. The results are shown in the upper portion of Table 10.4. All standardized factor loadings were greater than 0.6 and the z-values of freely estimated loadings were highly statistically significant. Similarly, all freely estimated error variances were statistically significant. Table 10.4 also indicates that some of the individual-item reliabilities are marginal, but overall the constructs which are indicated by multiple items seem to be measured adequately. Composite reliability was 0.73, 0.87, and 0.84 for attitude, subjective norms, and behavioral intentions, respectively, if the

Table 10.4 Results for the target model

(a) Measurement model:

Parameter	Parameter estimate	Standardized parameter estimate	z-value	Individual-item reliability
λ^x_{11}	1.00	0.73	—	0.54
λ^x_{21}	0.83	0.66	8.19	0.44
λ^x_{31}	0.92	0.67	8.25	0.45
λ^x_{42}	1.00	0.80	—	0.64
λ^x_{52}	1.32	0.90	11.48	0.81
λ^x_{62}	0.77	0.61	8.88	0.37
λ^x_{73}	1.00	1.00	—	1.00
θ^ε_{11}	1.23	0.31	7.06	—
θ^ε_{22}	0.87	0.24	5.70	—
θ^ε_{33}	0.00	0.00	—	—
λ^y_{11}	1.00	0.83	—	0.68
λ^y_{21}	1.00	0.87	—	0.76
λ^y_{32}	1.00	1.00	—	1.00
θ^δ_{11}	0.61	0.46	7.09	—
θ^δ_{22}	0.63	0.56	8.24	—
θ^δ_{33}	0.74	0.55	8.15	—
θ^δ_{44}	0.55	0.36	6.58	—
θ^δ_{55}	0.41	0.19	3.44	—
θ^δ_{66}	0.97	0.63	9.43	—
θ^δ_{77}	0.00	0.00	—	—

(b) Latent variable model:

Parameter	Parameter estimate	Standardized parameter estimate	Test of significance		
			LR	Wald	LM
β_{21}	0.21	0.44	32.26	33.59	29.89
γ_{11}	1.10	0.57	31.75	26.61	29.62
γ_{12}	−0.03	−0.02	0.03	0.03	0.03
γ_{13}	0.82	0.36	25.61	31.76	28.65
γ_{23}	0.23	0.22	9.40	9.79	9.52
φ_{11}	0.72	1.00	—	30.61	—
φ_{21}	0.49	0.59	—	30.59	—
φ_{22}	0.96	1.00	—	41.30	—
φ_{31}	0.18	0.29	—	12.41	—
φ_{32}	0.06	0.08	—	1.25	—
φ_{33}	0.52	1.00	—	109.00	—
ψ_{11}	1.18	0.44	—	35.25	—
ψ_{22}	0.40	0.66	—	98.93	—

formula for the reliability of a weighted composite of measures was used, and 0.73, 0.83, and 0.84 when the formula for an unweighted composite of measures was employed. The figures for average variance extracted were 0.48, 0.62, and 0.72. Note that composite reliability based on unweighted and weighted composites is essentially identical for attitude and behavioral intentions, which reflects the fact that the indicators of these constructs are more or less parallel, whereas for subjective norms the two kinds of reliabilities differ somewhat.

The lower portion of Table 10.4 presents the results for the latent variable model. It can be seen that consumers' behavioral intentions to eat at a fast food restaurant with friends are a function of attitudes and past behavior; subjective norms are not significant. Actual behavior, in turn, is determined by behavioral intentions and past behavior. Fifty-six percent of the variation in behavioral intentions is accounted for by the three exogenous constructs, and 34 percent of the variation in actual behavior is explained by intentions and past behavior. For purposes of comparison, Table 10.4 reports the significance of the structural coefficients based on likelihood ratio, Wald, and Lagrange multiplier tests; it is apparent that all three tests lead more or less to the same result.

Attitude was the most important determinant of behavioral intentions in terms of the size of the standardized regression coefficient (0.57) and the magnitude of the zero-order correlations between the two constructs (0.67, or 44 percent in terms of R^2). Past behavior explained roughly an additional 12 percent of the variance in behavioral intentions. For actual behavior, behavioral intentions were the primary antecedent, with a standardized regression coefficient of 0.44 and a zero-order correlation of 0.55 (or 30 percent in terms of R^2). Again, past behavior contributed a sizeable increment of 4 percent. Thus, the effects of attitude and past behavior on behavioral intentions and of behavioral intentions and past behavior on subsequent behavior are not only statistically but also practically significant. The effect of subjective norms on behavioral intentions was not significant and had the wrong sign. The three subjective norm measures are actually positively and significantly correlated with the two measures of behavioral intentions and the negative sign may be due to poor separation of attitude and subjective norms (the two factors are correlated 0.59) and multicollinearity.

The LISRES macro was also used to perform a residual analysis of the observed variable residuals and the equation residuals. Problems of nonnormality were apparent for the measurement errors of several of the observed variables (especially BI1, BI2, PB, and AA1), but the structural residuals were well behaved. There were no significant standardized equation residuals and only three significant standardized observed variable residuals, using a conservative Bonferroni adjusted p-value. The three standardized residuals were for three of the four outliers identified earlier.

When model M_t was rerun on the data with three outliers removed (the three cases which also had significant standardized residuals), the χ^2 statistic improved somewhat (χ^2 value of 45.41 with 30 degrees of freedom), but otherwise the results were essentially the same as for the model estimated on all data points. Only the path from past behavior to future behavior was affected and was only of borderline significance (z-value of 1.92). Thus, the relationship between past behavior and future behavior is apparently somewhat fragile.

Conclusion

The use of structural equation modeling in marketing research has increased considerably in recent years. Not everyone sees this as a positive development. In part, the dissatisfaction may be due to exaggerated initial expectations. For example, the techniques described in this chapter are sometimes referred to as causal modeling. The term is unfortunate because structural equation modeling, being based essentially on correlational data, *cannot* give a researcher privileged access to the causal mechanisms that may operate among a set of theoretical concepts (cf. Cliff, 1983). The only thing it *can* provide are possible parsimonious accounts of the nexus of relationships between constructs that take into account the inherent fallibility of all empirical measurement. In part, the antipathy toward structural equation modeling probably also results from a lack of understanding of the technique, both on the side of its critics and on the side of its users. It is hoped that this chapter will alleviate some of these difficulties.

Questions

1 Show that model M_t is identified and determine how many degrees of freedom are due to overidentifying restrictions at the measurement level and how many are due to overidentifying restrictions at the level of latent variables. Show that model M_{mi} is not identified unless the loadings of the two indicators of behavioral intentions are specified to be equal.

2 Use the covariance matrix in Table 10.2 to estimate a five-factor confirmatory factor analysis model with attitudes, subjective norms, past behavior, behavioral intentions, and behavior as factors. Interpret your results.

3 Use the decision tree in Anderson and Gerbing (1988) to show that model M_t provides the "best" approximation to the data in Table 10.2 (at least for the models considered as plausible alternatives). Interpret the results for model M_t.

4 Specify at least two models which are equivalent to model M_t. Do the conclusions derived from these models differ from the interpretations forwarded in the chapter? Can you think of a model that is nearly equivalent to model M_t and also provides a plausible account of the data?

Notes

1 That multiple measures of each construct are used should not be an issue.

2 In contrast to McDonald and Marsh (1990), the noncentrality parameter is rescaled here by (N–1) rather than N.
3 Homburg (1991) presents evidence that nonrandom splits may have advantages over random splits.

References

Akaike, H. 1987: Factor analysis and AIC. *Psychometrika*, 52, 317–32.

Alwin, D. F. and Jackson, D. J. 1979: Measurement models for response errors in surveys: issues and applications. In K.F. Schuessler (ed.), *Sociological Methodology 1980*, San Francisco: Jossey-Bass.

Anderson, J. C. and Gerbing, D. W. 1988: Structural equation modeling in practice: a review and recommended two-step approach. *Psychological Bulletin*, 103, 411–423.

Babakus, E., Ferguson, Jr., C. E. and Jöreskog, K. G. 1987: The sensitivity of confirmatory maximum likelihood factor analysis to violations of measurement scale and distributional assumptions. *Journal of Marketing Research*, 24, 222–8.

Bagozzi, R. P. 1981: Attitudes, intentions, and behavior: a test of some key hypotheses. *Journal of Personality and Social Psychology*, 41, 607–27.

Bagozzi, R. P., Baumgartner, H. and Yi, Y. 1992: State versus action orientation and the theory of reasoned action: an application to coupon usage. *Journal of Consumer Research*, 18, 505–18.

Bagozzi, R. P. and Yi, Y. 1988: On the evaluation of structural equation models. *Journal of the Academy of Marketing Science*, 16, 74–94.

Bagozzi, R. P. and Yi, Y. 1991: Multitrait–multimethod matrices in consumer research. *Journal of Consumer Research*, 17, 426–439.

Bassman, R. L. 1963: The causal interpretation of non-triangular systems of economic relations. *Econometrica*, 31, 439–48.

Baumgartner, H. and Bagozzi, R. P. 1993: Specification, estimation, and testing of moment structure models based on latent variates involving interactions among the exogenous constructs. Working Paper, The Pennsylvania State University.

Bentler, P. M. 1986: *Lagrange Multiplier and Wald Tests for EQS and EQS/PC*, Los Angeles: BMDP Statistical Software.

Bentler, P. M. 1989: *EQS: Structural Equations Program Manual*, Los Angeles, CA: BMDP Statistical Software.

Bentler, P. M. 1990: Comparative fit indexes in structural models, *Psychological Bulletin*, 107, 238–46.

Bentler, P. M. and Bonett, D. G. 1980: Significance tests and goodness of fit in the analysis of covariance structures. *Psychological Bulletin*, 88, 588–606.

Bentler, P. M. and Chou, C. P. 1987: Practical issues in structural modeling. *Sociological Methods and Research*, 16, 78–117.

Bentler, P. M. and Speckart, G. 1979: Models of attitude–behavior relations. *Psychological Review*, 86, 452–64.

Bentler, P. M. and Speckart, G. 1981: Attitudes cause behaviors: a structural equation analysis. *Journal of Personality and Social Psychology*, 40, 226–38.

Bentler, P. M. and Weeks, D. G. 1979: Interrelations among models for the analysis of moment structures. *Multivariate Behavioral Research*, 14, 169–86.

Bollen, K. A. 1986: Sample size and Bentler and Bonett's nonnormed fit index, *Psychometrika*, 51, 375–7.

Bollen, K. A. 1988: A new incremental fit index for general structural equation models. *Sociological Methods and Research*, 17, 303–16.
Bollen, K. A. 1989: *Structural Equations with Latent Variables*, New York: Wiley.
Bollen, K. A. and Arminger, G. 1991: Observational residuals in factor analysis and structural equation models. In *Sociological Methodology 1991*, Washington: American Sociological Association.
Bollen, K. A. and Jöreskog, K. G. 1985: Uniqueness does not imply identification, *Sociological Methods and Research*, 14, 155–63.
Bollen, K. and Lennox, R. 1991: Conventional wisdom on measurement: a structural equation perspective. *Psychological Bulletin*, 110, 305–14.
Bozdogan, H. 1987: Model selection and Akaike's Information Criterion (AIC): the general theory and its analytical extensions. *Psychometrika*, 52, 345–70.
Breckler, S. J. 1990: Applications of covariance structure modeling in psychology: cause for concern? *Psychological Bulletin*, 107, 260–73.
Browne, M. W. 1982: Covariance structures. In D. M. Hawkins (ed.), *Topics in Applied Multivariate Analysis*, Cambridge: Cambridge University Press, 72–141.
Browne, M. W. 1974: Generalized least squares estimators in the analysis of covariance structures. *South African Statistical Journal*, 8, 1–24.
Browne, M. W. 1982: Covariance structures. In D. M. Hawkins (ed.), *Topics in Multivariate Analysis*, Cambridge: Cambridge University Press.
Browne, M. W. 1984: Asymptotically distribution-free methods for the analysis of covariance structures. *British Journal of Mathematical and Statistical Psychology*, 37, 62–83.
Browne, M. W. and Cudeck, R. 1989: Single sample cross-validation indices for covariance structures. *Multivariate Behavioral Research*, 24, 445–55.
Browne, M. W. and Mels, G. 1992: *RAMONA User's Guide*; Department of Psychology, Ohio State University, Columbus, Ohio.
Buse, A. 1982: The likelihood ratio, Wald, and Lagrange multiplier tests: an expository note. *American Statistician*, 36, 153–7.
Cliff, N. 1983: Some cautions concerning the application of causal modeling methods. *Multivariate Behavioral Research*, 18, 115–26.
Cudeck, R. 1989: Analysis of correlation matrices using covariance structure models. *Psychological Bulletin*, 1989, 317–27.
Cudeck, R. and M. W. Browne 1983: Cross-validation of covariance structures. *Multivariate Behavioral Research*, 18, 147–67.
Davis, W. R. 1992: The LISRES macro. Unpublished manuscript, University of North Carolina.
Etezadi-Amoli, J. and McDonald, R. P. 1983: A second generation nonlinear factor analysis. *Psychometrika*, 48, 315–42.
Fishbein, M. and Ajzen, I. 1975: *Belief, Attitude, Intention and Behavior: An Introduction to Theory and Research*, Reading, MA: Addison-Wesley.
Fornell, C. and Bookstein, F. L. 1982: Two structural equation models: LISREL and PLS applied to consumer exit-voice theory. *Journal of Marketing Research*, 19, 440–520.
Fornell, C. and Larcker, D. F. 1981: Evaluating structural equation models with unobservable variables and measurement errors. *Journal of Marketing Research*, 18, 39–50.
Fornell, C. and Yi, Y. 1992: Assumptions of the two-step approach to latent variable modeling. *Sociological Methods and Research*, 20, 291–320.

Fraser, C. 1980: *COSAN User's Guide*. Centre for Behavioral Studies, University of New England, Armidale, New South Wales, Australia.

Fredricks, A. J. and Dossett, D. J. 1983: Attitude-behavior relations: a comparison of the Fishbein-Ajzen and Bentler-Speckart models. *Journal of Personality and Social Psychology*, 45, 501–12.

Gerbing, D. W. and Anderson, J. C. 1988: An updated paradigm for scale development incorporating unidimensionality and its assessment. *Journal of Marketing Research*, 25, 186–92.

Glymour, C., Scheines, R., Spirtes, P., and Kelly, R. 1987: *Discovering Causal Structure: Artificial Intelligence, Philosophy of Science, and Statistical Modeling*, Orlando, FL: Academic Press.

Hattie, J. A. 1985: Methodology review: assessing unidimensionality of tests and items. *Applied Psychological Measurement*, 9, 139–64.

Hayduk, L. A. 1987: *Structural Equation Modeling with LISREL: Essentials and Advances*, Baltimore: John Hopkins University Press.

Hoelter, J. W. 1983: The analysis of covariance structures: goodness-of-fit indices. *Sociological Methods and Research*, 11, 325–44.

Homburg, C. 1991: Cross-validation and information criteria in causal modeling. *Journal of Marketing Research*, 28, 137–44.

Homburg, C. and Dobratz, A. 1992: Covariance structure analysis via specification searches. *Statistical Papers*, 33, 119–42.

Hu, L., Bentler, P. M. and Kano, Y. 1992: Can test statistics in covariance structure analysis be trusted? *Psychological Bulletin*, 112, 351–62.

Jöreskog, K. G. 1973: A general method for estimating a linear structural equation System. In A. S. Goldberger and O. D. Duncan (eds), *Structural Equation Models in the Social Sciences*, New York: Seminar Press, 85–112.

Jöreskog, K. G. and Sörbom, D. 1989: *LISREL7: A Guide to the Program and Applications*. Chicago, IL: SPSS Inc.

Jöreskog, K. G. and Sörbom, D. 1993a: *LISREL8: Structural Equation Modeling with SIMPLIS Command Language*. Hillsdale, NJ: Lawrence Erlbaum Associates.

Jöreskog, K. G. and Sörbom, D. 1993b: *SPSS LISREL7 and PRELIS*. Chicago, IL: SPSS Inc.

Kano, Y., Berkane, M. and Bentler, P. M. 1990: Covariance structure analysis with heterogeneous kurtosis parameters. *Biometrika*, 77, 575–85.

Kaplan, D. 1989: Model modification in covariance structure analysis: application of the expected parameter change statistic. *Multivariate Behavioral Research*, 24, 285–305.

Kenny, D. A. 1979: *Correlation and Causality*, New York: Wiley.

Kenny, D. A. and Judd, C. M. 1984: Estimating the nonlinear and interactive effects of latent variables. *Psychological Bulletin*, 96, 201–10.

Lastovicka, J. L. and Thamodaran, K. 1991: Common factor score estimates in multiple regression. *Journal of Marketing Research*, 28, 105–12.

Lohmöller, J.-B. 1984: *LVPLS Program Manual: Latent Variables Path Analysis with Partial Least-Squares Estimation*, Köln, West Germany: Zentralarchiv für Empirische Sozialforschung.

Luijben, T. C. W. 1991: Equivalent models in covariance structure analysis. *Psychometrika*, 56, 653–65.

MacCallum, R. 1986: Specification searches in covariance structure modeling. *Psychological Bulletin*, 100, 107–20.

Marsh, H. W., Balla, J. R. and McDonald, R. P. 1988: Goodness-of-fit indexes in confirmatory factor analysis: the effect of sample size. *Psychological Bulletin*, 103, 391–410.

MacArdle, J. J. and McDonald, R. P. 1984: Some algebraic properties of the reticular action model for moment structures. *British Journal of Mathematical and Statistical Psychology*, 37, 234–51.

McDonald, R. P. 1978: A simple comprehensive model for the analysis of covariance structures. *British Journal of Mathematical and Statistical Psychology*, 31, 59–72.

McDonald, R. P. 1980: A simple comprehensive model for the analysis of covariance structures: some remarks on application. *British Journal of Mathematical and Statistical Psychology*, 33, 161–83.

McDonald, R. P. 1989: An index of goodness-of-fit based on noncentrality. *Journal of Classification*, 6, 97–103.

McDonald, R. P. and Marsh, H. 1990: Choosing a multivariate model: noncentrality and goodness of fit. *Psychological Bulletin*, 107, 247–55.

Mooijaart, A. and Bentler, P. M. 1986: Random polynomial factor analysis. In E. Diday, et al. (eds). *Data Analysis and Informatics*, Amsterdam: North-Holland.

Mulaik, S. A., James, L. R., Van Alstine, J., Bennett, N., Lind, S. and Stilwell, C. D. 1989: Evaluation of goodness-of-fit indices for structural equation models. *Psychological Bulletin*, 105, 430–45.

Muthén, B. O. 1987: *LISCOMP: Analysis of Linear Structural Relations Using a Comprehensive Measurement Model*, Mooresville, IN: Scientific Software.

Rigdon, E. E. and Ferguson, Jr. C. E. 1991: The performance of the polychoric correlation coefficient and selected fitting functions in confirmatory factor analysis with ordinal data. *Journal of Marketing Research*, 28, 491–7.

Rindskopf, D. 1984: Using phantom and imaginary latent variables to parameterize constraints in linear structural models. *Psychometrika*, 49, 37–47.

Saris, W. E. and Stronkhorst, L. H. 1984: *Casual Modeling in Nonexperimental Research*. Amsterdam, The Netherlands: Sociometric Research Foundation.

Saris, W. E., Den Ronden, J., and Satorra, A. 1987: Testing structural equation models. In P. Cuttance and R. Ecob (eds), *Structural Modeling by Example: Applications in Educational, Sociological, and Behavioral Research*, Cambridge: Cambridge University Press.

Satorra, A. and Bentler, P. M. 1991: Goodness-of-fit test under IV estimation: asymptotic robustness of a NT test statistic. In R. Erutierrez and M. J. Valderrrana (eds), *Applied Stochastic Models and Data Analysis*, London: World Scientific, 555–67.

Satorra, A. and Saris, W. E. 1985: Power of the likelihood ratio test in covariance structure analysis. *Psychometrika*, 50, 83–90.

Schaubroek, J. 1990: Investigating reciprocal causation in organizational behavior research. *Journal of Organizational Behavior*, 11, 17–28.

Schoenberg, R. 1987: *LINCS: Linear Covariance Structure Analysis Users' Guide*, Kensington, MD: RJS Software.

Schwarz, G. 1978: Estimating the dimension of a model. *Annals of Statistics*, 6, 461–4.

Sharma, S., Durvasula, S. and Dillon, W. R. 1989: Some results on the behavior of alternate covariance structure estimation procedures in the presence of non-normal data. *Journal of Marketing Research*, 26, 214–21.

Sobel, M. E. and Bohrnstedt, G. W. 1985: Use of null models in evaluating the fit of covariance structure models. In N. B. Tuma (ed.), *Sociological Methodology 1985*, San Francisco: Jossey-Bass, 152–78.

Steenkamp, J. B. and van Trijp, H. 1991: The use of LISREL in validating marketing constructs. *International Journal of Research in Marketing*, 8, 283–99.

Steiger, J. H. 1989: *EZPATH Causal Modelling: A Supplementary Module for SYSTAT and SYGRAPH*, Evanston, IL: SYSTAT.

Steiger, J. H., Shapiro, A., and Browne, M. W. 1985: On the multivariate asymptotic distribution of sequential chi-square statistics. *Psychometrika*, 50, 253–64.

Stelzl, I. 1986: Changing a causal hypothesis without changing the fit: some rules for generating equivalent path models. *Multivariate Behavioral Research*, 21, 309–31.

Strotz, R. H. and Wold, H. O. A. 1960: Recursive vs. nonrecursive systems: an attempt at synthesis. *Econometrica*, 28, 417–27.

Tucker, L. R. and Lewis, C. 1973: The reliability coefficient for maximum likelihood factor analysis. *Psychometrika*, 38, 1–10.

Vandaele, W. 1981: Wald, likelihood ratio, and Lagrange multiplier tests as an F test. *Economics Letters*, 8, 361–5.

Index

Page references to figures are italicized

academic work, place of 117, 222
ads, exposure to 207-8
affectivity, positive and negative 30-1
AHA (American Hospital
    Association) 132
algorithms 97
  objective 300-1, 304-5
ANCOVA (analysis of covariance)
    224, 250-2, 252, 253
  see also MANCOVA
ANOVA (analysis of variance)
    225-50, 253, 269-71, 270
  "contrasts" 242-6, 244
  effect-size 248-50
  fixed- versus random-effects 242
  one-way 227-33, 231
  simple effects 246-8
  three-way and higher-order 240-1, 241
  two-way 233-9
  see also MANOVA
area probability sampling 91-2
aroused conditions 328-31
ARS (acquiescence response sets) 29
association, measures of 394-5
attitude
  defined 2
  and intention 364-73, 410-12
  models of 334
  see also habit; questionnaires; responses
autocorrelation, error 165, 178-80

backfire effect 35-6
balanced repeated replication see BRR

Bass diffusion model 189
behavior, consumer 195-222
Bentler and Bonett index 400-1
beta coefficient β∗ 173
bias
  with different methodologies 127-8, 127
  negative affectivity 29-30
  nonresponse 142-5
  purchase 100
  research, and self-concept 28-9
  responses 121-3, 152
  sampling frames 77, 118
  social desirability 28-9
  specification 181
  telephone surveys 130, 133, 135
"blindfolded one-on-ones" 64
Bollen test 393, 412
brainstorming sessions 58, 60
brands
  awareness 219-20, 219
  choice 85
  ski parka survey 196-9, 212-17, 214, 219-21
breakeven, distance from 104, 106
BRR (balanced repeated replication) 97, 98, 99

Campbell and Fiske's procedure
    20-2, 23, 24-5, 343, 361
carryover effect 35, 36
CATI (computer aided telephone
    interviewing) 126
causality 195
  indicator models 320

424 INDEX

causation, mutual *see* reciprocal causation
Census Bureau, US 81, 91, 97, 100, 102
CEOs *347*, 348
CFA (confirmatory factor analysis) 413
  advantages 346, 348–9
  assessment techniques *361–3*
  and construct validity 343–50, *347*, 357–8
  hierarchical (HCFA) 355, 360–1, *362–3*
  model *344*
  pros and cons 346, 348–9, *361–2*
  second-order 339–41, *340*, *341*, 362
  see also MTMM
CFI (comparative fit index) 400–1
chi-squares 295, 325
  alternatives to *398*, 399–400
classic factor analysis *see* factor analysis, classic
clinical focus groups 57–8
clusters *see* sampling clusters
coefficient alpha *see* Cronbach alpha
coefficient of determination 168
cognitive abilities 32
comparative fit index *see* CFI
competitors, marketing efforts of 175
"completely crossed designs" 233
computers
  and BRR 99
  and factor analyses 310–12
  and focus groups 62
  programs and commands *see* CATI; EQS; LISREL; LISRES; MUTMUM; SAS; SPSSX
  responses via 156
  and rotations 300, 313
  and sampling errors from complex samples 96–9
  and SEMs 386, 393–5
  and telephone interviews (CATI) 126
concepts, *see also* "traits"
conceptual meaning 19, 318–20
confirmatory factor analysis *see* CFA
congeneric measurement model *324*, 325, *326*, *328*, *329–30*, 330, 331
construct validity 20, 201–2, 211, 342, 342–63
constructs 200–1, 212, 388–9
  unobservable 279–82

context, and attitude item interpretation 35–6, *36*, *37*
"contrasts" *see under* ANOVA; MANOVA
convergent validity 20–2, *23*, 24–5
corporate world, marketing research 117–25
correlated uniqueness model *see* CU
correlation matrices 292–4, 300, *302*, *303*, 304, 313–14, *326*, *329*, *340*
correspondence rules *4*, 5–6, *7*, 320–1
costs
  and gains, linear 106–7
  reducing 151–2
  sampling 81–8; fixed 108–9
  survey 83–5, 128, *128*, *129*
covariance *253*, 261–2, *413*
  see also ANCOVA; MANCOVA
credibility 213
criterion variables *see* dependent variables
criterion-related validity 19–20
Cronbach alpha 18, 152, *152*, 323, 325
cross-validation of models 408–9
CU (correlated uniqueness) model 350–1, *351*, *352*, 353, 357–8, 360, *362*
customer satisfaction data, variance and 237–9, *237–8*, *240*, 251, *259–60*, 268–9, 304–5

data collection
  methods 74–5, 119
  purposes 119–20
data screening issues 392–5
demand equations 9
demographic biases 100
dependent (criterion) variables 162, 184, 216, 227–8
  triangulation 203
  see also regression analysis
dependent measures, selecting 215–20
derived concepts 3–4, *4*
"design effect" 86
Dillman's guidelines 40
direct product model *see* DP model
discriminant validity 20–2, *23*, 24–5
distributed-lag regression model 190
DP (direct product) model 353–5, *356*, 357–8, *362*
dual frame sampling methods 94
dummy variable regression 182–6

Edwards' proscriptions 40
eigenvalues and eigenvectors 265-7, 282-8, 284, *285*, *287*, 293-4, *295*, *302*, 313
electricity 54-5
emotional states 29-30, 331
empiricism 3, *4*, 6, 8-9
  and meaning 320-1
EMSs ("expected mean squares") 230-1
EQS program 355, 394, 395, 403, 404
equalitative research *68*
error
  mail surveys 139
  measurement *see* measurement error
  non-sampling 99-102
  random 164-6, 321-2, 342, 360, *364*
  regression analysis 164-6, 177
  research 26-33, *27*
  sampling 26, 96-7, *98*, 99
  see also heteroscedasticity; homoscedasticity; random error; spurious meaning; variance
error, measurement *see* measurement error
estimation problems 396-7
ethics 43, 124
EV (expectancy-value) model 335-7, *336*, *338*
expected mean squares 264-5, *265*
experimental data
  analysis of 224-78
  summary 224-5
experimental design 195-223
  choice of context 204-8
  generalization approach 196-8
  laboratory or field? 204-6
  theoretical explanation approach 198-204
experiments, laboratory or field 205, 224
explanation, prediction and control 363-77
explanatory variables *see* independent variables
exploratory focus groups 58-9
exponential regression models 188

F-tests 229-31, *230*, 242
  and reliability 18
factor analysis
  classic 279-316
  computer commands 310-12
  conducting 291-309
  higher order 305-9, *306*
  logic of 288-91
  principal components and 286-8
  Q-factor and multi-mode 307-8
  sample size and 308-9
  variables, numbers of 309
factorials, completely randomized two-factor 233
factors, underlying *292*
field experiments OR testing 119, 120, 126
Fishbein model 335-6
"fixed- *versus* random-factors", and expected mean squares 264-5, *265*
focus groups 50-63, 147
  background to 51-3
  and mail/telephone surveys 127-9, *127-8*
  and miscellaneous surveys 153-4, *153-4*
  and one-on-one interviews 64-8
  procedural issues and analysis 60-2
  research into 62-3
  types 53-62
"focussed interviews" 51-2
FOMIMI model 361, *363*
forecasting 162
formative indicators 331-4, 388-9
Fornell and Larcker's index 402-3
frames *see* sampling frames
freedom, degrees of 229

gains, linear costs and 106-7
gains and losses, potential 103-4, 105
generalization
  and dependent measure selection 219-20
  and independent variable selection 214-15
  and theoretical explanation 220-2
geography
  and sample clustering 92-3
  and stratification 102
goal-directed attitudes 337
goodness-of-fit 325, *326*, 329-30, 330, 394, *398*, 399-401, *414*
  see also chi-squares
graphical rotations *see* rotations
"greater than one" rule 293-4
groups
  conformity 61

interaction within 63
interviewed *see* focus groups; theatre
polarization within 61

habit
  and questionnaire return 143–4
  and research behaviour 119
hard-to-reach populations *142*
HCFA *see* CFA, hierarchical
heteroscedasticity 165, 177, 178, *178*, 180
"Heywood cases" 397
history of marketing research 118–19
homogenous groups, and sample selection 208–9
homoscedasticity 165, 177
Hotelling–Lawley trace 267–8
Hotelling's T^2 tests 253–6, *255*, 268
household sampling 91–2

identification, model 390–2, 397
incomplete list sampling 93–4
independent (explanatory) variables 162, 184, 185–6, 201, 227–8
  selecting 210–15
  see also regression analysis
independent samples 97
individual interviews *see* one-on-one interviews
information
  motive for processing 211–12
  value of *see* value of information
intelligence, measuring 280–1
intention
  attitude and 364–73, 410–12
  see also habit
interaction centered focus groups 53–7
interaction regression model 190
interactions, two-way ANOVA 234, *235*
intercept term 172, 177, 183
internal consistency reliability 17
interpretational confounding 332
interval scales 12–15
interviews *see* focus groups; mail surveys; one-on-one; shopping mall intercepts; telephone surveys
item overlap errors 30–1

Kendall's Coefficient of Concordance 23, 24, 25
Koyck type specification 190
kurtosis 268, 393–4, 412

laboratory experiment 199, 200, 202
Lagrange multipliers 80–1, 82, 404
latent variables 331–3, 387–9, 403–4, *415*, 416
"law-cluster concepts" 18
least squares 172, 178, 182, 184, 395
likelihood, estimating maximum 306–7
Likert (summated rating) scale 14–15, 219
linear costs and gains 106–7
linear model, general 263
linear regression model 164–71
  with non-linear features 186–90
  statistical testing of 168–70
LISREL program 355, 386, 395, 397, 402, 403, 404, 407
LISRES macro 393–4, 407, 412, 416
Literary Digest surveys 77, 118
log-linear regression models 188
long-term memory 33, 35
losses, gains and, potential 103–4, 105
low-income consumers 54–5

mail surveys 137–48
  disadvantages 137
  enhanced return rates 138–42, *139*
  errors 138–9
  and miscellaneous other methods 153–4, *153–4*
  panels 94, 138
  response stages hypothesized *145*
  and telephone surveys 125–48, *127–8*, *129*
"main effects" 233–4
mall intercepts *see* shopping mall intercepts
managers, marketing 103, 162–3
MANCOVA (multi-variate analysis of covariance) 224, *253*, 261–3
manipulated independent variables 210–12
MANOVA (multi-variate analysis of variance) 252–3, *253*, 256–63, *257*, 271–2
  and ANOVA 256–9, *257*
  "contrasts" and followup testing 260–1
  repeated measures via 261
  statistics Λ, T, and R 267–9
  see also MANCOVA
matrix algebra 265–7, 282–314, 313

mean squares 229
  see also EMSs
meaning
  the three types of *318*
  see also conceptual; spurious *and under* empiricism
measured independent variables 210–12
measurement
  defined 2–3
  reliability 16–18, 19, 26–33
  scales of 10–16
  validity 18–22, 24–33
measurement error 342
  attitudes and *364*
  in substantive research 364–7, *364, 366–8*, 369
  and unobservable constructs 279–82
  see also random error
measurement models 331, 401–3
"measures of process" 217
medical services 55–6
  return rates and those in 140–2, *141, 143*
method
  error 342
  see also MTMM
methods, "traits" and 342–51, *344, 352*, 353–4
military recruitment 64–8
MIMIC (multiple indicator, multiple cause) models 333
"mini-focus groups" 60
misspecification of models 178, 182, 389–90, 406
mobile special populations 95–6
models
  identification of 390–2, 397
  specifications *411*
  see also theoretical
moderators 50, 58, 61, 147
Motivation Research 52–3
MTMM (multitrait-multimethod) matrix 21–2, *21, 23*
  and construct validity 342–63
  data analysis 358–60, *359*
multicollinearity, variables and 172, 180–2, 189
multidimensionality 334–41, *336, 338*
multiple regression analysis 171–7
multitrait-multimethod matrix *see* MTMM

multivariate analysis 18
  see also MANCOVA; MANOVA
MUTMUM program 355, 357
mutual causation 374–7, *374, 376, 377*

negative affectivity biases 29–30
network samples 95
no treatment controls 212, 213
nominal scales 10–12
nomological network 205
nomological validity 25–6
non-centrality 400–1
non-linear regression models 186–90
non-observational propositions 4
non-recursive relationships 374–7, *374, 376, 377*, 389
non-response bias 142–5
non-sampling errors, types 26–7
non-zero clusters 93, 94
null hypotheses 174, 175, 176, 177, 226, 228, 252–3

OBLIMIN 301, 314
oblique rotations 299–301, 314
one-on-one interviews 63–8, 145–6
  compared with other methods 64–8, 153–4, *153–4*
  see also shopping mall intercepts; telephone surveys
one-way mirrors 50, 147
ordinal scales 11–12
orthogonality 245, 300–1, *303*
outliers 393, 408, 412
overlap *see* item overlap

panel studies 389
parallel forms model 325, *326*, 329–30, 330
"parsimonious" processes 201–3, 205, 250, 407
Pearson product-moment correlations 25, 309
personalized service, perception of 55–6
phenomenological focus groups 53–7
Pillai–Bartlett trace V 258–9
polynomial regression models 189
positive and negative attitudes 337–9
post hoc processes 203–4, 245–6, 250
post-stratification 101–2
power 404–5

PPS (probabilities proportionate to size) 88, 89
predicted explanations 203–4
predictive validity 26
predictors *see* independent variables
presidential election 1936 77, 118
pricing 196–7, 199, *200*, 212
   elasticity *123*
   and sales 167–8
primary sampling units *see* PSUs
principal components 285–8, *287*
   and factor analysis 286–8
probability sampling methods 73–115
   see also PPS
products *see* brands
professional market researchers 123–5
projective techniques 64
projects, specific, and value of information 104
pseudoreplication 97, 99
PSUs (primary sampling units) 91–2, 96, 99
purchase biases 100

Q-factor analysis 307
qualitative marketing research 50–72
   background to 51–3
   defined 69–70
   and quantitative marketing research 68–70, *68*
   see also focus groups
quantitative marketing research 68–70, *68*
questionnaires
   designing and developing 33, 35–43, *40*
   form, and interview mode 121–2
   how answered 33, *34*, 35–6
   polarity of items 41
   pretesting of 42–3
   semantics of 39
   see also attitude; responses

random digit dialing *see* RDD
random error 164–6, 321–2, 342, 360, *364*
random factors *see* fixed-
randomized factorials 233
ratio estimates 102
ratio scales 15–16
RDD (random digit dialing) 118, 126, 130, 132

reasoned action theory, tests *366*
reciprocal causation 374–7, *374*, *376*, *377*
reciprocal regression model 189
recursive models 389, 391
   see also non-recursive
reflective indicators 331–4, 388–9
regression
   coefficients 172–6
   dummy variable 182–6
   estimated line *167*
regression analysis 162–94
   diagnostic checks in 177–82
   multiple 171–7
   summarized 190–2
regression models
   functional forms 186–90
   with no intercept term 170
   random error term 164–6
   restricted and unrestricted 175–7
   units of measurement 170
   see also linear regression; multiple; non-linear
regression parameters
   estimating 166–8
   significance 174–7
reinforcement structures 117
reliability 16–18, 323–31, *326*, 402–3
   double- and multiple-factor models 326–31
   single-factor model 323–5
   see also under measurement
repeated measures data 269
repetition of message *207*
replications 97, *98*, 99, 248
research
   amount of? 107
   justification for? 108–10
   see also surveys
researchers
   decision-making styles of 218
   see also surveyors
residual analysis 407–8
resources
   using limitations 110–11
   see also costs
respondents, talkativeness 61, 64
responses 33, *34*, 35–6
   alternative, attitudes and 32–3
   biases in 121–3, 152
   thought processes behind *34*
   see also non-response

return rates
    enhanced 138–42, 139
    hard-to-reach populations *142*
ridge regression 182
role-play 58
rotations 281, 297–303, *298, 299, 303*
"Roy's greatest characteristic root" 268

sales, and pricing 167–8
sample biases, bounding the effects 101–2
sample cooperation, measuring 100
sample selection, experimental design and 208–10
sample sizes 107–10, *115*, 241–2
    "classical" approach 102
    factor analysis and 308–9
    previous 110
    typical 110, *110*
    value of information and 102–7
sampling 73–115
    costs 81–8
    methods, taxonomy of 74–5
    optimized 79–83, 107–10, *115*
    pre-research questions 107, 108–9
    stratification 79–83
    variances 80–1
sampling clusters 83–99, *84*
    optimum size 86–8
    unequally-sized 88–92
    variances 85–6, 99
sampling error 26, 96–7, *98*, 99
    and telephone call-backs *134*
sampling frames 75
    biased 77, 118
    evaluating 75–8
    problem correction 76–8
    telephone surveys 78–9, 118
SAS commands 310
scales of measurement *see* measurement, scales of
scanner panels 146
"scree" tests 294, *295*
secondary sources 119
self-concept, and research bias 28–9
semantics
    differential 13–14, *13*, 39, 219
    questionnaires 29, 39–41, *40*
SEMS (structural equation models) 317–85
    evaluation 409–17

and hypothesis testing 386–422
Jöreskog's specification 386–7
structure of theory and 318–23
shopping mall intercepts 87–8, 89–91, 129, 145
    sample sizes 87–8
    venues selected for 89
simple effects 247–8, *247*
"simple structure", goal of 297–8
simultaneity 374–7, *374, 376, 377*
social desirability biases 28–9
special populations, screening for 92–6
"specific" factors 289–91
specification
    bias 181
    issues related to initial 387–93
sponsorship 139
SPSSX commands 310–12
spurious meaning 321–3
squares *see* EMSs; least; mean; sums of
stability, reliability 17
standards, research 124
    see also ethics
statistical assumptions 392
structural equation models *see* SEMs
structure coefficients 300, 304
subconscious motivation 57
summated rating scale *see* Likert
sums of squares 229–31, *232*
survey methodologies 120–3, *121*, 156
    compared 125–48, *127, 153–4*
    see also focus groups; mail; one-on-one interviews; telephone
surveyors
    surveyed 148–9, *149, 150*, 151–5, *151*
    variations among 154–5
surveys
    basics of conducting 126
    costs 83–5, 128, *128, 129*
    history 118–19
    in marketing research context 119–25
    methods other than mail or telephone 145–7
    risks to quality of 124–5
    see also interviews; questionnaires; researchers; respondents
Surveys of Business 81
Swain's model 354
syndicated sources of purchase data 119, 120
systematic error 321–2, 342

430 INDEX

T^2 tests 252, 268
  one-sample 253–4, *255*
  two-sample 254–6, *255*
t-tests 169, 224–5, 230
  one-sample 225–7
  two-sample 227
  see also ANOVAs
tape recordings 61–2
tau-equivalent model 325, *326*
Taylorized deviations 97
technology
  advances in 125
  see also computers
telephone surveys 129–37, *134*, *136*
  advantages 129–30
  biases 133, 135, 130
  call-back, and sampling error *134*
  CATI programs 126
  compared with mail surveys 125–48, *127–8*, 129
  completion rates 132–3
  dialings, disposition of 130–2, *131*, *132*
  high return rates 133, 135–7
  and miscellaneous other surveys 153–4, *153–4*
  regulations 130
  research into 120
  ring policies 135, 137
telephones, sample frames 78–9, 118
test–retest reliability 17
theater testing procedure 206–8
theoretical concepts 3, 4, 9
theoretical definitions 4, 5
theoretical explanation, and generalization 220–2
theoretical explanations, dependent measure selection and 216–19
theoretical model of interest
  estimation and testing issues 395–409
  goodness of fit 399–401
  initial specification issues 387–92
  modification 405–7
theoretical relationships 200–4, 212
theory, structure of 3–10, *4*
  and SEMs 318–23
  and source credibility effects *7*
time sampling 90
trade conventions 147
"traits" 21–5
  see also MTMM
triangulation, variables 203, 211

true-score theory 17–18
Tucker–Lewis index (TFI) 400–1

uncertainty, estimating prior 103, 105–6
unidimensional view of attitudes 334–5
unit normal loss integral *115*
unobservable constructs and measurement error 279–82

validity
  construct 20, 201–2, 211, 342–63
  external 198
  internal 197–8, 211
  measurement 18–22, 24–33
  types 19–26
value of information 102–7
  decline in 107
  factors related to 103–4
variables
  with common variance 296
  constructs and 201
  criterion *vis-à-vis* explanatory *see* regression analysis
  dependent (criterion) *see* dependent variables
  elasticities 172–3
  independent (explanatory) *see* independent variables
  moment matrix 394–5
  normality assessment 393–4
  in substantive research 369–72, *370*, *372–3*
  triangulation 203, 211
  see also dummy; error; variance
variance, sampling 96–7, *98*, 99
variance analysis models *253*, 261–2
  see also ANOVA; covariance; Hotelling T^2 tests; MANOVA; *t*-tests
VARIMAX 301

Waksberg–Mitofsky method 78–9
Wald tests 404
Wilks' Likelihood Ratio Test Statistic 267
wording of questionnaires 29, 39–41, *40*

"yea- and nay-saying" 29

zero
  segments 92–3
  see also null hypothesis